Drawing Manga for Beginners

# LEARN TO DRAW
# MANGA POSES

FOR KIDS

LEARN TO DRAW
WITH EASY-TO-FOLLOW
DRAWING LESSONS IN
A MANGA STORY!

YUYU KOUHARA

QUARRY

# PROLOGUE

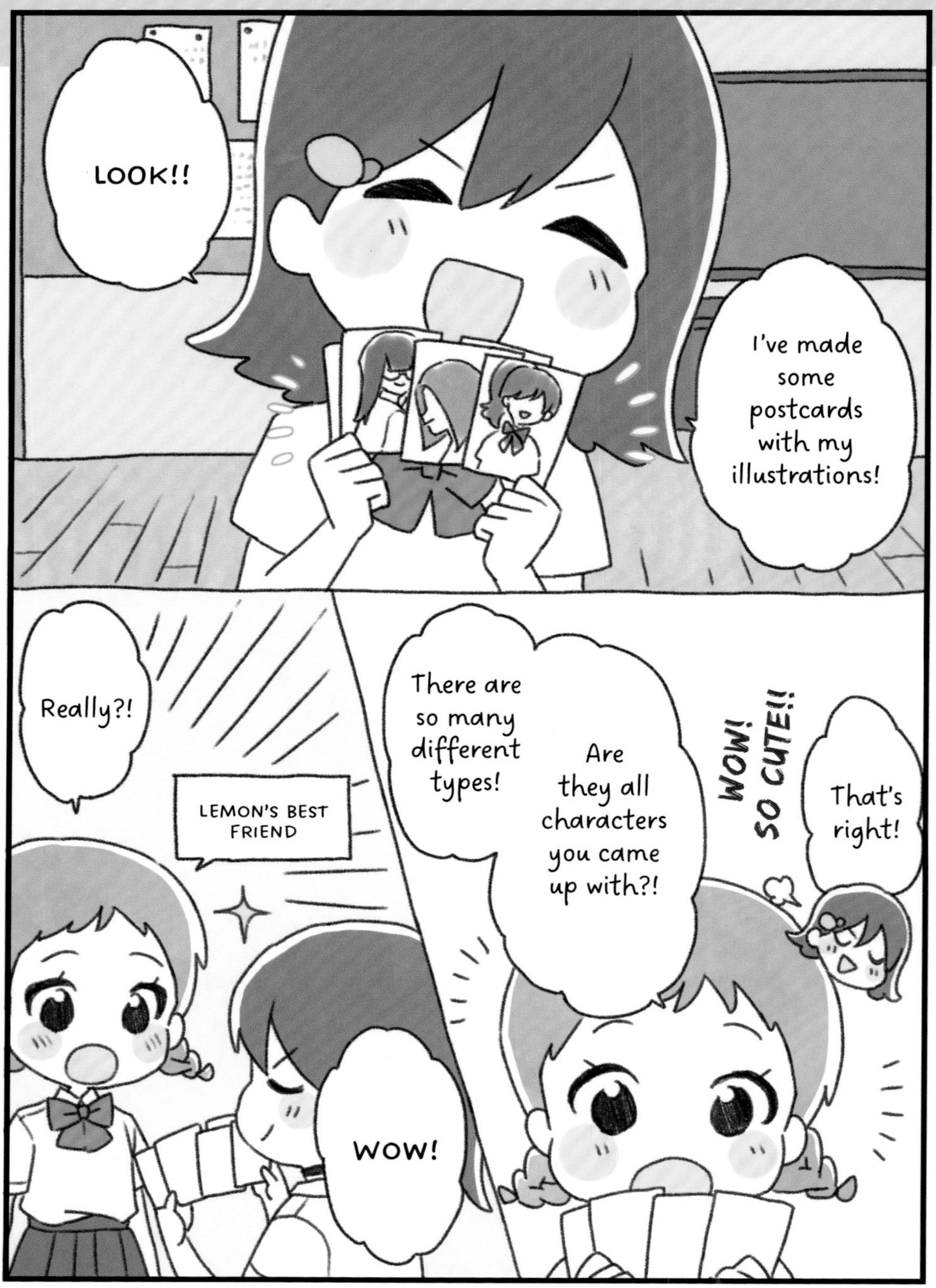
LOOK!!
I've made some postcards with my illustrations!
Really?!
LEMON'S BEST FRIEND
There are so many different types!
Are they all characters you came up with?!
WOW! SO CUTE!!
That's right!
WOW!

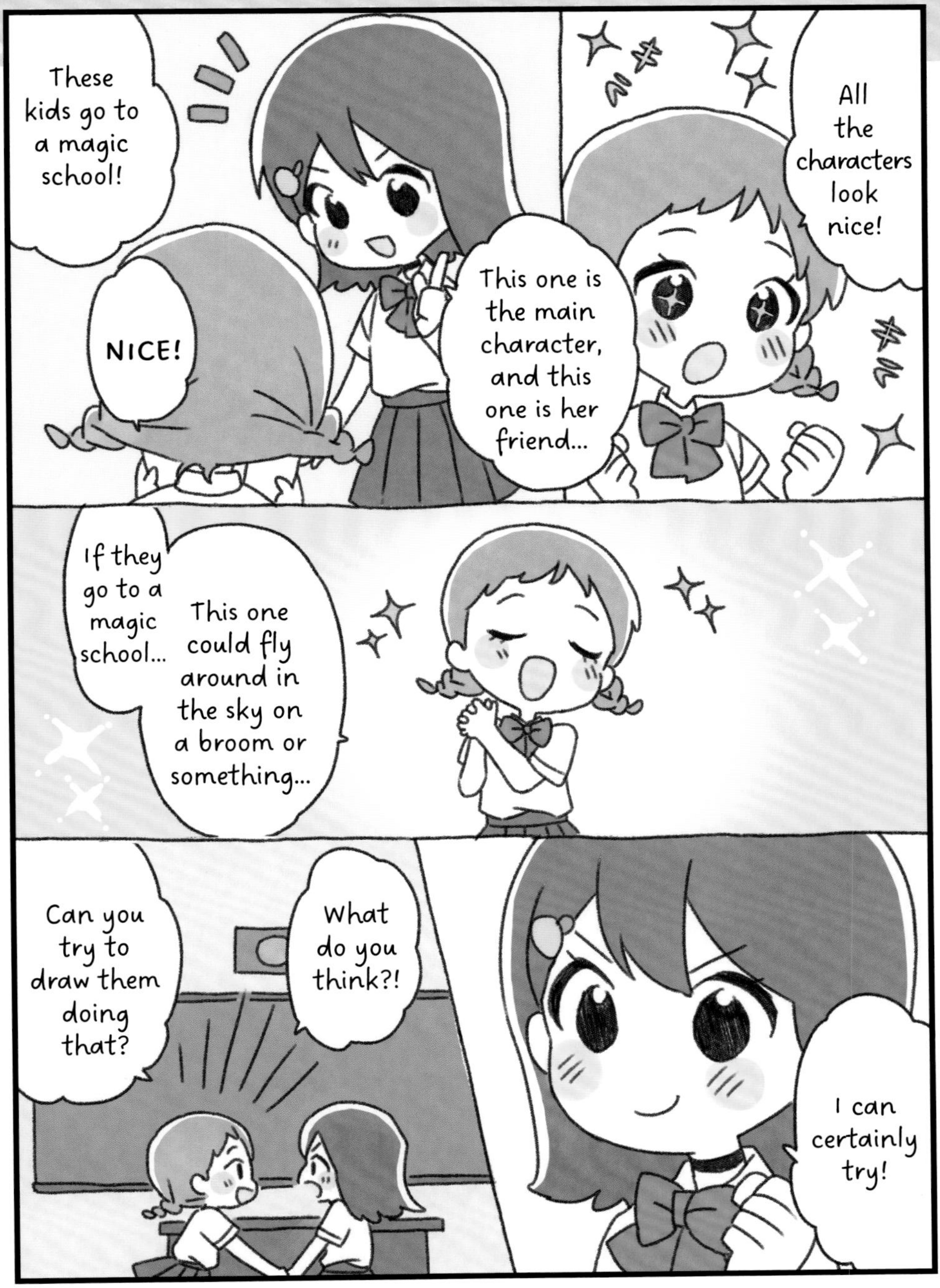
These kids go to a magic school!
NICE!
This one is the main character, and this one is her friend...
All the characters look nice!
If they go to a magic school...
This one could fly around in the sky on a broom or something...
Can you try to draw them doing that?
What do you think?!
I can certainly try!

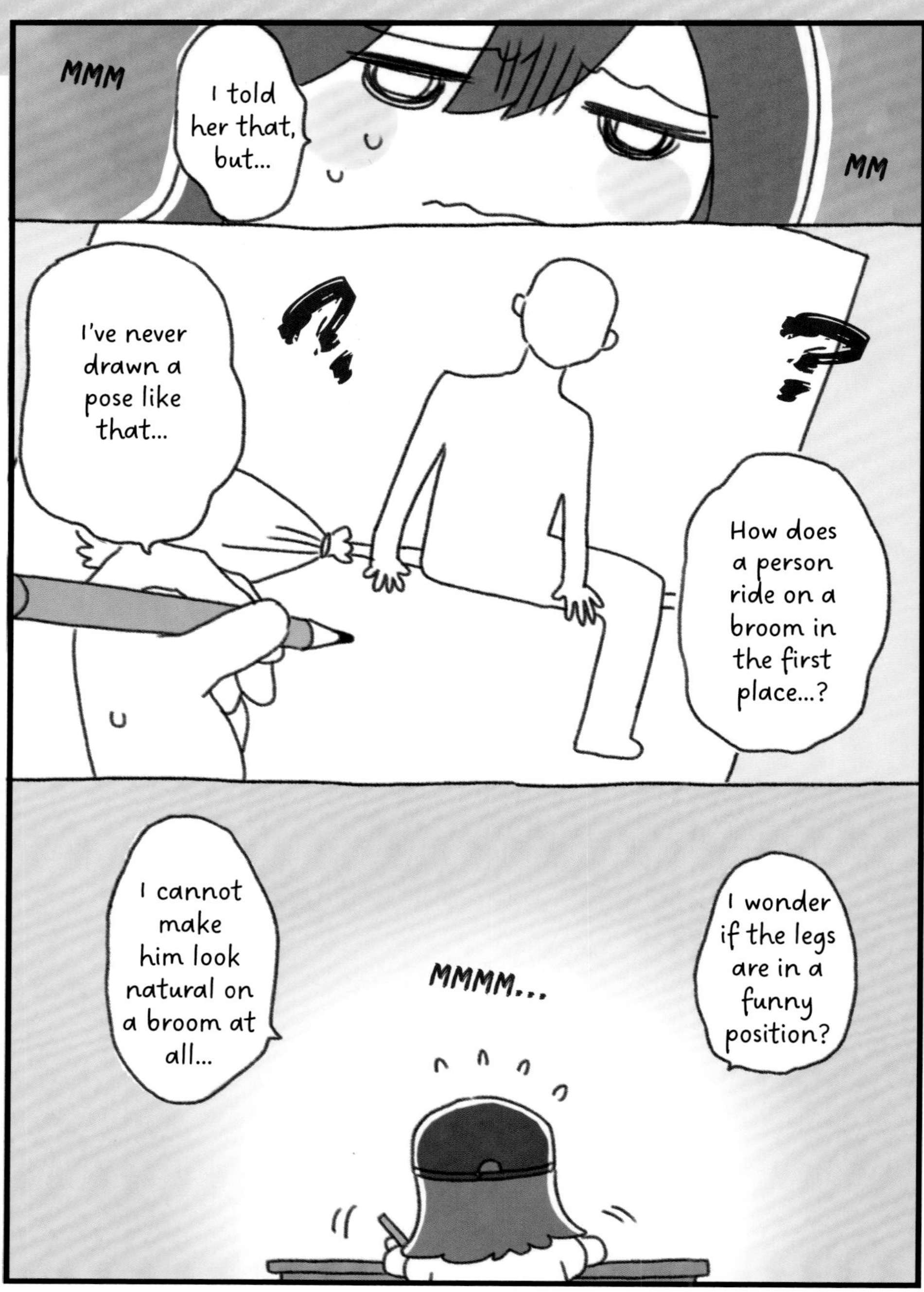
MMM
I told her that, but...
MM
I've never drawn a pose like that...
How does a person ride on a broom in the first place...?
I cannot make him look natural on a broom at all...
MMMM...
I wonder if the legs are in a funny position?

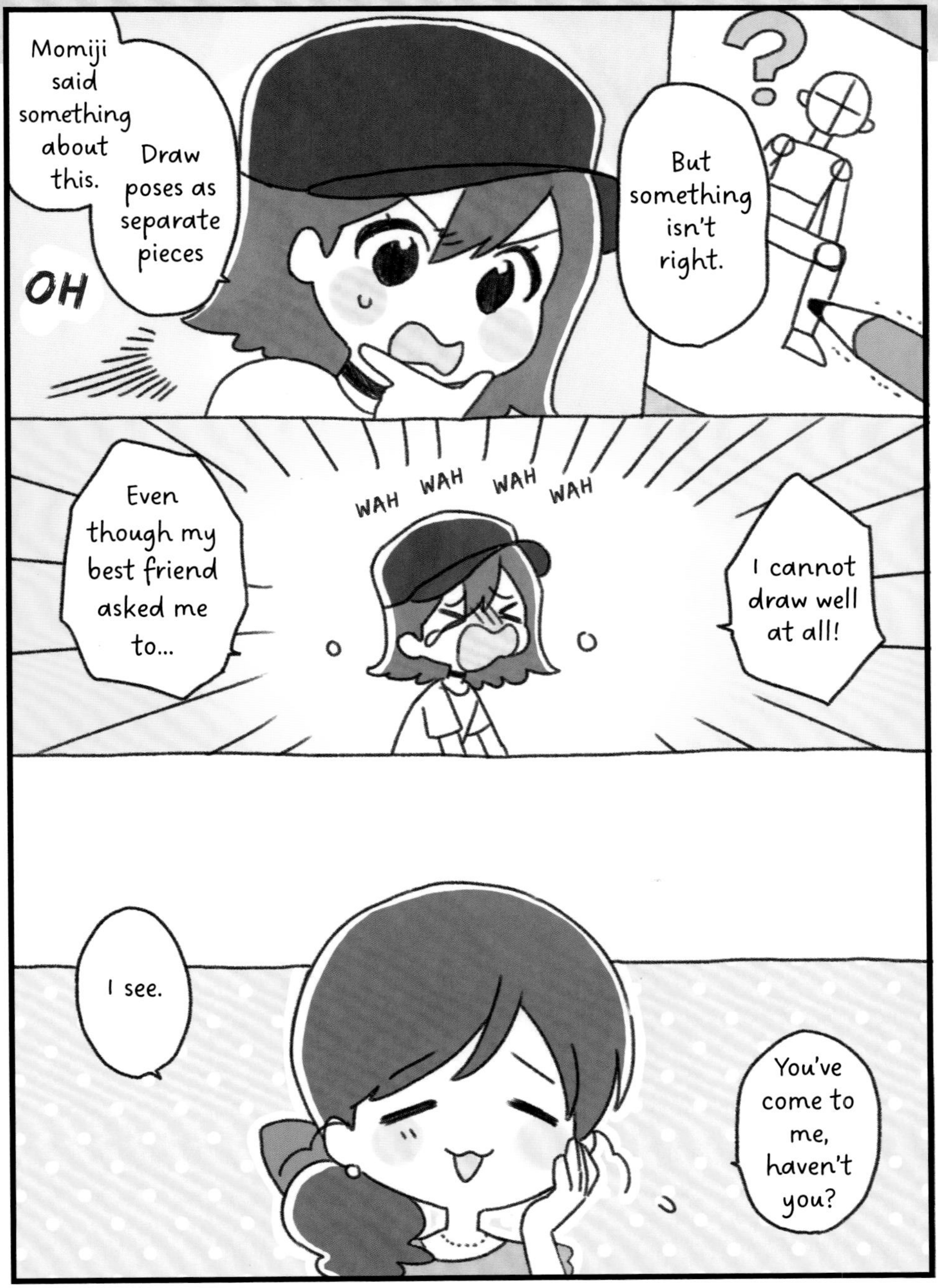
Momiji said something about this.
Draw poses as separate pieces
OH
But something isn't right.
?
Even though my best friend asked me to...
WAH WAH WAH WAH
I cannot draw well at all!
I see.
You've come to me, haven't you?

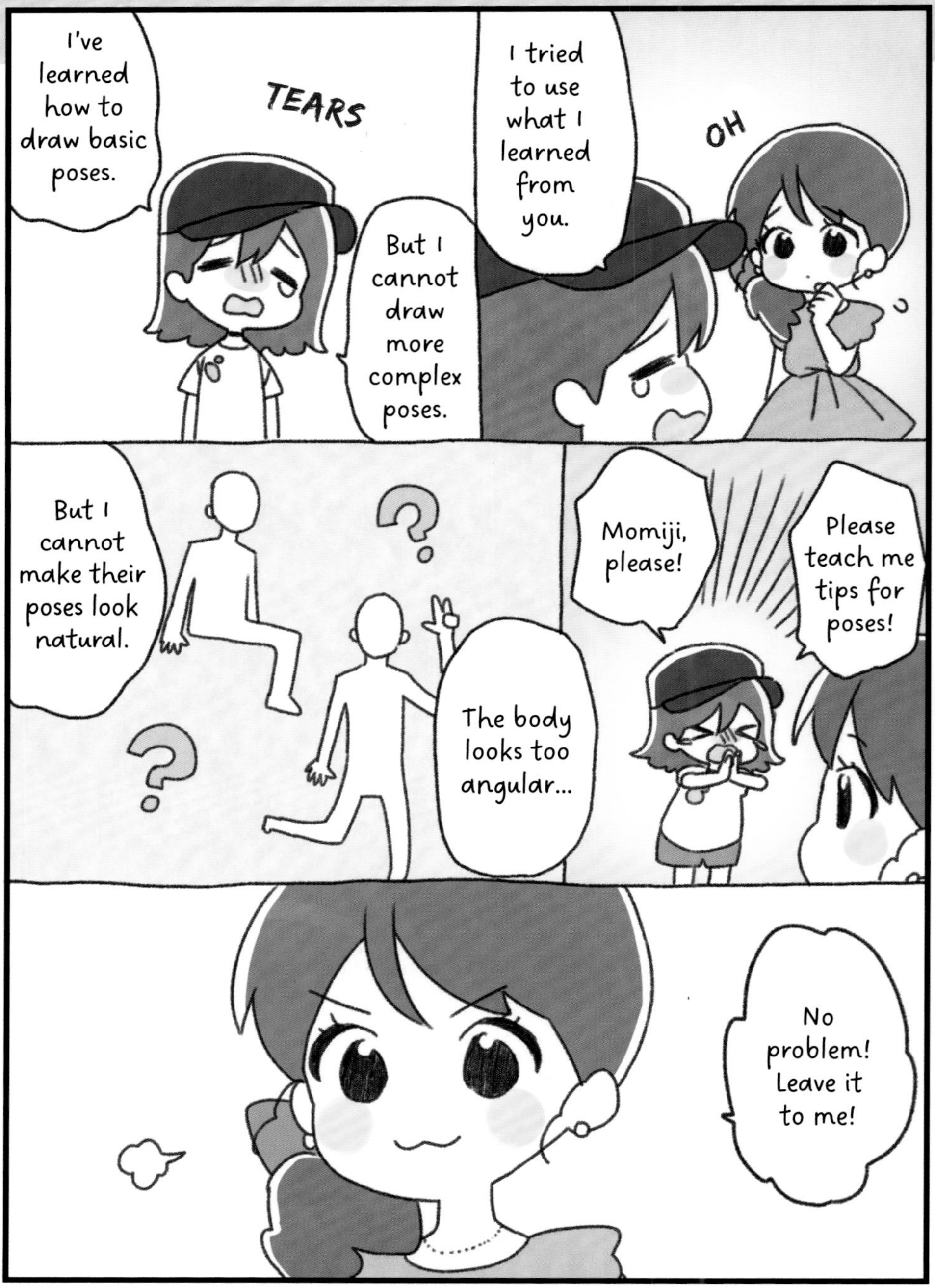
I've learned how to draw basic poses.
TEARS
But I cannot draw more complex poses.
I tried to use what I learned from you.
OH
But I cannot make their poses look natural.
The body looks too angular...
Momiji, please!
Please teach me tips for poses!
No problem! Leave it to me!

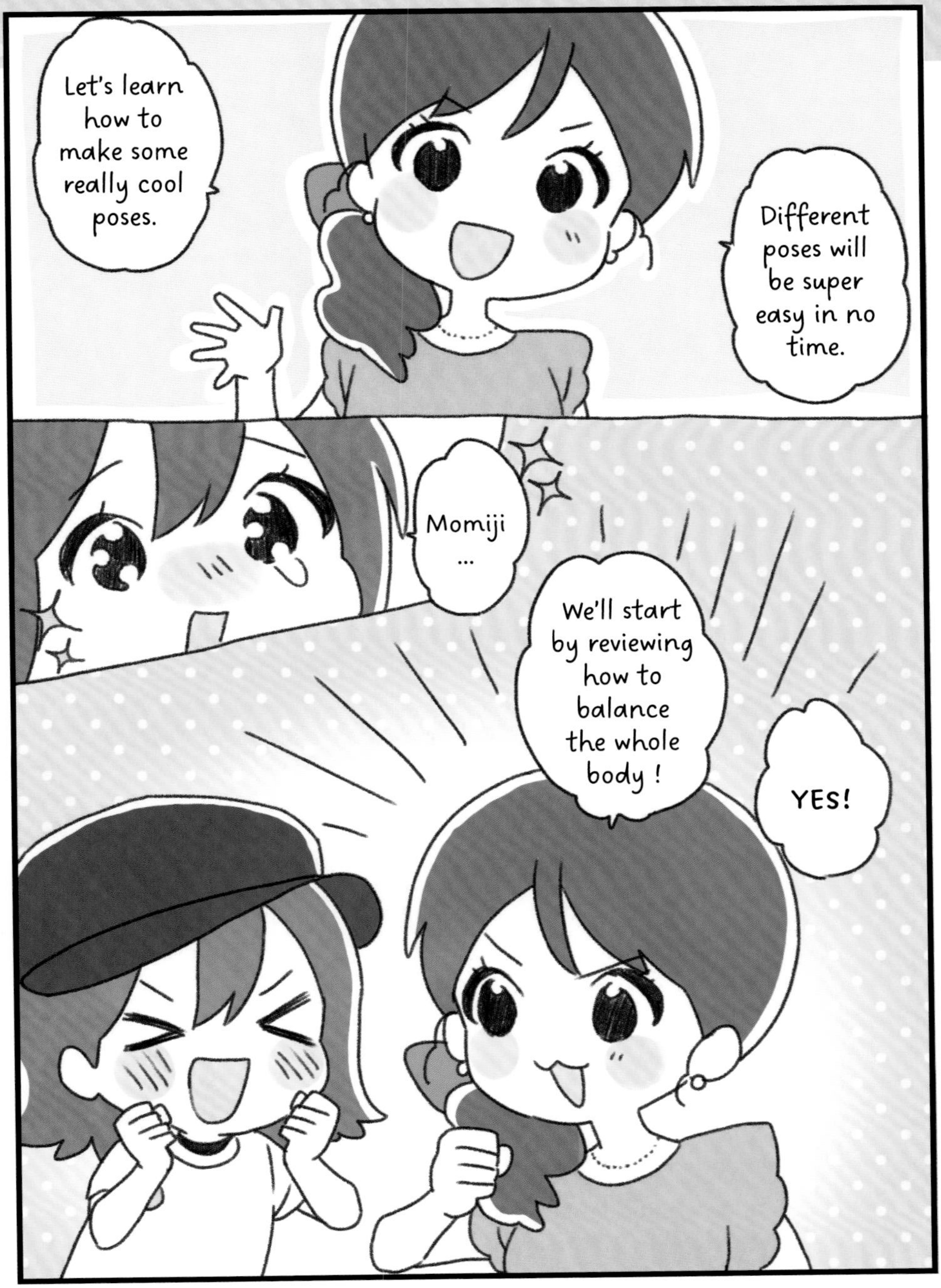
Let's learn how to make some really cool poses.
Different poses will be super easy in no time.
Momiji ...
We'll start by reviewing how to balance the whole body !
YES!

# CONTENTS



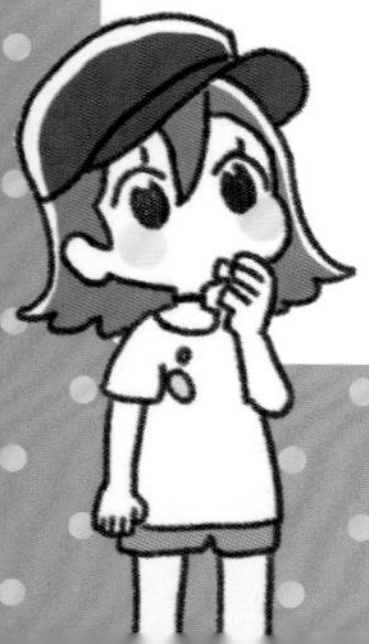

# THE MAIN CHARACTERS

Lemon is a 7th grader who doesn't stop when she gets onto something. She also has a cheerful and goofy side. She likes drawing and wants to be able to draw amazing pictures like her cousin Momiji.

Momiji, Lemon's cousin, is an illustrator in her 20s. Although she's sweet, she's also very reliable and can be strict sometimes too. She thinks Lemon is cute.

# WHAT TO DO WHEN YOU CANNOT DRAW POSES WELL

# CONSIDER THE BASIC WHOLE BODY BALANCE

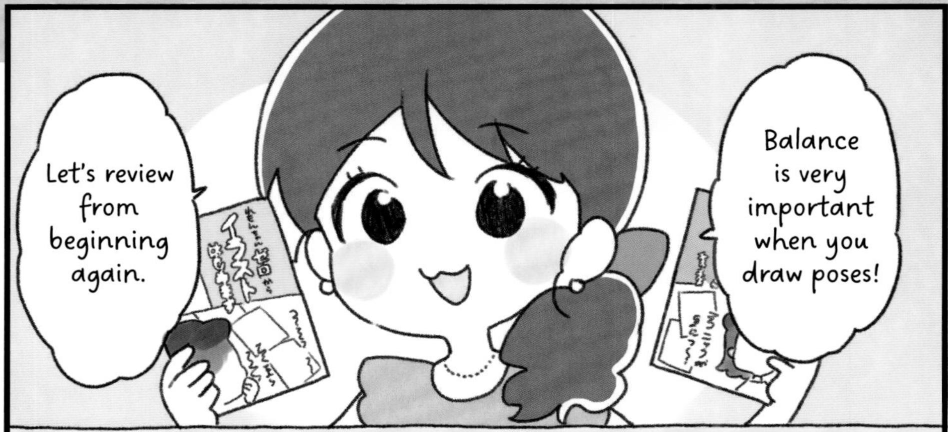
Let's review from beginning again.
Balance is very important when you draw poses!

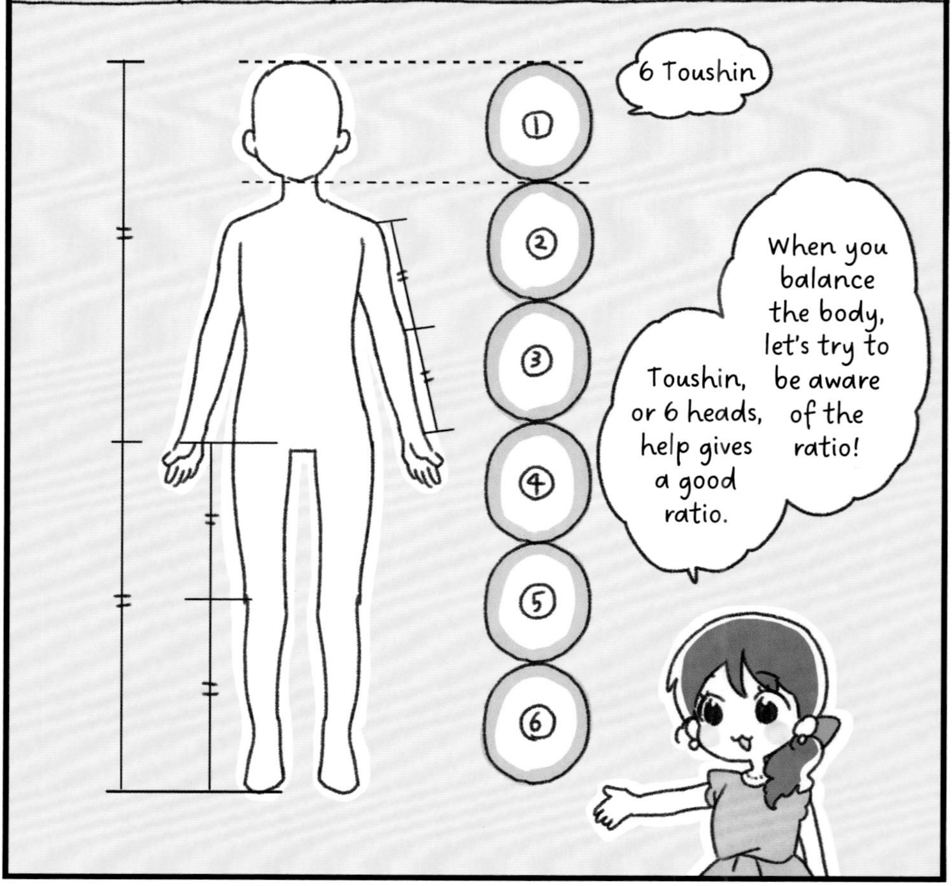
6 Toushin
①
②
③
④
⑤
⑥
When you balance the body, let's try to be aware of the ratio!
Toushin, or 6 heads, help gives a good ratio.

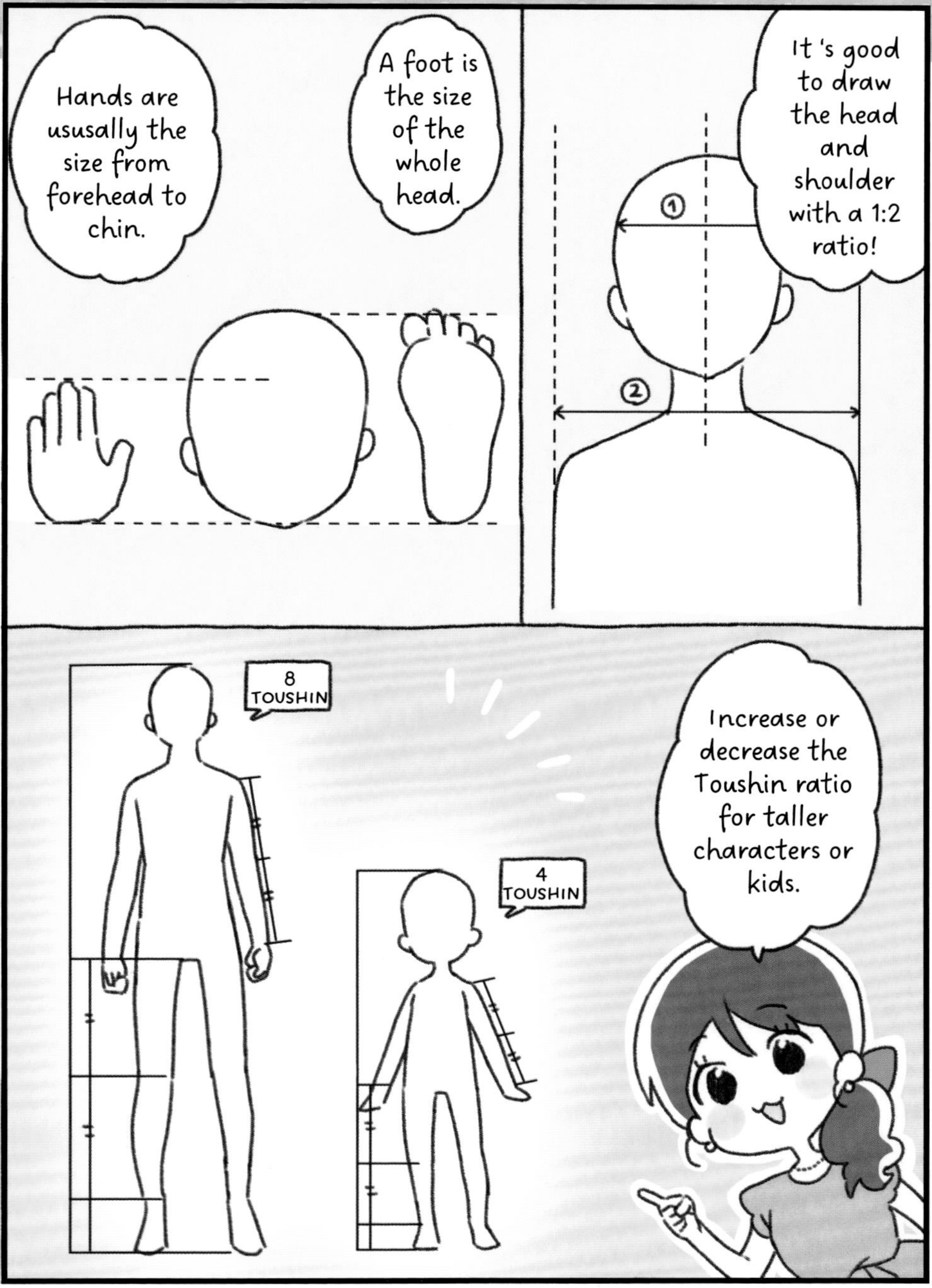
Hands are ususally the size from forehead to chin.
A foot is the size of the whole head.
It's good to draw the head and shoulder with a 1:2 ratio!
①
②
8 TOUSHIN
4 TOUSHIN
Increase or decrease the Toushin ratio for taller characters or kids.

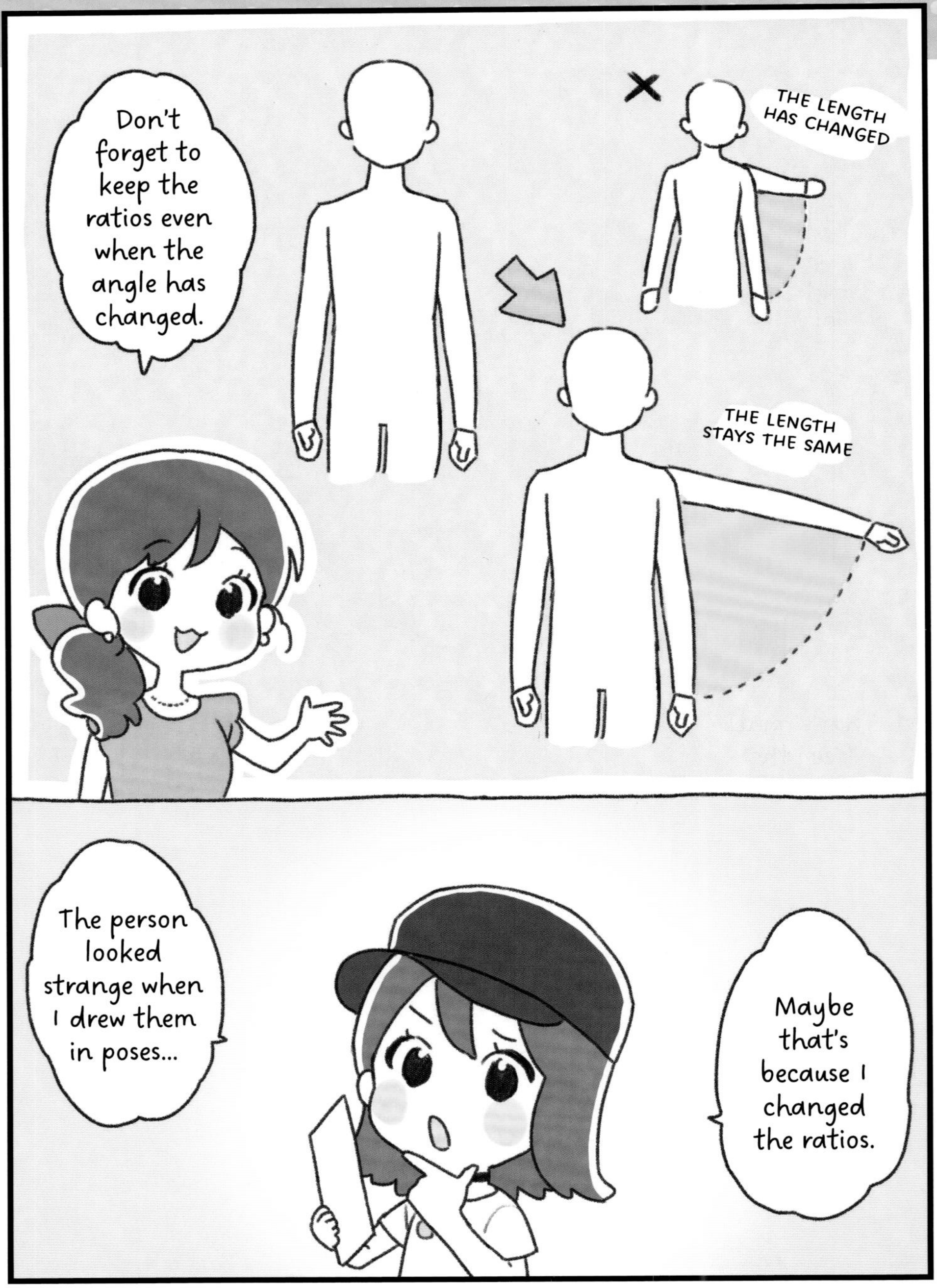
Don't forget to keep the ratios even when the angle has changed.
THE LENGTH HAS CHANGED
THE LENGTH STAYS THE SAME
The person looked strange when I drew them in poses...
Maybe that's because I changed the ratios.

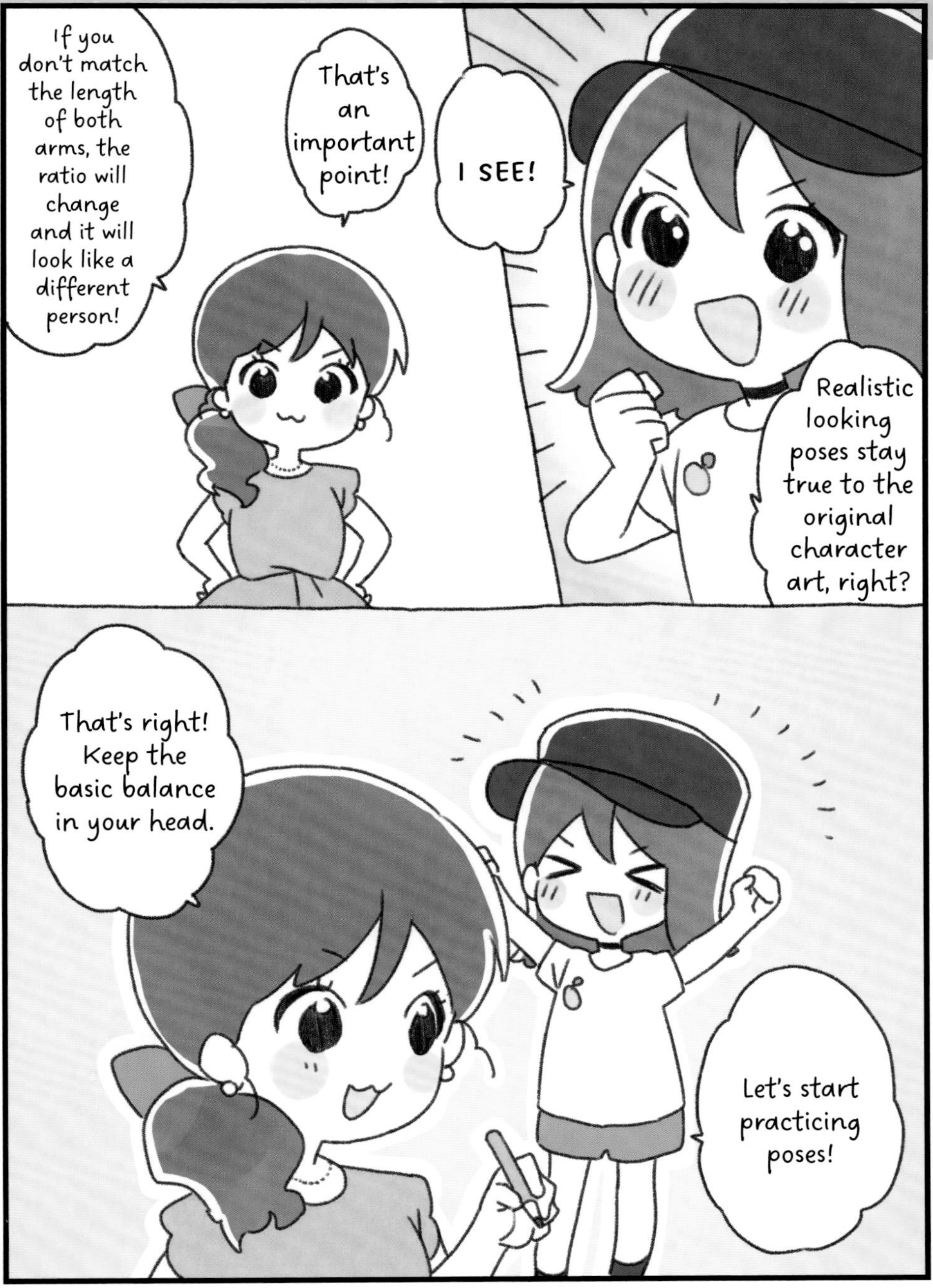
If you don't match the length of both arms, the ratio will change and it will look like a different person!
That's an important point!
I SEE!
Realistic looking poses stay true to the original character art, right?
That's right! Keep the basic balance in your head.
Let's start practicing poses!

# POSE BY YOURSELF

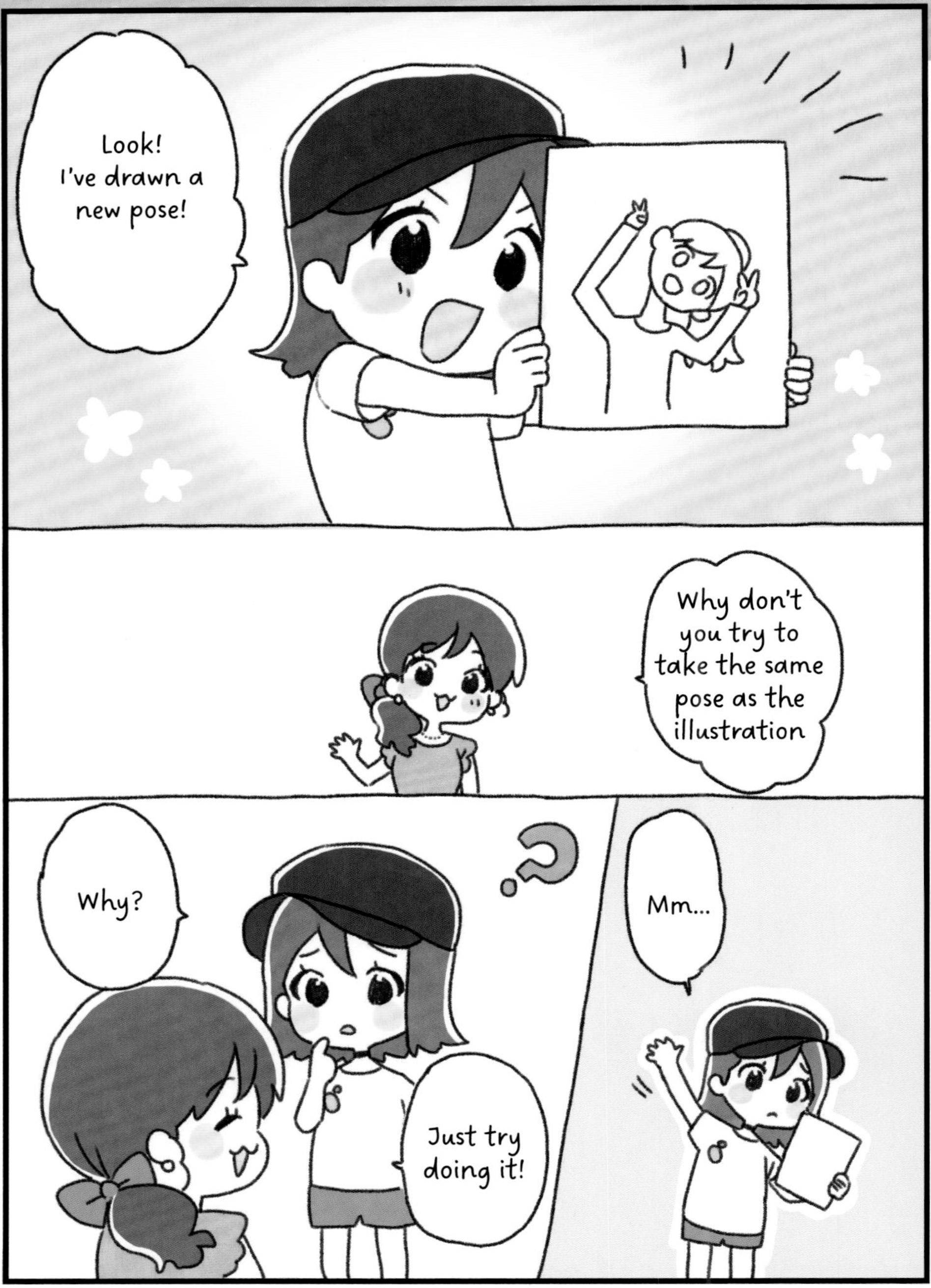
Look! I've drawn a new pose!
Why don't you try to take the same pose as the illustration
Why?
Just try doing it!
Mm...

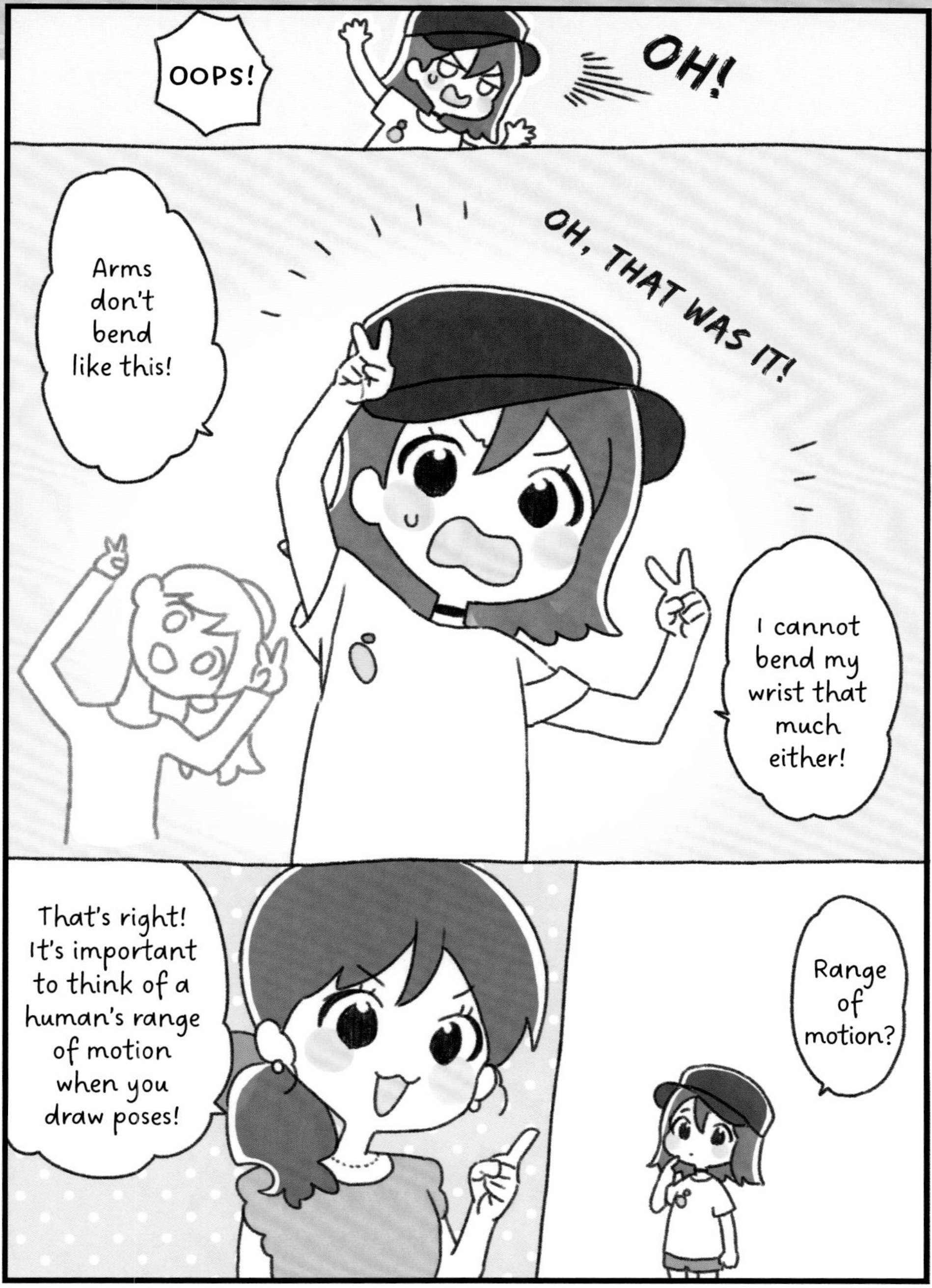
OOPS!
OH!
OH, THAT WAS IT!
Arms don't bend like this!
I cannot bend my wrist that much either!
That's right! It's important to think of a human's range of motion when you draw poses!
Range of motion?

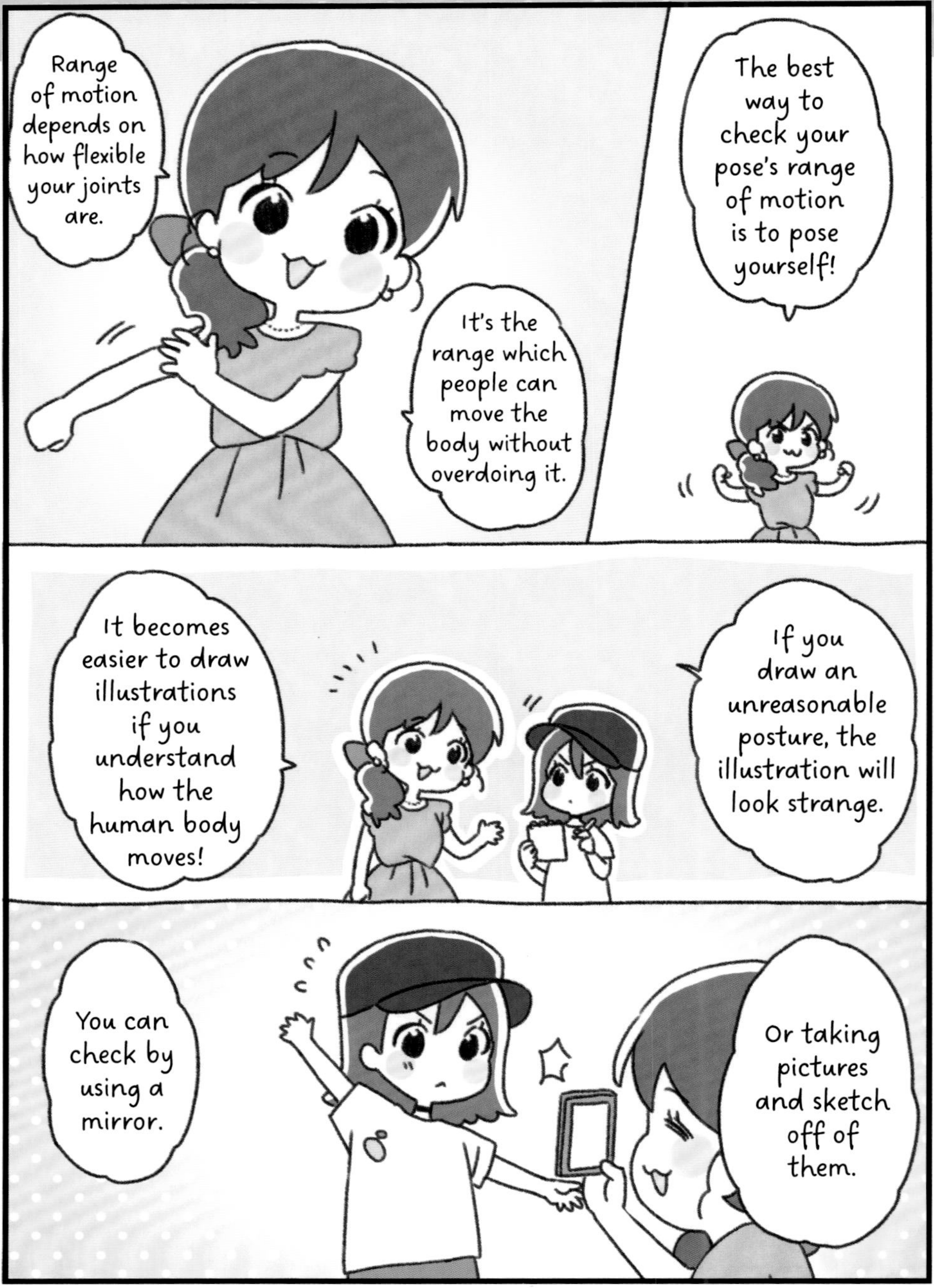
Range of motion depends on how flexible your joints are.
It's the range which people can move the body without overdoing it.
The best way to check your pose's range of motion is to pose yourself!
It becomes easier to draw illustrations if you understand how the human body moves!
If you draw an unreasonable posture, the illustration will look strange.
You can check by using a mirror.
Or taking pictures and sketch off of them.

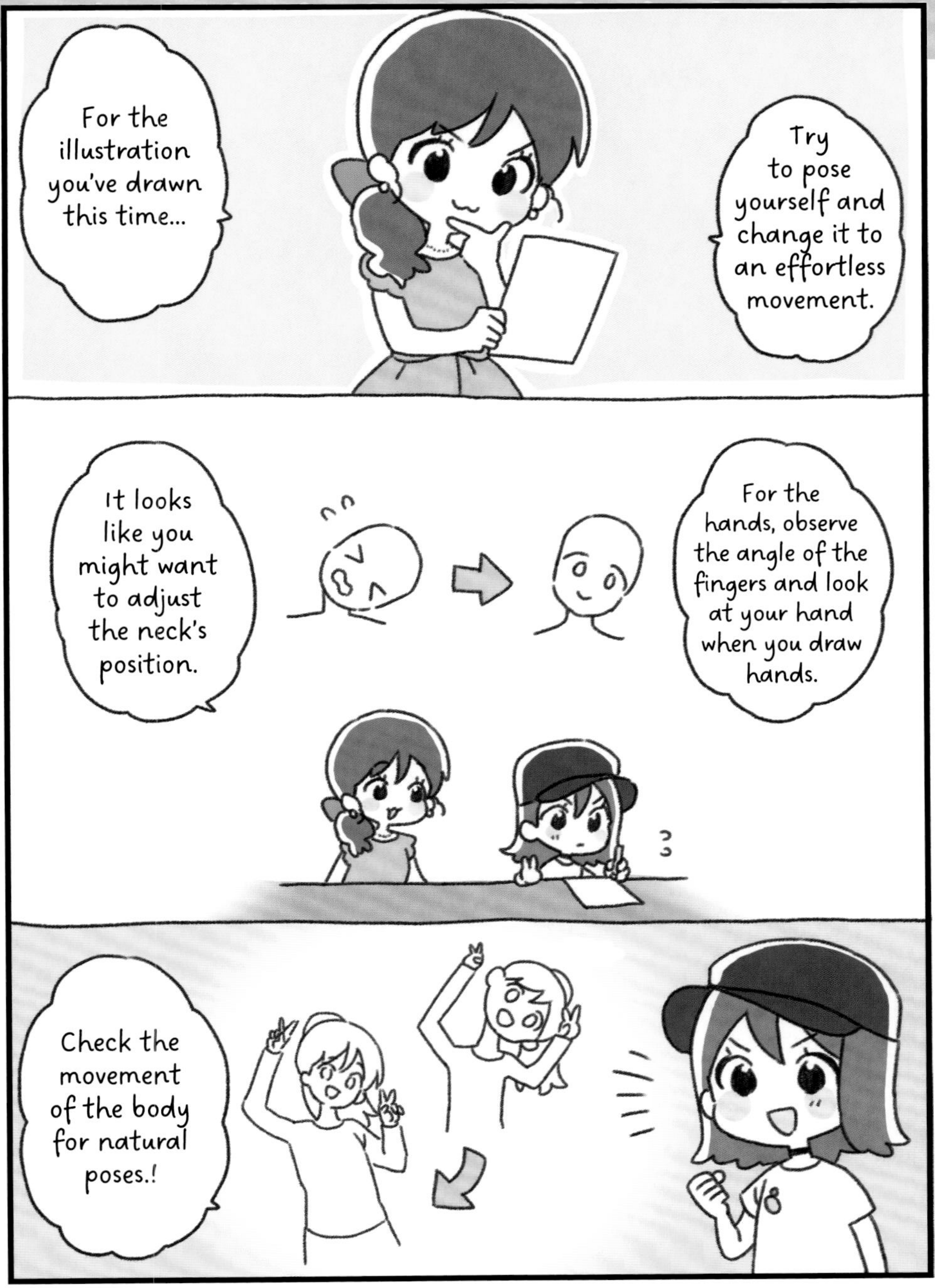
For the illustration you've drawn this time...
Try to pose yourself and change it to an effortless movement.
It looks like you might want to adjust the neck's position.
For the hands, observe the angle of the fingers and look at your hand when you draw hands.
Check the movement of the body for natural poses.!

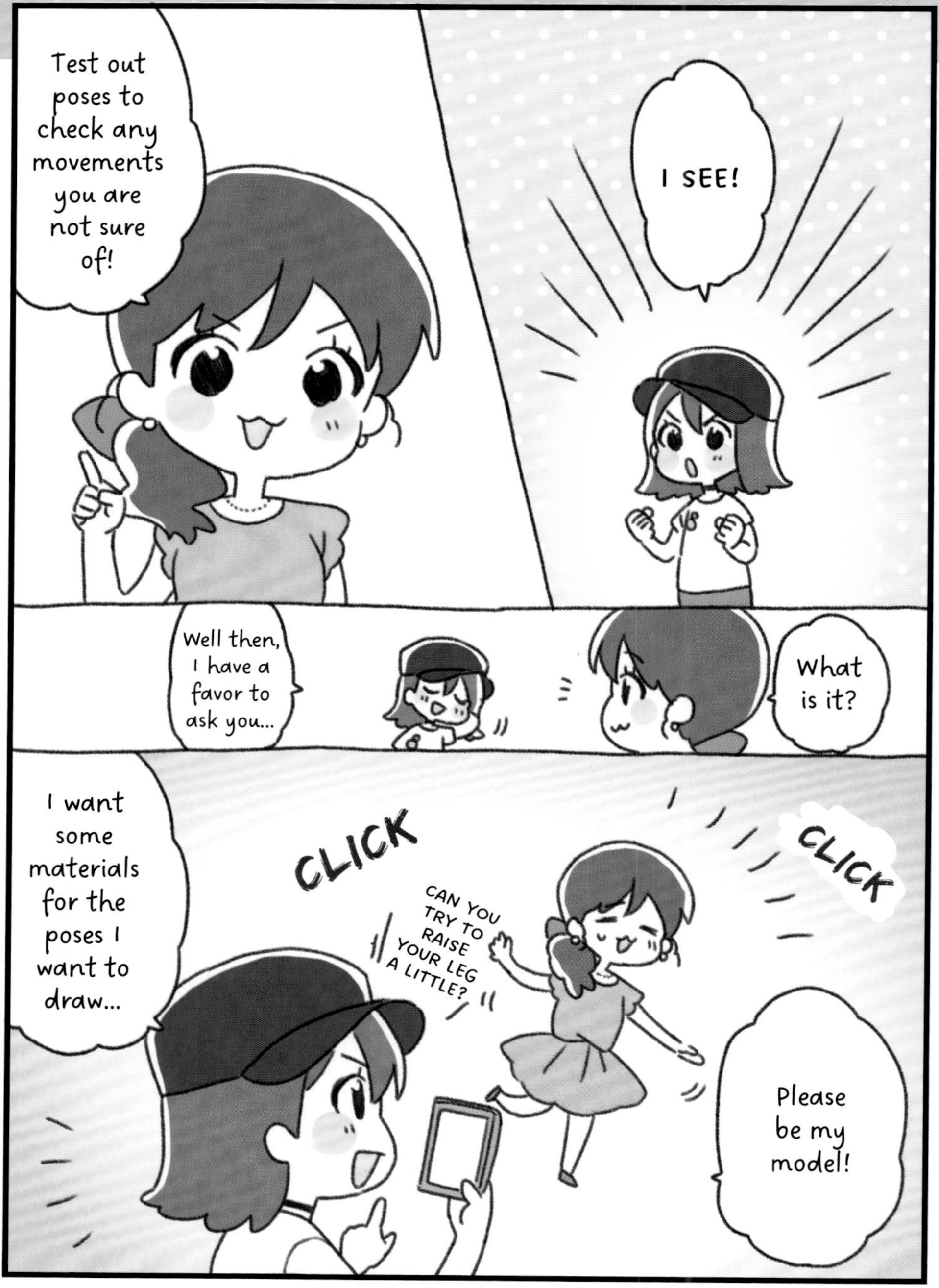
Test out poses to check any movements you are not sure of!
I SEE!
Well then, I have a favor to ask you...
What is it?
I want some materials for the poses I want to draw...
CLICK
CLICK
CAN YOU TRY TO RAISE YOUR LEG A LITTLE?
Please be my model!

## SUMMARY

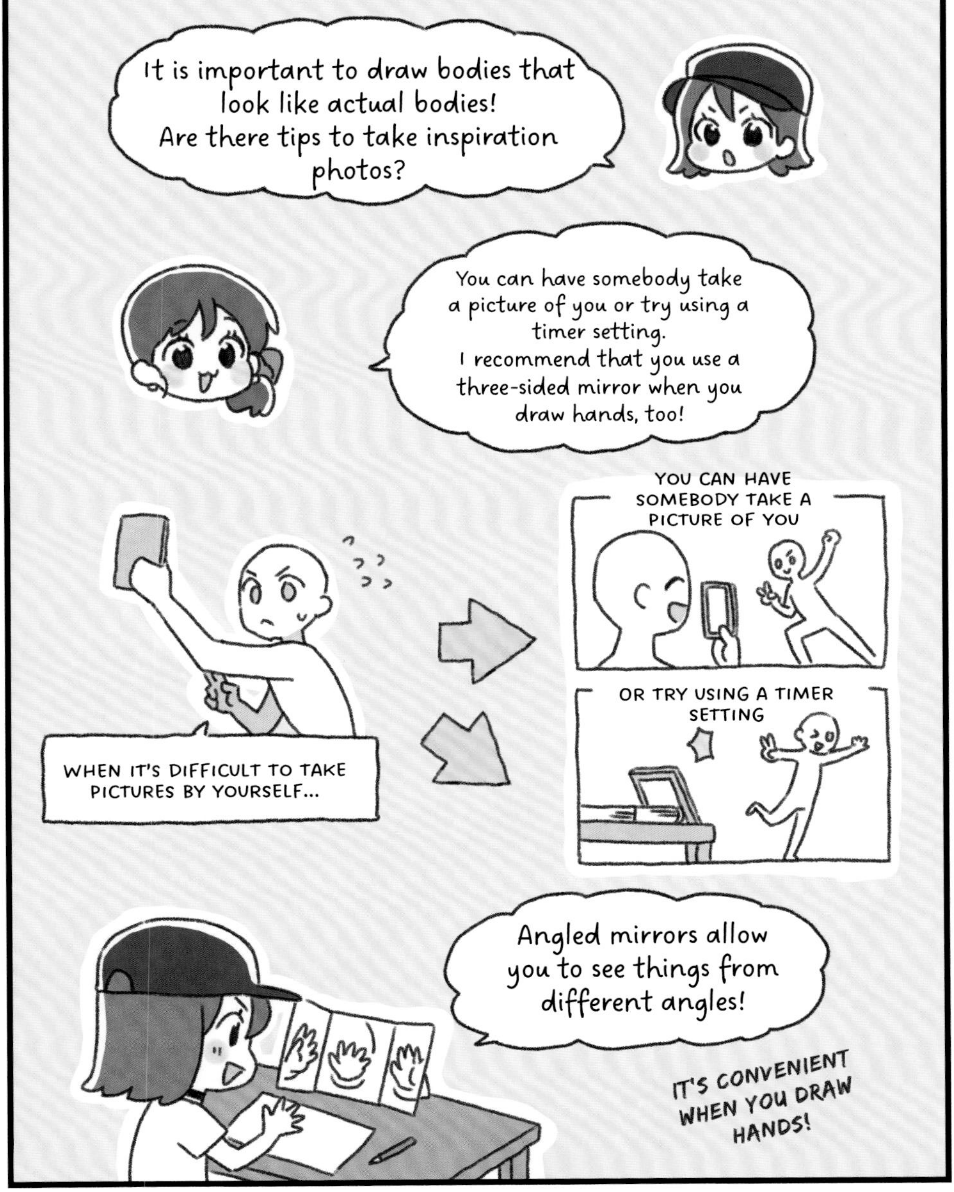
It is important to draw bodies that look like actual bodies! Are there tips to take inspiration photos?
You can have somebody take a picture of you or try using a timer setting. I recommend that you use a three-sided mirror when you draw hands, too!
WHEN IT'S DIFFICULT TO TAKE PICTURES BY YOURSELF...
YOU CAN HAVE SOMEBODY TAKE A PICTURE OF YOU
OR TRY USING A TIMER SETTING
Angled mirrors allow you to see things from different angles!
IT'S CONVENIENT WHEN YOU DRAW HANDS!

# DIFFERENTIATING BETWEEN MEN'S AND WOMEN'S BALANCE

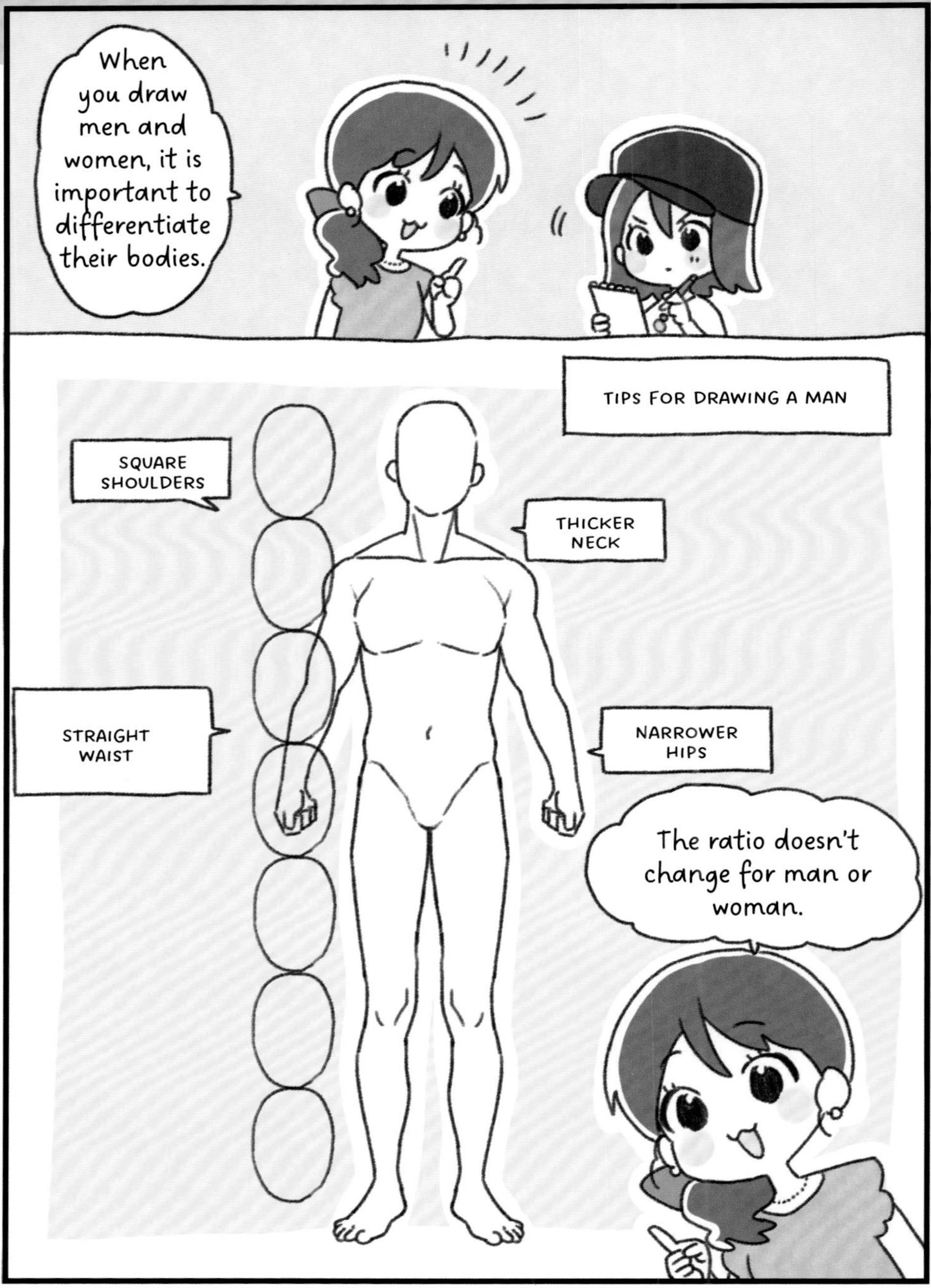
When you draw men and women, it is important to differentiate their bodies.
TIPS FOR DRAWING A MAN
SQUARE SHOULDERS
THICKER NECK
STRAIGHT WAIST
NARROWER HIPS
The ratio doesn't change for man or woman.

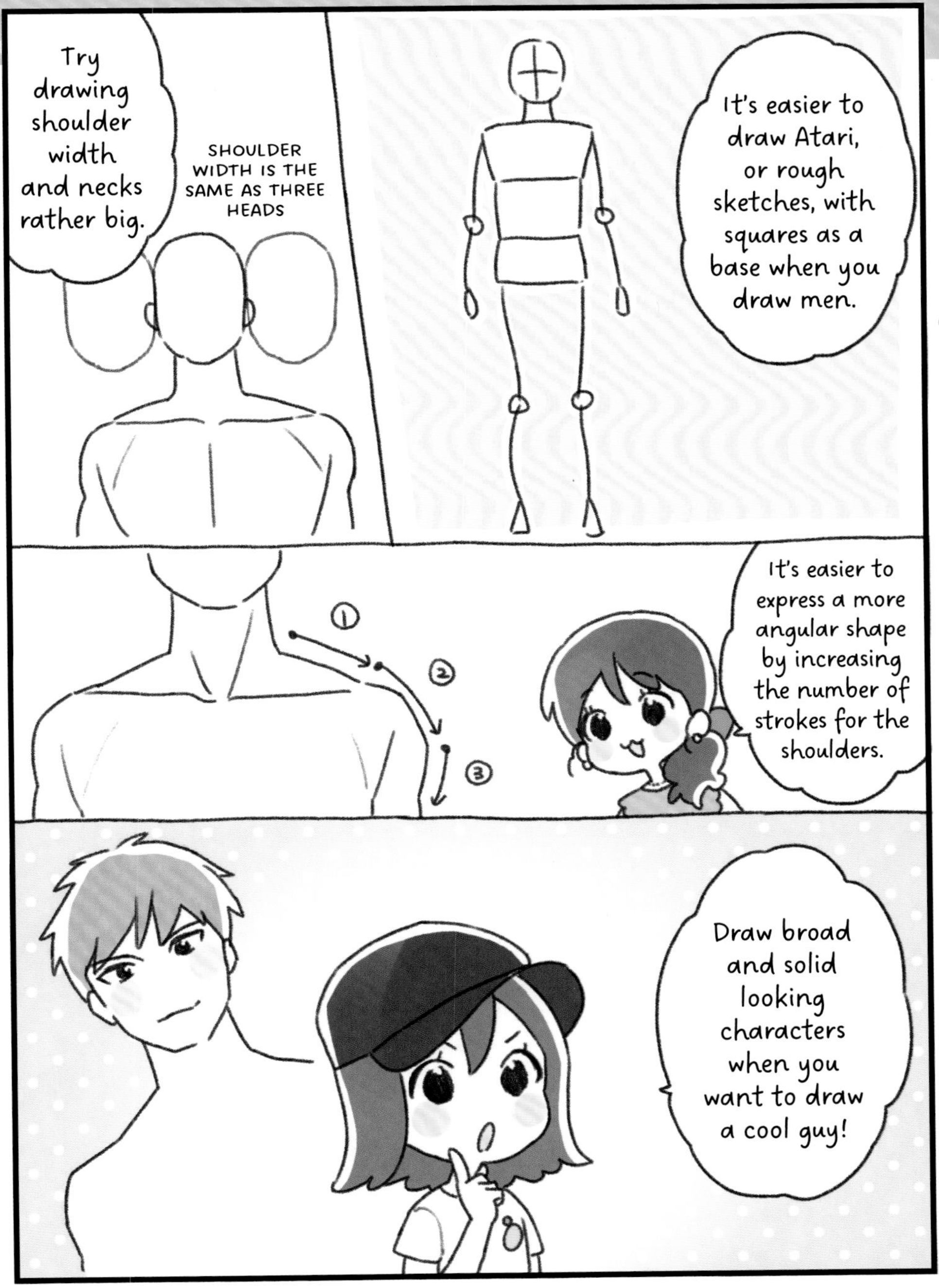
Try drawing shoulder width and necks rather big.
SHOULDER WIDTH IS THE SAME AS THREE HEADS
It's easier to draw Atari, or rough sketches, with squares as a base when you draw men.
①
②
③
It's easier to express a more angular shape by increasing the number of strokes for the shoulders.
Draw broad and solid looking characters when you want to draw a cool guy!

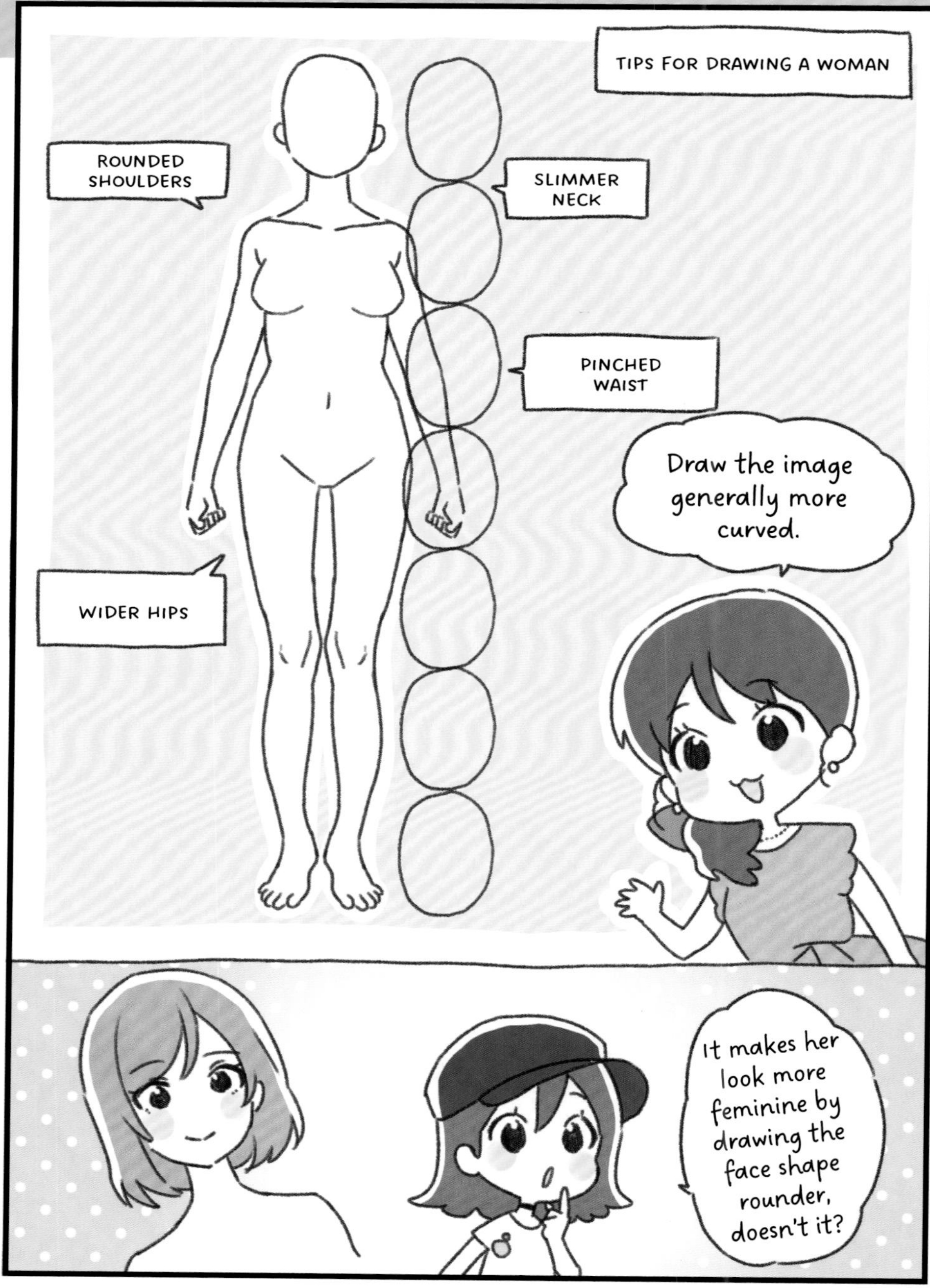
TIPS FOR DRAWING A WOMAN
ROUNDED SHOULDERS
SLIMMER NECK
PINCHED WAIST
WIDER HIPS
Draw the image generally more curved.
It makes her look more feminine by drawing the face shape rounder, doesn't it?

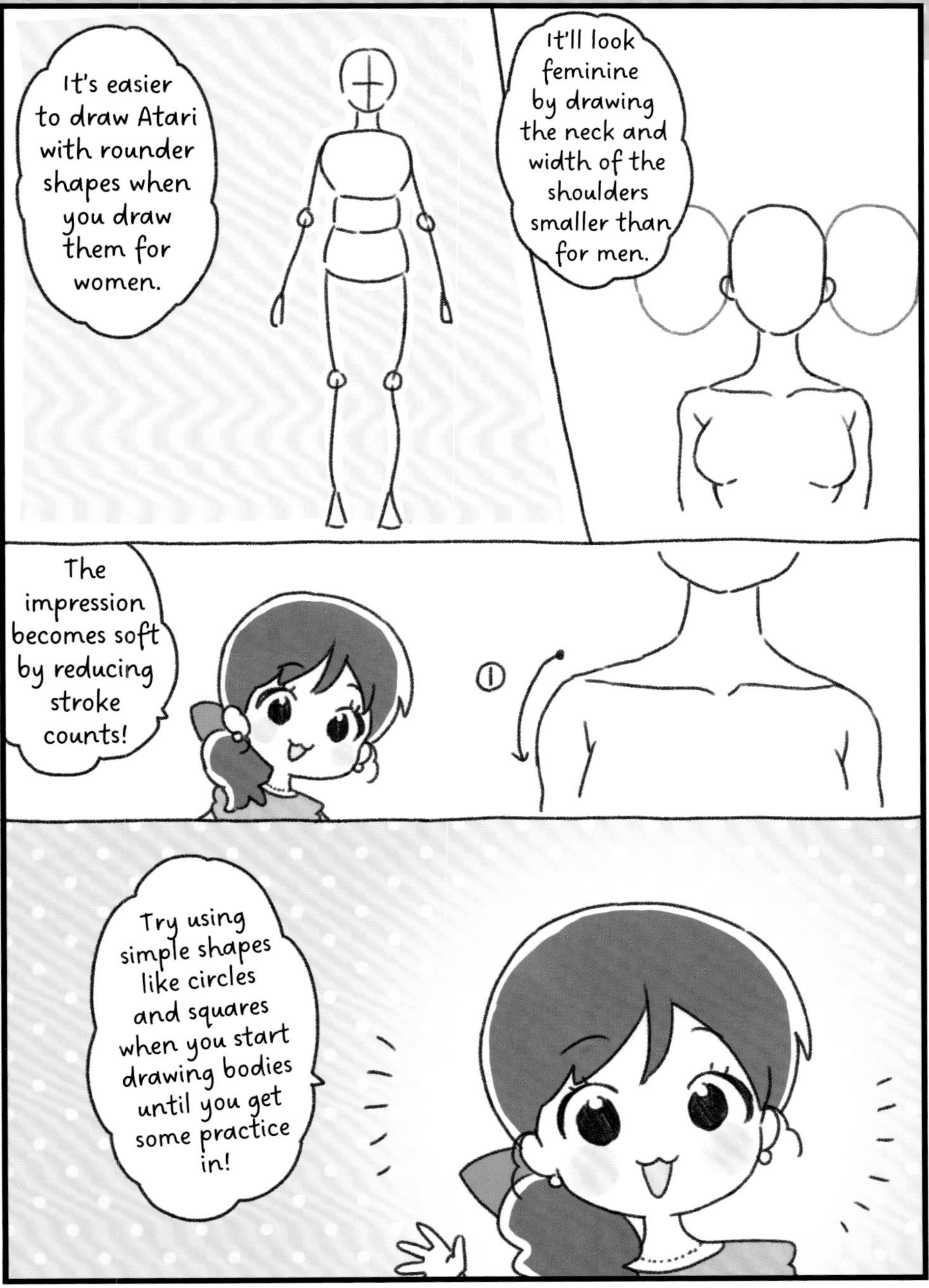
It's easier to draw Atari with rounder shapes when you draw them for women.
It'll look feminine by drawing the neck and width of the shoulders smaller than for men.
The impression becomes soft by reducing stroke counts!
①
Try using simple shapes like circles and squares when you start drawing bodies until you get some practice in!

# SUMMARY

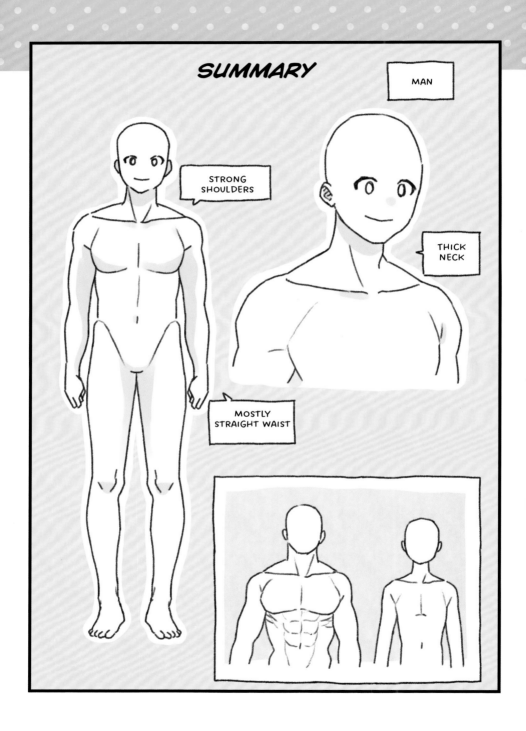

MAN

STRONG SHOULDERS

THICK NECK

MOSTLY STRAIGHT WAIST

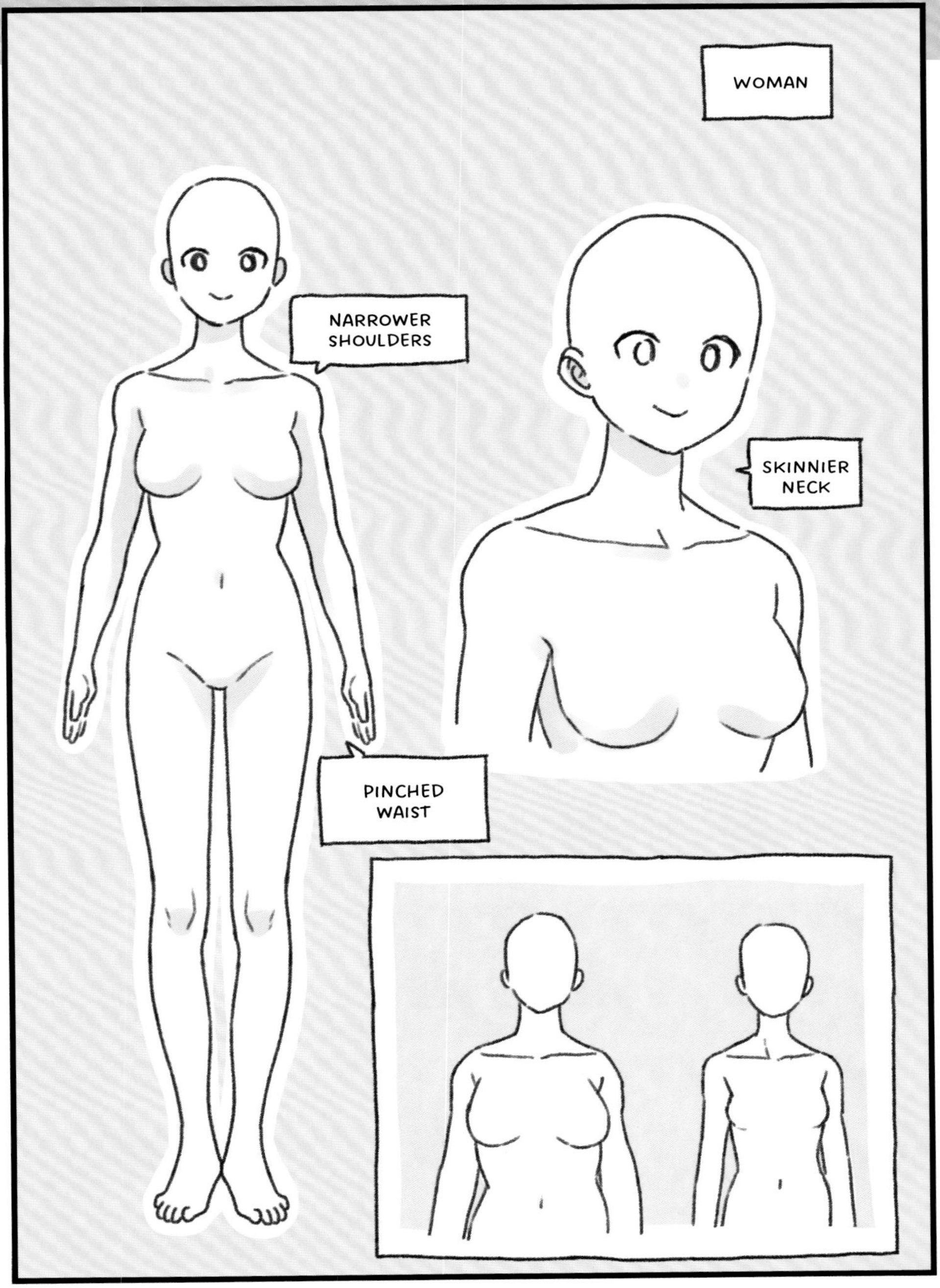
WOMAN
NARROWER SHOULDERS
SKINNIER NECK
PINCHED WAIST

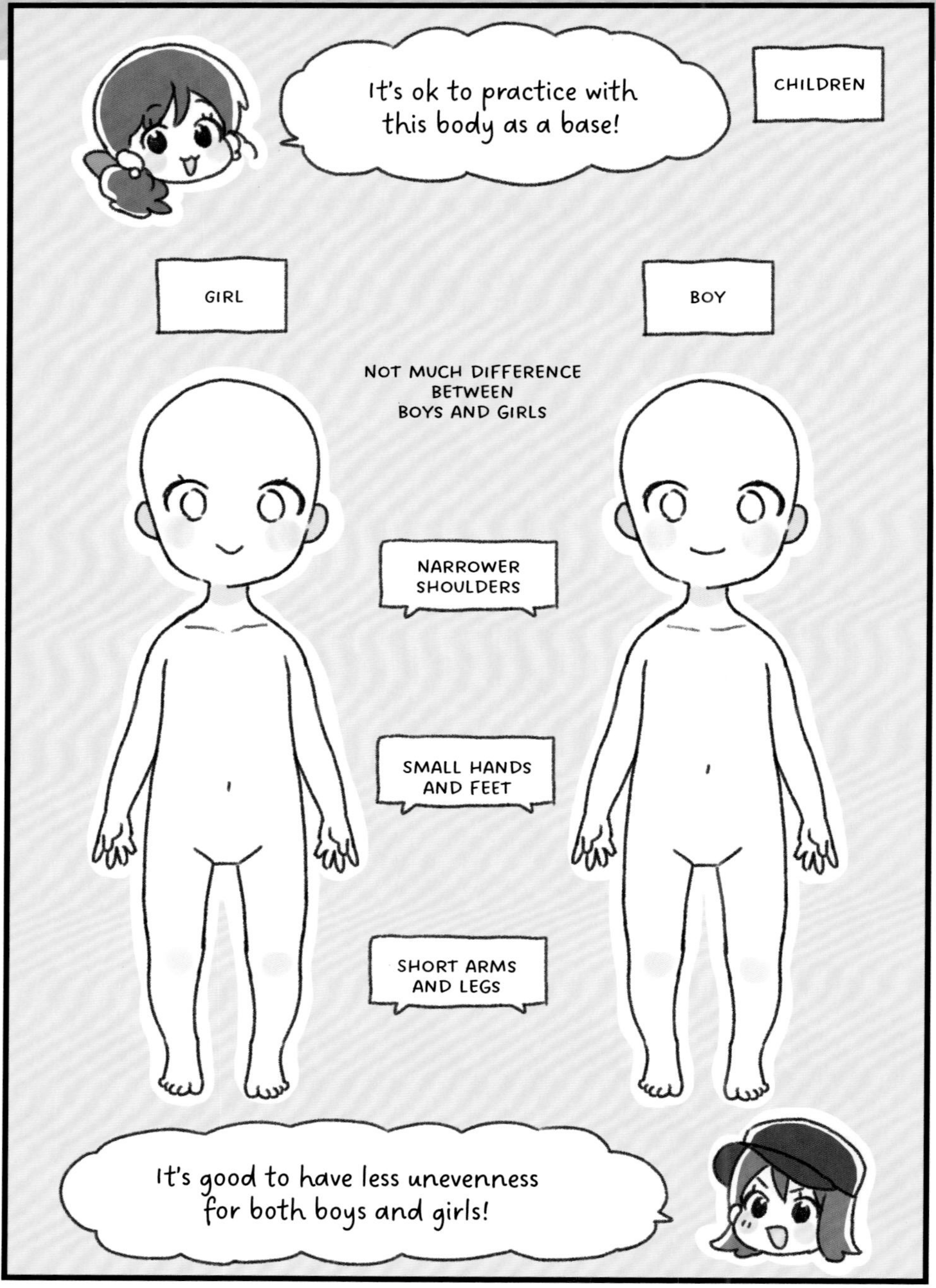
It's ok to practice with this body as a base!
CHILDREN
GIRL
BOY
NOT MUCH DIFFERENCE BETWEEN BOYS AND GIRLS
NARROWER SHOULDERS
SMALL HANDS AND FEET
SHORT ARMS AND LEGS
It's good to have less unevenness for both boys and girls!

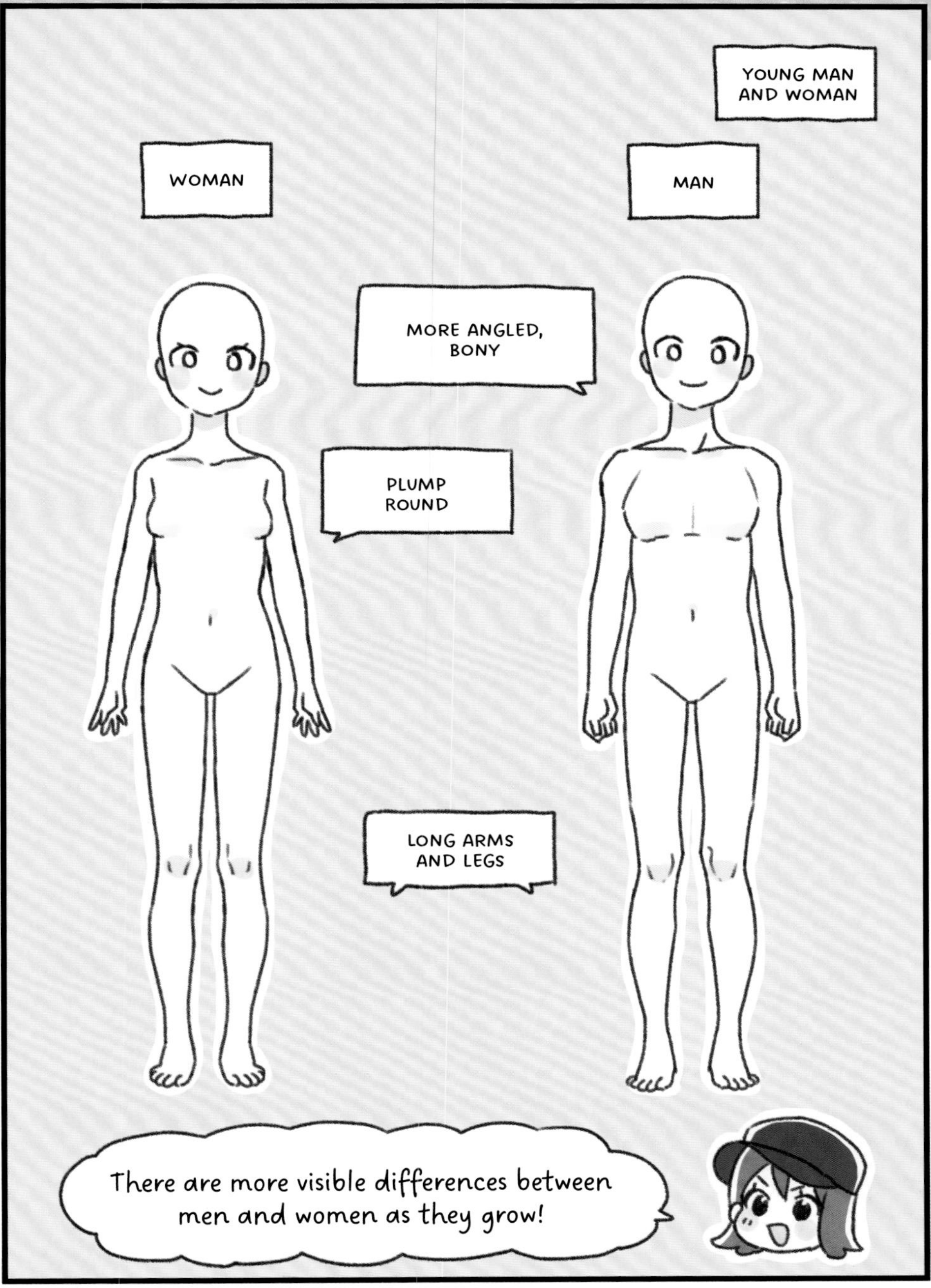
YOUNG MAN AND WOMAN
WOMAN
MAN
MORE ANGLED, BONY
PLUMP ROUND
LONG ARMS AND LEGS
There are more visible differences between men and women as they grow!

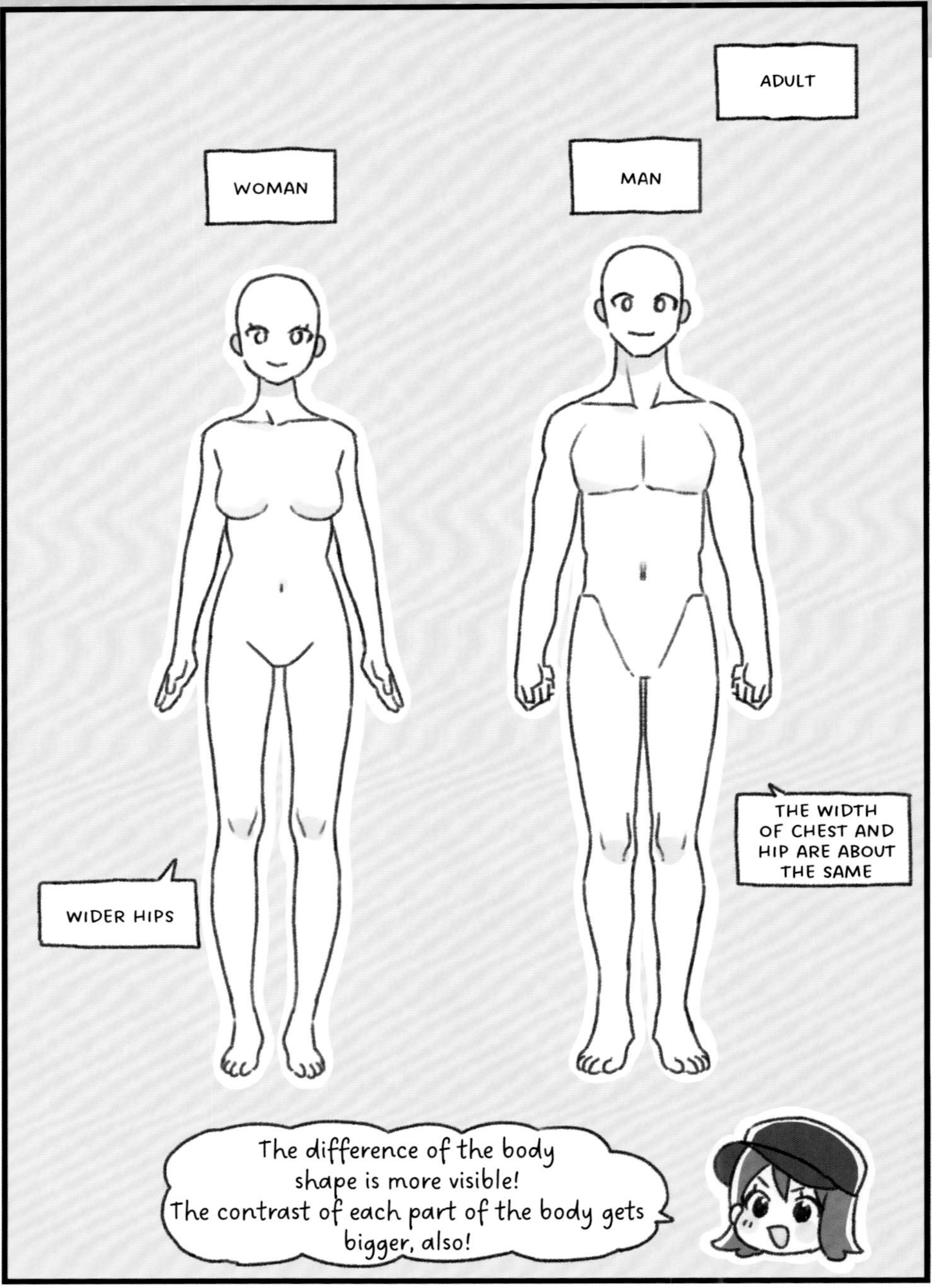
ADULT
WOMAN
MAN
THE WIDTH OF CHEST AND HIP ARE ABOUT THE SAME
WIDER HIPS
The difference of the body shape is more visible! The contrast of each part of the body gets bigger, also!

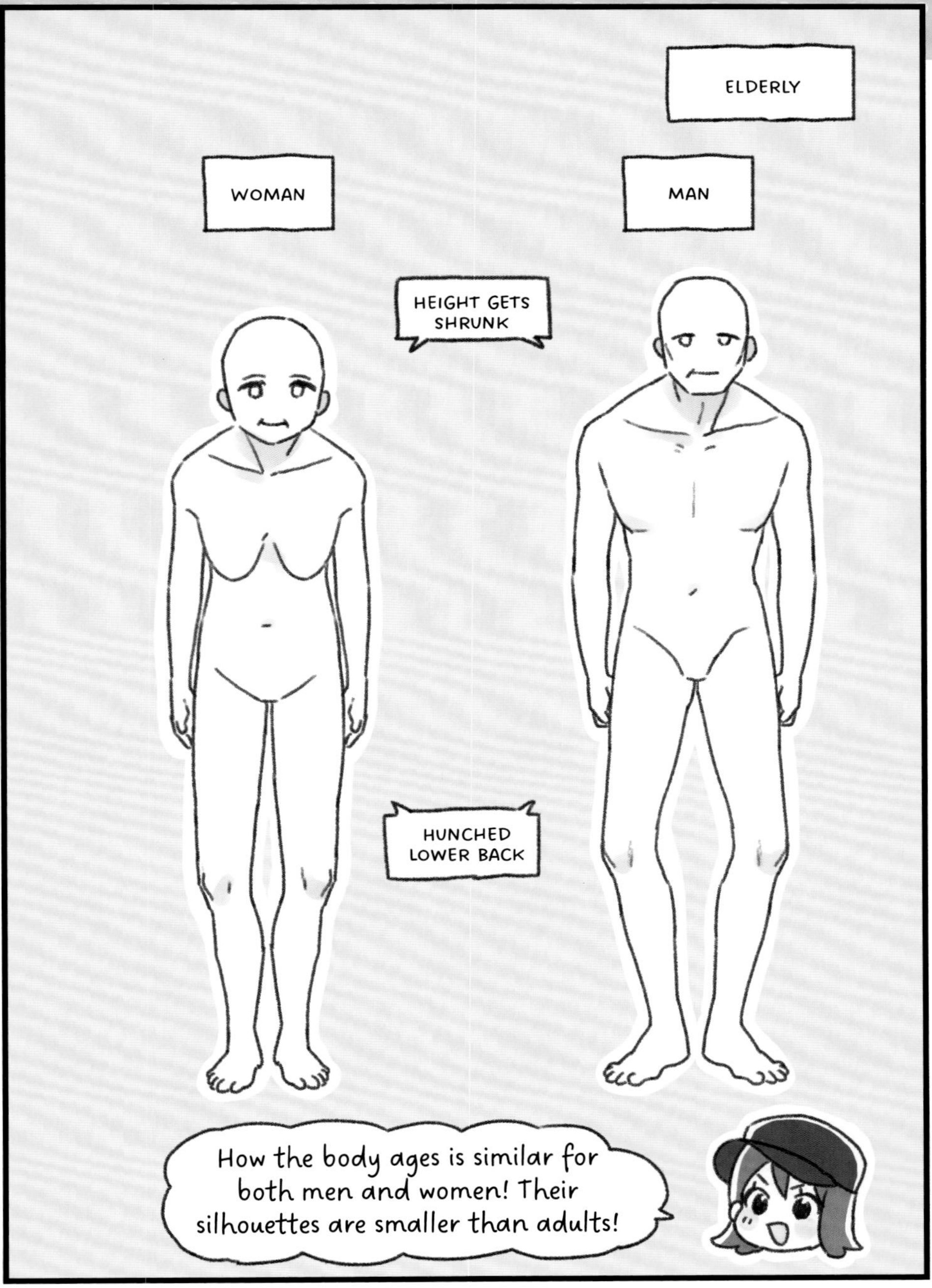
ELDERLY
WOMAN
MAN
HEIGHT GETS SHRUNK
HUNCHED LOWER BACK
How the body ages is similar for both men and women! Their silhouettes are smaller than adults!

# SURPRISINGLY, PEOPLE DO NOT STAND STRAIGHT

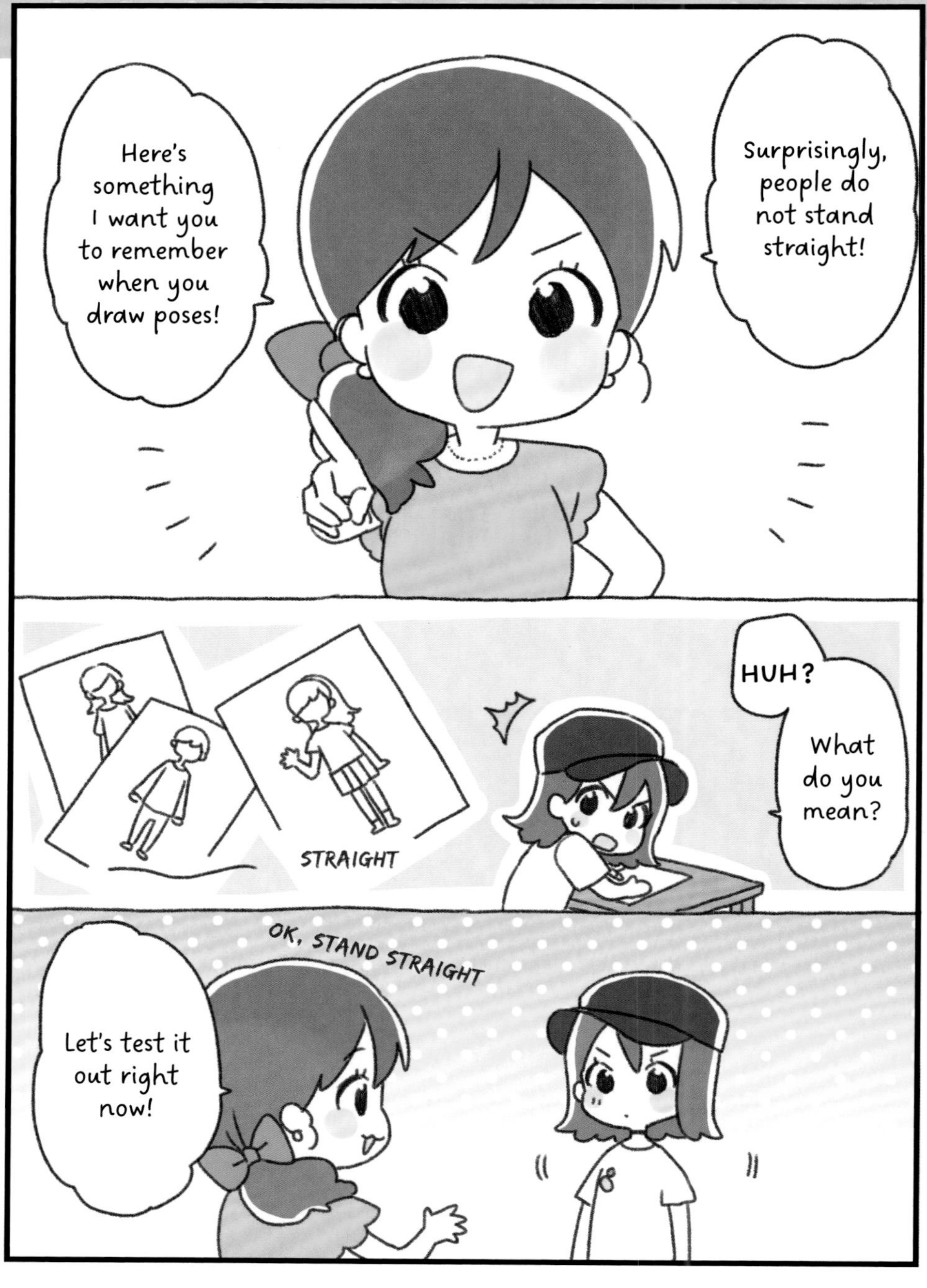
Here's something I want you to remember when you draw poses!
Surprisingly, people do not stand straight!
HUH?
What do you mean?
STRAIGHT
OK, STAND STRAIGHT
Let's test it out right now!

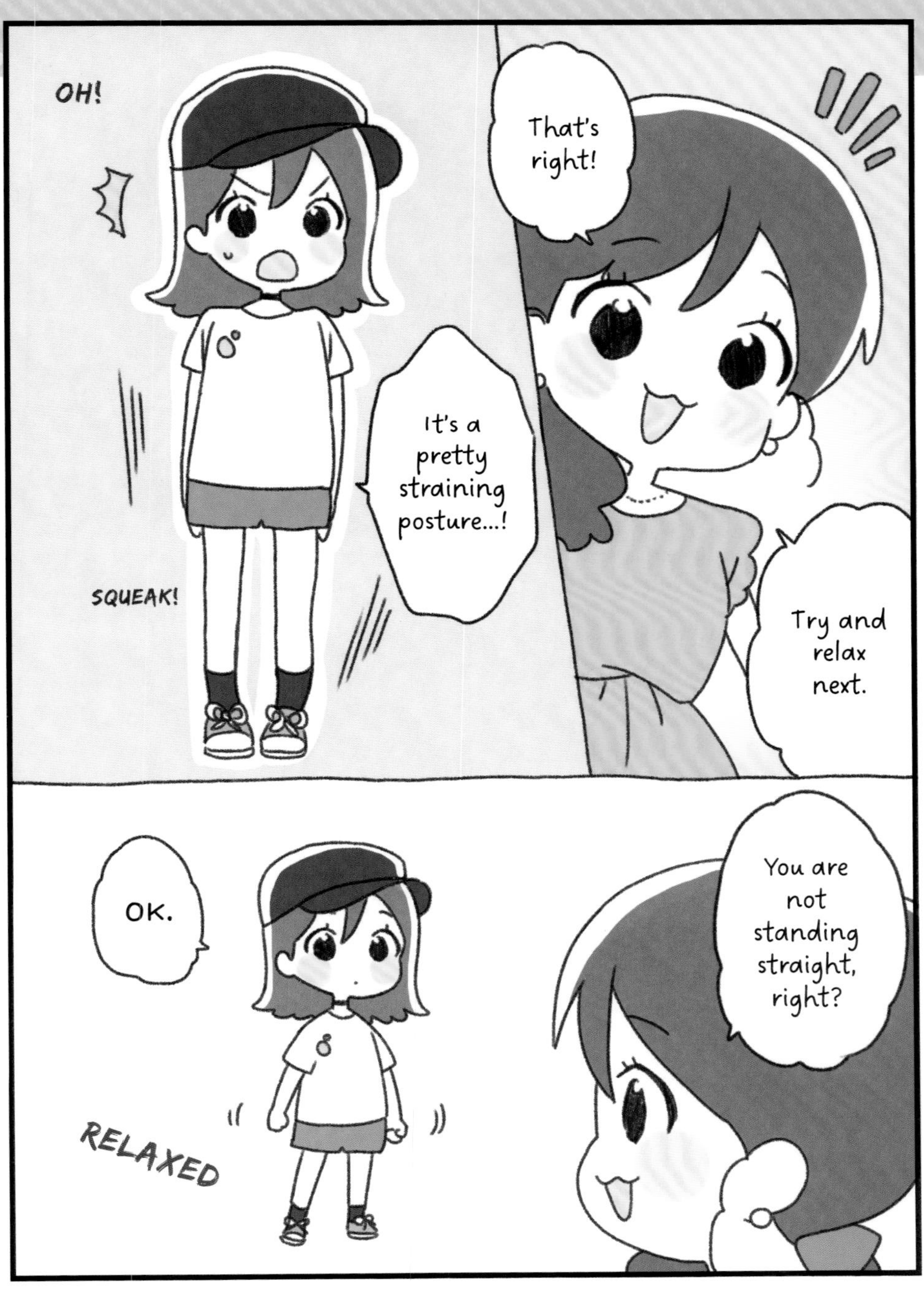
That's right!
OH!
It's a pretty straining posture...!
SQUEAK!
Try and relax next.
You are not standing straight, right?
OK.
RELAXED

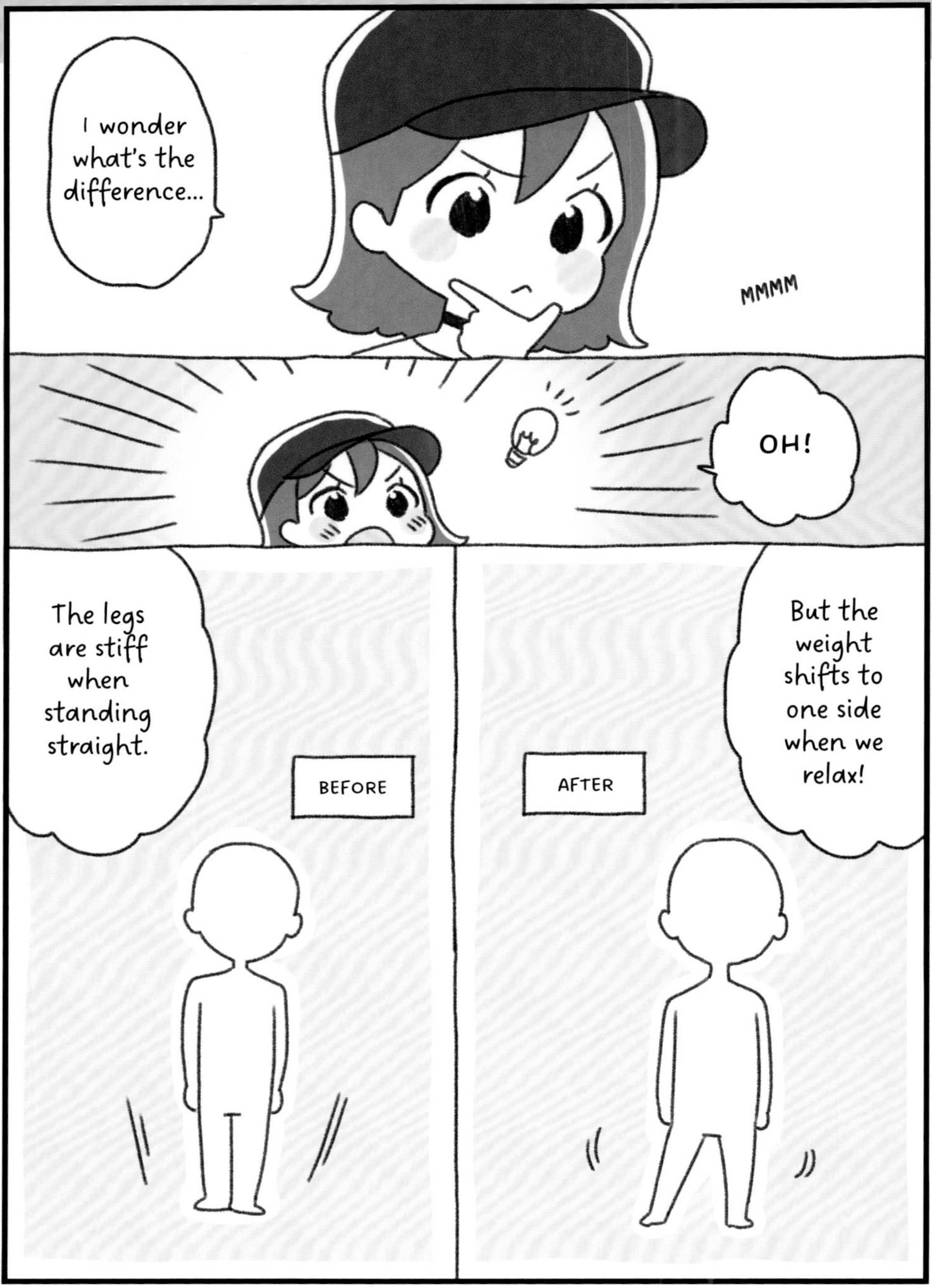
I wonder what's the difference...
MMMM
OH!
The legs are stiff when standing straight.
BEFORE
AFTER
But the weight shifts to one side when we relax!

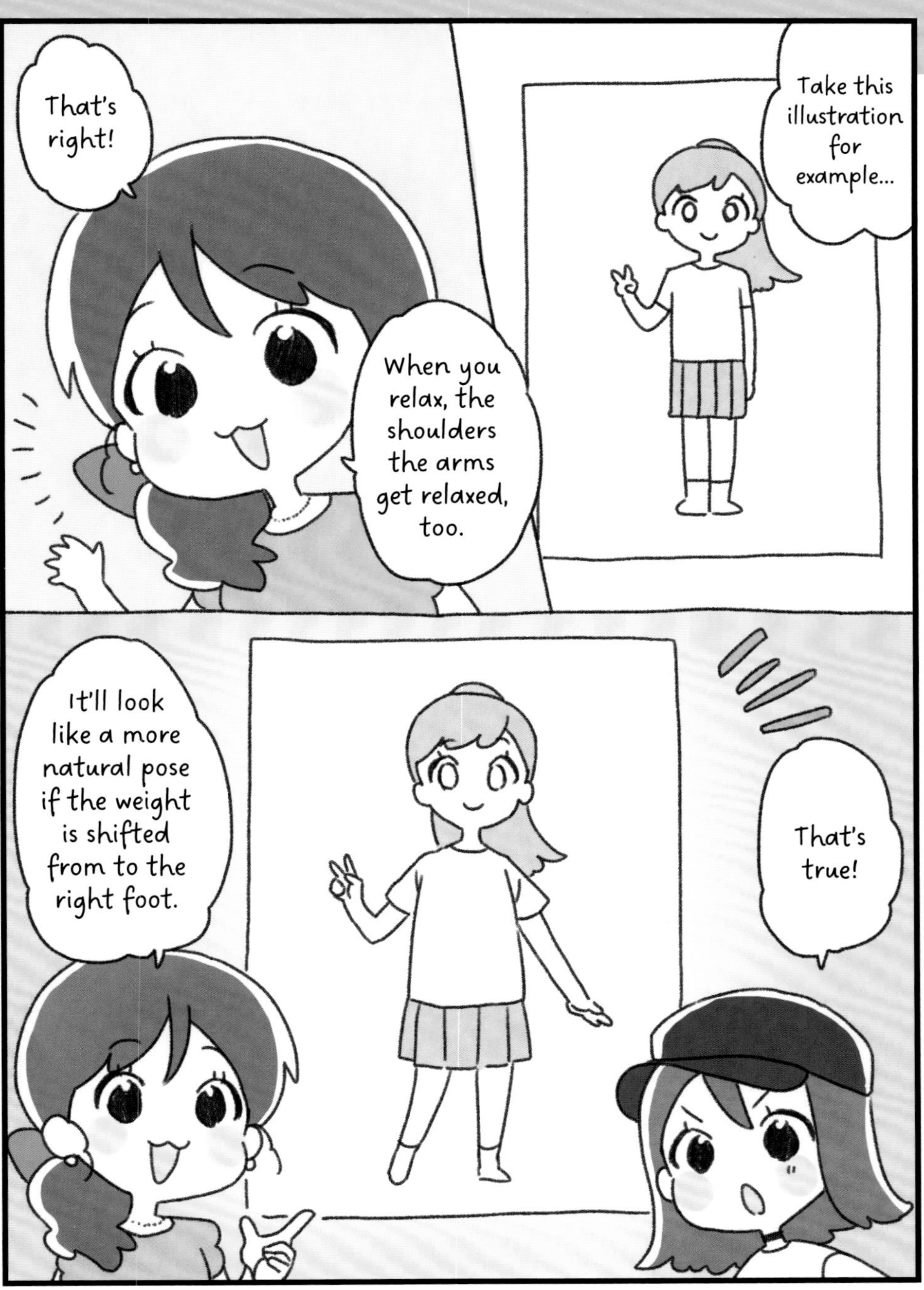
That's right!
Take this illustration for example...
When you relax, the shoulders the arms get relaxed, too.
It'll look like a more natural pose if the weight is shifted from to the right foot.
That's true!

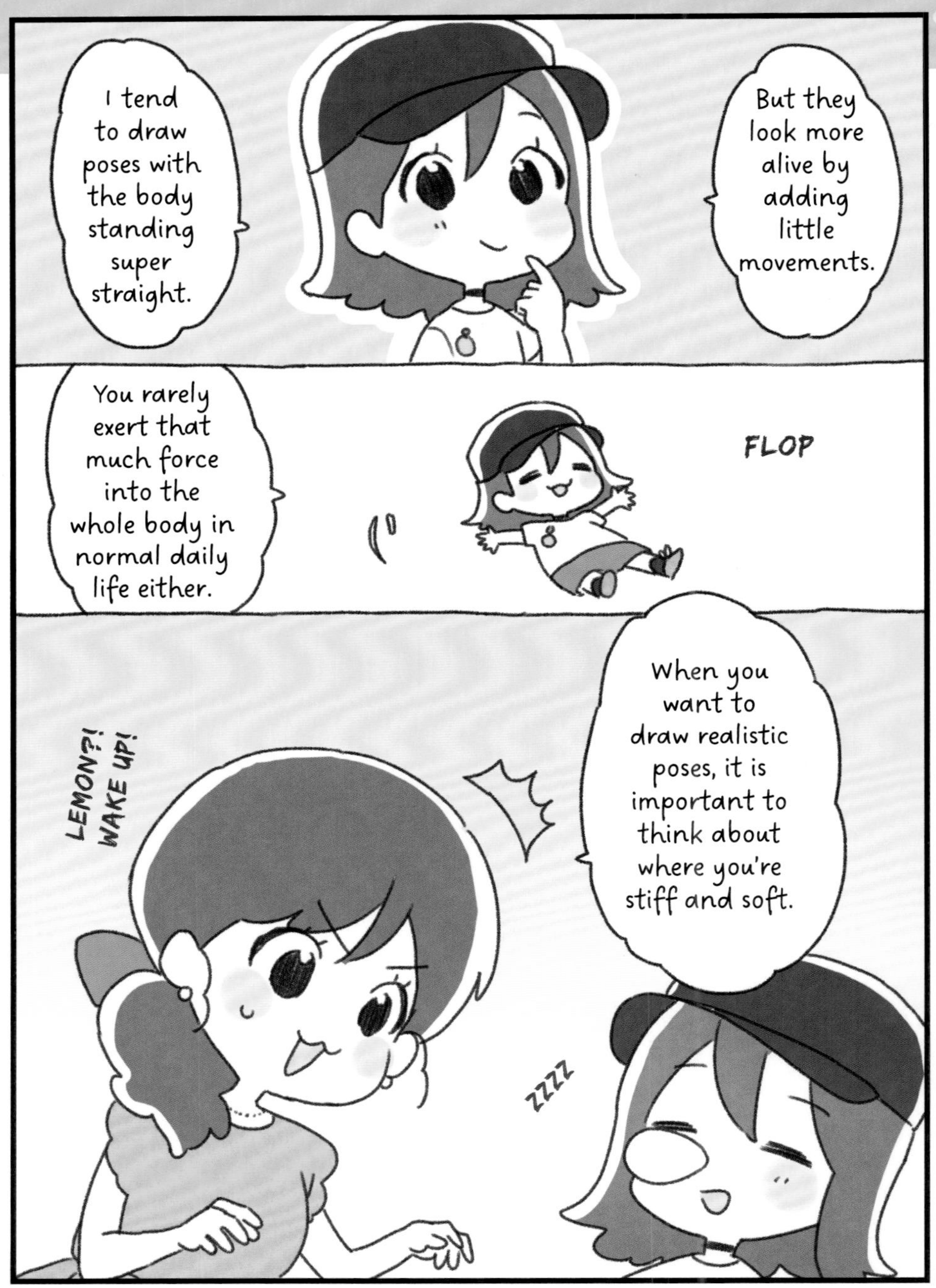
I tend to draw poses with the body standing super straight.
But they look more alive by adding little movements.
You rarely exert that much force into the whole body in normal daily life either.
FLOP
When you want to draw realistic poses, it is important to think about where you're stiff and soft.
LEMON?! WAKE UP!
ZZZZ

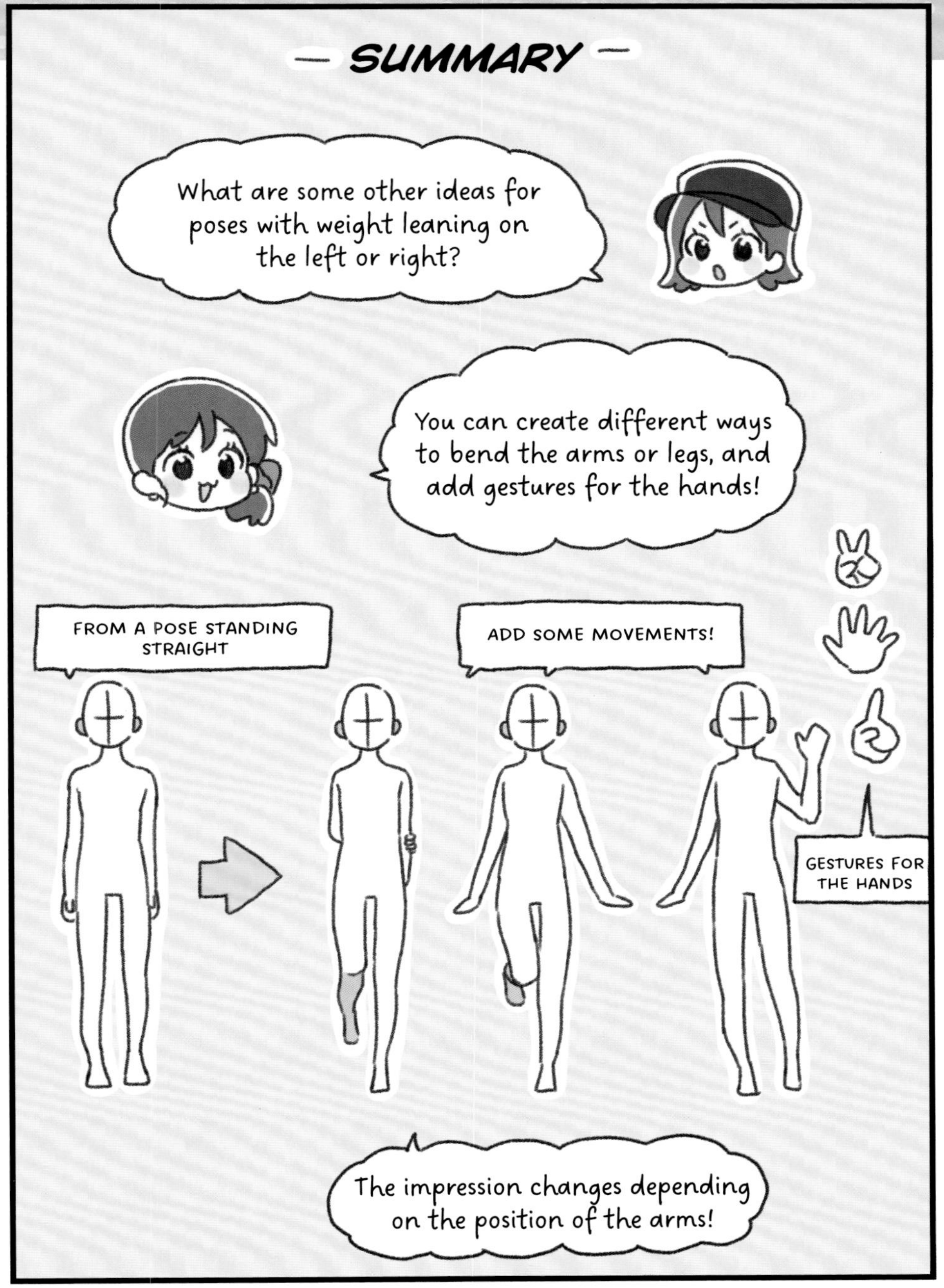
— SUMMARY —
What are some other ideas for poses with weight leaning on the left or right?
You can create different ways to bend the arms or legs, and add gestures for the hands!
FROM A POSE STANDING STRAIGHT
ADD SOME MOVEMENTS!
GESTURES FOR THE HANDS
The impression changes depending on the position of the arms!

# PARTS NECESSARY FOR DRAWING POSES

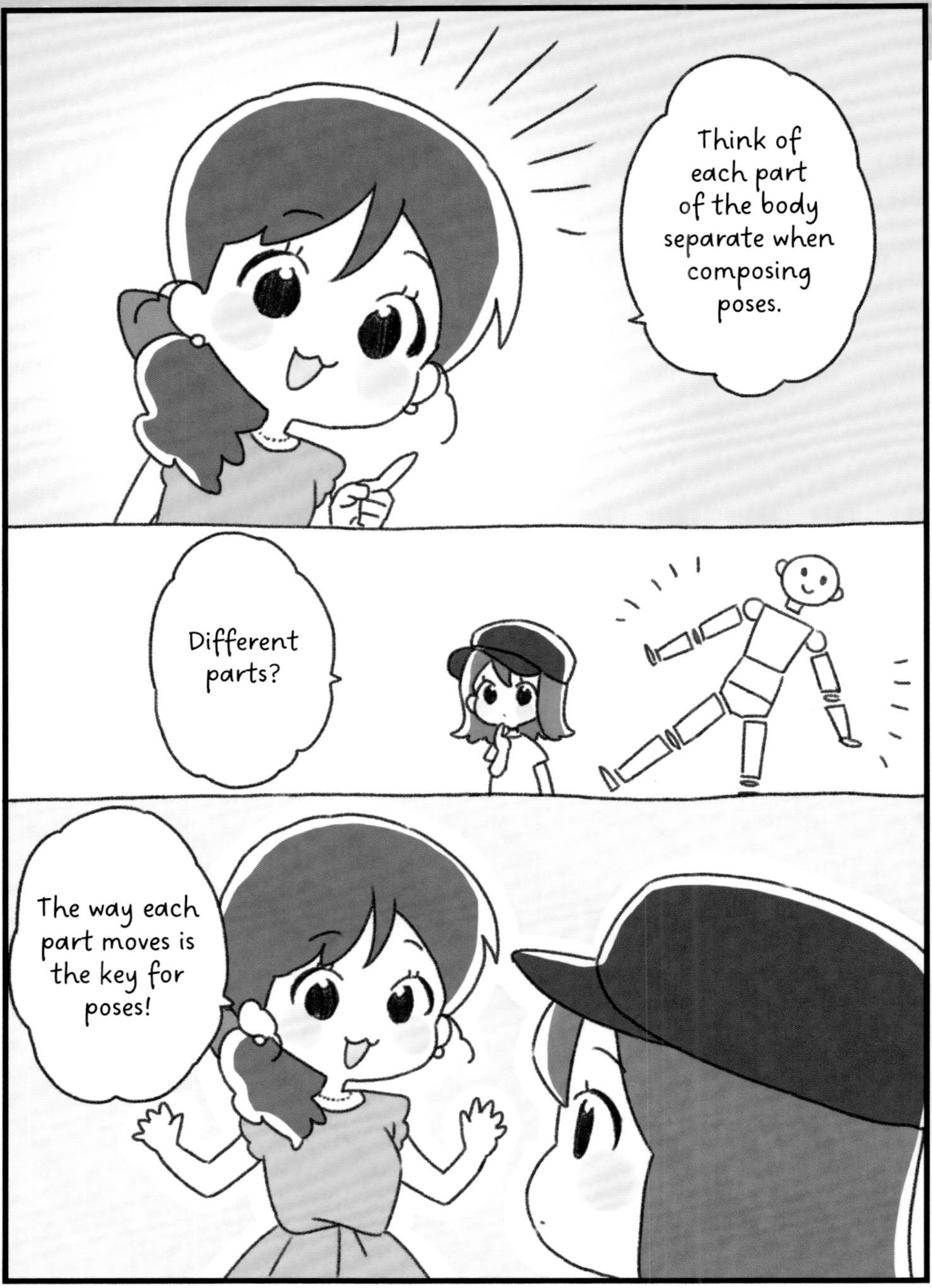

Think of each part of the body separate when composing poses.
Different parts?
The way each part moves is the key for poses!

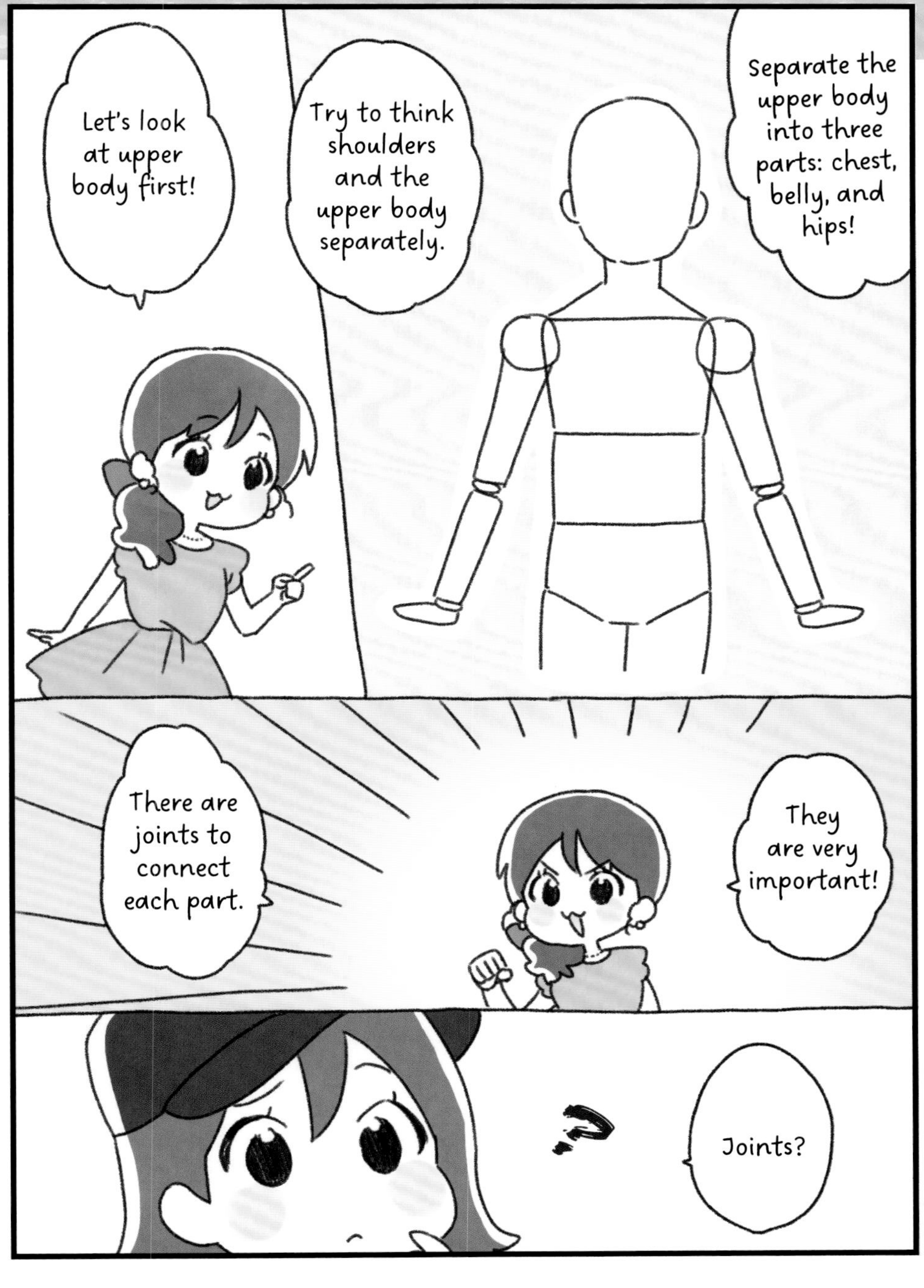
Let's look at upper body first!
Try to think shoulders and the upper body separately.
Separate the upper body into three parts: chest, belly, and hips!
There are joints to connect each part.
They are very important!
Joints?

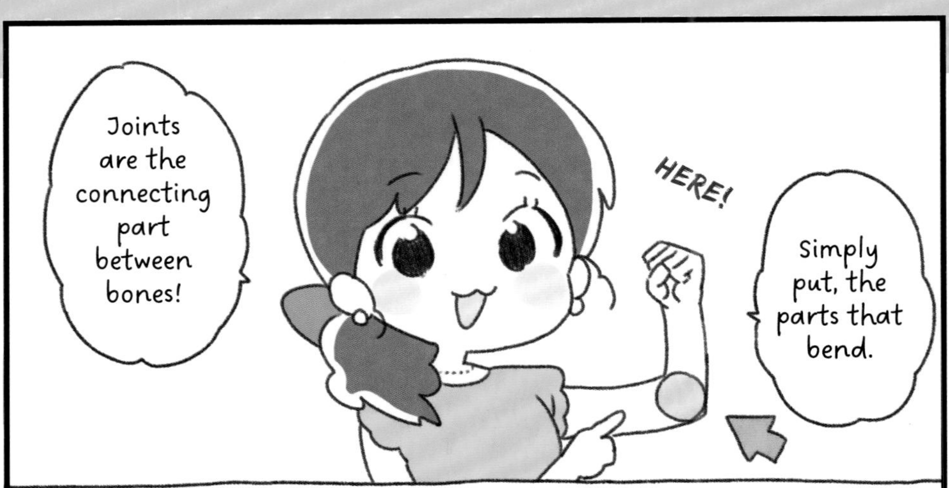
Joints are the connecting part between bones!
HERE!
Simply put, the parts that bend.

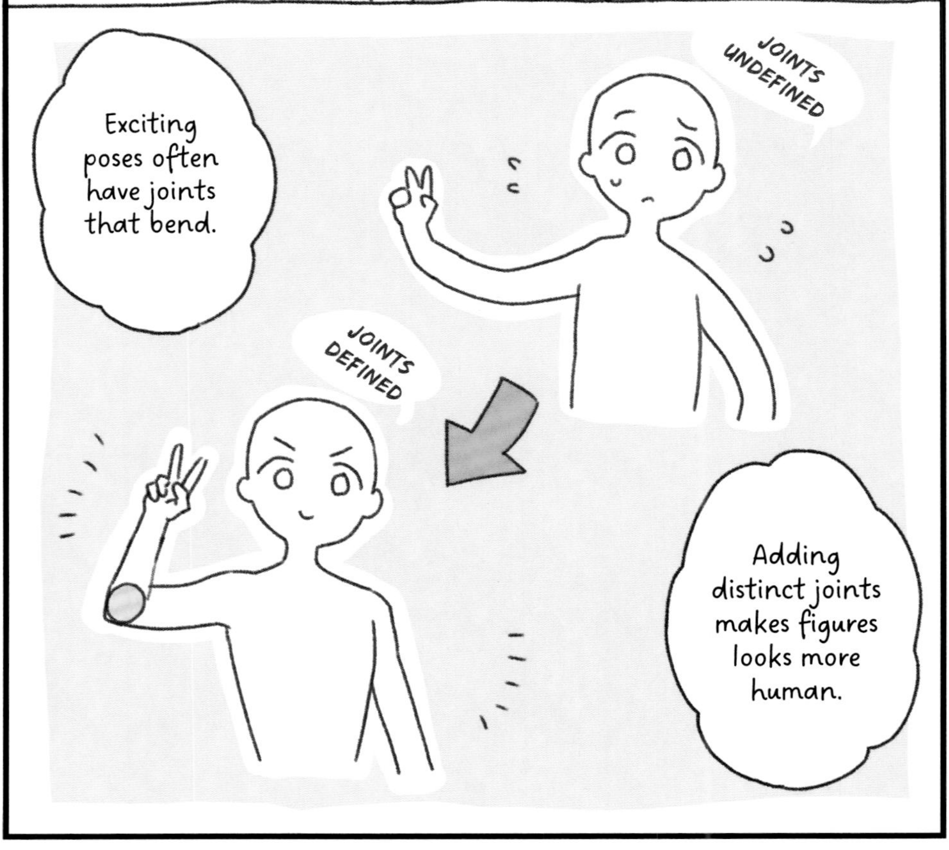
Exciting poses often have joints that bend.
JOINTS UNDEFINED
JOINTS DEFINED
Adding distinct joints makes figures looks more human.

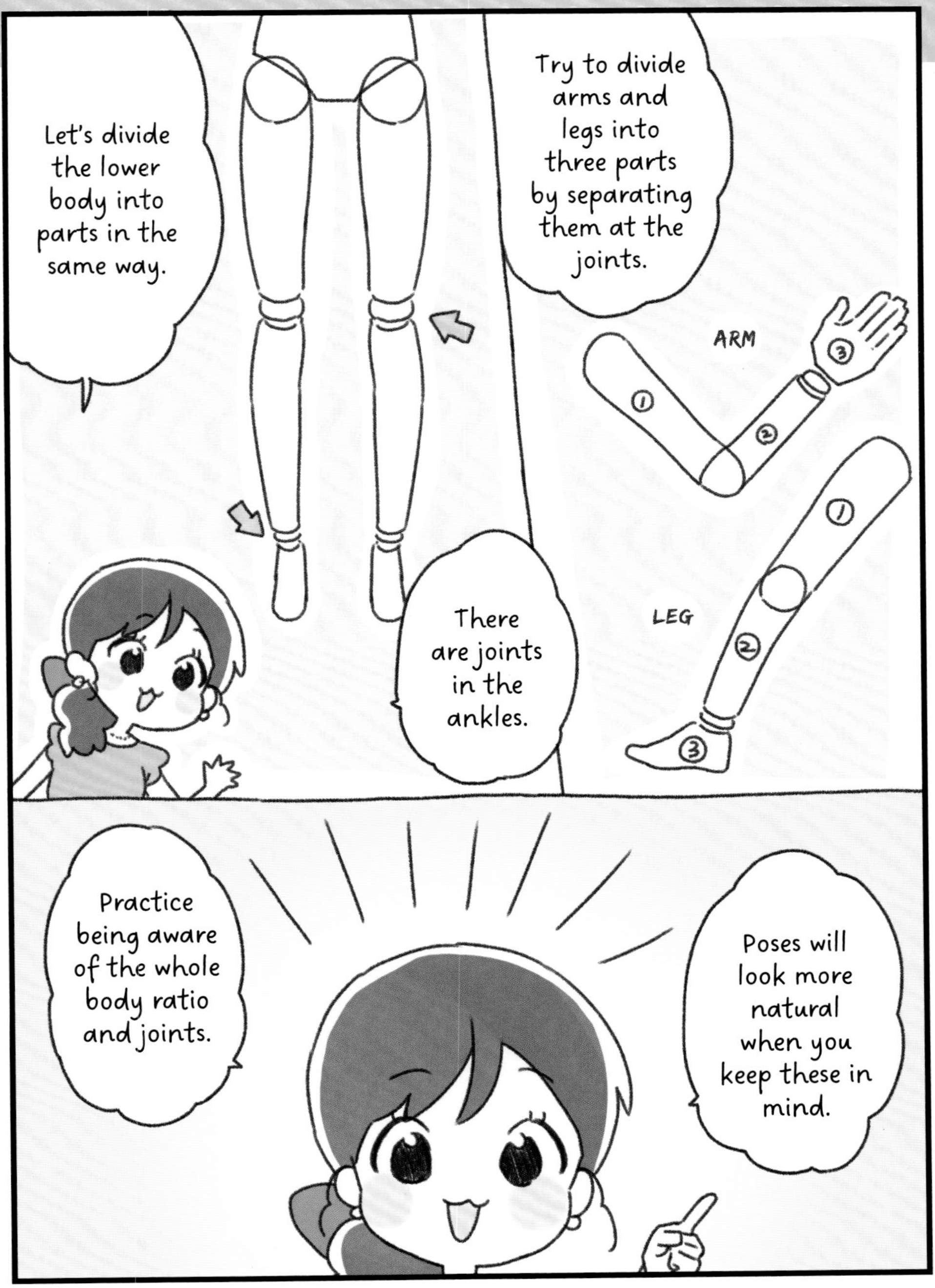
Let's divide the lower body into parts in the same way.
Try to divide arms and legs into three parts by separating them at the joints.
ARM
①
②
③
LEG
①
②
③
There are joints in the ankles.
Practice being aware of the whole body ratio and joints.
Poses will look more natural when you keep these in mind.

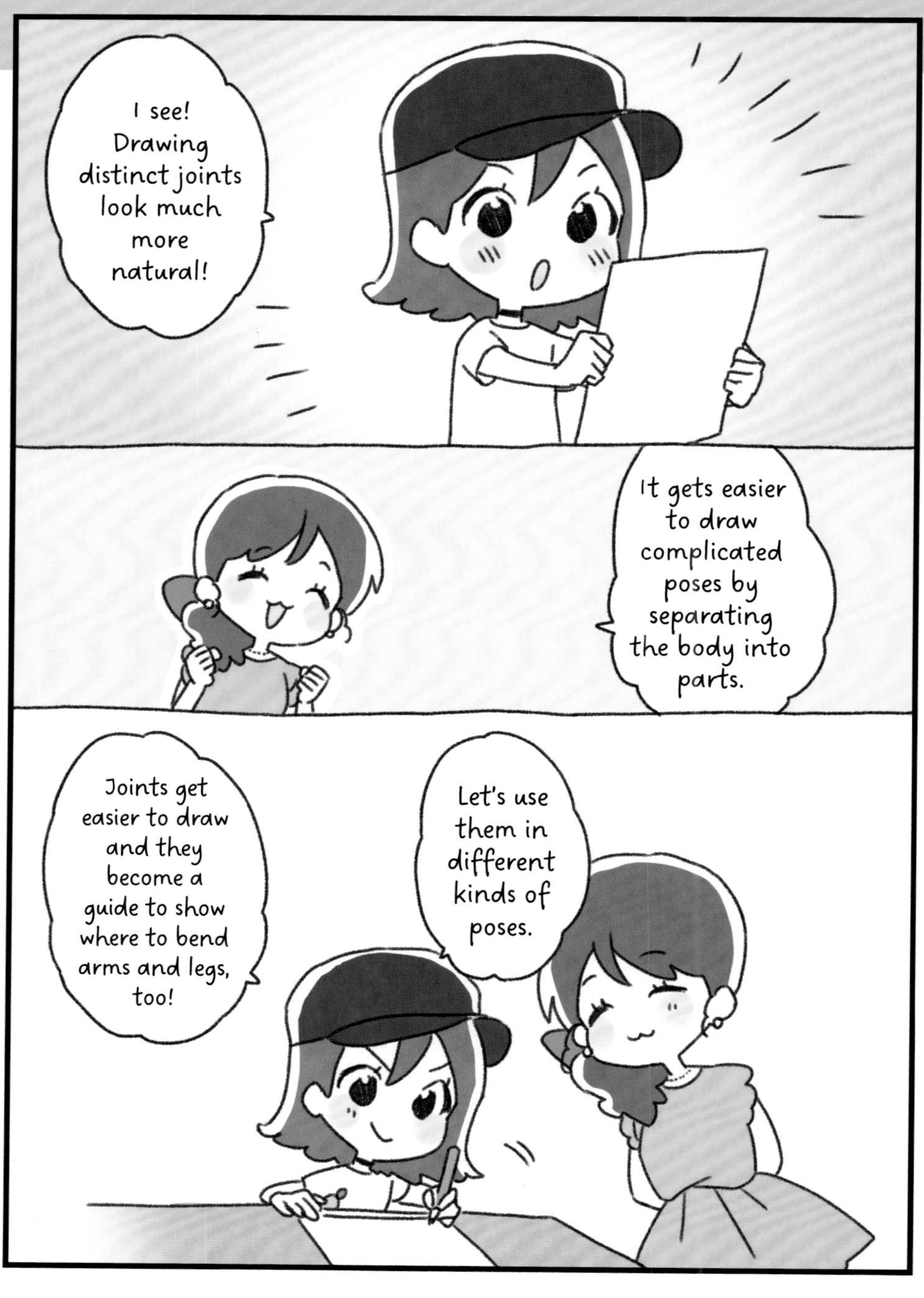
I see! Drawing distinct joints look much more natural!
It gets easier to draw complicated poses by separating the body into parts.
Joints get easier to draw and they become a guide to show where to bend arms and legs, too!
Let's use them in different kinds of poses.

CHAPTER
2

# LET'S TRY TO DRAW UPPER BODIES

# UNDERSTANDING THE SKELETON AND JOINTS

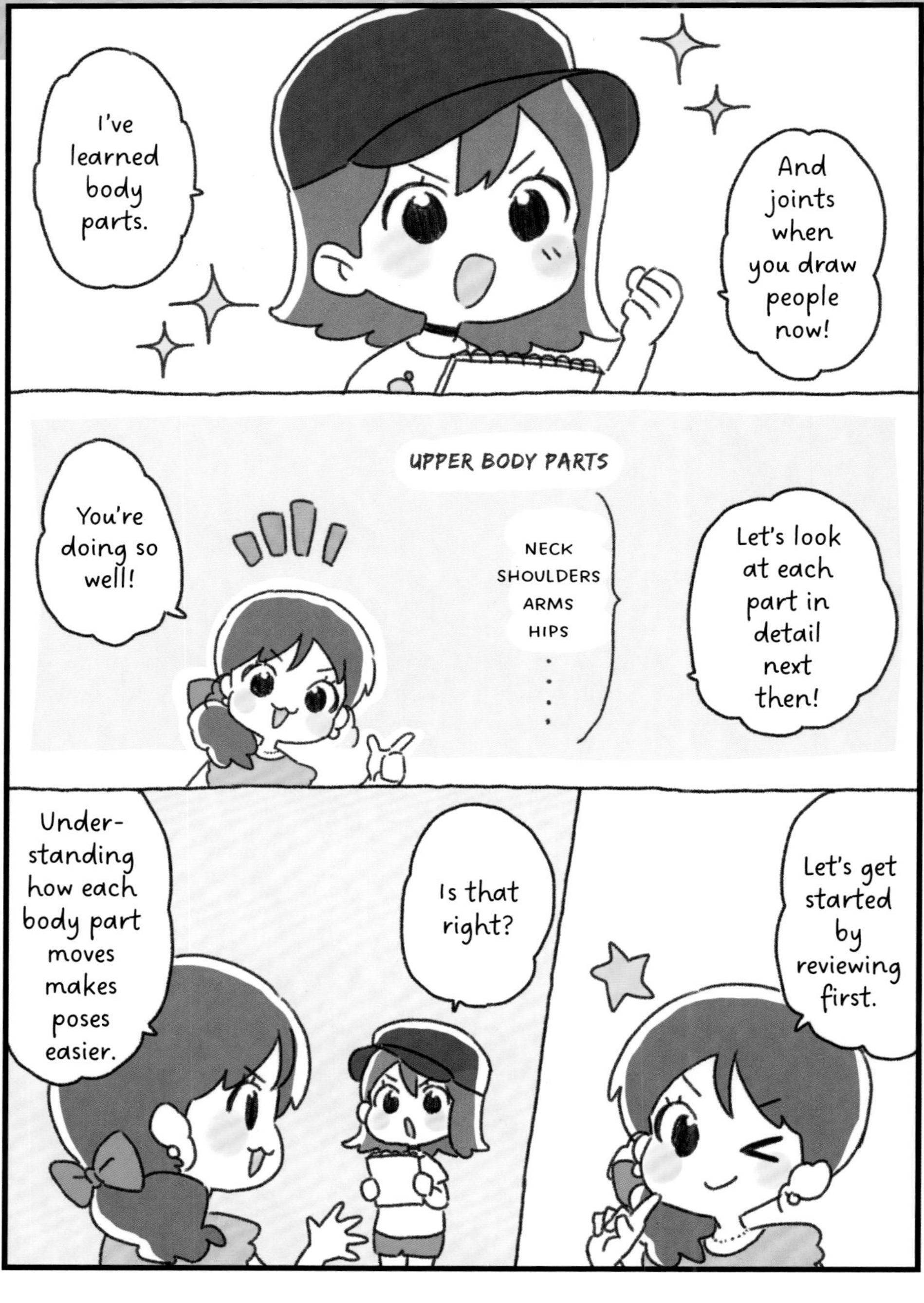
I've learned body parts.
And joints when you draw people now!
You're doing so well!
UPPER BODY PARTS
NECK
SHOULDERS
ARMS
HIPS
Let's look at each part in detail next then!
Under-standing how each body part moves makes poses easier.
Is that right?
Let's get started by reviewing first.

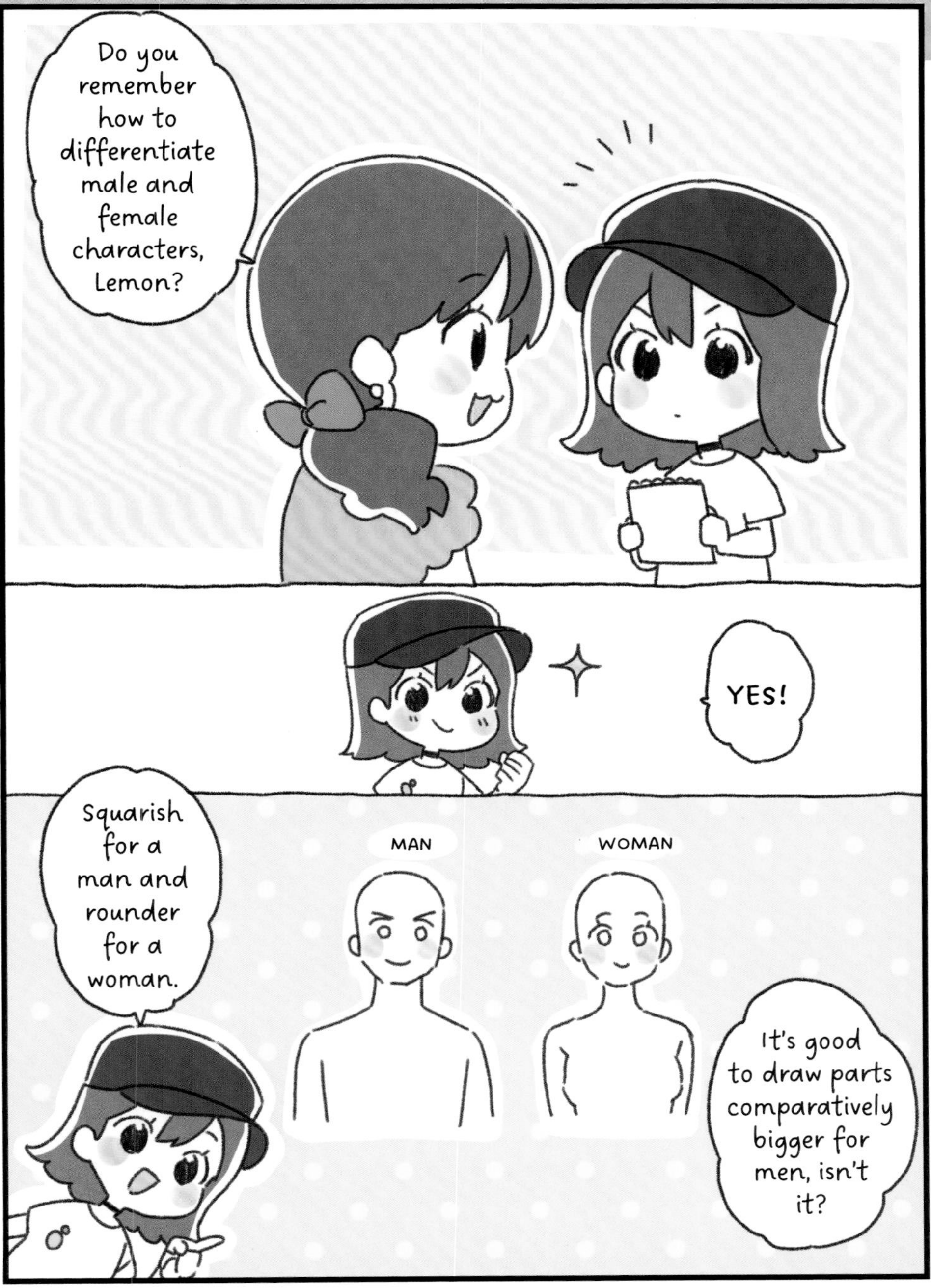
Do you remember how to differentiate male and female characters, Lemon?
YES!
Squarish for a man and rounder for a woman.
MAN
WOMAN
It's good to draw parts comparatively bigger for men, isn't it?

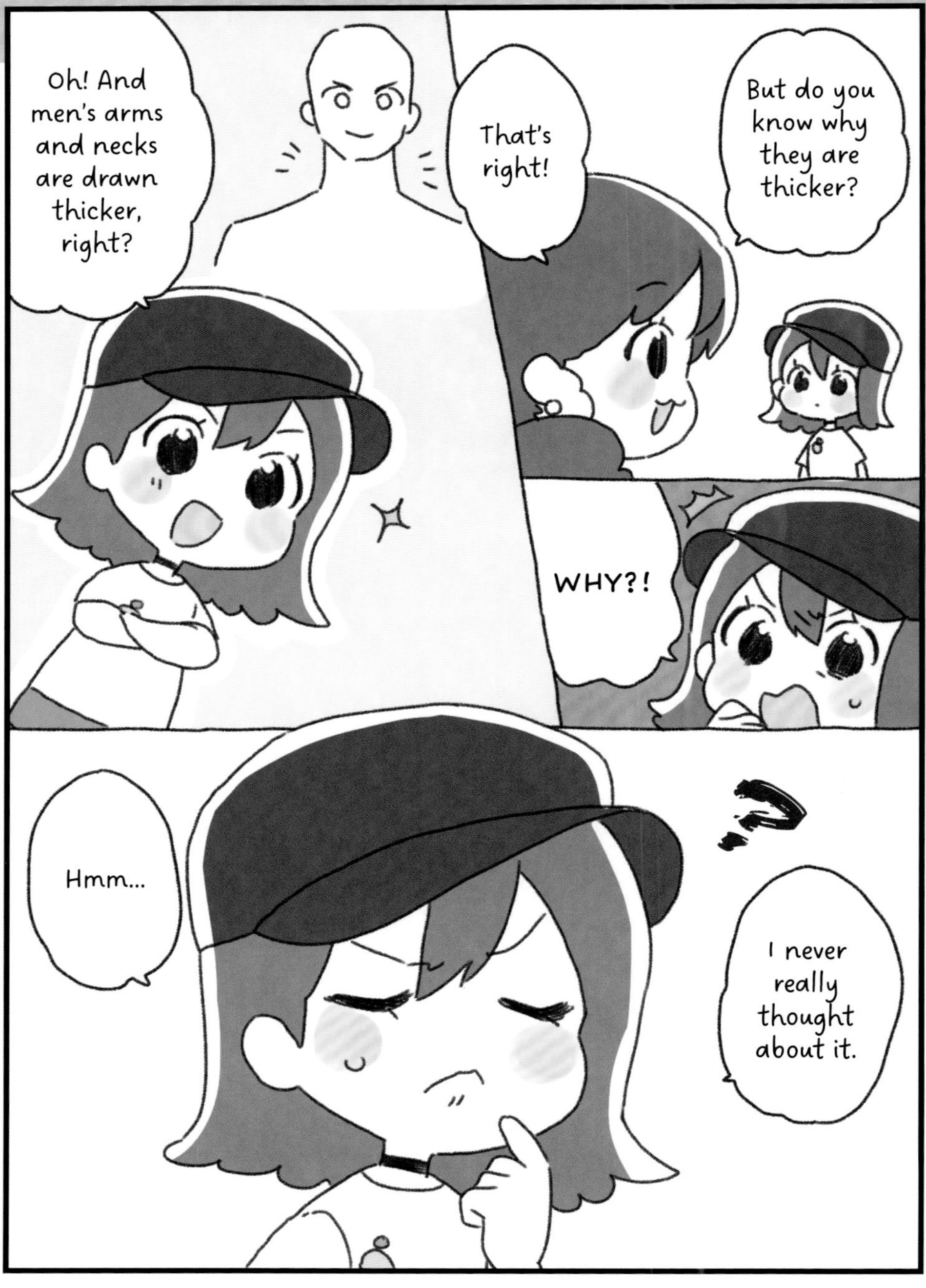
Oh! And men's arms and necks are drawn thicker, right?
That's right!
But do you know why they are thicker?
WHY?!
Hmm...
I never really thought about it.

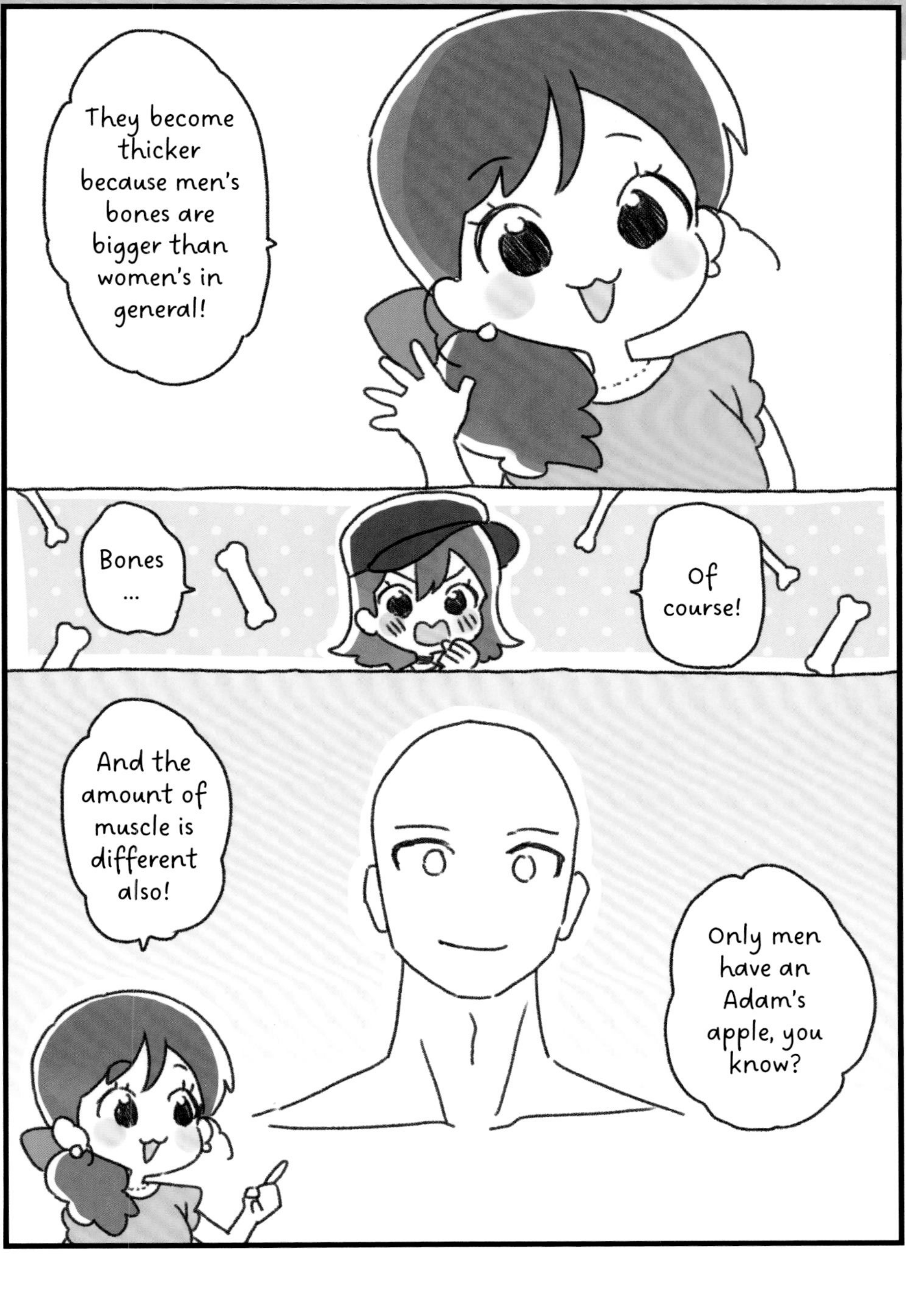
They become thicker because men's bones are bigger than women's in general!
Bones …
Of course!
And the amount of muscle is different also!
Only men have an Adam's apple, you know?

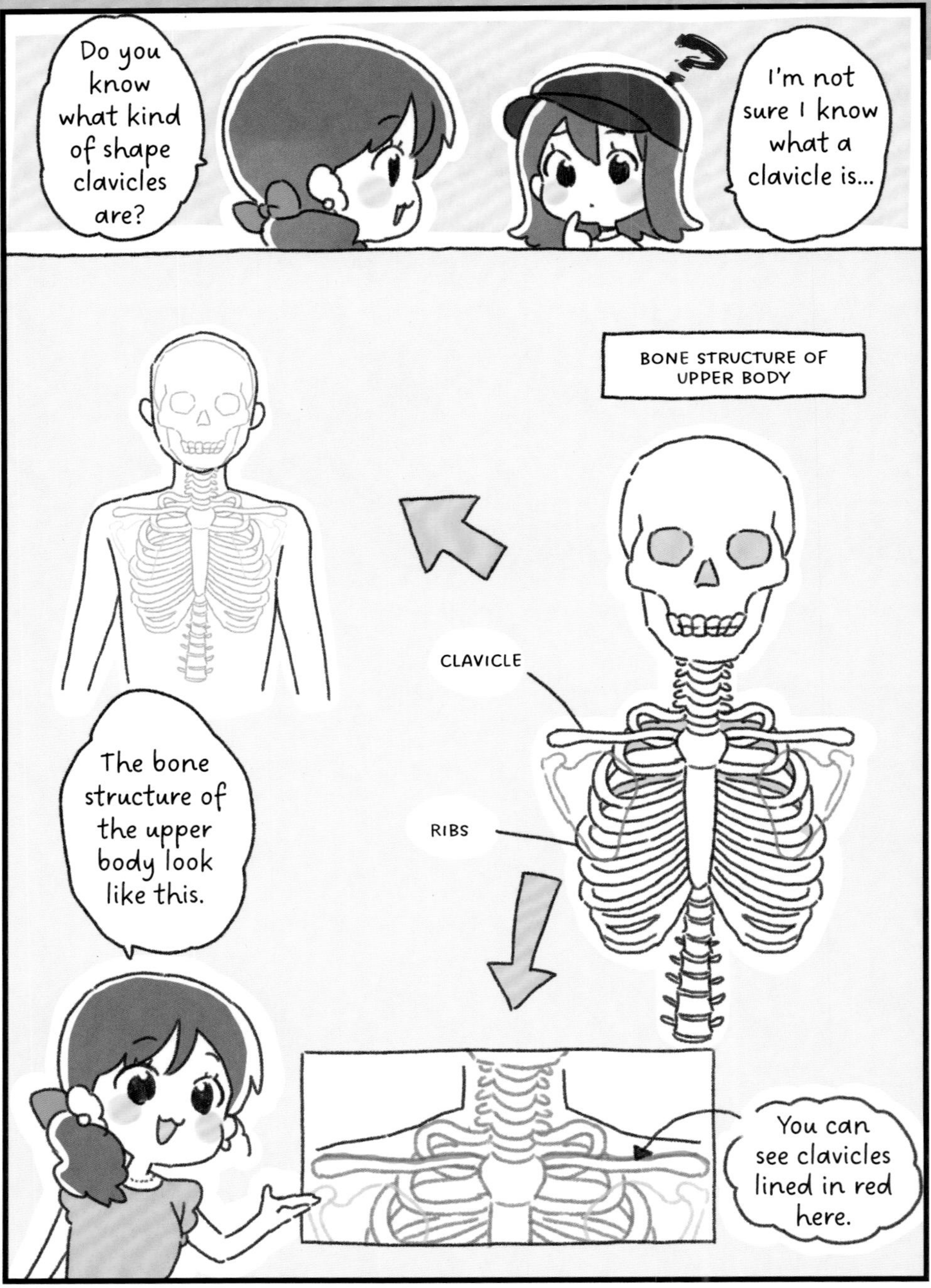
Do you know what kind of shape clavicles are?
I'm not sure I know what a clavicle is...
BONE STRUCTURE OF UPPER BODY
CLAVICLE
RIBS
The bone structure of the upper body look like this.
You can see clavicles lined in red here.

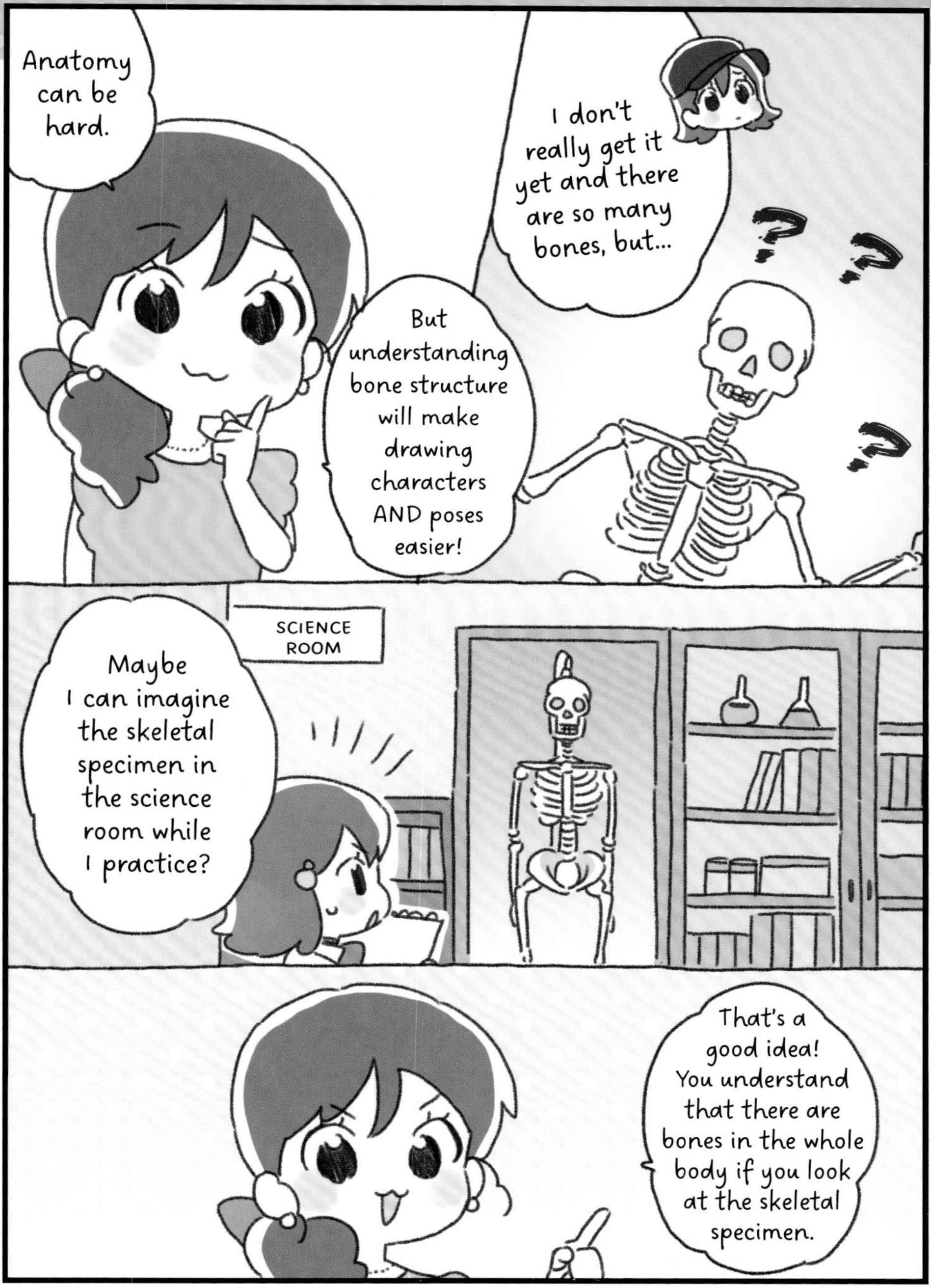
Anatomy can be hard.
I don't really get it yet and there are so many bones, but...
But understanding bone structure will make drawing characters AND poses easier!
SCIENCE ROOM
Maybe I can imagine the skeletal specimen in the science room while I practice?
That's a good idea! You understand that there are bones in the whole body if you look at the skeletal specimen.

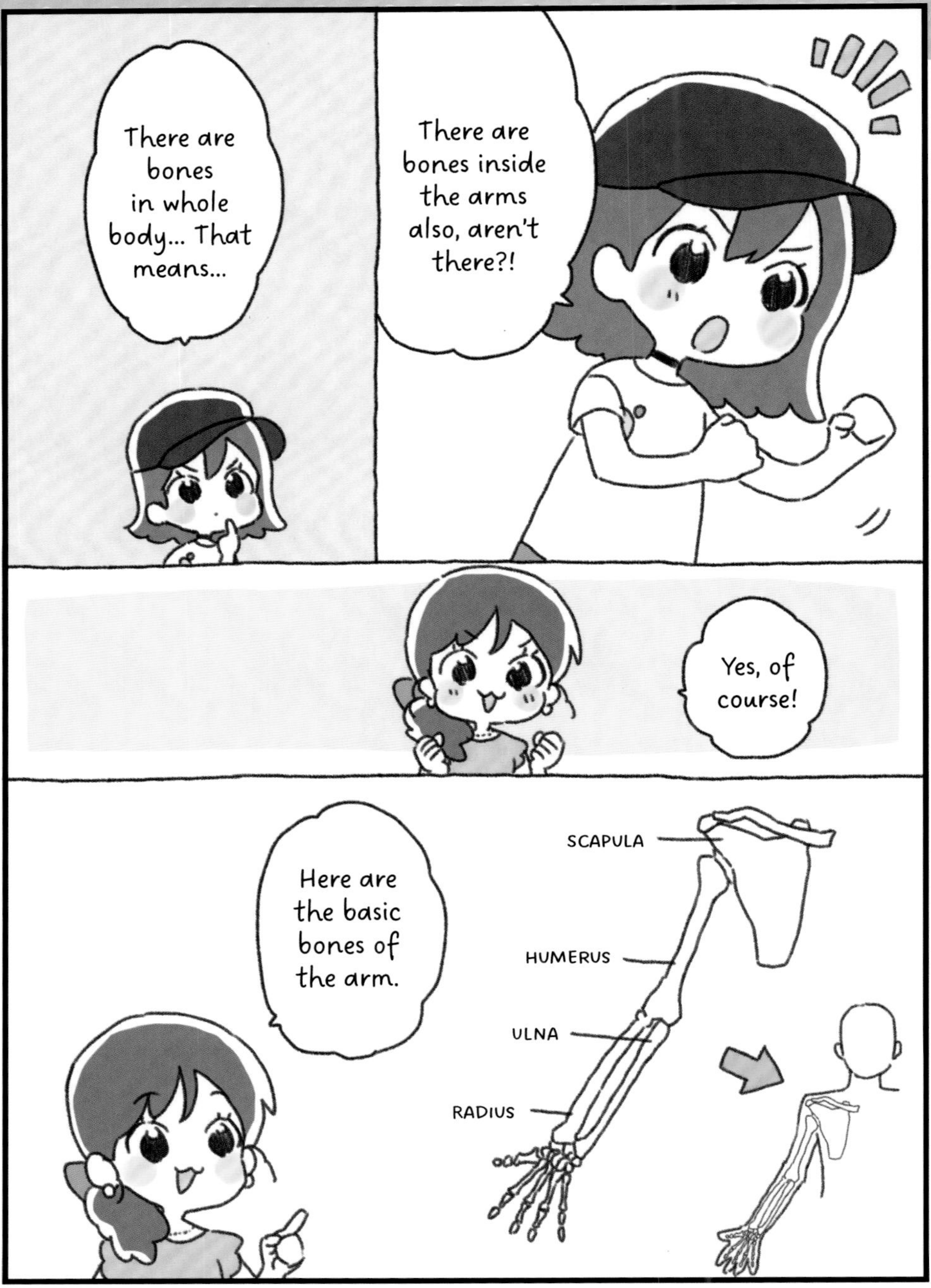
There are bones in whole body... That means...
There are bones inside the arms also, aren't there?!
Yes, of course!
Here are the basic bones of the arm.
SCAPULA
HUMERUS
ULNA
RADIUS

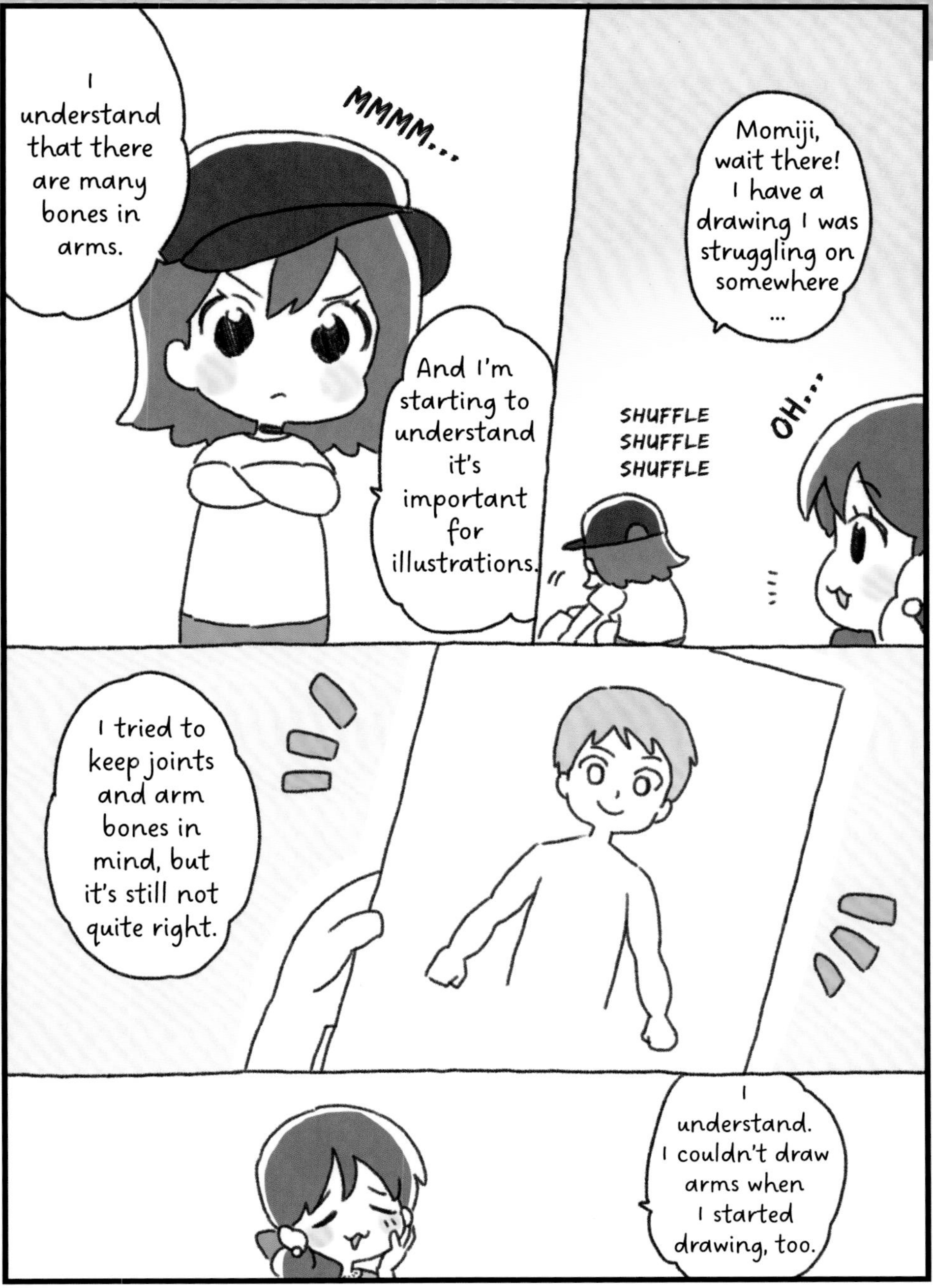
I understand that there are many bones in arms.
MMMM...
And I'm starting to understand it's important for illustrations.
Momiji, wait there! I have a drawing I was struggling on somewhere ...
SHUFFLE SHUFFLE SHUFFLE
OH...
I tried to keep joints and arm bones in mind, but it's still not quite right.
I understand. I couldn't draw arms when I started drawing, too.

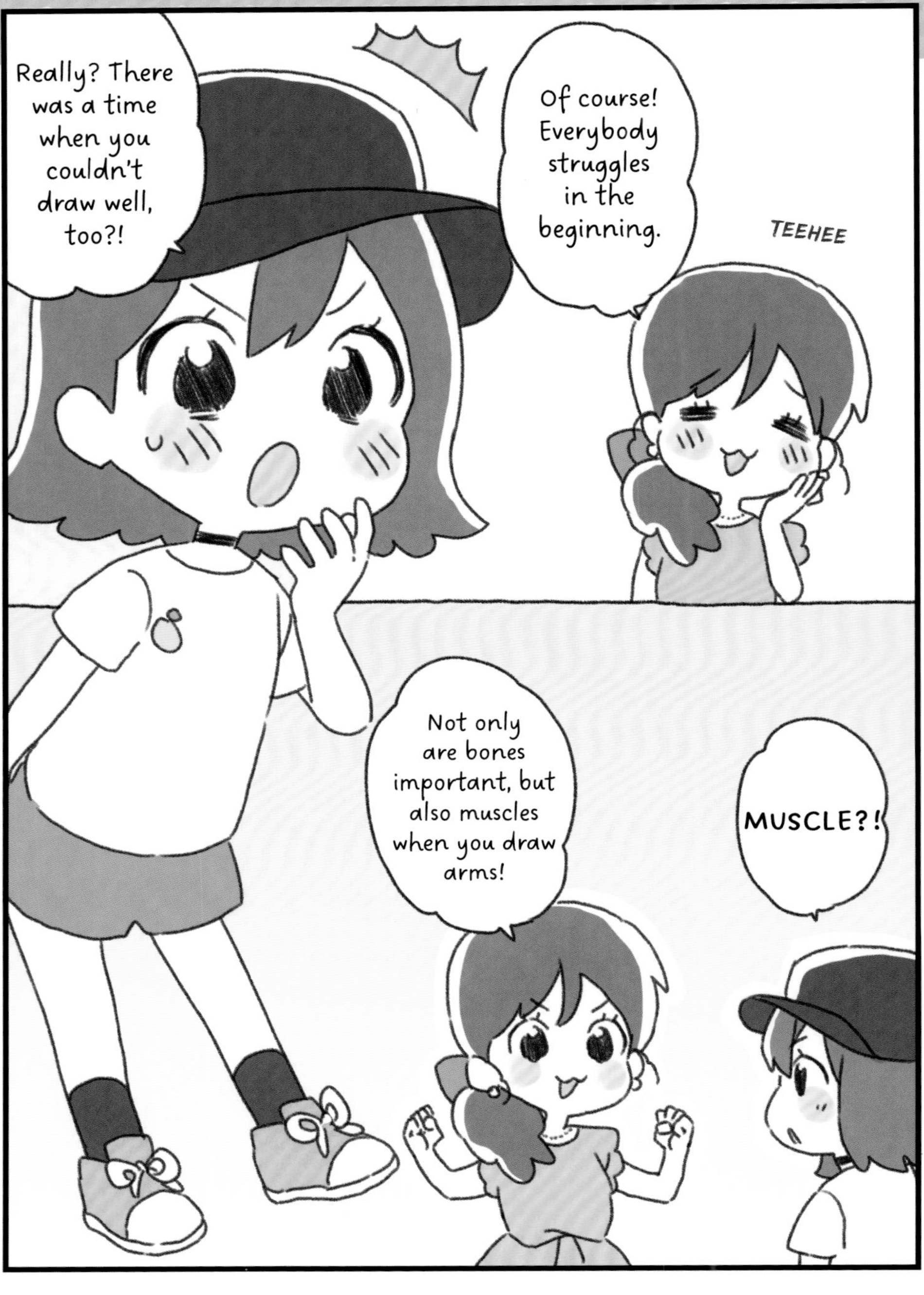

Really? There was a time when you couldn't draw well, too?!
Of course! Everybody struggles in the beginning.
TEEHEE
Not only are bones important, but also muscles when you draw arms!
MUSCLE?!

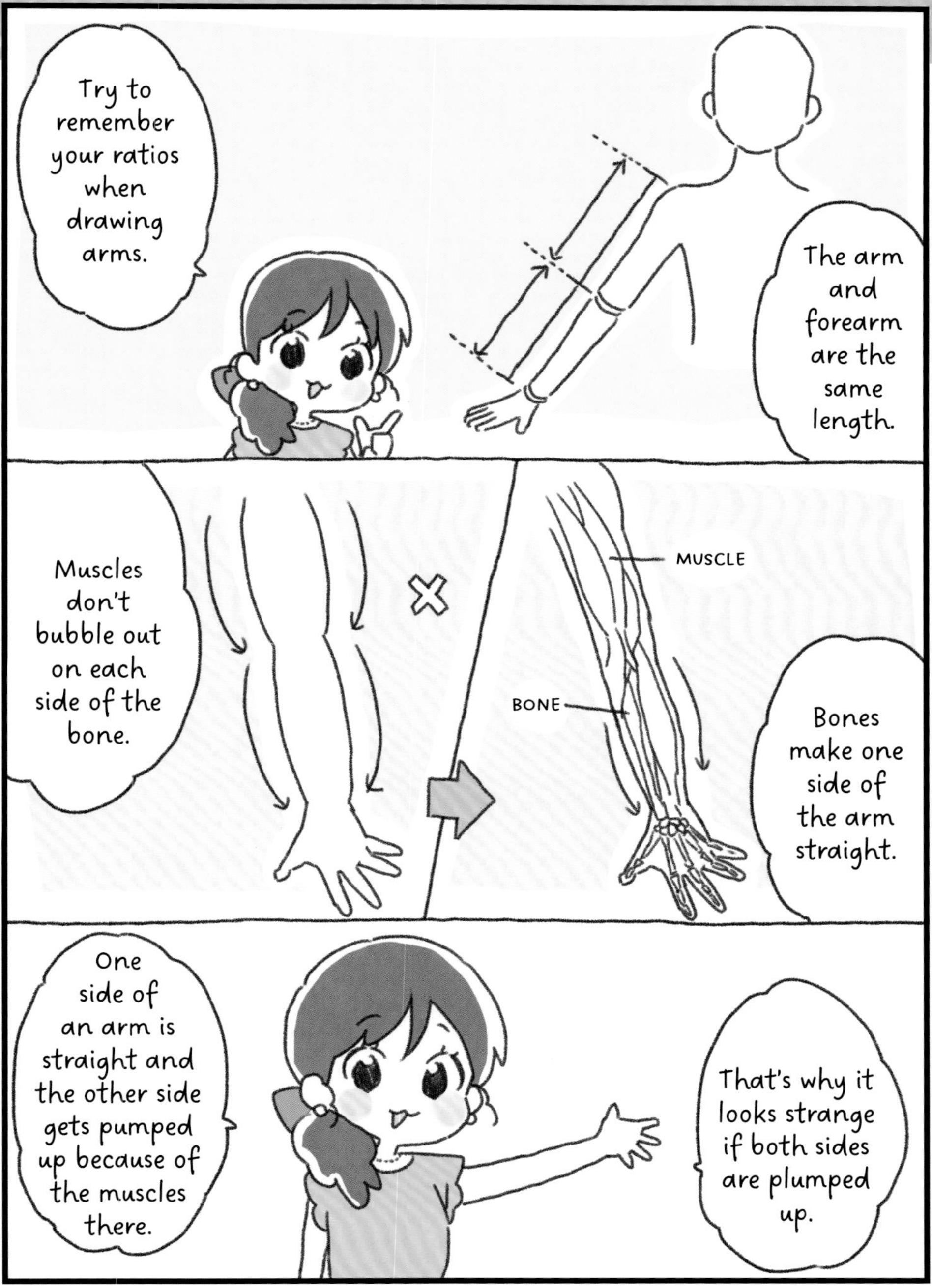
Try to remember your ratios when drawing arms.
The arm and forearm are the same length.
Muscles don't bubble out on each side of the bone.
MUSCLE
BONE
Bones make one side of the arm straight.
One side of an arm is straight and the other side gets pumped up because of the muscles there.
That's why it looks strange if both sides are plumped up.

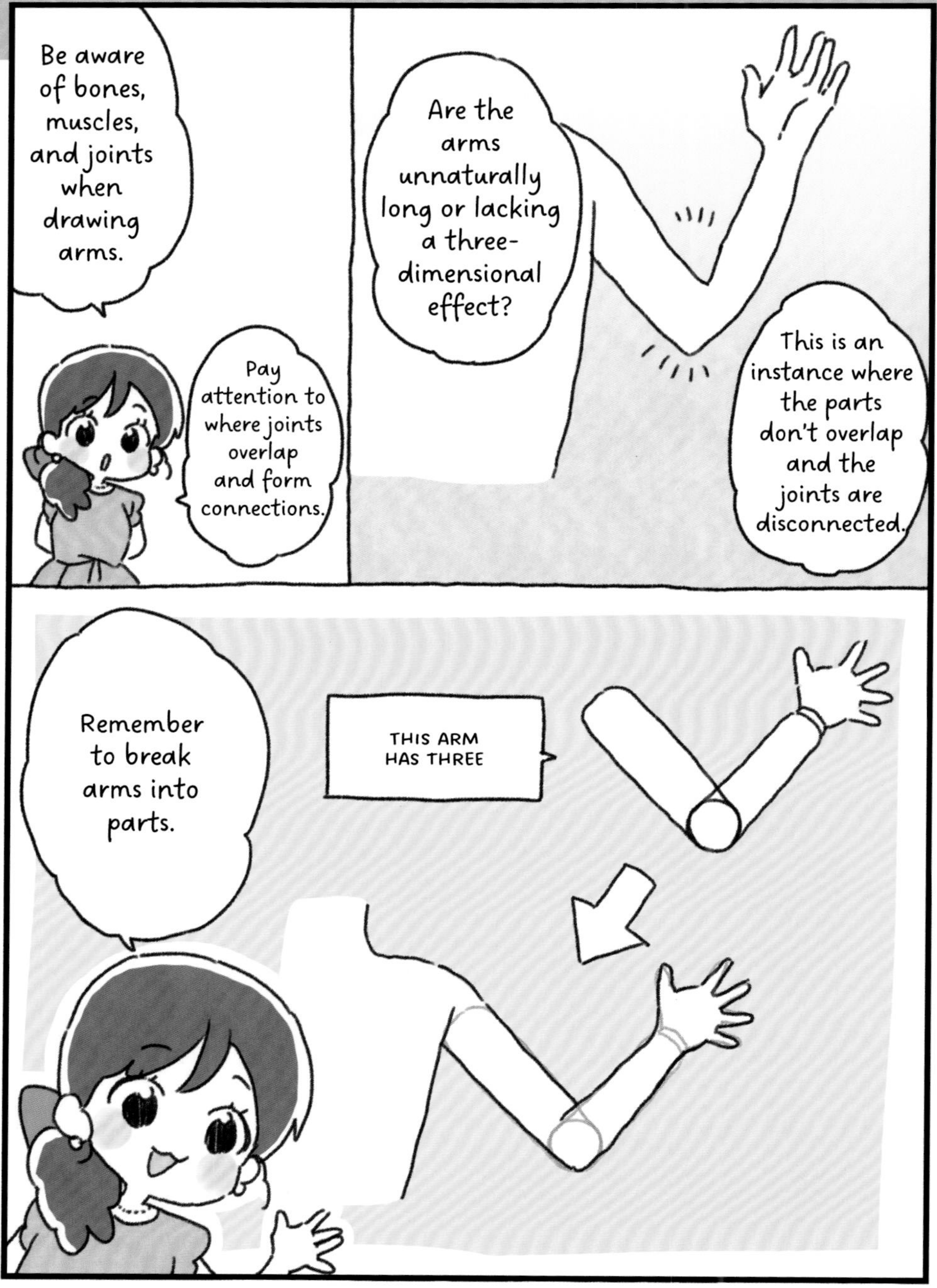
Be aware of bones, muscles, and joints when drawing arms.
Pay attention to where joints overlap and form connections.
Are the arms unnaturally long or lacking a three-dimensional effect?
This is an instance where the parts don't overlap and the joints are disconnected.
Remember to break arms into parts.
THIS ARM HAS THREE

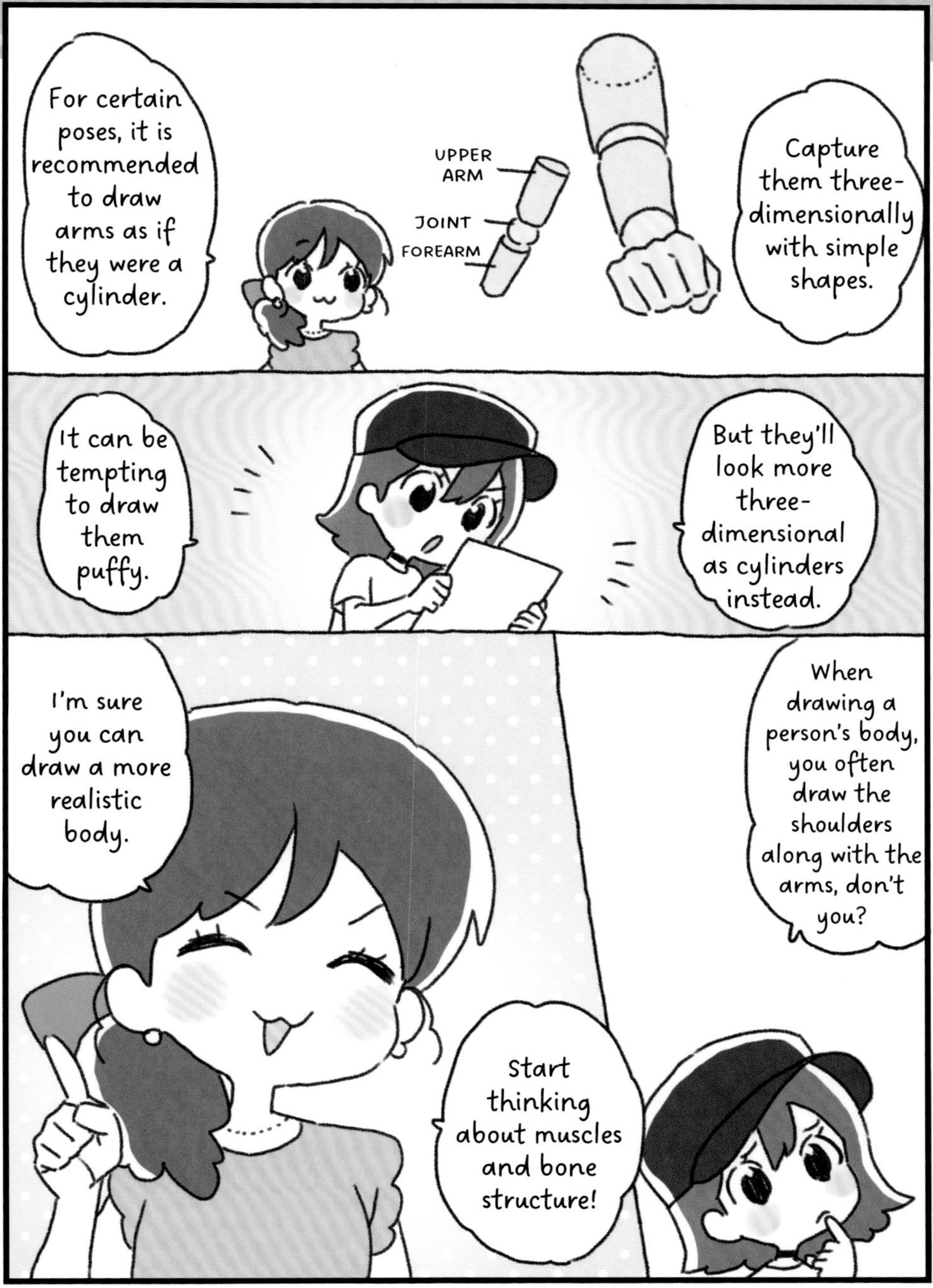
For certain poses, it is recommended to draw arms as if they were a cylinder.
UPPER ARM
JOINT
FOREARM
Capture them three-dimensionally with simple shapes.
It can be tempting to draw them puffy.
But they'll look more three-dimensional as cylinders instead.
I'm sure you can draw a more realistic body.
When drawing a person's body, you often draw the shoulders along with the arms, don't you?
Start thinking about muscles and bone structure!

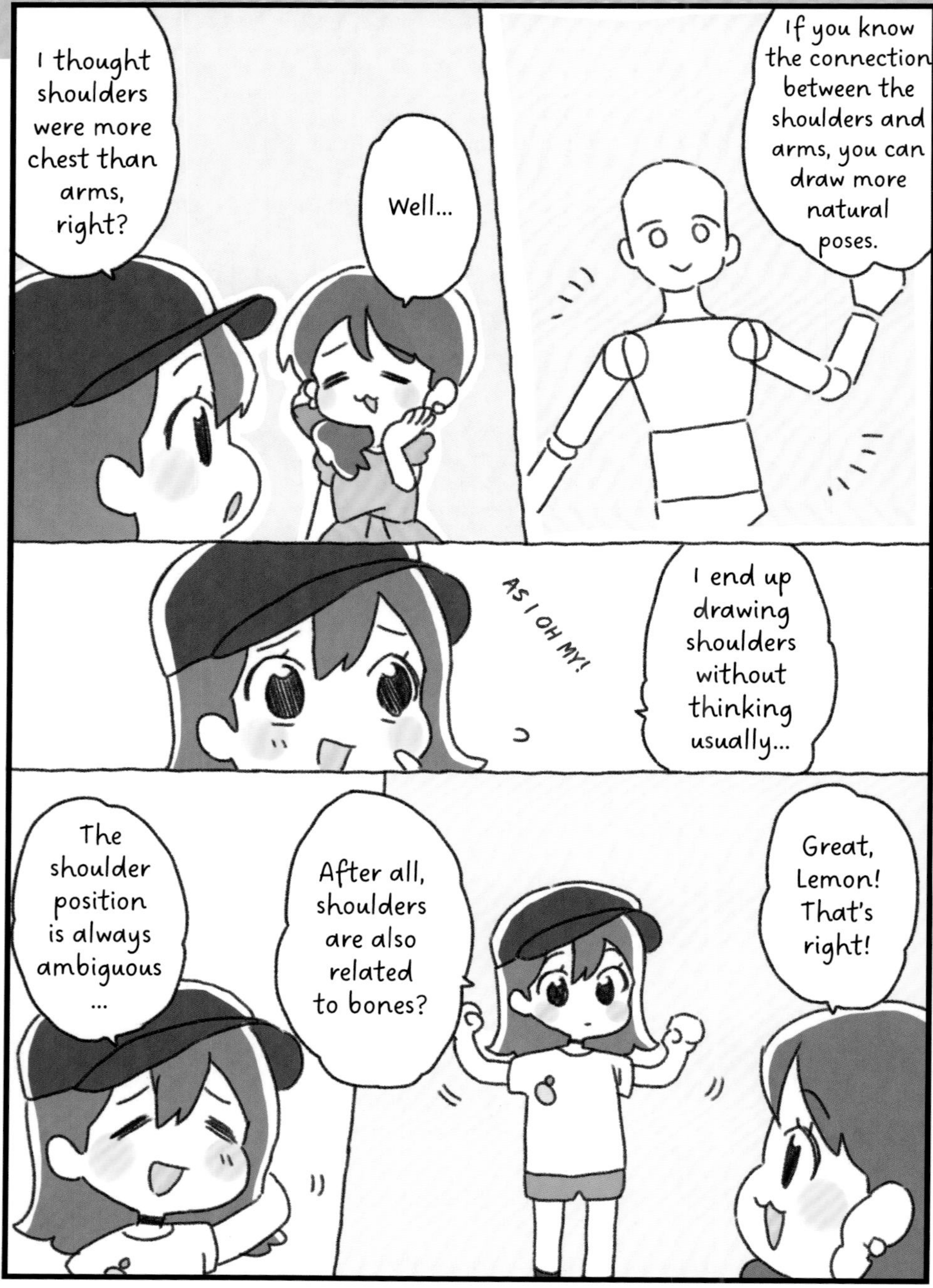

If you know the connection between the shoulders and arms, you can draw more natural poses.
Well...
I thought shoulders were more chest than arms, right?
I end up drawing shoulders without thinking usually...
AS I OH MY!
Great, Lemon! That's right!
After all, shoulders are also related to bones?
The shoulder position is always ambiguous ...

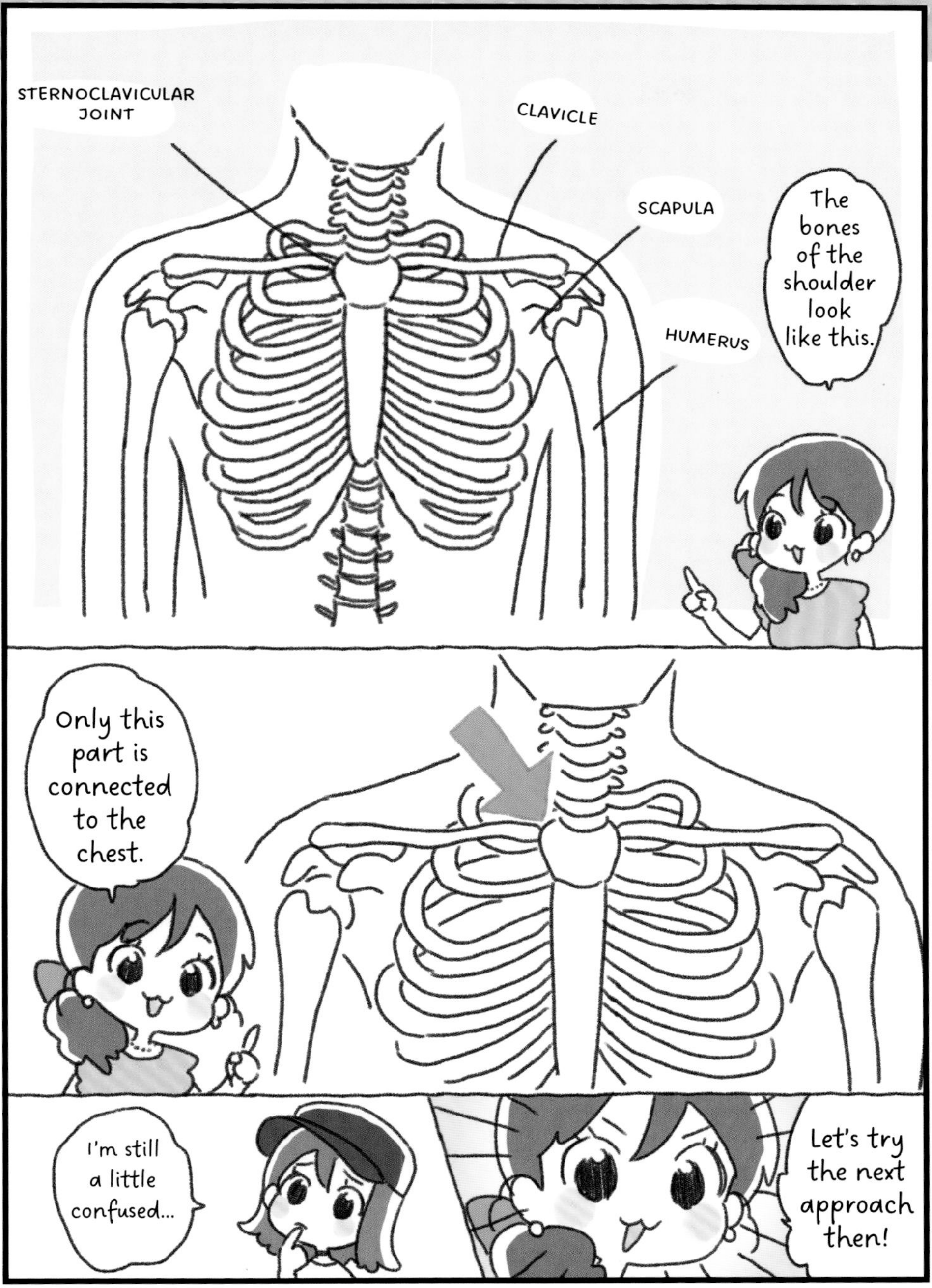
STERNOCLAVICULAR JOINT
CLAVICLE
SCAPULA
HUMERUS
The bones of the shoulder look like this.
Only this part is connected to the chest.
I'm still a little confused...
Let's try the next approach then!

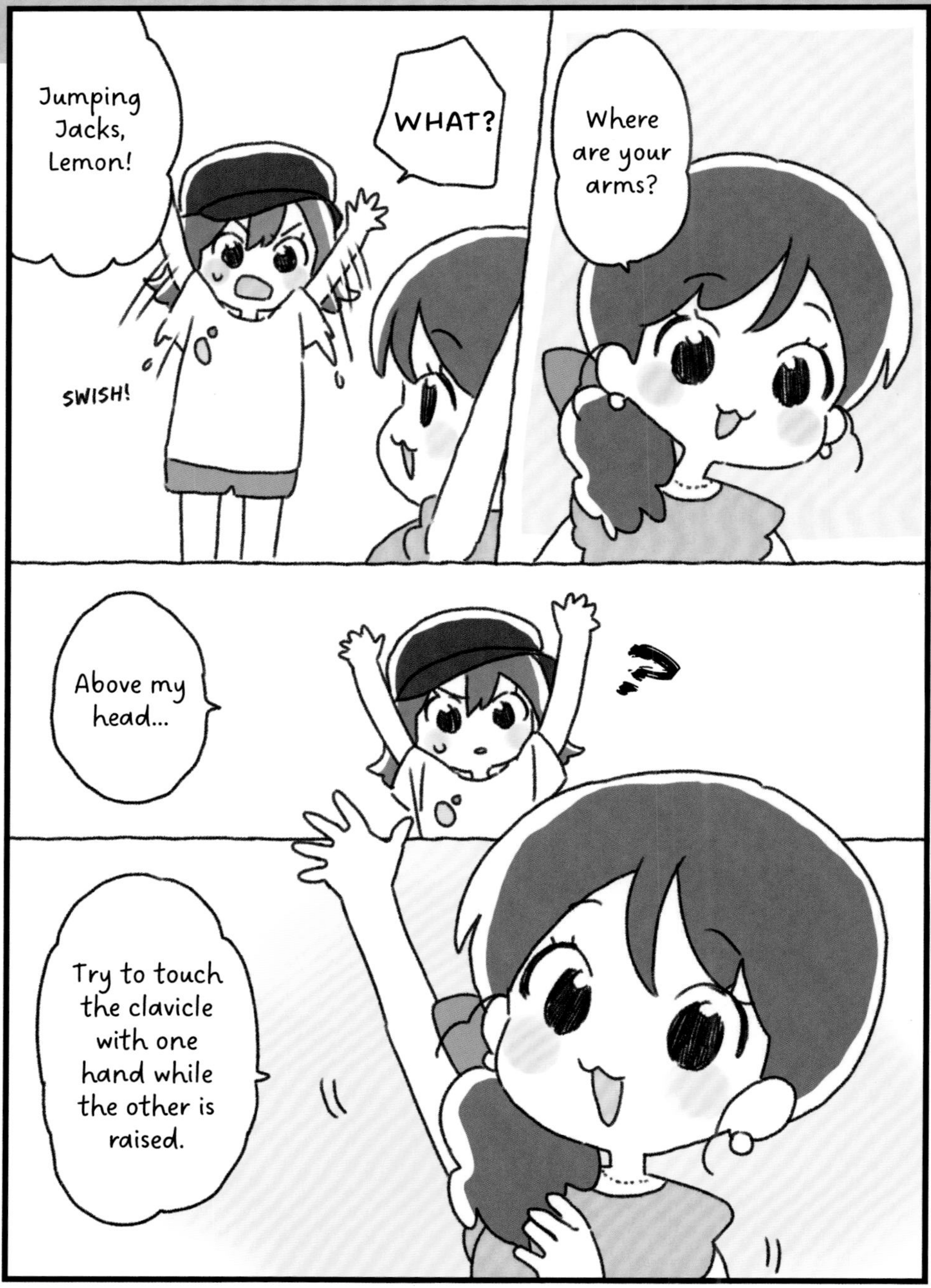
Jumping Jacks, Lemon!
WHAT?
SWISH!
Where are your arms?
Above my head...
?
Try to touch the clavicle with one hand while the other is raised.

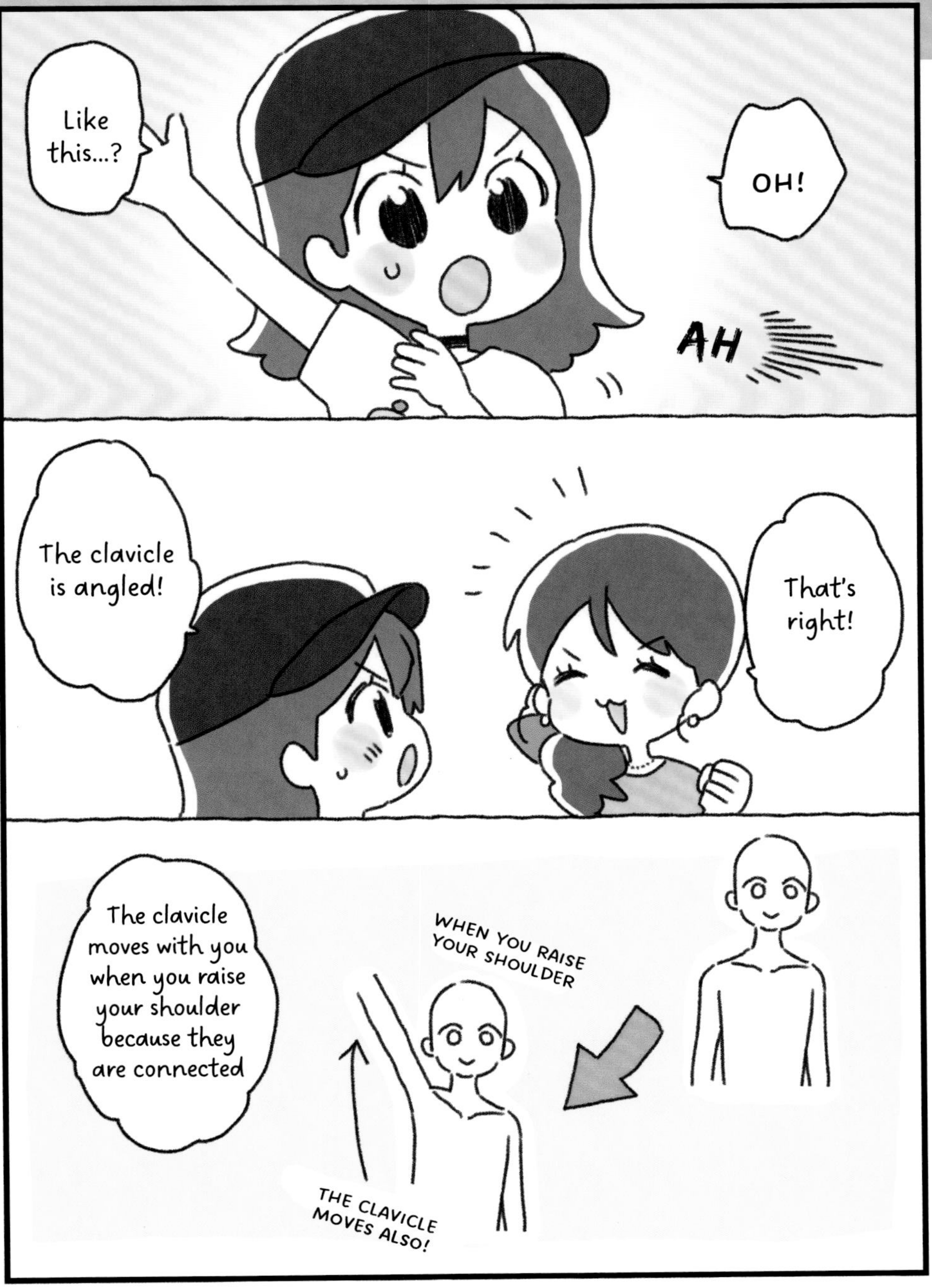
Like this...?
OH!
AH
The clavicle is angled!
That's right!
The clavicle moves with you when you raise your shoulder because they are connected
WHEN YOU RAISE YOUR SHOULDER
THE CLAVICLE MOVES ALSO!

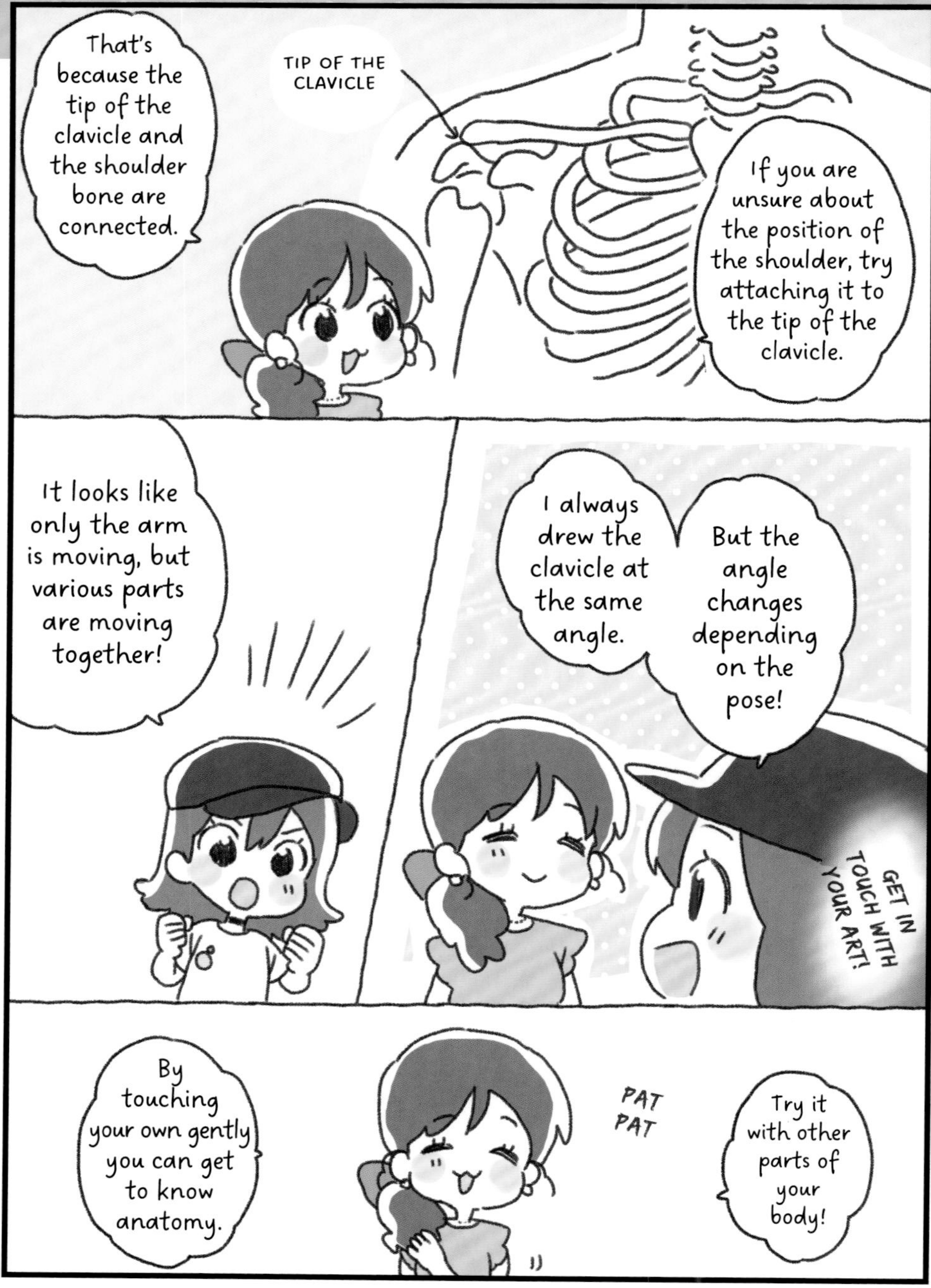
That's because the tip of the clavicle and the shoulder bone are connected.
TIP OF THE CLAVICLE
If you are unsure about the position of the shoulder, try attaching it to the tip of the clavicle.
It looks like only the arm is moving, but various parts are moving together!
I always drew the clavicle at the same angle.
But the angle changes depending on the pose!
GET IN TOUCH WITH YOUR ART!
By touching your own gently you can get to know anatomy.
PAT PAT
Try it with other parts of your body!

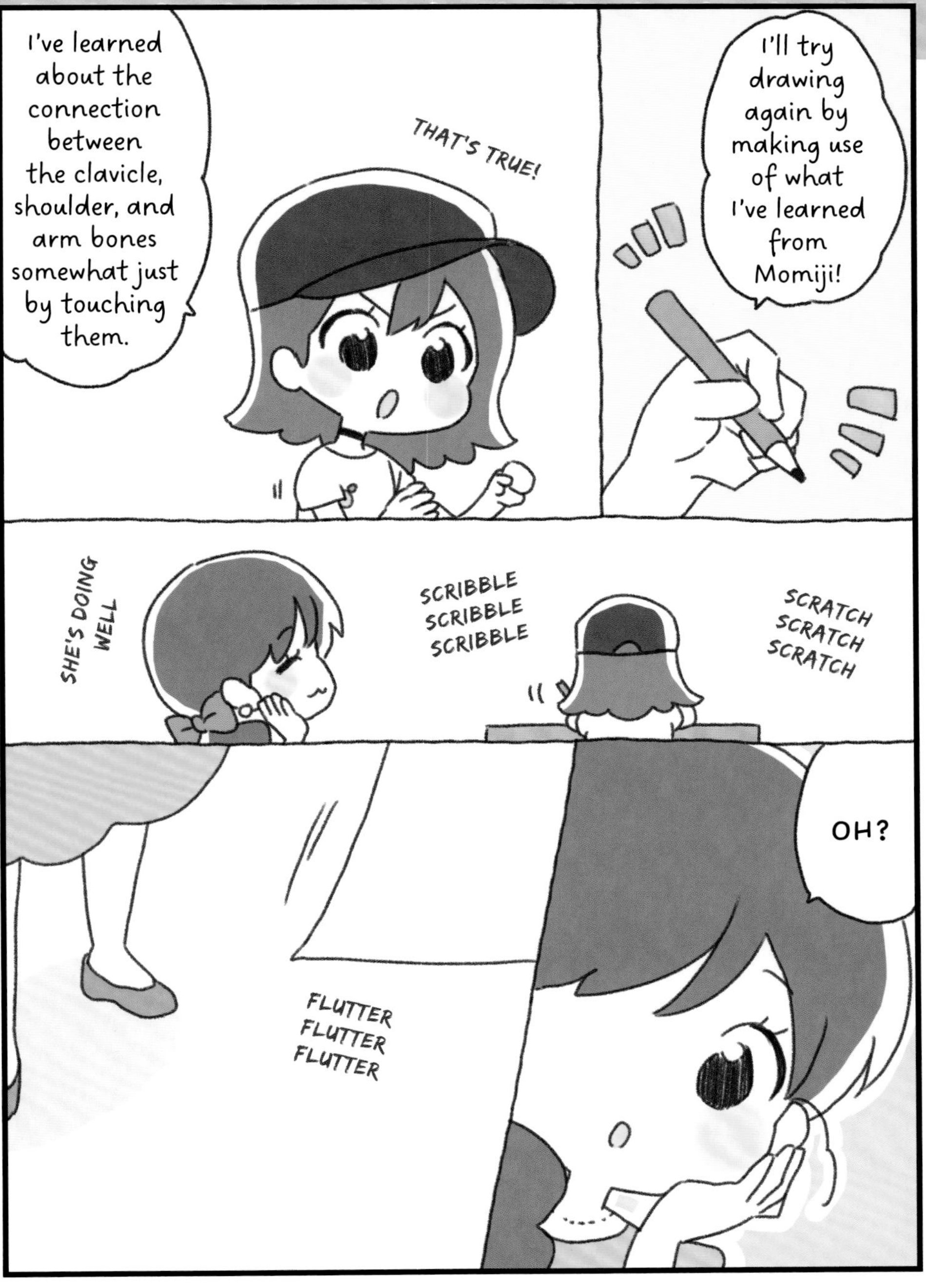
I've learned about the connection between the clavicle, shoulder, and arm bones somewhat just by touching them.
THAT'S TRUE!
I'll try drawing again by making use of what I've learned from Momiji!
SCRATCH SCRATCH SCRATCH
SCRIBBLE SCRIBBLE SCRIBBLE
SHE'S DOING WELL
OH?
FLUTTER FLUTTER FLUTTER

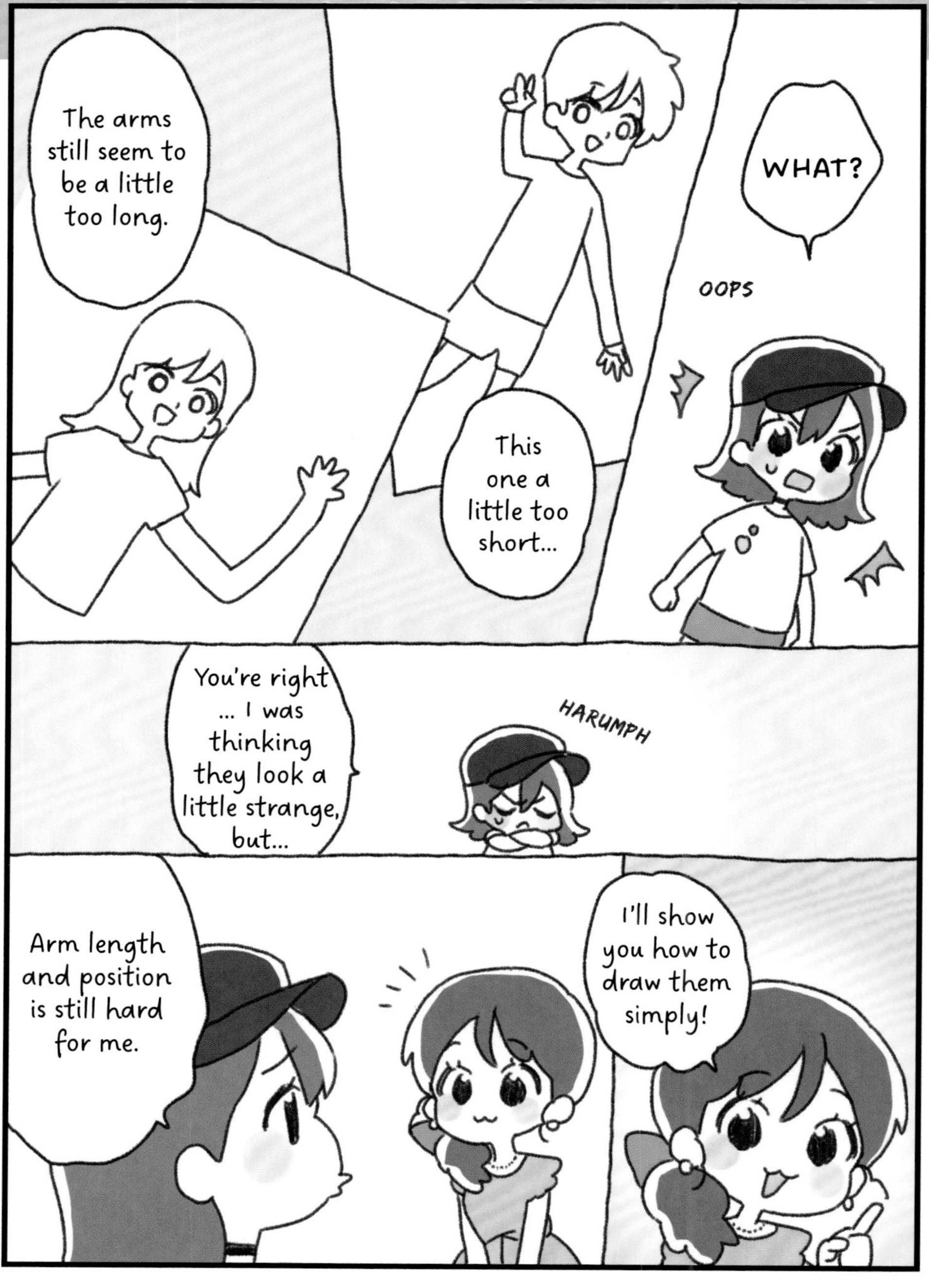
The arms still seem to be a little too long.
WHAT?
OOPS
This one a little too short...
You're right ... I was thinking they look a little strange, but...
HARUMPH
Arm length and position is still hard for me.
I'll show you how to draw them simply!

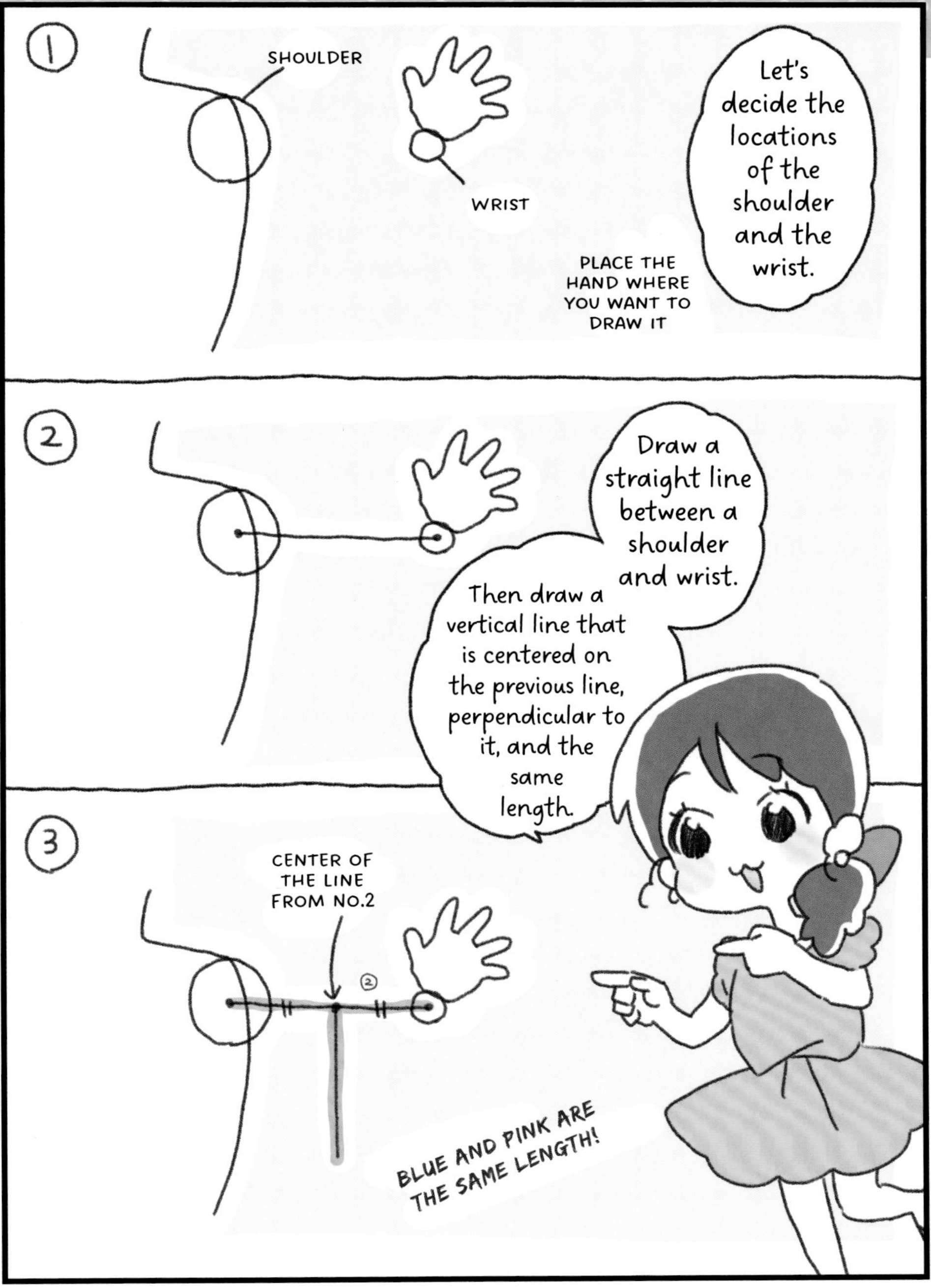
①
SHOULDER
WRIST
Let's decide the locations of the shoulder and the wrist.
PLACE THE HAND WHERE YOU WANT TO DRAW IT
②
Draw a straight line between a shoulder and wrist.
Then draw a vertical line that is centered on the previous line, perpendicular to it, and the same length.
③
CENTER OF THE LINE FROM NO.2
②
BLUE AND PINK ARE THE SAME LENGTH!

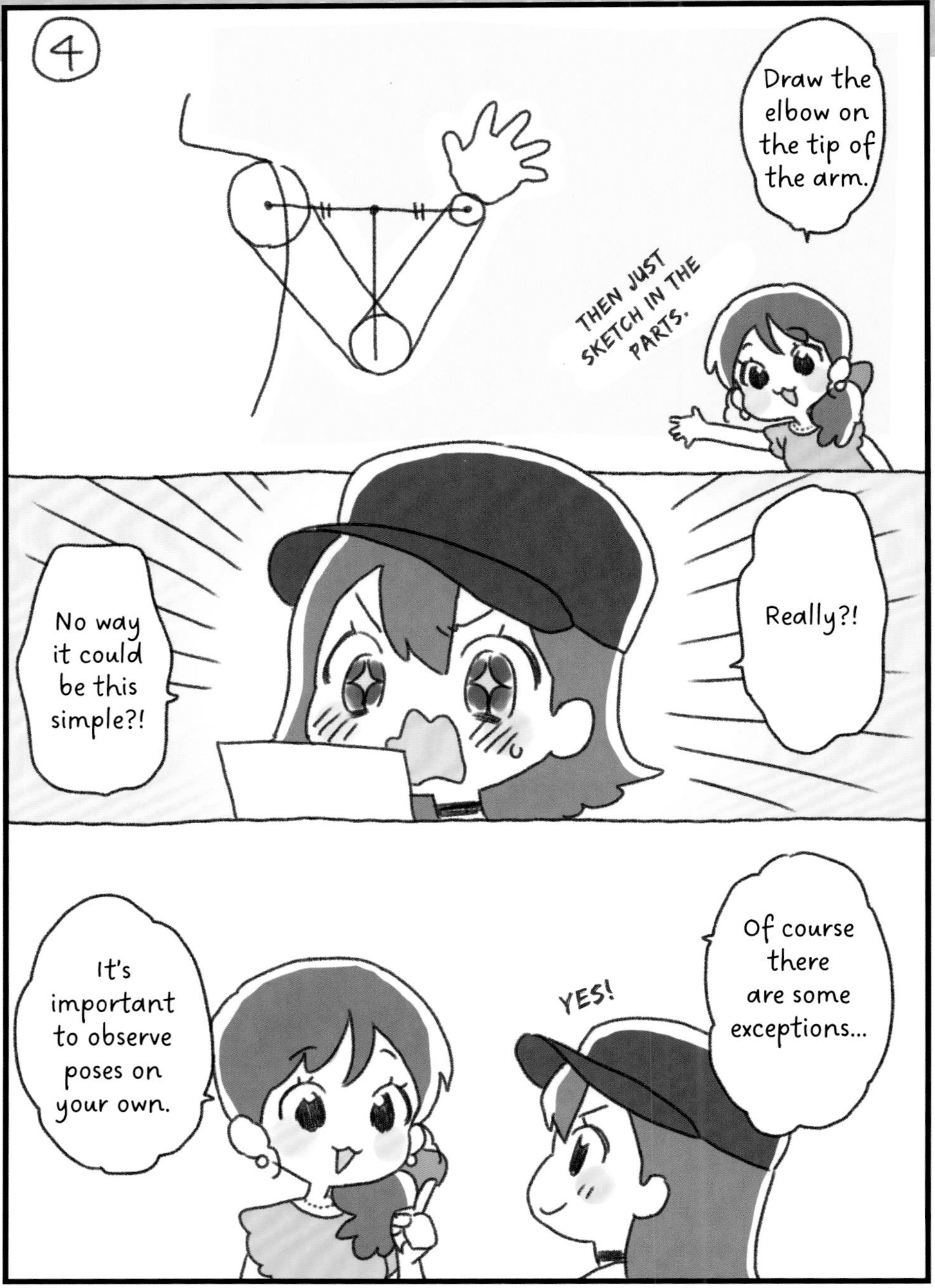
4
Draw the elbow on the tip of the arm.
THEN JUST SKETCH IN THE PARTS.
Really?!
No way it could be this simple?!
Of course there are some exceptions...
YES!
It's important to observe poses on your own.

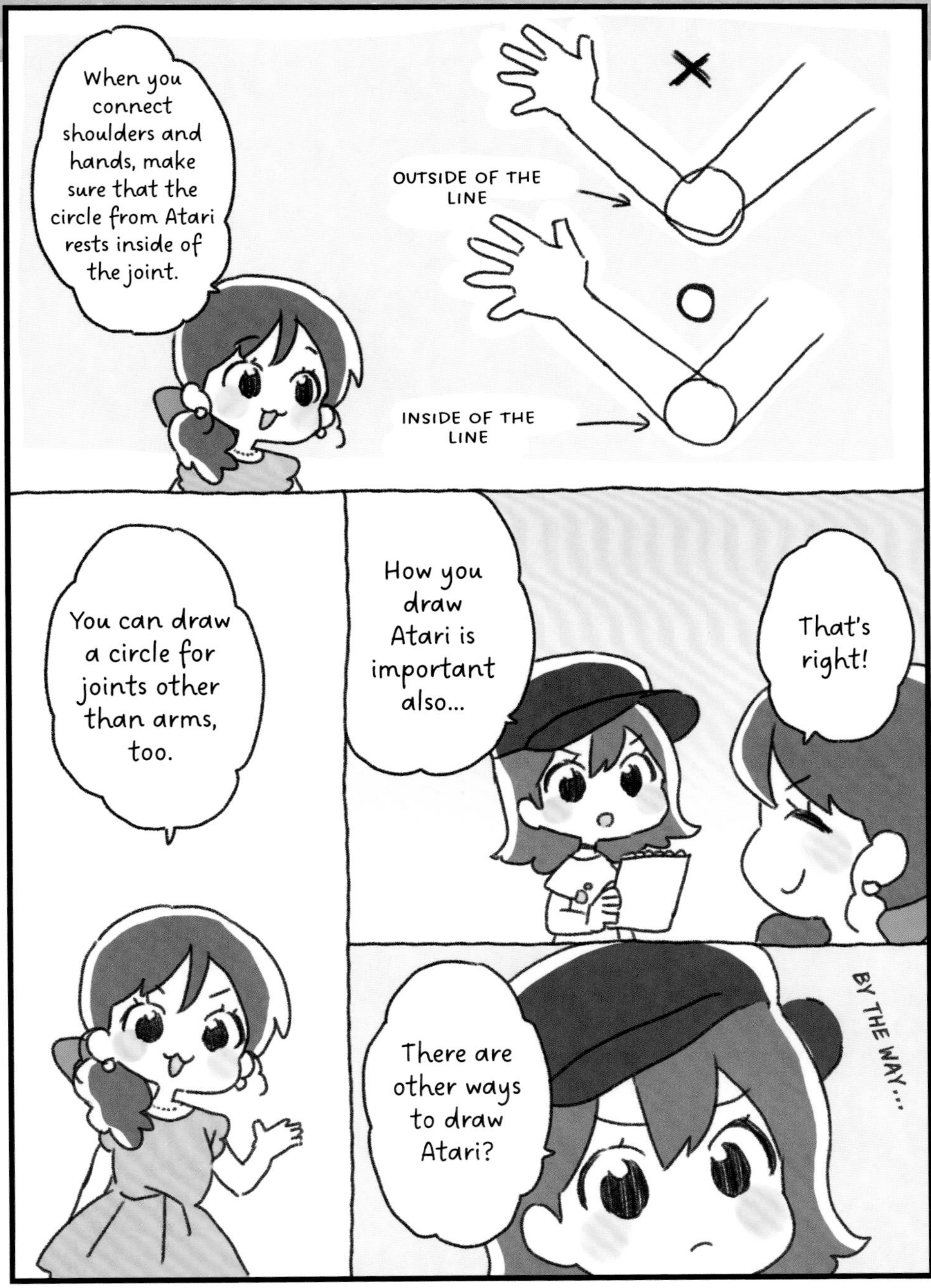
When you connect shoulders and hands, make sure that the circle from Atari rests inside of the joint.
OUTSIDE OF THE LINE
INSIDE OF THE LINE
You can draw a circle for joints other than arms, too.
How you draw Atari is important also...
That's right!
BY THE WAY...
There are other ways to draw Atari?

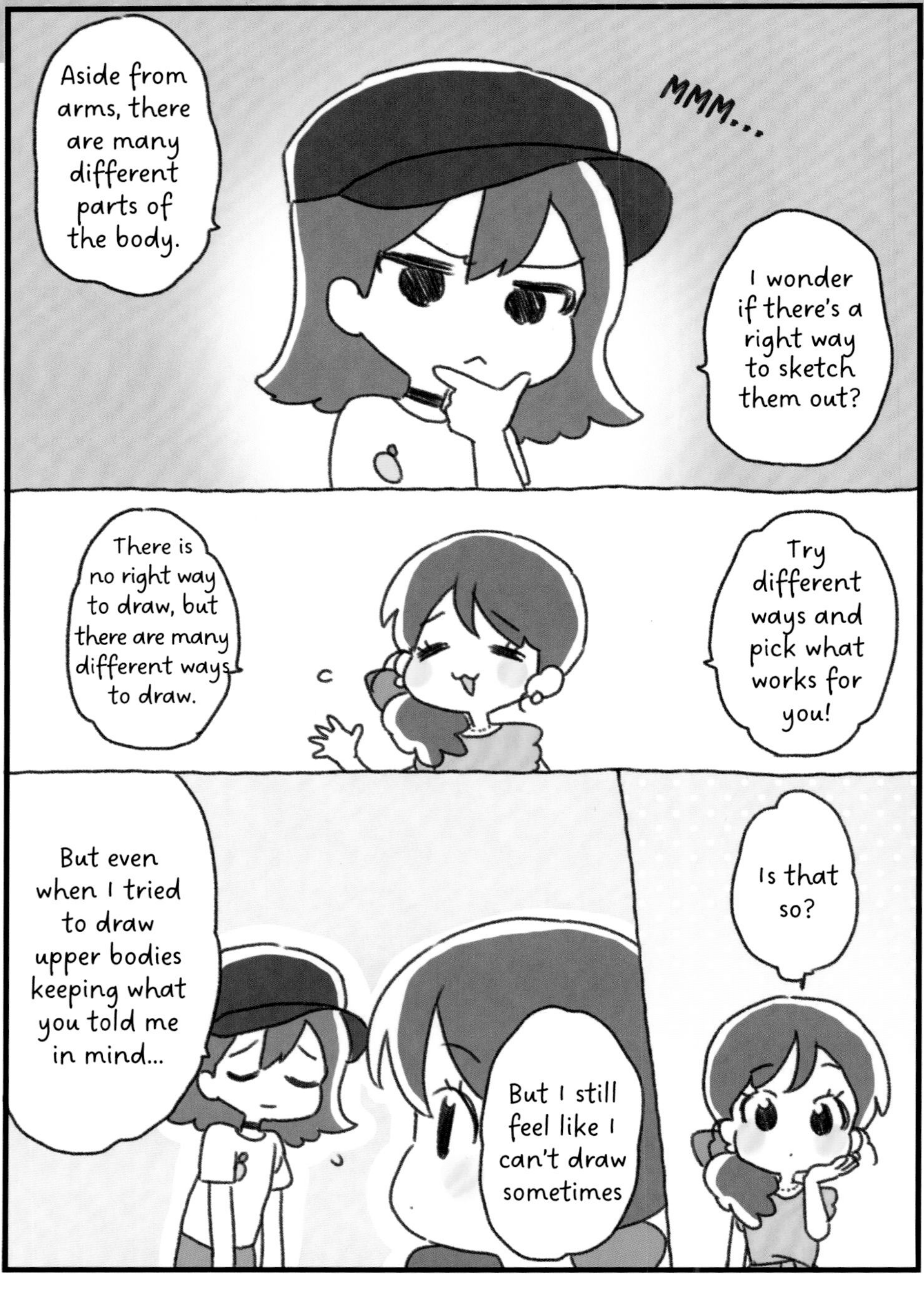
Aside from arms, there are many different parts of the body.
MMM...
I wonder if there's a right way to sketch them out?
There is no right way to draw, but there are many different ways to draw.
Try different ways and pick what works for you!
But even when I tried to draw upper bodies keeping what you told me in mind...
But I still feel like I can't draw sometimes
Is that so?

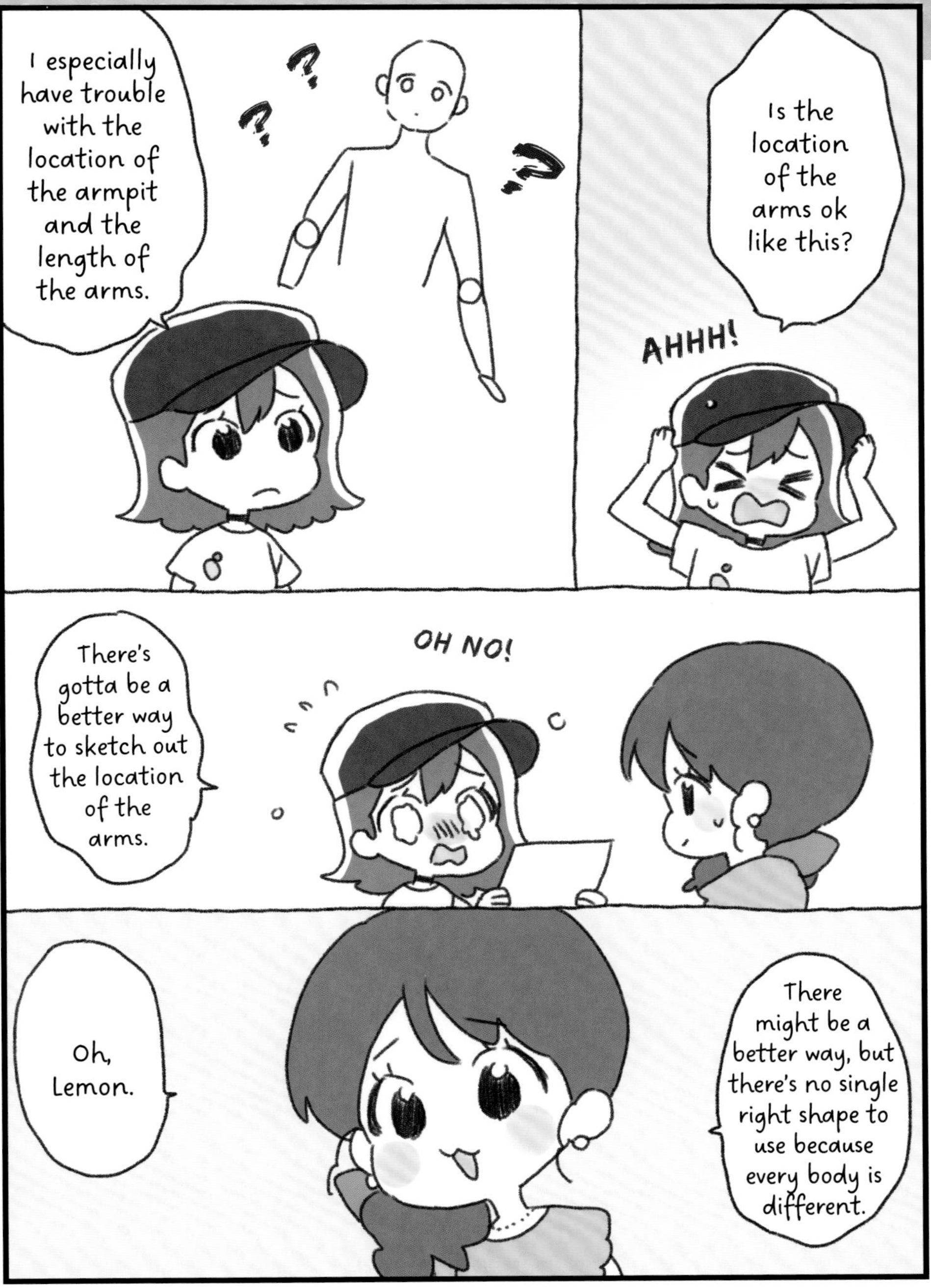
I especially have trouble with the location of the armpit and the length of the arms.
Is the location of the arms ok like this?
AHHH!
There's gotta be a better way to sketch out the location of the arms.
OH NO!
Oh, Lemon.
There might be a better way, but there's no single right shape to use because every body is different.

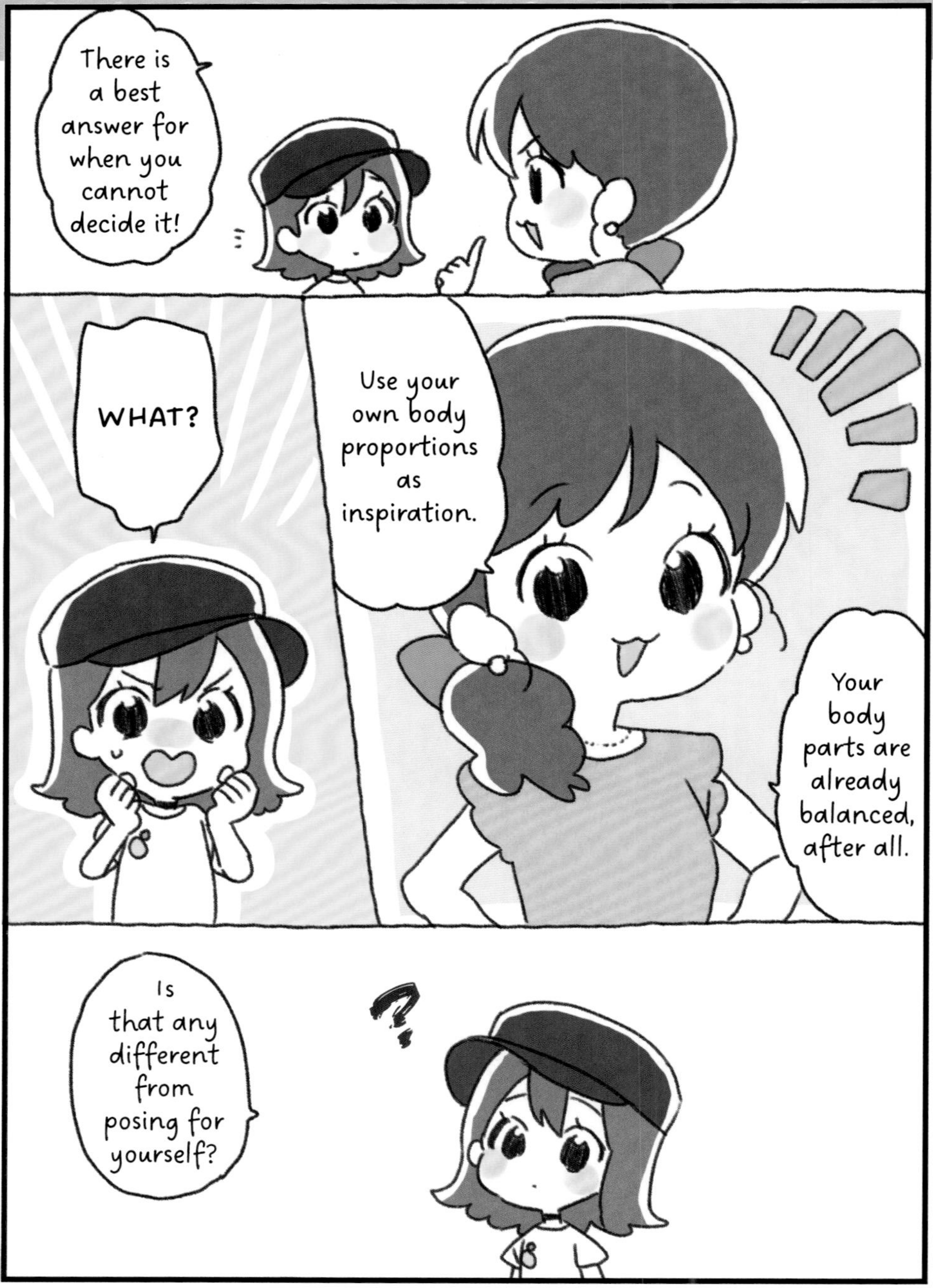
There is a best answer for when you cannot decide it!
WHAT?
Use your own body proportions as inspiration.
Your body parts are already balanced, after all.
Is that any different from posing for yourself?

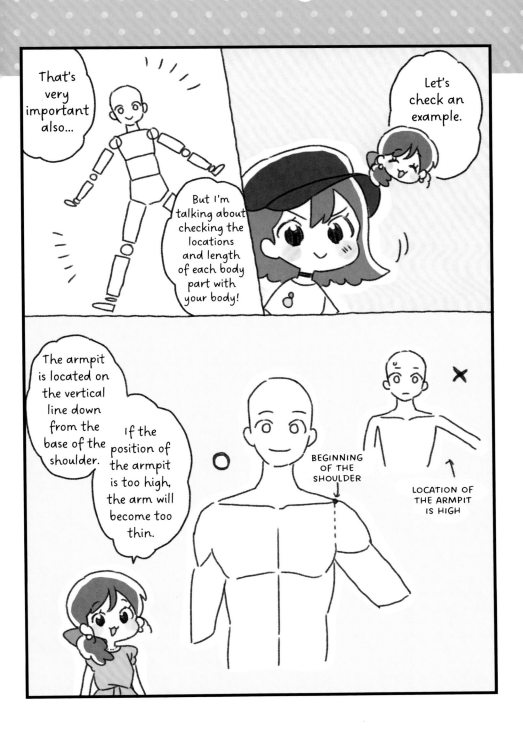

That's very important also...

But I'm talking about checking the locations and length of each body part with your body!

Let's check an example.

The armpit is located on the vertical line down from the base of the shoulder.

If the position of the armpit is too high, the arm will become too thin.

BEGINNING OF THE SHOULDER

×

LOCATION OF THE ARMPIT IS HIGH

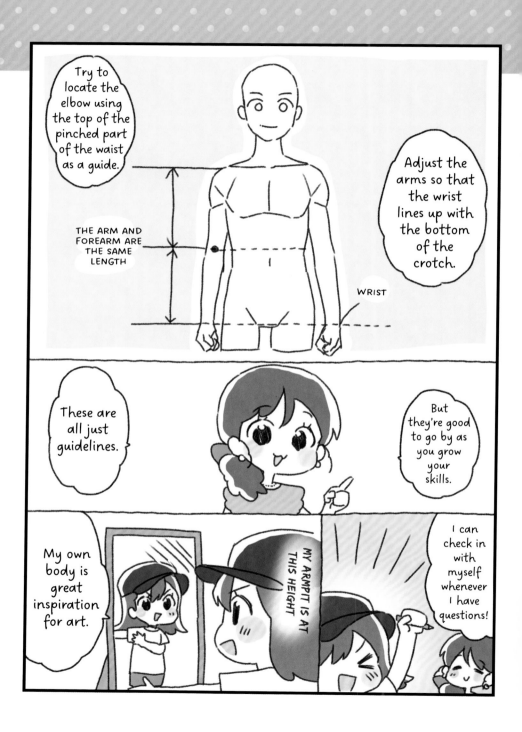

Try to locate the elbow using the top of the pinched part of the waist as a guide.

Adjust the arms so that the wrist lines up with the bottom of the crotch.

THE ARM AND FOREARM ARE THE SAME LENGTH

WRIST

These are all just guidelines.

But they're good to go by as you grow your skills.

My own body is great inspiration for art.

MY ARMPIT IS AT THIS HEIGHT

I can check in with myself whenever I have questions!

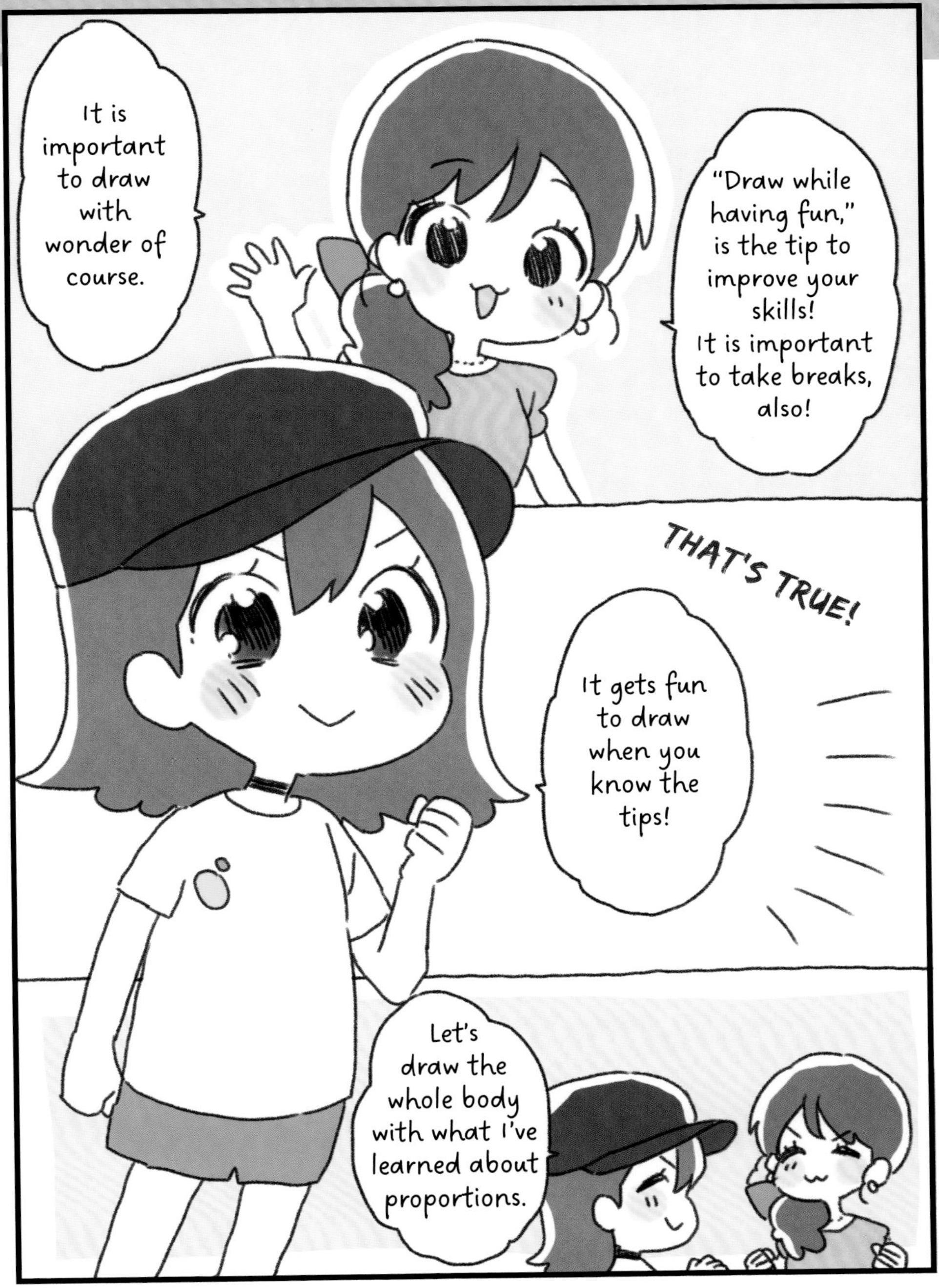
It is important to draw with wonder of course.
"Draw while having fun," is the tip to improve your skills! It is important to take breaks, also!
THAT'S TRUE!
It gets fun to draw when you know the tips!
Let's draw the whole body with what I've learned about proportions.

# LEVEL UP

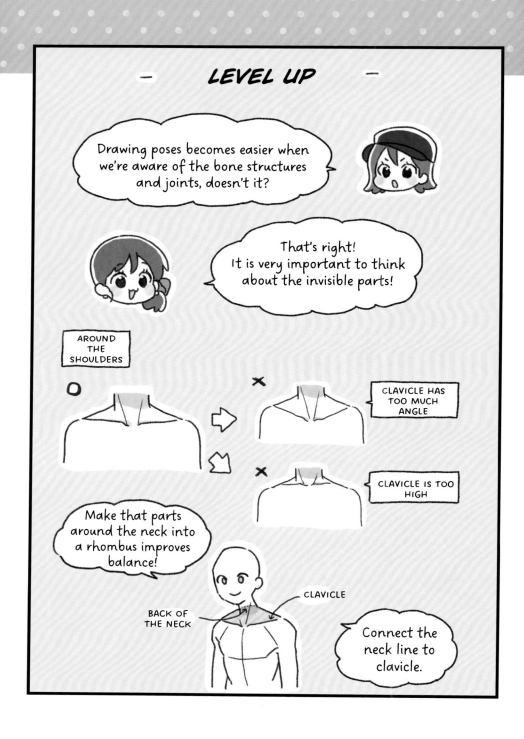

Drawing poses becomes easier when we're aware of the bone structures and joints, doesn't it?

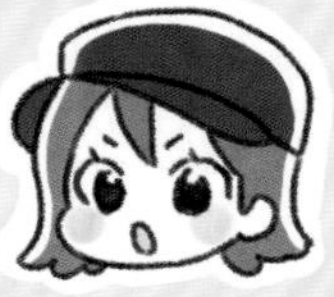

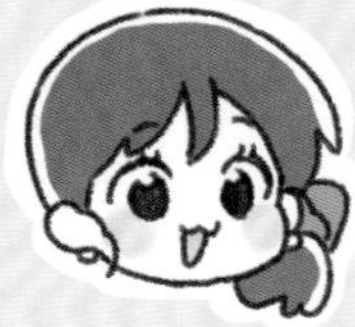

That's right!
It is very important to think about the invisible parts!

AROUND THE SHOULDERS

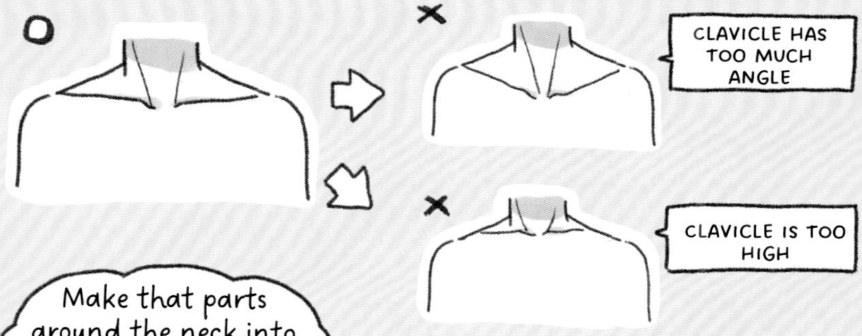

O
×
CLAVICLE HAS TOO MUCH ANGLE
×
CLAVICLE IS TOO HIGH


Make that parts around the neck into a rhombus improves balance!

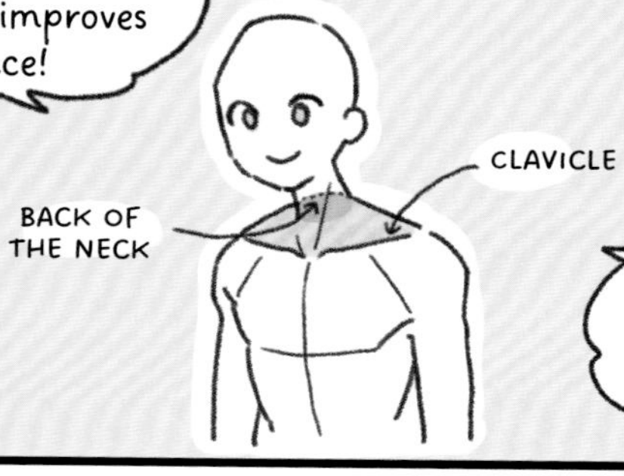

CLAVICLE
BACK OF THE NECK


Connect the neck line to clavicle.

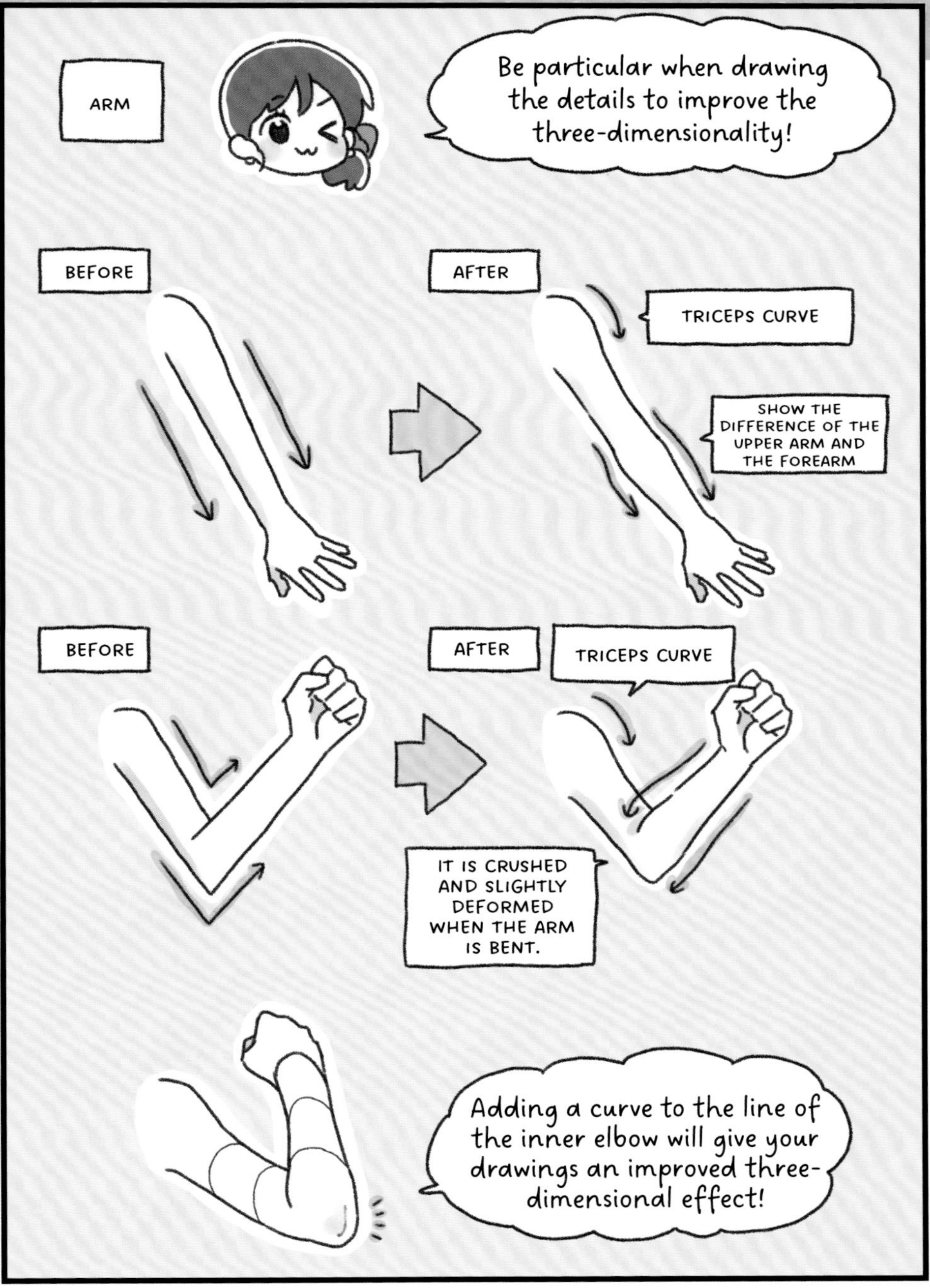
ARM
Be particular when drawing the details to improve the three-dimensionality!
BEFORE
AFTER
TRICEPS CURVE
SHOW THE DIFFERENCE OF THE UPPER ARM AND THE FOREARM
BEFORE
AFTER
TRICEPS CURVE
IT IS CRUSHED AND SLIGHTLY DEFORMED WHEN THE ARM IS BENT.
Adding a curve to the line of the inner elbow will give your drawings an improved three-dimensional effect!

# RANGE OF MOTION FOR THE WHOLE BODY

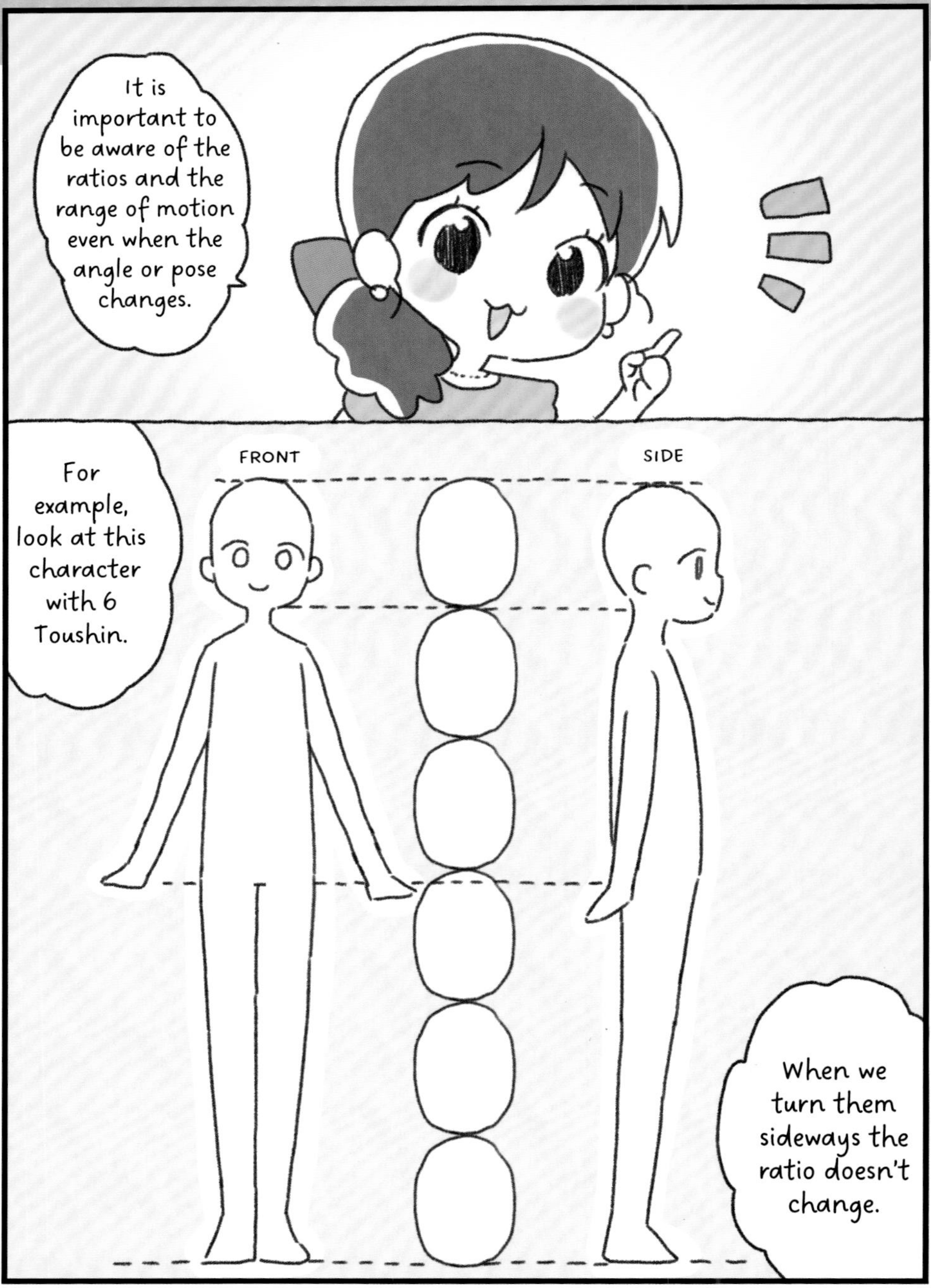

It is important to be aware of the ratios and the range of motion even when the angle or pose changes.
For example, look at this character with 6 Toushin.
FRONT
SIDE
When we turn them sideways the ratio doesn't change.

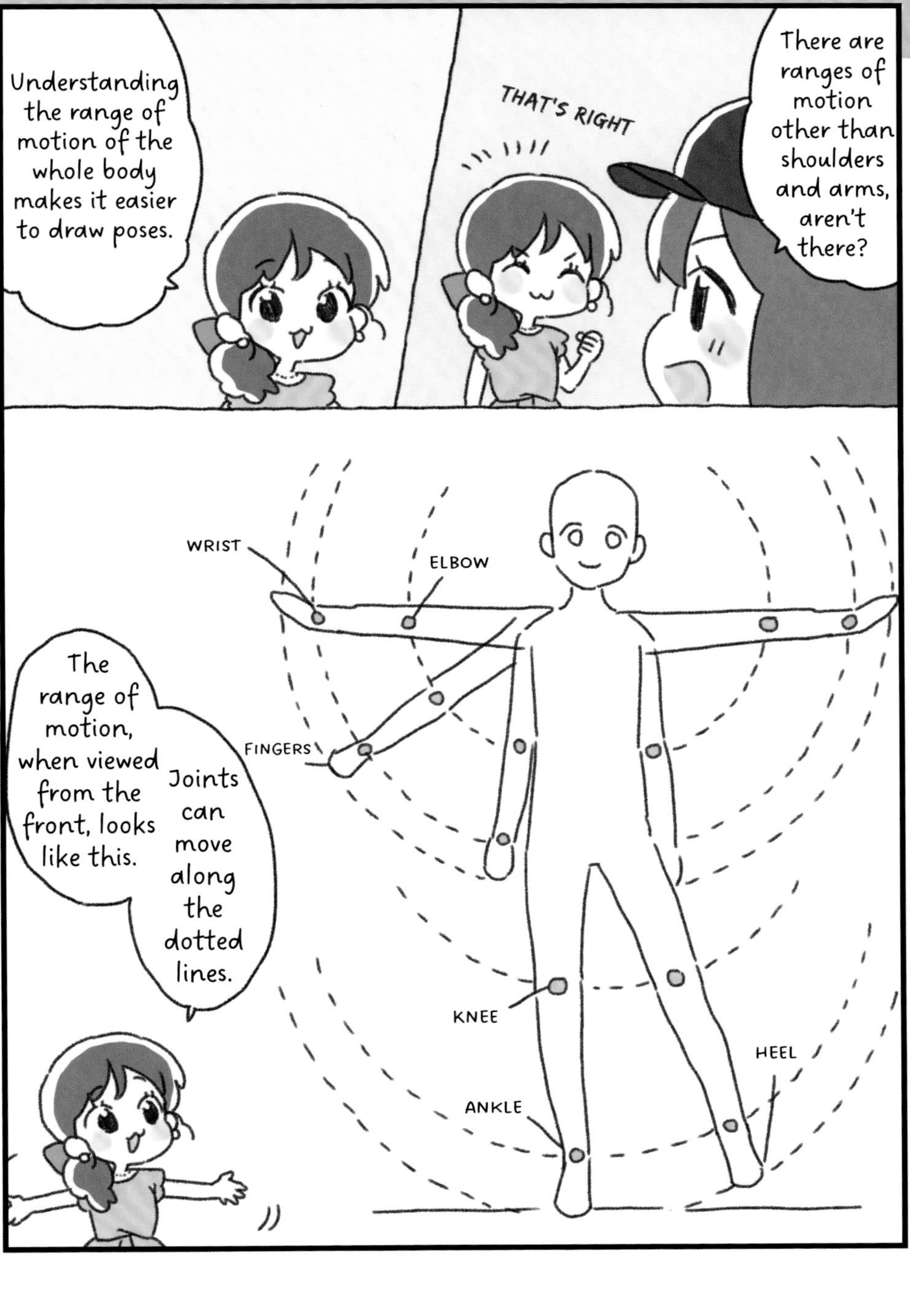

Understanding the range of motion of the whole body makes it easier to draw poses.
THAT'S RIGHT
There are ranges of motion other than shoulders and arms, aren't there?
The range of motion, when viewed from the front, looks like this.
Joints can move along the dotted lines.
WRIST
ELBOW
FINGERS
KNEE
HEEL
ANKLE

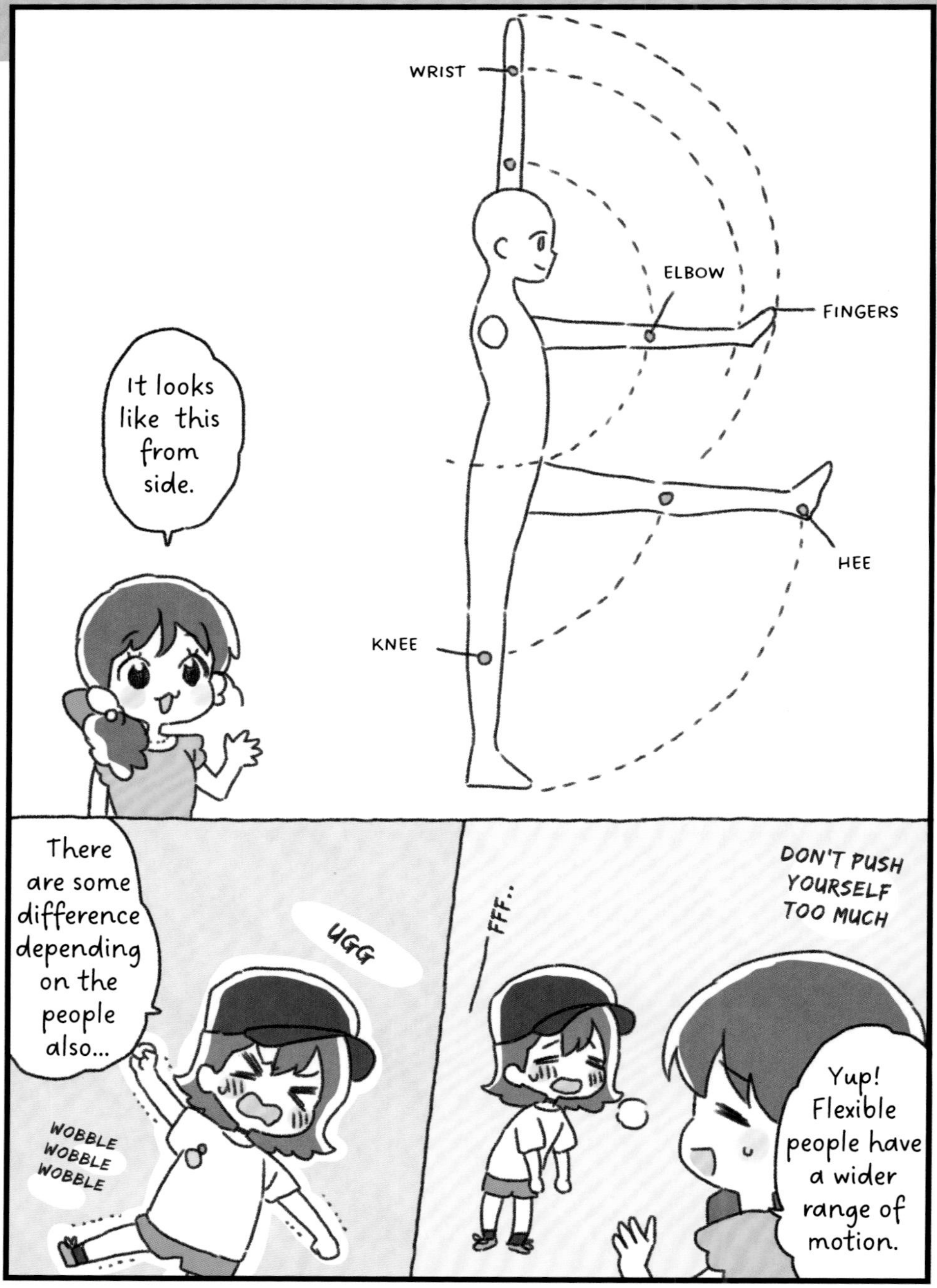
WRIST
ELBOW
FINGERS
HEE
KNEE
It looks like this from side.
There are some difference depending on the people also...
UGG
WOBBLE WOBBLE WOBBLE
FFF..
DON'T PUSH YOURSELF TOO MUCH
Yup! Flexible people have a wider range of motion.

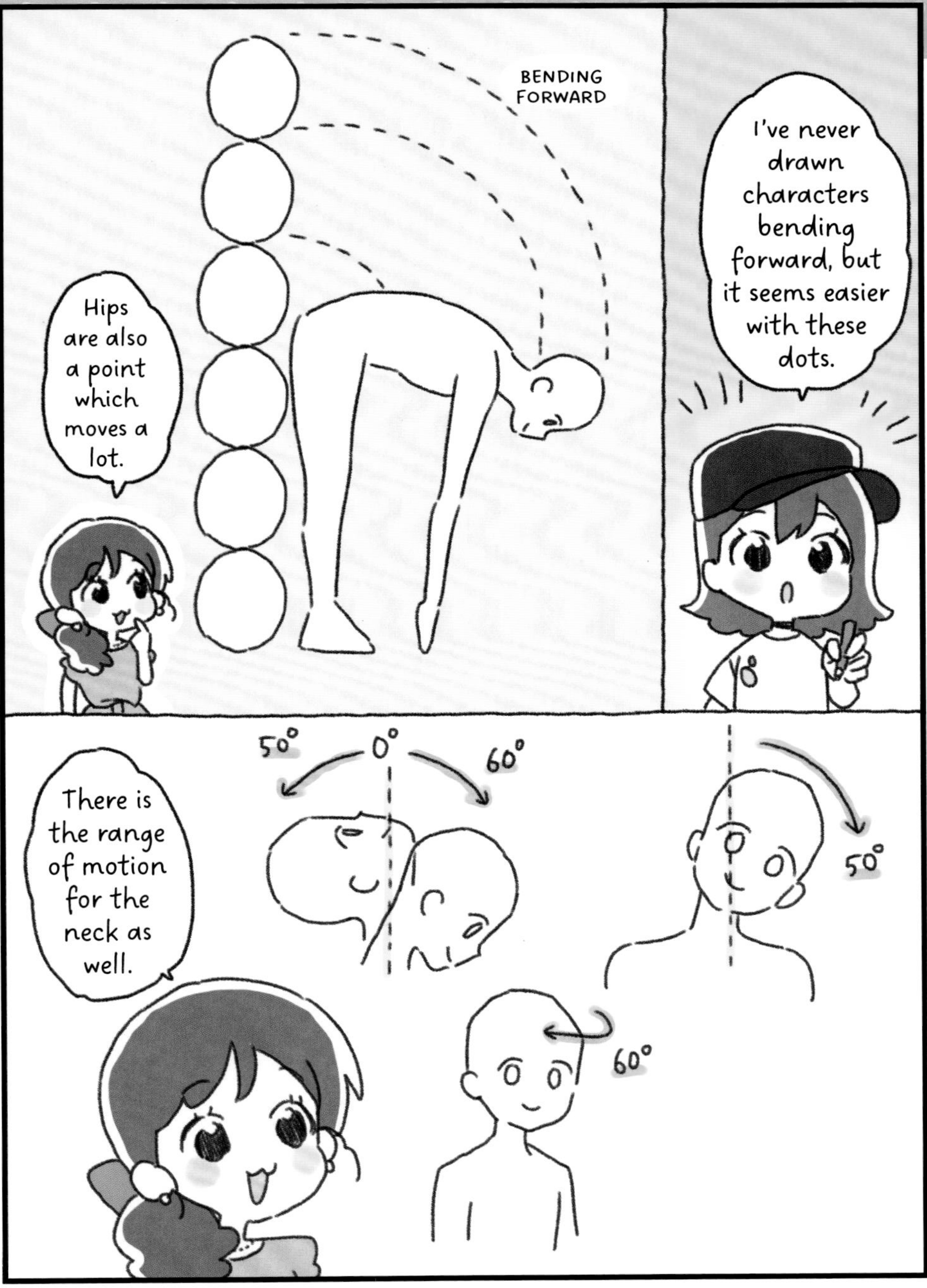
BENDING FORWARD
I've never drawn characters bending forward, but it seems easier with these dots.
Hips are also a point which moves a lot.
50°
0°
60°
50°
There is the range of motion for the neck as well.
60°

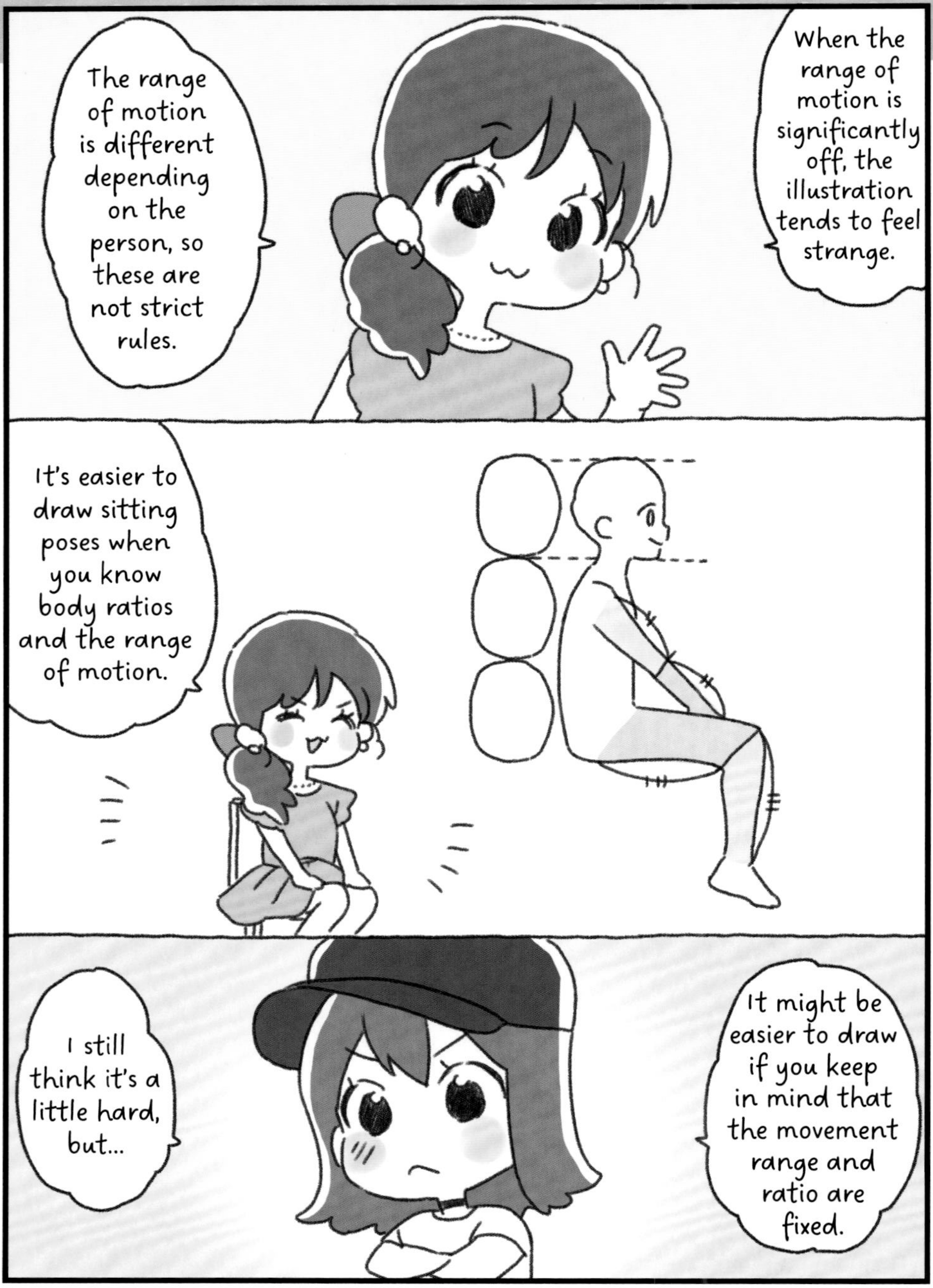
The range of motion is different depending on the person, so these are not strict rules.
When the range of motion is significantly off, the illustration tends to feel strange.
It's easier to draw sitting poses when you know body ratios and the range of motion.
I still think it's a little hard, but...
It might be easier to draw if you keep in mind that the movement range and ratio are fixed.

## — SUMMARY —

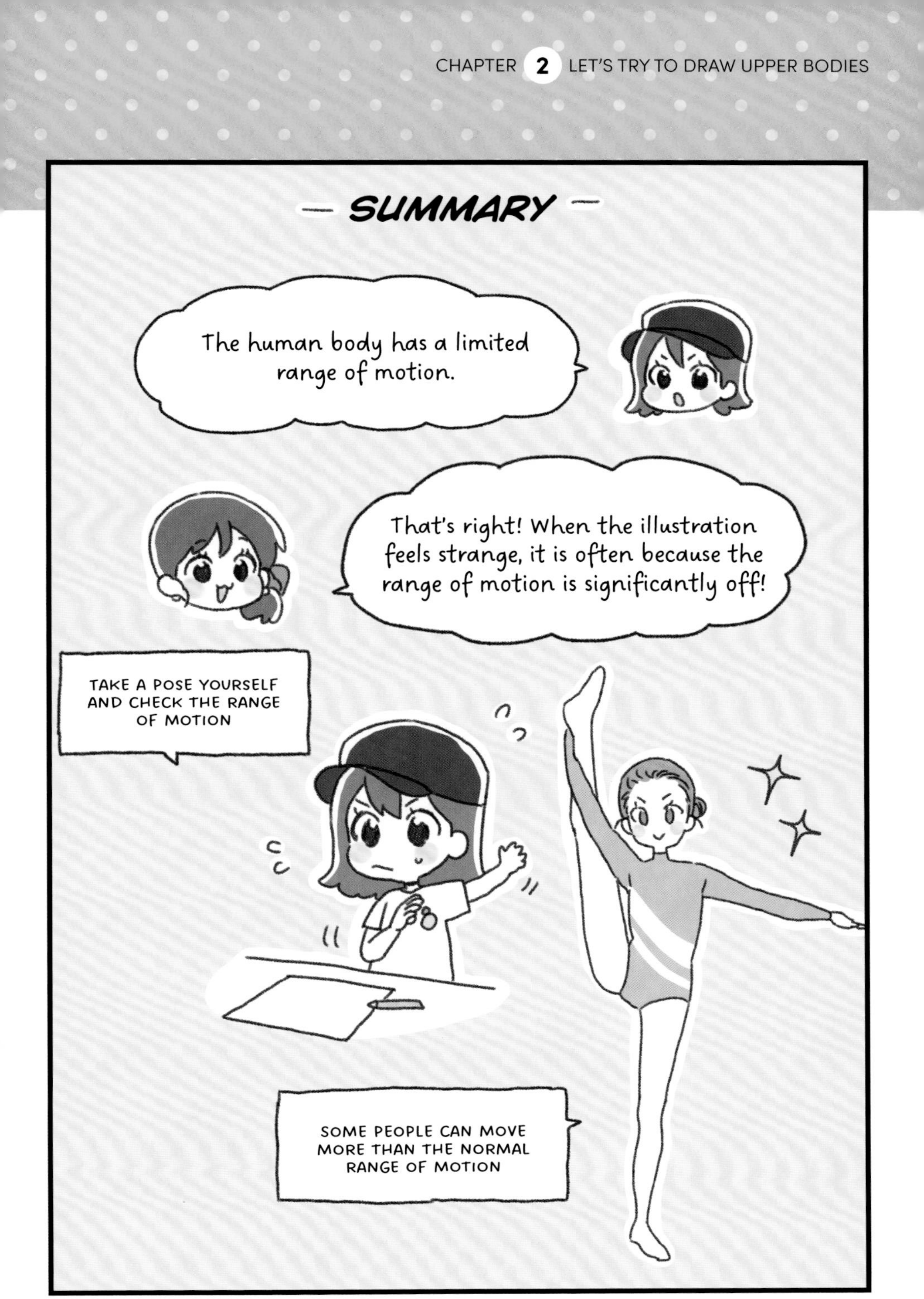
The human body has a limited range of motion.
That's right! When the illustration feels strange, it is often because the range of motion is significantly off!
TAKE A POSE YOURSELF AND CHECK THE RANGE OF MOTION
SOME PEOPLE CAN MOVE MORE THAN THE NORMAL RANGE OF MOTION

# DIFFERENTIATING BETWEEN MEN'S AND WOMEN'S ARMS

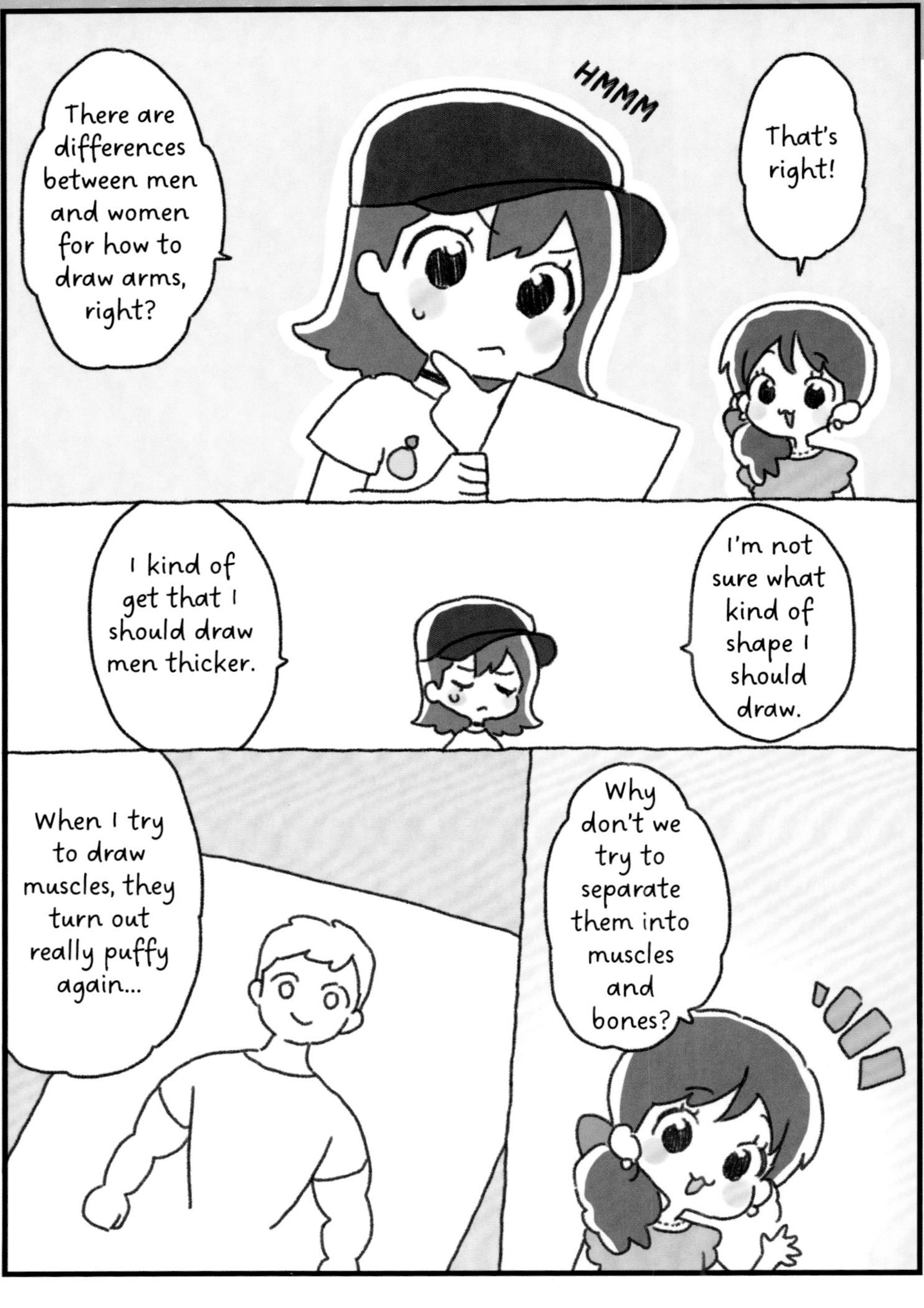
There are differences between men and women for how to draw arms, right?
HMMM
That's right!
I kind of get that I should draw men thicker.
I'm not sure what kind of shape I should draw.
When I try to draw muscles, they turn out really puffy again...
Why don't we try to separate them into muscles and bones?

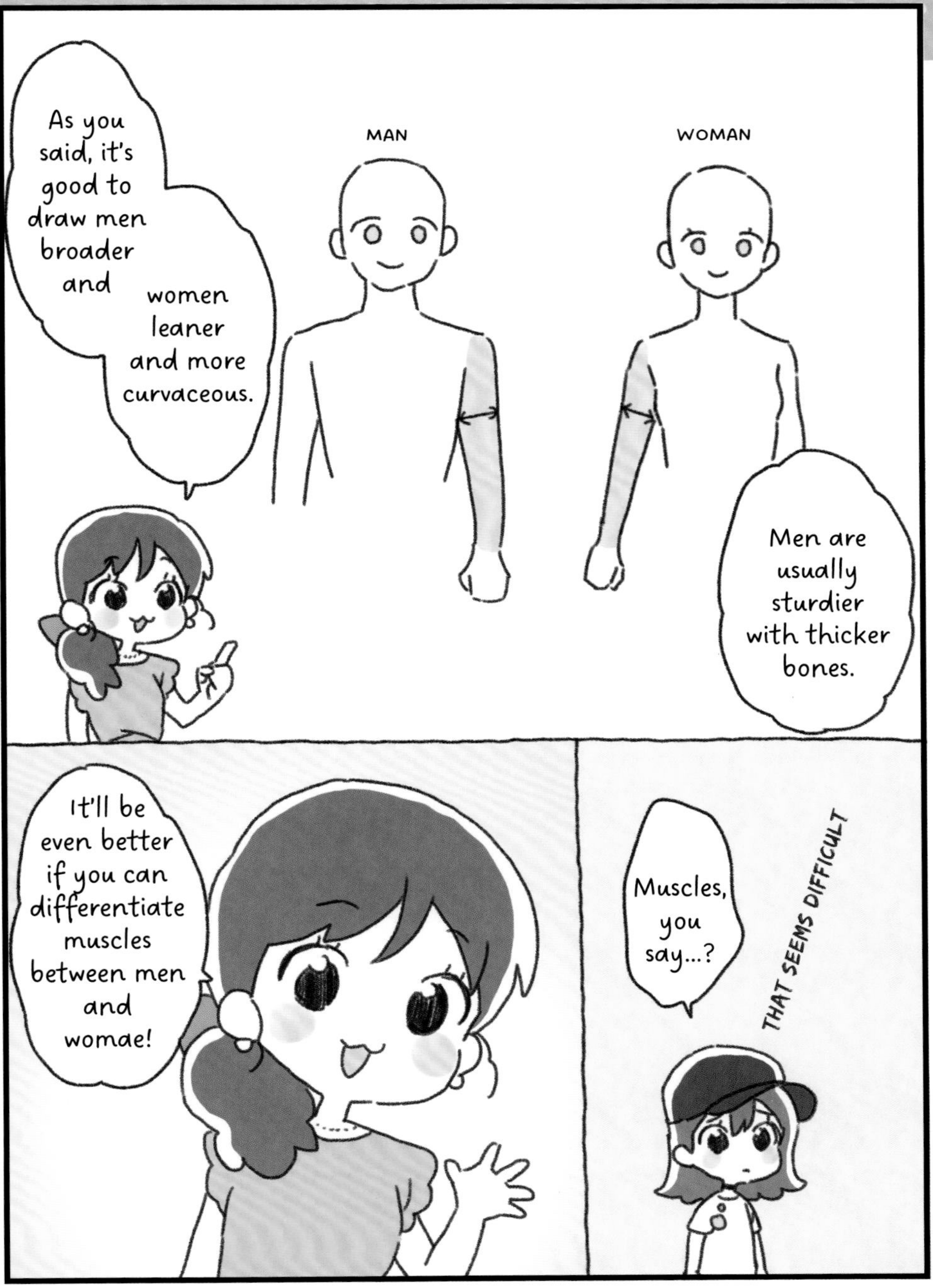
As you said, it's good to draw men broader and
MAN
WOMAN
women leaner and more curvaceous.
Men are usually sturdier with thicker bones.
It'll be even better if you can differentiate muscles between men and womae!
Muscles, you say...?
THAT SEEMS DIFFICULT

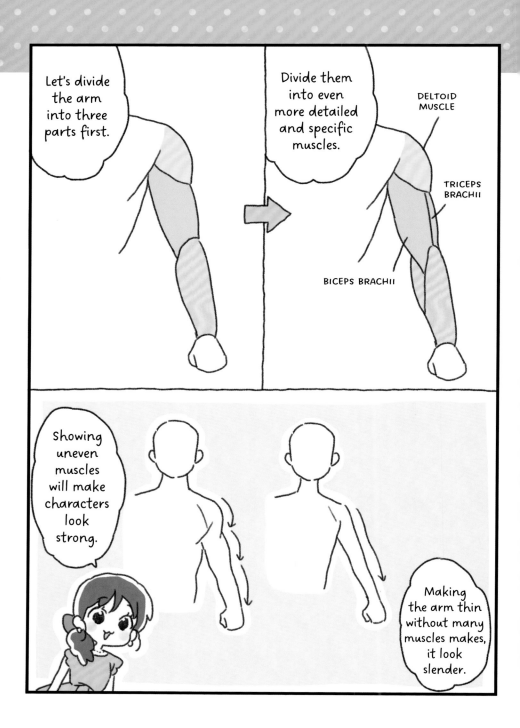

Let's divide the arm into three parts first.

Divide them into even more detailed and specific muscles.

DELTOID MUSCLE

TRICEPS BRACHII

BICEPS BRACHII

Showing uneven muscles will make characters look strong.

Making the arm thin without many muscles makes, it look slender.

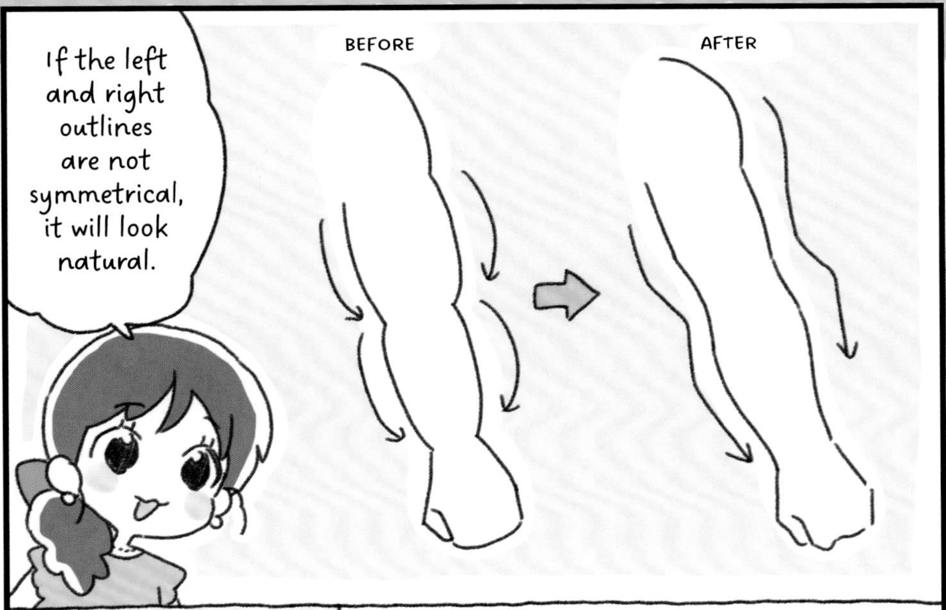
If the left and right outlines are not symmetrical, it will look natural.
BEFORE
AFTER

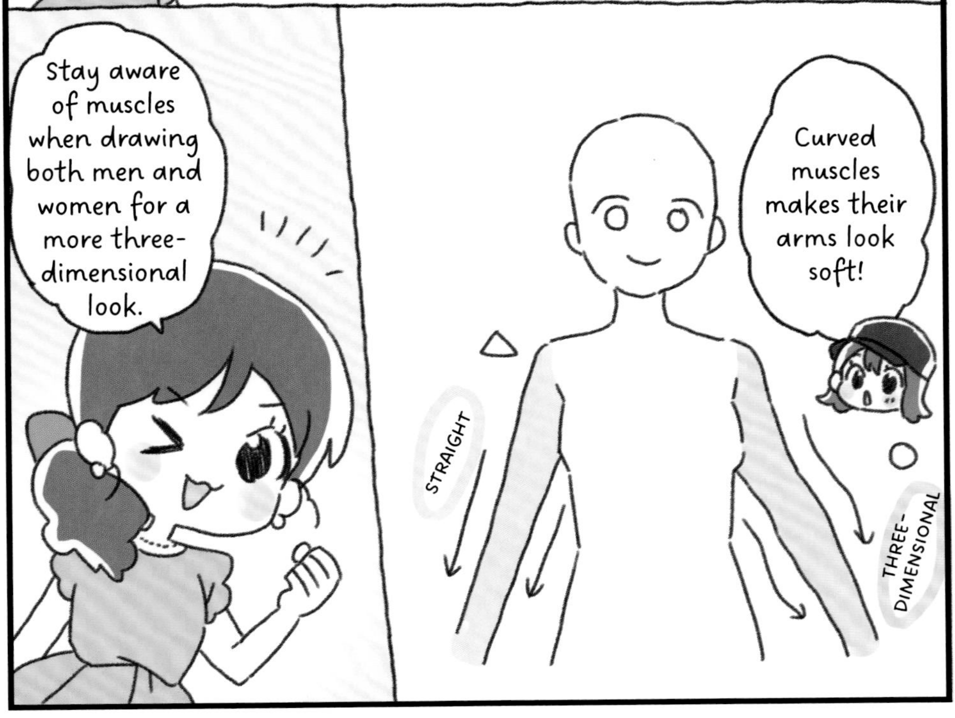
Stay aware of muscles when drawing both men and women for a more three-dimensional look.
Curved muscles makes their arms look soft!
STRAIGHT
THREE-DIMENSIONAL

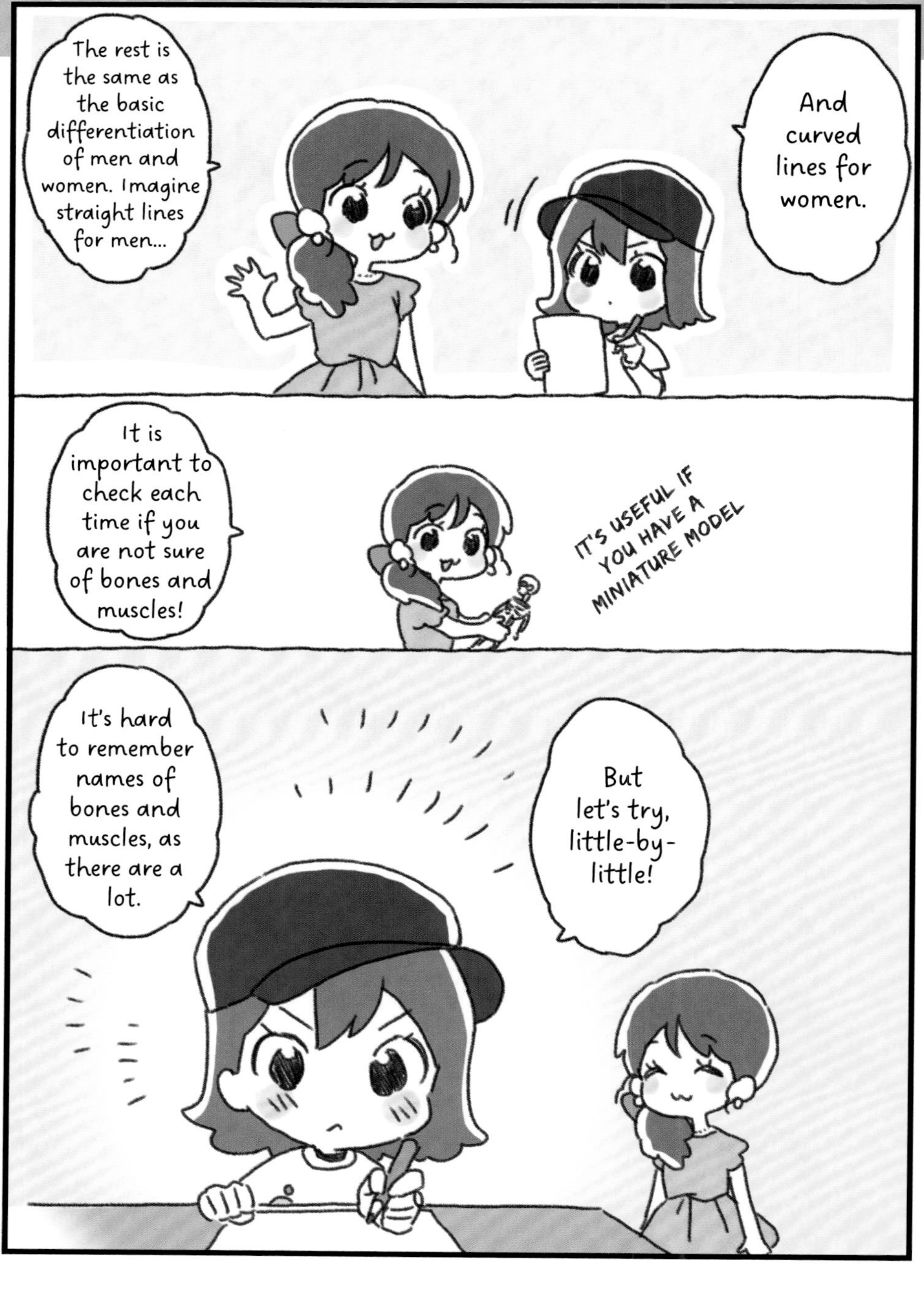
The rest is the same as the basic differentiation of men and women. Imagine straight lines for men...
And curved lines for women.
It is important to check each time if you are not sure of bones and muscles!
IT'S USEFUL IF YOU HAVE A MINIATURE MODEL
It's hard to remember names of bones and muscles, as there are a lot.
But let's try, little-by-little!

## — SUMMARY —

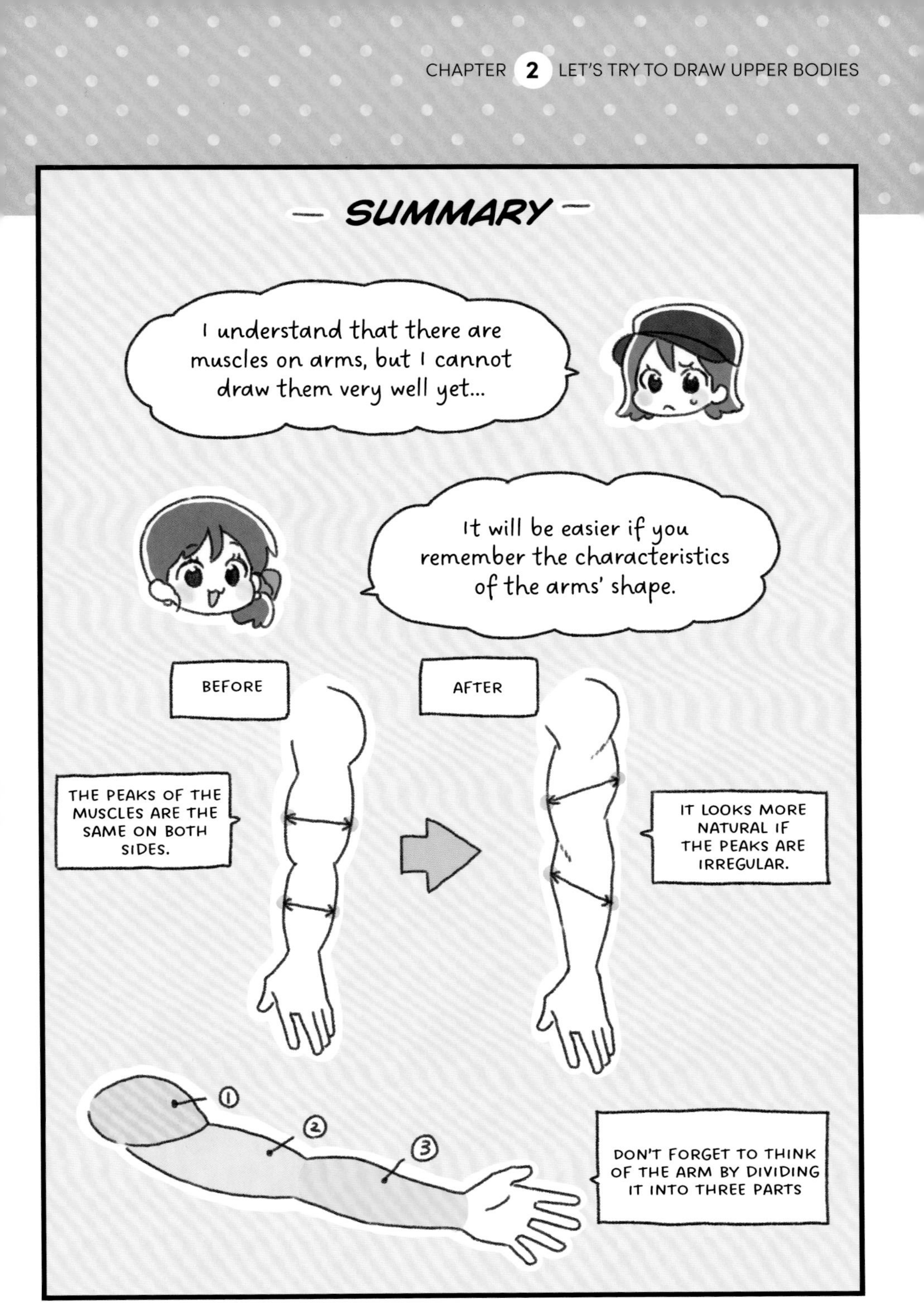
I understand that there are muscles on arms, but I cannot draw them very well yet...
It will be easier if you remember the characteristics of the arms' shape.
BEFORE
AFTER
THE PEAKS OF THE MUSCLES ARE THE SAME ON BOTH SIDES.
IT LOOKS MORE NATURAL IF THE PEAKS ARE IRREGULAR.
①
②
③
DON'T FORGET TO THINK OF THE ARM BY DIVIDING IT INTO THREE PARTS

# HOW TO DRAW HANDS

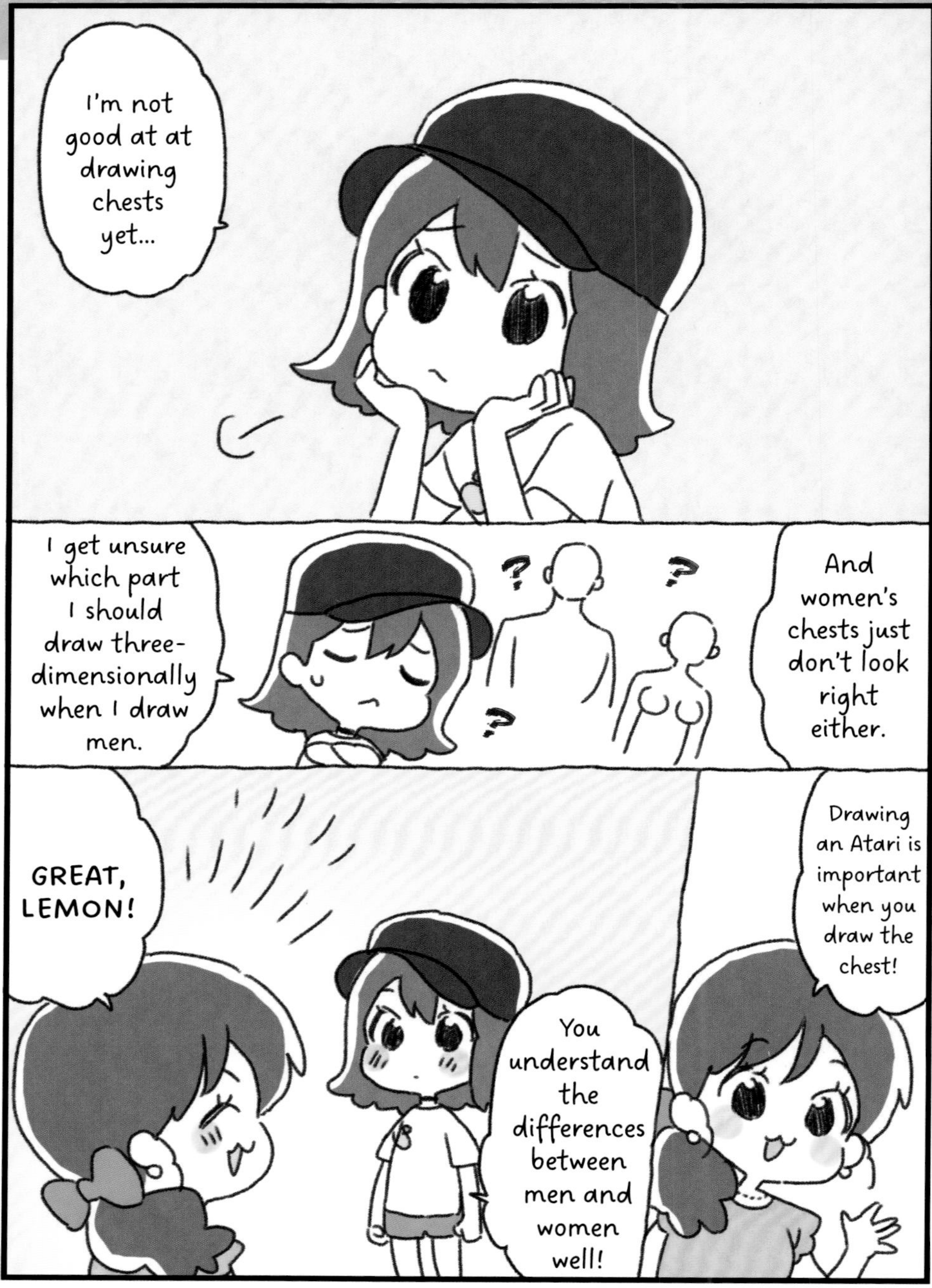

I'm not good at at drawing chests yet...
I get unsure which part I should draw three-dimensionally when I draw men.
And women's chests just don't look right either.
GREAT, LEMON!
You understand the differences between men and women well!
Drawing an Atari is important when you draw the chest!

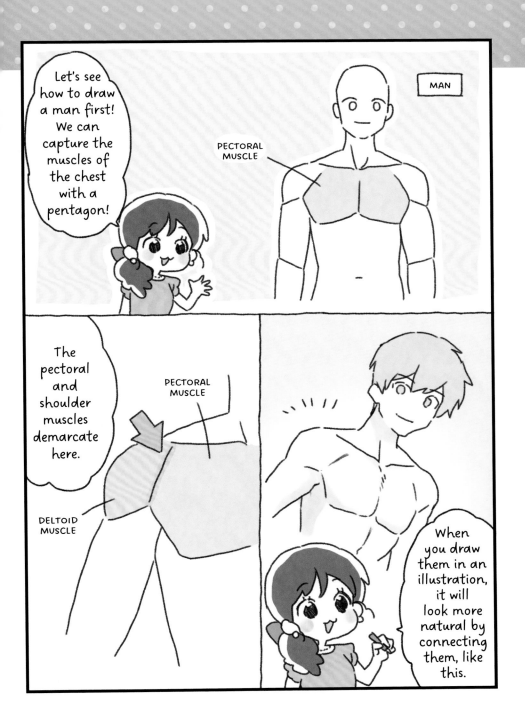

Let's see how to draw a man first! We can capture the muscles of the chest with a pentagon!

MAN

PECTORAL MUSCLE

The pectoral and shoulder muscles demarcate here.

PECTORAL MUSCLE

DELTOID MUSCLE

When you draw them in an illustration, it will look more natural by connecting them, like this.

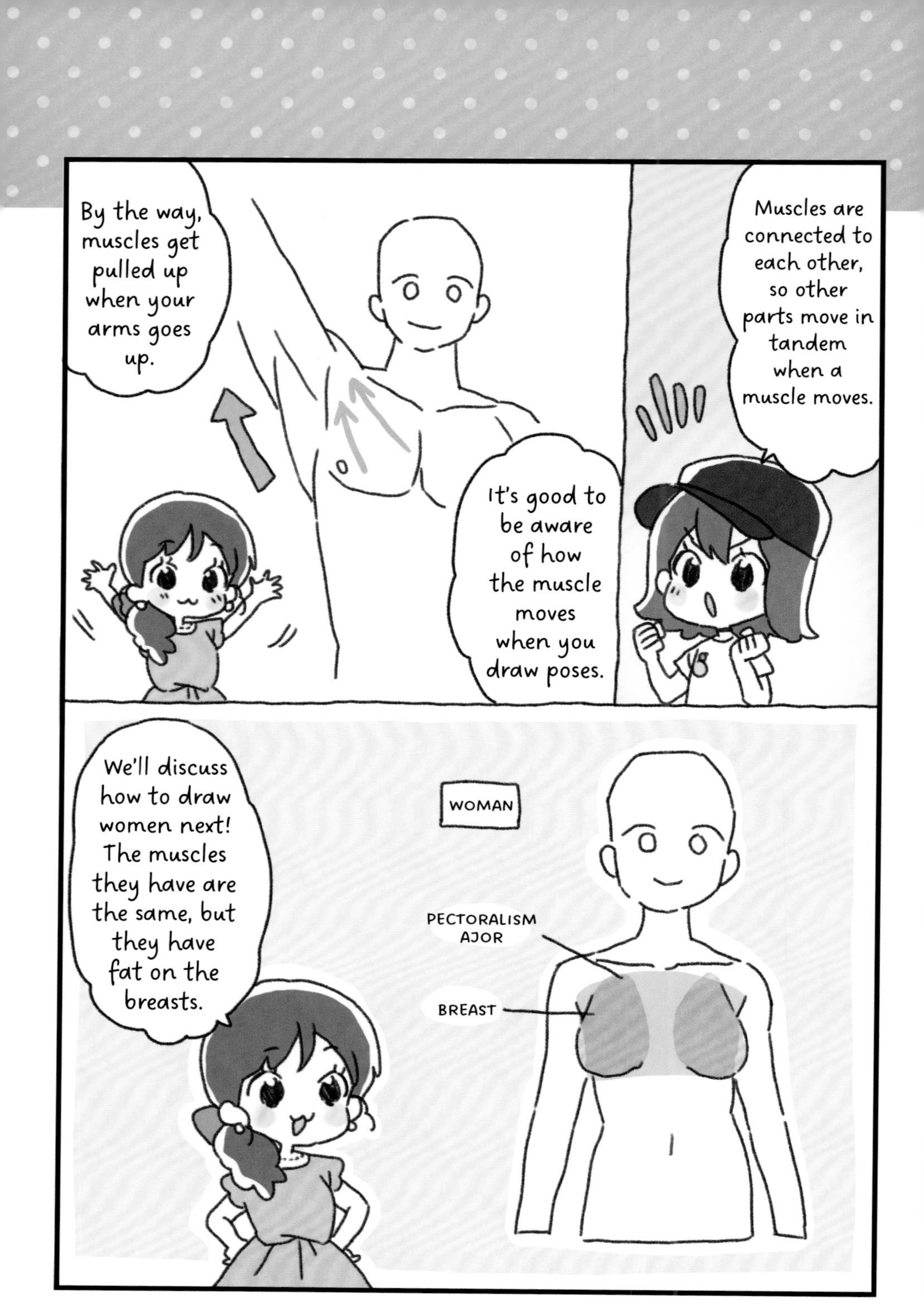
By the way, muscles get pulled up when your arms goes up.
Muscles are connected to each other, so other parts move in tandem when a muscle moves.
It's good to be aware of how the muscle moves when you draw poses.
We'll discuss how to draw women next! The muscles they have are the same, but they have fat on the breasts.
WOMAN
PECTORALISM AJOR
BREAST

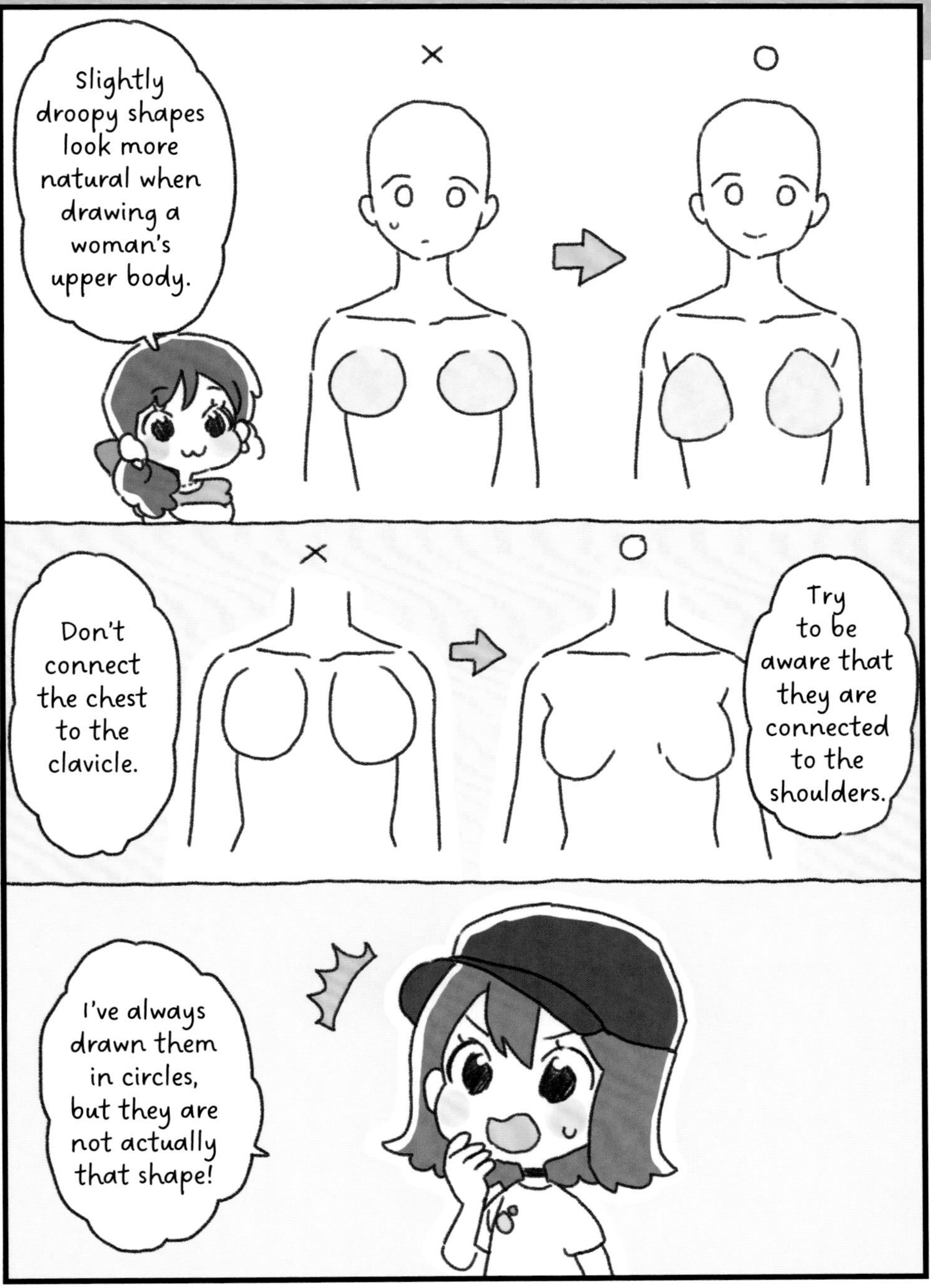
Slightly droopy shapes look more natural when drawing a woman's upper body.
×
○
×
○
Don't connect the chest to the clavicle.
Try to be aware that they are connected to the shoulders.
I've always drawn them in circles, but they are not actually that shape!

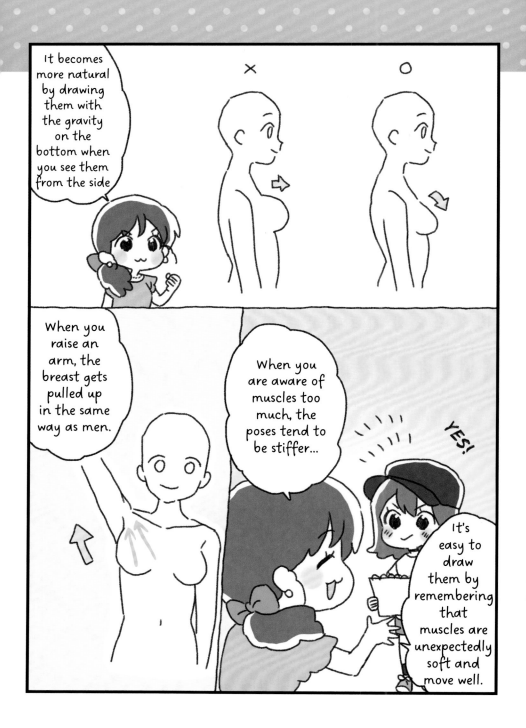

It becomes more natural by drawing them with the gravity on the bottom when you see them from the side

×

○

When you raise an arm, the breast gets pulled up in the same way as men.

When you are aware of muscles too much, the poses tend to be stiffer...

YES!

It's easy to draw them by remembering that muscles are unexpectedly soft and move well.

## SUMMARY

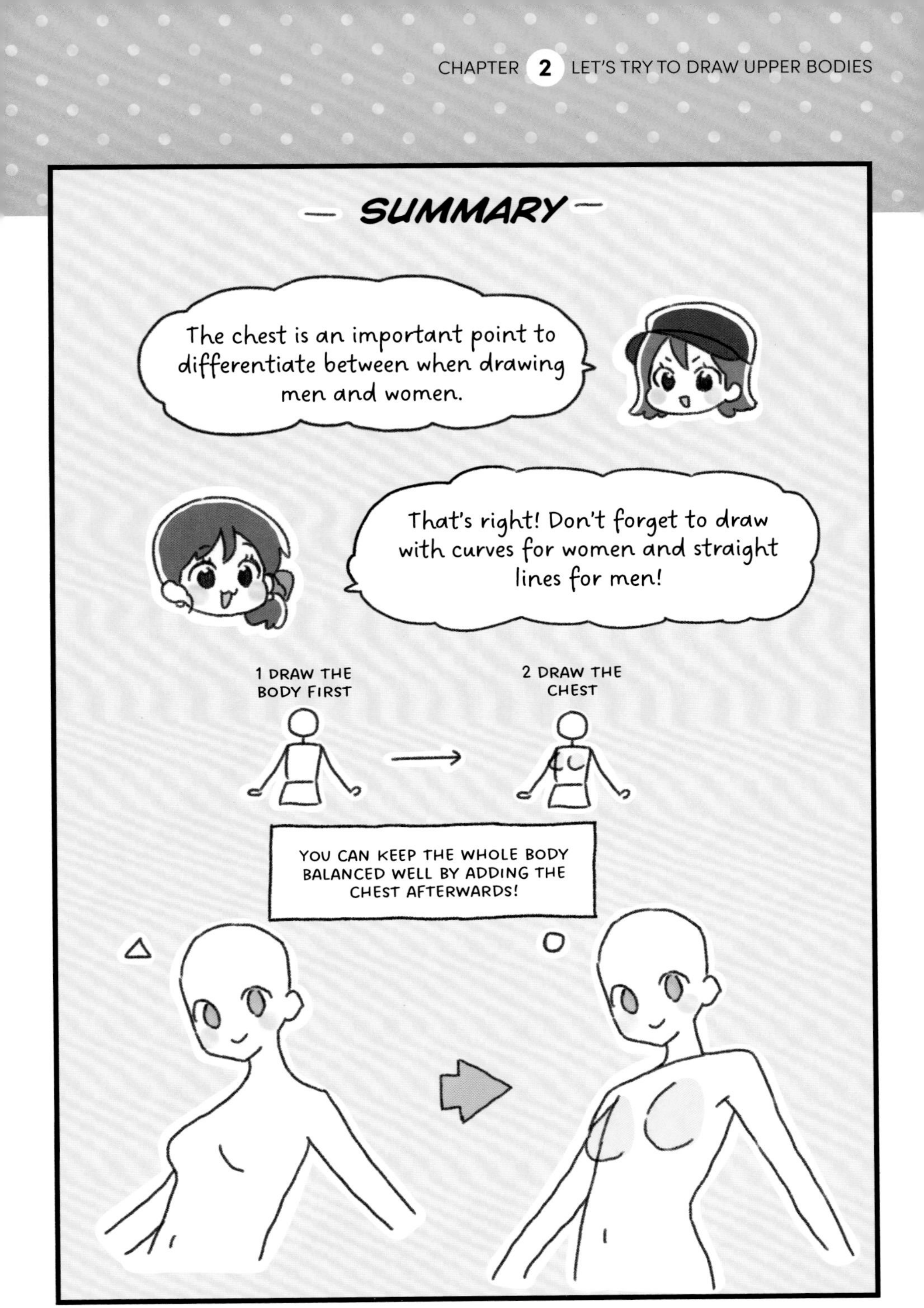
The chest is an important point to differentiate between when drawing men and women.
That's right! Don't forget to draw with curves for women and straight lines for men!
1 DRAW THE BODY FIRST
2 DRAW THE CHEST
YOU CAN KEEP THE WHOLE BODY BALANCED WELL BY ADDING THE CHEST AFTERWARDS!

# CONSIDER VARIOUS BODY TYPES

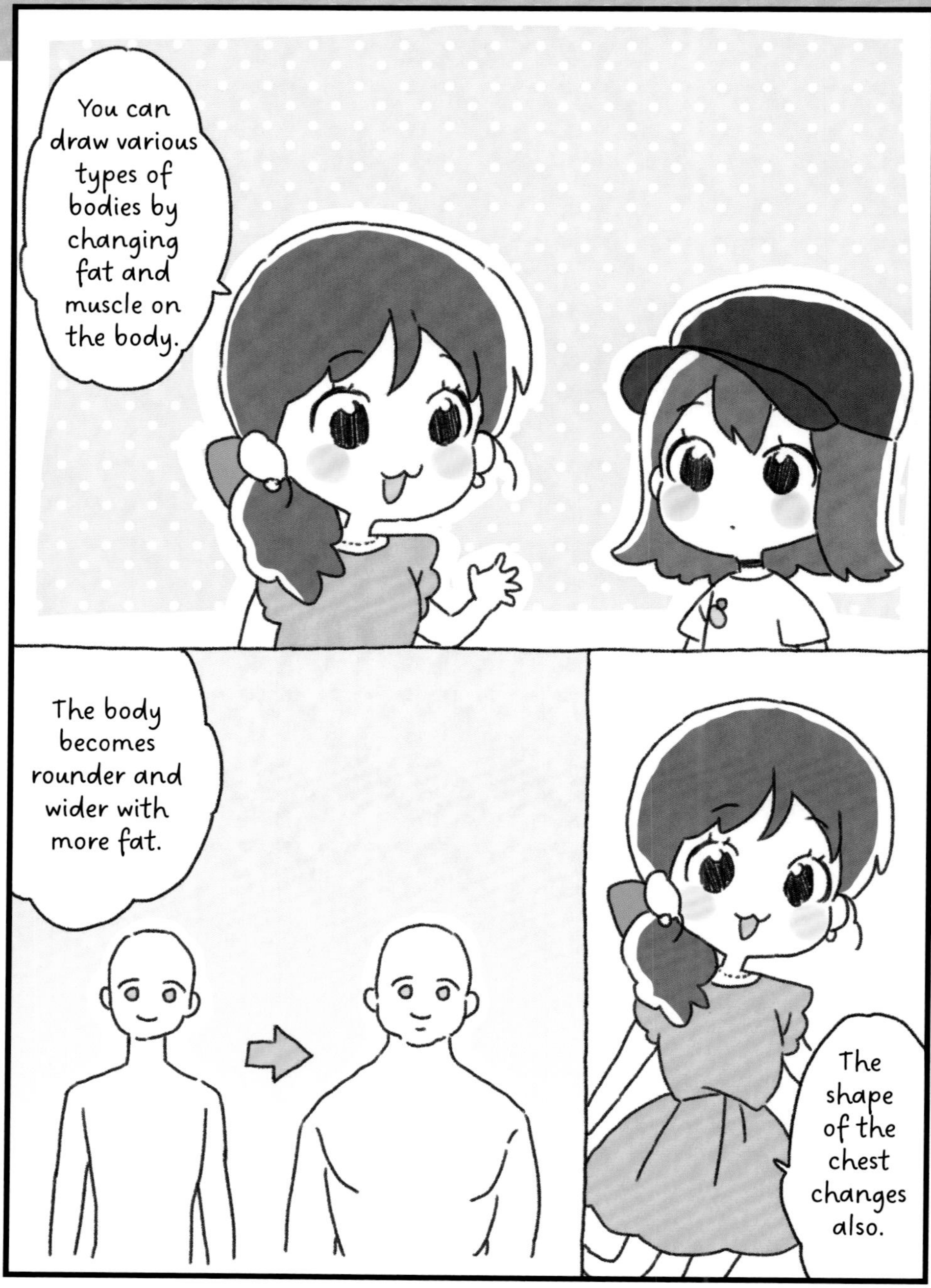
You can draw various types of bodies by changing fat and muscle on the body.
The body becomes rounder and wider with more fat.
The shape of the chest changes also.

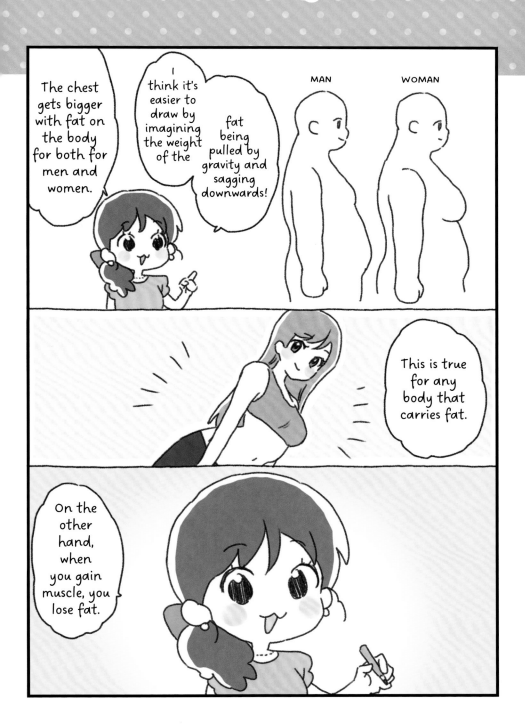

The chest gets bigger with fat on the body for both for men and women.

I think it's easier to draw by imagining the weight of the fat being pulled by gravity and sagging downwards!

MAN

WOMAN

This is true for any body that carries fat.

On the other hand, when you gain muscle, you lose fat.

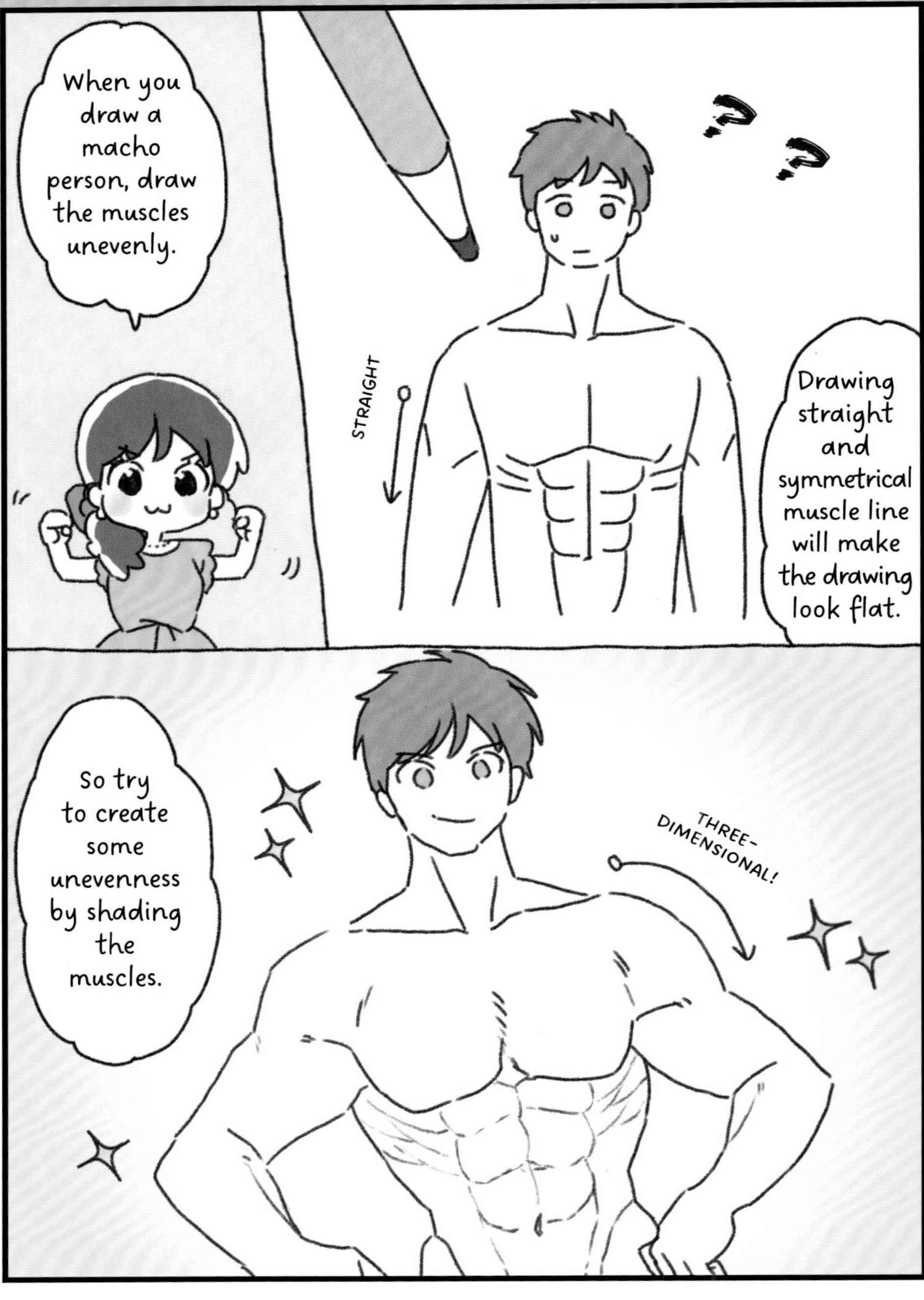
When you draw a macho person, draw the muscles unevenly.
STRAIGHT
Drawing straight and symmetrical muscle line will make the drawing look flat.
So try to create some unevenness by shading the muscles.
THREE-DIMENSIONAL!

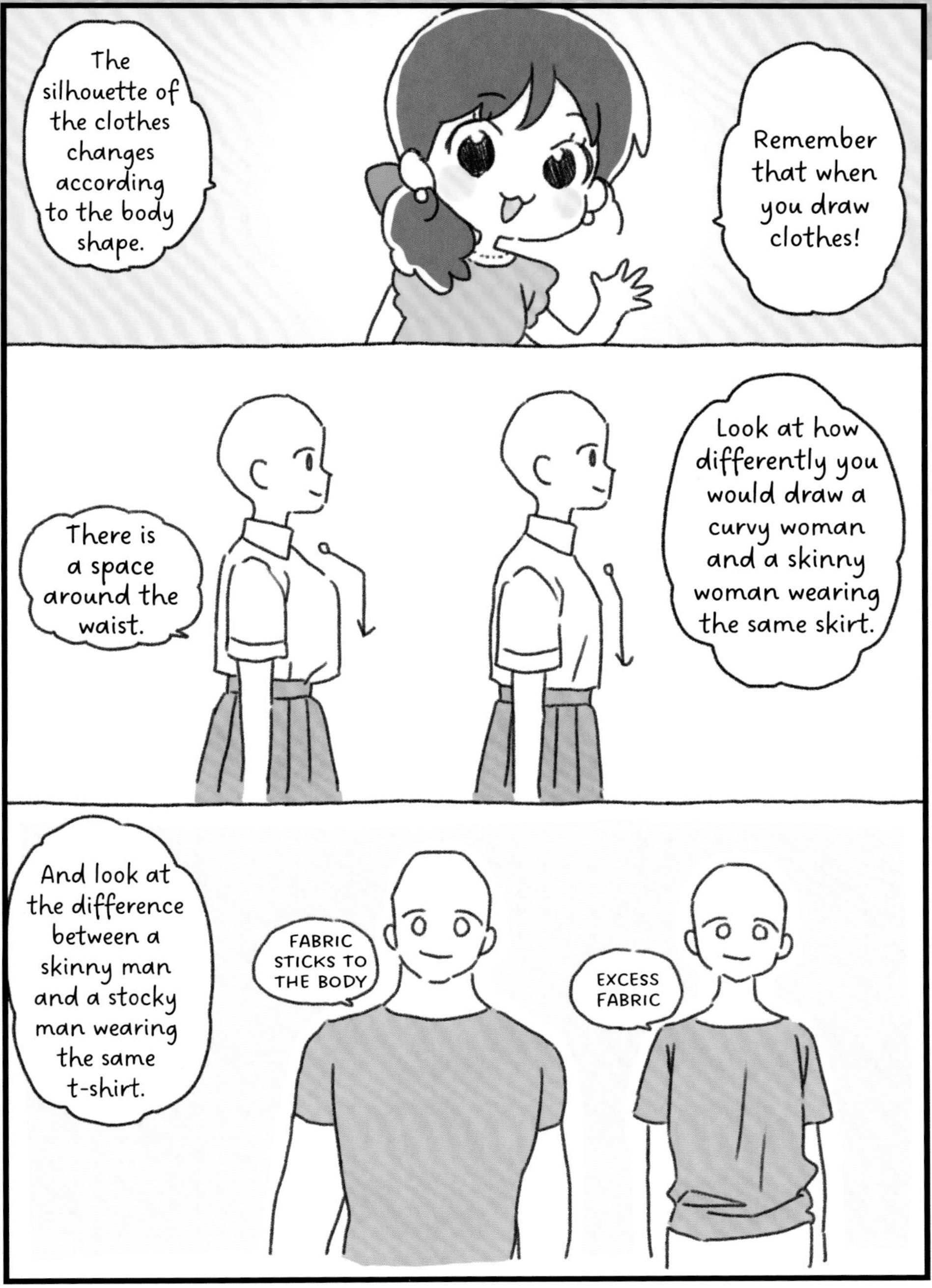
The silhouette of the clothes changes according to the body shape.
Remember that when you draw clothes!
Look at how differently you would draw a curvy woman and a skinny woman wearing the same skirt.
There is a space around the waist.
And look at the difference between a skinny man and a stocky man wearing the same t-shirt.
FABRIC STICKS TO THE BODY
EXCESS FABRIC

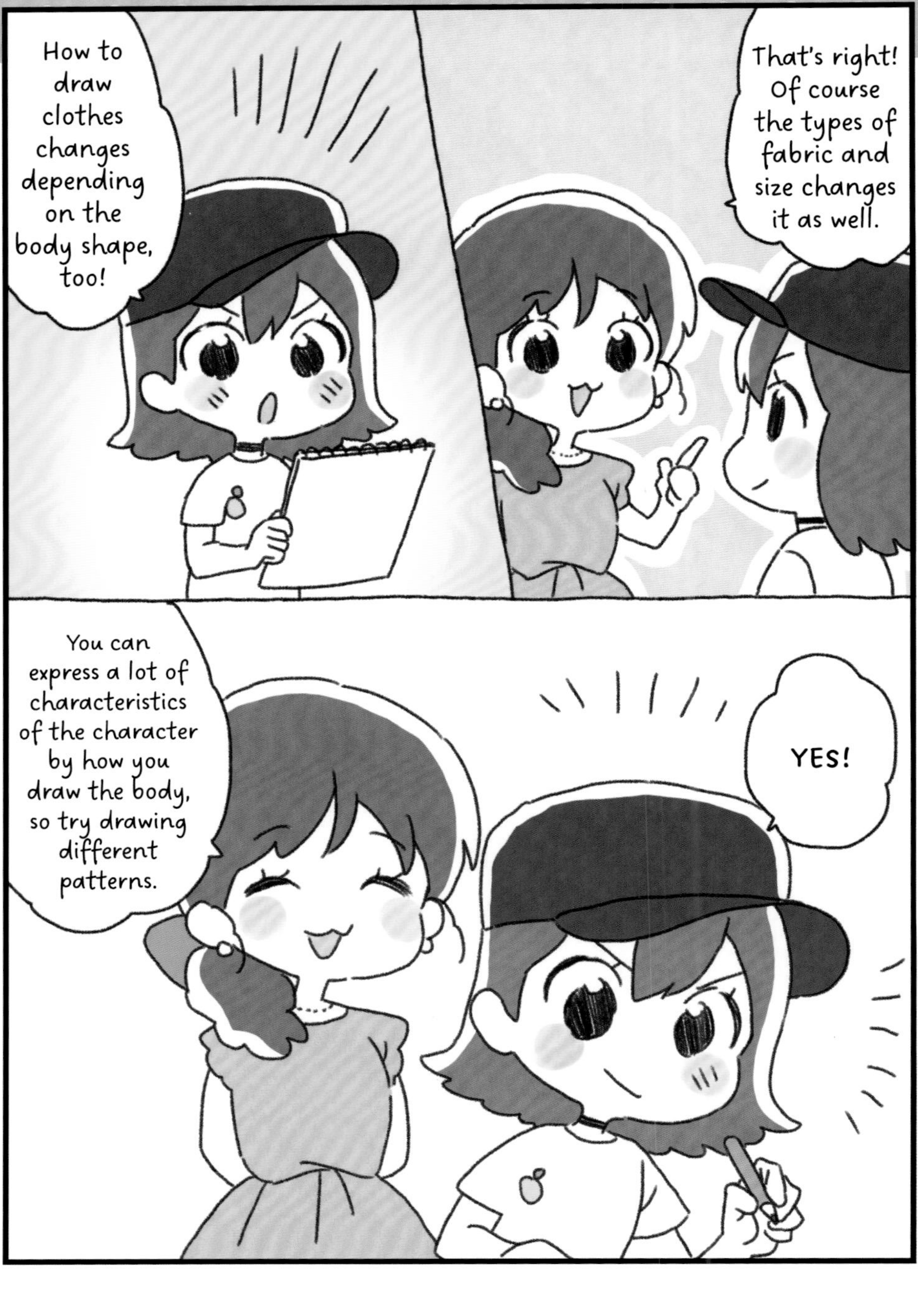
How to draw clothes changes depending on the body shape, too!
That's right! Of course the types of fabric and size changes it as well.
You can express a lot of characteristics of the character by how you draw the body, so try drawing different patterns.
YES!

# — *SUMMARY* —

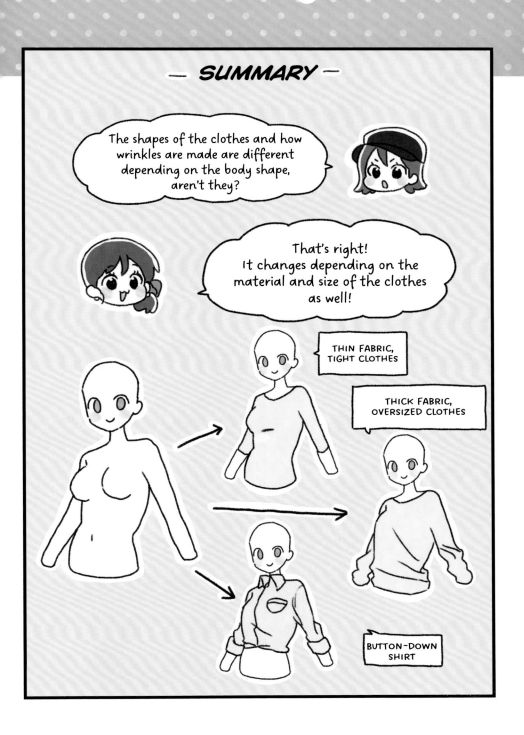

The shapes of the clothes and how wrinkles are made are different depending on the body shape, aren't they?

That's right! It changes depending on the material and size of the clothes as well!

THIN FABRIC, TIGHT CLOTHES

THICK FABRIC, OVERSIZED CLOTHES

BUTTON-DOWN SHIRT

# CONSIDER WHAT YOU CAN'T SEE

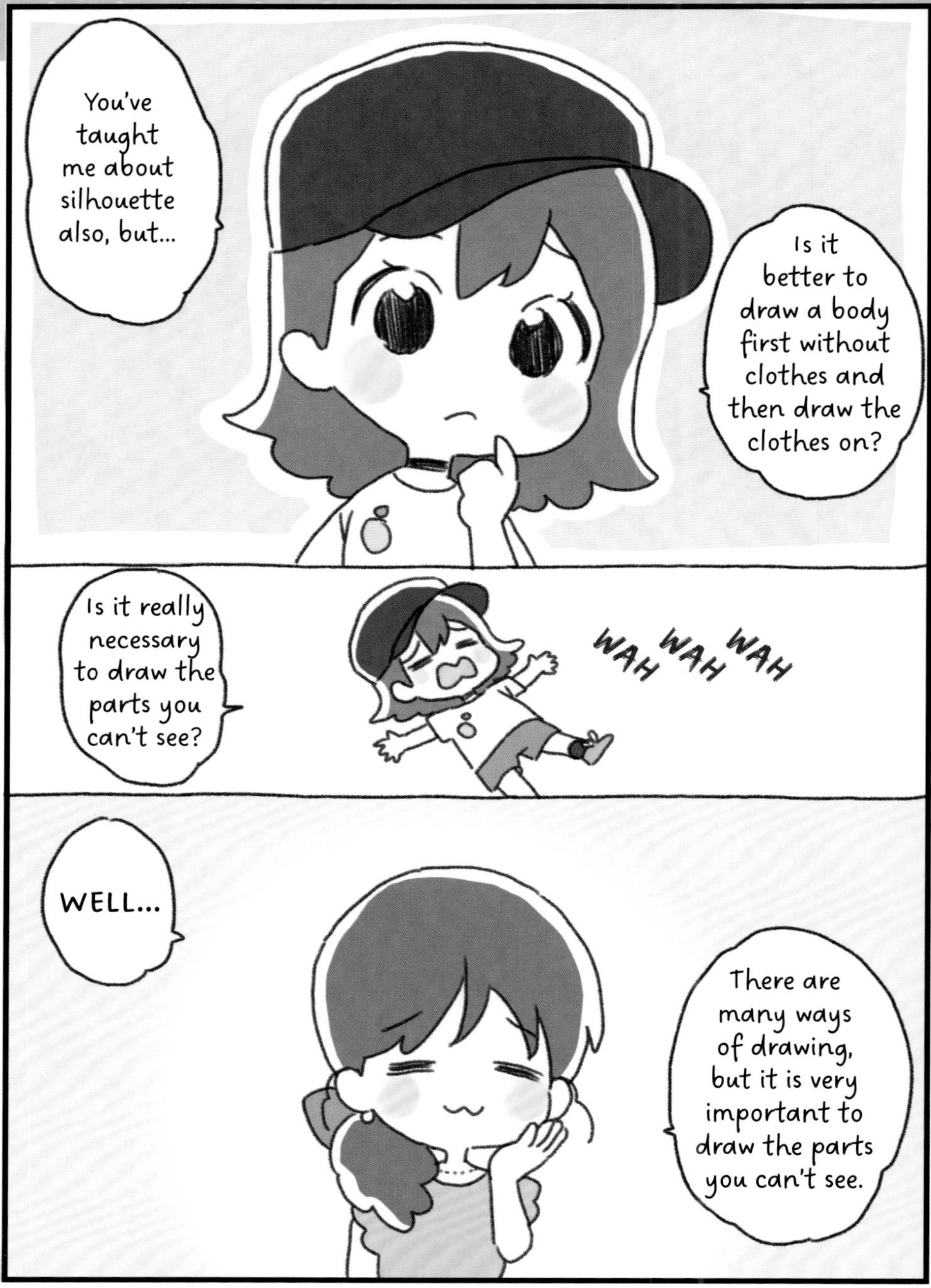

You've taught me about silhouette also, but...
Is it better to draw a body first without clothes and then draw the clothes on?
Is it really necessary to draw the parts you can't see?
WAH WAH WAH
WELL...
There are many ways of drawing, but it is very important to draw the parts you can't see.

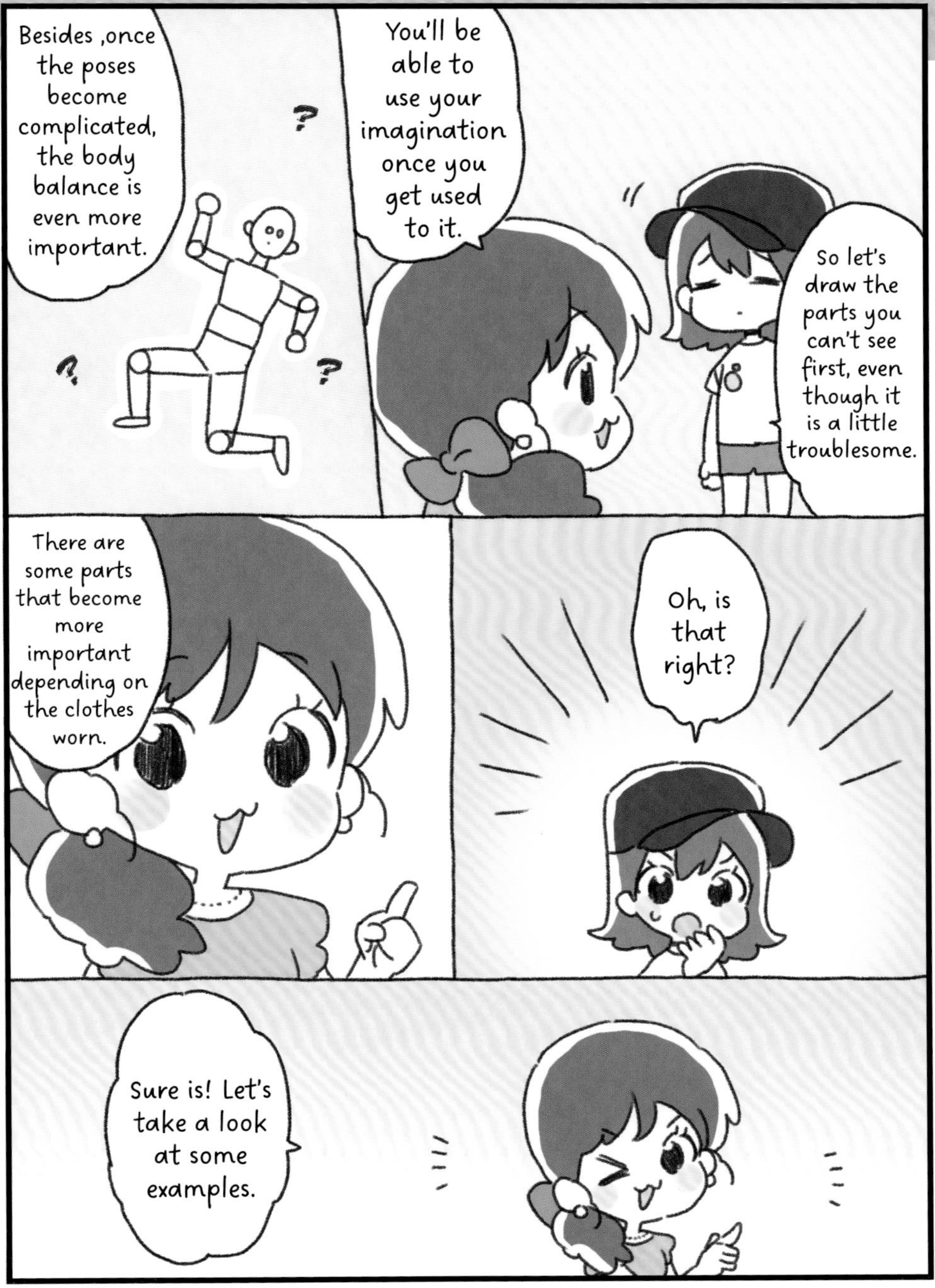
Besides ,once the poses become complicated, the body balance is even more important.
You'll be able to use your imagination once you get used to it.
So let's draw the parts you can't see first, even though it is a little troublesome.
There are some parts that become more important depending on the clothes worn.
Oh, is that right?
Sure is! Let's take a look at some examples.

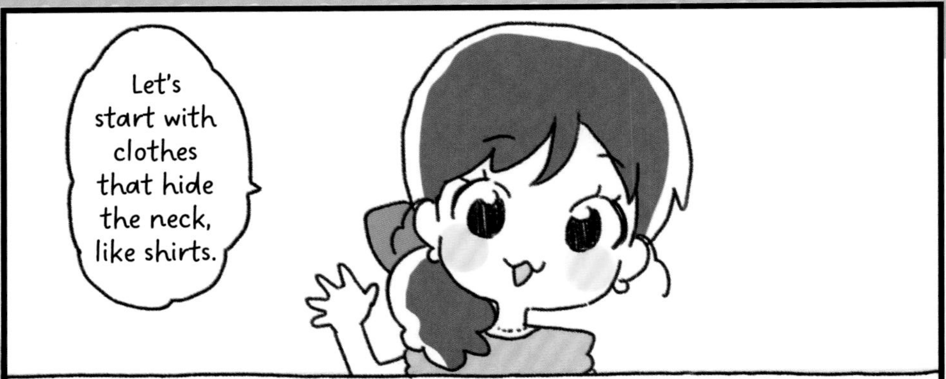
Let's start with clothes that hide the neck, like shirts.

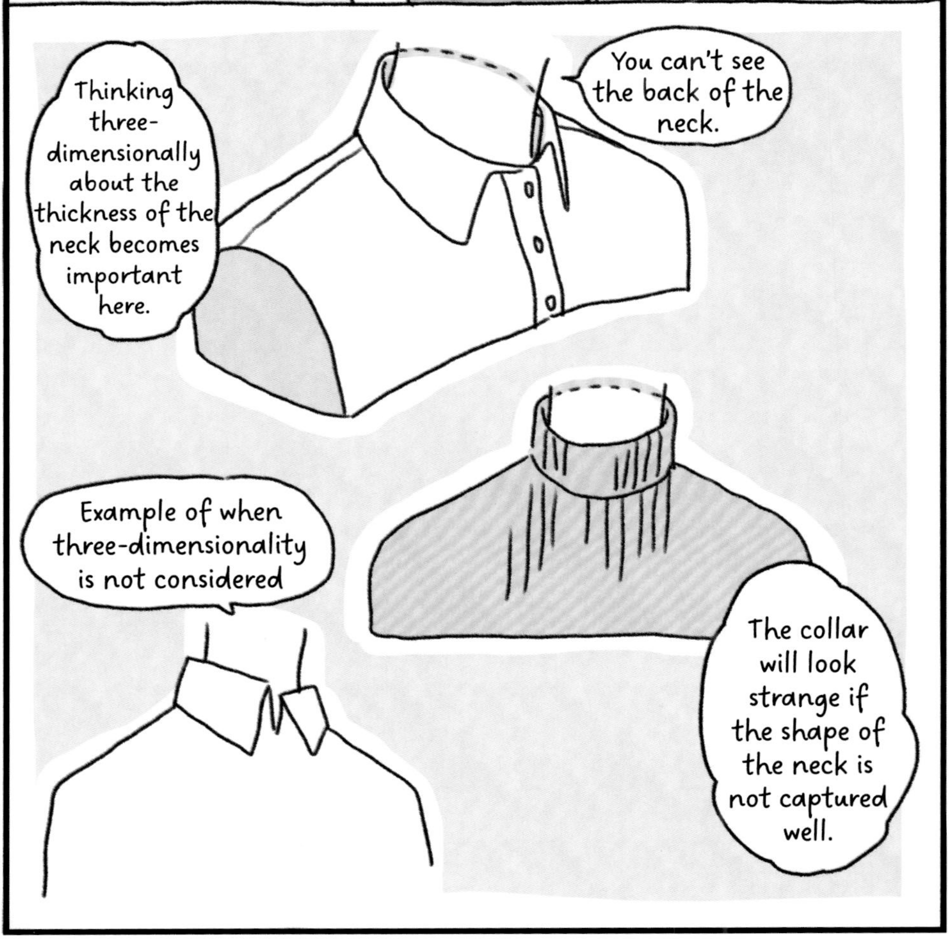
Thinking three-dimensionally about the thickness of the neck becomes important here.
You can't see the back of the neck.
Example of when three-dimensionality is not considered
The collar will look strange if the shape of the neck is not captured well.

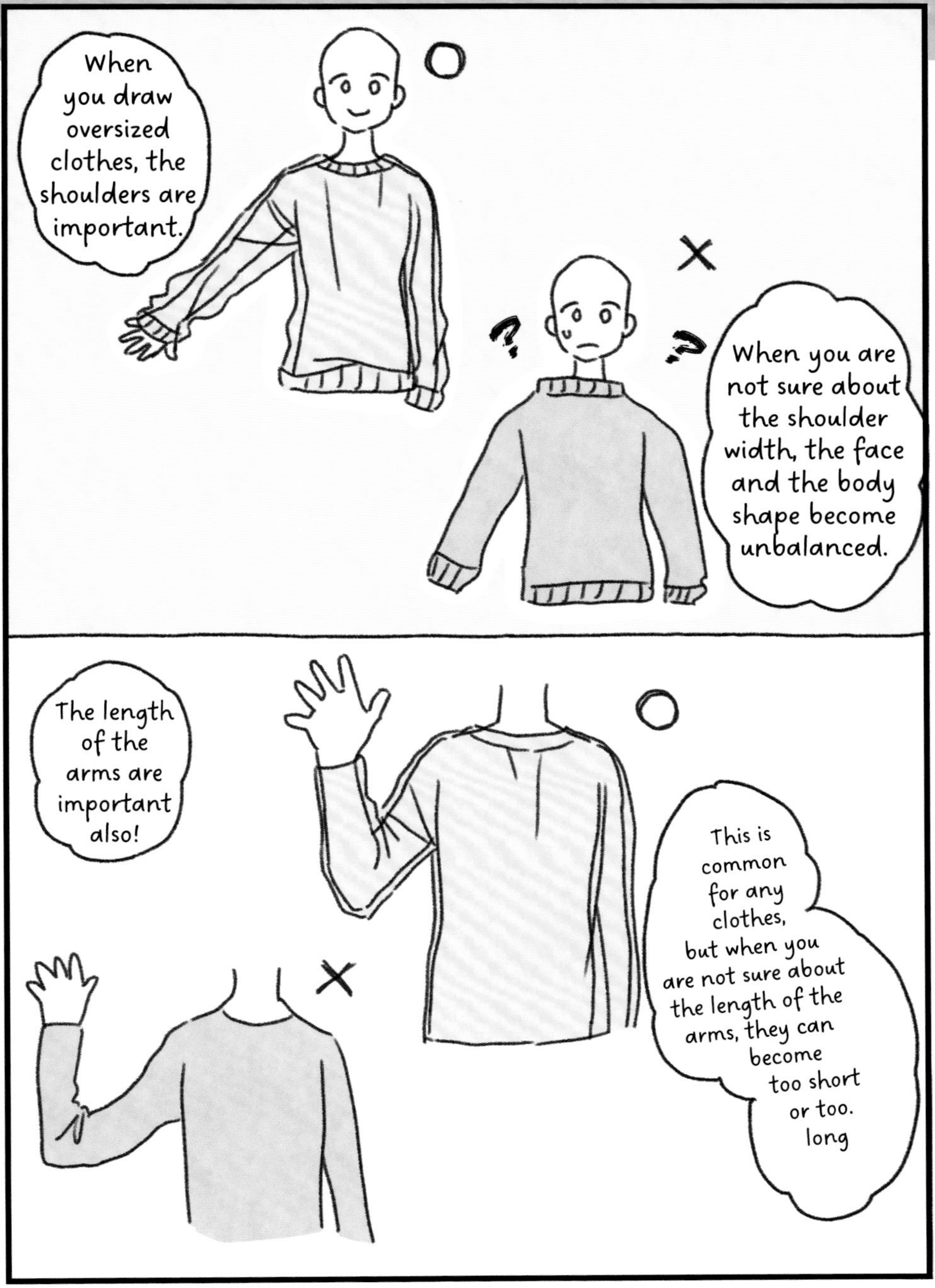
When you draw oversized clothes, the shoulders are important.
When you are not sure about the shoulder width, the face and the body shape become unbalanced.
The length of the arms are important also!
This is common for any clothes, but when you are not sure about the length of the arms, they can become too short or too. long

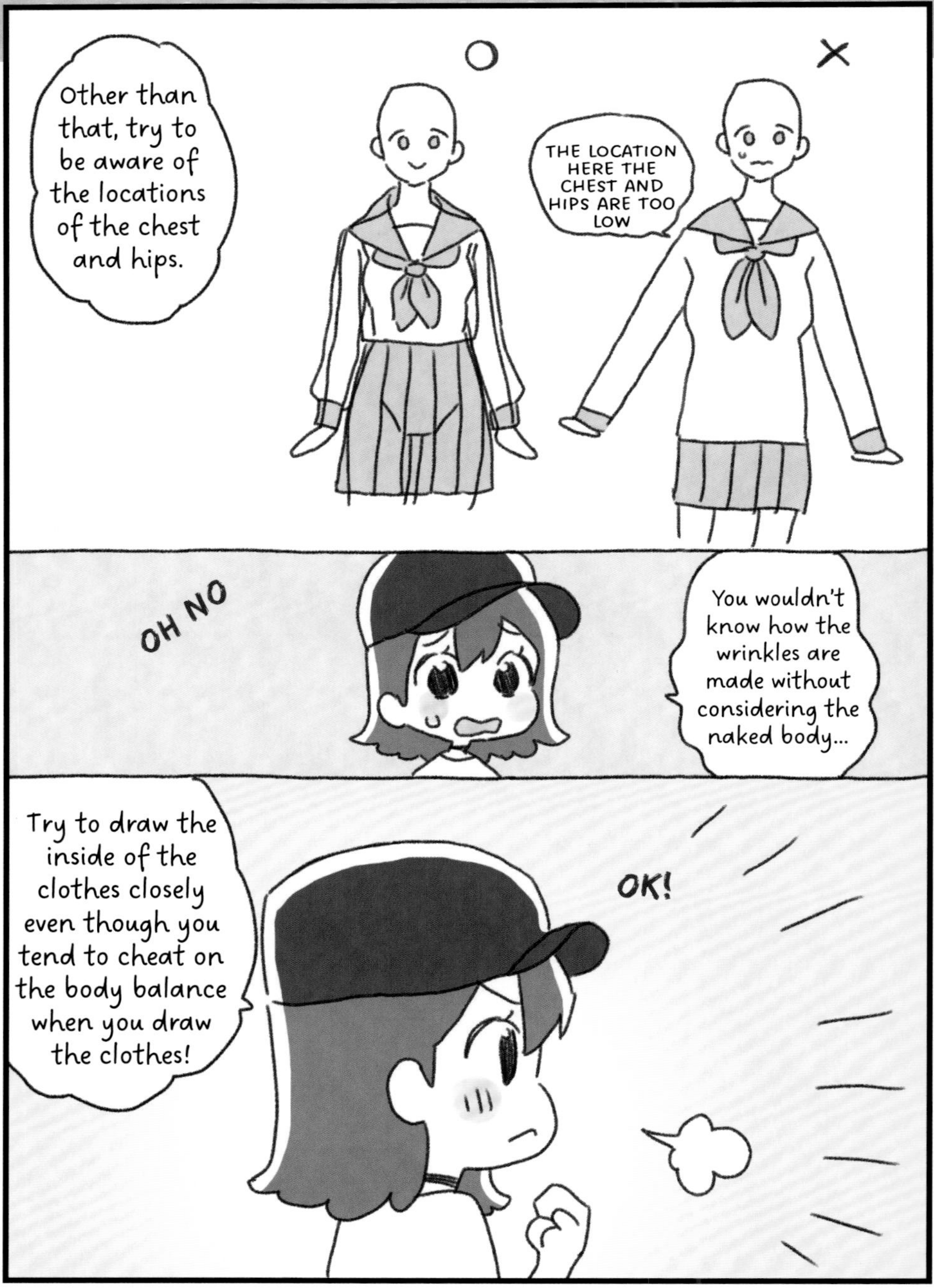
Other than that, try to be aware of the locations of the chest and hips.
○
×
THE LOCATION HERE THE CHEST AND HIPS ARE TOO LOW
You wouldn't know how the wrinkles are made without considering the naked body...
OH NO
Try to draw the inside of the clothes closely even though you tend to cheat on the body balance when you draw the clothes!
OK!

## — SUMMARY —

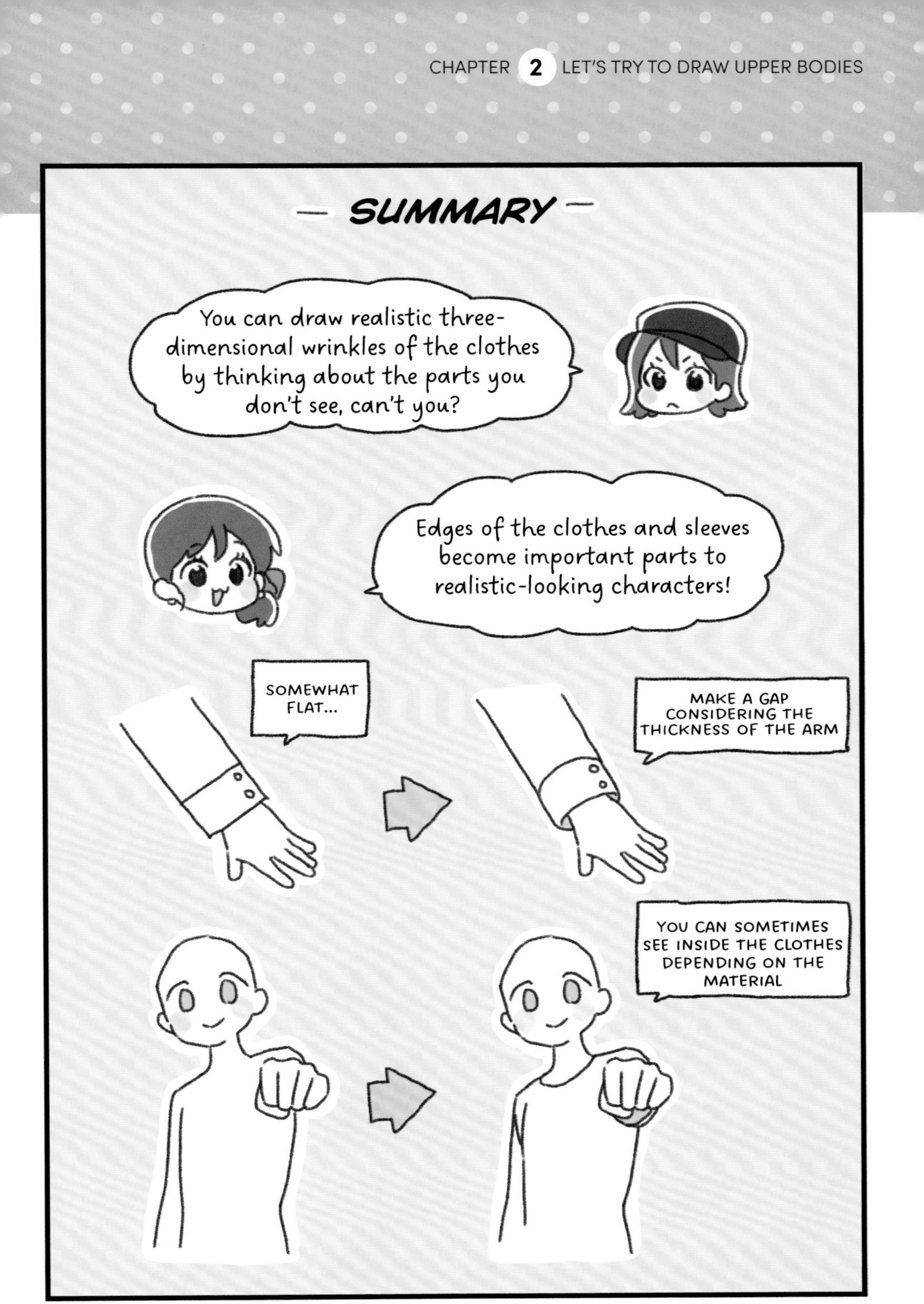
You can draw realistic three-dimensional wrinkles of the clothes by thinking about the parts you don't see, can't you?
Edges of the clothes and sleeves become important parts to realistic-looking characters!
SOMEWHAT FLAT...
MAKE A GAP CONSIDERING THE THICKNESS OF THE ARM
YOU CAN SOMETIMES SEE INSIDE THE CLOTHES DEPENDING ON THE MATERIAL

# HOW TO DRAW HANDS

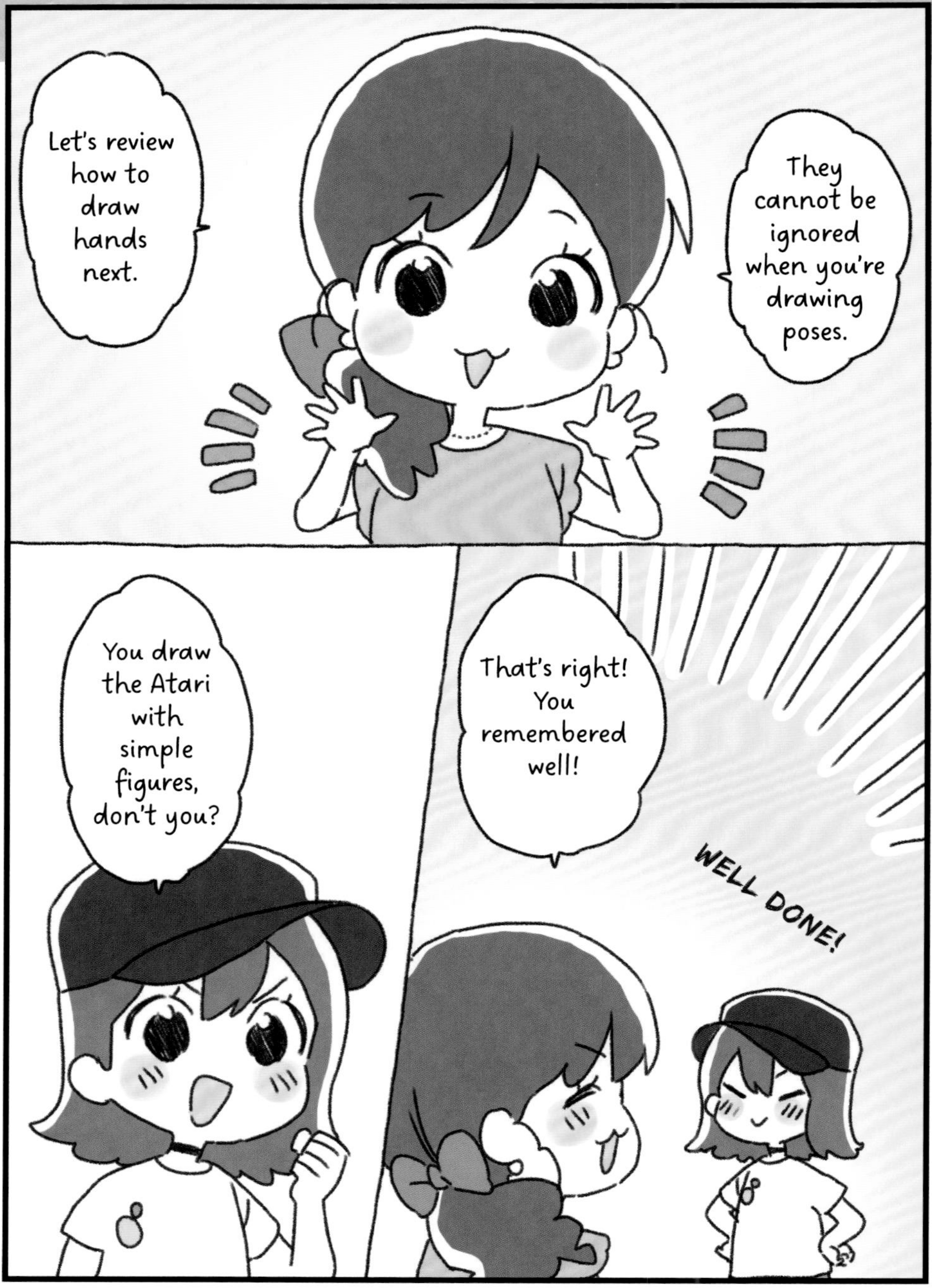

Let's review how to draw hands next.
They cannot be ignored when you're drawing poses.
You draw the Atari with simple figures, don't you?
That's right! You remembered well!
WELL DONE!

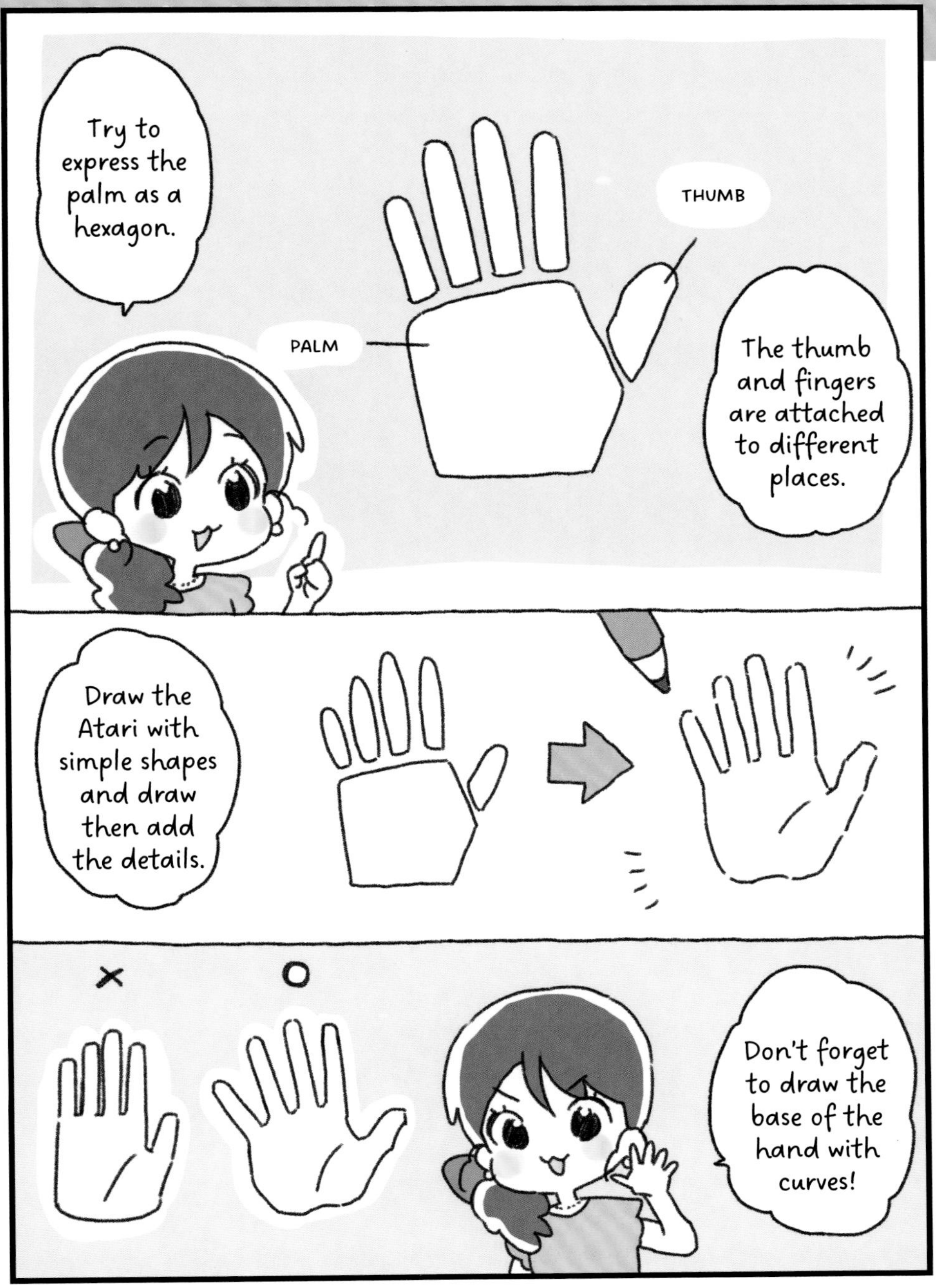
Try to express the palm as a hexagon.
THUMB
PALM
The thumb and fingers are attached to different places.
Draw the Atari with simple shapes and draw then add the details.
×
O
Don't forget to draw the base of the hand with curves!

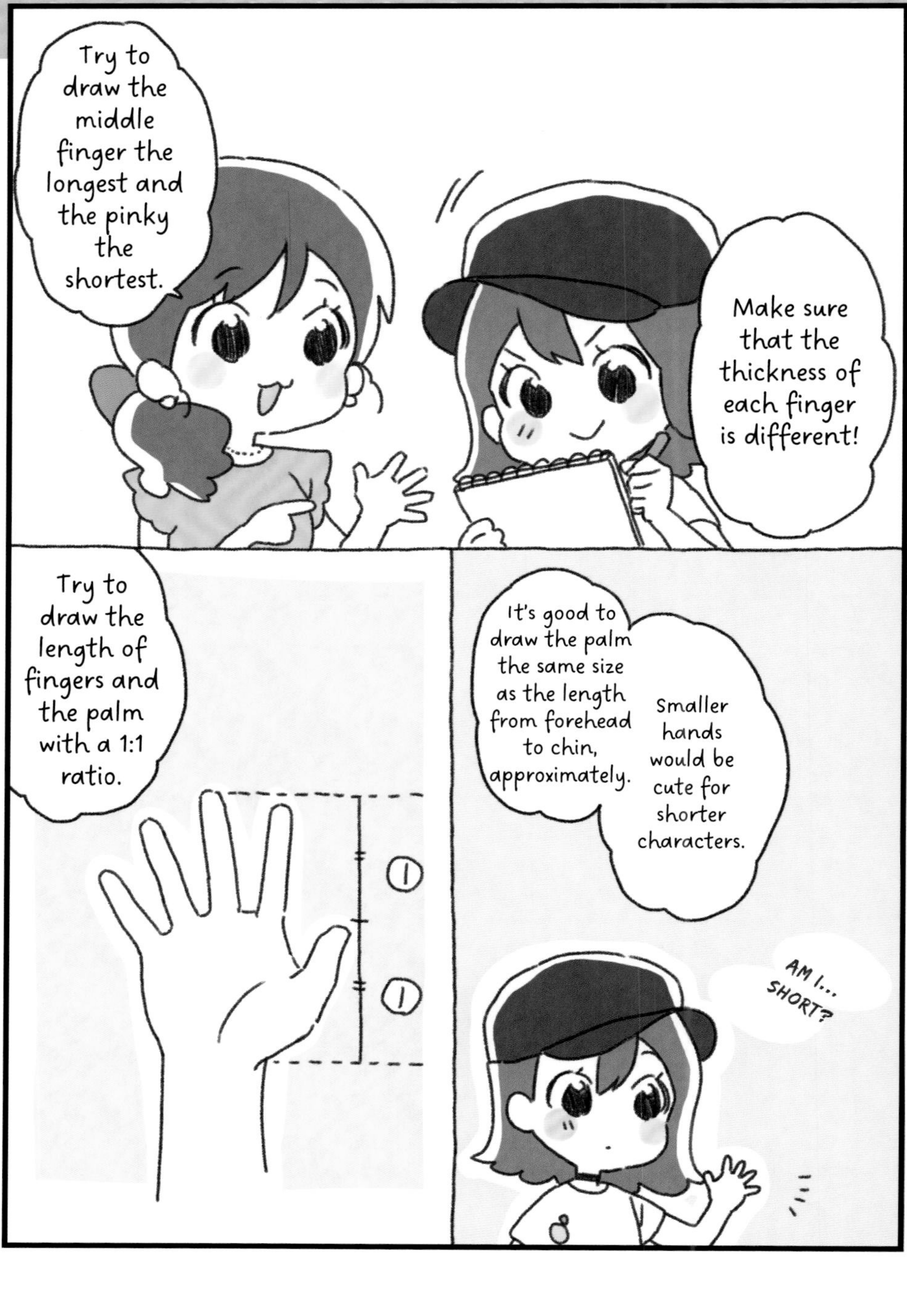
Try to draw the middle finger the longest and the pinky the shortest.
Make sure that the thickness of each finger is different!
Try to draw the length of fingers and the palm with a 1:1 ratio.
1
1
It's good to draw the palm the same size as the length from forehead to chin, approximately.
Smaller hands would be cute for shorter characters.
AM I... SHORT?

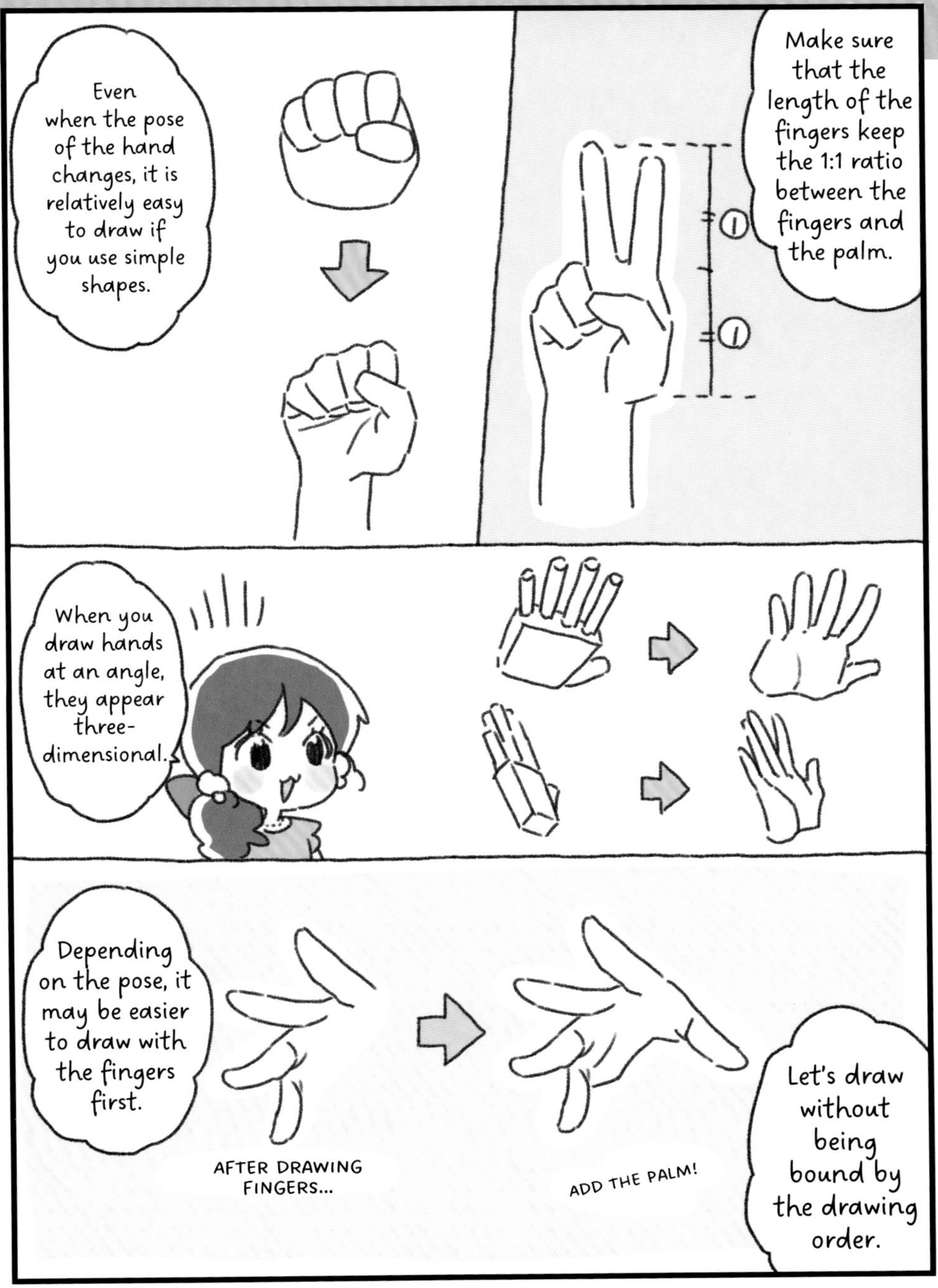
Even when the pose of the hand changes, it is relatively easy to draw if you use simple shapes.
Make sure that the length of the fingers keep the 1:1 ratio between the fingers and the palm.
1
1
When you draw hands at an angle, they appear three-dimensional.
Depending on the pose, it may be easier to draw with the fingers first.
AFTER DRAWING FINGERS...
ADD THE PALM!
Let's draw without being bound by the drawing order.

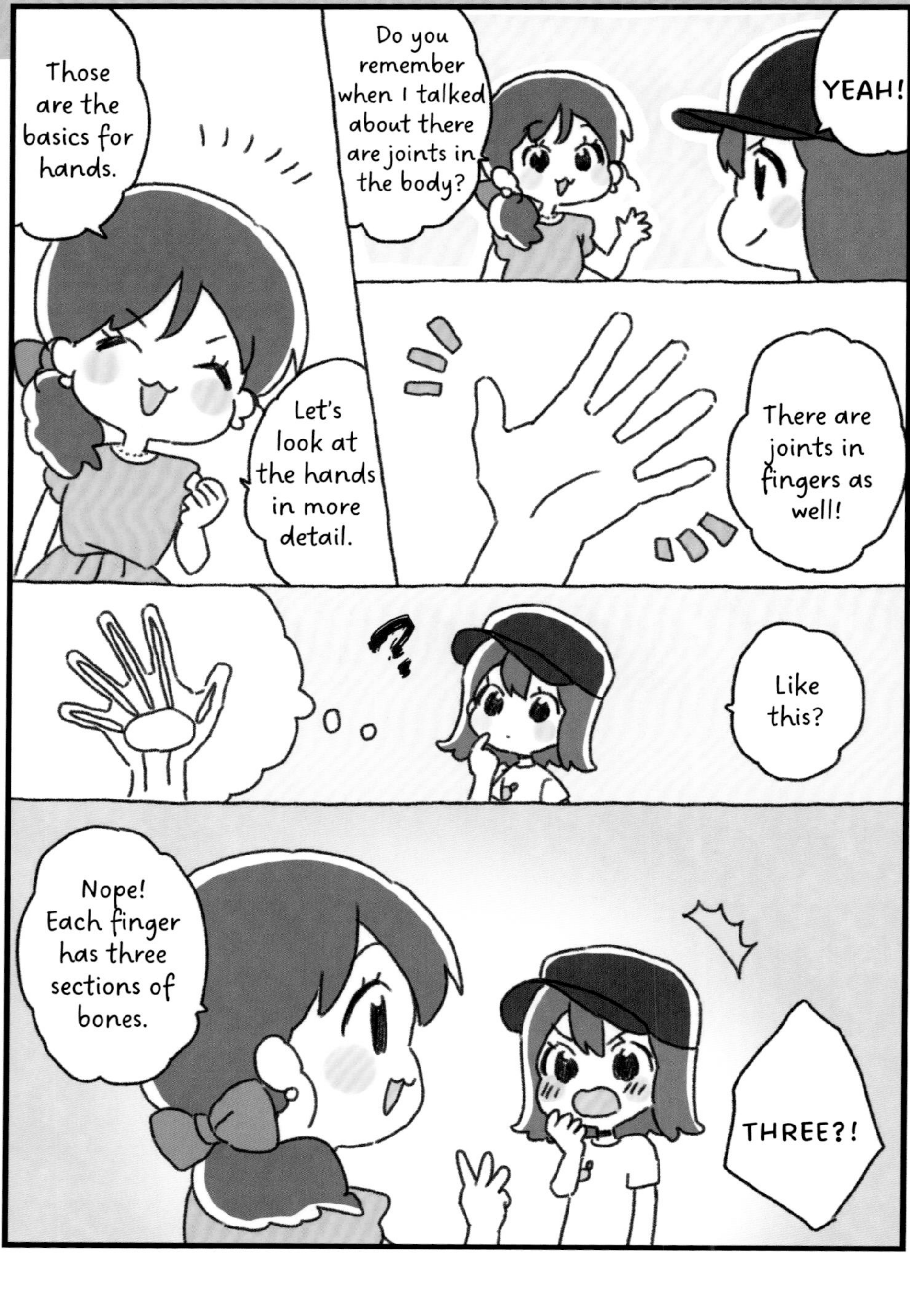
Those are the basics for hands.
Let's look at the hands in more detail.
Do you remember when I talked about there are joints in the body?
YEAH!
There are joints in fingers as well!
Like this?
Nope! Each finger has three sections of bones.
THREE?!

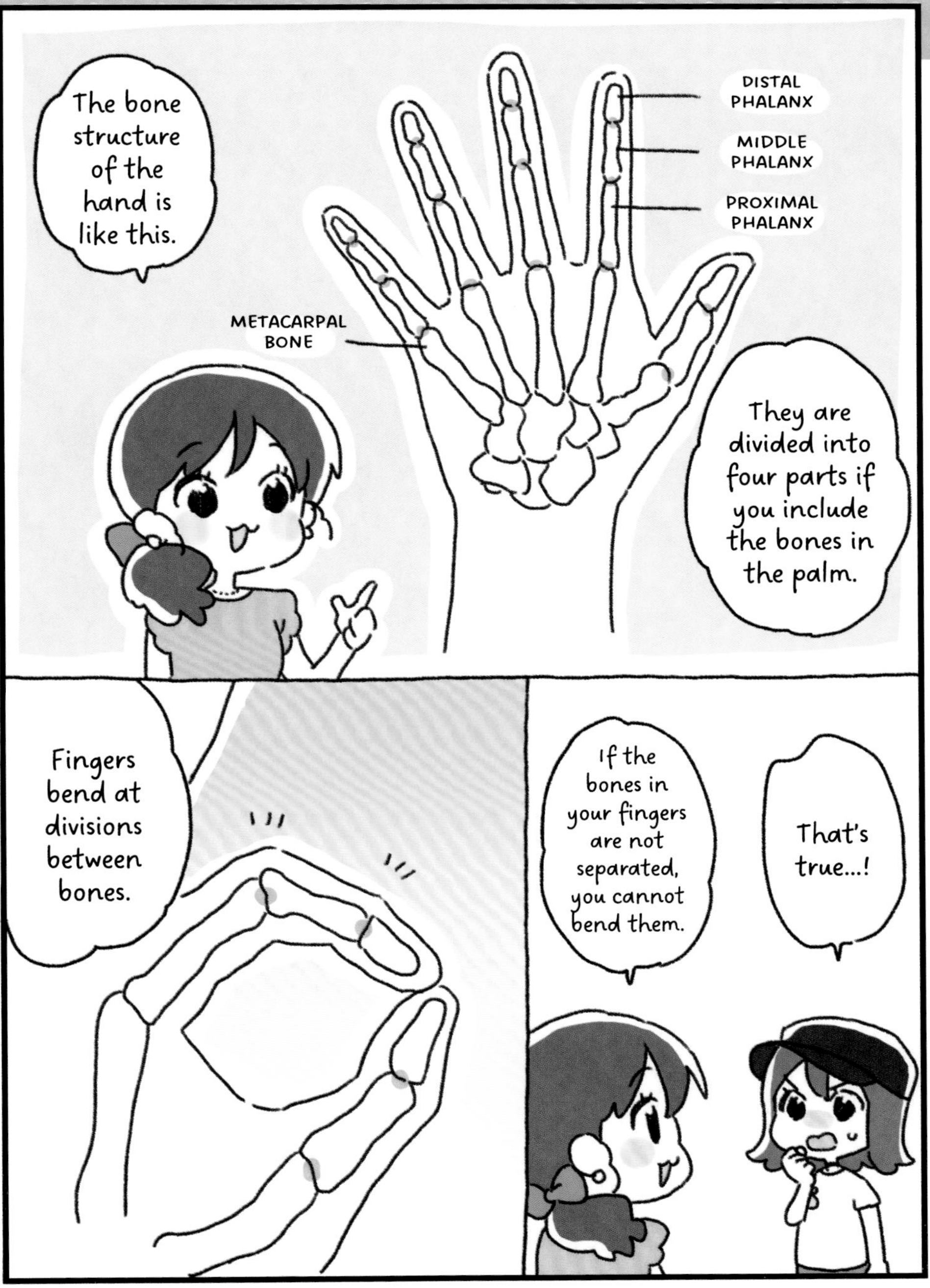

The bone structure of the hand is like this.
DISTAL PHALANX
MIDDLE PHALANX
PROXIMAL PHALANX
METACARPAL BONE
They are divided into four parts if you include the bones in the palm.
Fingers bend at divisions between bones.
If the bones in your fingers are not separated, you cannot bend them.
That's true...!

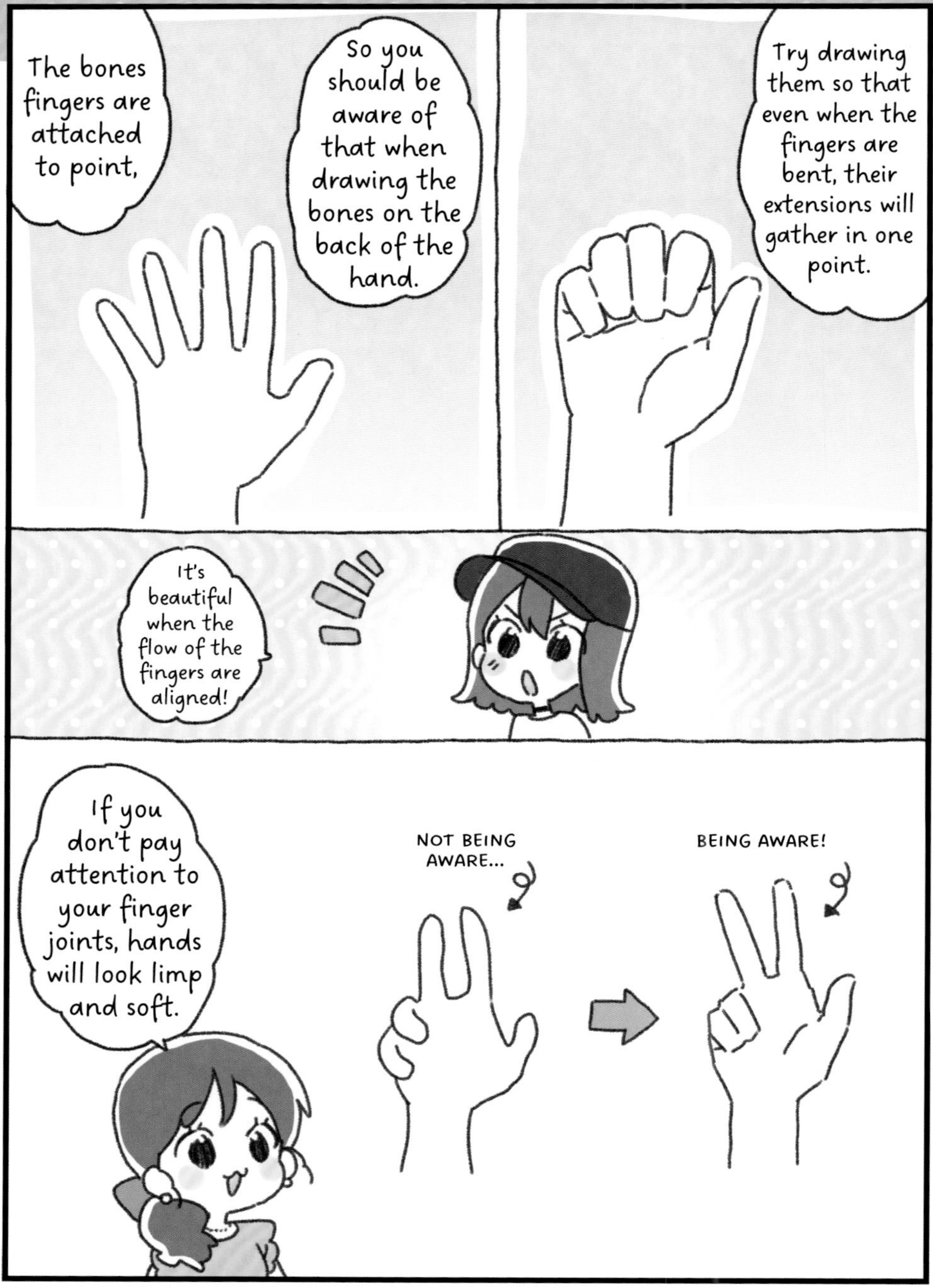

The bones fingers are attached to point,
So you should be aware of that when drawing the bones on the back of the hand.
Try drawing them so that even when the fingers are bent, their extensions will gather in one point.
It's beautiful when the flow of the fingers are aligned!
If you don't pay attention to your finger joints, hands will look limp and soft.
NOT BEING AWARE...
BEING AWARE!

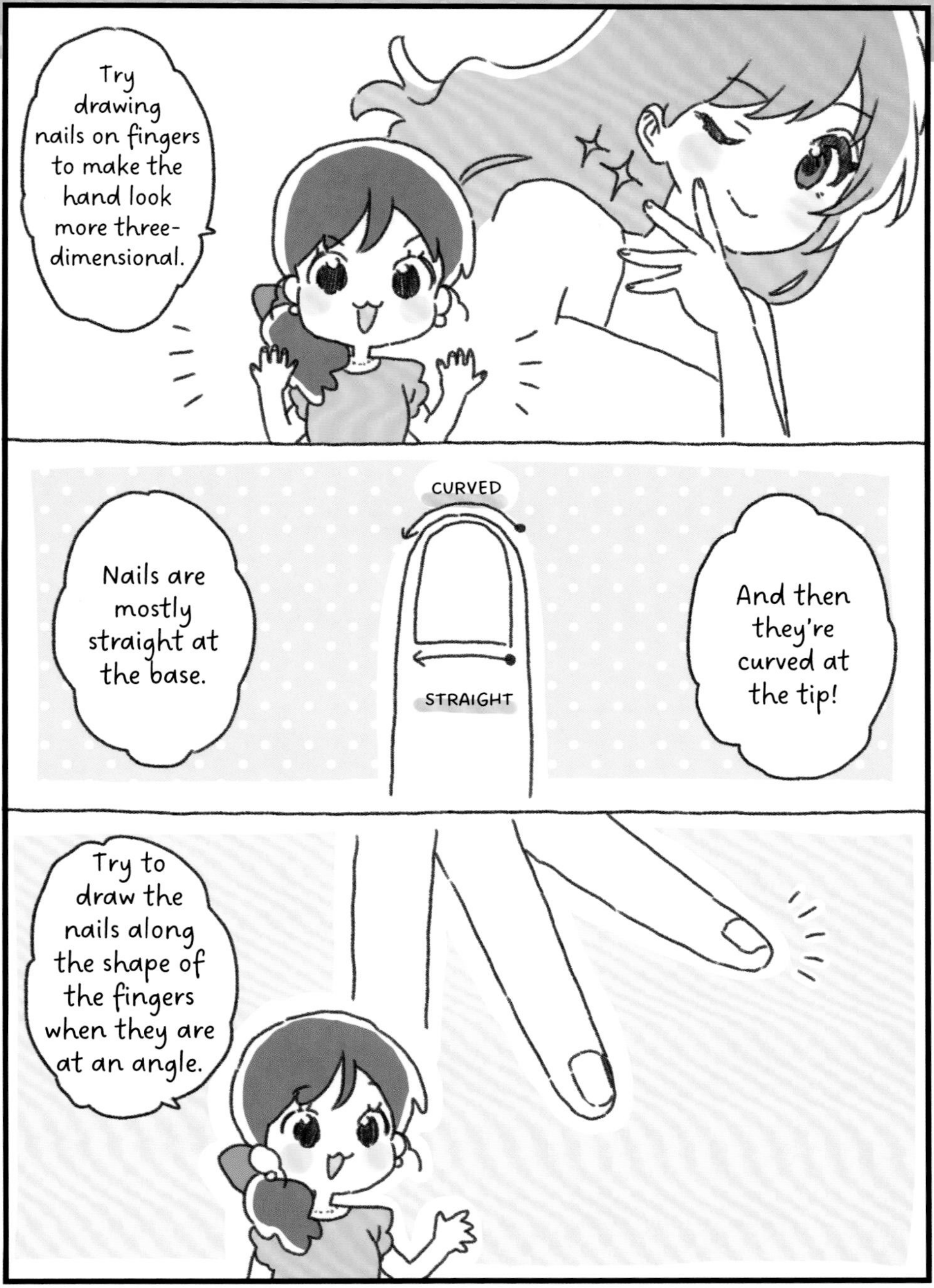
Try drawing nails on fingers to make the hand look more three-dimensional.
CURVED
Nails are mostly straight at the base.
STRAIGHT
And then they're curved at the tip!
Try to draw the nails along the shape of the fingers when they are at an angle.

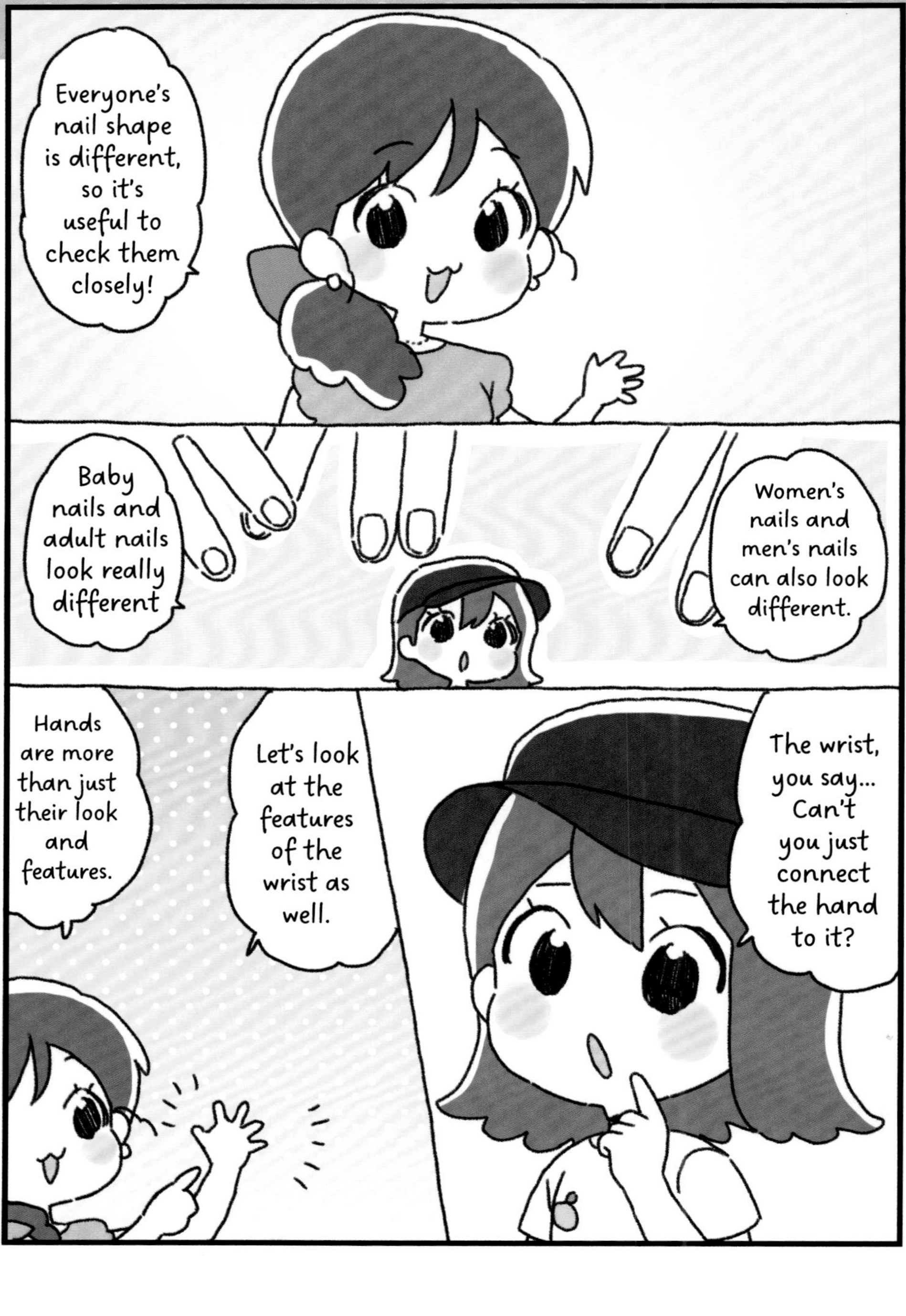

Everyone's nail shape is different, so it's useful to check them closely!
Baby nails and adult nails look really different
Women's nails and men's nails can also look different.
Hands are more than just their look and features.
Let's look at the features of the wrist as well.
The wrist, you say... Can't you just connect the hand to it?

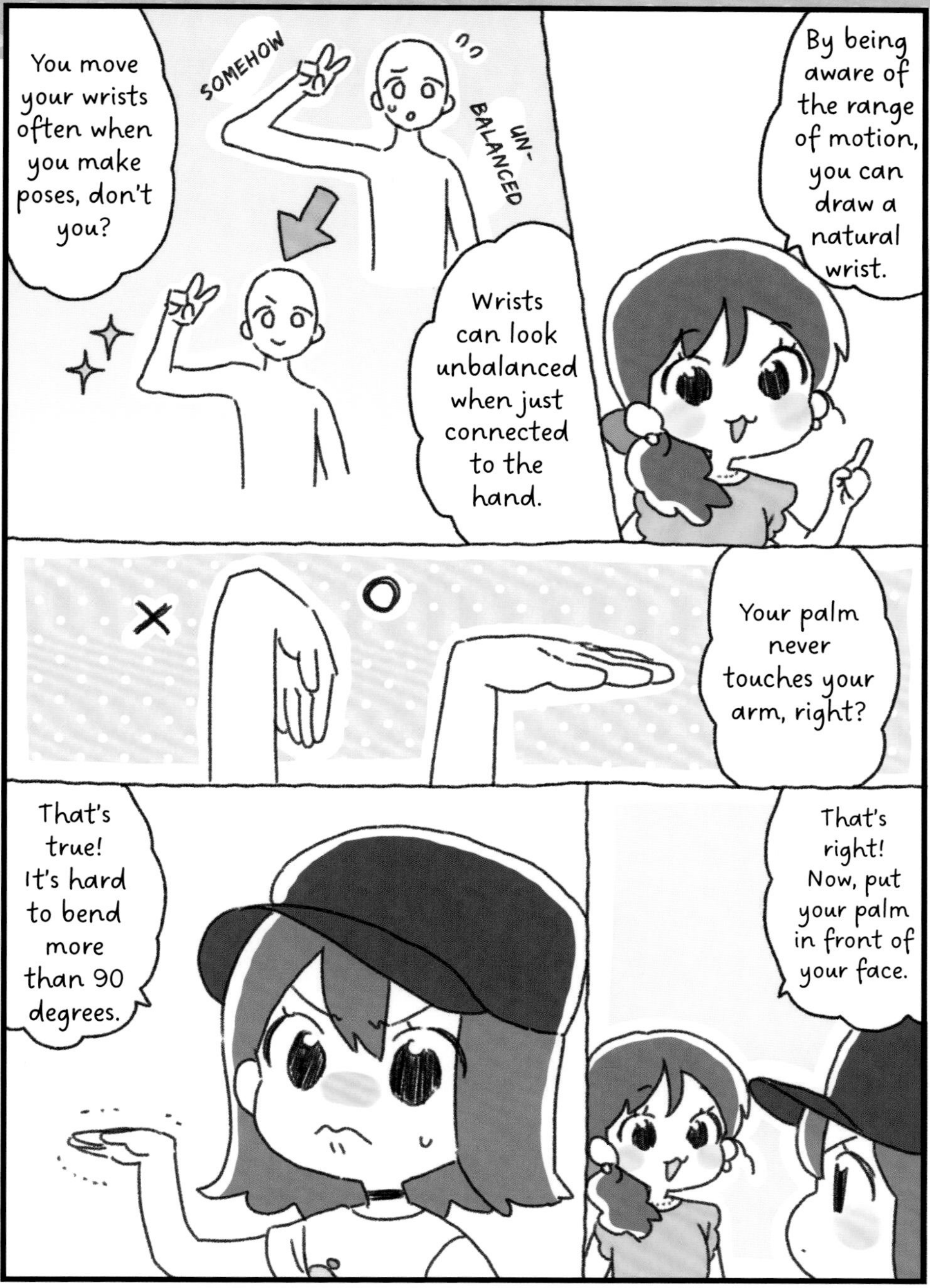
You move your wrists often when you make poses, don't you?
SOMEHOW
UN-BALANCED
Wrists can look unbalanced when just connected to the hand.
By being aware of the range of motion, you can draw a natural wrist.
×
○
Your palm never touches your arm, right?
That's true! It's hard to bend more than 90 degrees.
That's right! Now, put your palm in front of your face.

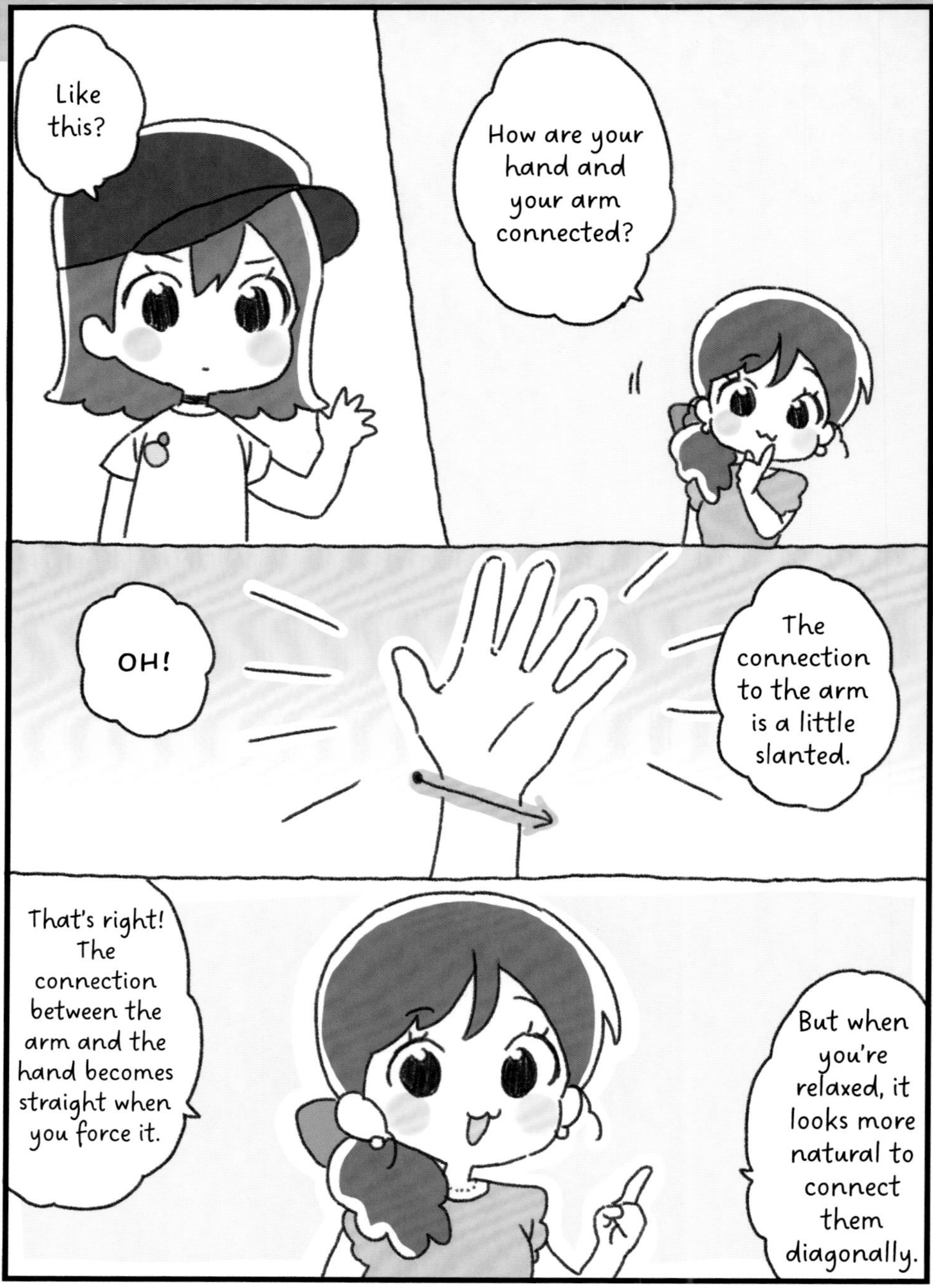
Like this?
How are your hand and your arm connected?
OH!
The connection to the arm is a little slanted.
That's right! The connection between the arm and the hand becomes straight when you force it.
But when you're relaxed, it looks more natural to connect them diagonally.

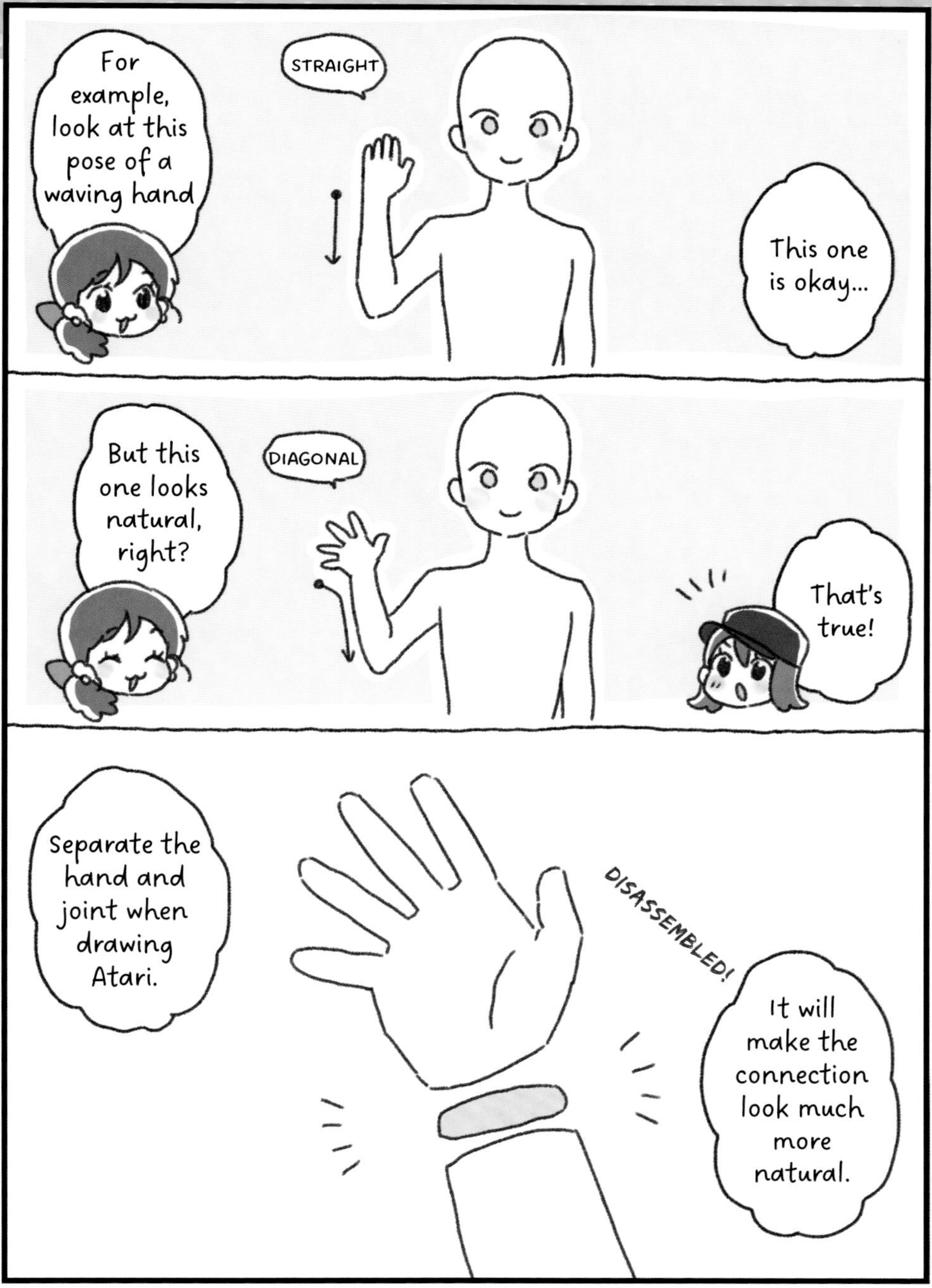
For example, look at this pose of a waving hand
STRAIGHT
This one is okay...
But this one looks natural, right?
DIAGONAL
That's true!
Separate the hand and joint when drawing Atari.
DISASSEMBLED!
It will make the connection look much more natural.

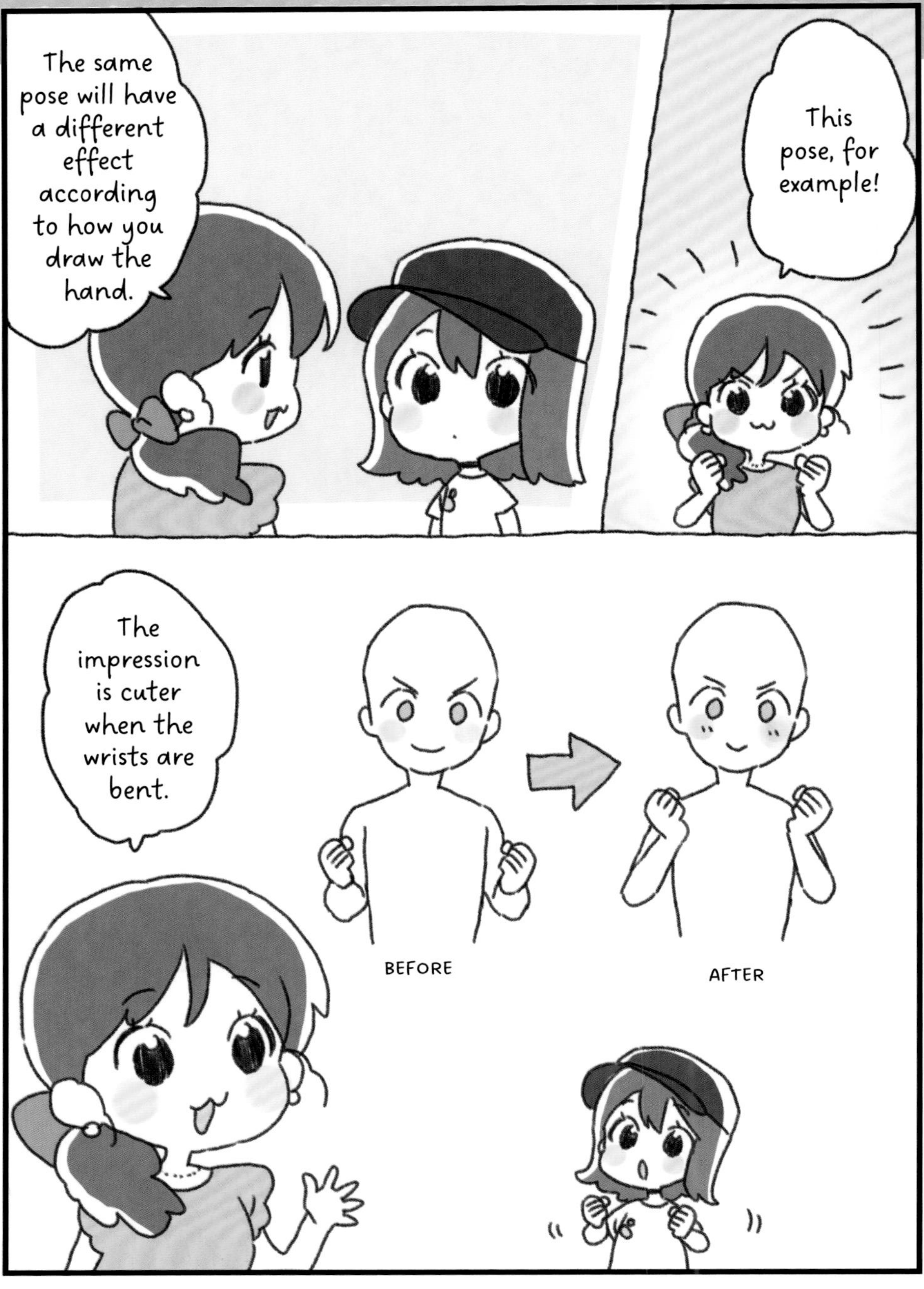
The same pose will have a different effect according to how you draw the hand.
This pose, for example!
The impression is cuter when the wrists are bent.
BEFORE
AFTER

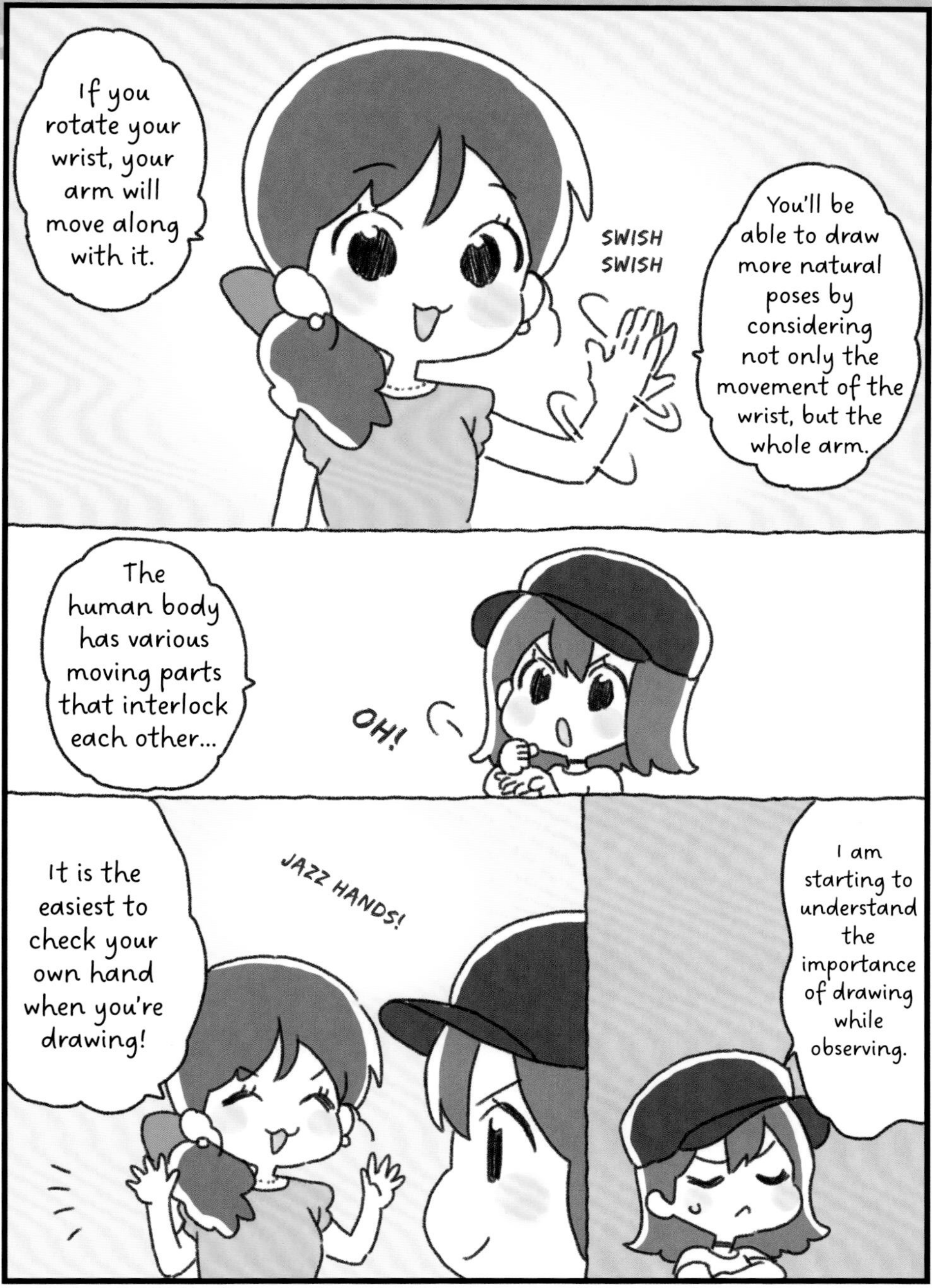
If you rotate your wrist, your arm will move along with it.
SWISH SWISH
You'll be able to draw more natural poses by considering not only the movement of the wrist, but the whole arm.
The human body has various moving parts that interlock each other...
OH!
It is the easiest to check your own hand when you're drawing!
JAZZ HANDS!
I am starting to understand the importance of drawing while observing.

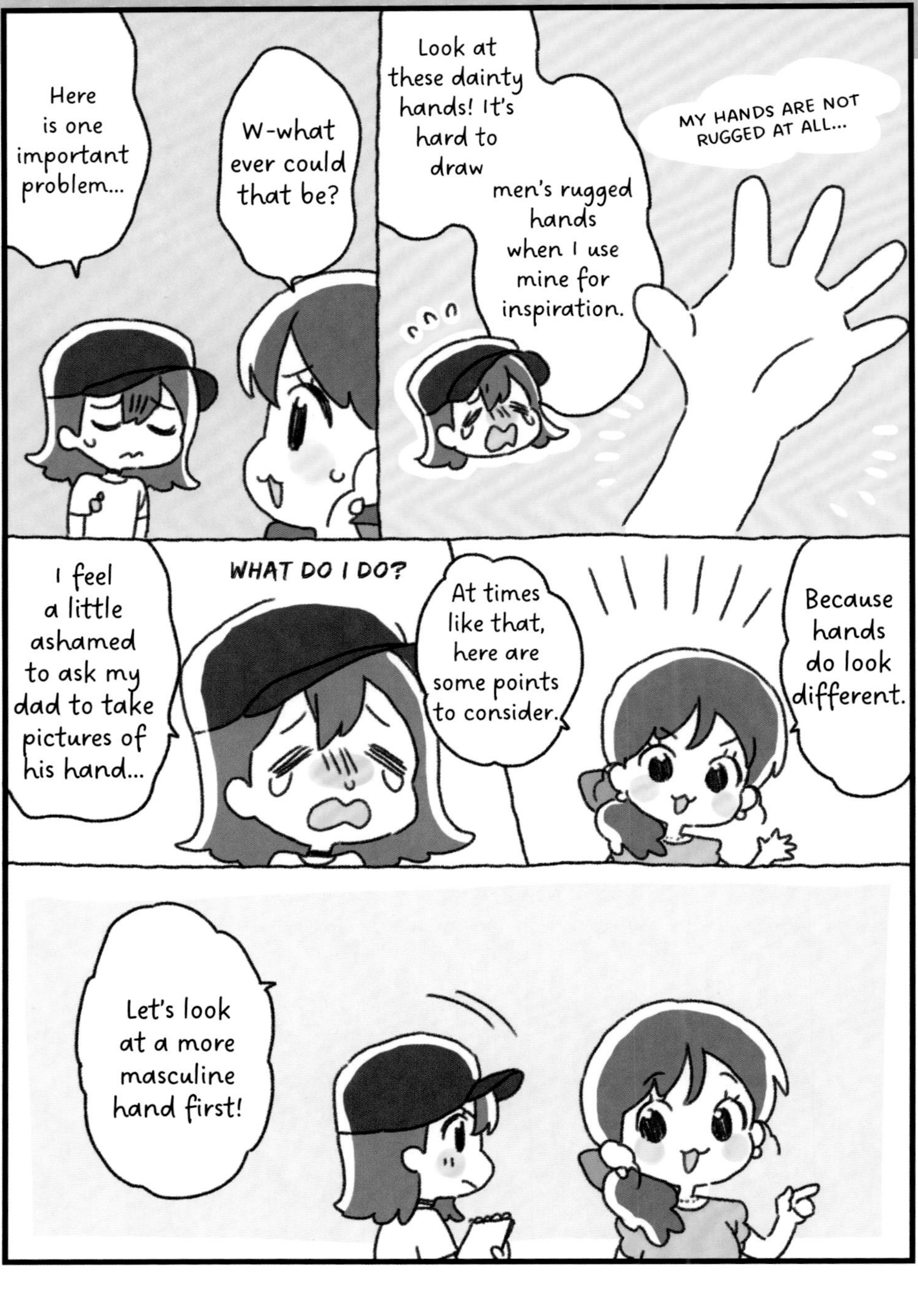
Here is one important problem...
W-what ever could that be?
Look at these dainty hands! It's hard to draw men's rugged hands when I use mine for inspiration.
MY HANDS ARE NOT RUGGED AT ALL...
I feel a little ashamed to ask my dad to take pictures of his hand...
WHAT DO I DO?
At times like that, here are some points to consider.
Because hands do look different.
Let's look at a more masculine hand first!

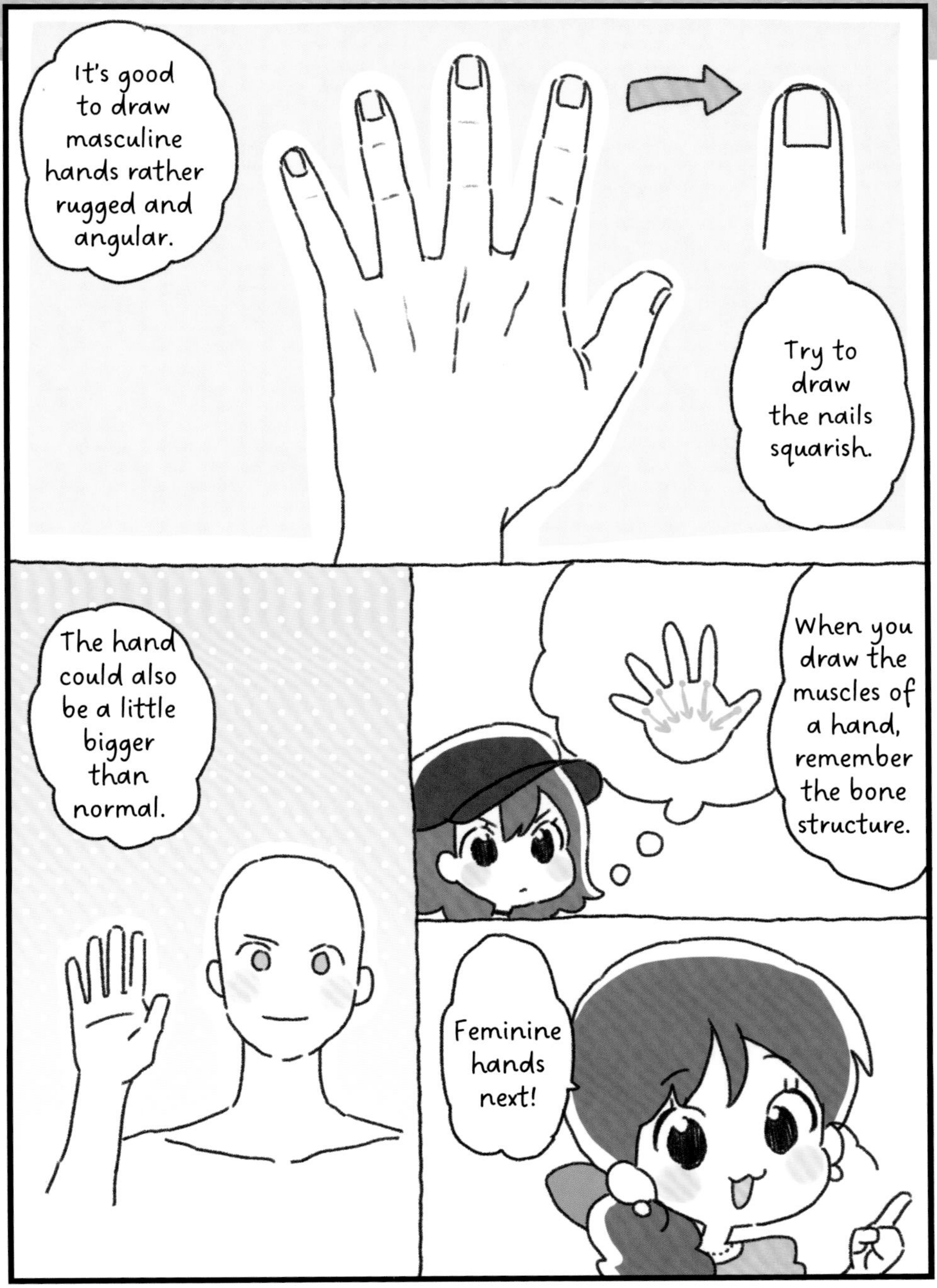
It's good to draw masculine hands rather rugged and angular.
Try to draw the nails squarish.
The hand could also be a little bigger than normal.
When you draw the muscles of a hand, remember the bone structure.
Feminine hands next!

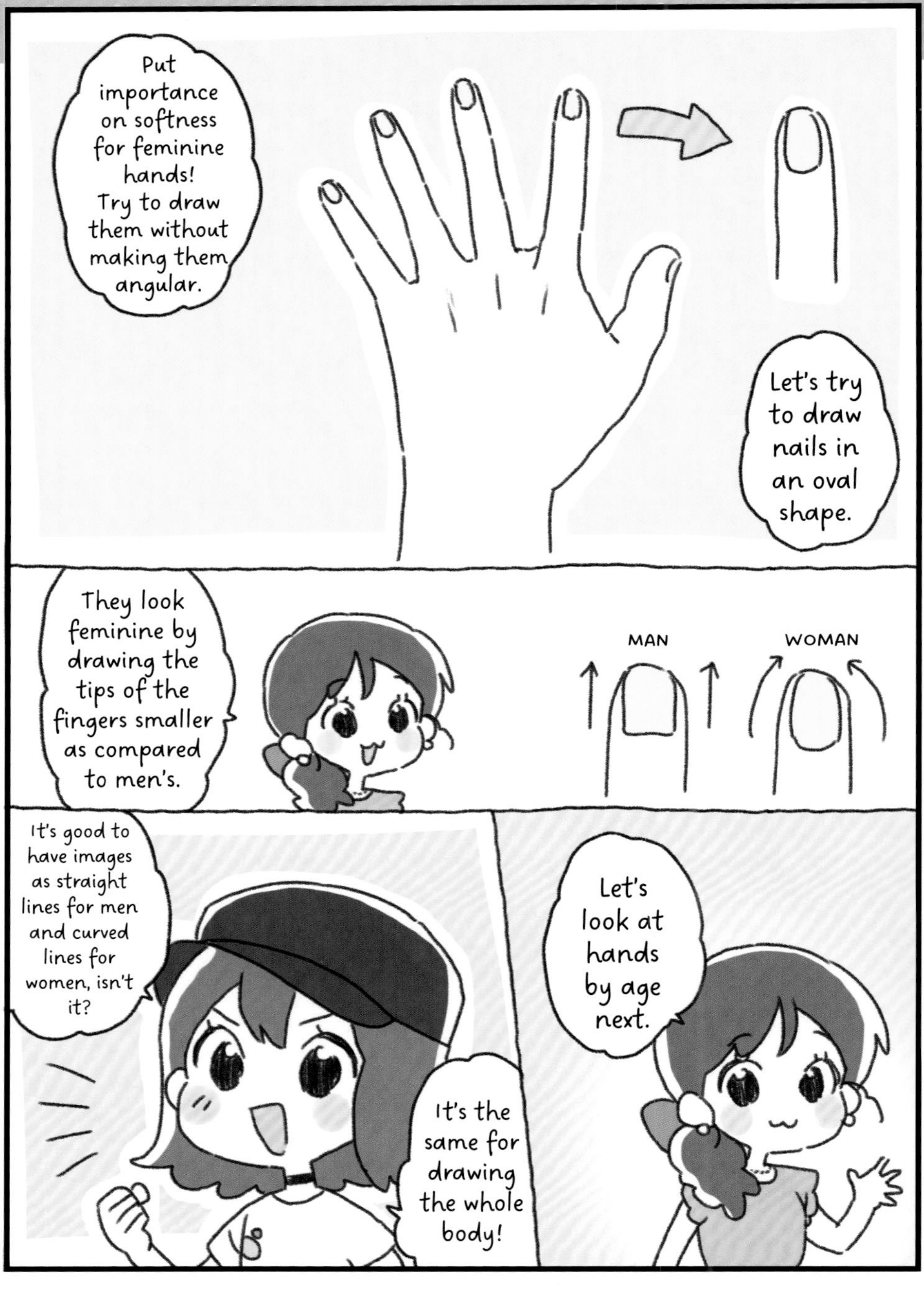
Put importance on softness for feminine hands! Try to draw them without making them angular.
Let's try to draw nails in an oval shape.
They look feminine by drawing the tips of the fingers smaller as compared to men's.
MAN
WOMAN
It's good to have images as straight lines for men and curved lines for women, isn't it?
It's the same for drawing the whole body!
Let's look at hands by age next.

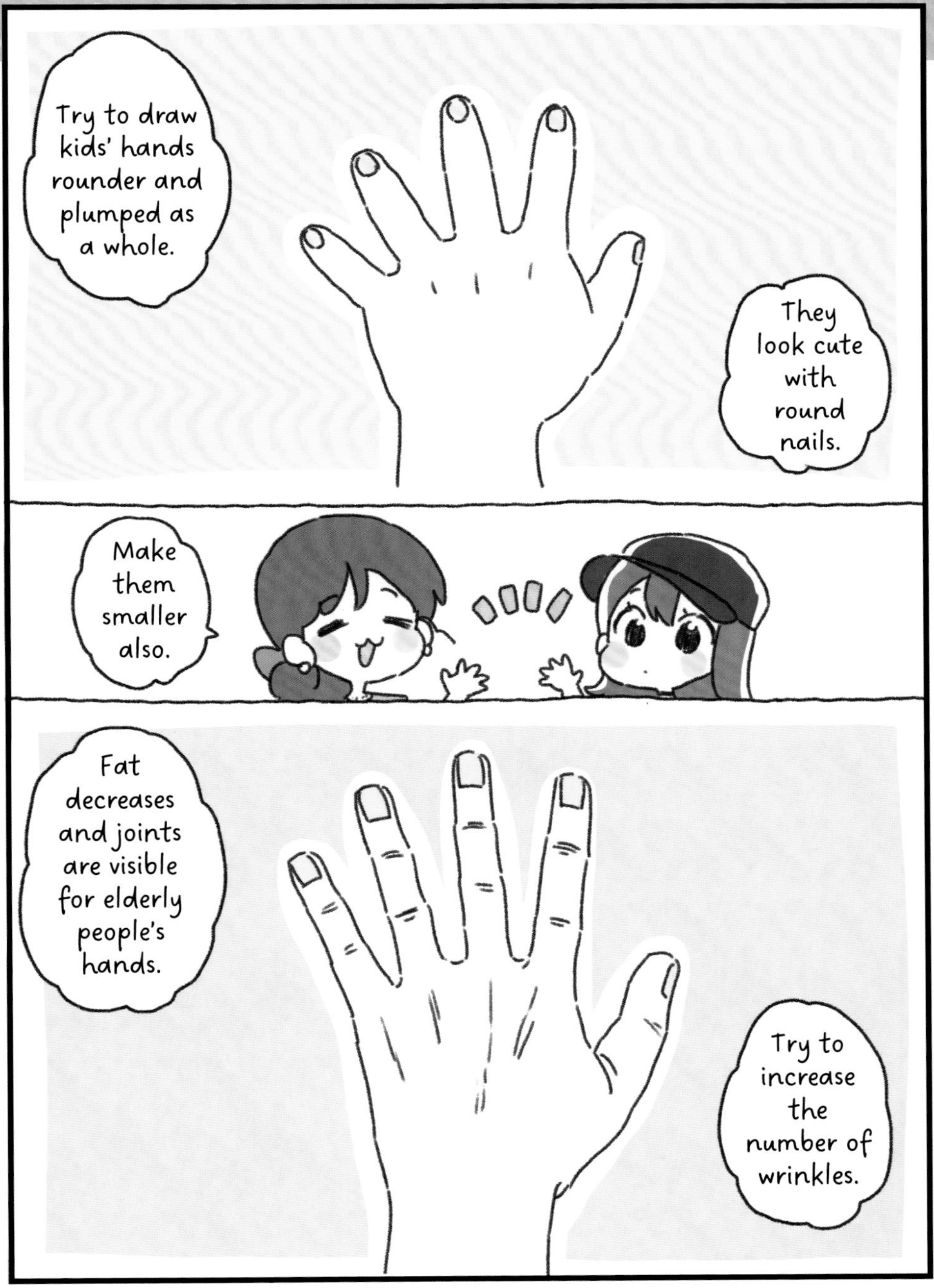
Try to draw kids' hands rounder and plumped as a whole.
They look cute with round nails.
Make them smaller also.
Fat decreases and joints are visible for elderly people's hands.
Try to increase the number of wrinkles.

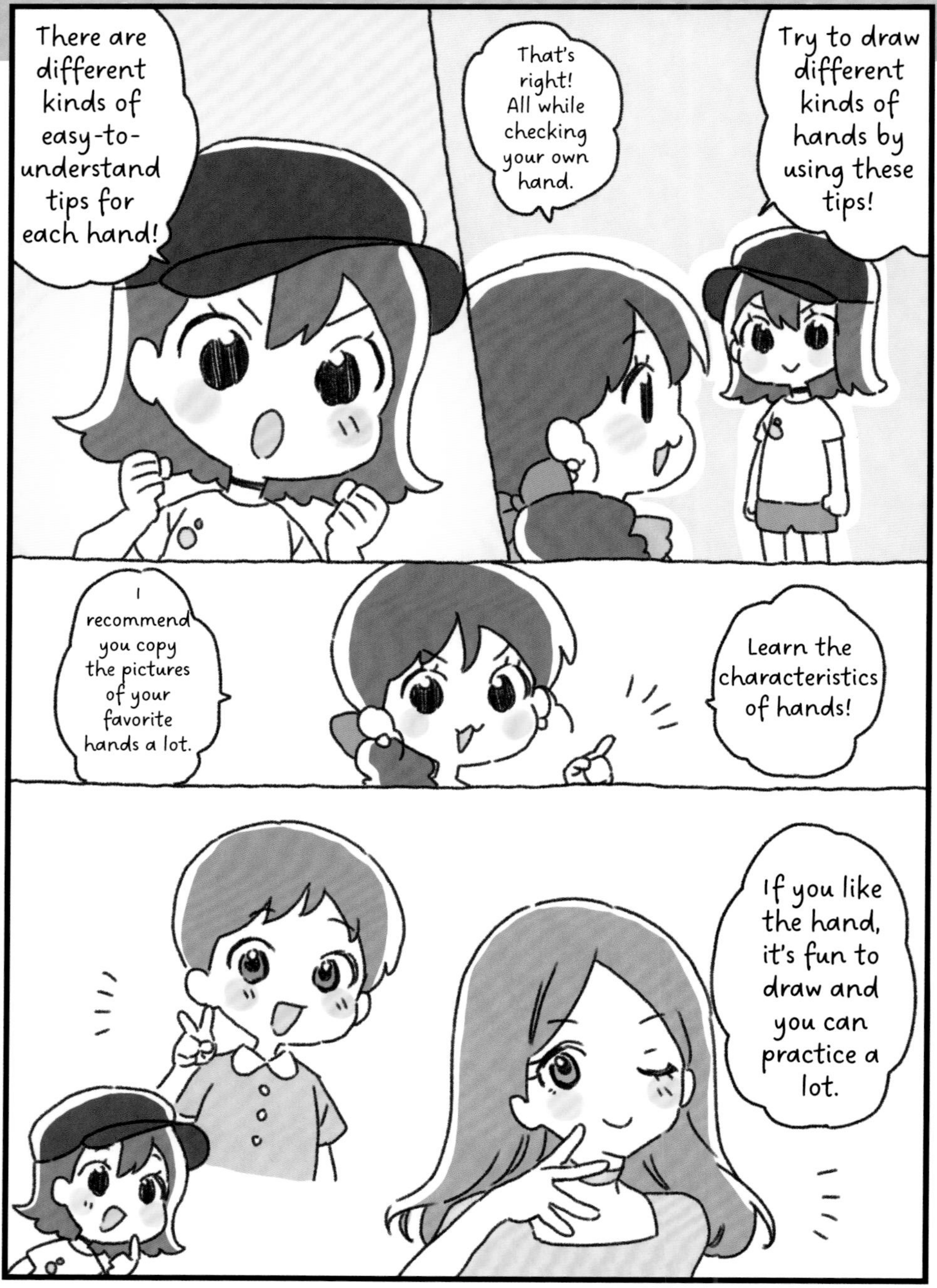
There are different kinds of easy-to-understand tips for each hand!
That's right! All while checking your own hand.
Try to draw different kinds of hands by using these tips!
I recommend you copy the pictures of your favorite hands a lot.
Learn the characteristics of hands!
If you like the hand, it's fun to draw and you can practice a lot.

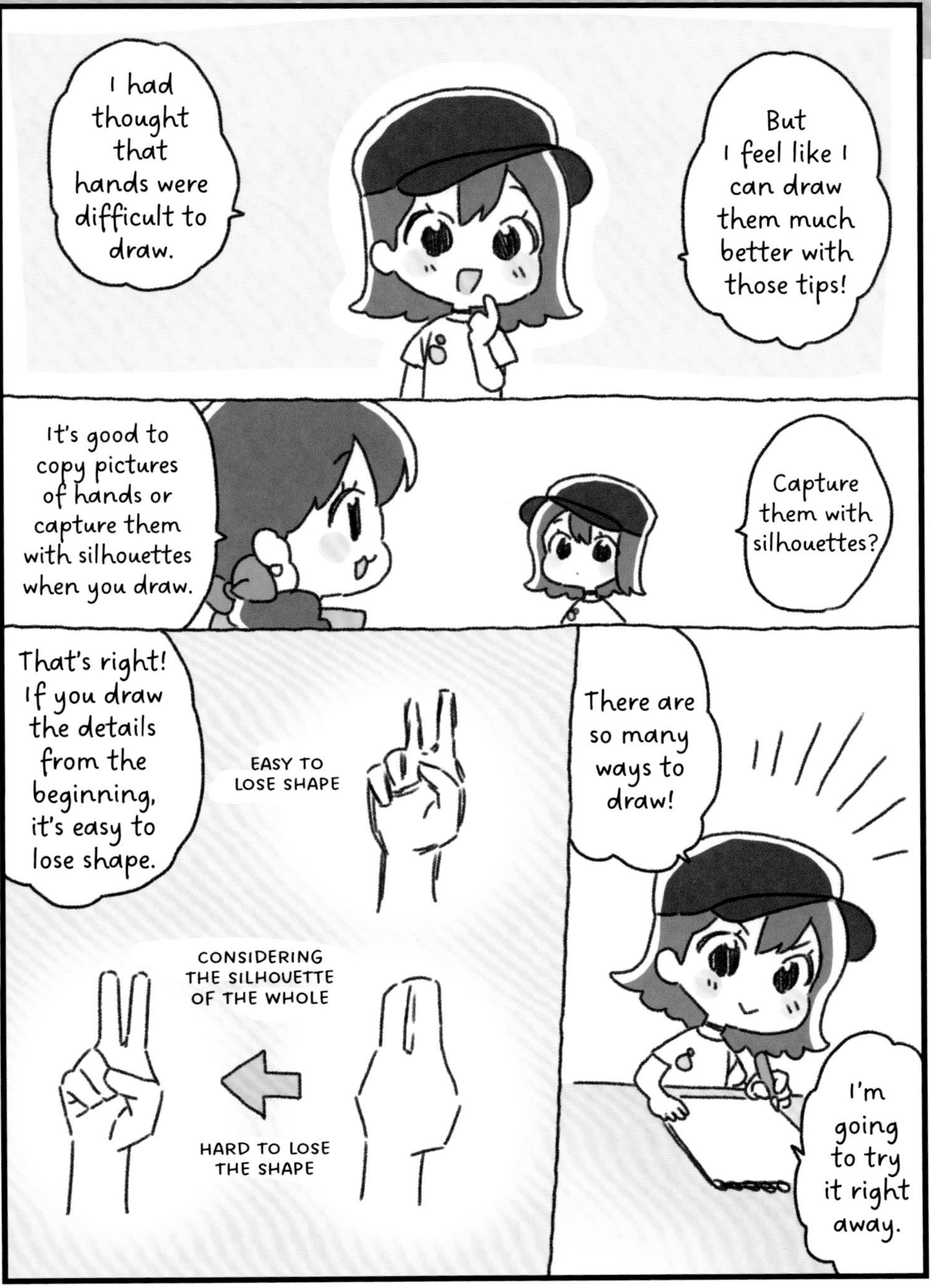
I had thought that hands were difficult to draw.
But I feel like I can draw them much better with those tips!
It's good to copy pictures of hands or capture them with silhouettes when you draw.
Capture them with silhouettes?
That's right! If you draw the details from the beginning, it's easy to lose shape.
EASY TO LOSE SHAPE
CONSIDERING THE SILHOUETTE OF THE WHOLE
HARD TO LOSE THE SHAPE
There are so many ways to draw!
I'm going to try it right away.

## LEVEL UP

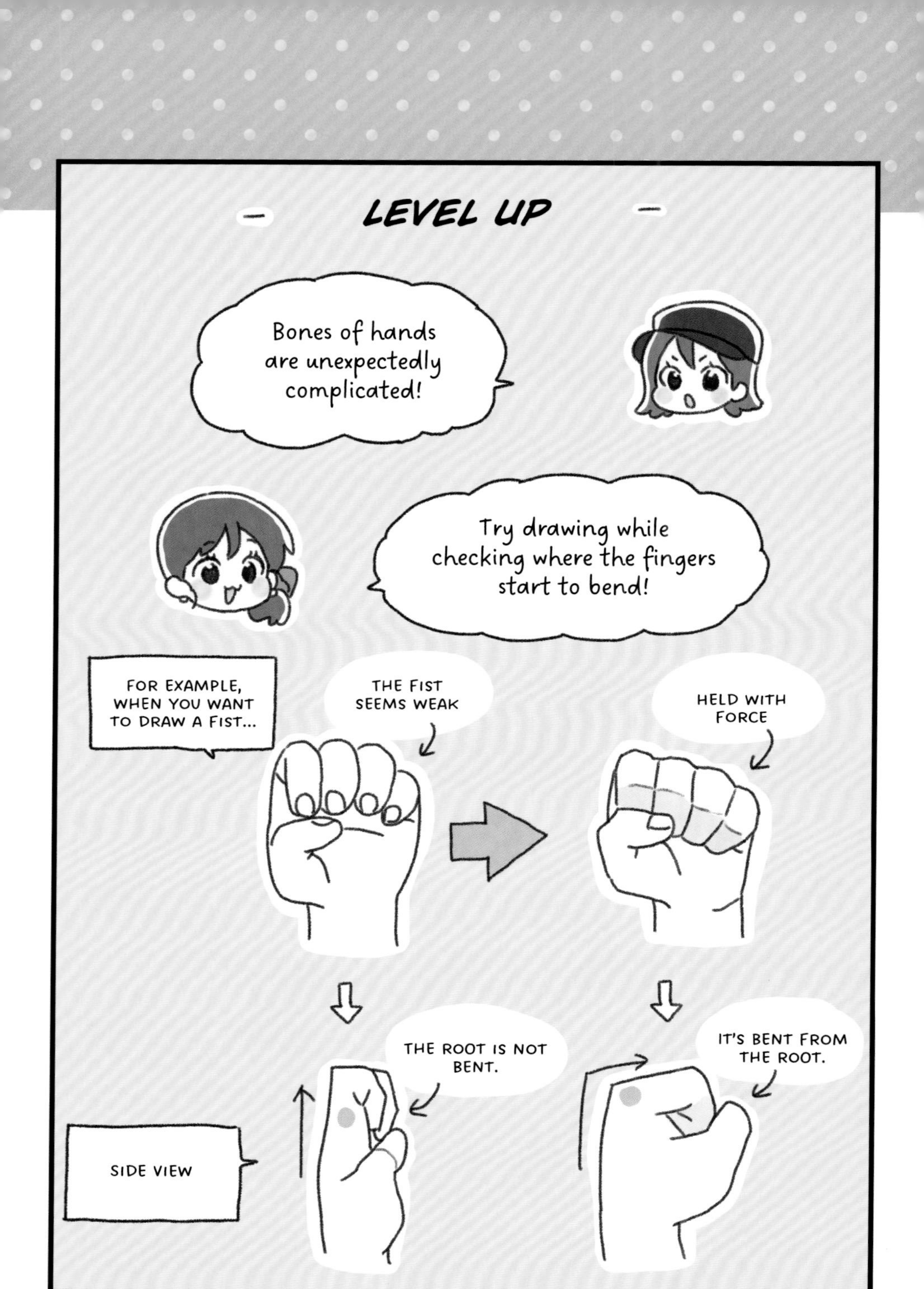

Bones of hands are unexpectedly complicated!
Try drawing while checking where the fingers start to bend!
FOR EXAMPLE, WHEN YOU WANT TO DRAW A FIST...
THE FIST SEEMS WEAK
HELD WITH FORCE
SIDE VIEW
THE ROOT IS NOT BENT.
IT'S BENT FROM THE ROOT.

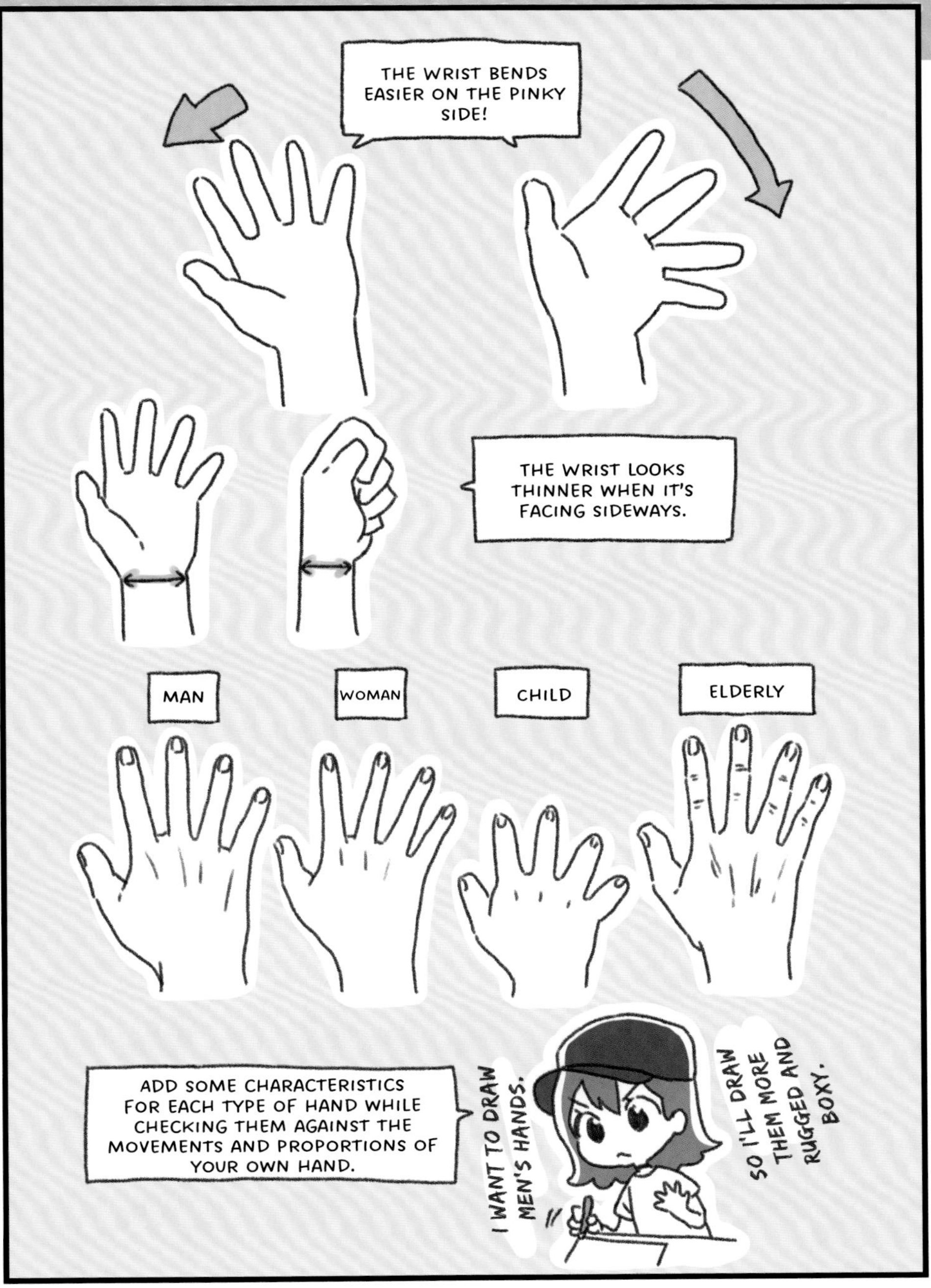
THE WRIST BENDS EASIER ON THE PINKY SIDE!
THE WRIST LOOKS THINNER WHEN IT'S FACING SIDEWAYS.
MAN
WOMAN
CHILD
ELDERLY
ADD SOME CHARACTERISTICS FOR EACH TYPE OF HAND WHILE CHECKING THEM AGAINST THE MOVEMENTS AND PROPORTIONS OF YOUR OWN HAND.
I WANT TO DRAW MEN'S HANDS.
SO I'LL DRAW THEM MORE RUGGED AND BOXY.

# VARIOUS HAND POSE SAMPLES

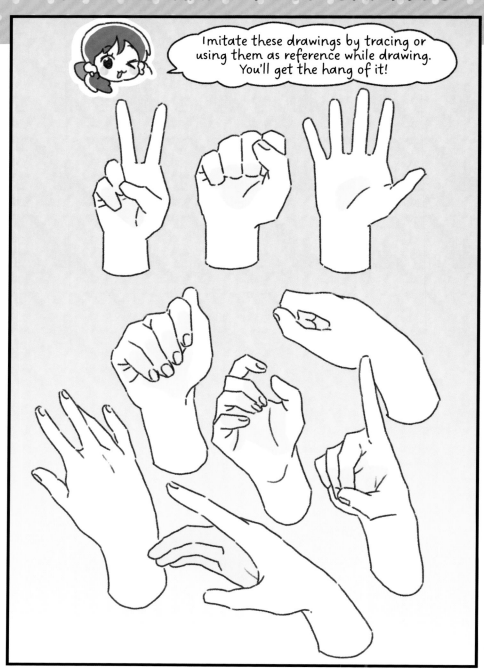

Imitate these drawings by tracing or using them as reference while drawing. You'll get the hang of it!

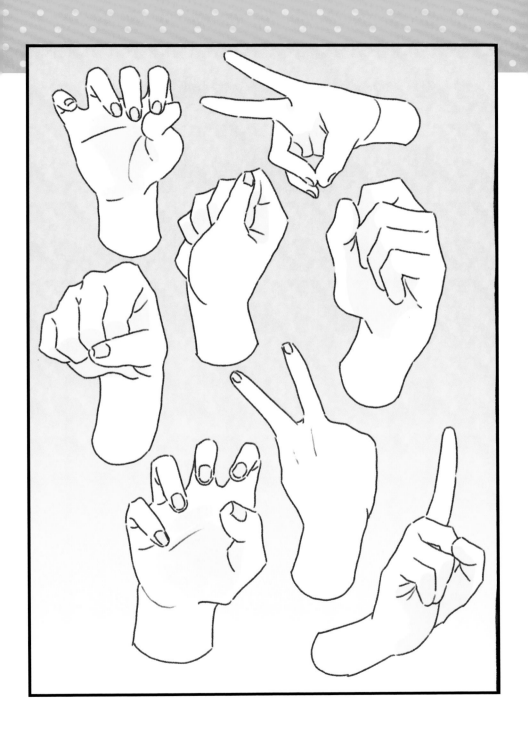

# HOW TO DRAW GLOVES AND ACCESSORIES

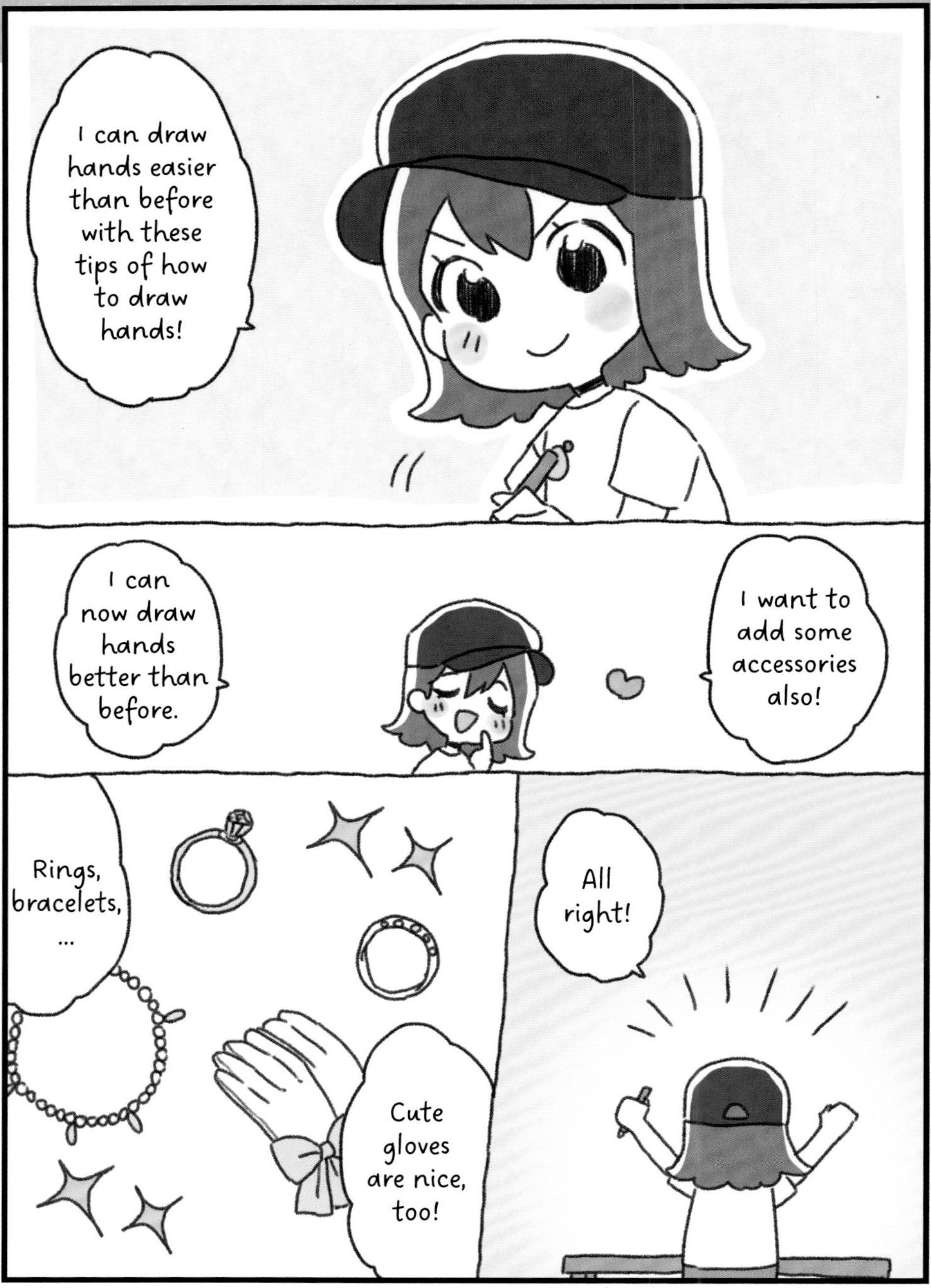
I can draw hands easier than before with these tips of how to draw hands!
I can now draw hands better than before.
I want to add some accessories also!
Rings, bracelets, ...
Cute gloves are nice, too!
All right!

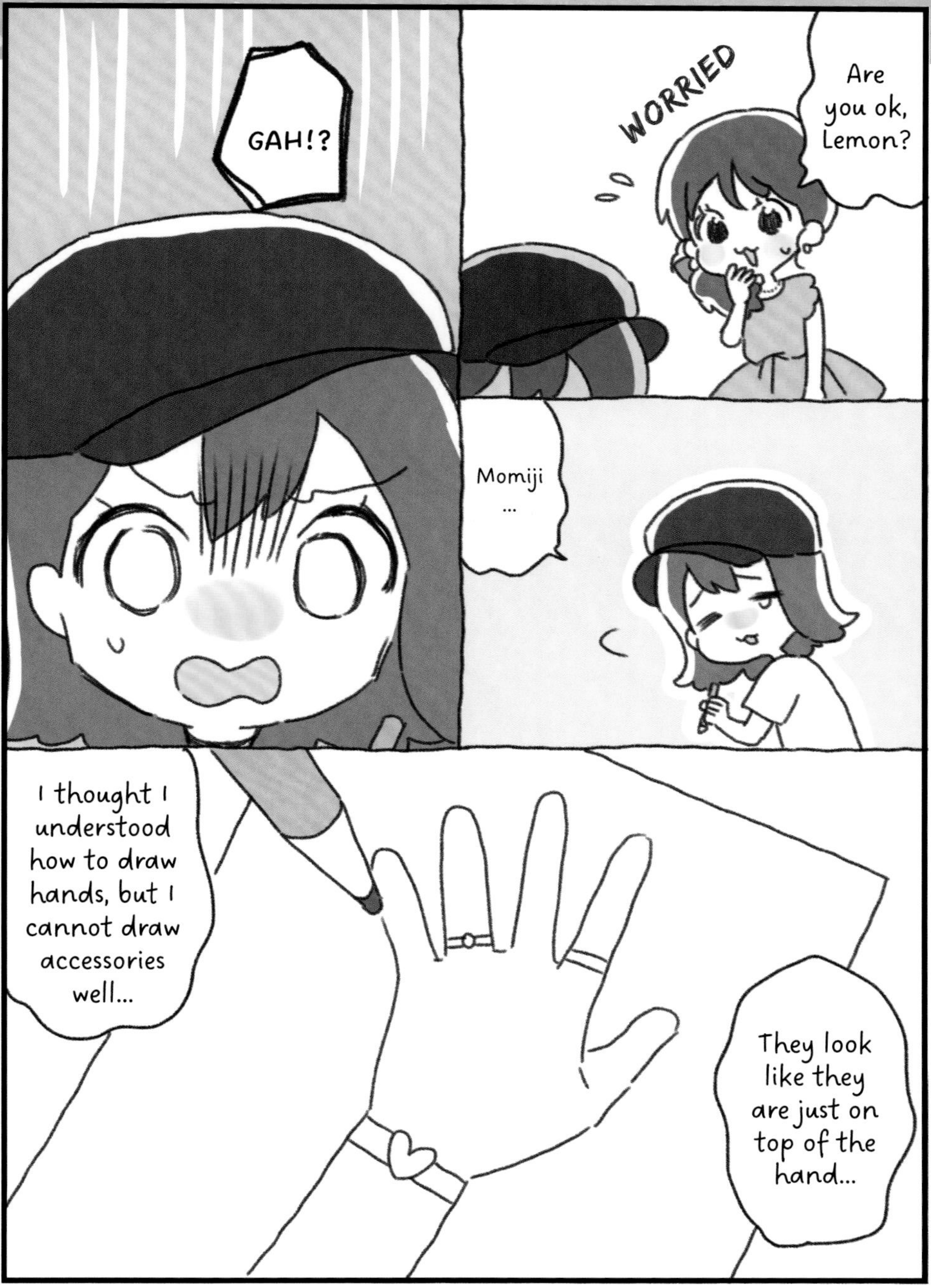
GAH!?
WORRIED
Are you ok, Lemon?
Momiji ...
I thought I understood how to draw hands, but I cannot draw accessories well...
They look like they are just on top of the hand...

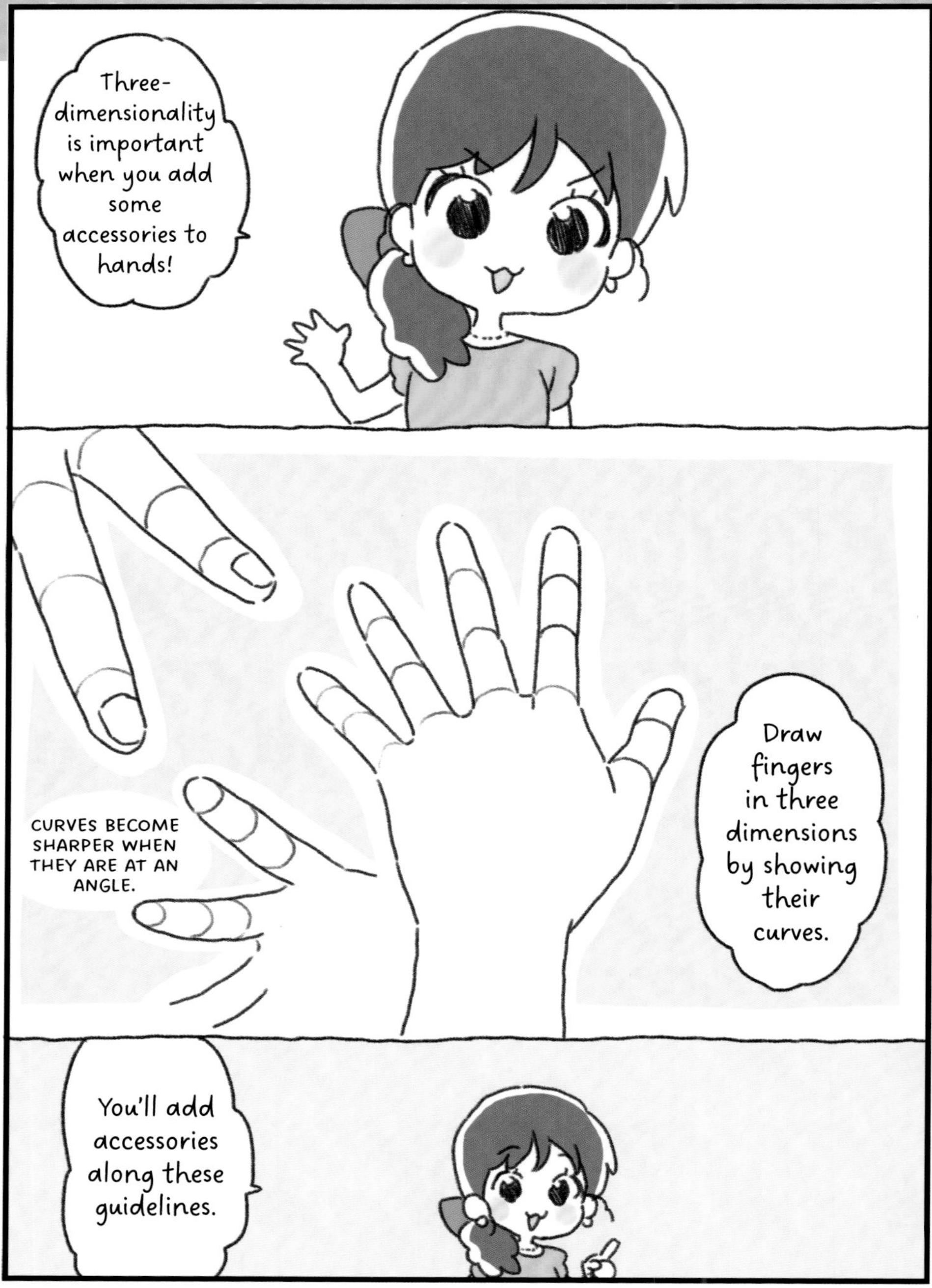
Three-dimensionality is important when you add some accessories to hands!
Draw fingers in three dimensions by showing their curves.
CURVES BECOME SHARPER WHEN THEY ARE AT AN ANGLE.
You'll add accessories along these guidelines.

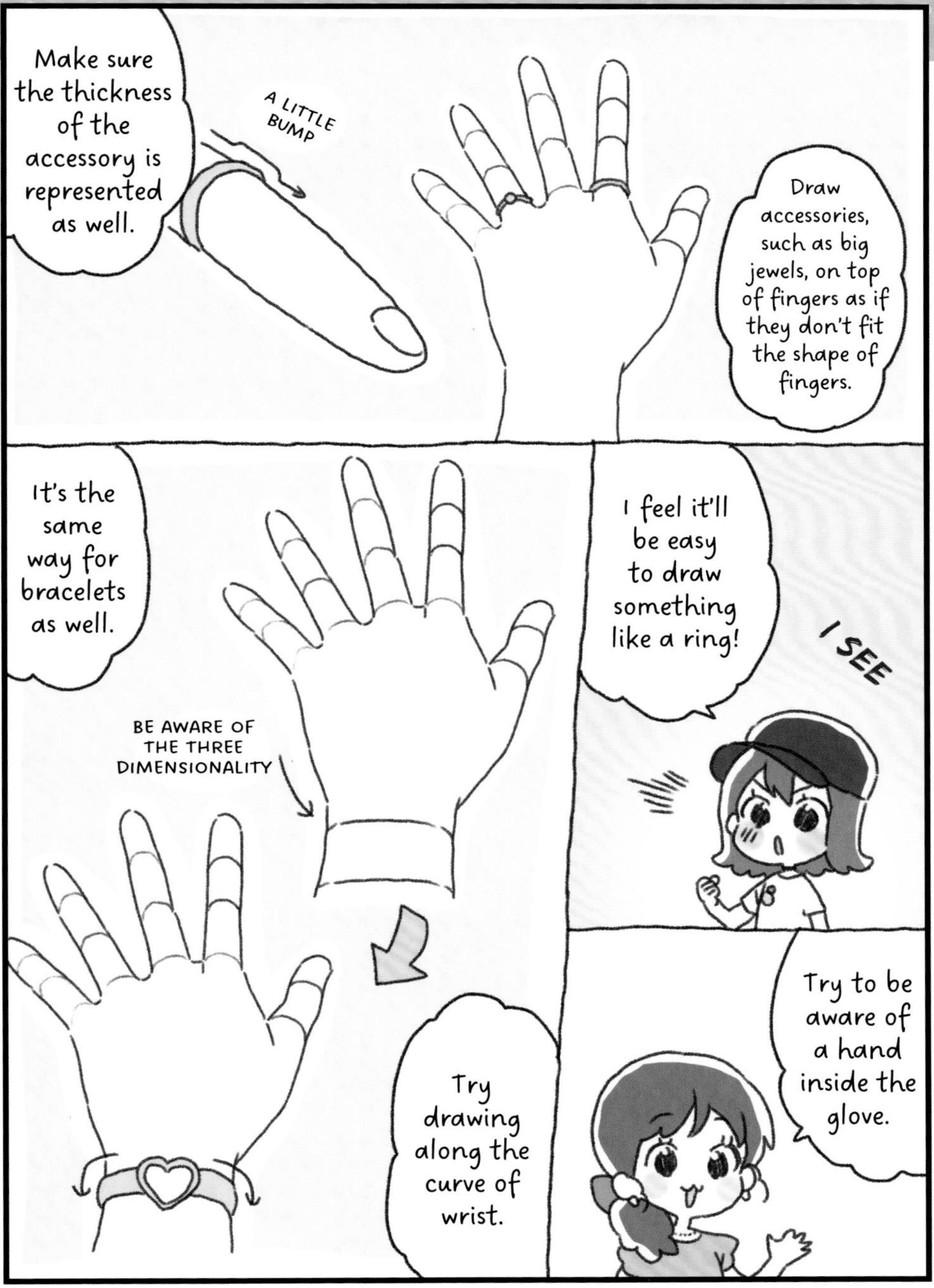
Make sure the thickness of the accessory is represented as well.
A LITTLE BUMP
Draw accessories, such as big jewels, on top of fingers as if they don't fit the shape of fingers.
It's the same way for bracelets as well.
BE AWARE OF THE THREE DIMENSIONALITY
I feel it'll be easy to draw something like a ring!
I SEE
Try drawing along the curve of wrist.
Try to be aware of a hand inside the glove.

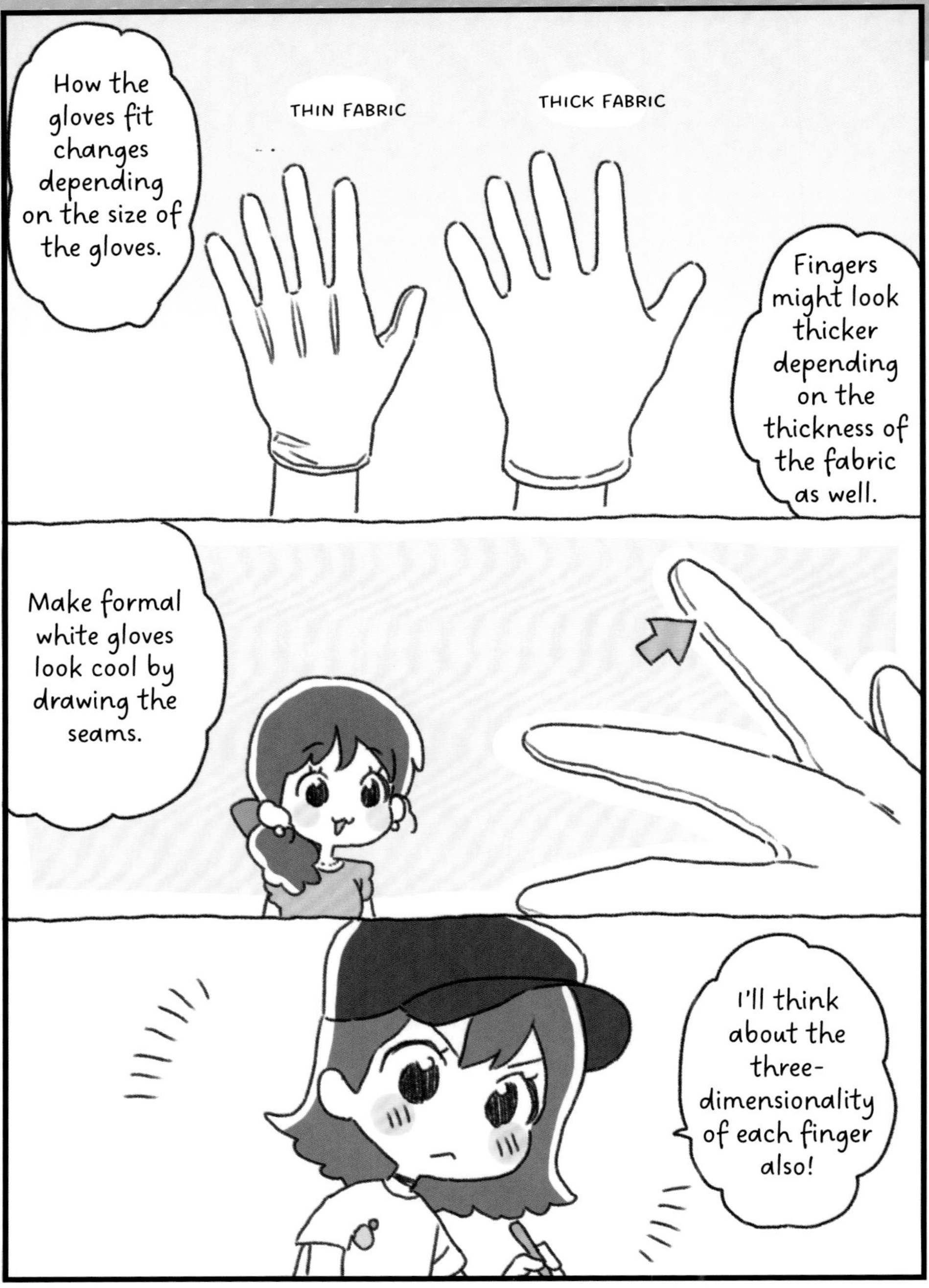
How the gloves fit changes depending on the size of the gloves.
THIN FABRIC
THICK FABRIC
Fingers might look thicker depending on the thickness of the fabric as well.
Make formal white gloves look cool by drawing the seams.
I'll think about the three-dimensionality of each finger also!

# — SUMMARY —

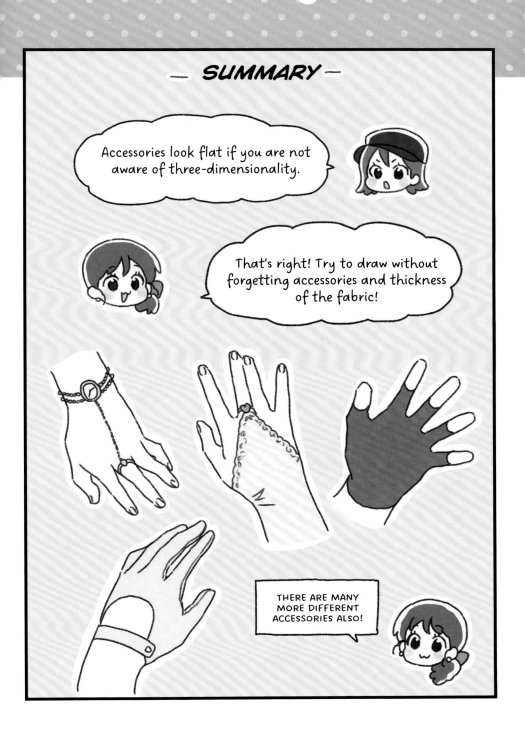

Accessories look flat if you are not aware of three-dimensionality.

That's right! Try to draw without forgetting accessories and thickness of the fabric!

THERE ARE MANY MORE DIFFERENT ACCESSORIES ALSO!

## TRY DRAWING UPPER BODY POSES

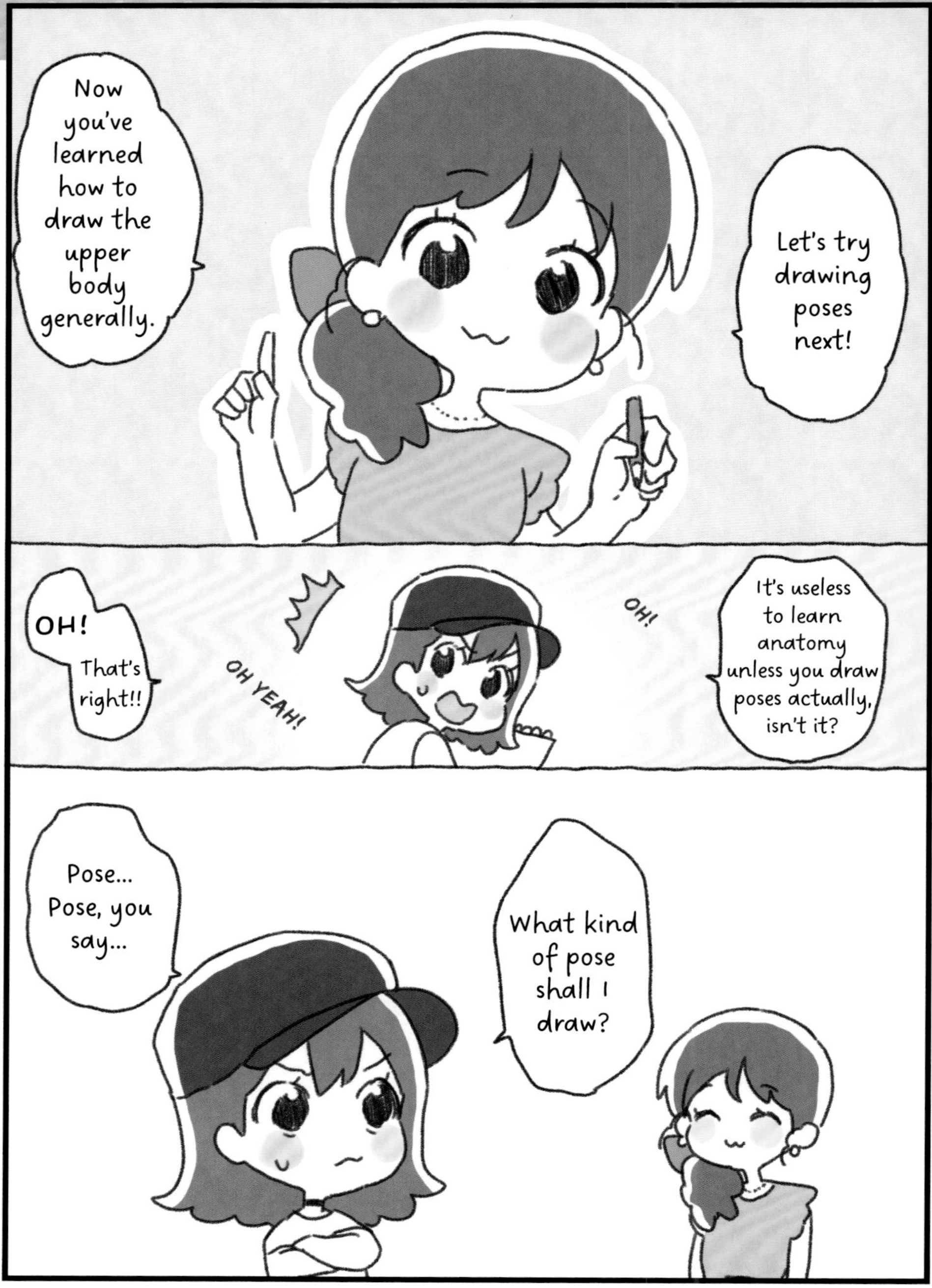

Now you've learned how to draw the upper body generally.
Let's try drawing poses next!
OH! That's right!!
OH YEAH!
OH!
It's useless to learn anatomy unless you draw poses actually, isn't it?
Pose... Pose, you say...
What kind of pose shall I draw?

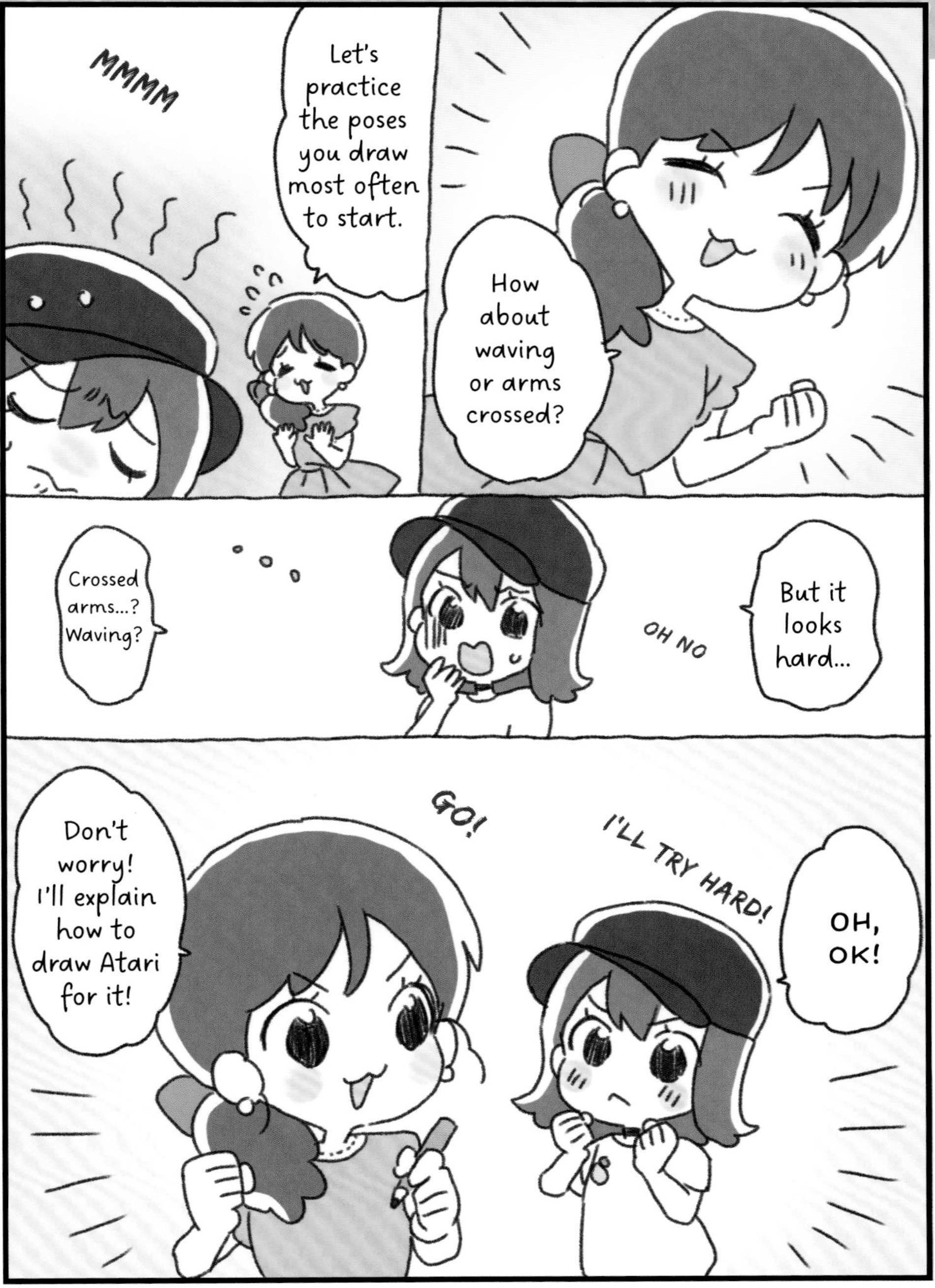
MMMM
Let's practice the poses you draw most often to start.
How about waving or arms crossed?
Crossed arms...? Waving?
OH NO
But it looks hard...
Don't worry! I'll explain how to draw Atari for it!
GO!
I'LL TRY HARD!
OH, OK!

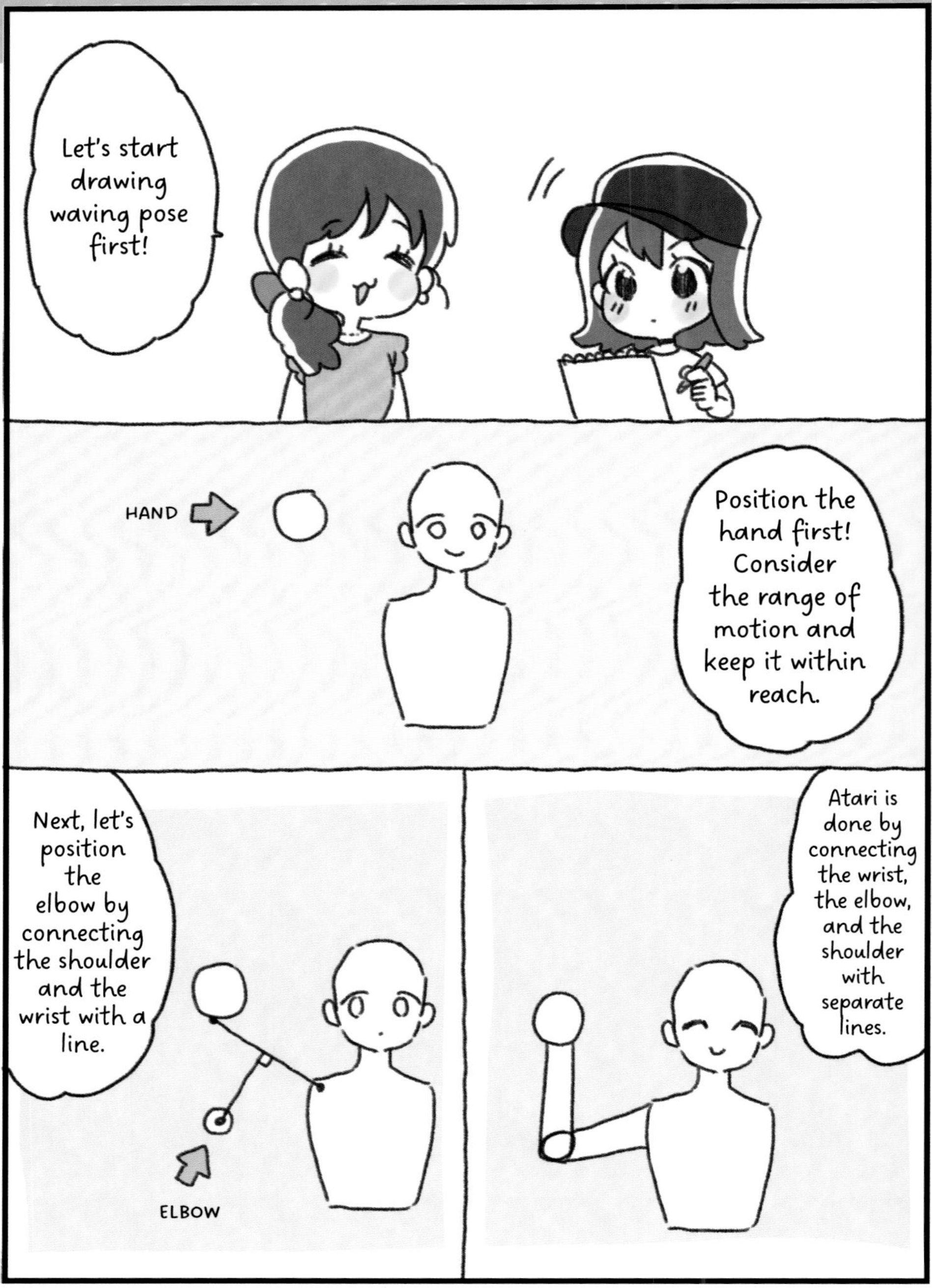
Let's start drawing waving pose first!
HAND
Position the hand first! Consider the range of motion and keep it within reach.
Next, let's position the elbow by connecting the shoulder and the wrist with a line.
ELBOW
Atari is done by connecting the wrist, the elbow, and the shoulder with separate lines.

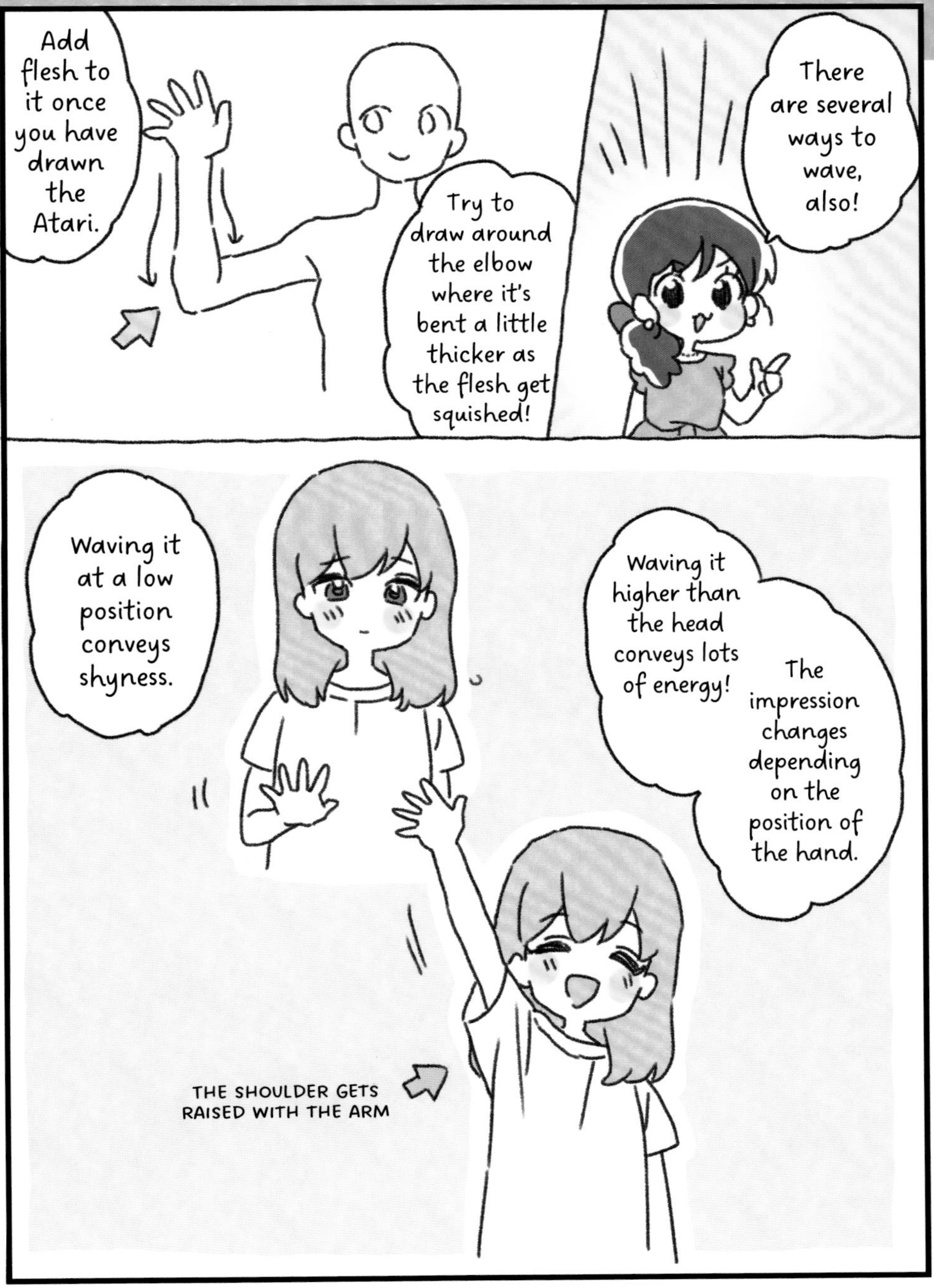
Add flesh to it once you have drawn the Atari.
Try to draw around the elbow where it's bent a little thicker as the flesh get squished!
There are several ways to wave, also!
Waving it at a low position conveys shyness.
Waving it higher than the head conveys lots of energy!
The impression changes depending on the position of the hand.
THE SHOULDER GETS RAISED WITH THE ARM

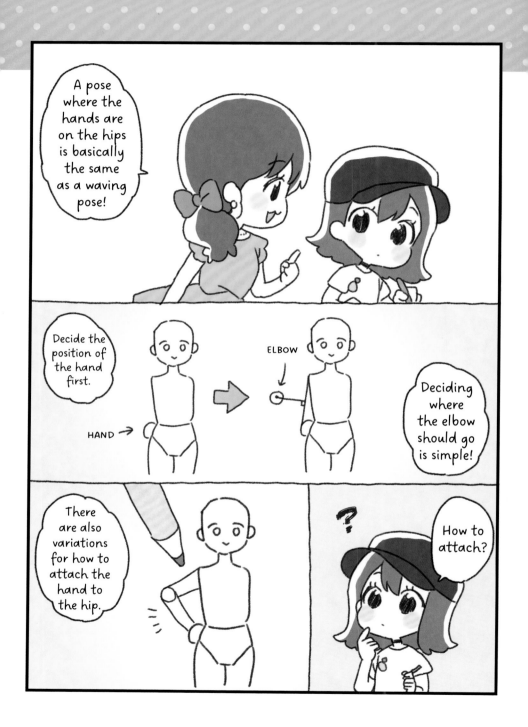

A pose where the hands are on the hips is basically the same as a waving pose!

Decide the position of the hand first.

HAND →

ELBOW

Deciding where the elbow should go is simple!

There are also variations for how to attach the hand to the hip.

How to attach?

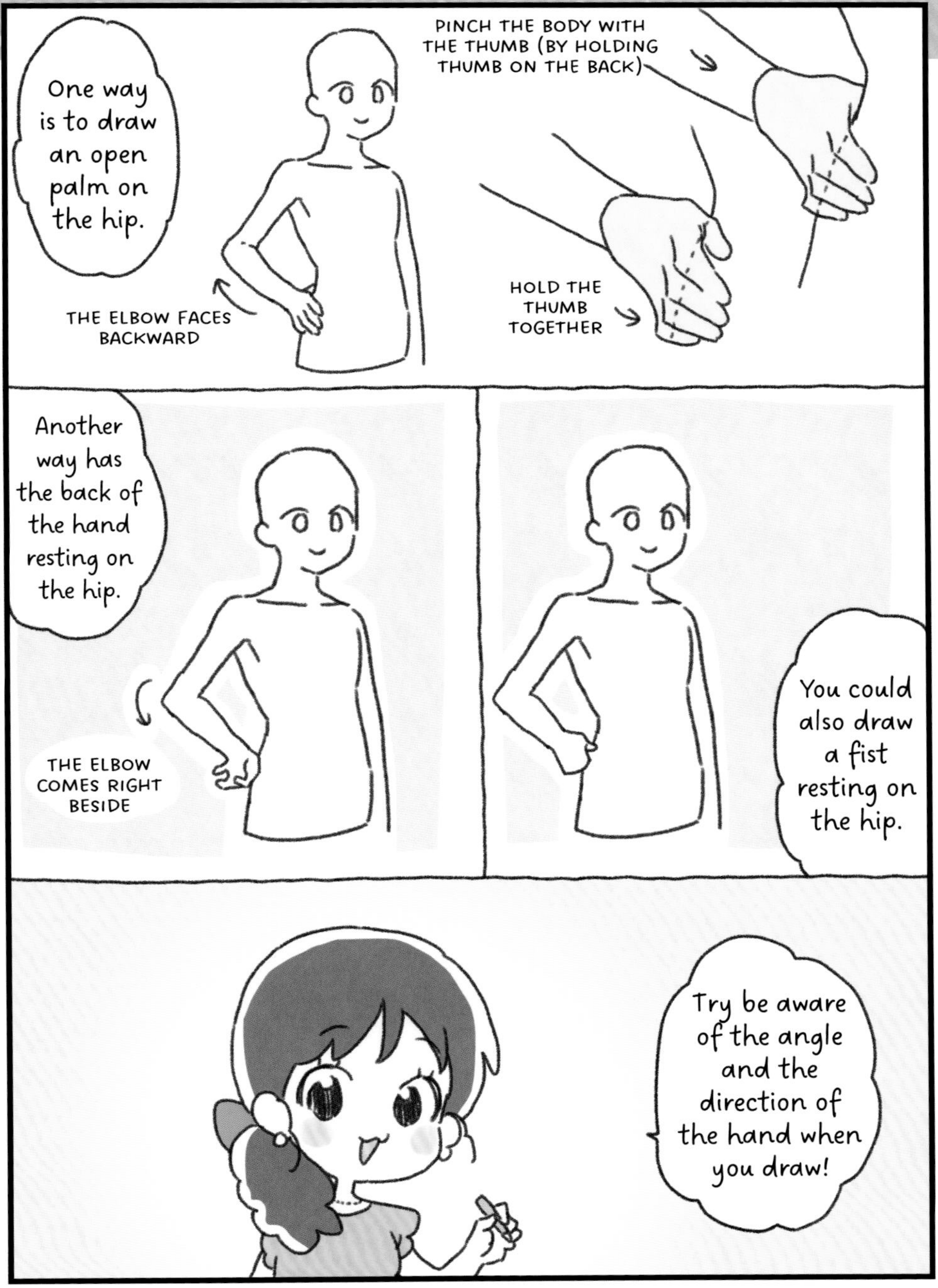
One way is to draw an open palm on the hip.
THE ELBOW FACES BACKWARD
PINCH THE BODY WITH THE THUMB (BY HOLDING THUMB ON THE BACK)
HOLD THE THUMB TOGETHER
Another way has the back of the hand resting on the hip.
THE ELBOW COMES RIGHT BESIDE
You could also draw a fist resting on the hip.
Try be aware of the angle and the direction of the hand when you draw!

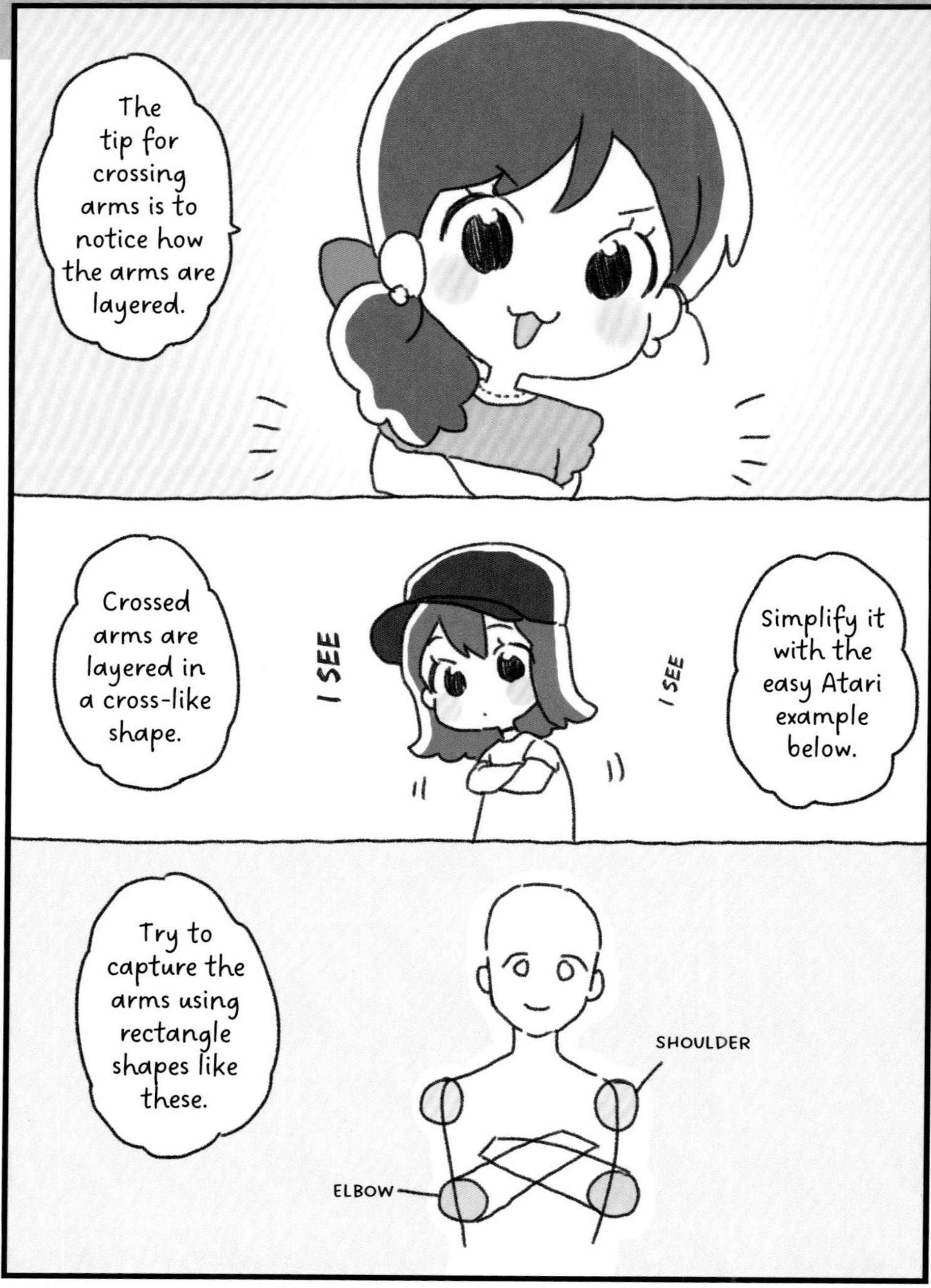
The tip for crossing arms is to notice how the arms are layered.
Crossed arms are layered in a cross-like shape.
I SEE
I SEE
Simplify it with the easy Atari example below.
Try to capture the arms using rectangle shapes like these.
SHOULDER
ELBOW

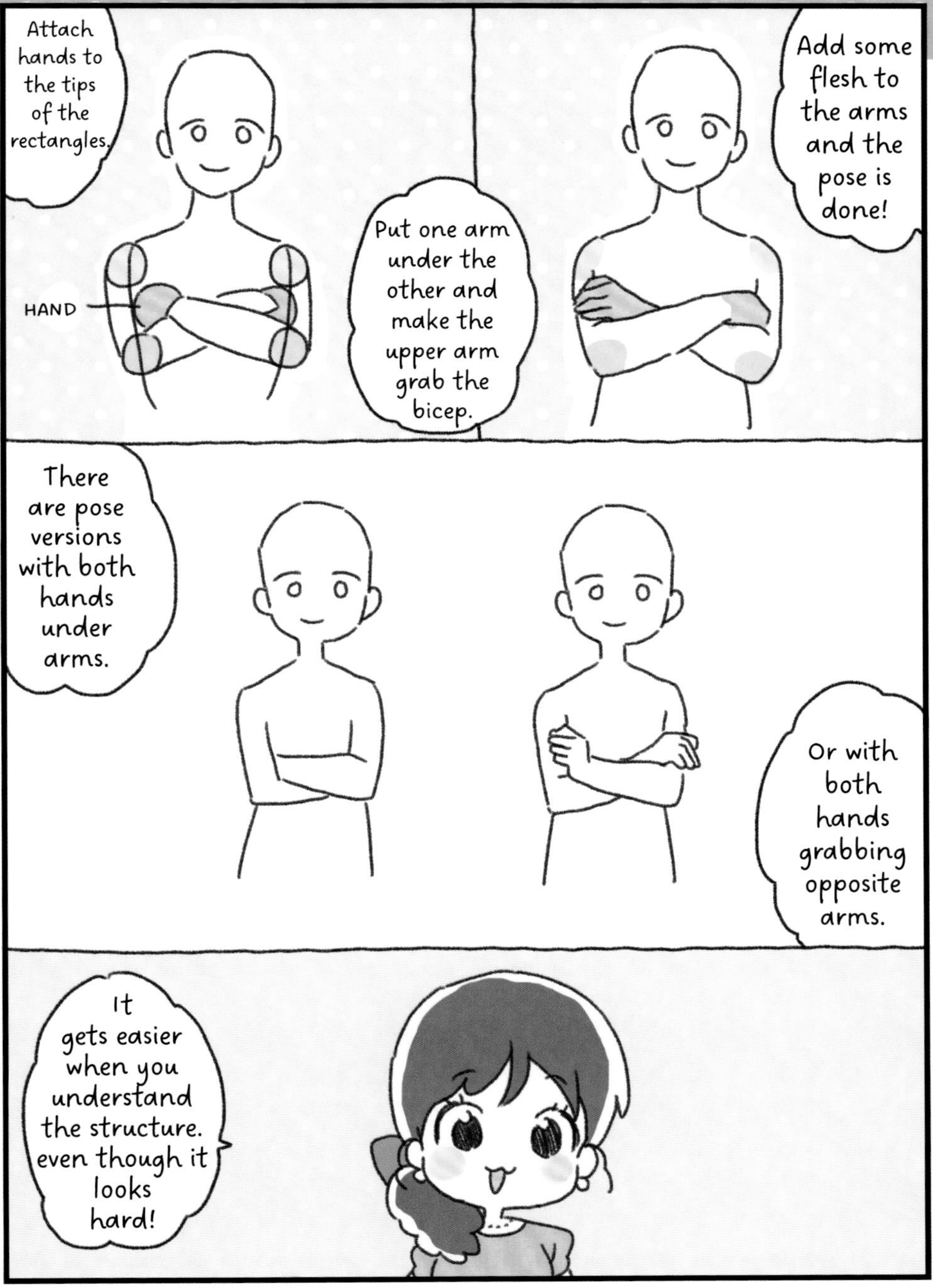
Attach hands to the tips of the rectangles.
HAND
Put one arm under the other and make the upper arm grab the bicep.
Add some flesh to the arms and the pose is done!
There are pose versions with both hands under arms.
Or with both hands grabbing opposite arms.
It gets easier when you understand the structure. even though it looks hard!

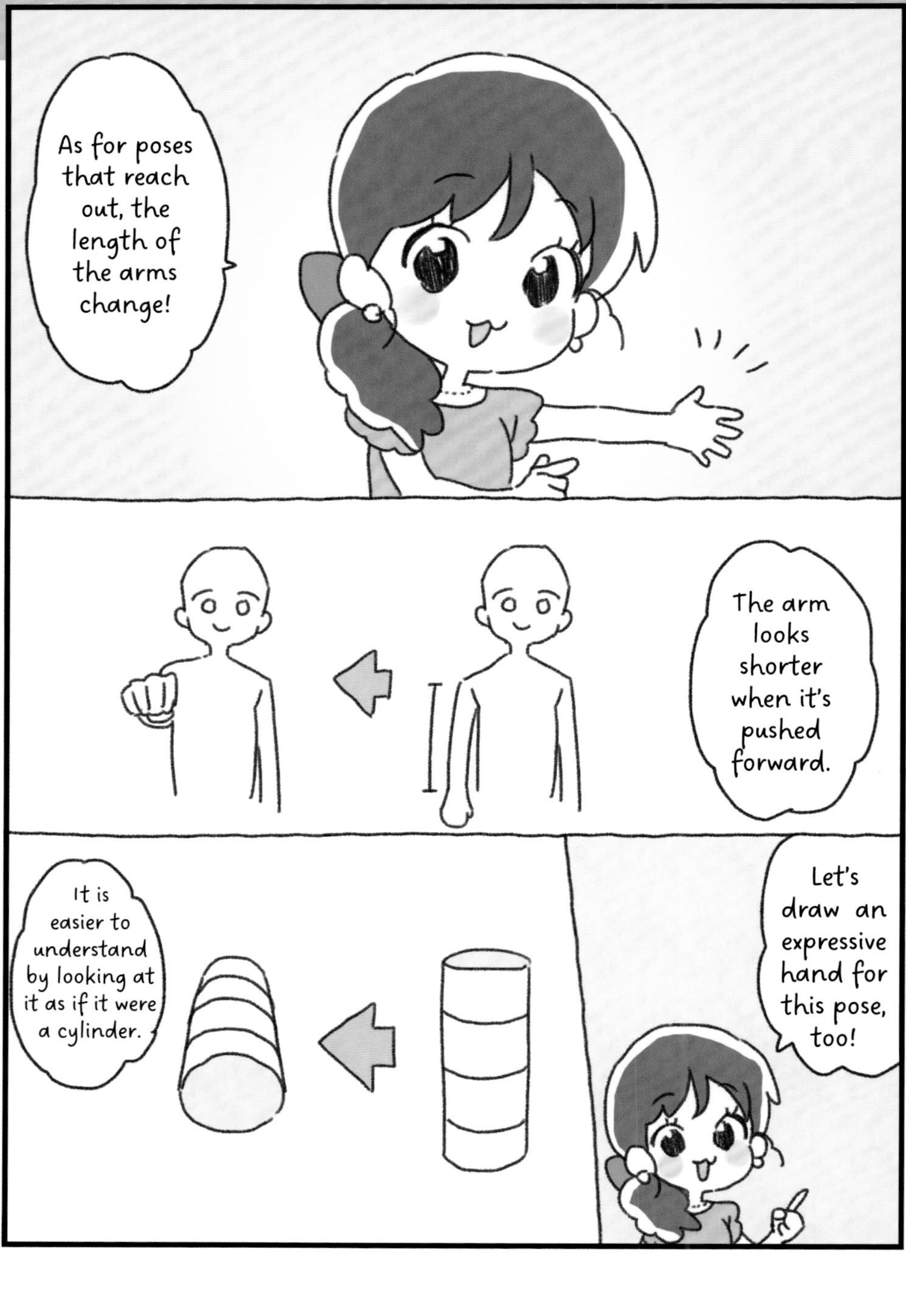
As for poses that reach out, the length of the arms change!
The arm looks shorter when it's pushed forward.
Let's draw an expressive hand for this pose, too!
It is easier to understand by looking at it as if it were a cylinder.

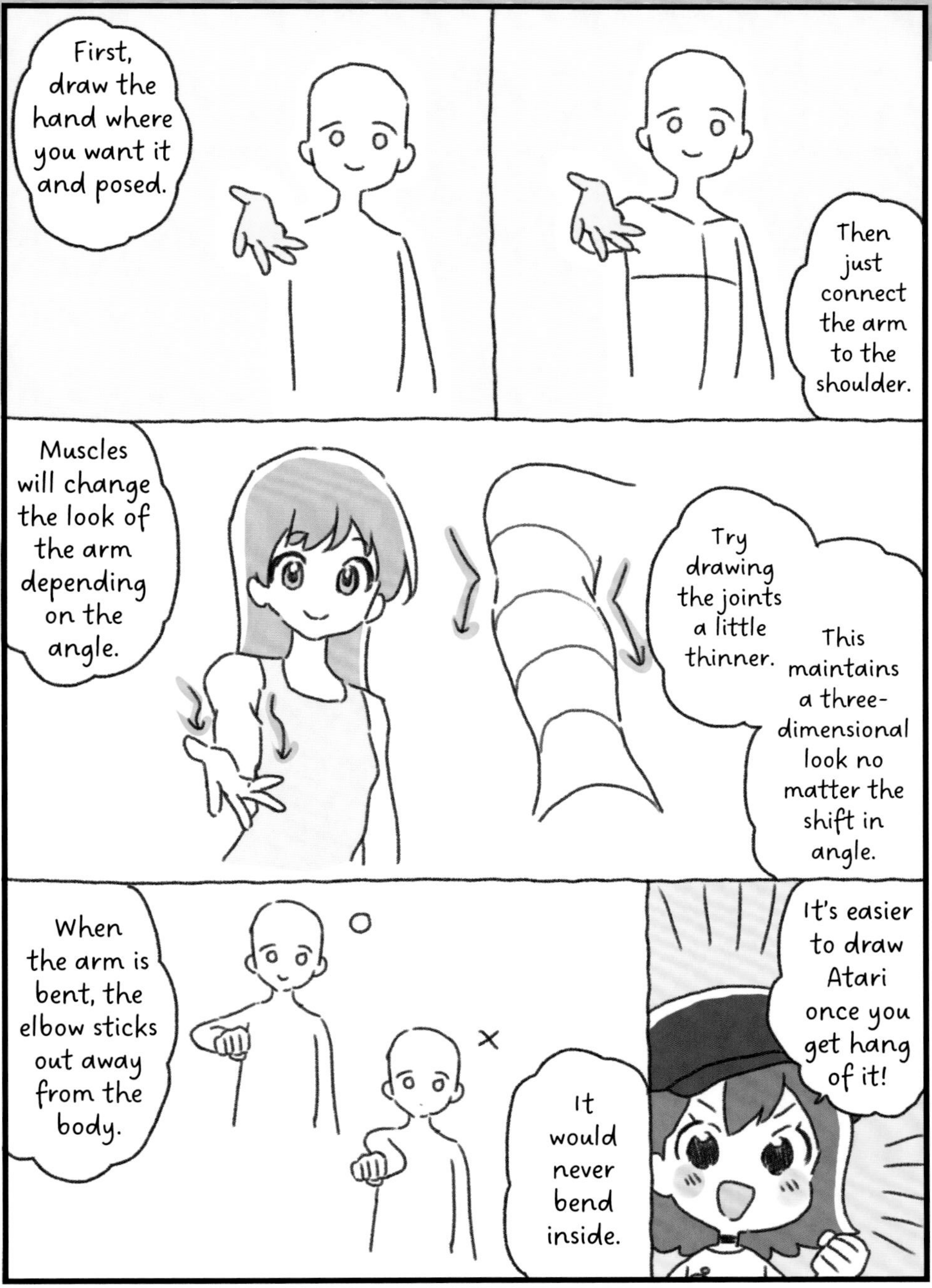
First, draw the hand where you want it and posed.
Then just connect the arm to the shoulder.
Muscles will change the look of the arm depending on the angle.
Try drawing the joints a little thinner.
This maintains a three-dimensional look no matter the shift in angle.
When the arm is bent, the elbow sticks out away from the body.
It would never bend inside.
It's easier to draw Atari once you get hang of it!

# CONSIDER THE PARTS YOU CANNOT SEE

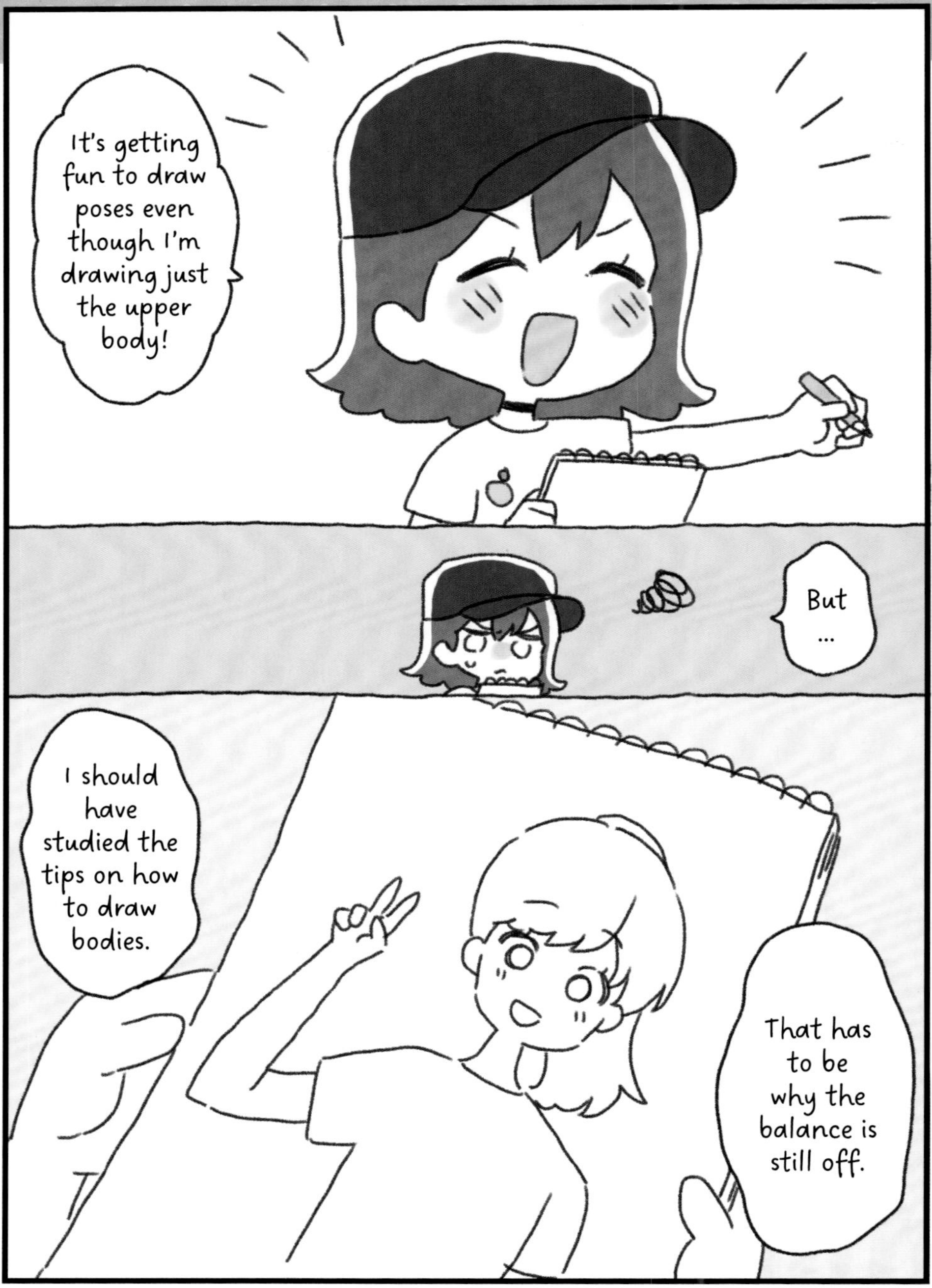
It's getting fun to draw poses even though I'm drawing just the upper body!
But ...
I should have studied the tips on how to draw bodies.
That has to be why the balance is still off.

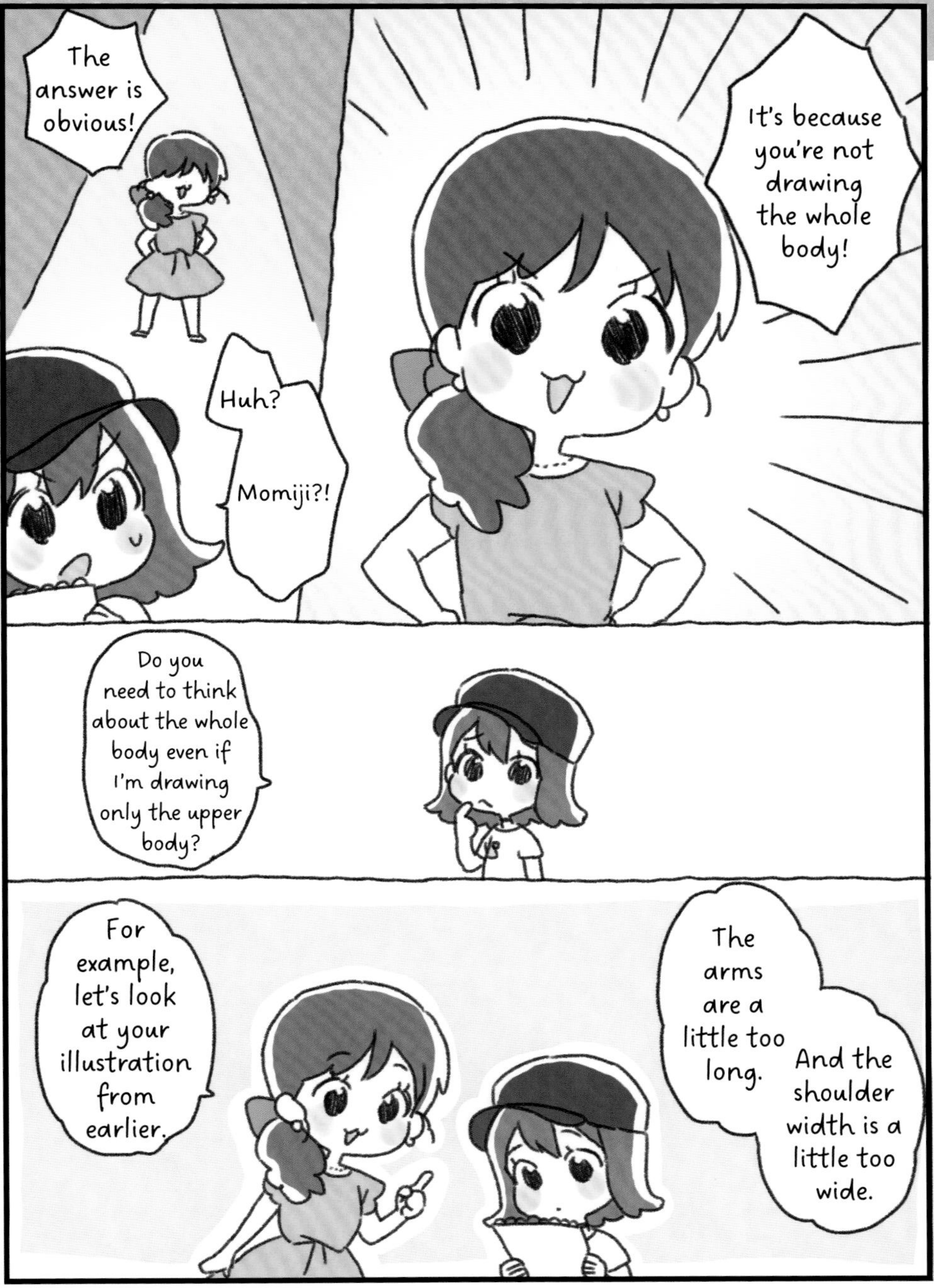
The answer is obvious!
It's because you're not drawing the whole body!
Huh?
Momiji?!
Do you need to think about the whole body even if I'm drawing only the upper body?
For example, let's look at your illustration from earlier.
The arms are a little too long.
And the shoulder width is a little too wide.

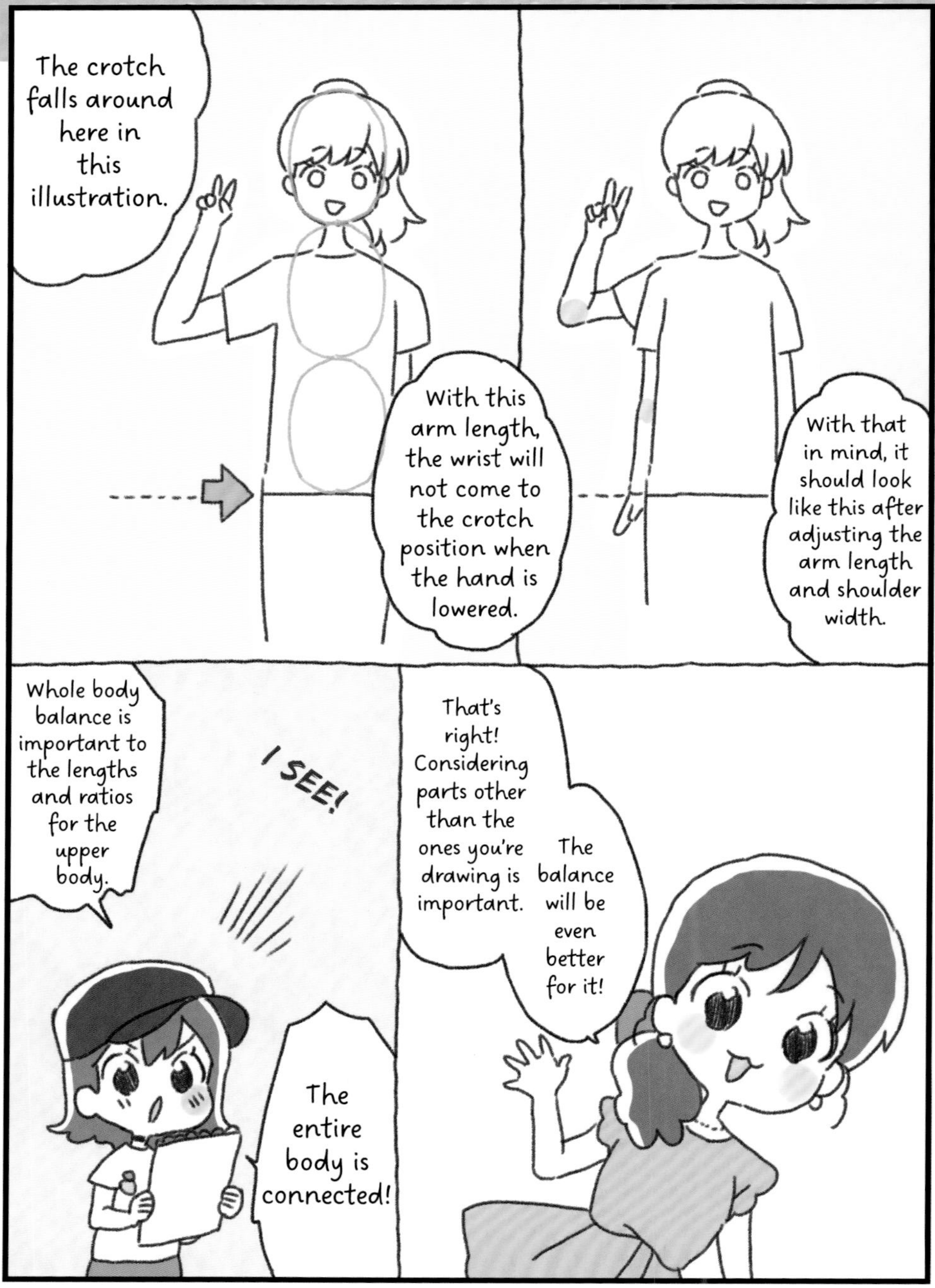
The crotch falls around here in this illustration.
With this arm length, the wrist will not come to the crotch position when the hand is lowered.
With that in mind, it should look like this after adjusting the arm length and shoulder width.
Whole body balance is important to the lengths and ratios for the upper body.
I SEE!
The entire body is connected!
That's right! Considering parts other than the ones you're drawing is important.
The balance will be even better for it!

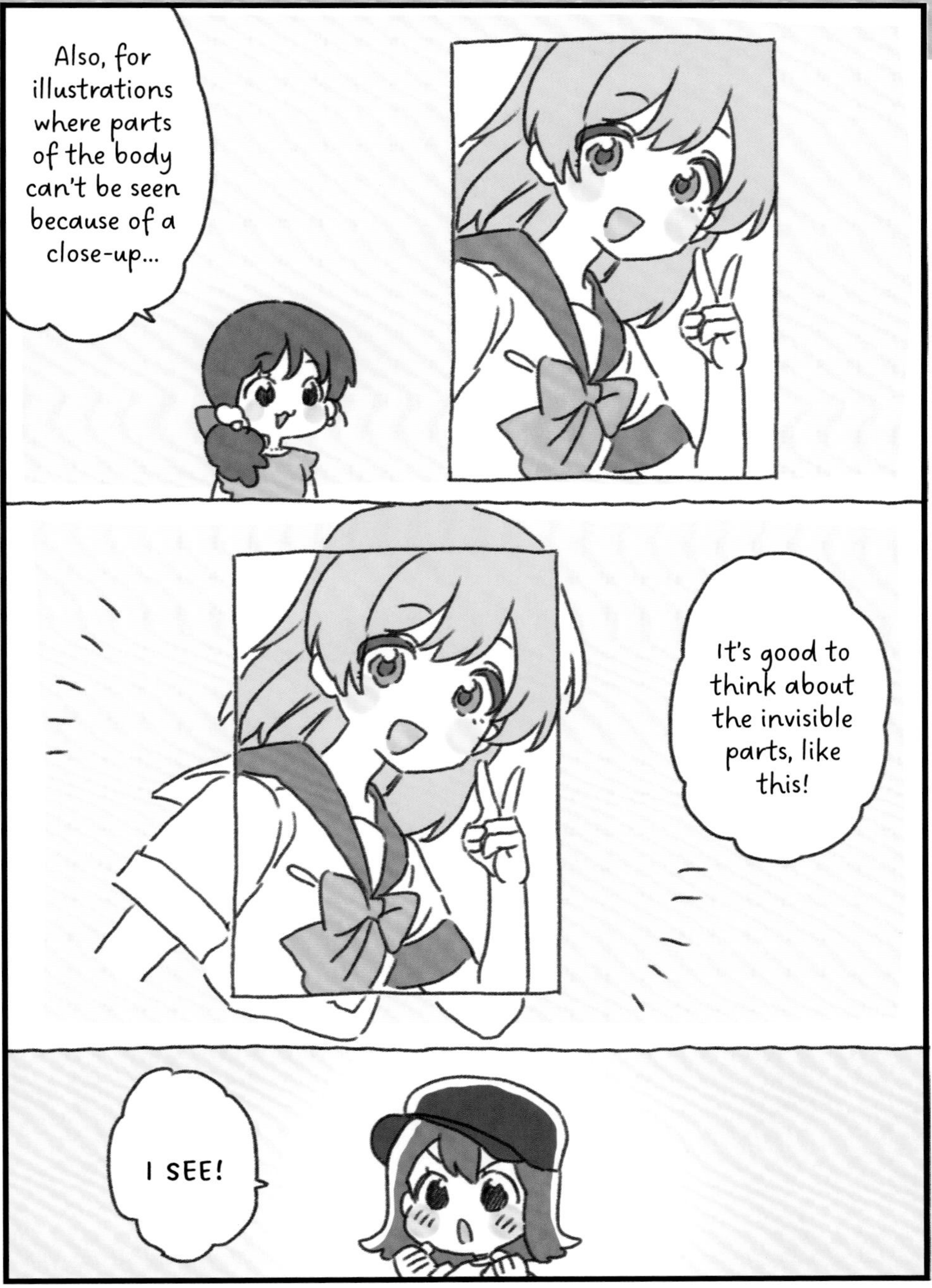
Also, for illustrations where parts of the body can't be seen because of a close-up...
It's good to think about the invisible parts, like this!
I SEE!

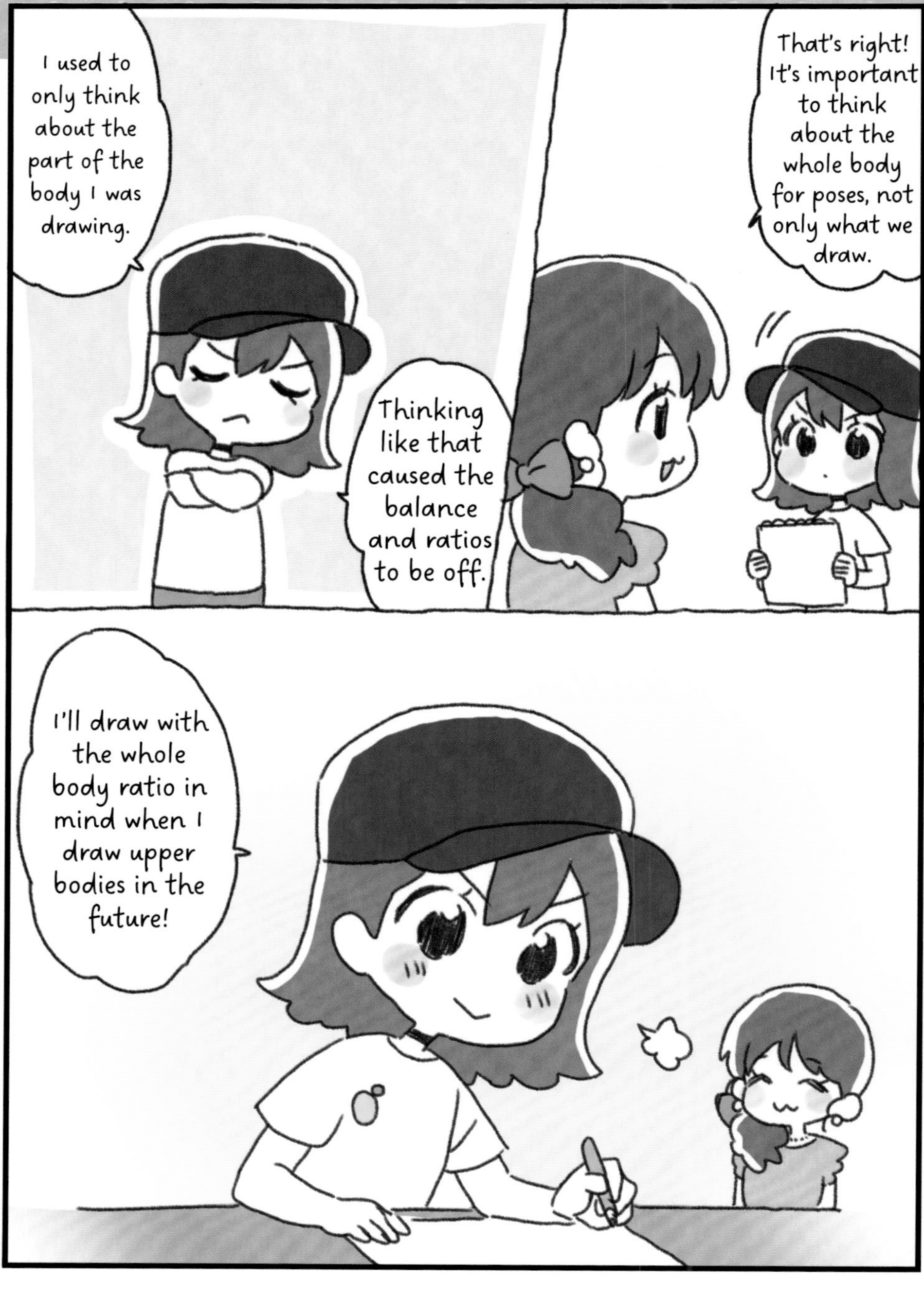
I used to only think about the part of the body I was drawing.
Thinking like that caused the balance and ratios to be off.
That's right! It's important to think about the whole body for poses, not only what we draw.
I'll draw with the whole body ratio in mind when I draw upper bodies in the future!

# LET'S TRY TO DRAW LOWER BODIES

# LOWER BODY BALANCE AND PARTS

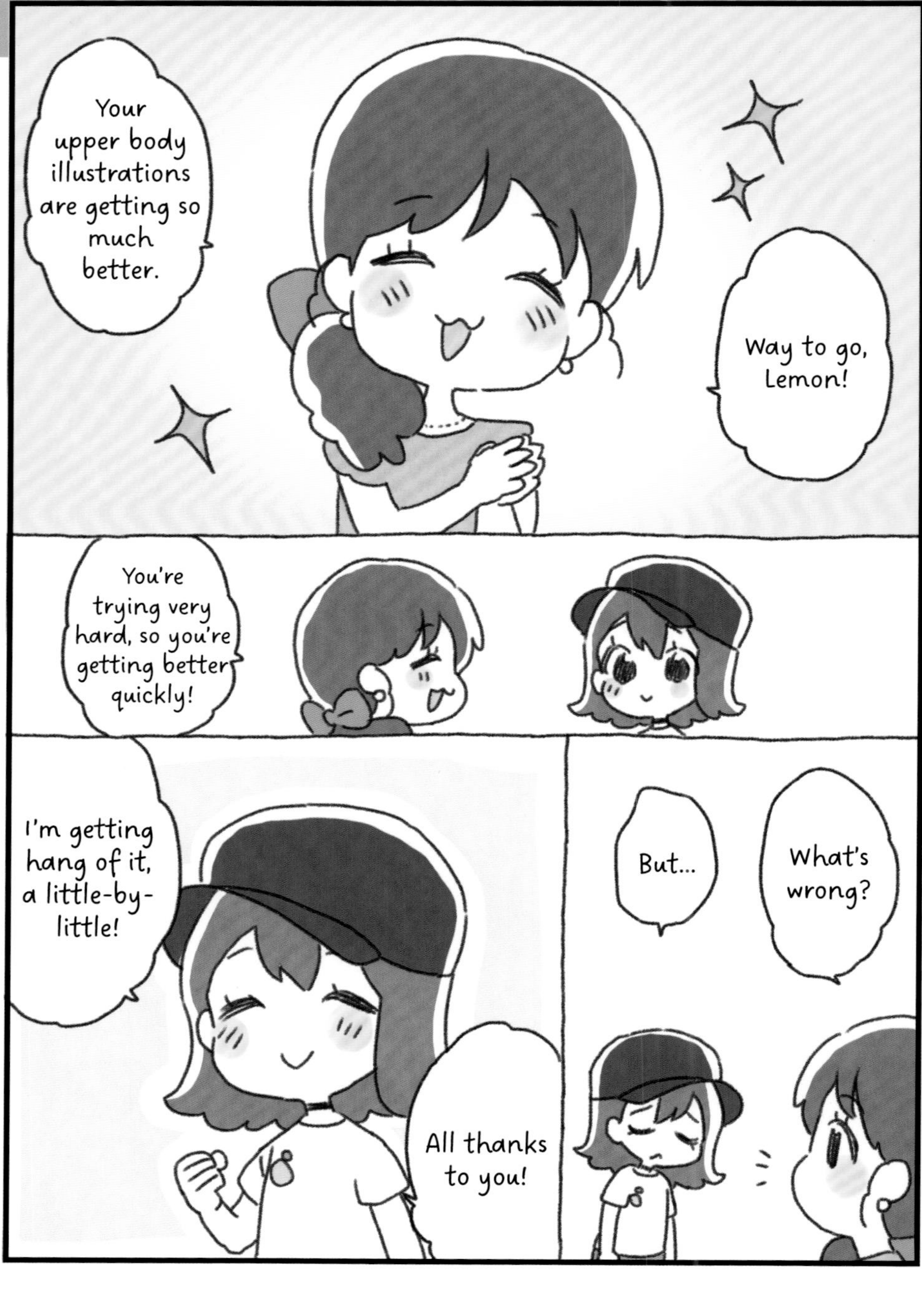
Your upper body illustrations are getting so much better.
Way to go, Lemon!
You're trying very hard, so you're getting better quickly!
I'm getting hang of it, a little-by-little!
All thanks to you!
What's wrong?
But...

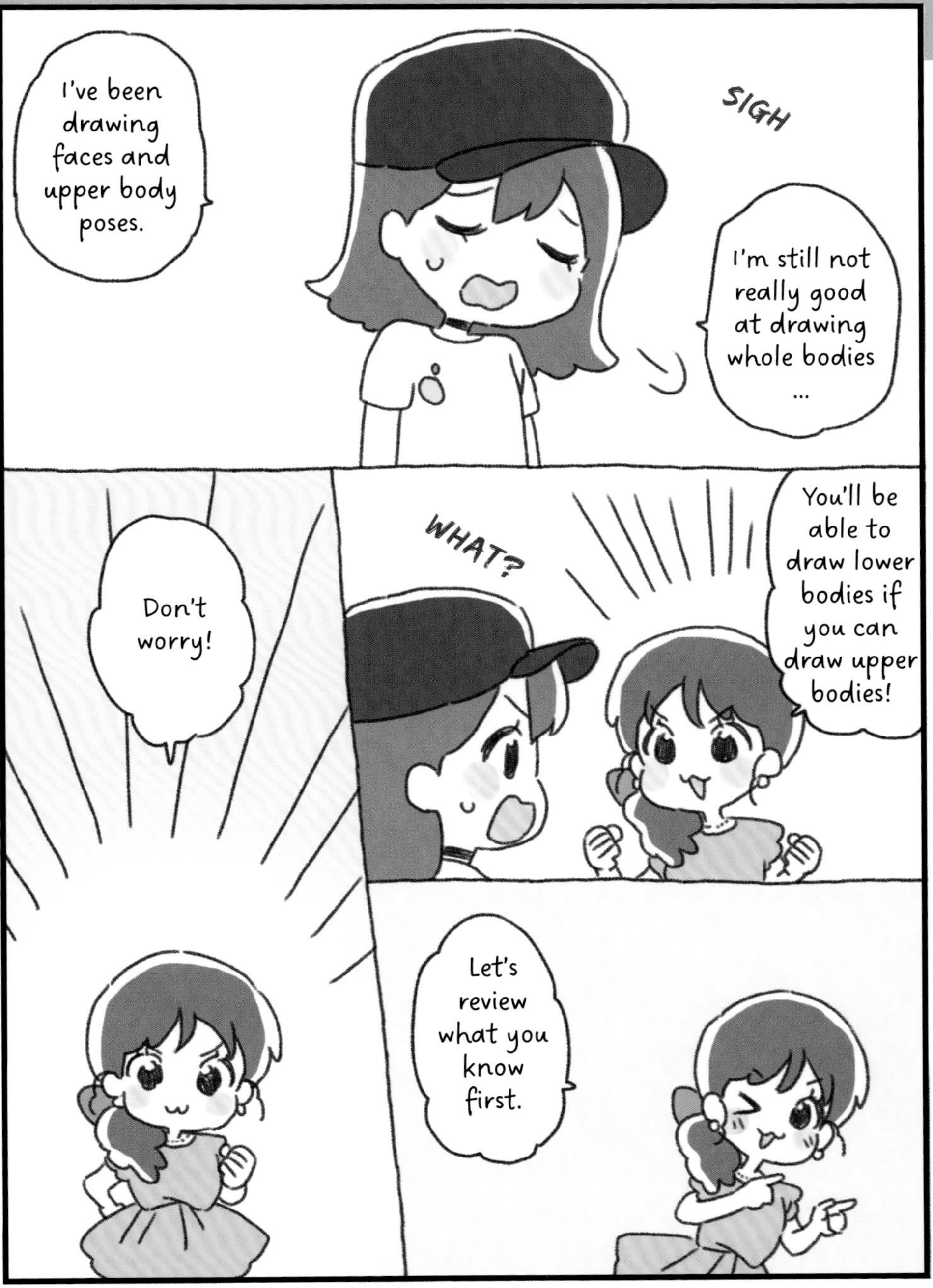
I've been drawing faces and upper body poses.
SIGH
I'm still not really good at drawing whole bodies ...
You'll be able to draw lower bodies if you can draw upper bodies!
WHAT?
Don't worry!
Let's review what you know first.

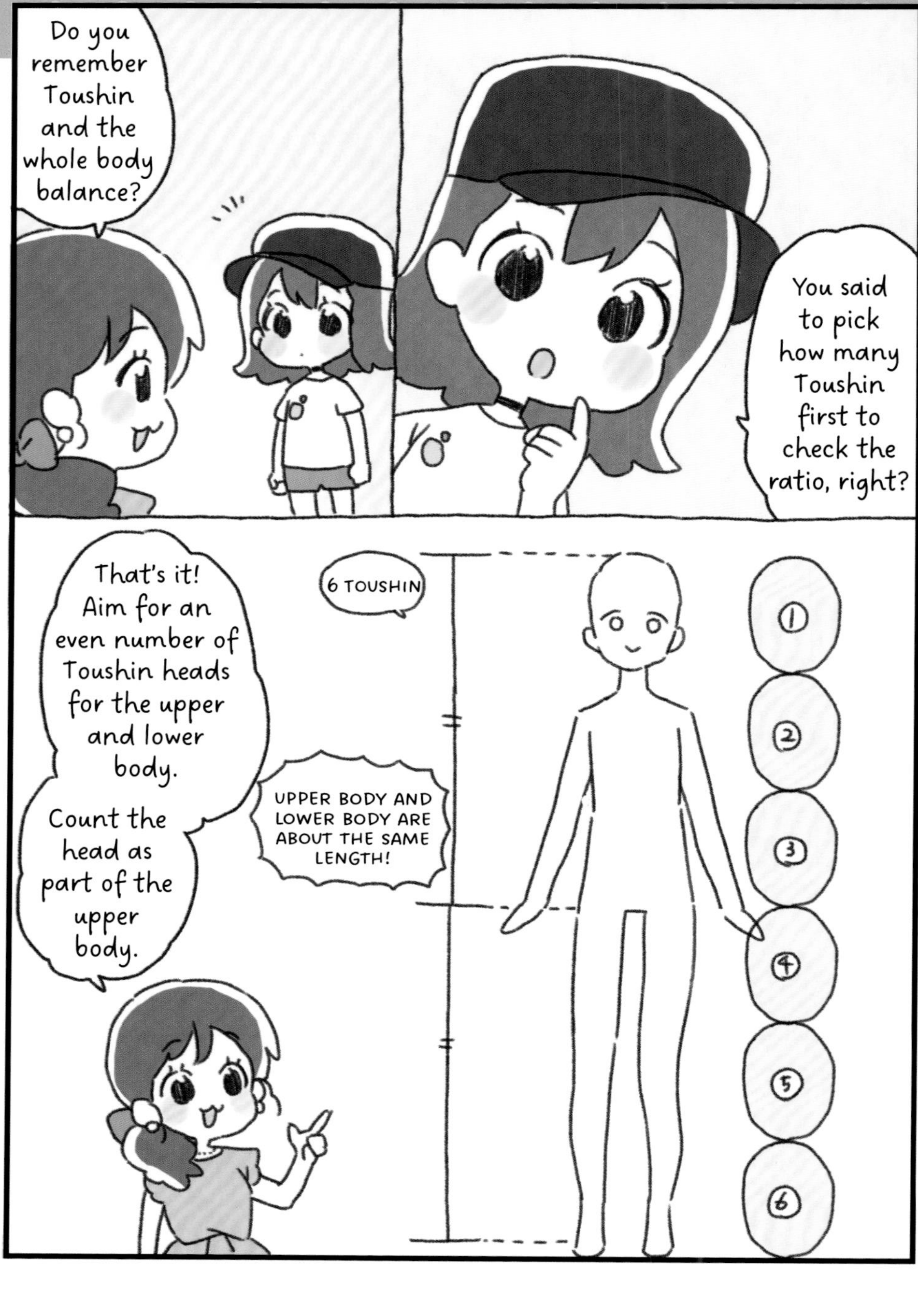
Do you remember Toushin and the whole body balance?
You said to pick how many Toushin first to check the ratio, right?
That's it! Aim for an even number of Toushin heads for the upper and lower body.
Count the head as part of the upper body.
6 TOUSHIN
UPPER BODY AND LOWER BODY ARE ABOUT THE SAME LENGTH!
1
2
3
4
5
6

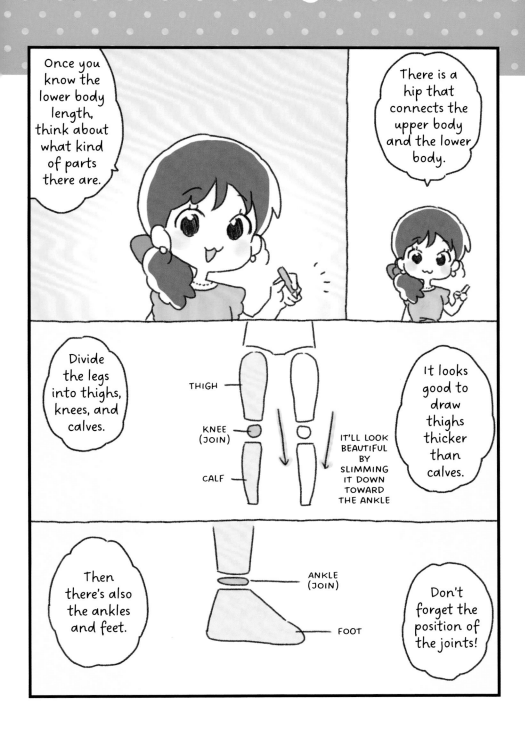

Once you know the lower body length, think about what kind of parts there are.

There is a hip that connects the upper body and the lower body.

Divide the legs into thighs, knees, and calves.

THIGH

KNEE (JOIN)

CALF

IT'LL LOOK BEAUTIFUL BY SLIMMING IT DOWN TOWARD THE ANKLE

It looks good to draw thighs thicker than calves.

Then there's also the ankles and feet.

ANKLE (JOIN)

FOOT

Don't forget the position of the joints!

153

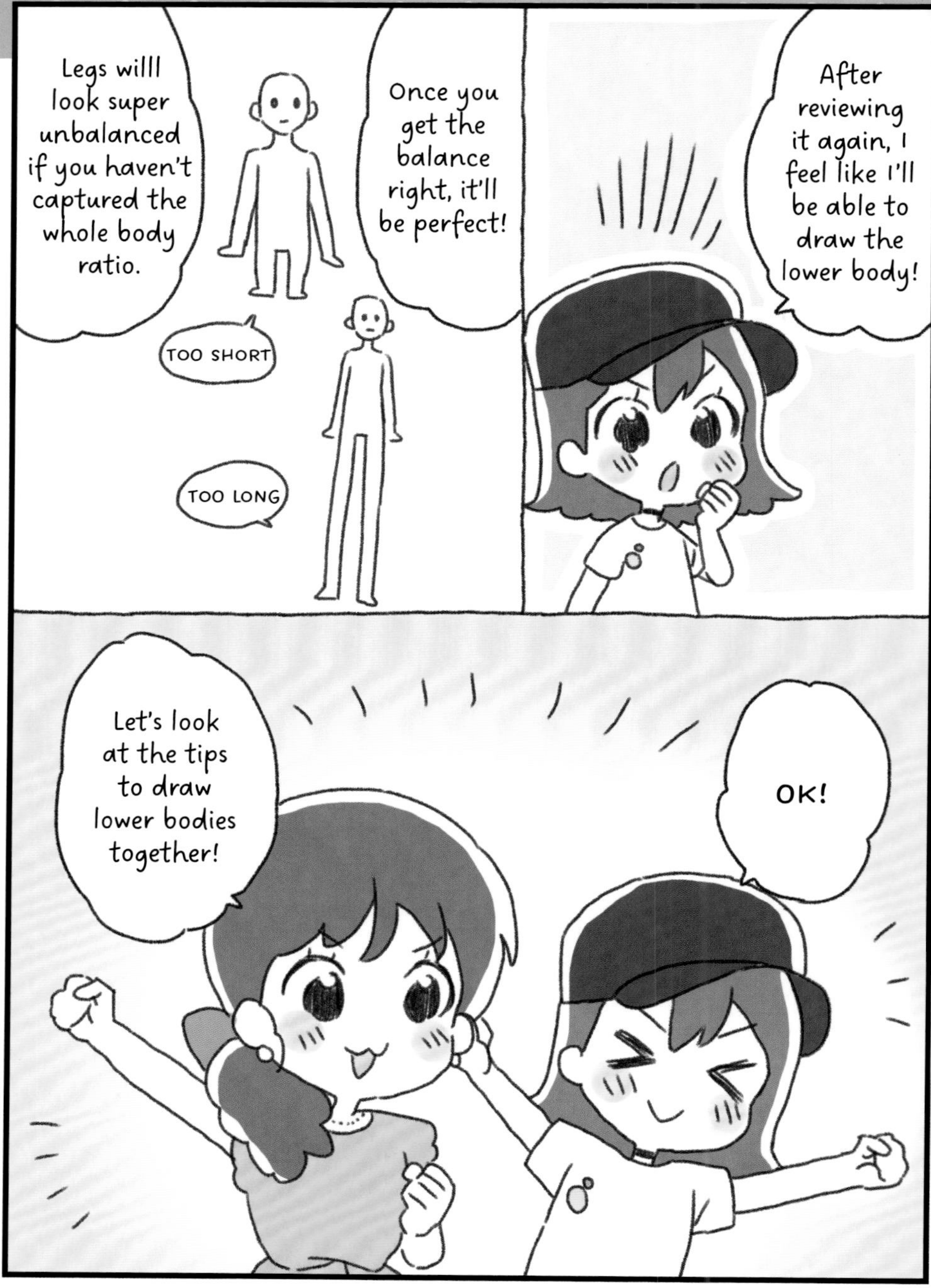
Legs willl look super unbalanced if you haven't captured the whole body ratio.
Once you get the balance right, it'll be perfect!
TOO SHORT
TOO LONG
After reviewing it again, I feel like I'll be able to draw the lower body!
Let's look at the tips to draw lower bodies together!
OK!

## — SUMMARY —

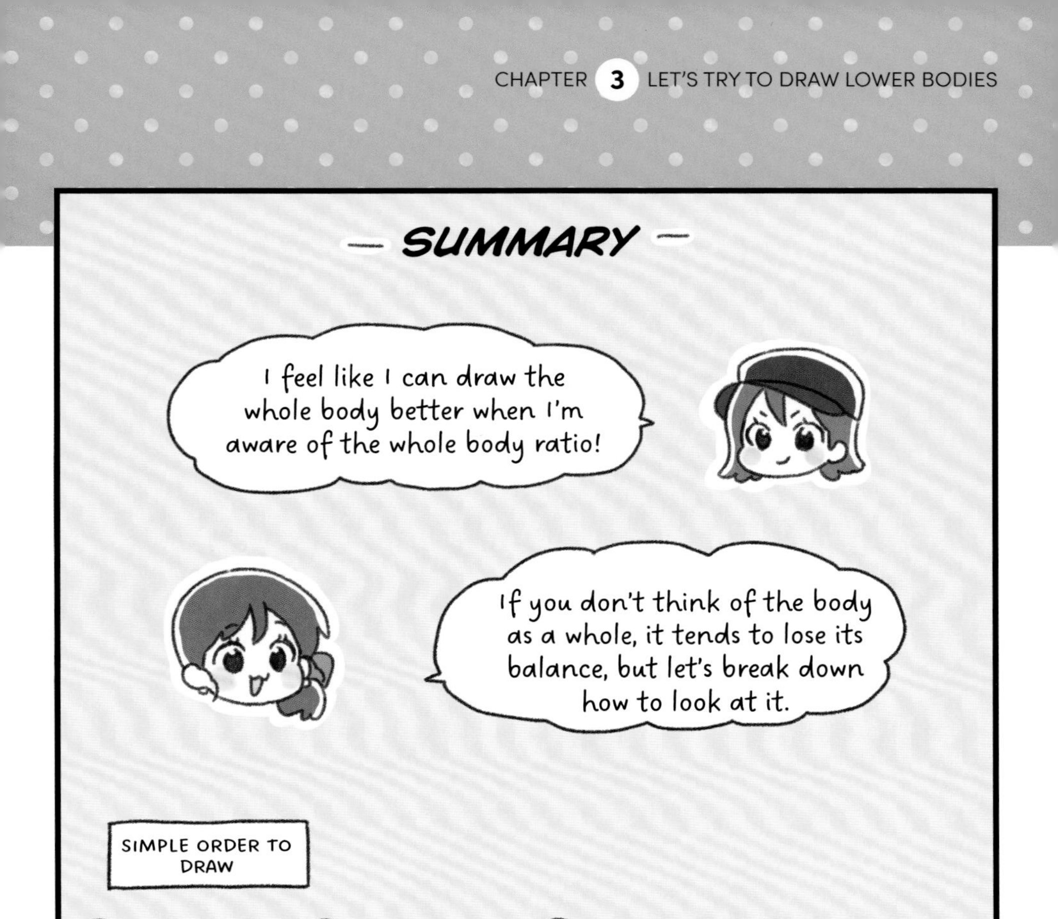
I feel like I can draw the whole body better when I'm aware of the whole body ratio!
If you don't think of the body as a whole, it tends to lose its balance, but let's break down how to look at it.

SIMPLE ORDER TO DRAW

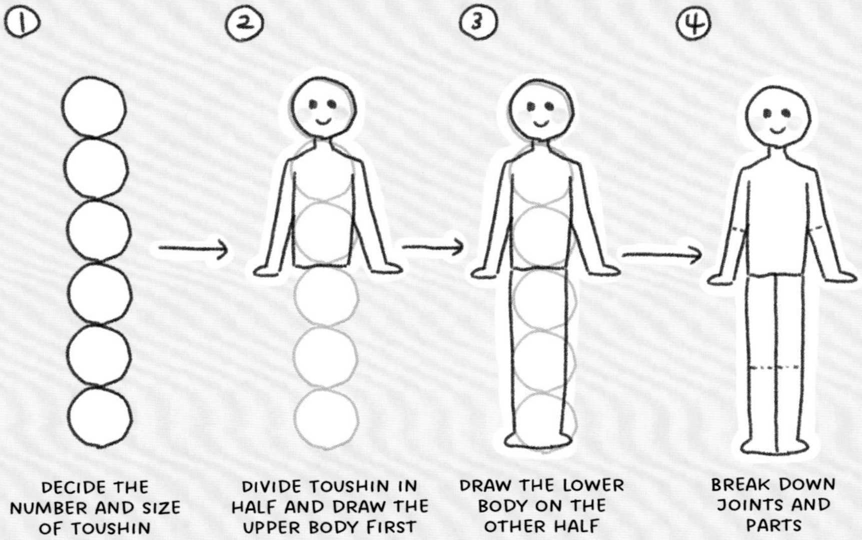
①
②
③
④
DECIDE THE NUMBER AND SIZE OF TOUSHIN
DIVIDE TOUSHIN IN HALF AND DRAW THE UPPER BODY FIRST
DRAW THE LOWER BODY ON THE OTHER HALF
BREAK DOWN JOINTS AND PARTS

# SPINE LINE

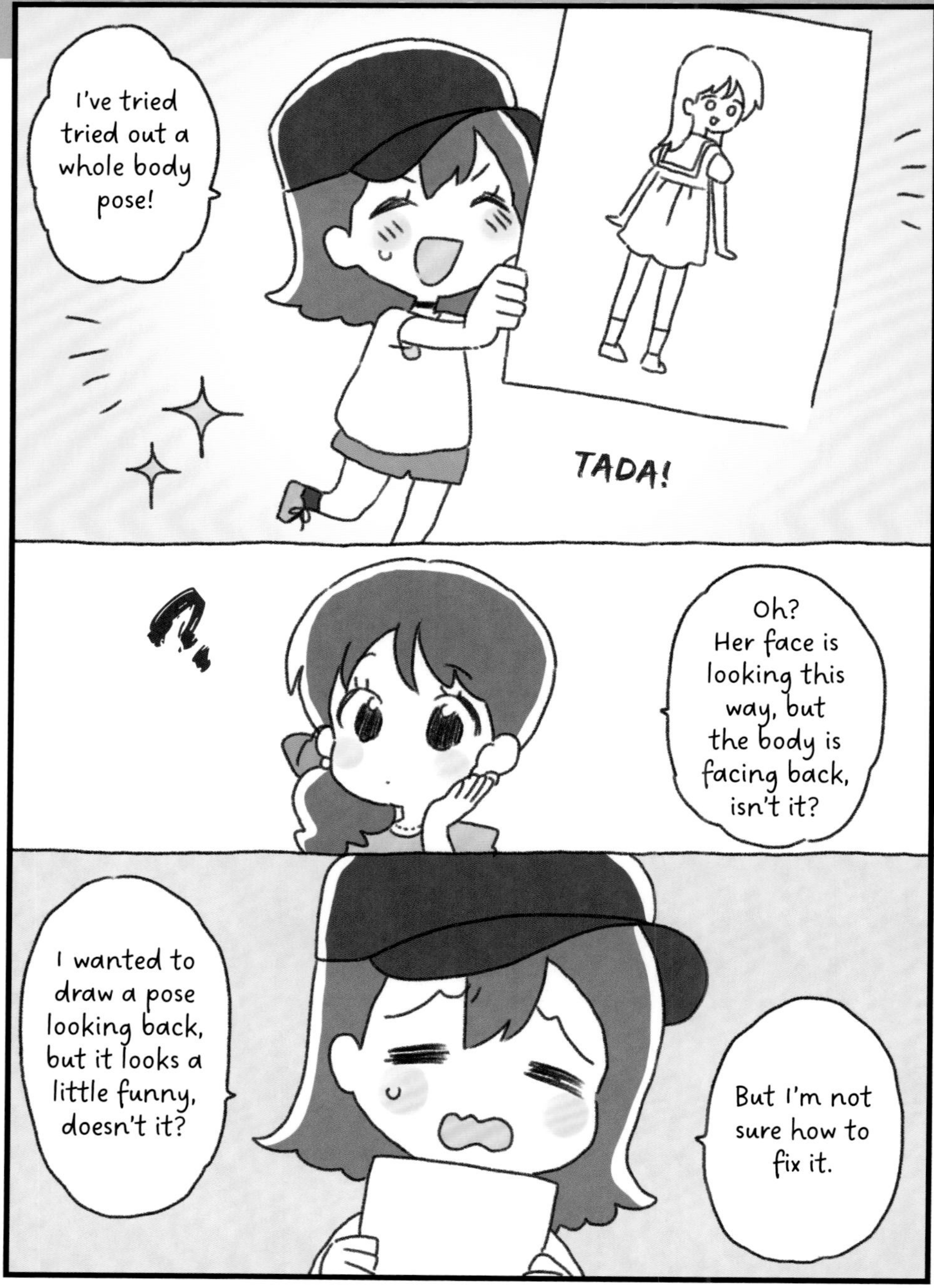
I've tried tried out a whole body pose!
TADA!
Oh? Her face is looking this way, but the body is facing back, isn't it?
I wanted to draw a pose looking back, but it looks a little funny, doesn't it?
But I'm not sure how to fix it.

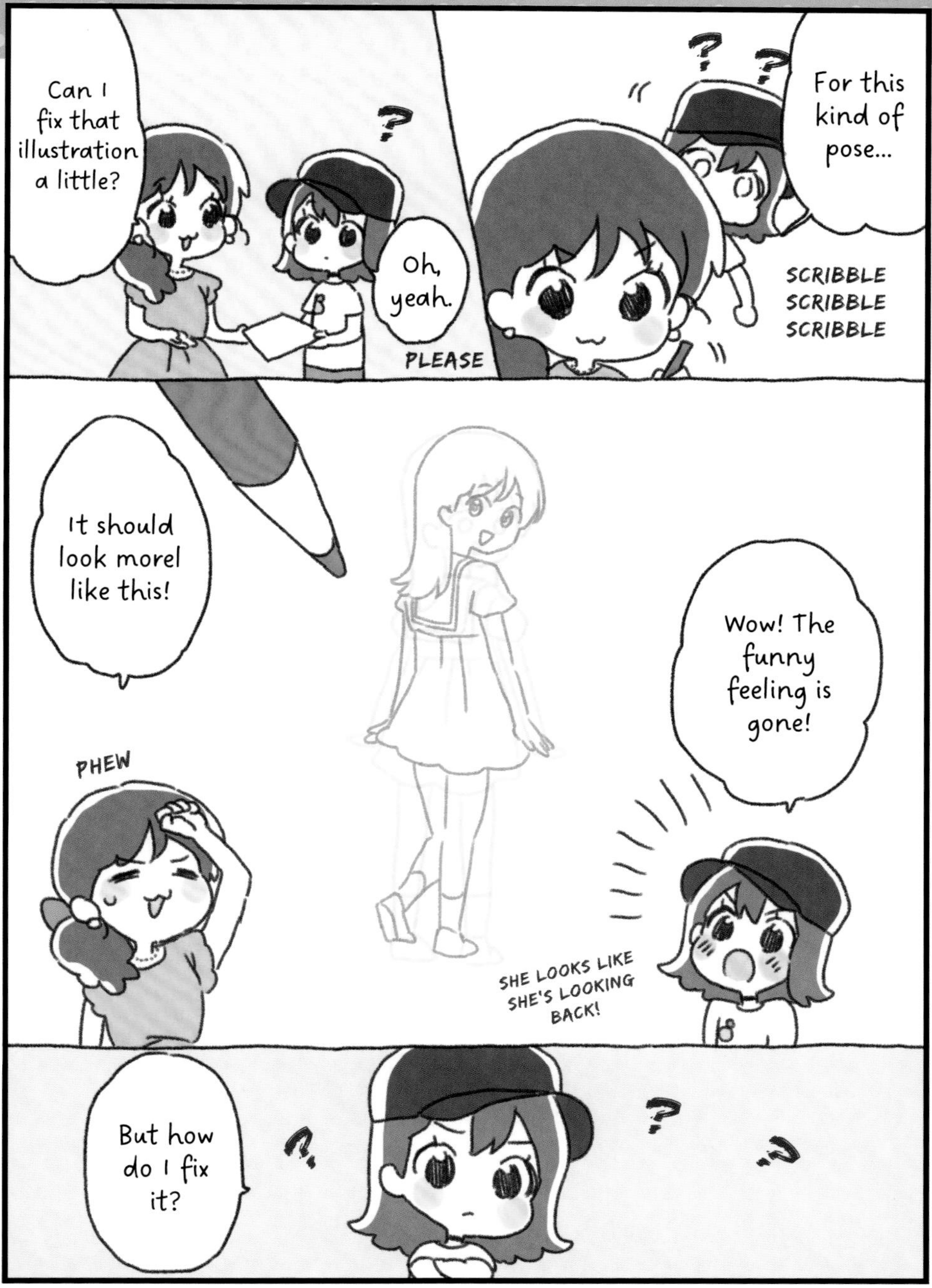
Can I fix that illustration a little?
Oh, yeah.
PLEASE
For this kind of pose...
SCRIBBLE SCRIBBLE SCRIBBLE
It should look morel like this!
Wow! The funny feeling is gone!
PHEW
SHE LOOKS LIKE SHE'S LOOKING BACK!
But how do I fix it?

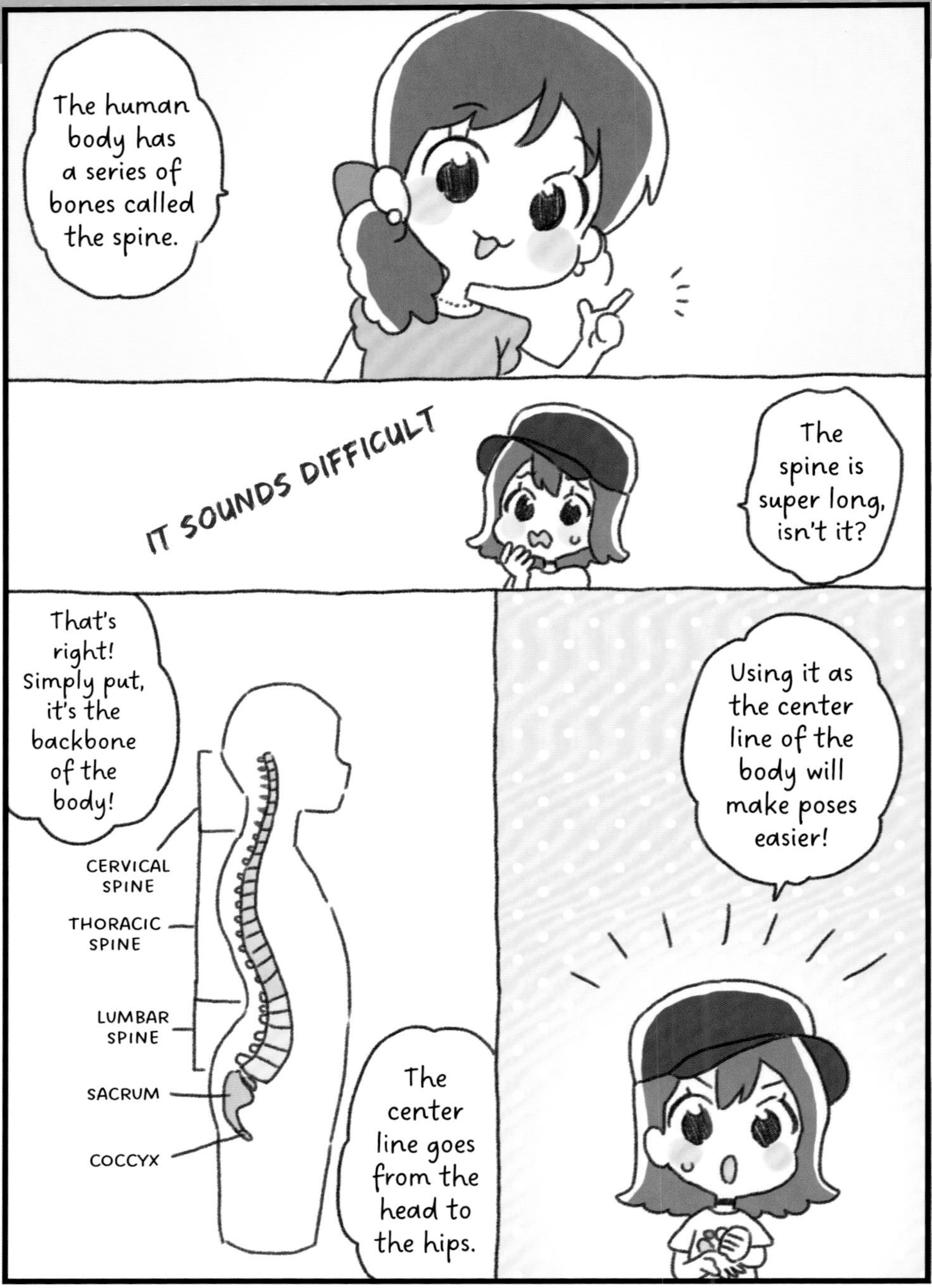
The human body has a series of bones called the spine.
IT SOUNDS DIFFICULT
The spine is super long, isn't it?
That's right! Simply put, it's the backbone of the body!
CERVICAL SPINE
THORACIC SPINE
LUMBAR SPINE
SACRUM
COCCYX
The center line goes from the head to the hips.
Using it as the center line of the body will make poses easier!

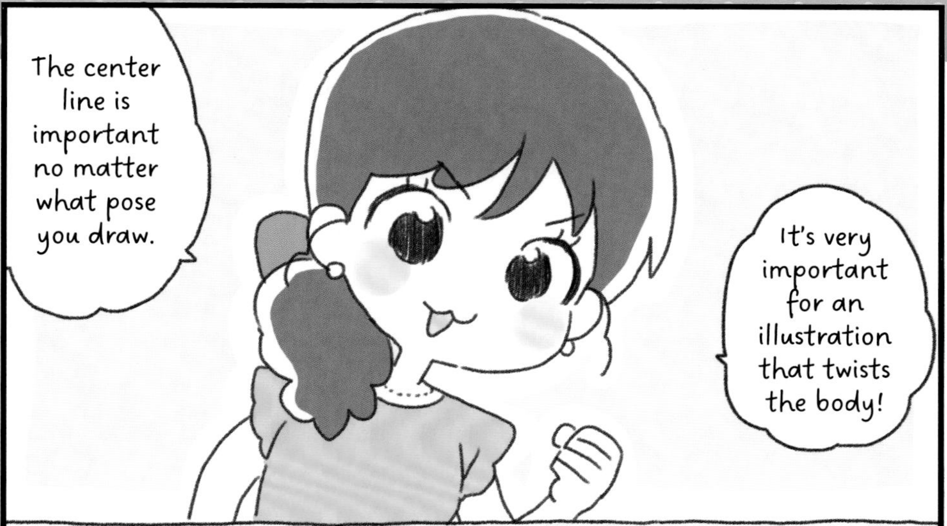
The center line is important no matter what pose you draw.
It's very important for an illustration that twists the body!

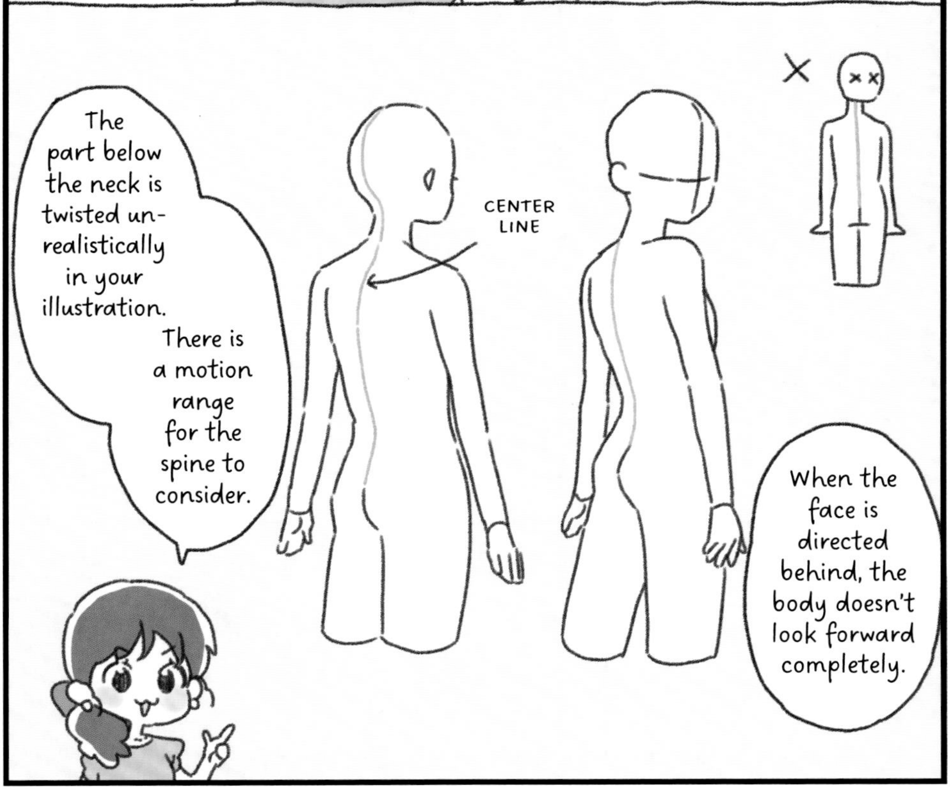
The part below the neck is twisted un-realistically in your illustration. There is a motion range for the spine to consider.
CENTER LINE
When the face is directed behind, the body doesn't look forward completely.

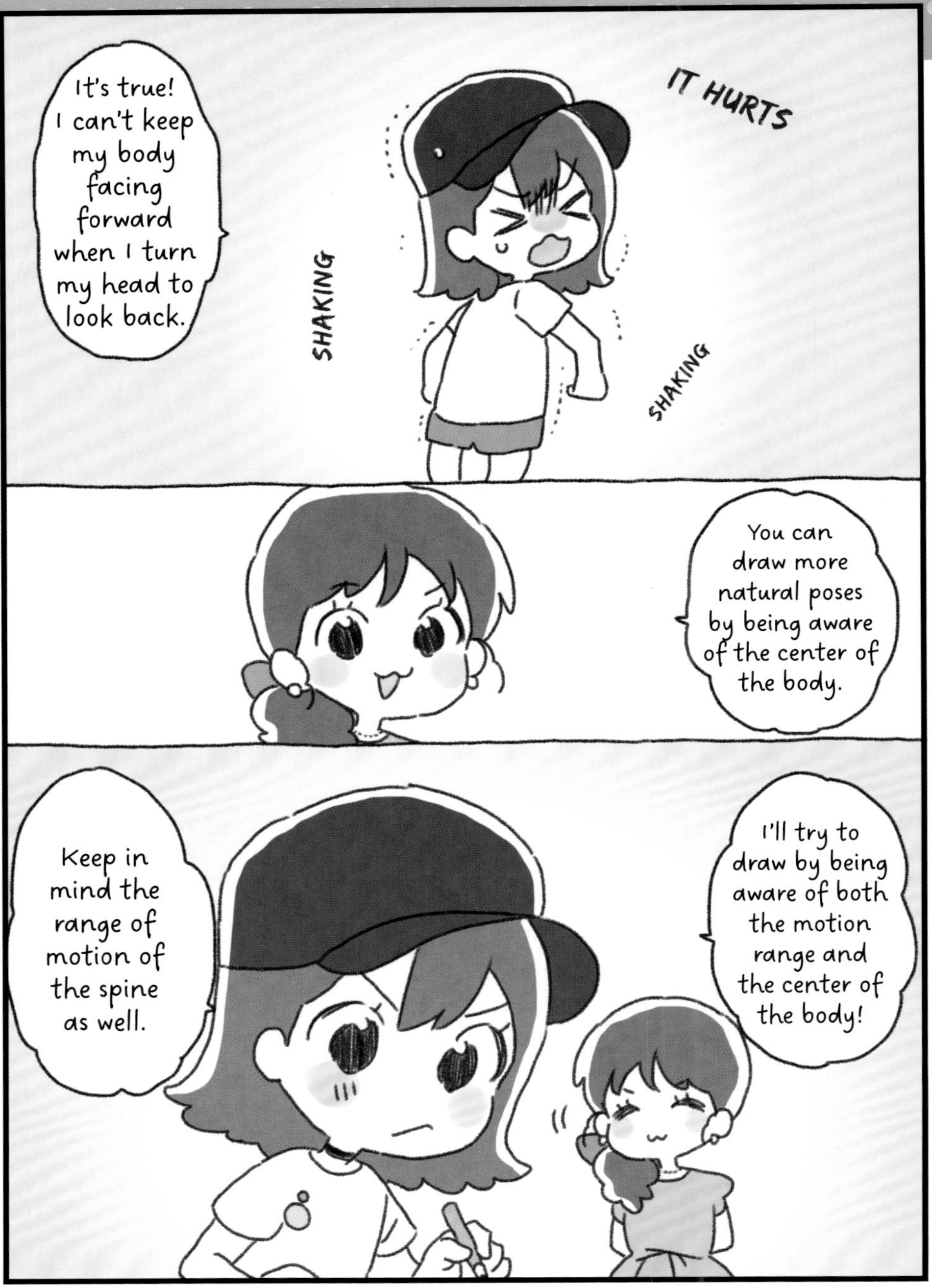
It's true! I can't keep my body facing forward when I turn my head to look back.
IT HURTS
SHAKING
SHAKING
You can draw more natural poses by being aware of the center of the body.
I'll try to draw by being aware of both the motion range and the center of the body!
Keep in mind the range of motion of the spine as well.

## LEVEL UP

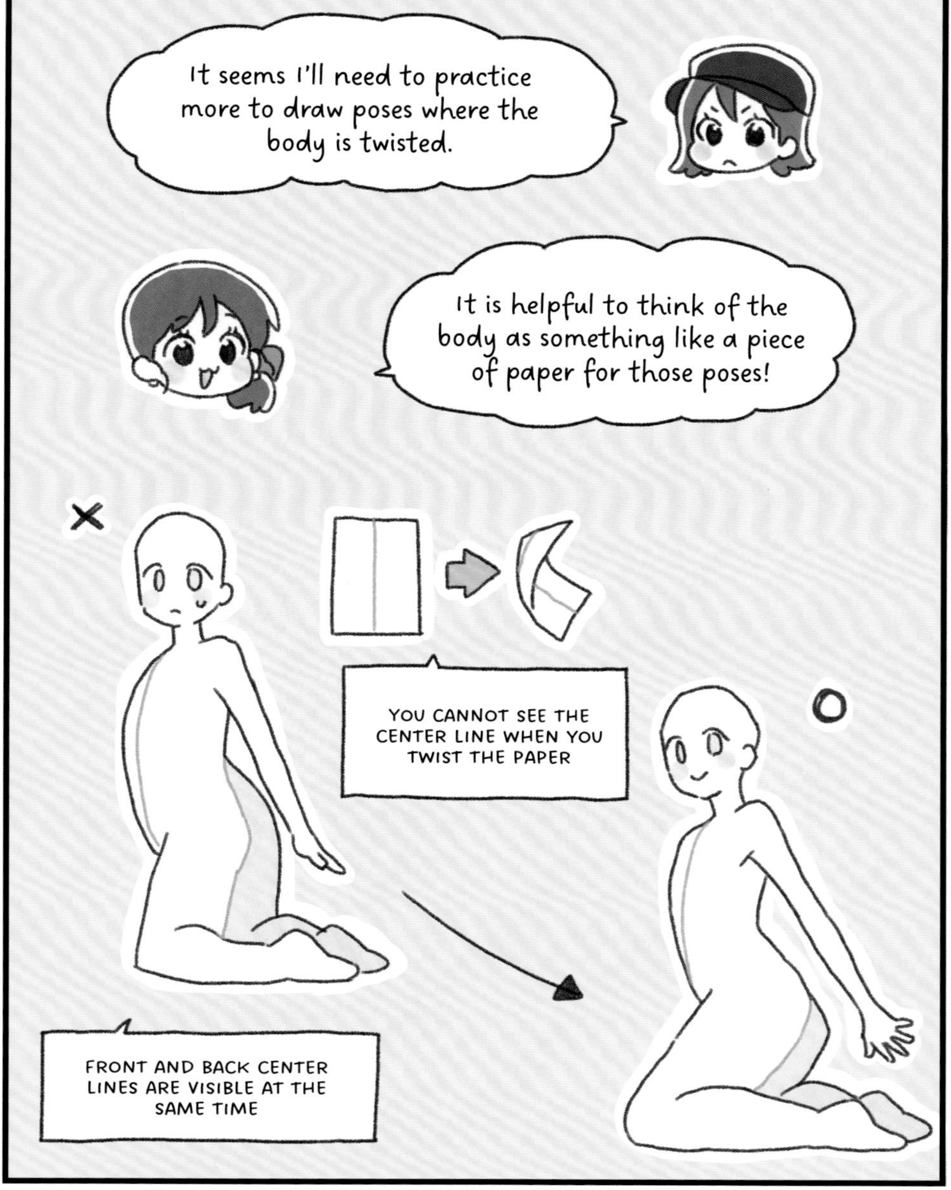
It seems I'll need to practice more to draw poses where the body is twisted.
It is helpful to think of the body as something like a piece of paper for those poses!
YOU CANNOT SEE THE CENTER LINE WHEN YOU TWIST THE PAPER
FRONT AND BACK CENTER LINES ARE VISIBLE AT THE SAME TIME

# HOW TO THINK OF A SITTING POSE

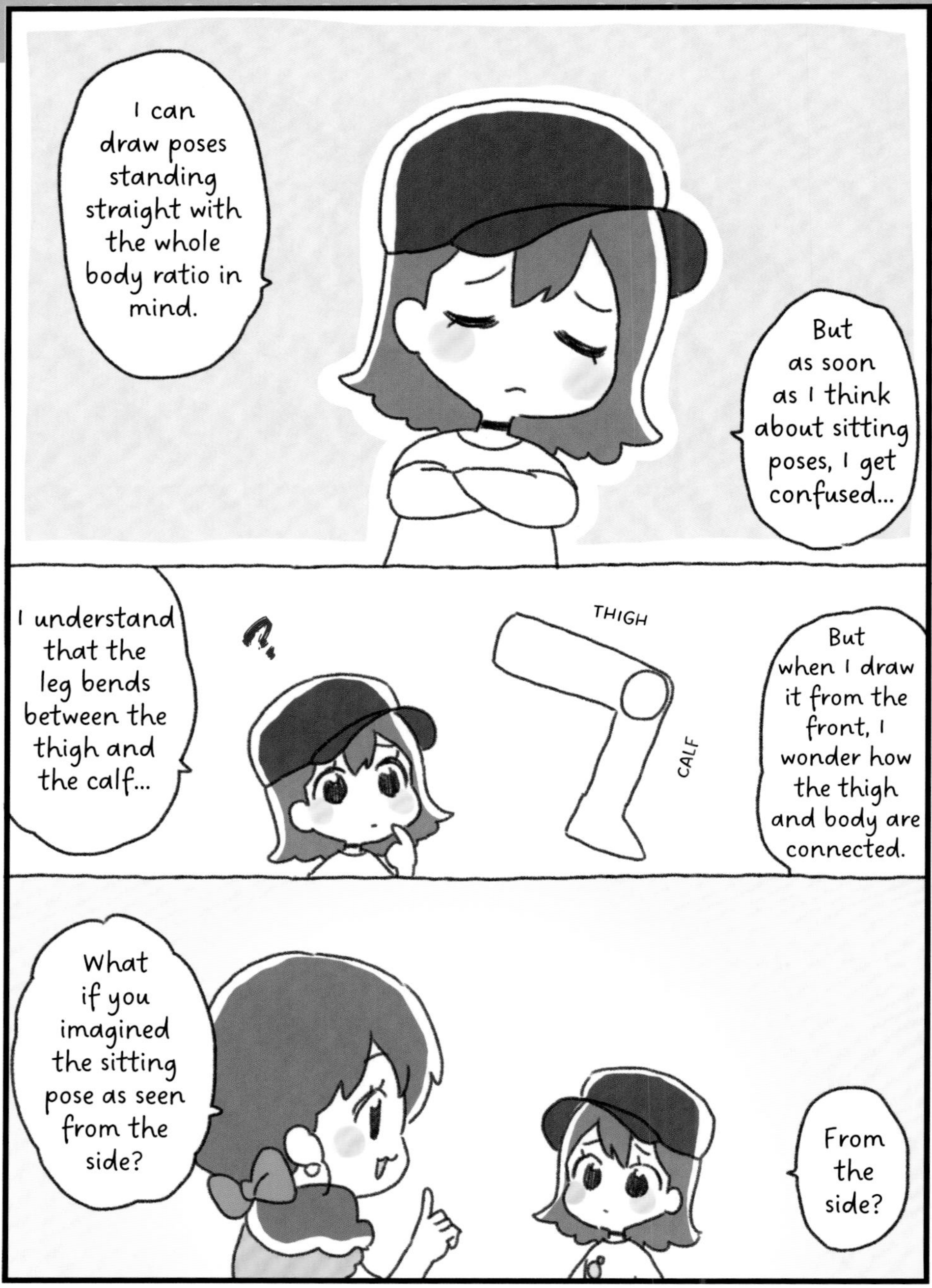
I can draw poses standing straight with the whole body ratio in mind.
But as soon as I think about sitting poses, I get confused...
I understand that the leg bends between the thigh and the calf...
THIGH
CALF
But when I draw it from the front, I wonder how the thigh and body are connected.
What if you imagined the sitting pose as seen from the side?
From the side?

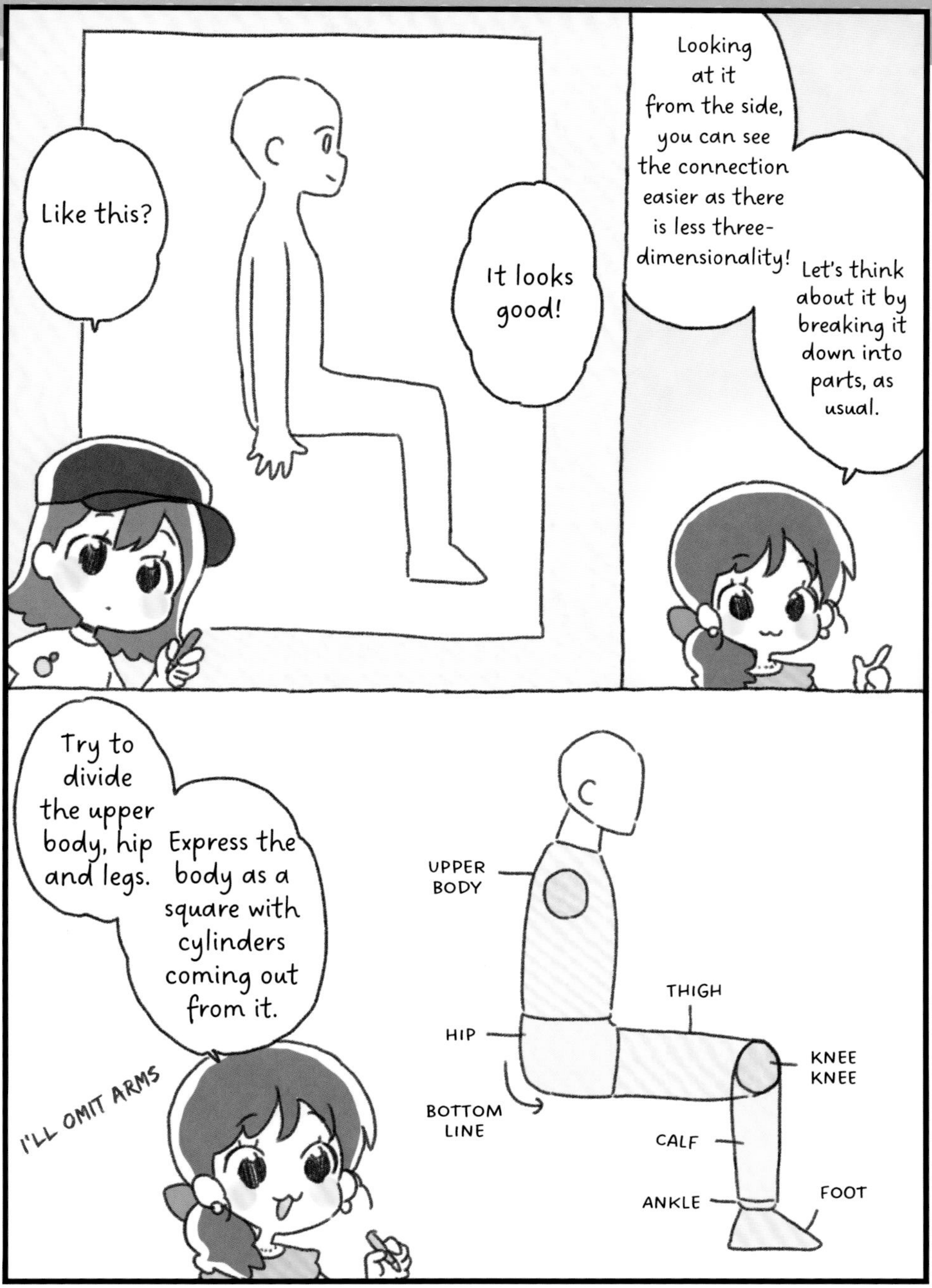
Like this?
It looks good!
Looking at it from the side, you can see the connection easier as there is less three-dimensionality!
Let's think about it by breaking it down into parts, as usual.
Try to divide the upper body, hip and legs.
Express the body as a square with cylinders coming out from it.
I'LL OMIT ARMS
UPPER BODY
THIGH
HIP
KNEE
KNEE
BOTTOM LINE
CALF
ANKLE
FOOT

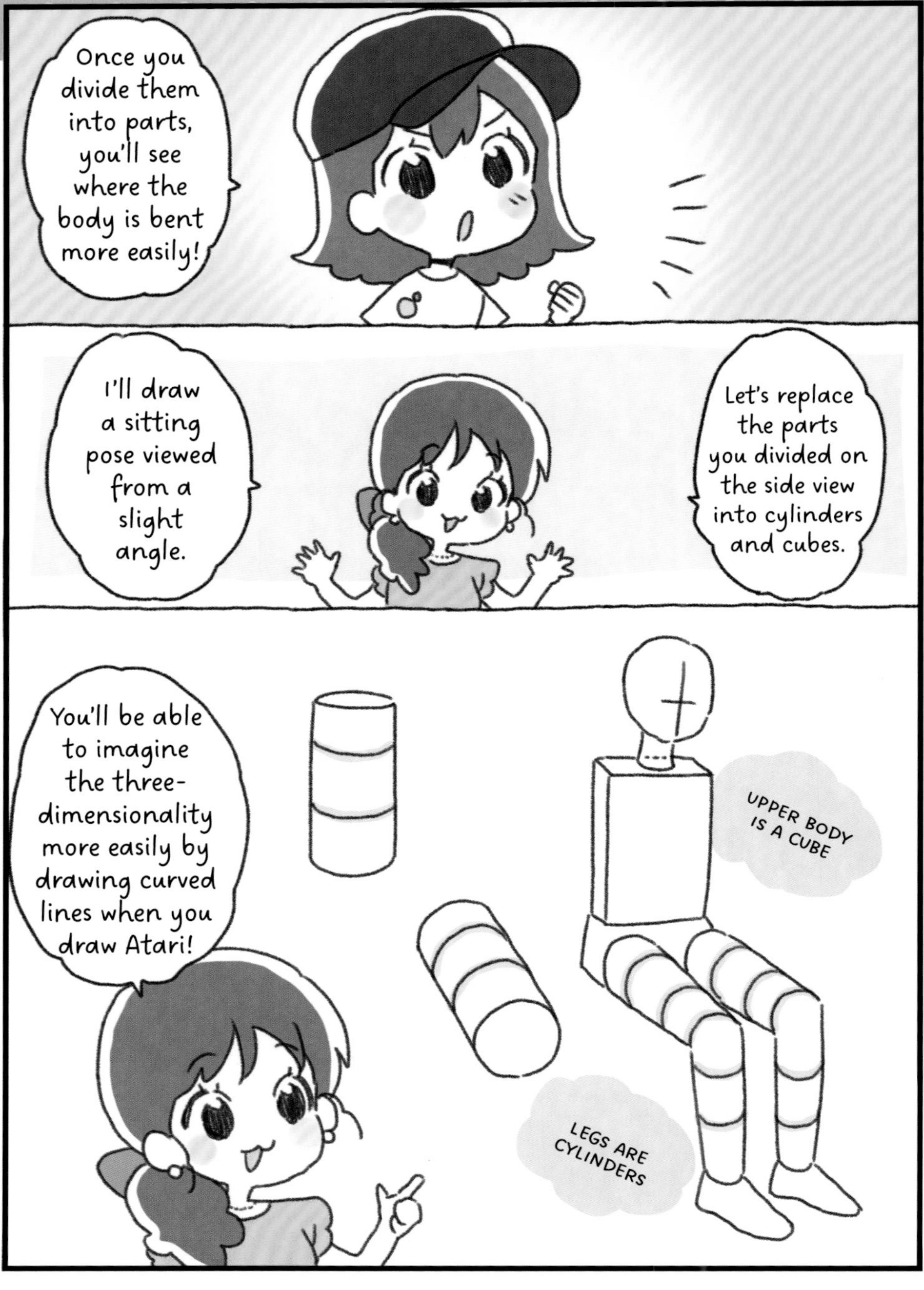
Once you divide them into parts, you'll see where the body is bent more easily!
I'll draw a sitting pose viewed from a slight angle.
Let's replace the parts you divided on the side view into cylinders and cubes.
You'll be able to imagine the three-dimensionality more easily by drawing curved lines when you draw Atari!
UPPER BODY IS A CUBE
LEGS ARE CYLINDERS

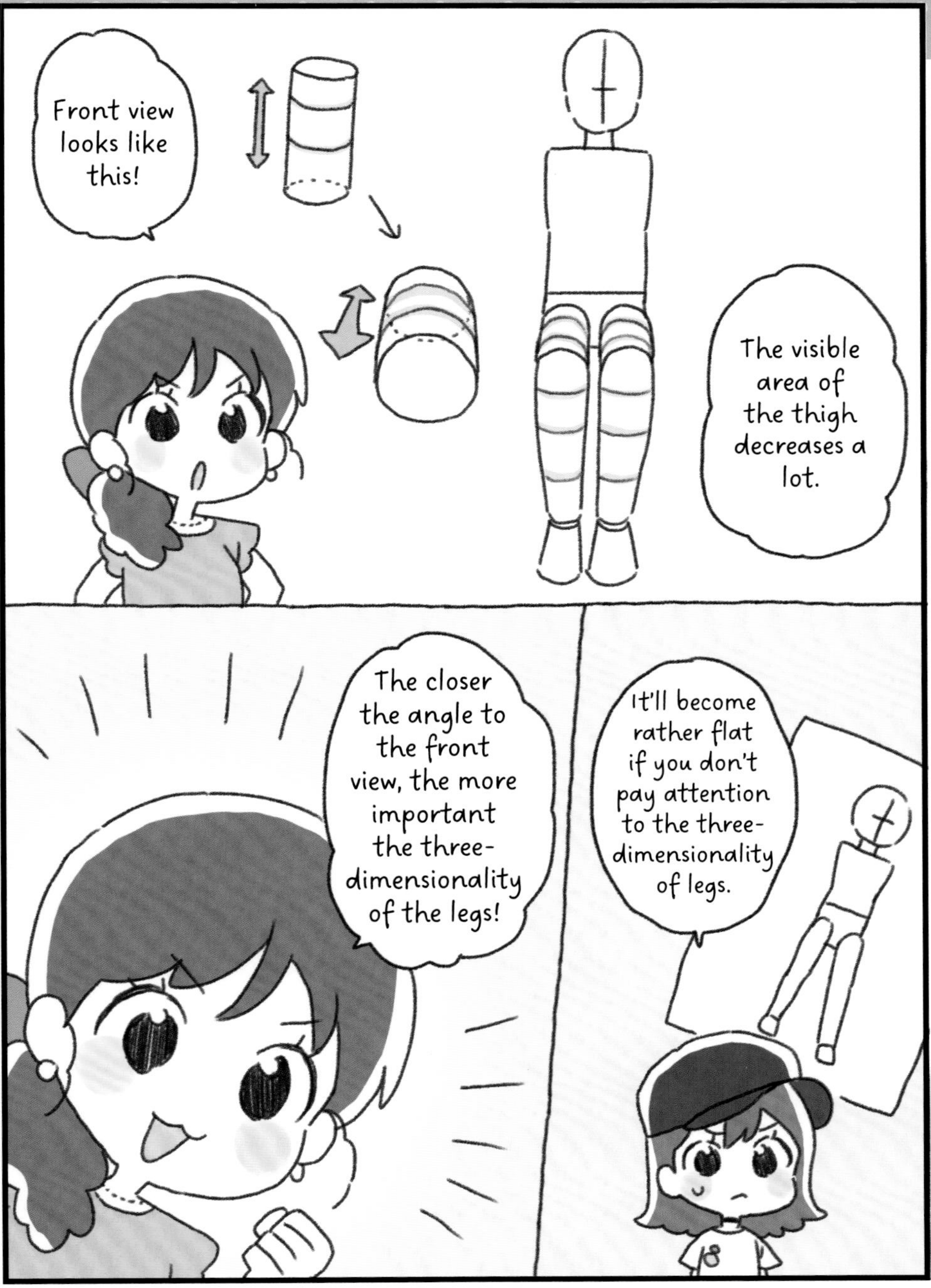
Front view looks like this!
The visible area of the thigh decreases a lot.
The closer the angle to the front view, the more important the three-dimensionality of the legs!
It'll become rather flat if you don't pay attention to the three-dimensionality of legs.

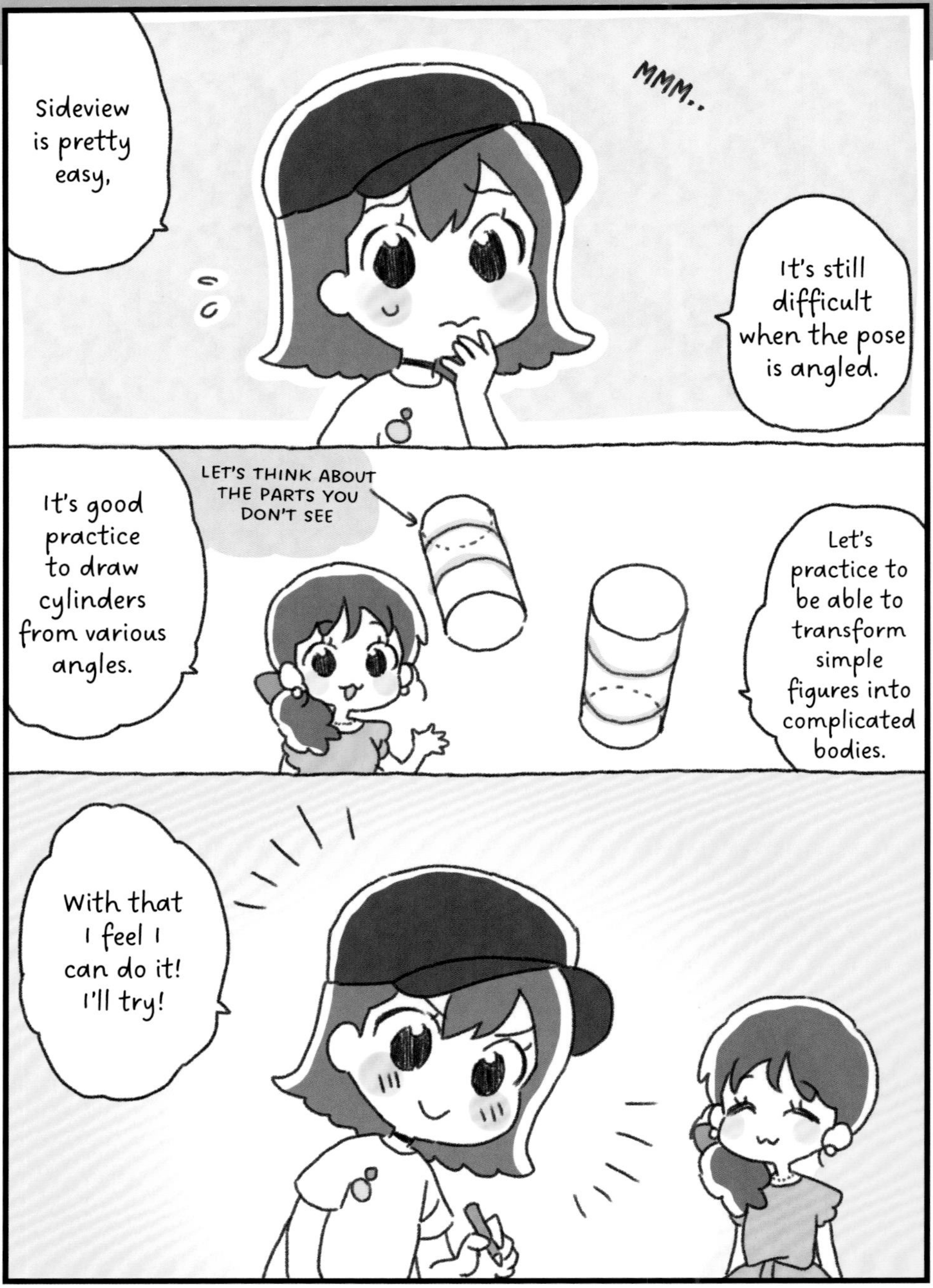
Sideview is pretty easy,
MMM..
It's still difficult when the pose is angled.
It's good practice to draw cylinders from various angles.
LET'S THINK ABOUT THE PARTS YOU DON'T SEE
Let's practice to be able to transform simple figures into complicated bodies.
With that I feel I can do it! I'll try!

## LEVEL UP

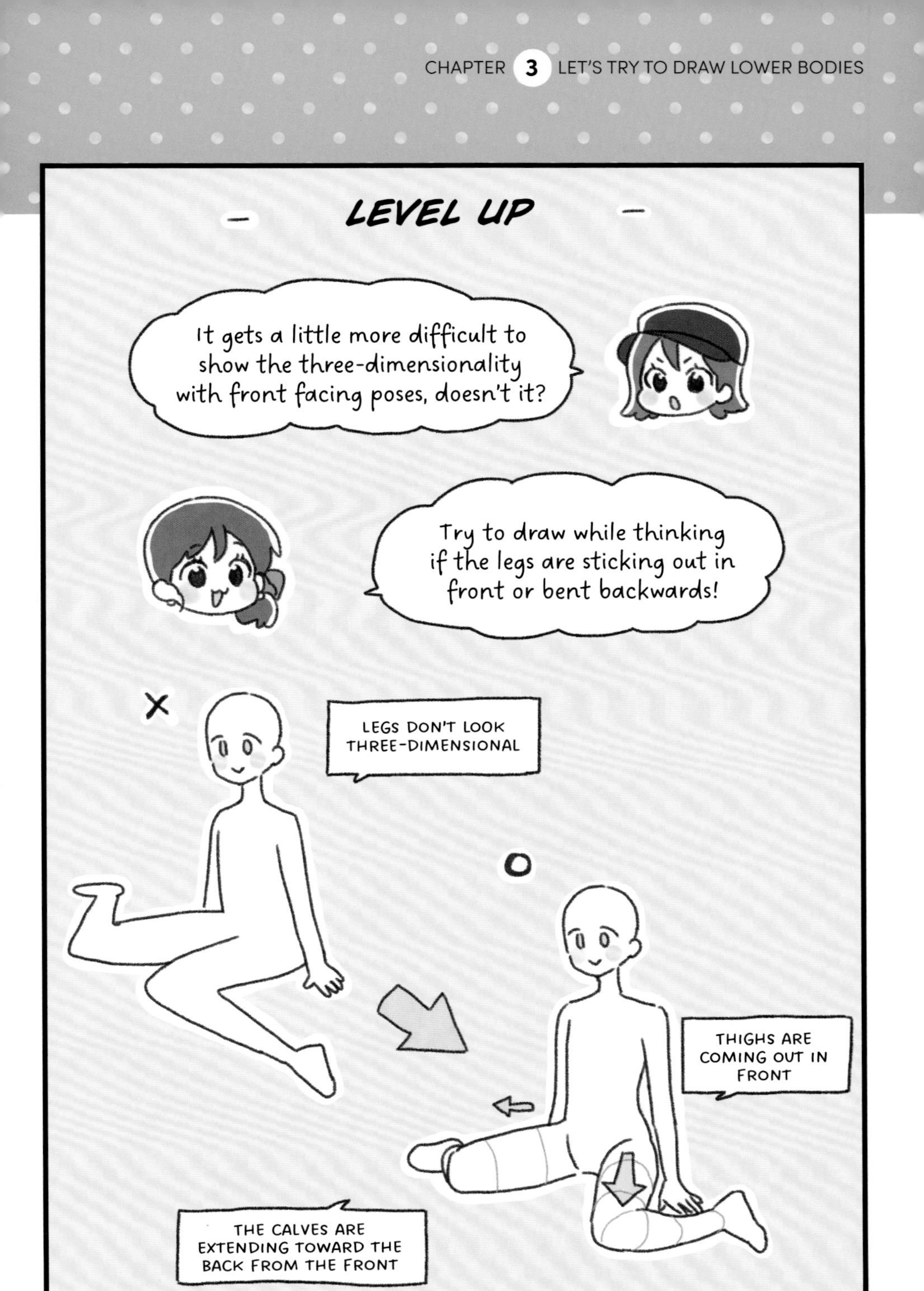
It gets a little more difficult to show the three-dimensionality with front facing poses, doesn't it?
Try to draw while thinking if the legs are sticking out in front or bent backwards!
×
LEGS DON'T LOOK THREE-DIMENSIONAL
○
THIGHS ARE COMING OUT IN FRONT
THE CALVES ARE EXTENDING TOWARD THE BACK FROM THE FRONT

# HOW TO DRAW LEGS

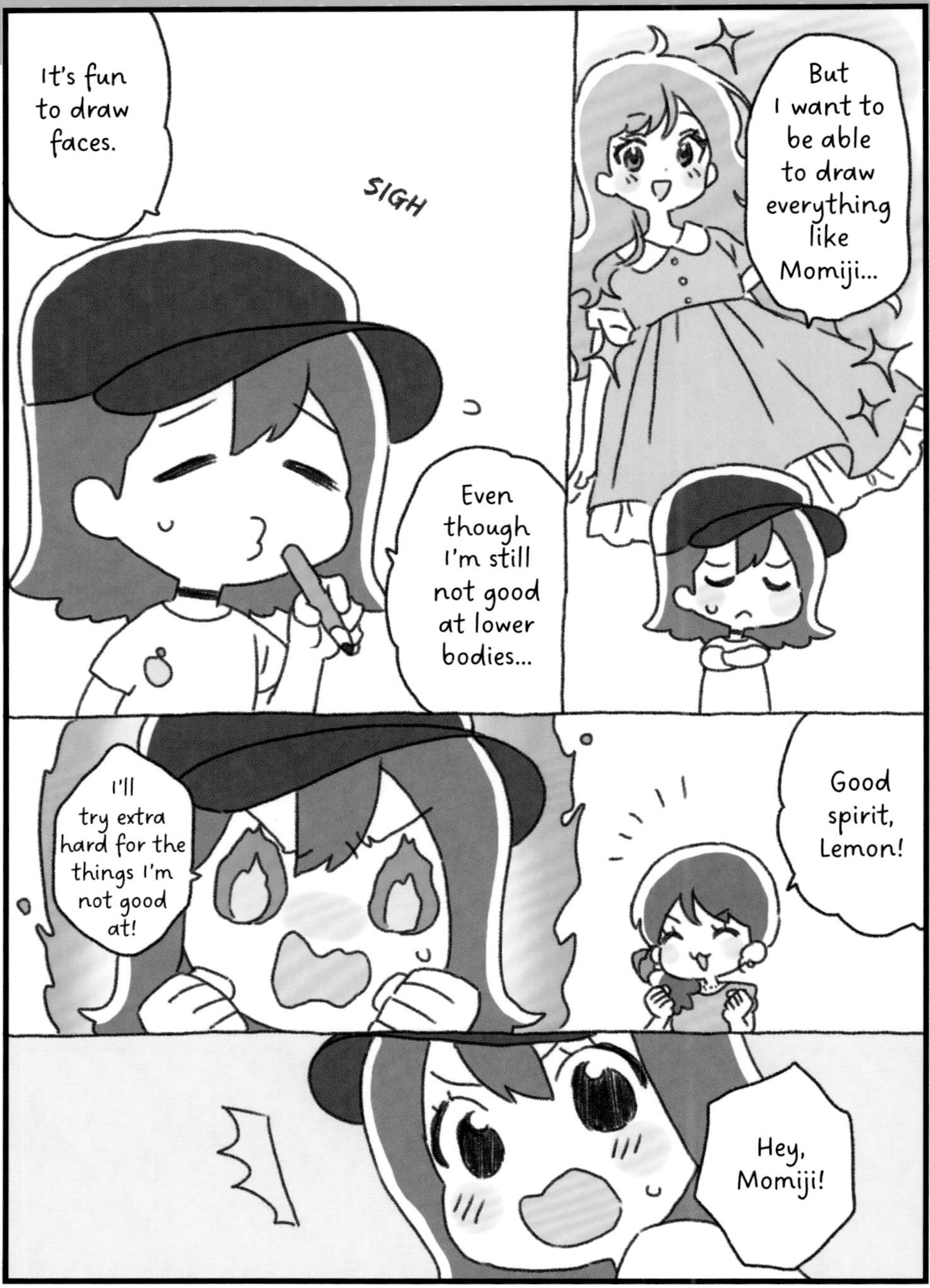
It's fun to draw faces.
SIGH
Even though I'm still not good at lower bodies...
But I want to be able to draw everything like Momiji...
I'll try extra hard for the things I'm not good at!
Good spirit, Lemon!
Hey, Momiji!

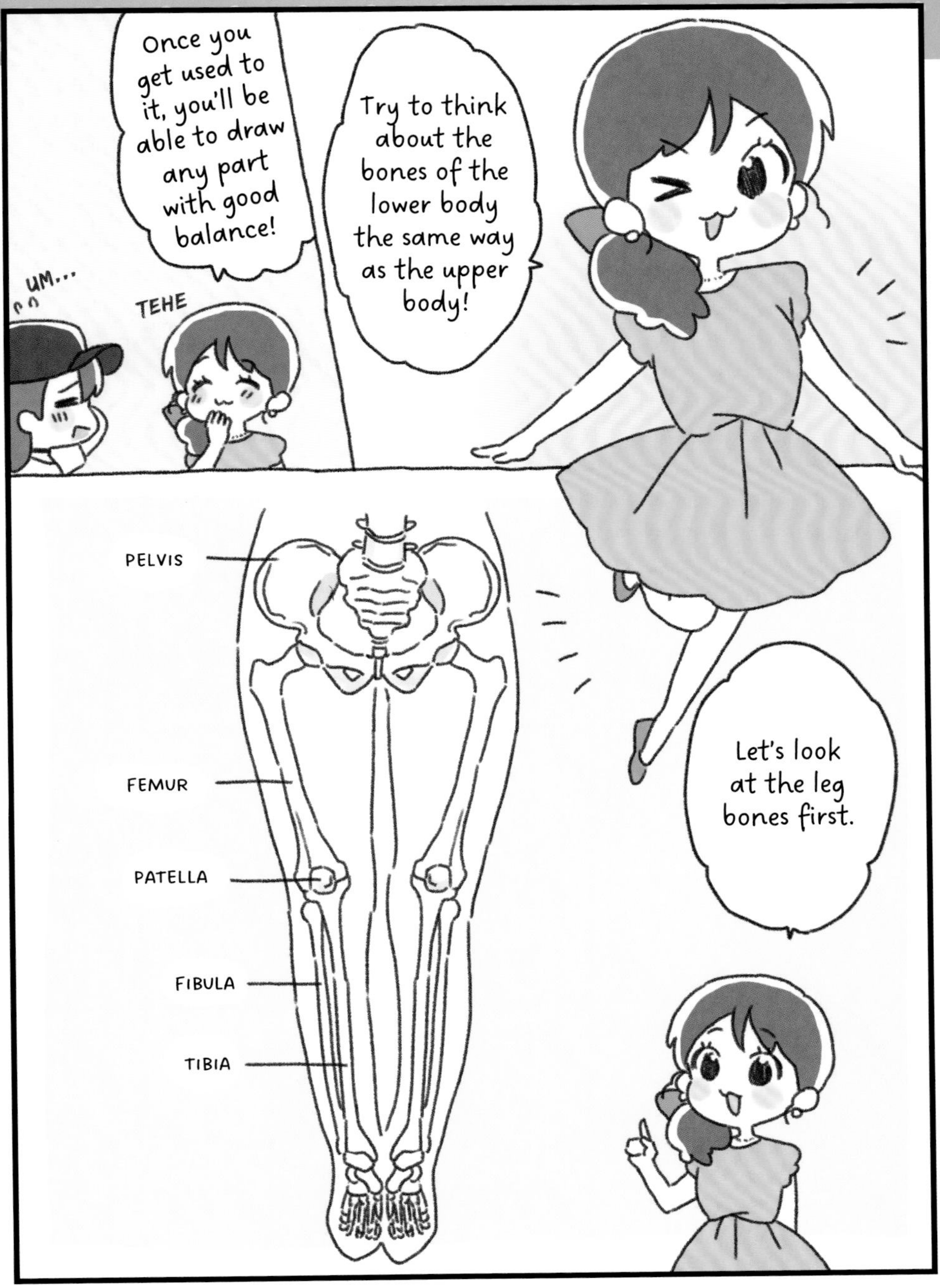
Once you get used to it, you'll be able to draw any part with good balance!
UM...
TEHE
Try to think about the bones of the lower body the same way as the upper body!
PELVIS
FEMUR
PATELLA
FIBULA
TIBIA
Let's look at the leg bones first.

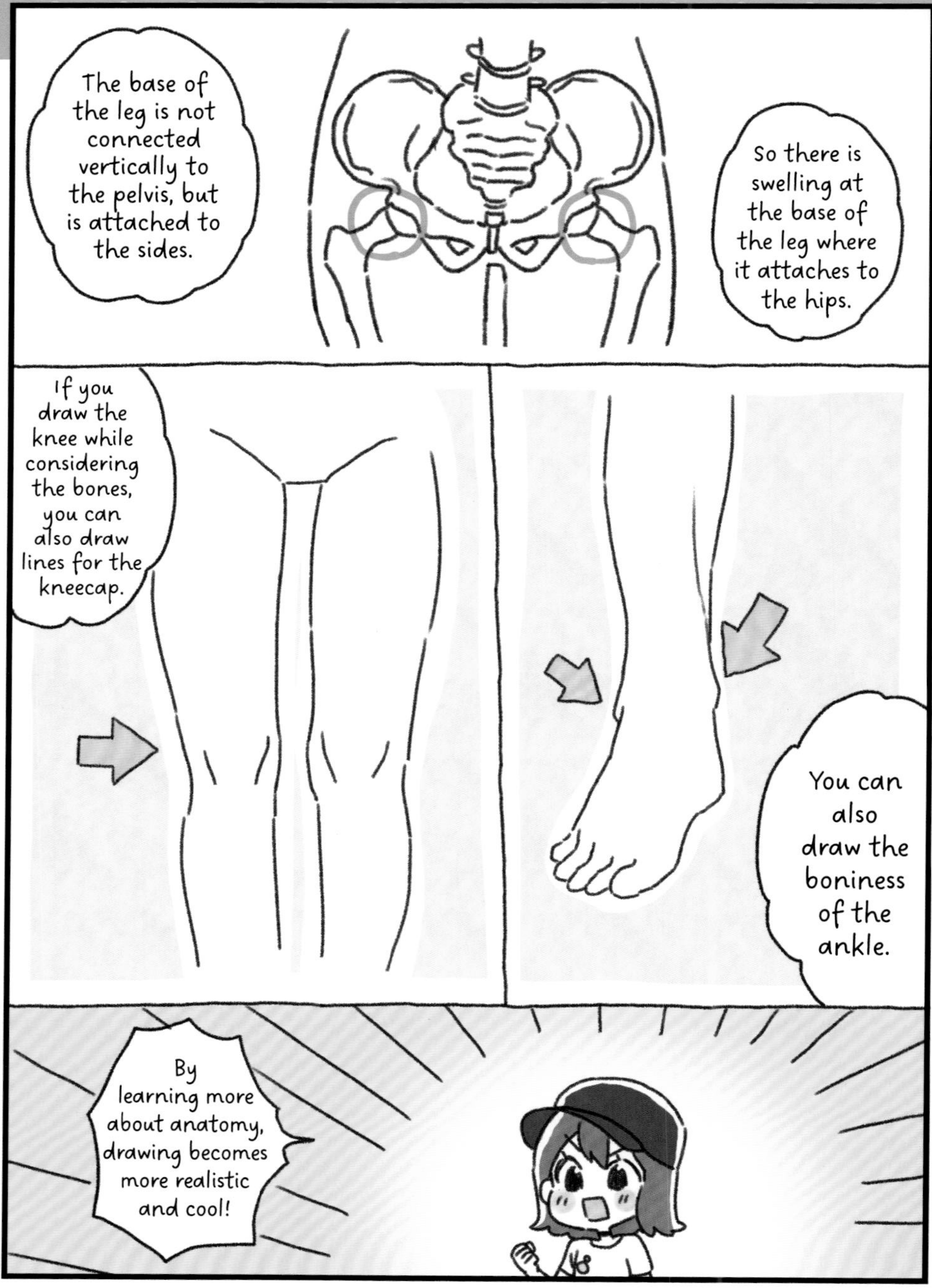
The base of the leg is not connected vertically to the pelvis, but is attached to the sides.
So there is swelling at the base of the leg where it attaches to the hips.
If you draw the knee while considering the bones, you can also draw lines for the kneecap.
You can also draw the boniness of the ankle.
By learning more about anatomy, drawing becomes more realistic and cool!

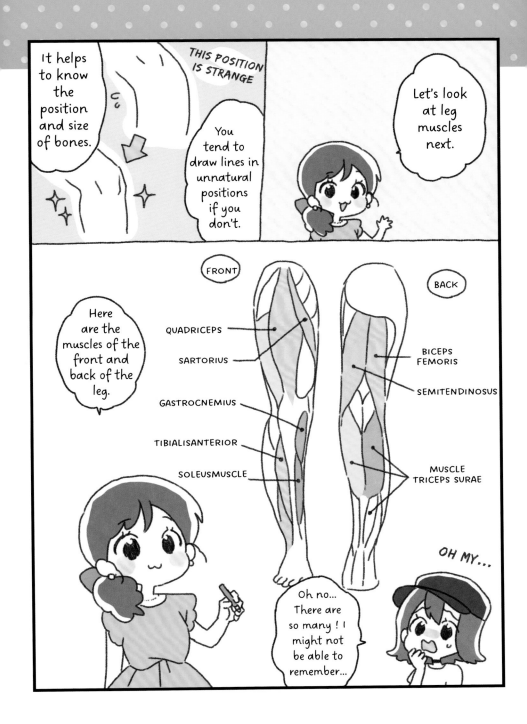

It helps to know the position and size of bones.

THIS POSITION IS STRANGE

You tend to draw lines in unnatural positions if you don't.

Let's look at leg muscles next.

Here are the muscles of the front and back of the leg.

FRONT

BACK

QUADRICEPS

SARTORIUS

GASTROCNEMIUS

TIBIALISANTERIOR

SOLEUSMUSCLE

BICEPS FEMORIS

SEMITENDINOSUS

MUSCLE TRICEPS SURAE

OH MY...

Oh no... There are so many! I might not be able to remember...

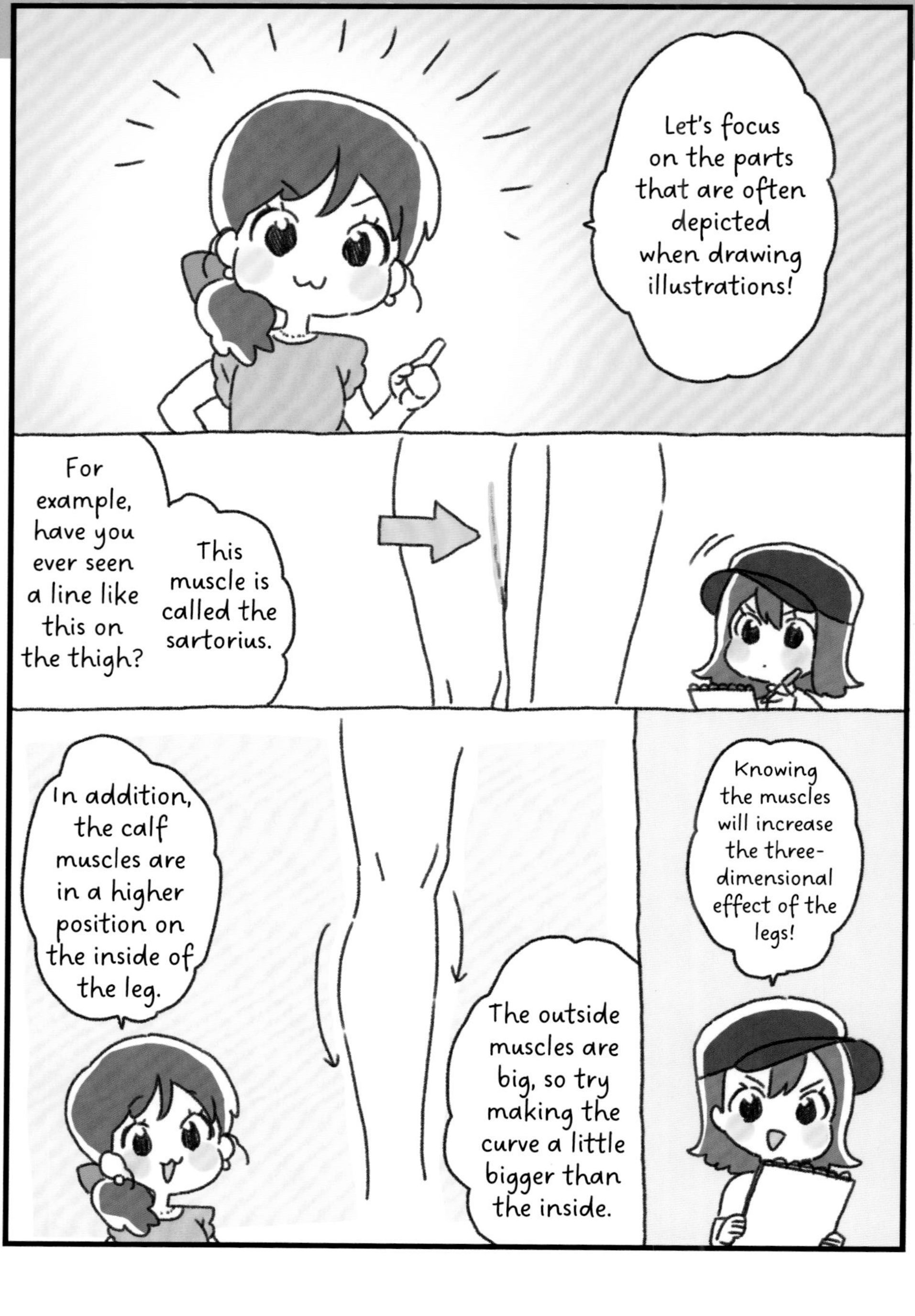
Let's focus on the parts that are often depicted when drawing illustrations!
For example, have you ever seen a line like this on the thigh?
This muscle is called the sartorius.
Knowing the muscles will increase the three-dimensional effect of the legs!
In addition, the calf muscles are in a higher position on the inside of the leg.
The outside muscles are big, so try making the curve a little bigger than the inside.

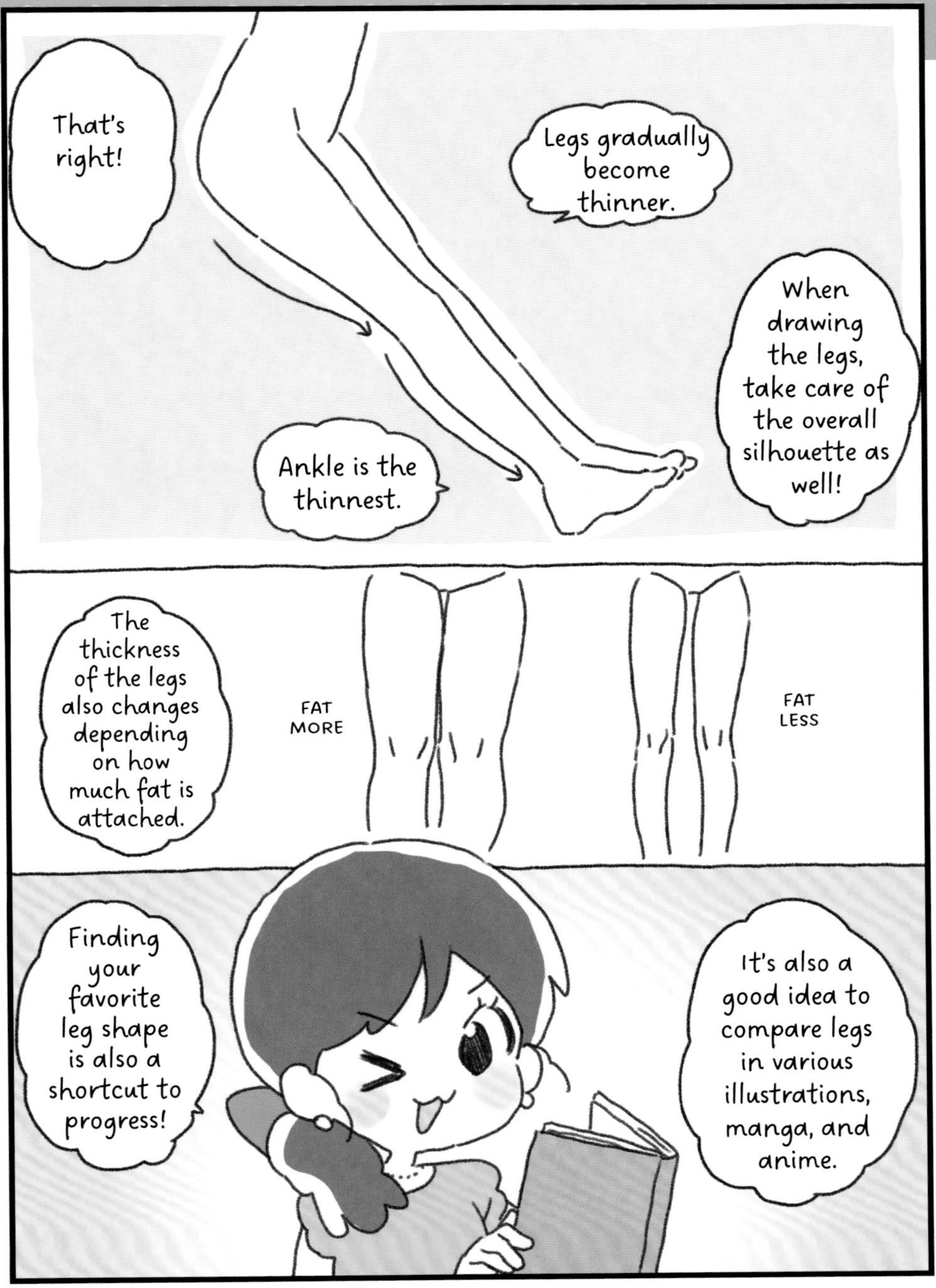
That's right!
Legs gradually become thinner.
When drawing the legs, take care of the overall silhouette as well!
Ankle is the thinnest.
The thickness of the legs also changes depending on how much fat is attached.
MORE FAT
LESS FAT
It's also a good idea to compare legs in various illustrations, manga, and anime.
Finding your favorite leg shape is also a shortcut to progress!

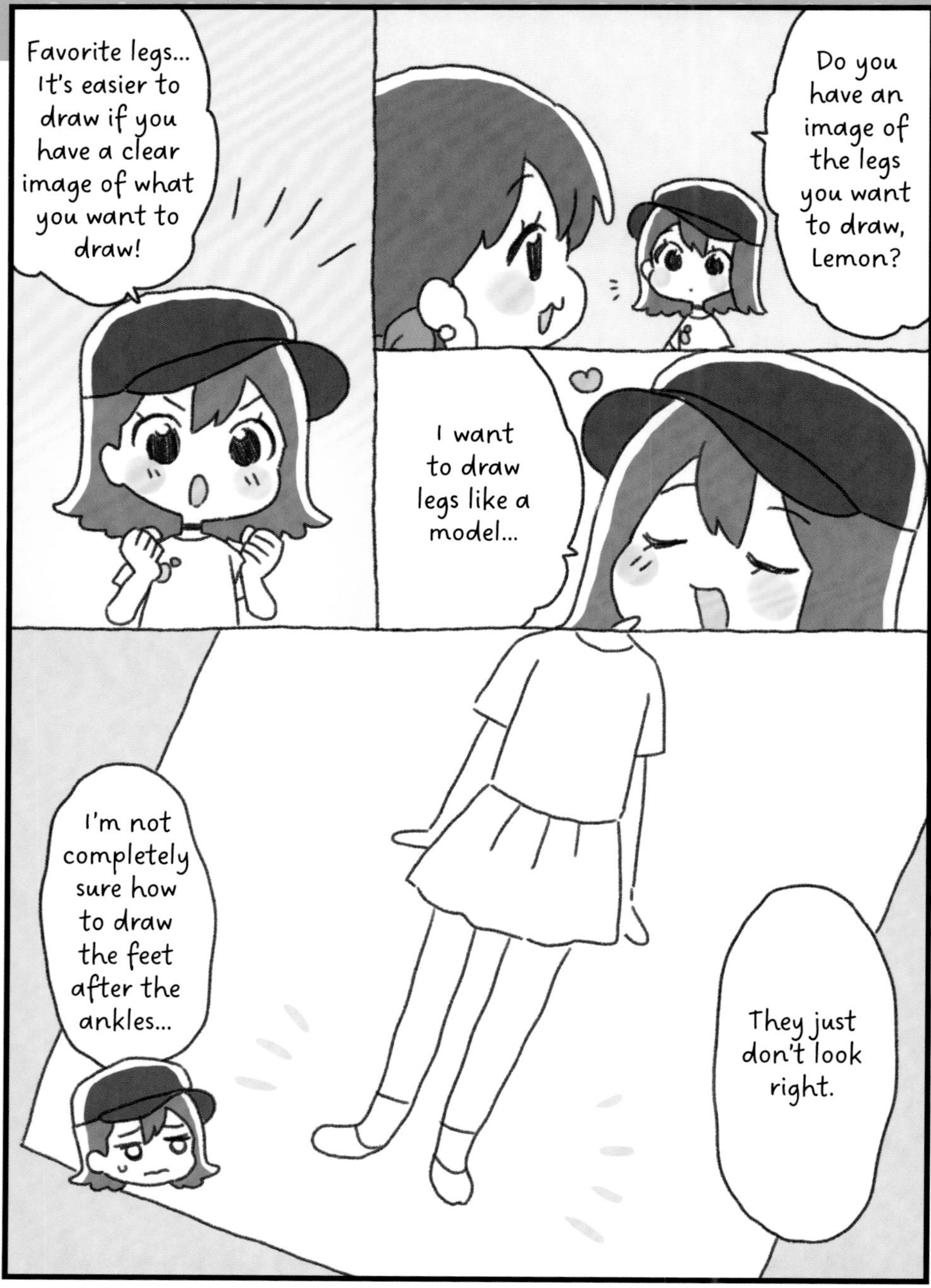
Favorite legs... It's easier to draw if you have a clear image of what you want to draw!
Do you have an image of the legs you want to draw, Lemon?
I want to draw legs like a model...
I'm not completely sure how to draw the feet after the ankles...
They just don't look right.

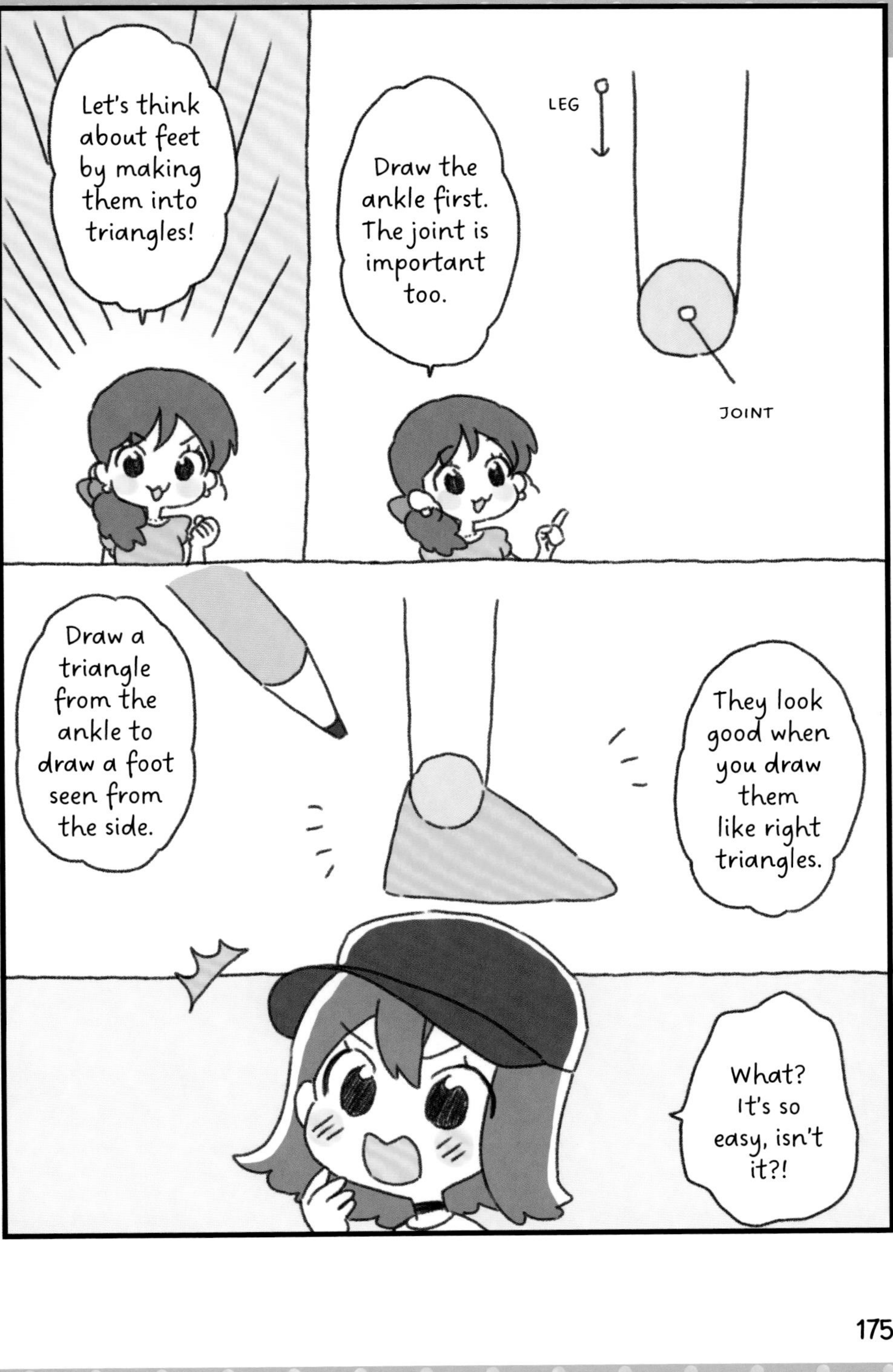
Let's think about feet by making them into triangles!
Draw the ankle first. The joint is important too.
LEG
JOINT
Draw a triangle from the ankle to draw a foot seen from the side.
They look good when you draw them like right triangles.
What? It's so easy, isn't it?!

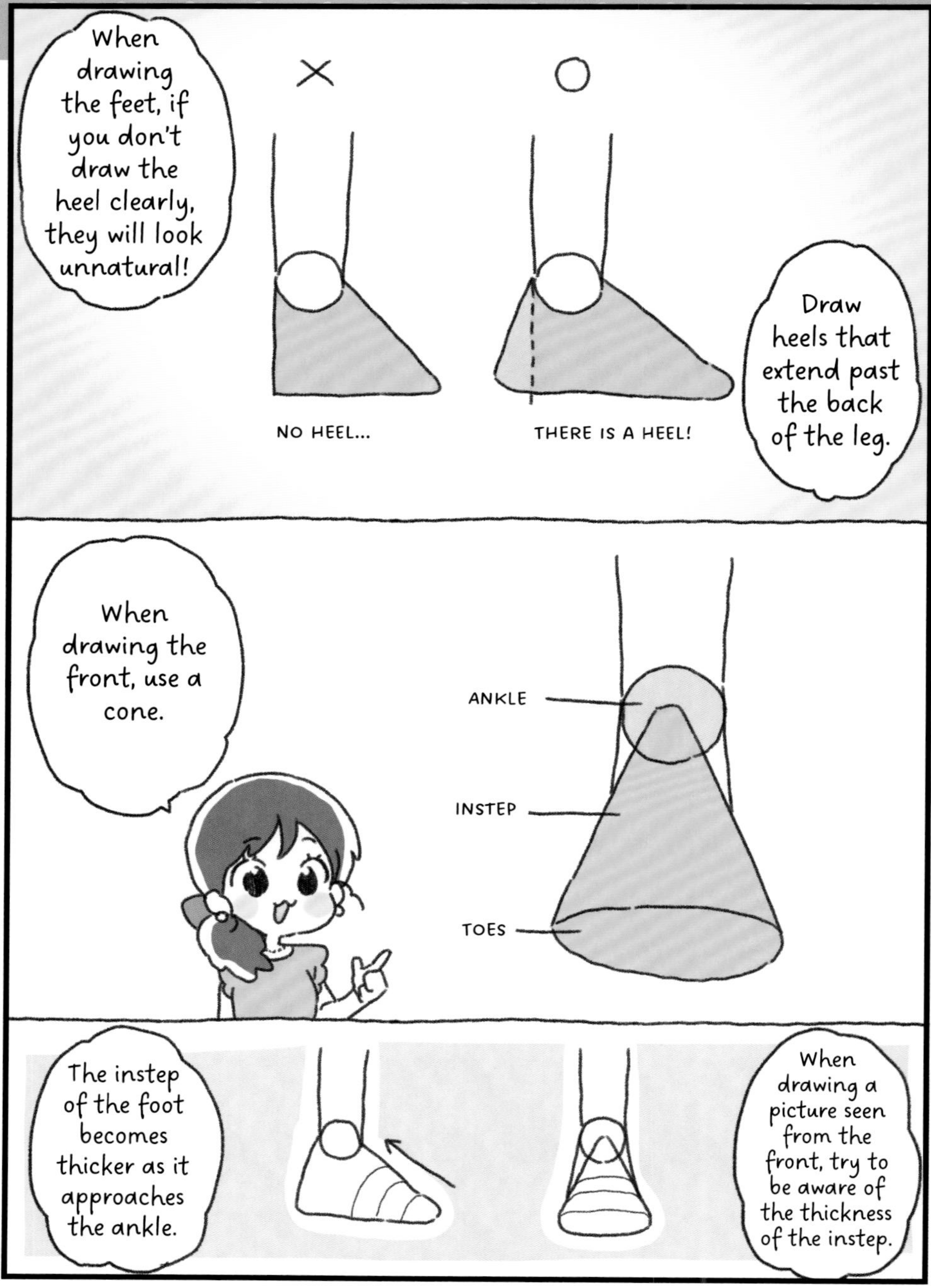
When drawing the feet, if you don't draw the heel clearly, they will look unnatural!
×
○
NO HEEL...
THERE IS A HEEL!
Draw heels that extend past the back of the leg.
When drawing the front, use a cone.
ANKLE
INSTEP
TOES
The instep of the foot becomes thicker as it approaches the ankle.
When drawing a picture seen from the front, try to be aware of the thickness of the instep.

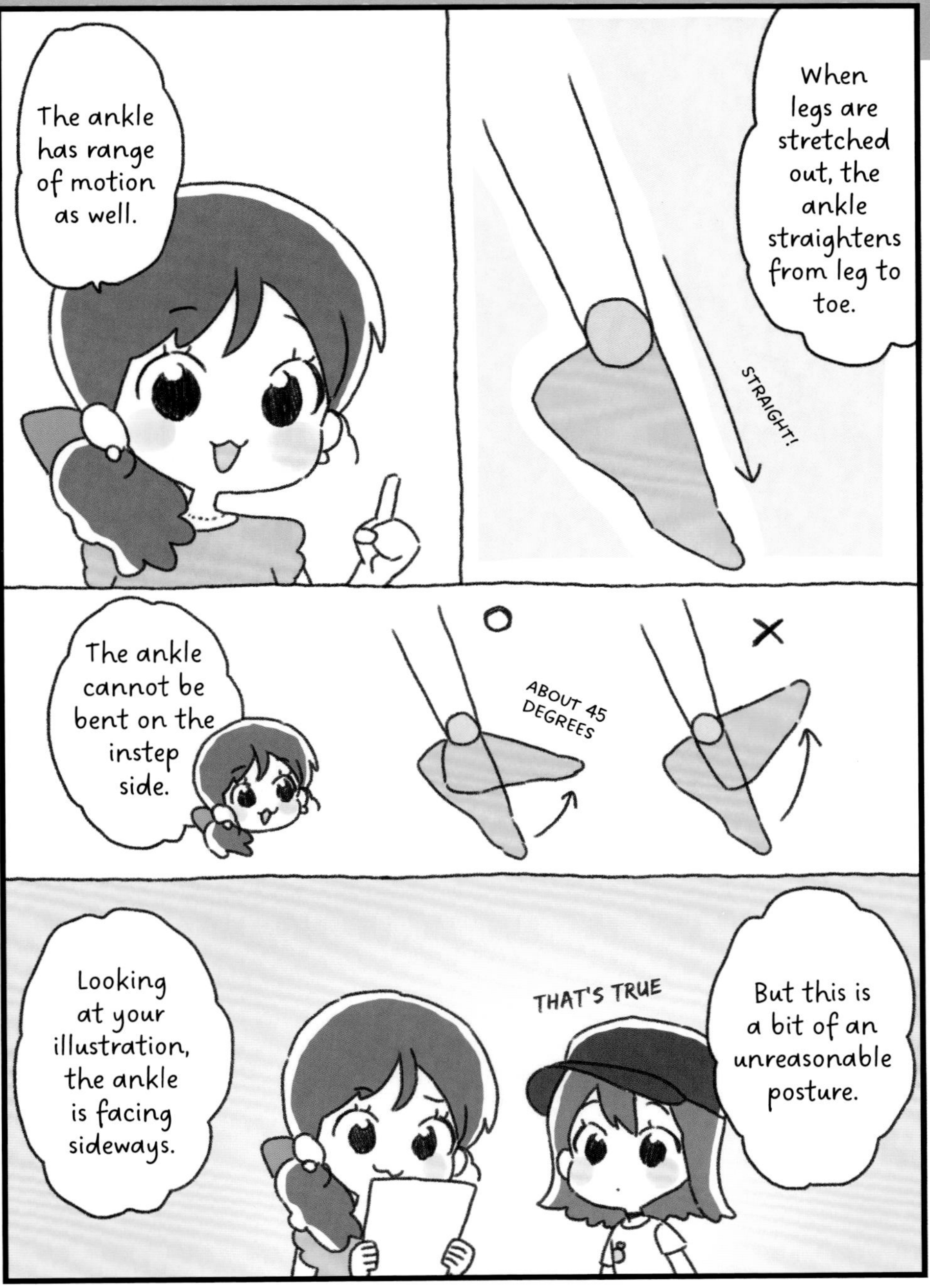
The ankle has range of motion as well.
When legs are stretched out, the ankle straightens from leg to toe.
STRAIGHT!
The ankle cannot be bent on the instep side.
O
ABOUT 45 DEGREES
X
Looking at your illustration, the ankle is facing sideways.
THAT'S TRUE
But this is a bit of an unreasonable posture.

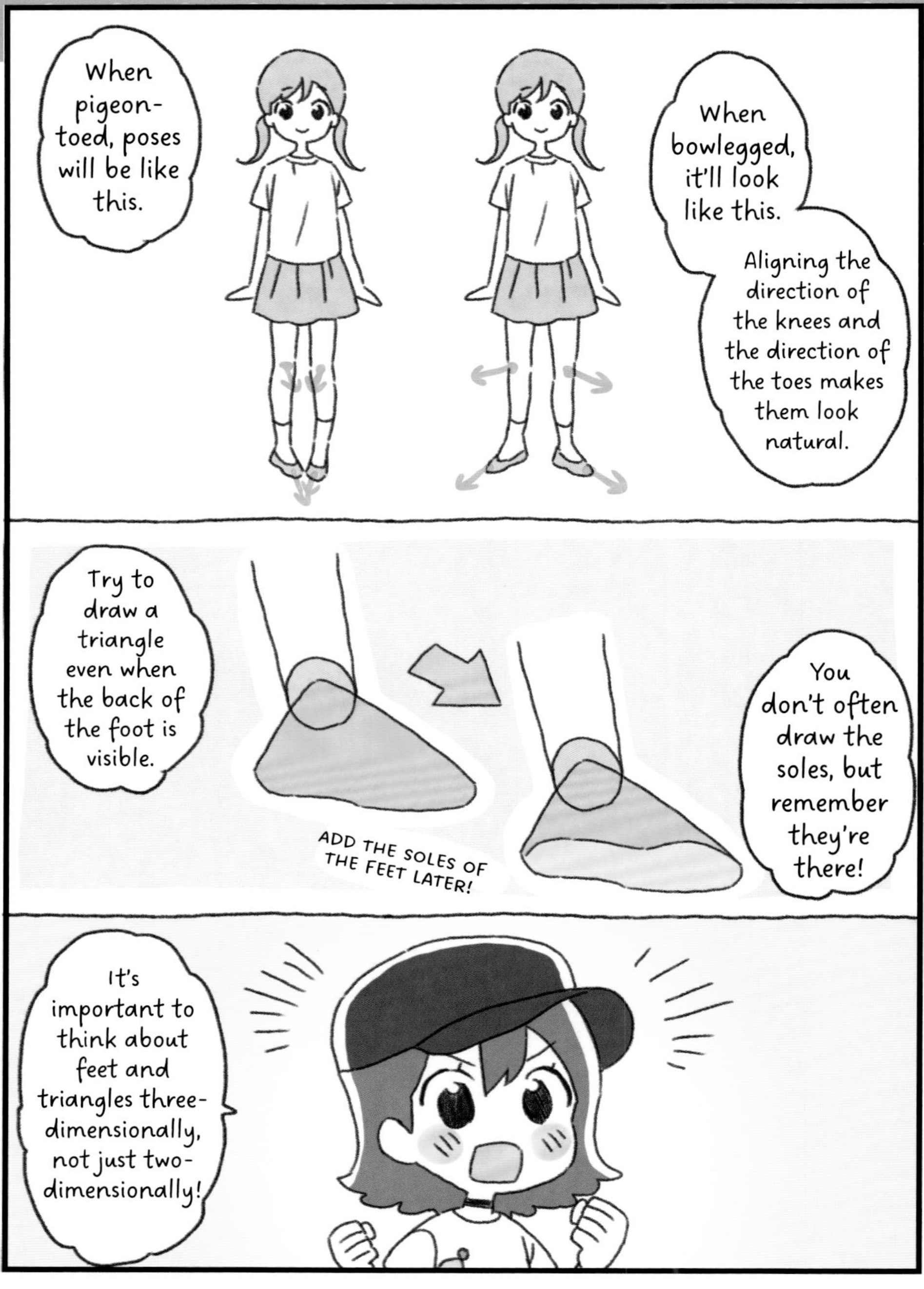
When pigeon-toed, poses will be like this.
When bowlegged, it'll look like this.
Aligning the direction of the knees and the direction of the toes makes them look natural.
Try to draw a triangle even when the back of the foot is visible.
ADD THE SOLES OF THE FEET LATER!
You don't often draw the soles, but remember they're there!
It's important to think about feet and triangles three-dimensionally, not just two-dimensionally!

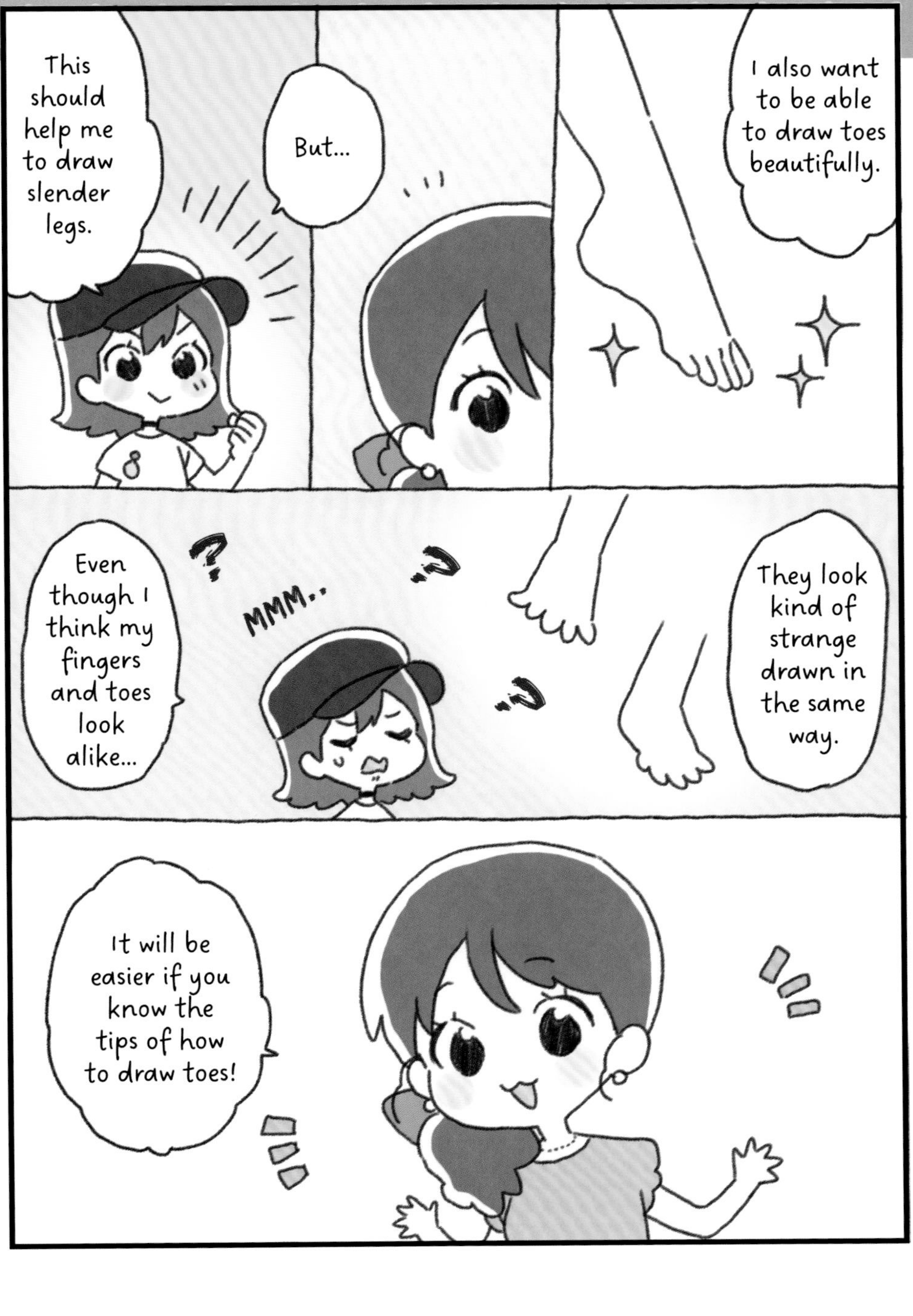
This should help me to draw slender legs.
But...
I also want to be able to draw toes beautifully.
Even though I think my fingers and toes look alike...
MMM..
They look kind of strange drawn in the same way.
It will be easier if you know the tips of how to draw toes!

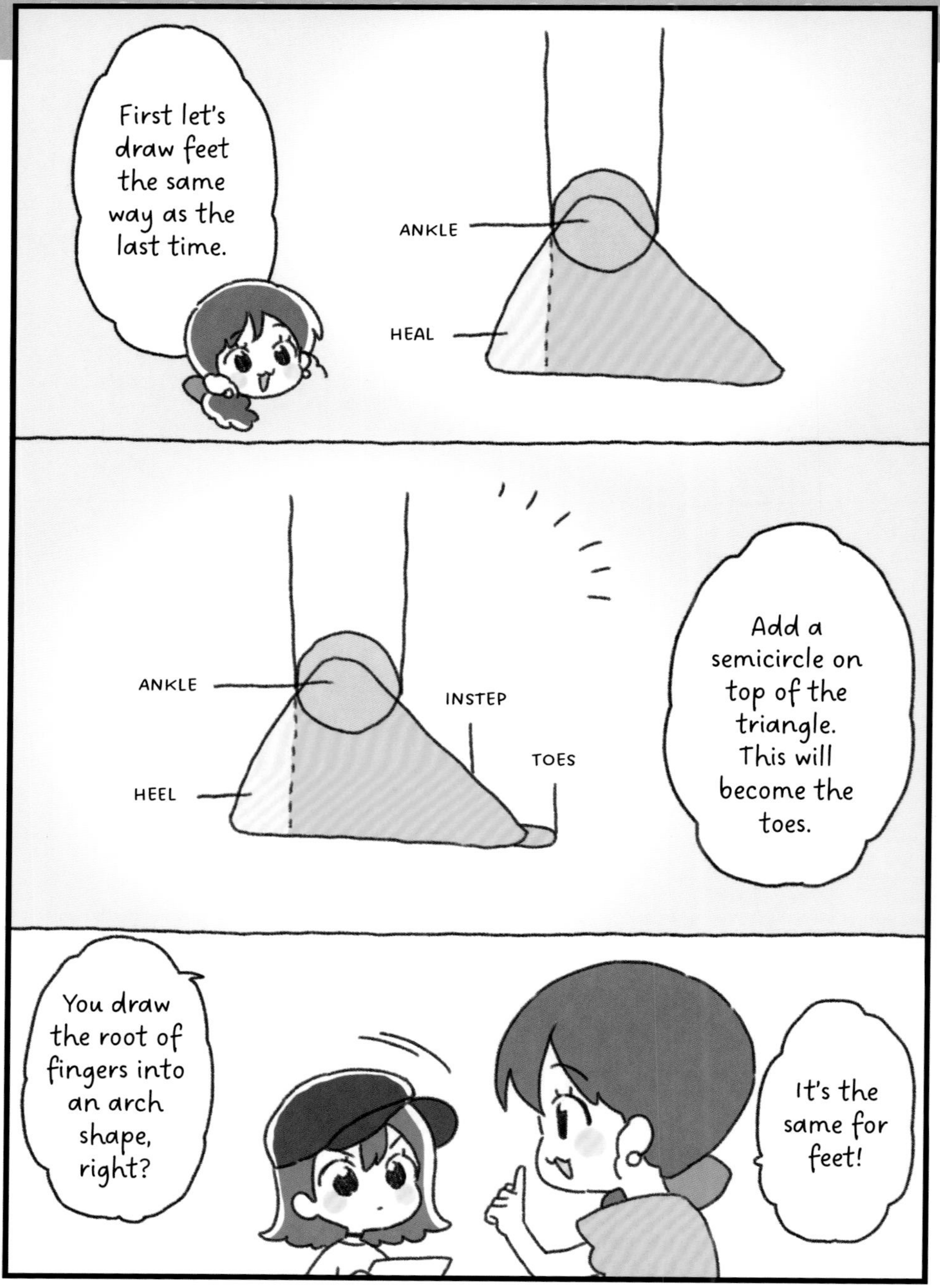
First let's draw feet the same way as the last time.
ANKLE
HEAL
ANKLE
INSTEP
TOES
HEEL
Add a semicircle on top of the triangle. This will become the toes.
You draw the root of fingers into an arch shape, right?
It's the same for feet!

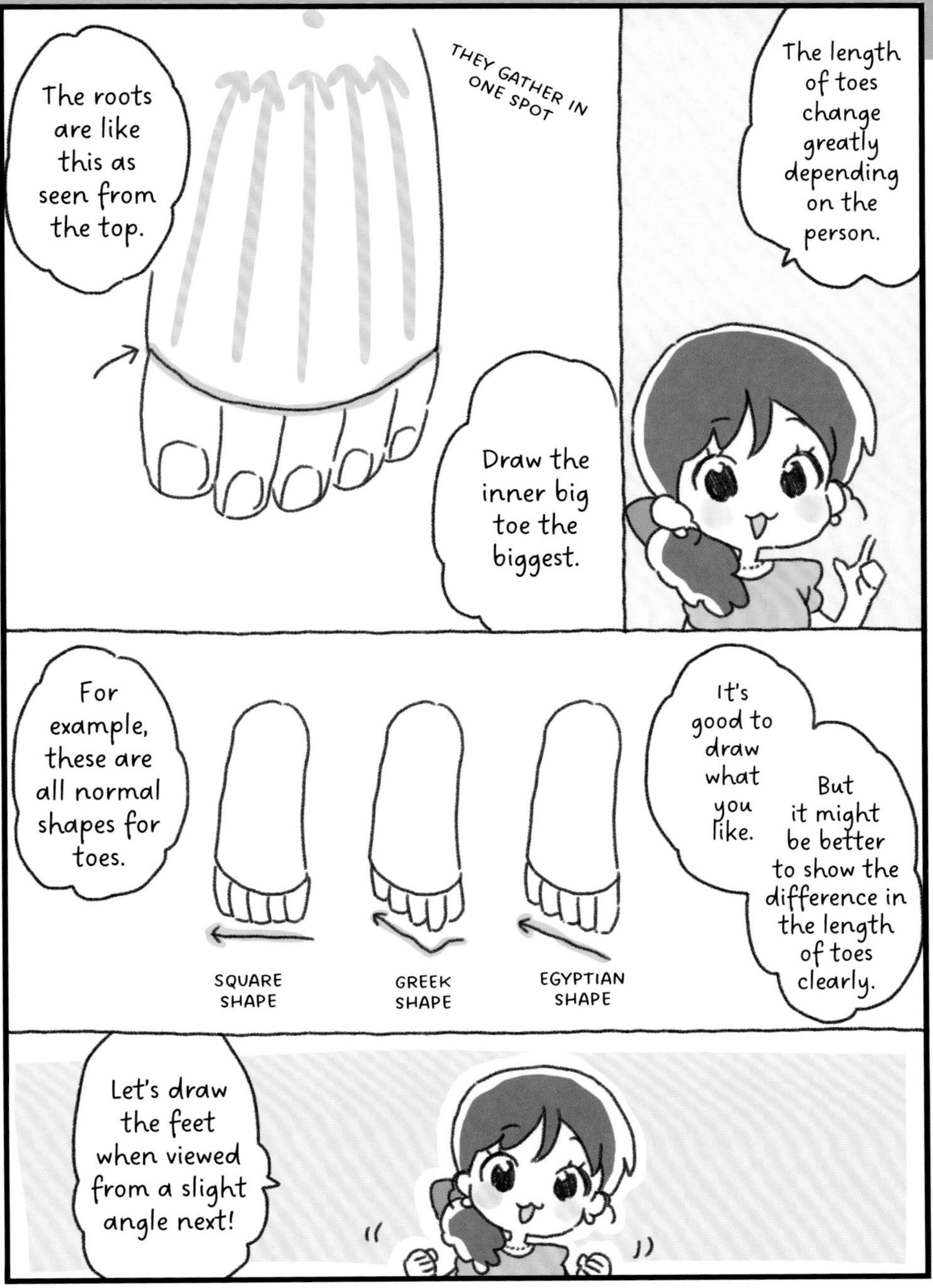
The roots are like this as seen from the top.
THEY GATHER IN ONE SPOT
Draw the inner big toe the biggest.
The length of toes change greatly depending on the person.
For example, these are all normal shapes for toes.
SQUARE SHAPE
GREEK SHAPE
EGYPTIAN SHAPE
It's good to draw what you like.
But it might be better to show the difference in the length of toes clearly.
Let's draw the feet when viewed from a slight angle next!

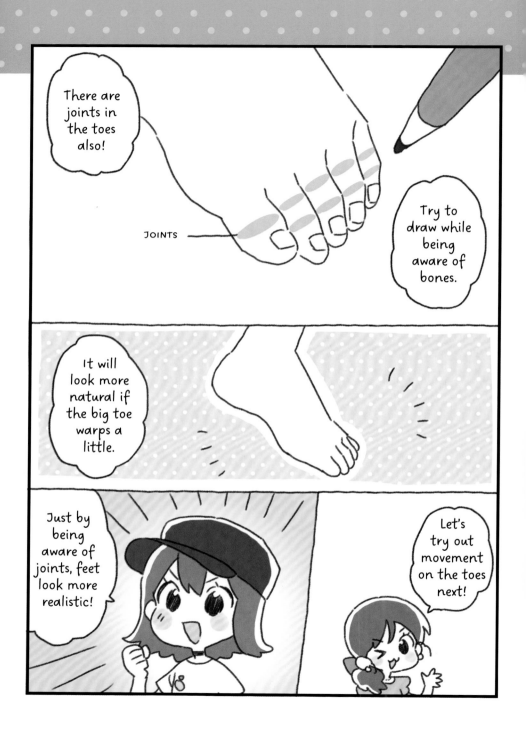

There are joints in the toes also!

JOINTS

Try to draw while being aware of bones.

It will look more natural if the big toe warps a little.

Just by being aware of joints, feet look more realistic!

Let's try out movement on the toes next!

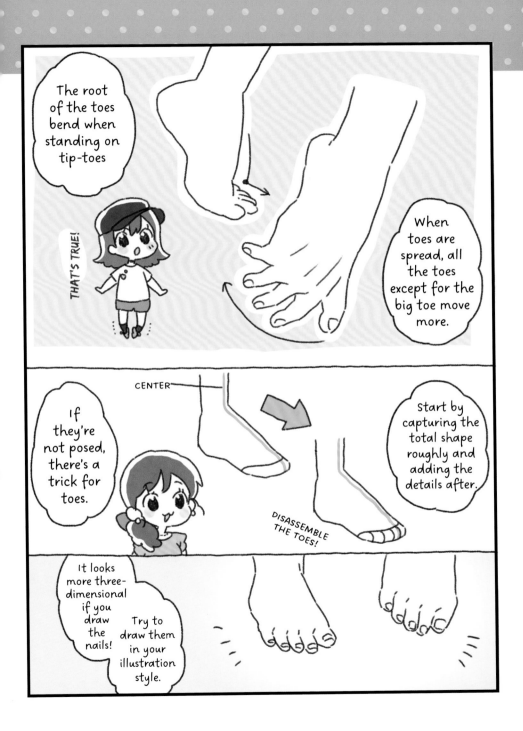

The root of the toes bend when standing on tip-toes

THAT'S TRUE!

When toes are spread, all the toes except for the big toe move more.

If they're not posed, there's a trick for toes.

CENTER

DISASSEMBLE THE TOES!

Start by capturing the total shape roughly and adding the details after.

It looks more three-dimensional if you draw the nails!

Try to draw them in your illustration style.

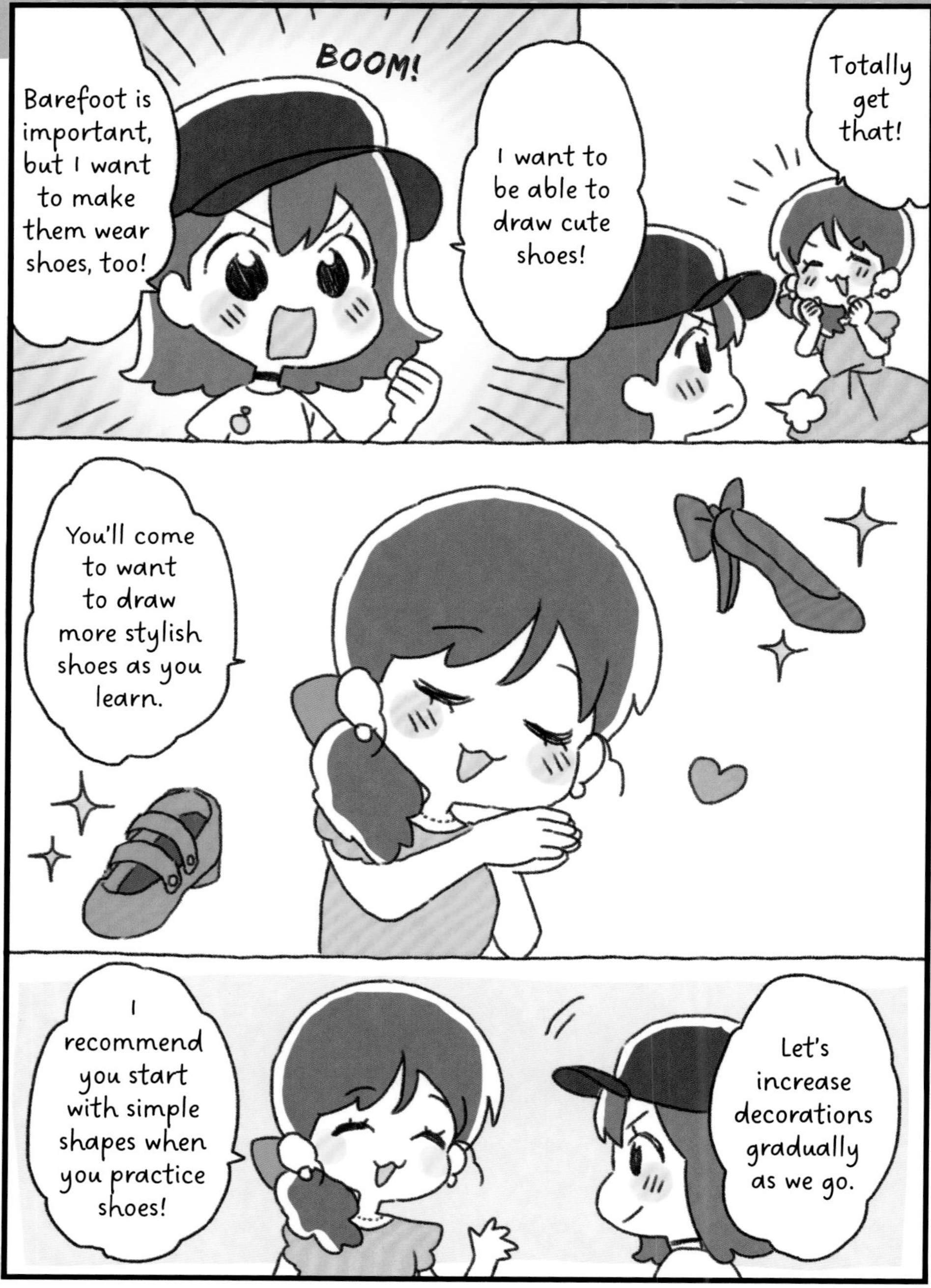
BOOM!
Barefoot is important, but I want to make them wear shoes, too!
I want to be able to draw cute shoes!
Totally get that!
You'll come to want to draw more stylish shoes as you learn.
I recommend you start with simple shapes when you practice shoes!
Let's increase decorations gradually as we go.

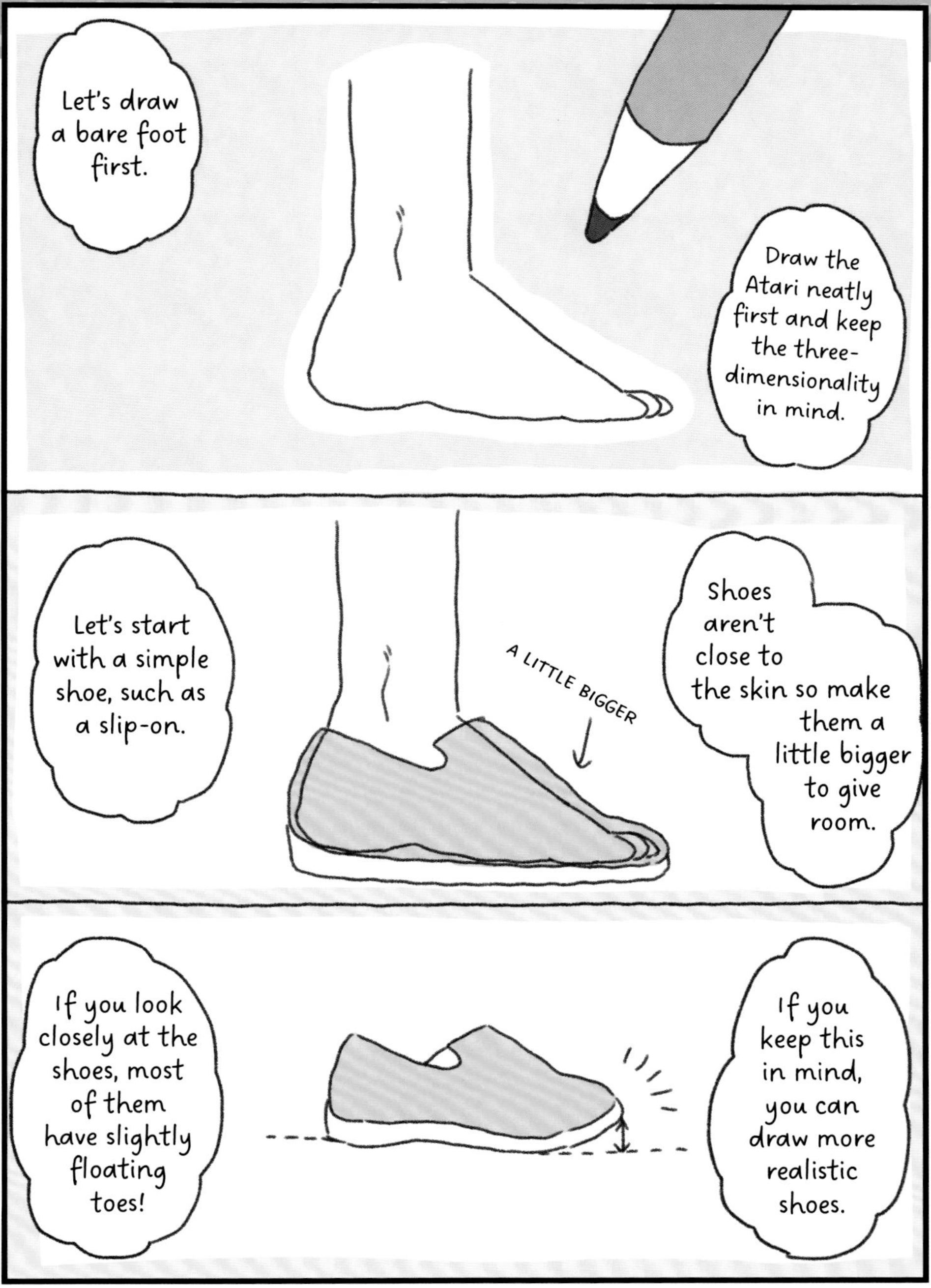
Let's draw a bare foot first.
Draw the Atari neatly first and keep the three-dimensionality in mind.
Let's start with a simple shoe, such as a slip-on.
A LITTLE BIGGER
Shoes aren't close to the skin so make them a little bigger to give room.
If you look closely at the shoes, most of them have slightly floating toes!
If you keep this in mind, you can draw more realistic shoes.

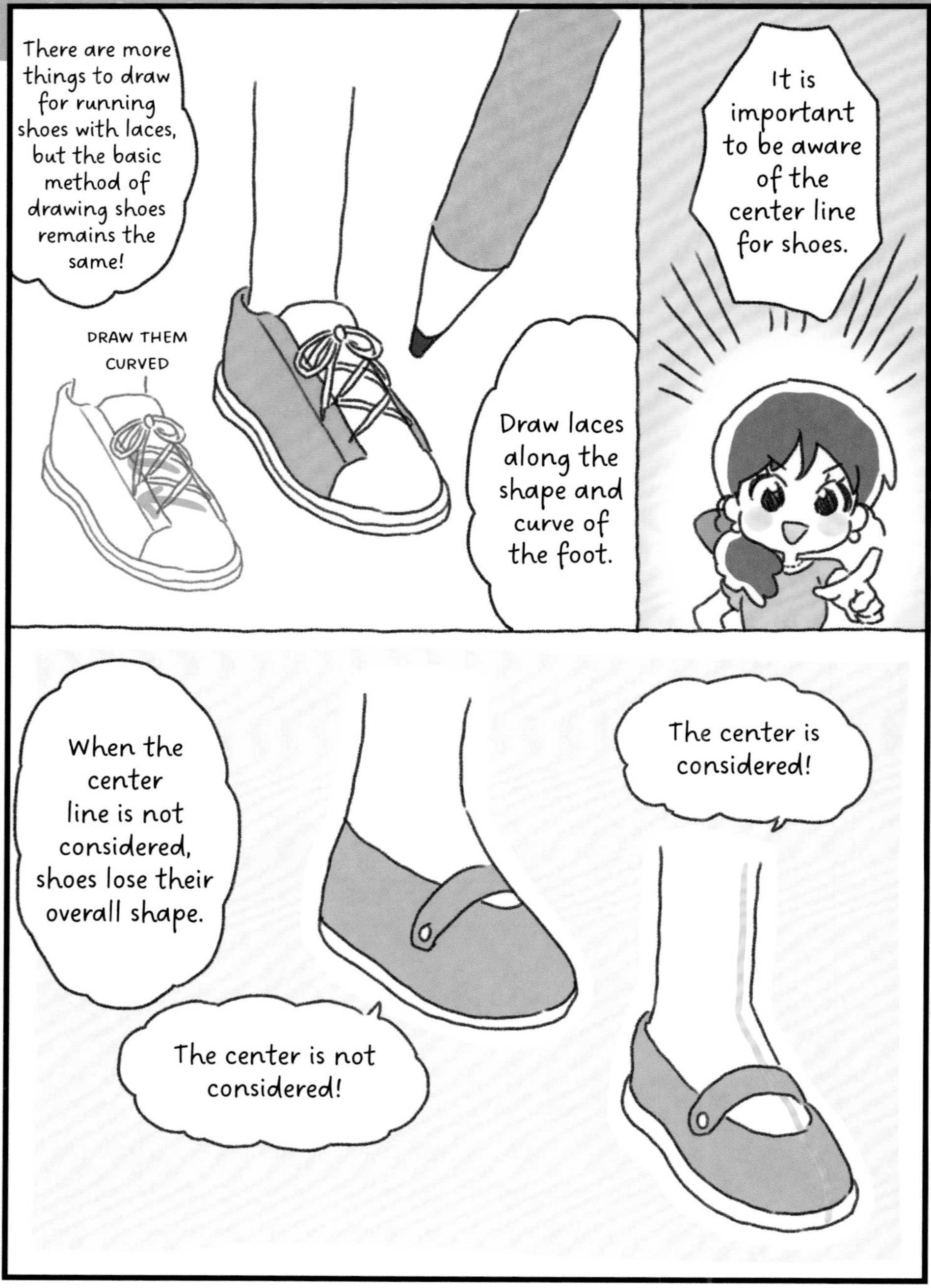
There are more things to draw for running shoes with laces, but the basic method of drawing shoes remains the same!
DRAW THEM CURVED
Draw laces along the shape and curve of the foot.
It is important to be aware of the center line for shoes.
When the center line is not considered, shoes lose their overall shape.
The center is not considered!
The center is considered!

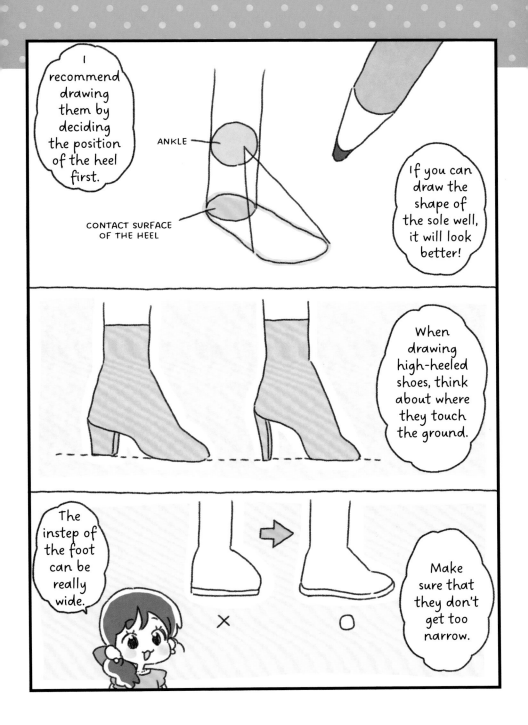

I recommend drawing them by deciding the position of the heel first.

ANKLE

CONTACT SURFACE OF THE HEEL

If you can draw the shape of the sole well, it will look better!

When drawing high-heeled shoes, think about where they touch the ground.

The instep of the foot can be really wide.

×

○

Make sure that they don't get too narrow.

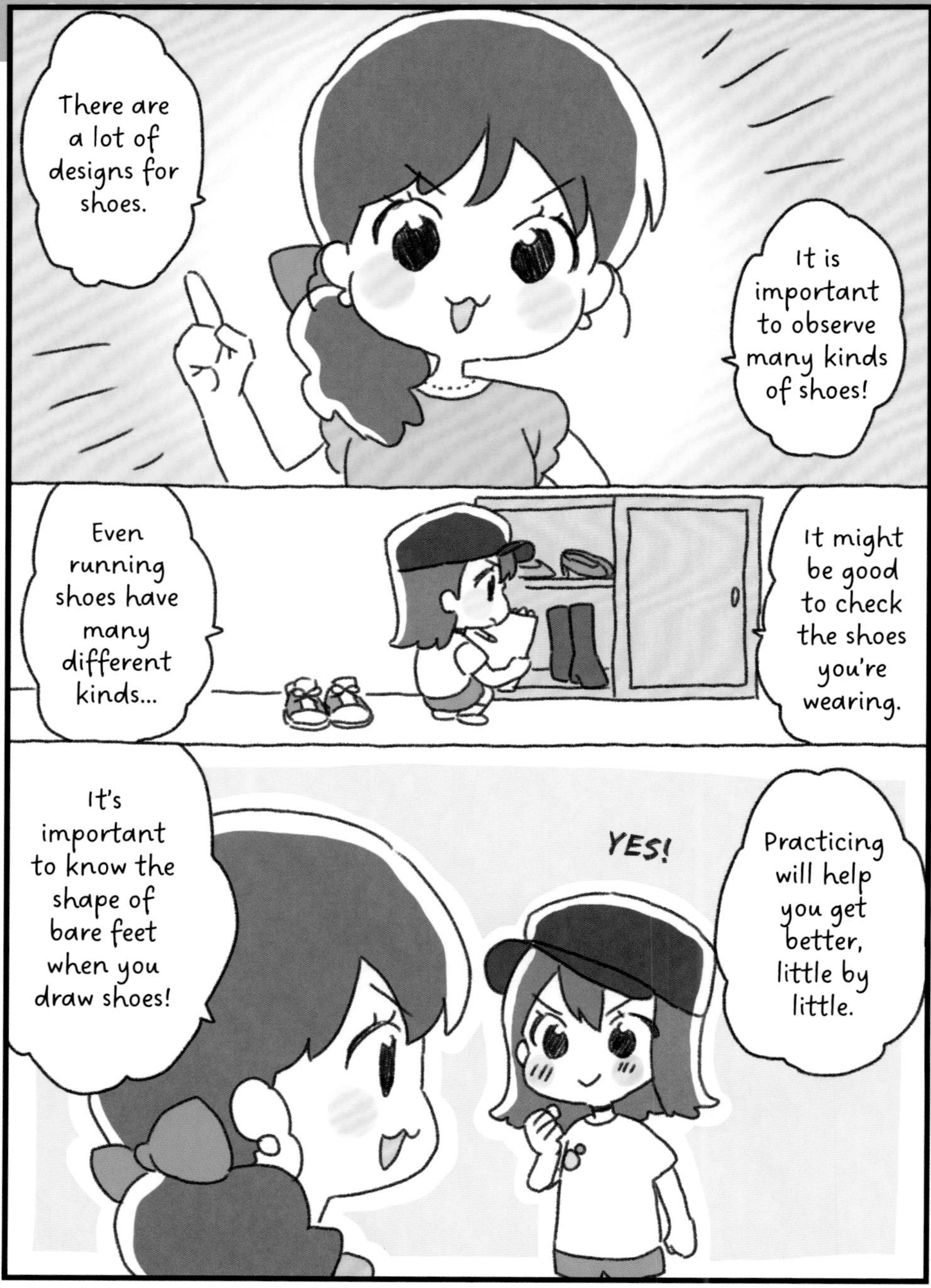
There are a lot of designs for shoes.
It is important to observe many kinds of shoes!
Even running shoes have many different kinds...
It might be good to check the shoes you're wearing.
It's important to know the shape of bare feet when you draw shoes!
YES!
Practicing will help you get better, little by little.

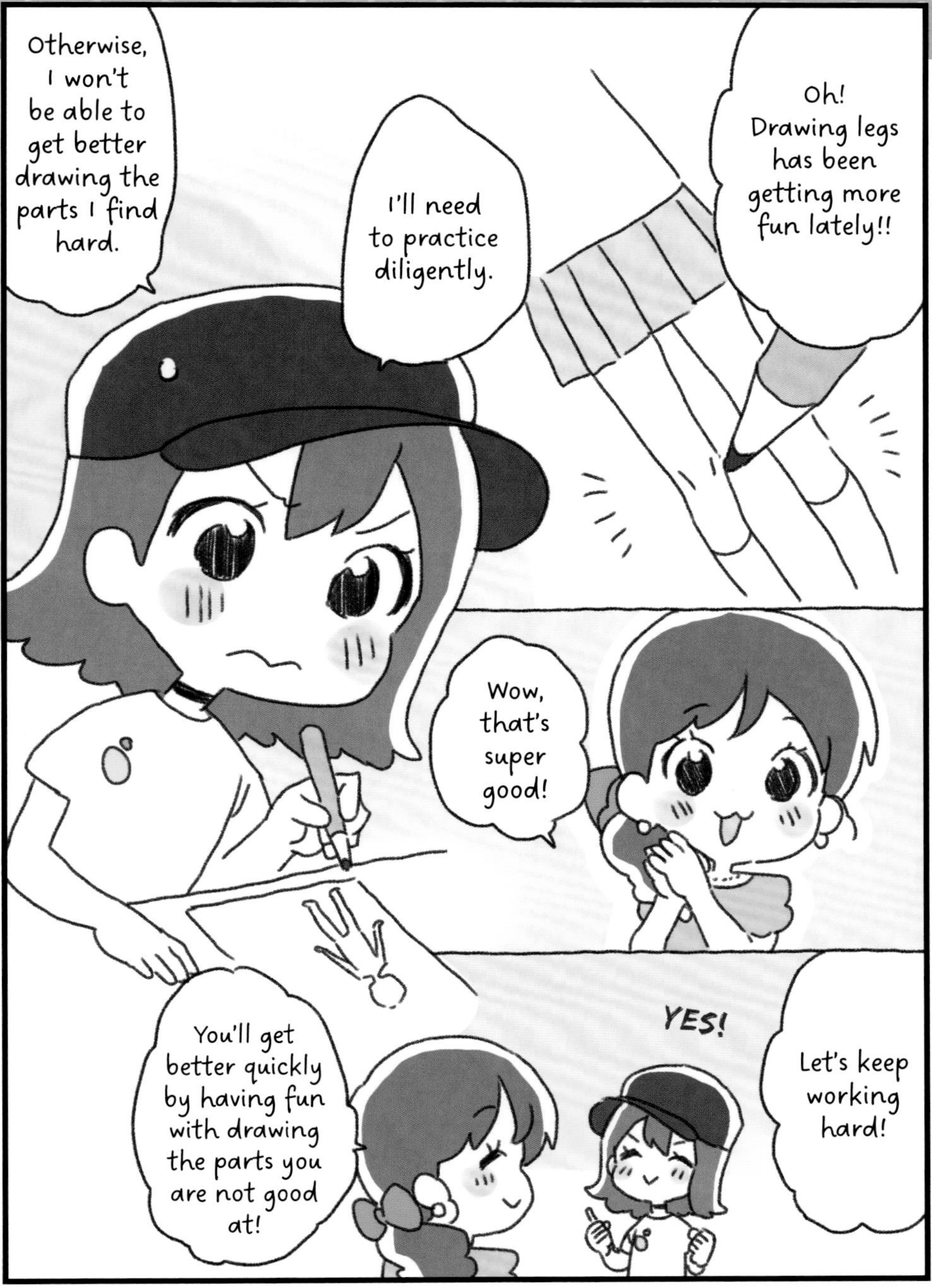
Oh! Drawing legs has been getting more fun lately!!
I'll need to practice diligently.
Otherwise, I won't be able to get better drawing the parts I find hard.
Wow, that's super good!
Let's keep working hard!
YES!
You'll get better quickly by having fun with drawing the parts you are not good at!

# LEVEL UP

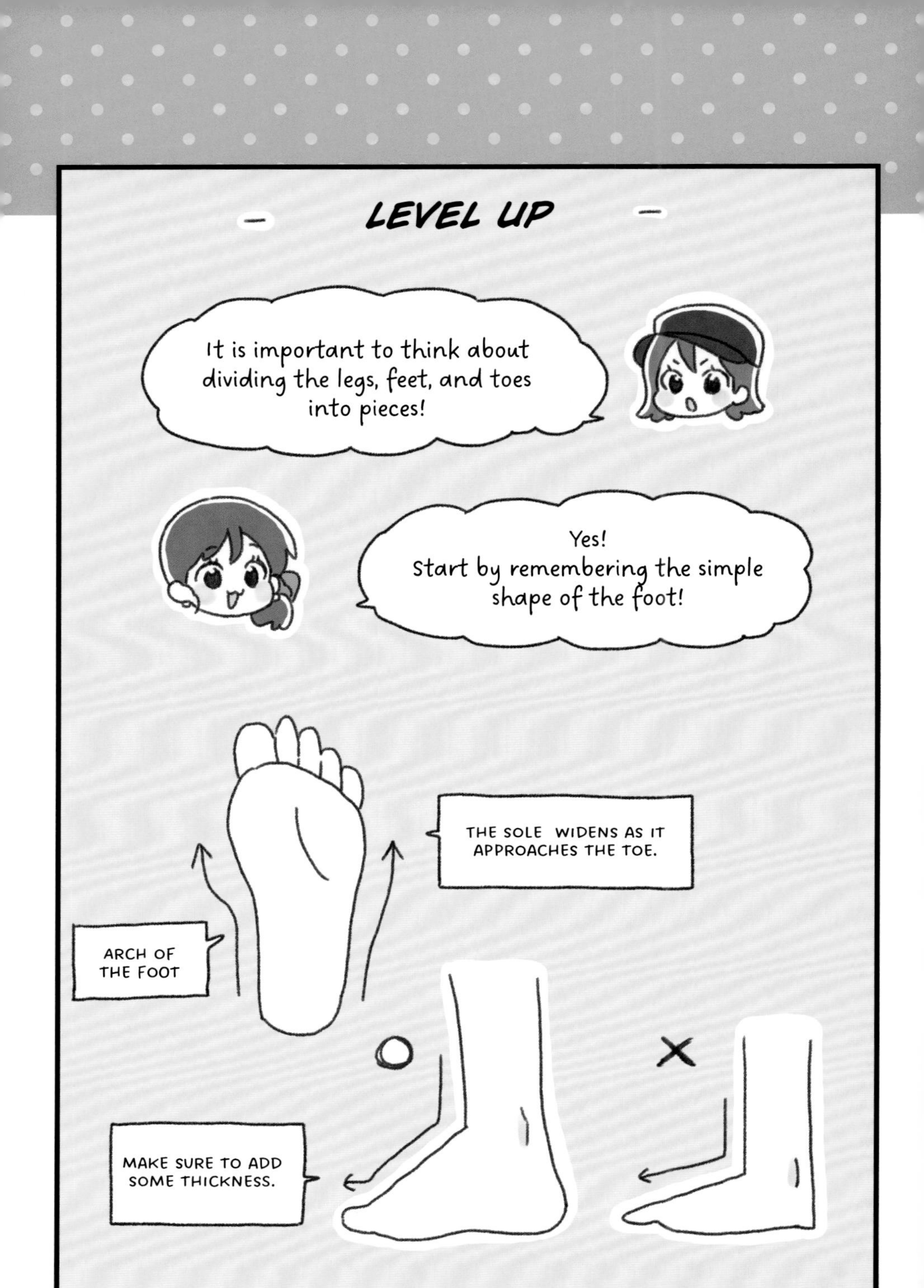

It is important to think about dividing the legs, feet, and toes into pieces!
Yes! Start by remembering the simple shape of the foot!
THE SOLE WIDENS AS IT APPROACHES THE TOE.
ARCH OF THE FOOT
MAKE SURE TO ADD SOME THICKNESS.

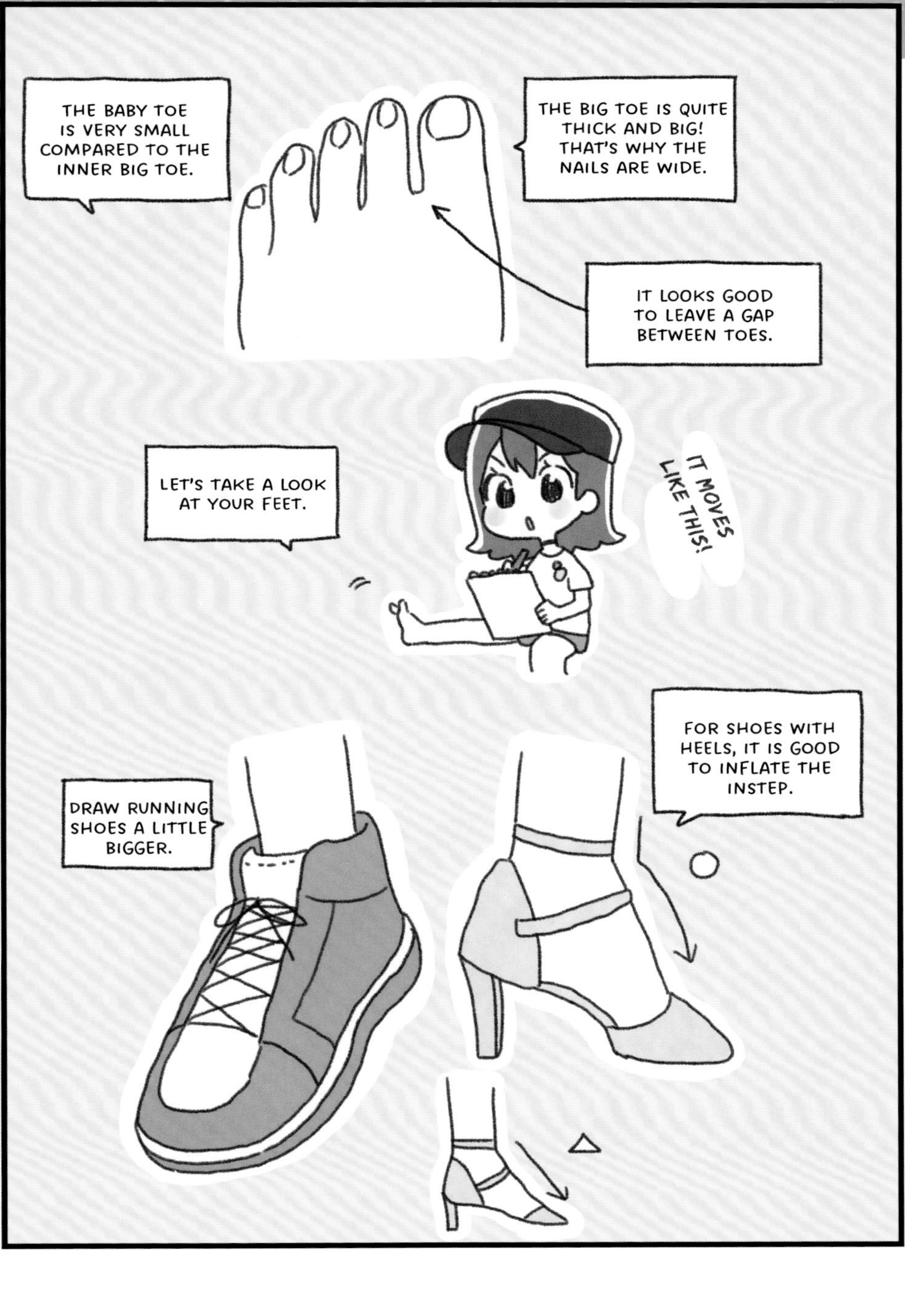
THE BABY TOE IS VERY SMALL COMPARED TO THE INNER BIG TOE.
THE BIG TOE IS QUITE THICK AND BIG! THAT'S WHY THE NAILS ARE WIDE.
IT LOOKS GOOD TO LEAVE A GAP BETWEEN TOES.
LET'S TAKE A LOOK AT YOUR FEET.
IT MOVES LIKE THIS!
FOR SHOES WITH HEELS, IT IS GOOD TO INFLATE THE INSTEP.
DRAW RUNNING SHOES A LITTLE BIGGER.

# DIFFERENT KINDS OF SHOES

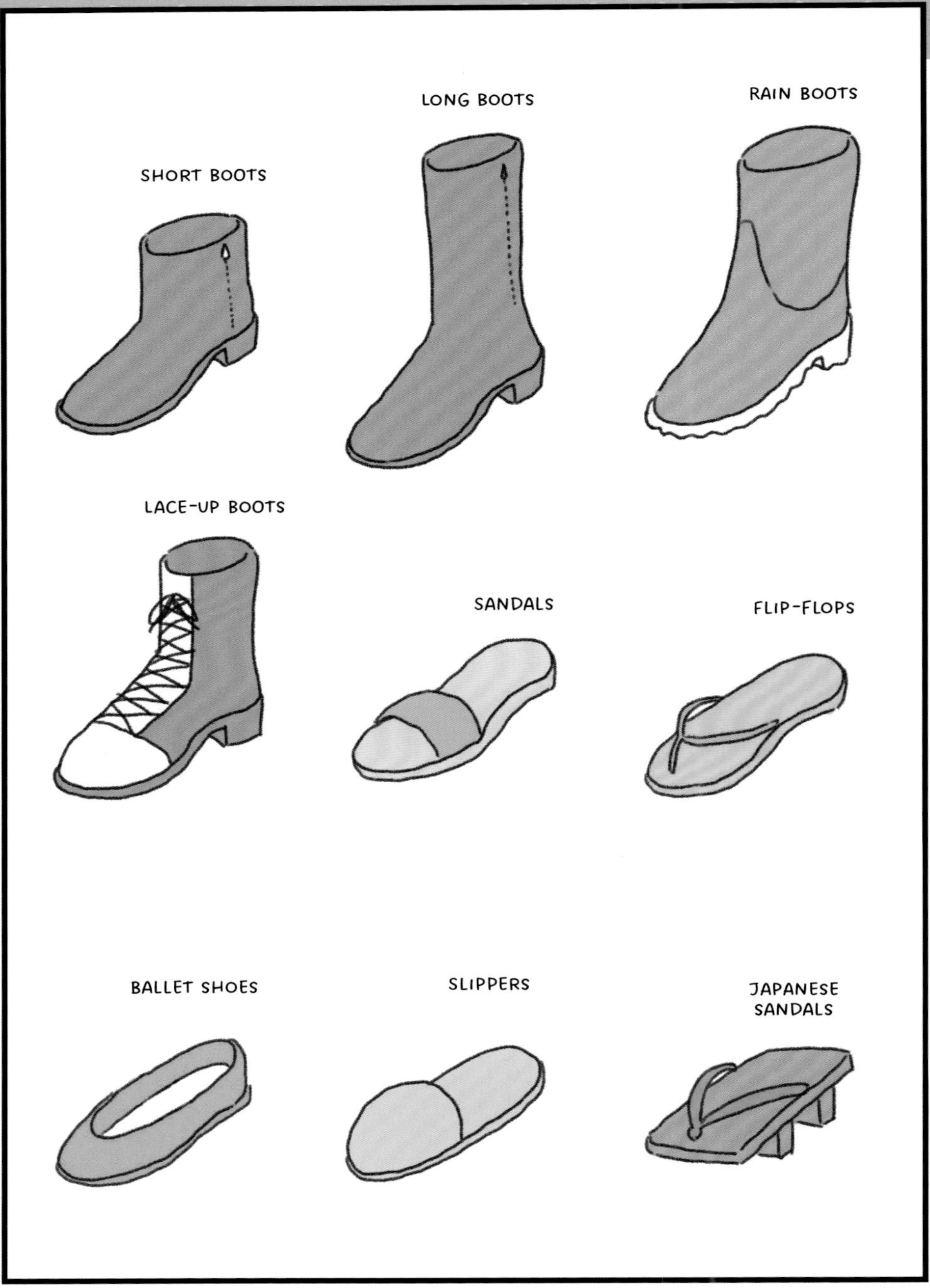
LONG BOOTS
RAIN BOOTS
SHORT BOOTS
LACE-UP BOOTS
SANDALS
FLIP-FLOPS
BALLET SHOES
SLIPPERS
JAPANESE SANDALS

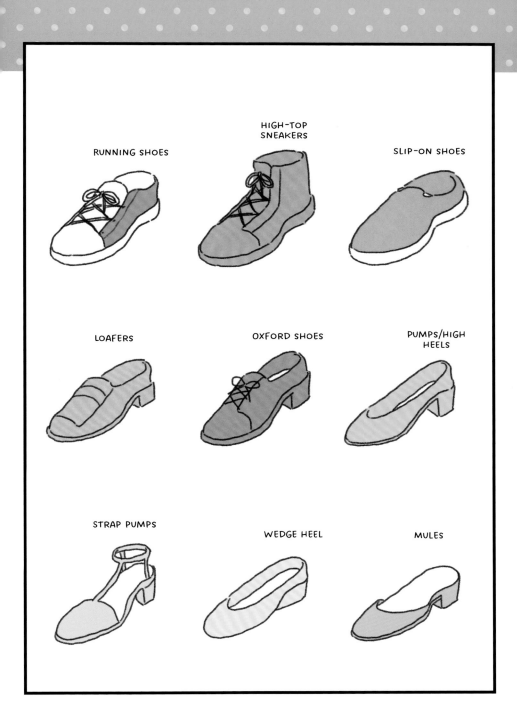

RUNNING SHOES

HIGH-TOP
SNEAKERS

SLIP-ON SHOES

LOAFERS

OXFORD SHOES

PUMPS/HIGH
HEELS

STRAP PUMPS

WEDGE HEEL

MULES

# DRAWING POSES FOR A LOWER BODY

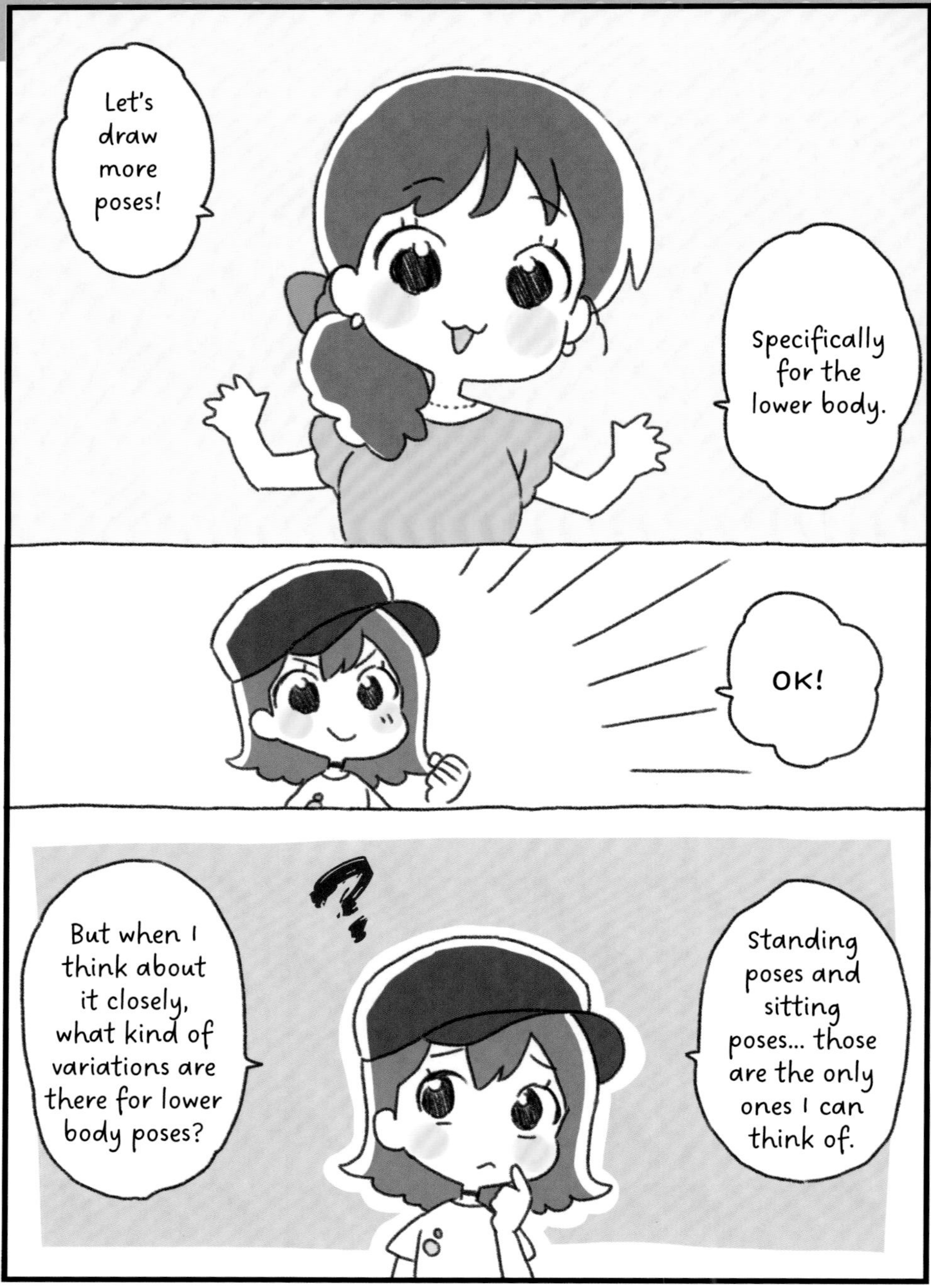
Let's draw more poses!
Specifically for the lower body.
OK!
But when I think about it closely, what kind of variations are there for lower body poses?
Standing poses and sitting poses... those are the only ones I can think of.

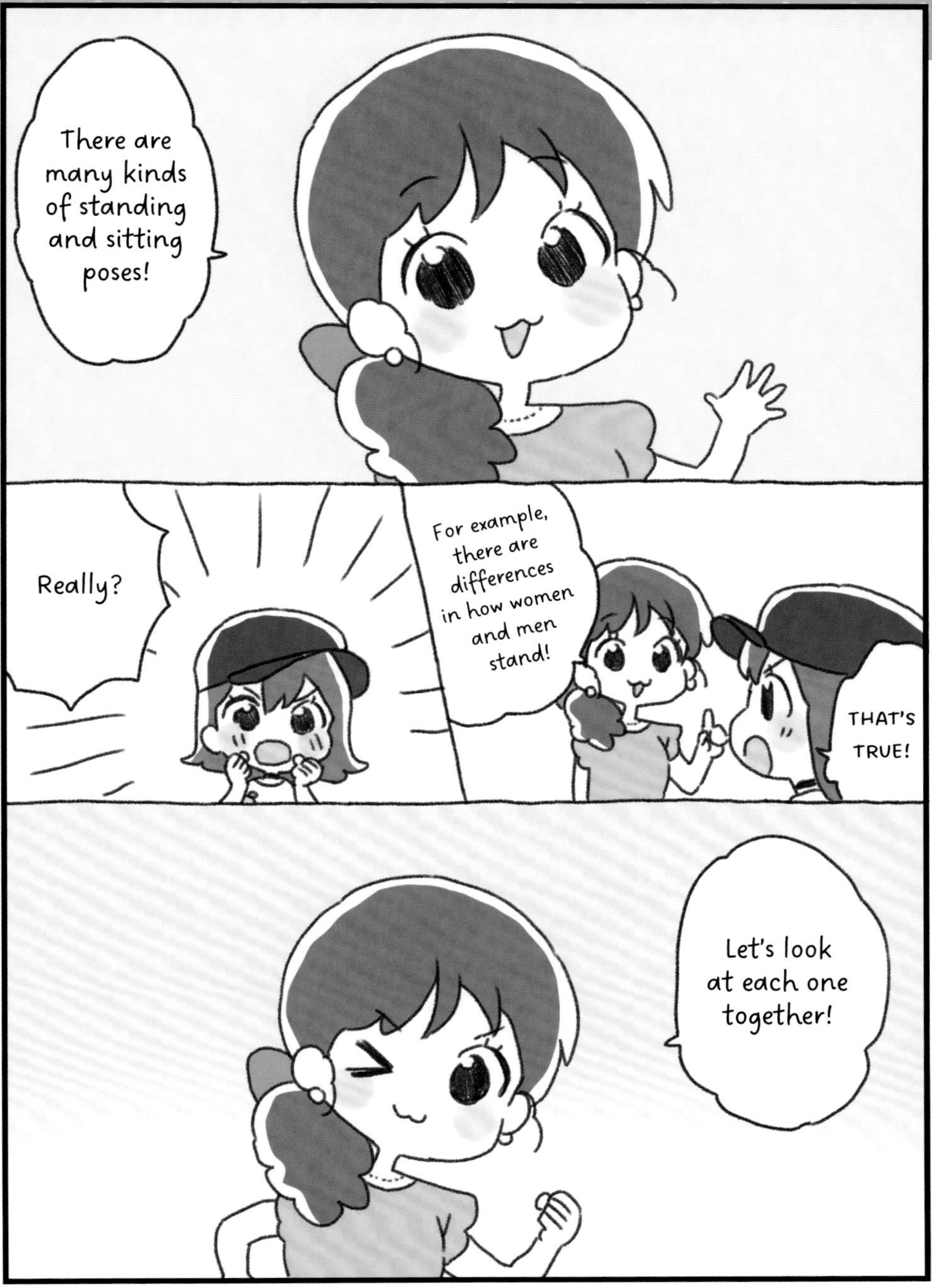
There are many kinds of standing and sitting poses!
Really?
For example, there are differences in how women and men stand!
THAT'S TRUE!
Let's look at each one together!

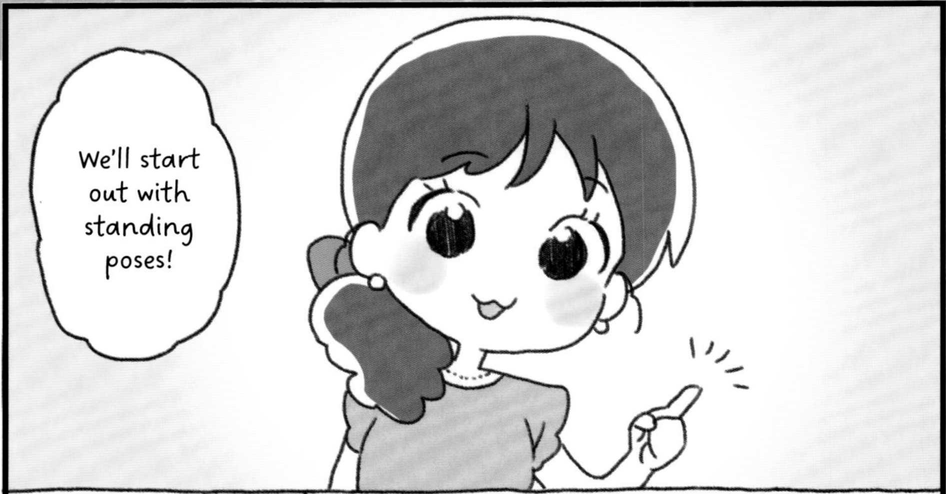
We'll start out with standing poses!

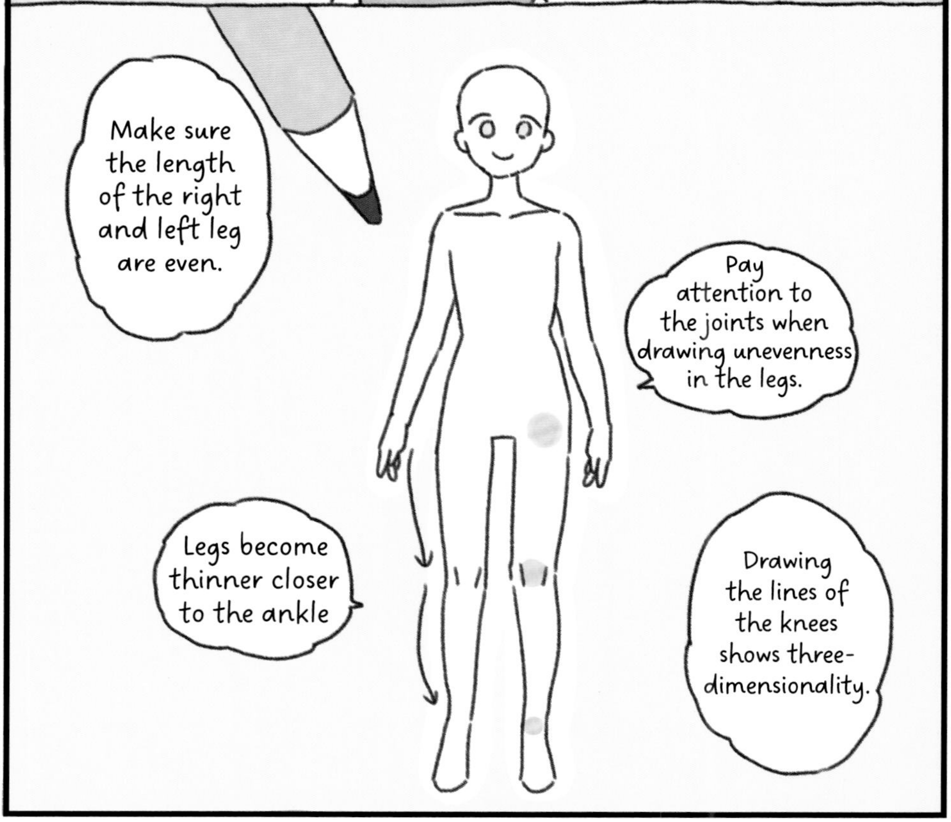
Make sure the length of the right and left leg are even.
Pay attention to the joints when drawing unevenness in the legs.
Legs become thinner closer to the ankle
Drawing the lines of the knees shows three-dimensionality.

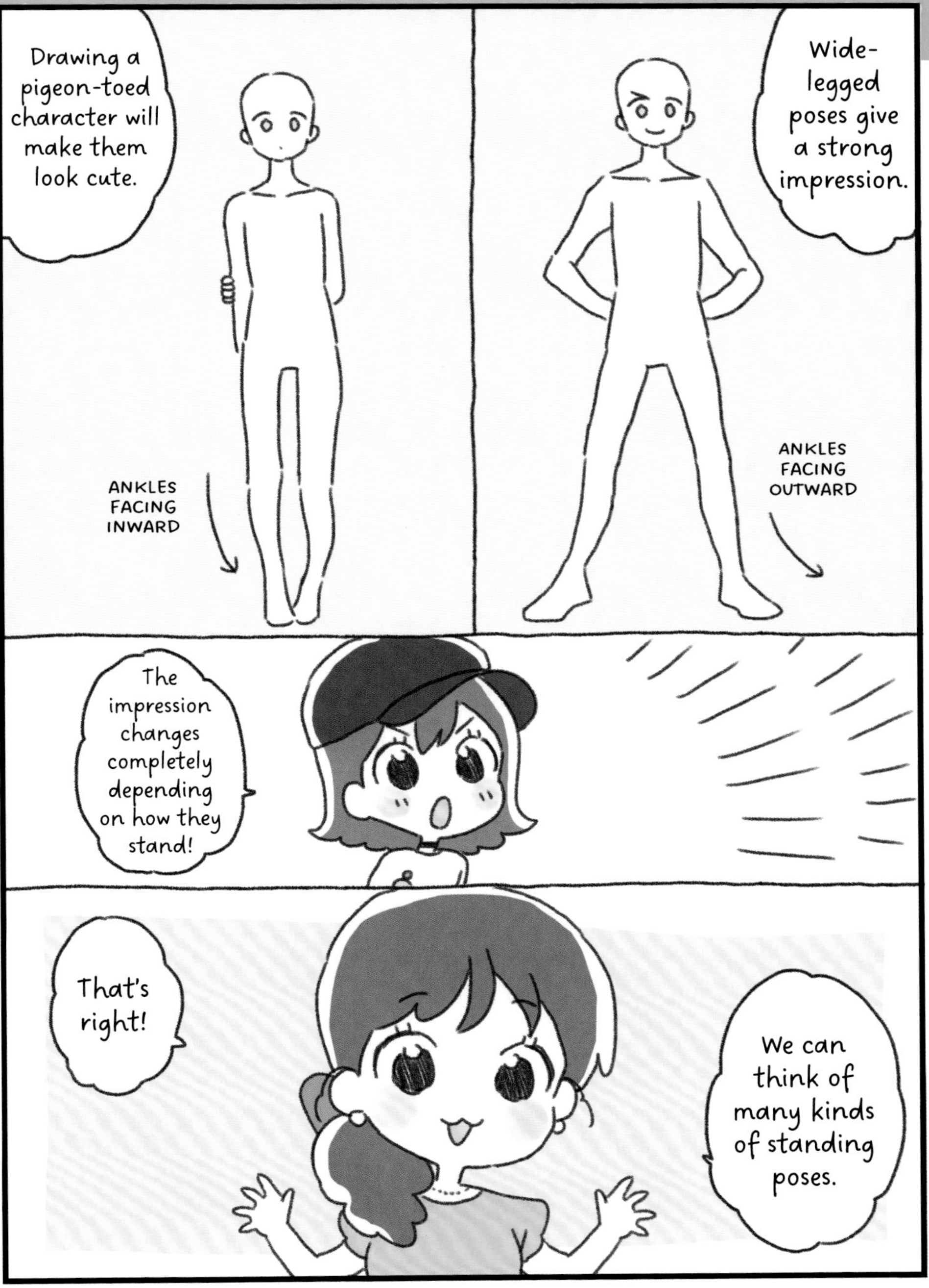
Drawing a pigeon-toed character will make them look cute.
ANKLES FACING INWARD
Wide-legged poses give a strong impression.
ANKLES FACING OUTWARD
The impression changes completely depending on how they stand!
That's right!
We can think of many kinds of standing poses.

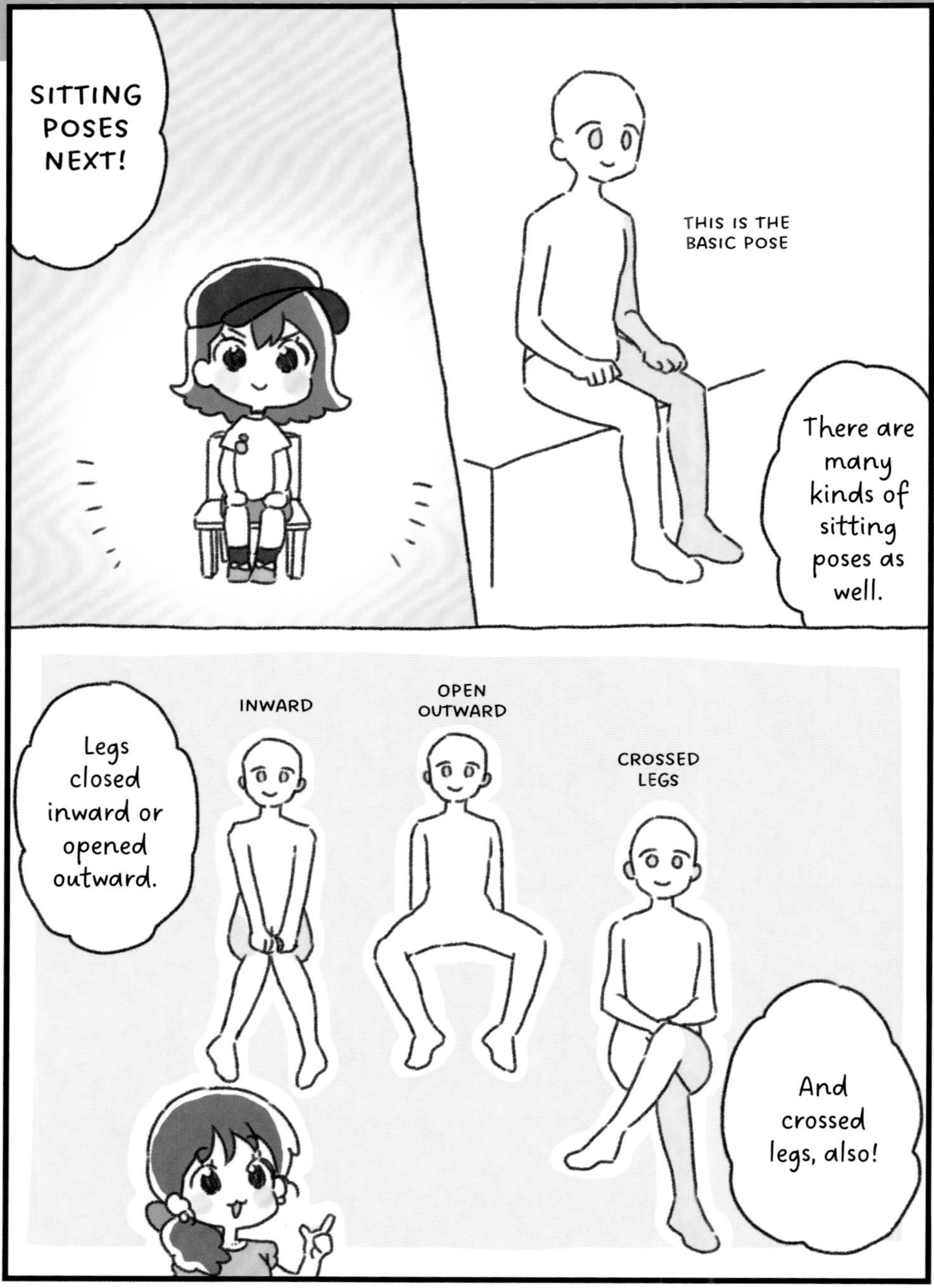
SITTING POSES NEXT!
THIS IS THE BASIC POSE
There are many kinds of sitting poses as well.
Legs closed inward or opened outward.
INWARD
OPEN OUTWARD
CROSSED LEGS
And crossed legs, also!

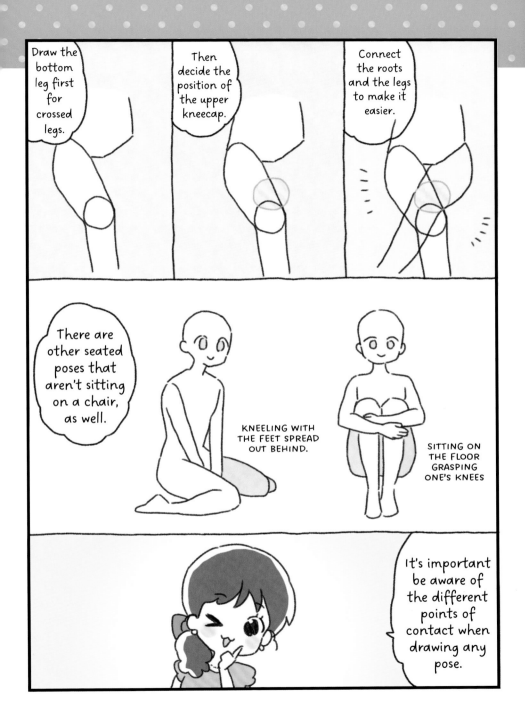

Draw the bottom leg first for crossed legs.

Then decide the position of the upper kneecap.

Connect the roots and the legs to make it easier.

There are other seated poses that aren't sitting on a chair, as well.

KNEELING WITH THE FEET SPREAD OUT BEHIND.

SITTING ON THE FLOOR GRASPING ONE'S KNEES

It's important be aware of the different points of contact when drawing any pose.

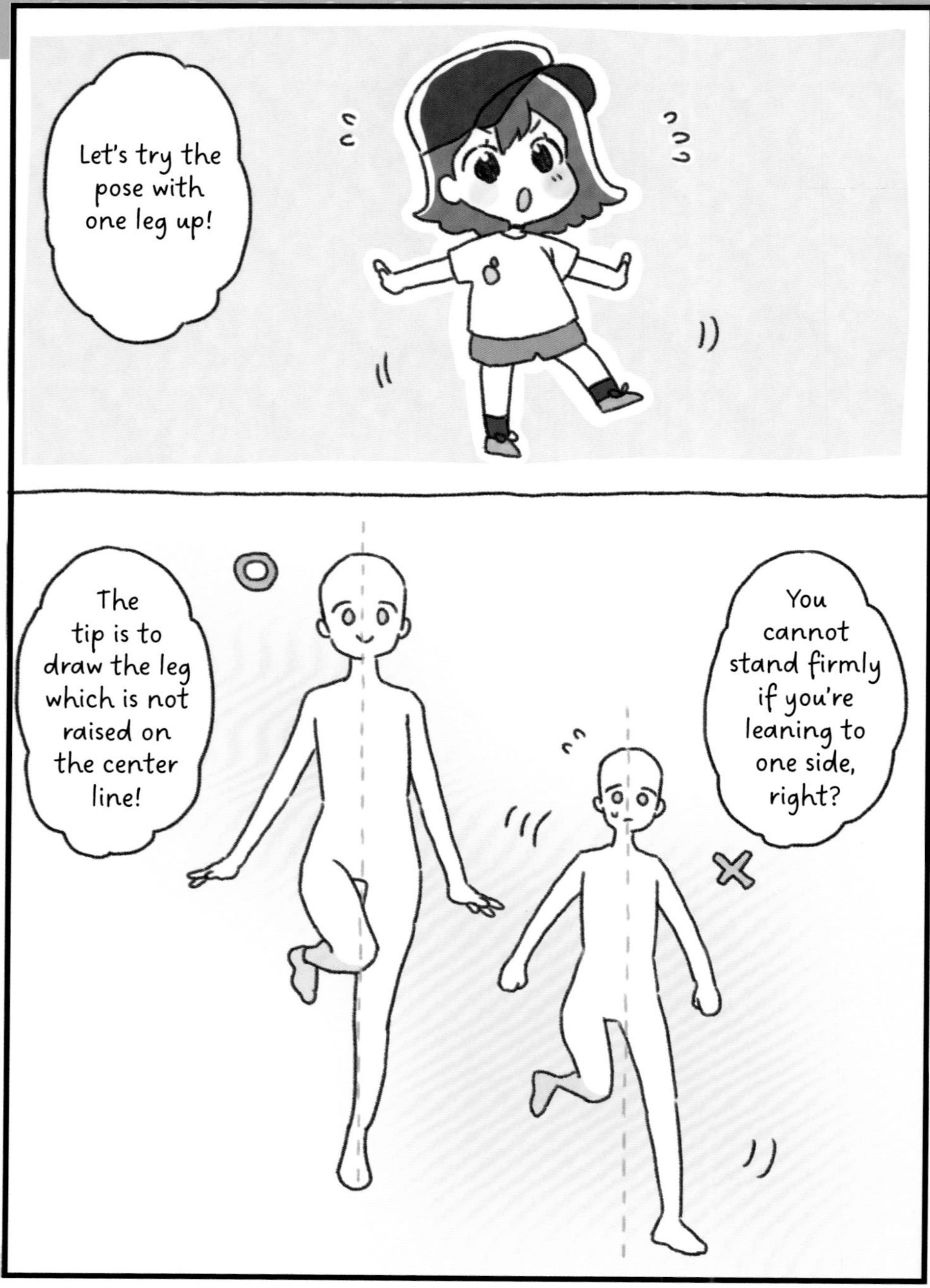
Let's try the pose with one leg up!
The tip is to draw the leg which is not raised on the center line!
You cannot stand firmly if you're leaning to one side, right?

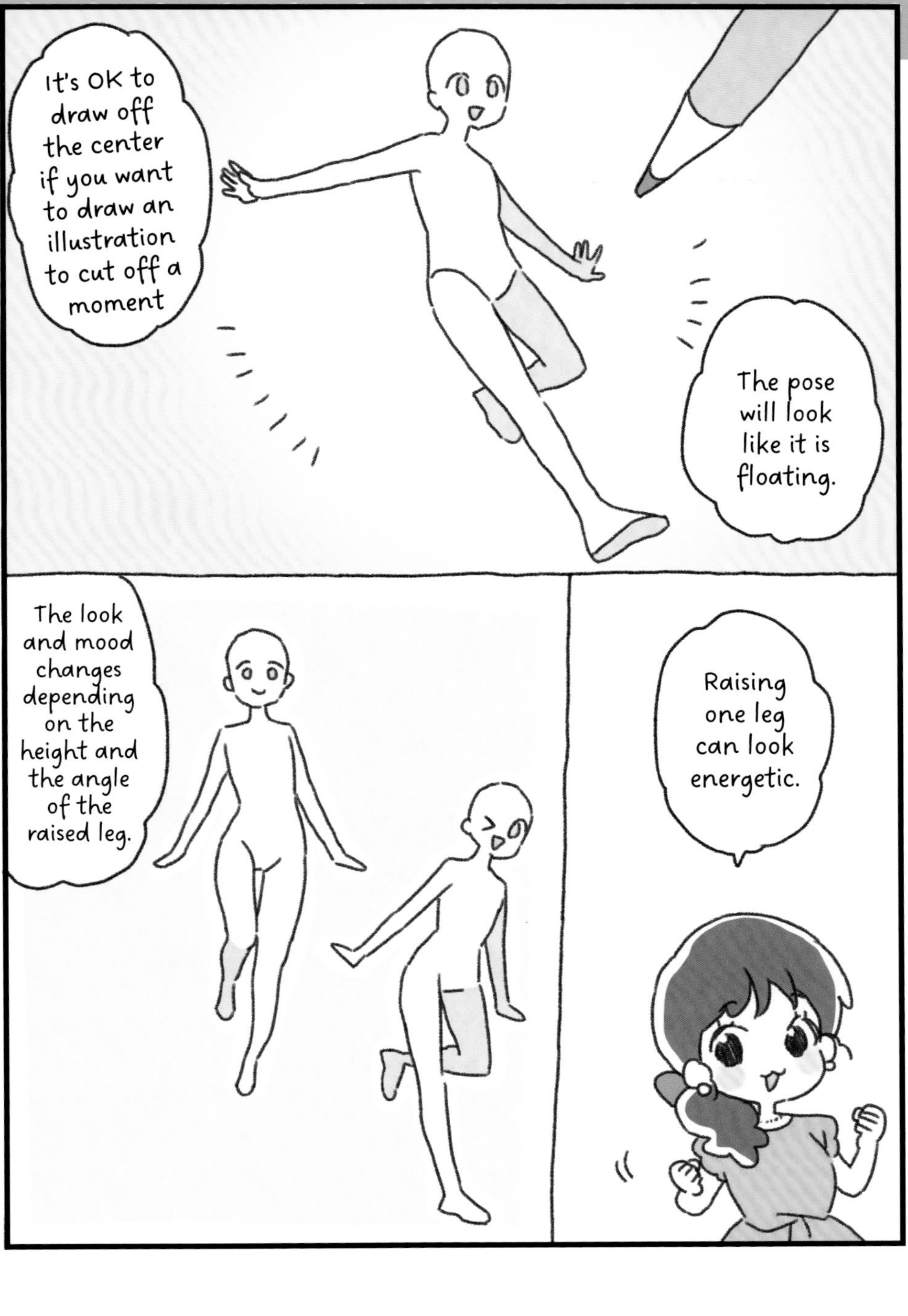
It's OK to draw off the center if you want to draw an illustration to cut off a moment
The pose will look like it is floating.
The look and mood changes depending on the height and the angle of the raised leg.
Raising one leg can look energetic.

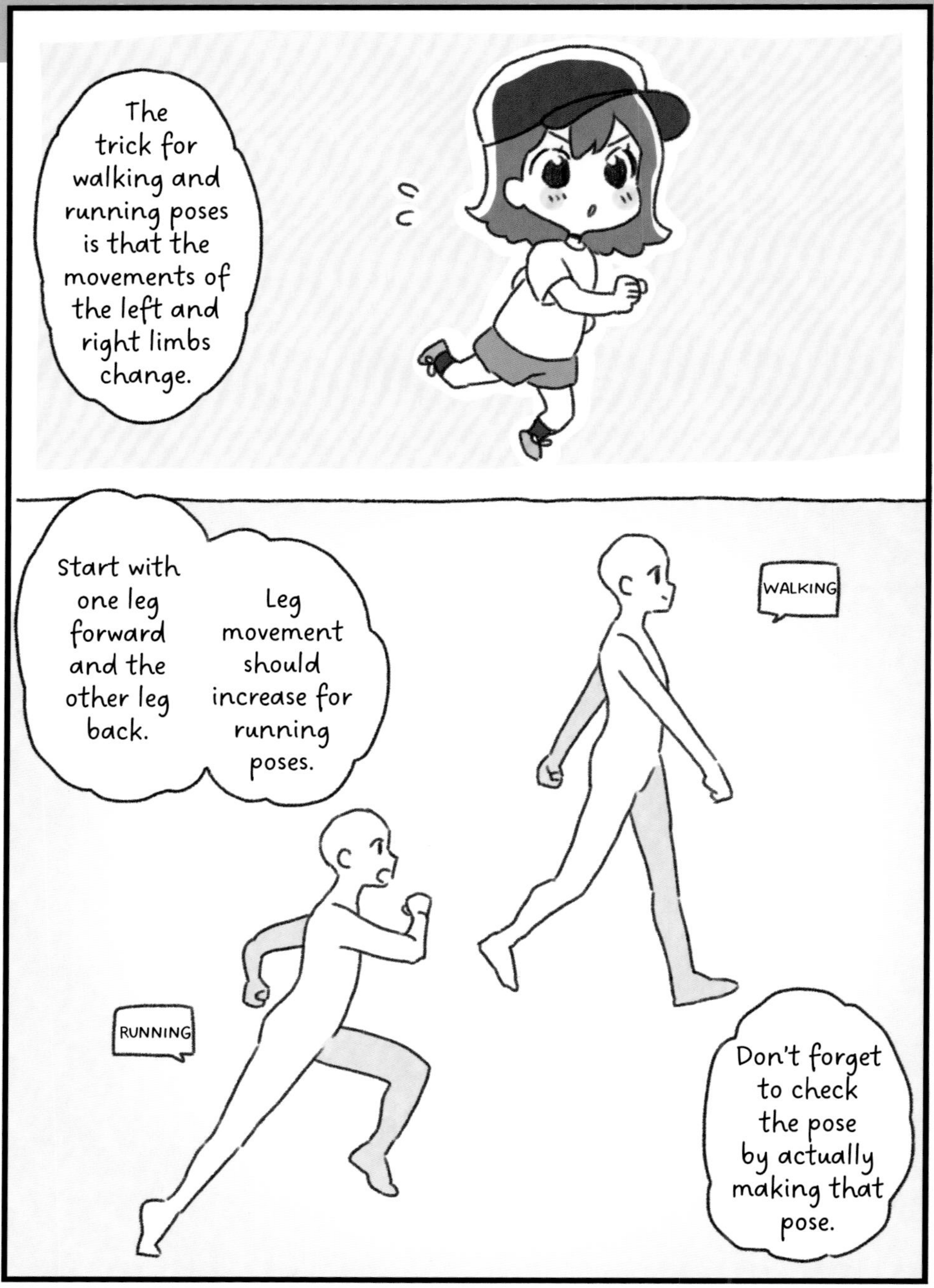
The trick for walking and running poses is that the movements of the left and right limbs change.
Start with one leg forward and the other leg back.
Leg movement should increase for running poses.
WALKING
RUNNING
Don't forget to check the pose by actually making that pose.

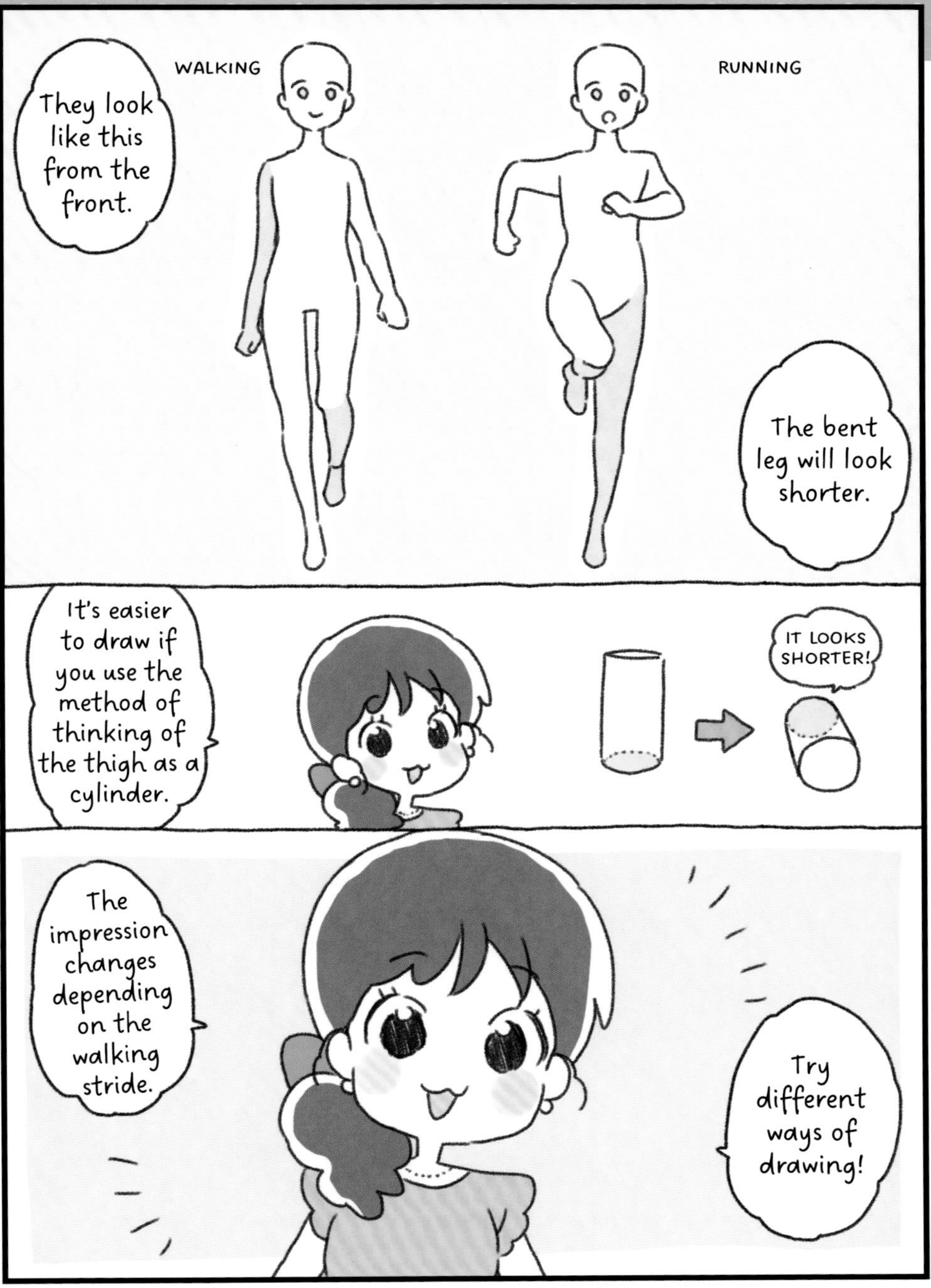
They look like this from the front.
WALKING
RUNNING
The bent leg will look shorter.
It's easier to draw if you use the method of thinking of the thigh as a cylinder.
IT LOOKS SHORTER!
The impression changes depending on the walking stride.
Try different ways of drawing!

# BALANCE OF THE WHOLE BODY IN PROFILE

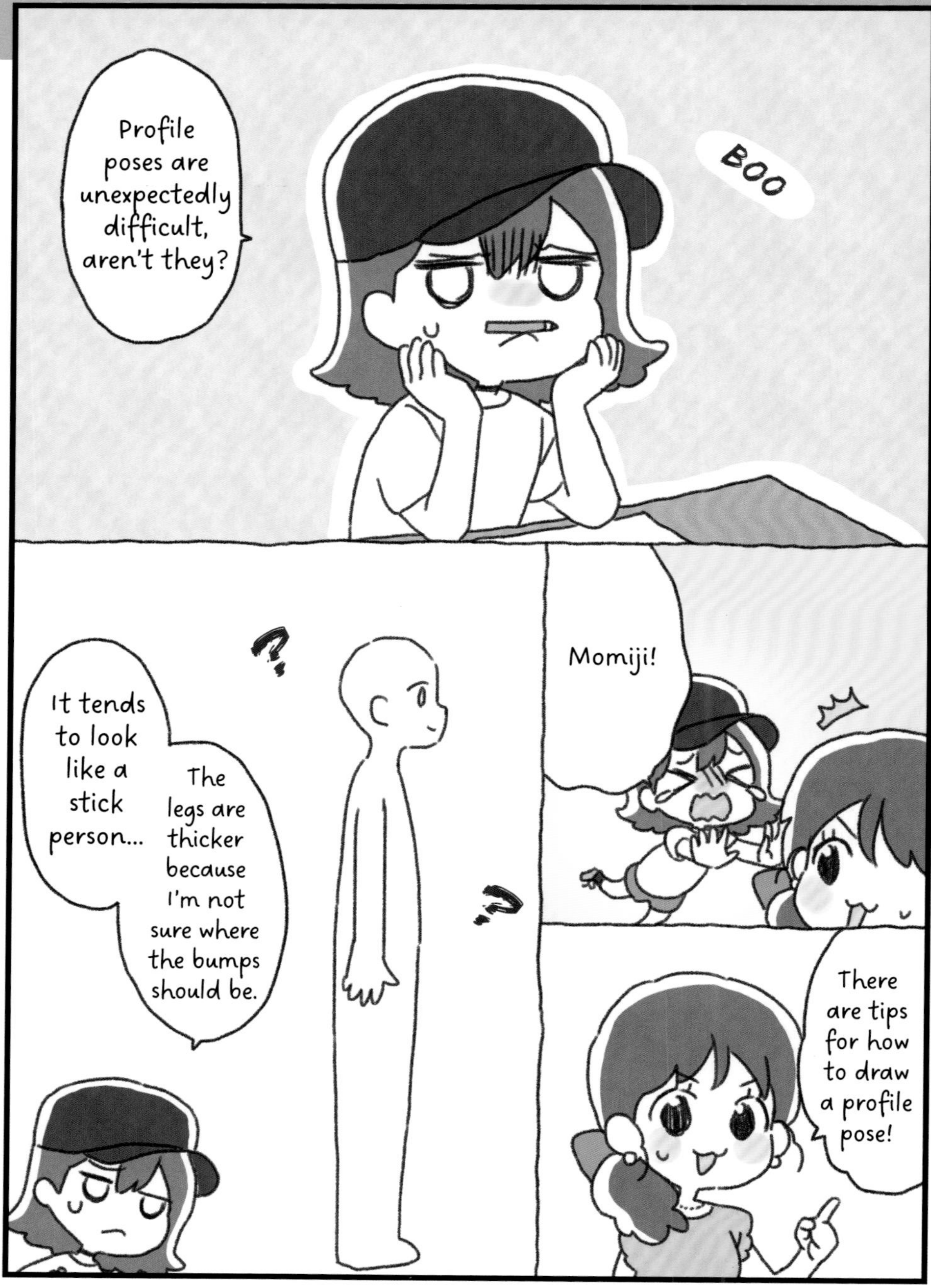
Profile poses are unexpectedly difficult, aren't they?
BOO
It tends to look like a stick person...
The legs are thicker because I'm not sure where the bumps should be.
Momiji!
There are tips for how to draw a profile pose!

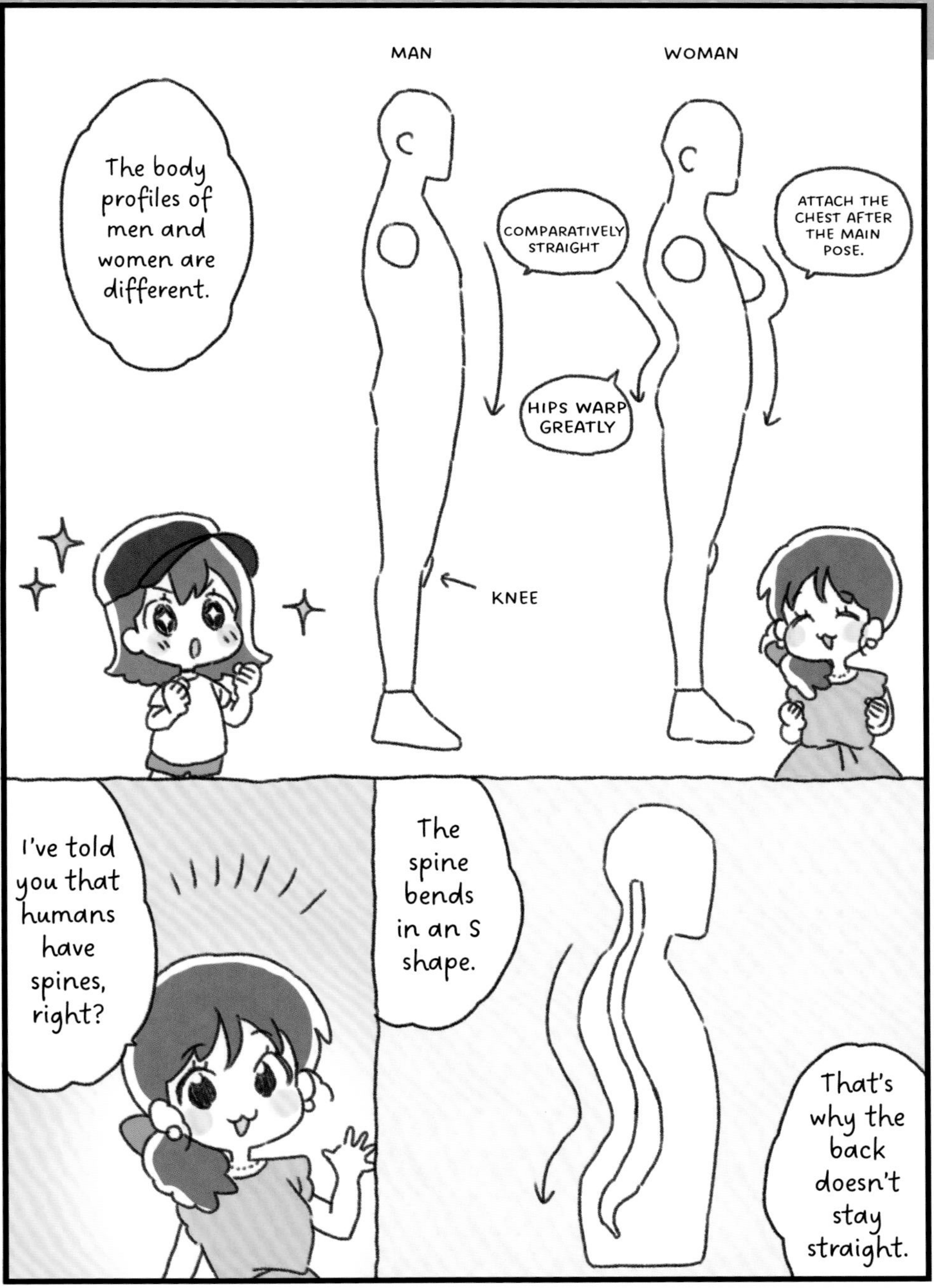
MAN
WOMAN
The body profiles of men and women are different.
COMPARATIVELY STRAIGHT
ATTACH THE CHEST AFTER THE MAIN POSE.
HIPS WARP GREATLY
KNEE
I've told you that humans have spines, right?
The spine bends in an S shape.
That's why the back doesn't stay straight.

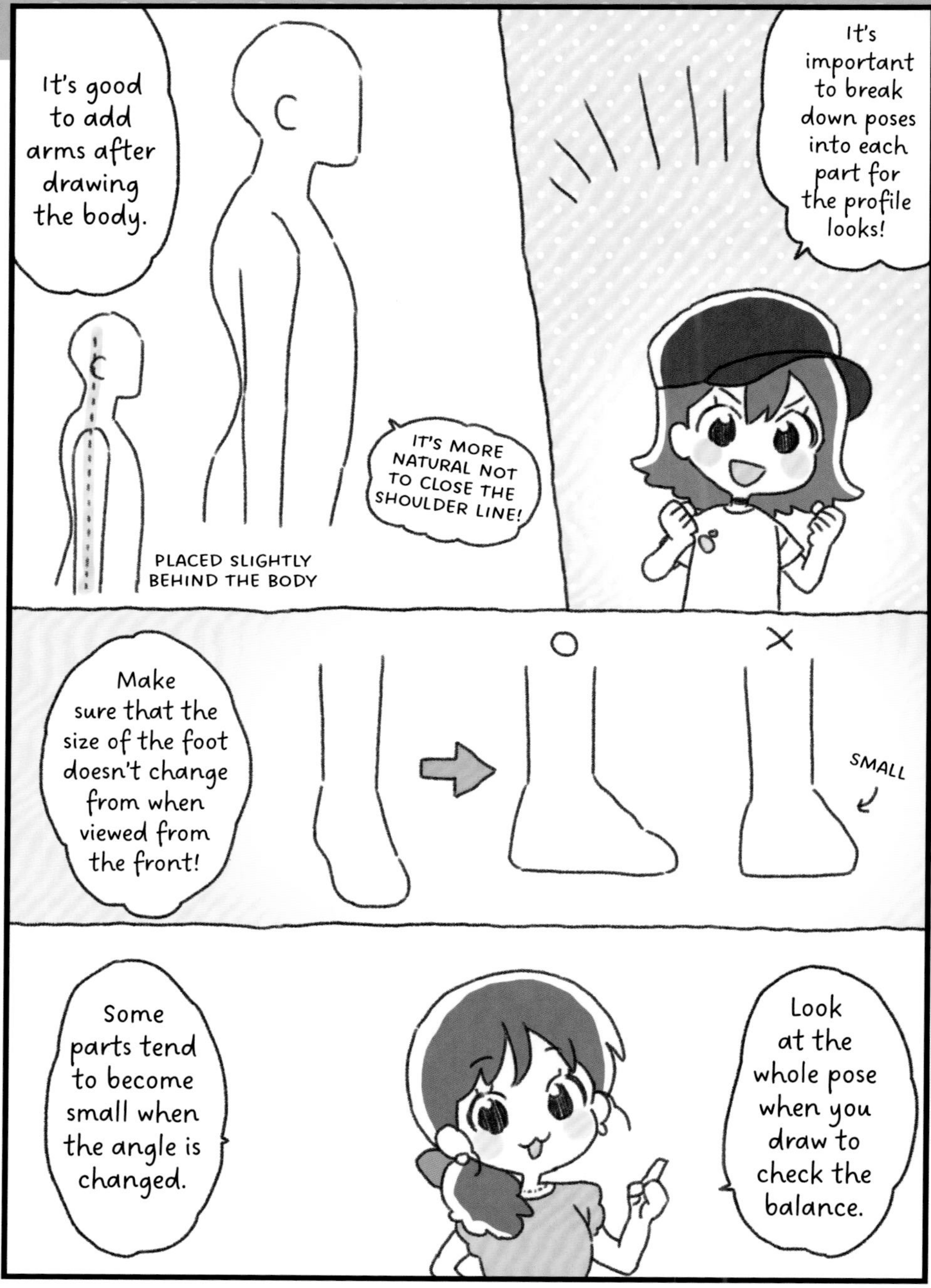
It's good to add arms after drawing the body.
Placed slightly behind the body
It's more natural not to close the shoulder line!
It's important to break down poses into each part for the profile looks!
Make sure that the size of the foot doesn't change from when viewed from the front!
Small
Some parts tend to become small when the angle is changed.
Look at the whole pose when you draw to check the balance.

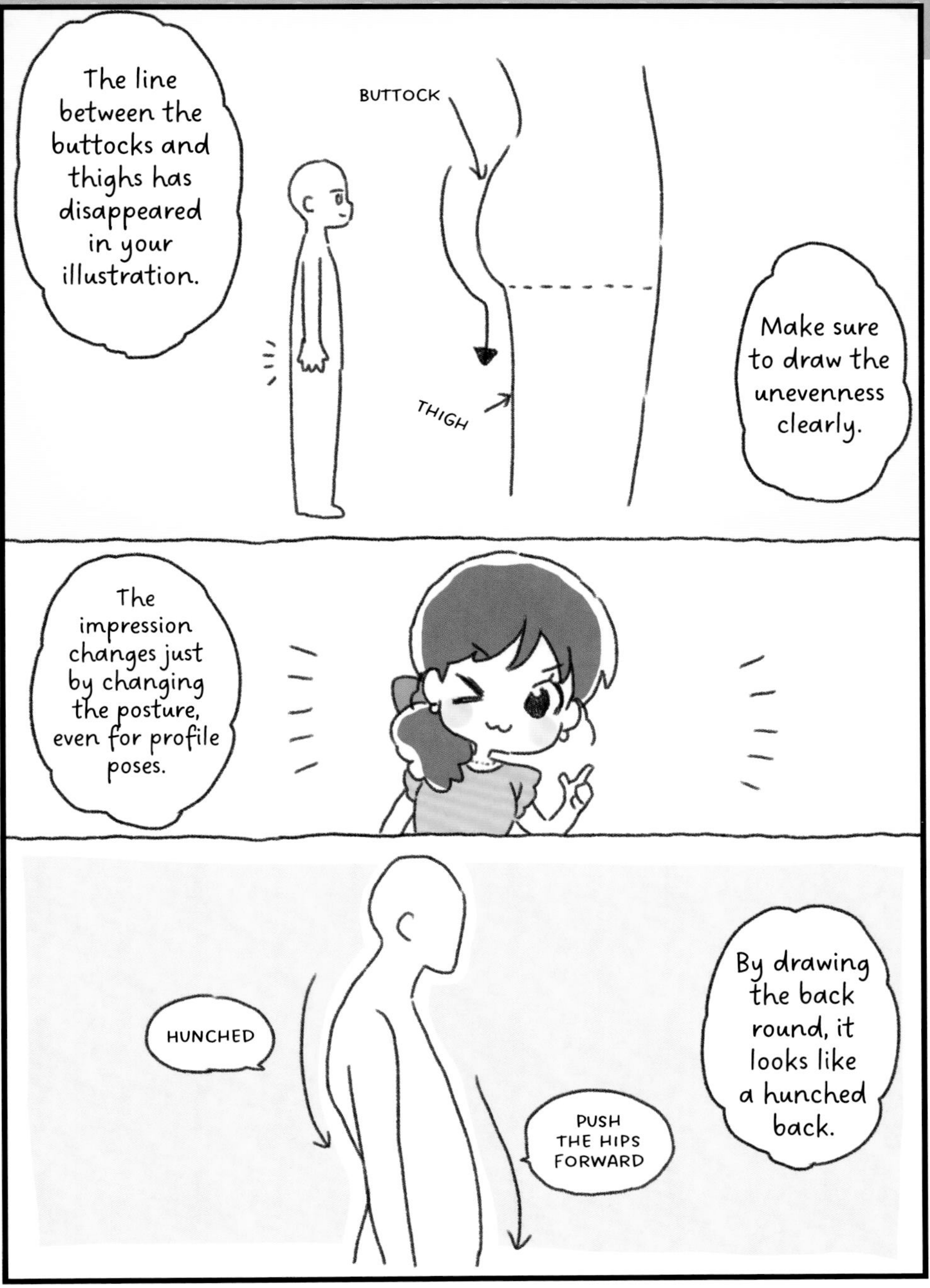
The line between the buttocks and thighs has disappeared in your illustration.
BUTTOCK
THIGH
Make sure to draw the unevenness clearly.
The impression changes just by changing the posture, even for profile poses.
HUNCHED
PUSH THE HIPS FORWARD
By drawing the back round, it looks like a hunched back.

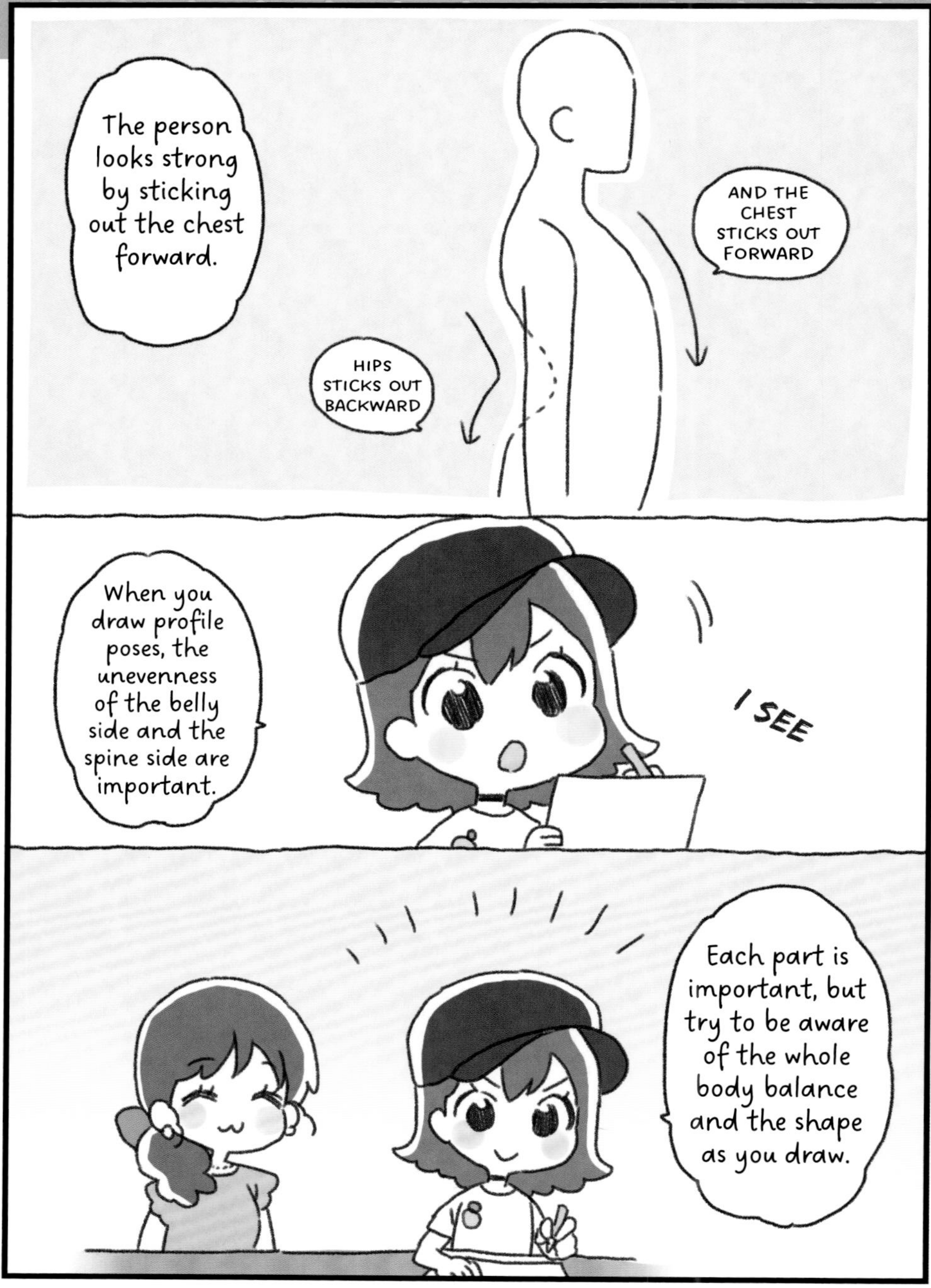
The person looks strong by sticking out the chest forward.
AND THE CHEST STICKS OUT FORWARD
HIPS STICKS OUT BACKWARD
When you draw profile poses, the unevenness of the belly side and the spine side are important.
I SEE
Each part is important, but try to be aware of the whole body balance and the shape as you draw.

## — SUMMARY —

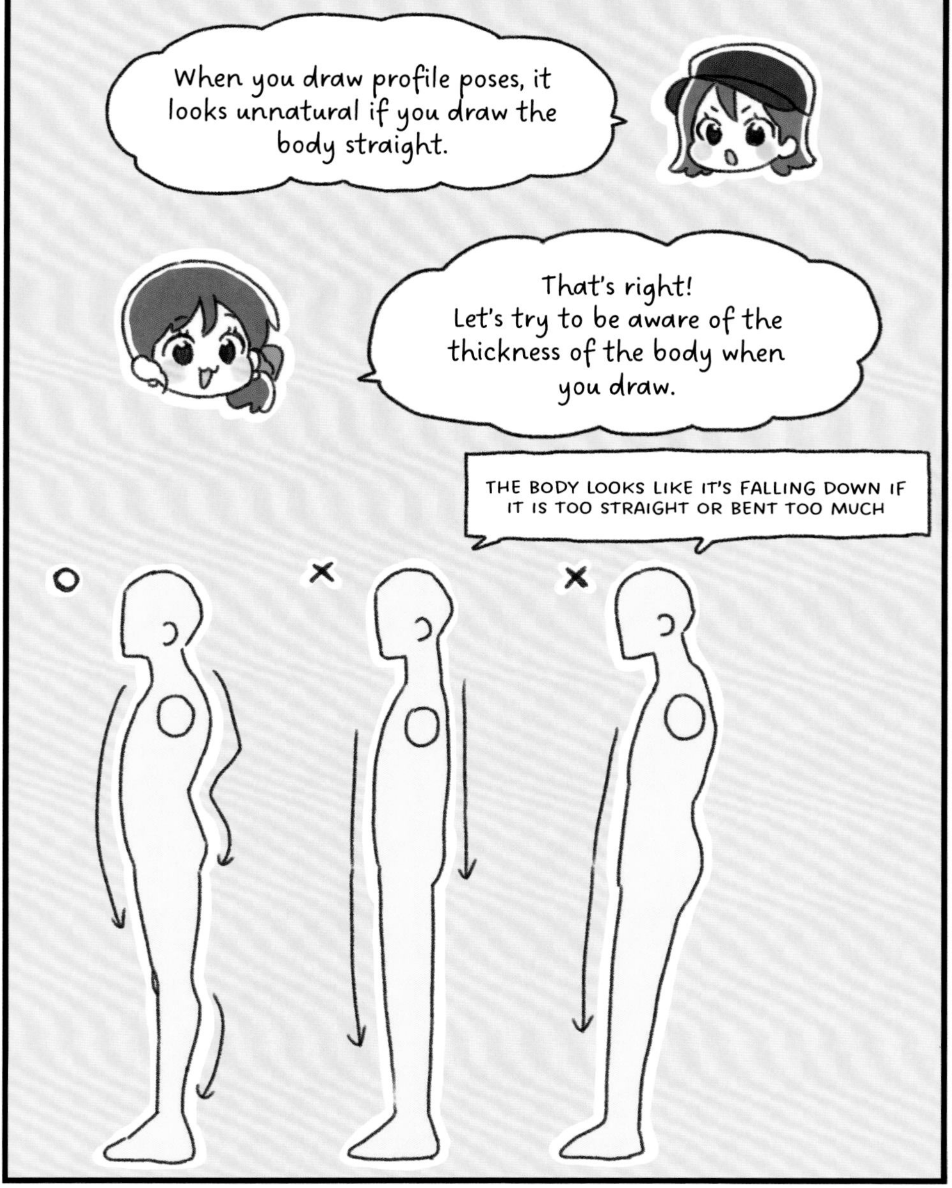
When you draw profile poses, it looks unnatural if you draw the body straight.
That's right! Let's try to be aware of the thickness of the body when you draw.
THE BODY LOOKS LIKE IT'S FALLING DOWN IF IT IS TOO STRAIGHT OR BENT TOO MUCH
O
×
×

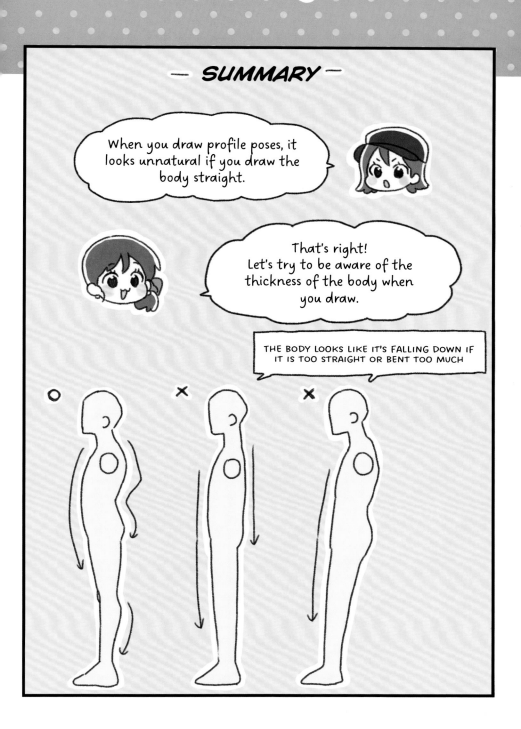

# MOMIJI'S
~ *TIP* ~
## TIPS FOR USING REFERENCE MATERIALS

I've understood that it is important to look for reference materials, but I wonder how I should collect them or check them?

I recommend that you take pictures or look at magazines for inspiration!

## TAKE PICTURES

TRY A POSE BY YOURSELF AND TAKE PICTURES!
IT'S OK TO TRACE IT, AS WELL!

CLICK

IT'S EASIER TO CREATE A SAMPLE BY TAKING THE PICTURE WITH A SIMILAR ANGLE TO THE POSE OF THE ILLUSTRATION THAT YOU WANT TO DRAW.

TAKE A LOOK IN THE MIRROR
SO YOU CAN SEE THE PARTS THAT
YOU CAN'T NORMALLY SEE.

DEPENDING ON THE INSPIRATION YOU NEED, LOOK
FOR CLOTHES ADS, FASHION MAGAZINES, AND
ONLINE FOR MATERIAL.

REFER TO ITEMS YOU OWN.
CHECK BY ACTUALLY TOUCHING THEM.
THIS CAN BE REFLECTED IN THE
ILLUSTRATION.

THE FABRIC OF THIS HOODIE IS THICK.

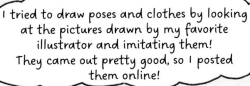

I tried to draw poses and clothes by looking at the pictures drawn by my favorite illustrator and imitating them! They came out pretty good, so I posted them online!

Wait, Lemon! You cannot do that!

PEOPLE'S ART, LIKE ILLUSTRATIONS AND PHOTOGRAPHS, ARE COPYRIGHTED! IF YOU IMITATE SOMEONE ELSE'S WORK, YOU CAN KEEP THE ART FOR PRACTICE, BUT IT COULD BE A BIG PROBLEM IF YOU SHARE IT ONLINE.

I DIDN'T MEAN TO

# THE POSE I'VE DRAWN LOOKS A LITTLE STRANGE

# THINK AGAIN ABOUT THE POSE YOU WANT TO DRAW

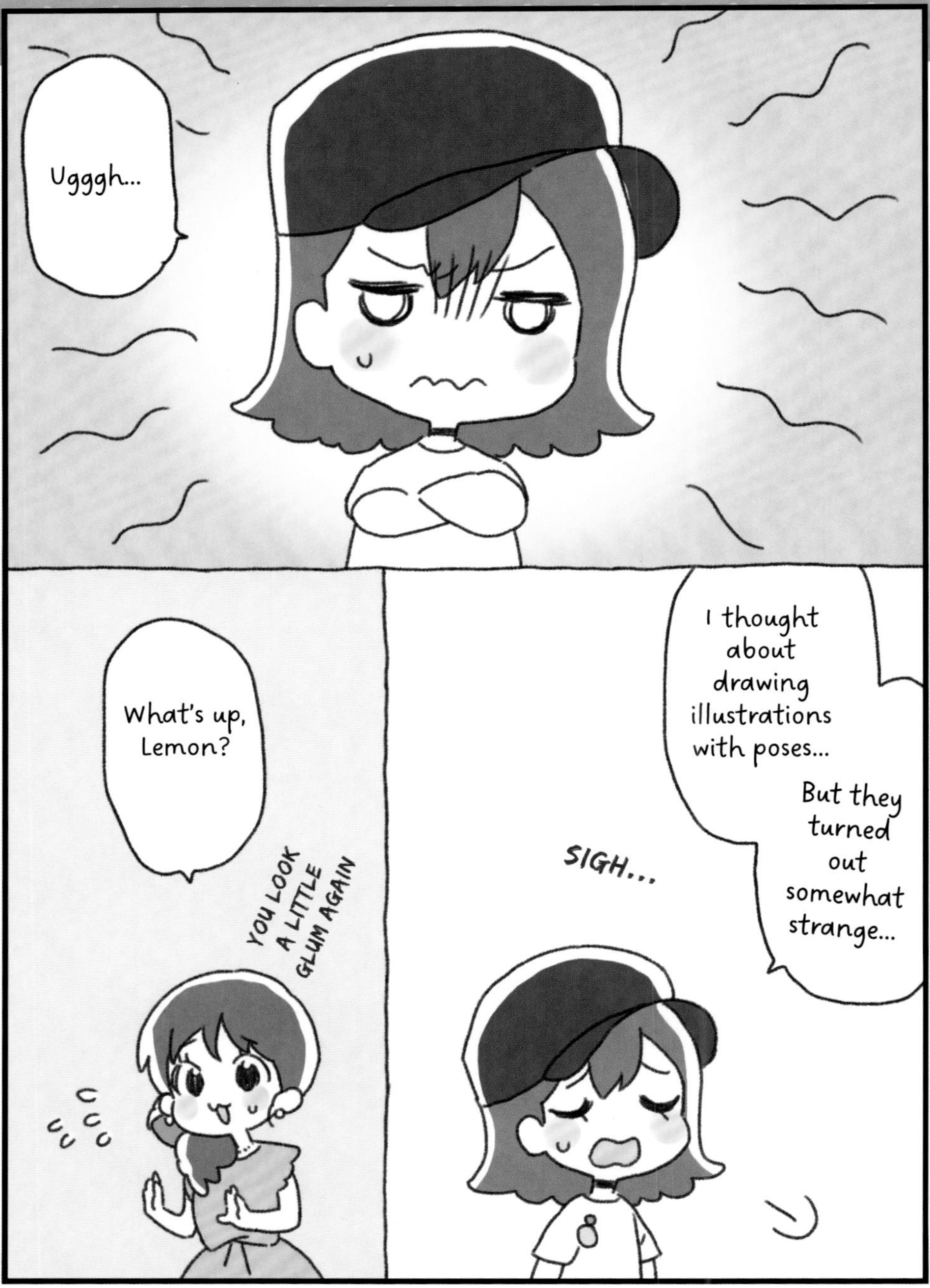
Ugggh...
What's up, Lemon?
YOU LOOK A LITTLE GLUM AGAIN
I thought about drawing illustrations with poses...
But they turned out somewhat strange...
SIGH...

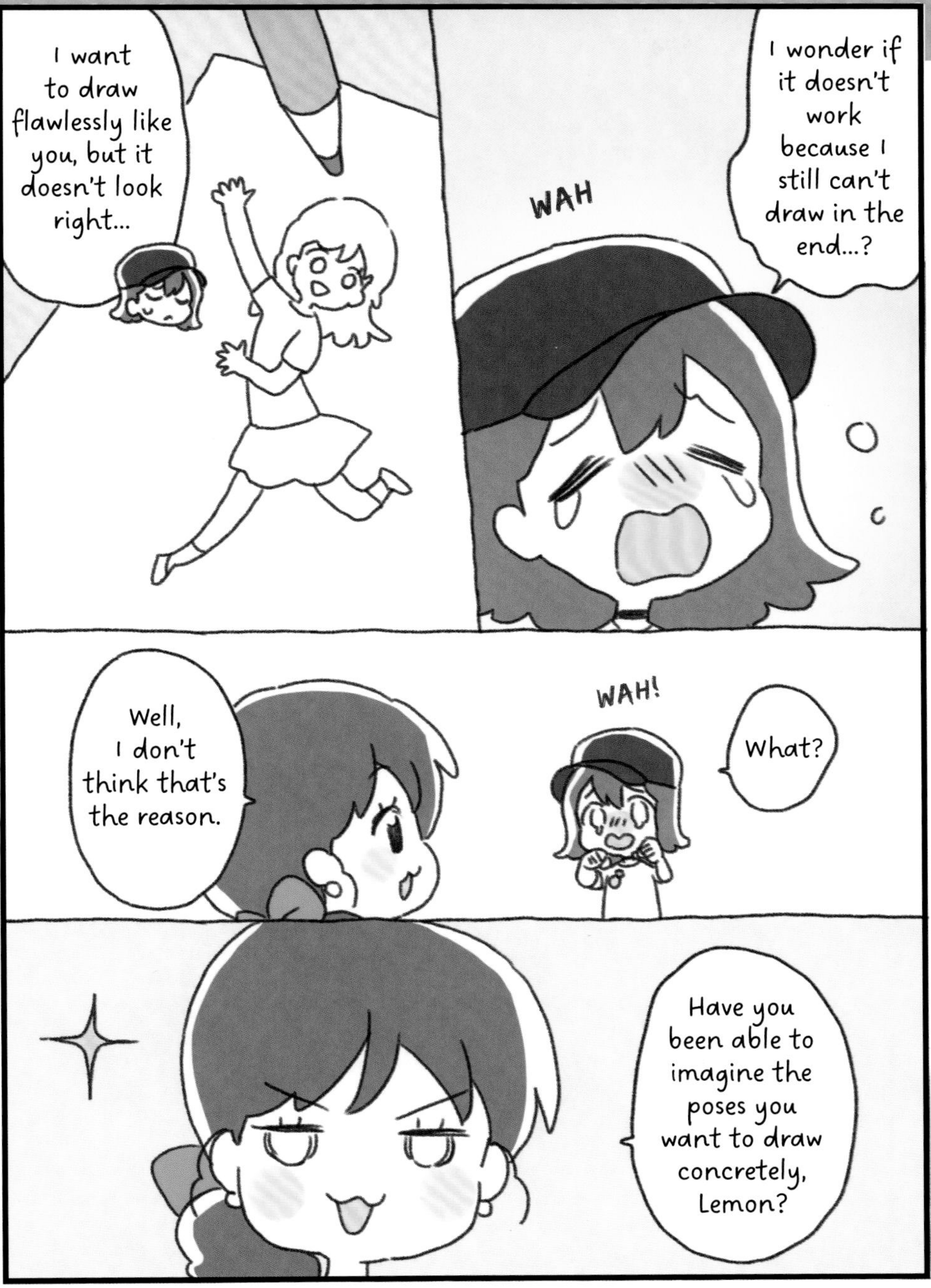
I wonder if it doesn't work because I still can't draw in the end...?
WAH
I want to draw flawlessly like you, but it doesn't look right...
What?
WAH!
Well, I don't think that's the reason.
Have you been able to imagine the poses you want to draw concretely, Lemon?

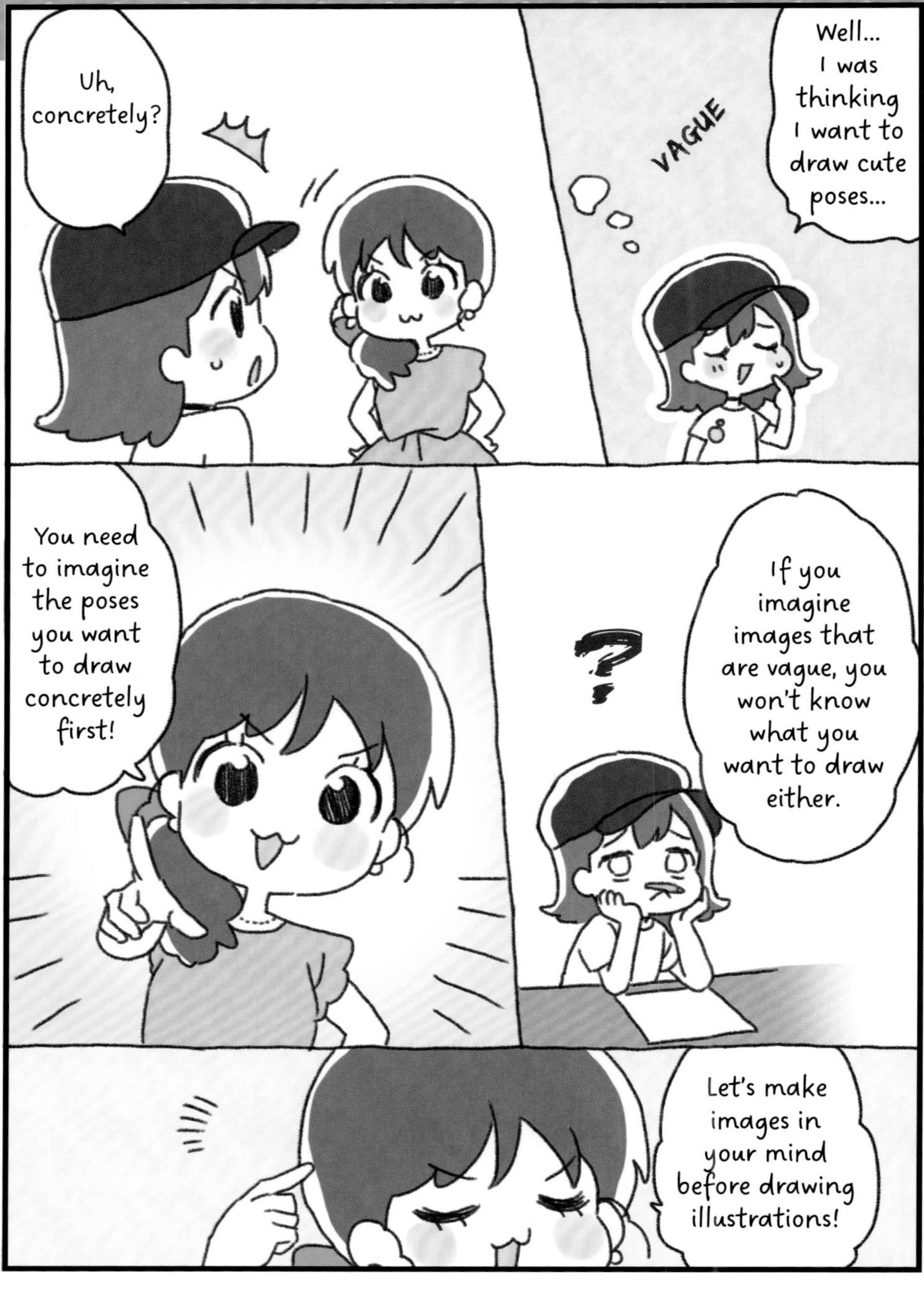

Uh, concretely?
Well... I was thinking I want to draw cute poses...
VAGUE
You need to imagine the poses you want to draw concretely first!
If you imagine images that are vague, you won't know what you want to draw either.
Let's make images in your mind before drawing illustrations!

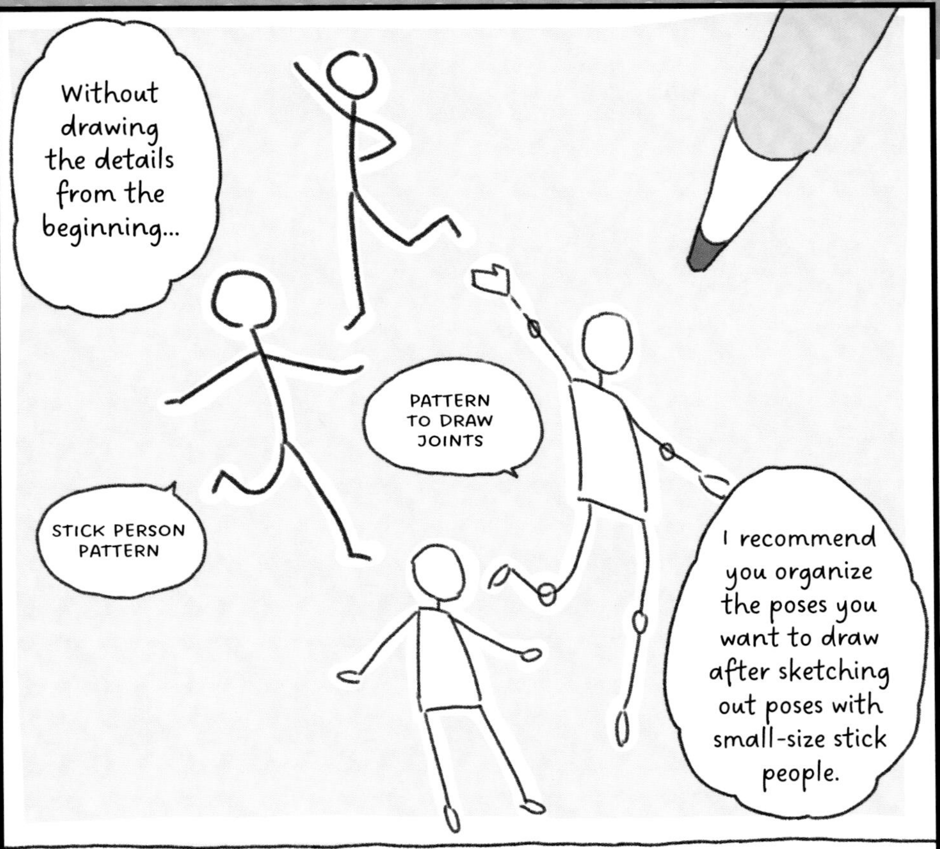
Without drawing the details from the beginning...
PATTERN TO DRAW JOINTS
STICK PERSON PATTERN
I recommend you organize the poses you want to draw after sketching out poses with small-size stick people.

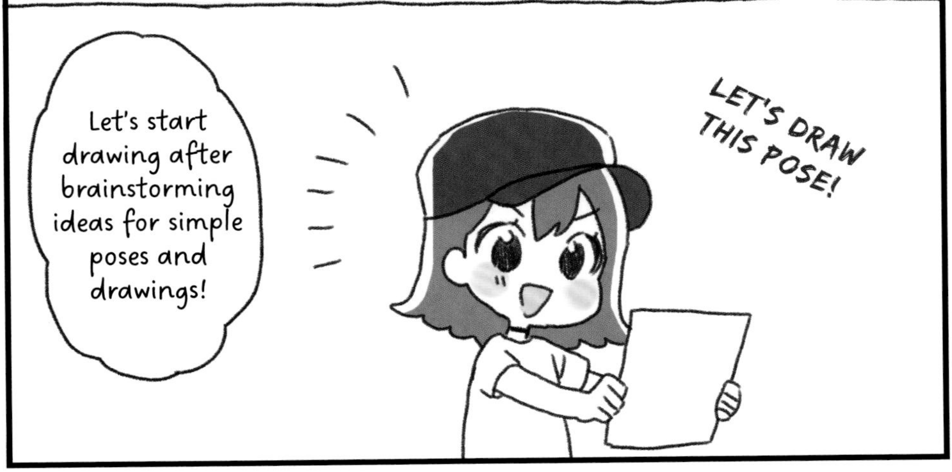
Let's start drawing after brainstorming ideas for simple poses and drawings!
LET'S DRAW THIS POSE!

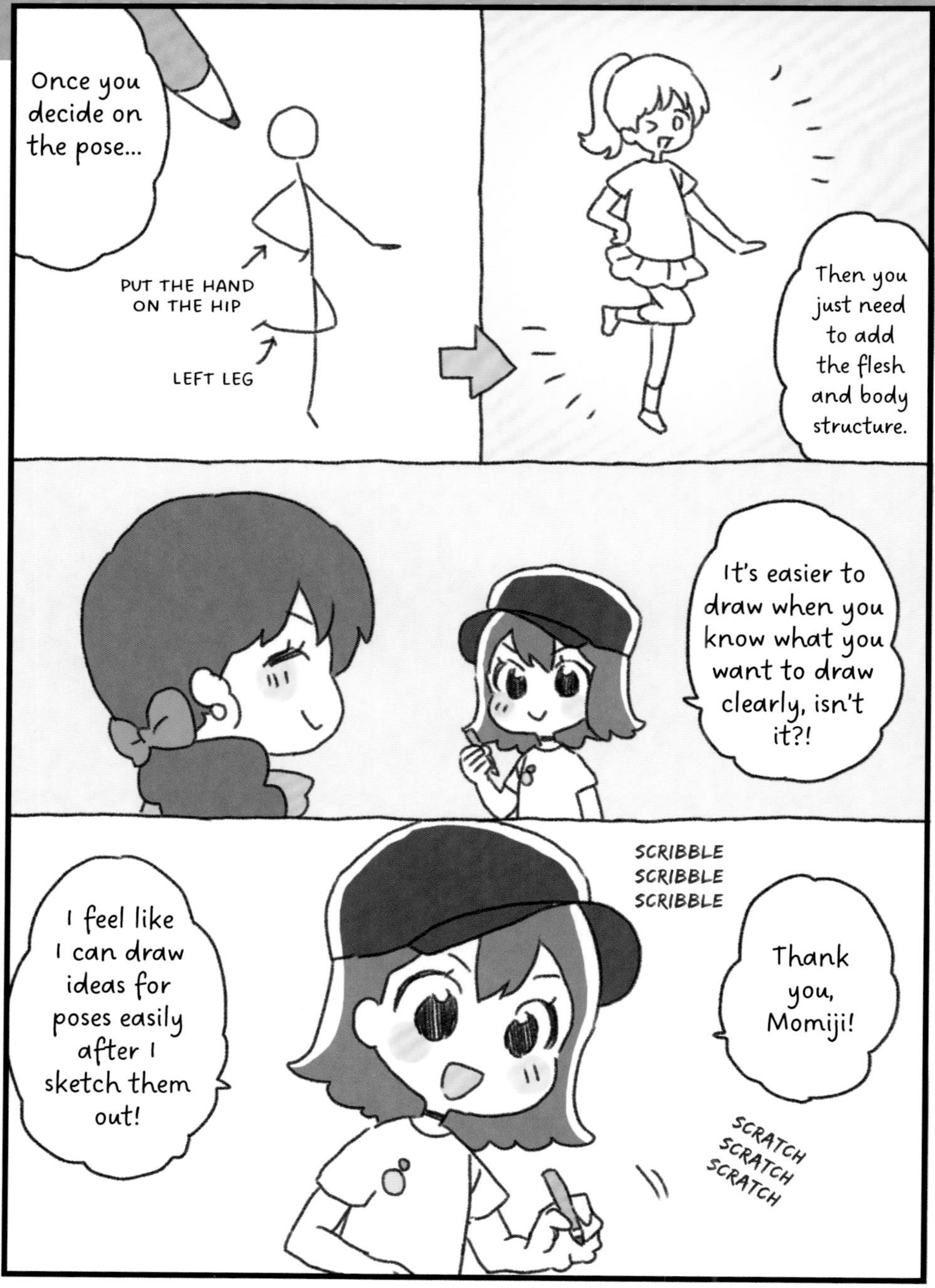
Once you decide on the pose...
PUT THE HAND ON THE HIP
LEFT LEG
Then you just need to add the flesh and body structure.
It's easier to draw when you know what you want to draw clearly, isn't it?!
SCRIBBLE SCRIBBLE SCRIBBLE
Thank you, Momiji!
I feel like I can draw ideas for poses easily after I sketch them out!
SCRATCH SCRATCH SCRATCH

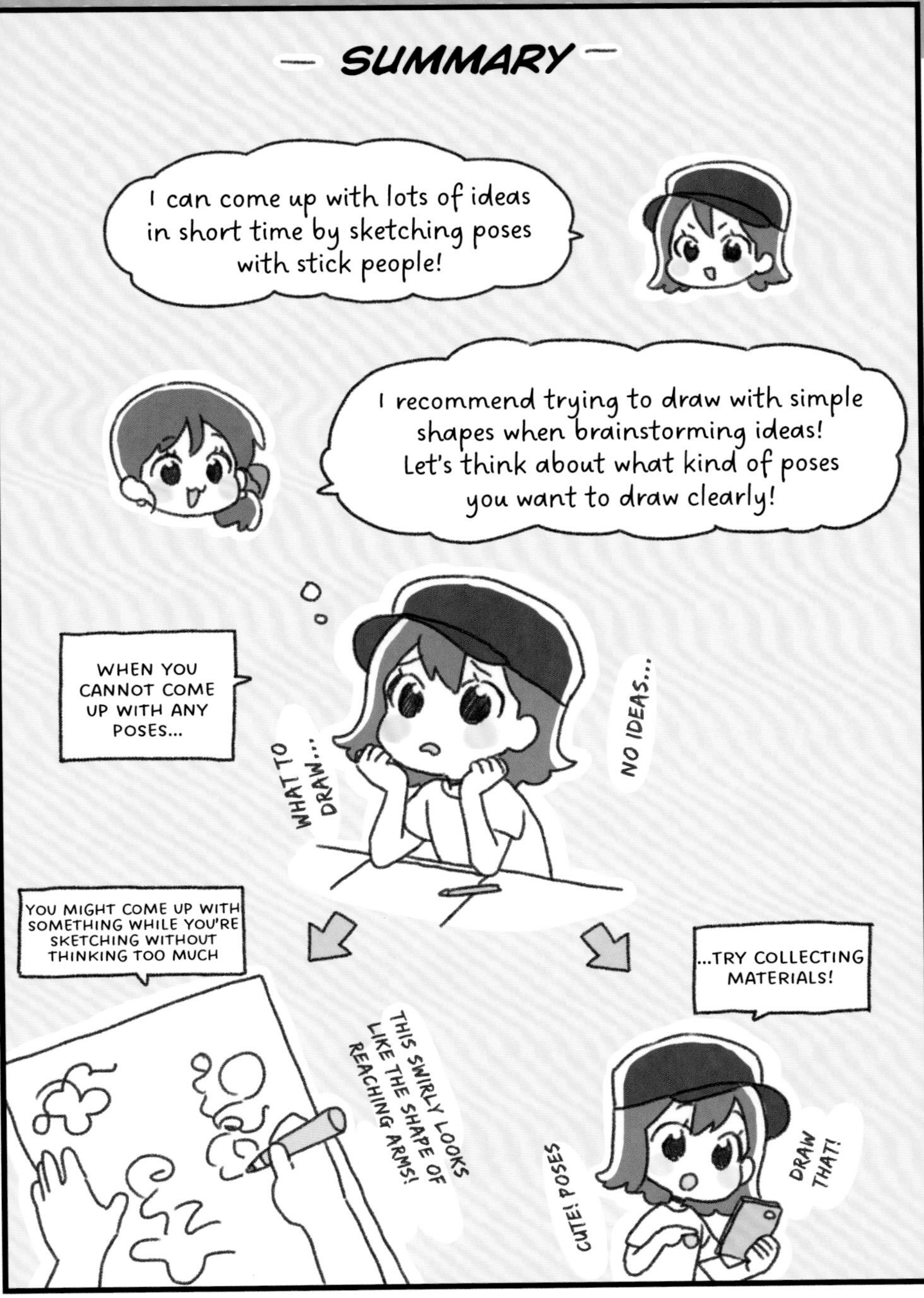
SUMMARY
I can come up with lots of ideas in short time by sketching poses with stick people!
I recommend trying to draw with simple shapes when brainstorming ideas! Let's think about what kind of poses you want to draw clearly!
WHEN YOU CANNOT COME UP WITH ANY POSES...
WHAT TO DRAW...
NO IDEAS...
YOU MIGHT COME UP WITH SOMETHING WHILE YOU'RE SKETCHING WITHOUT THINKING TOO MUCH
THIS SWIRLY LOOKS LIKE THE SHAPE OF REACHING ARMS!
...TRY COLLECTING MATERIALS!
DRAW THAT!
CUTE! POSES

# HOW TO CONNECT THE UPPER AND LOWER BODY

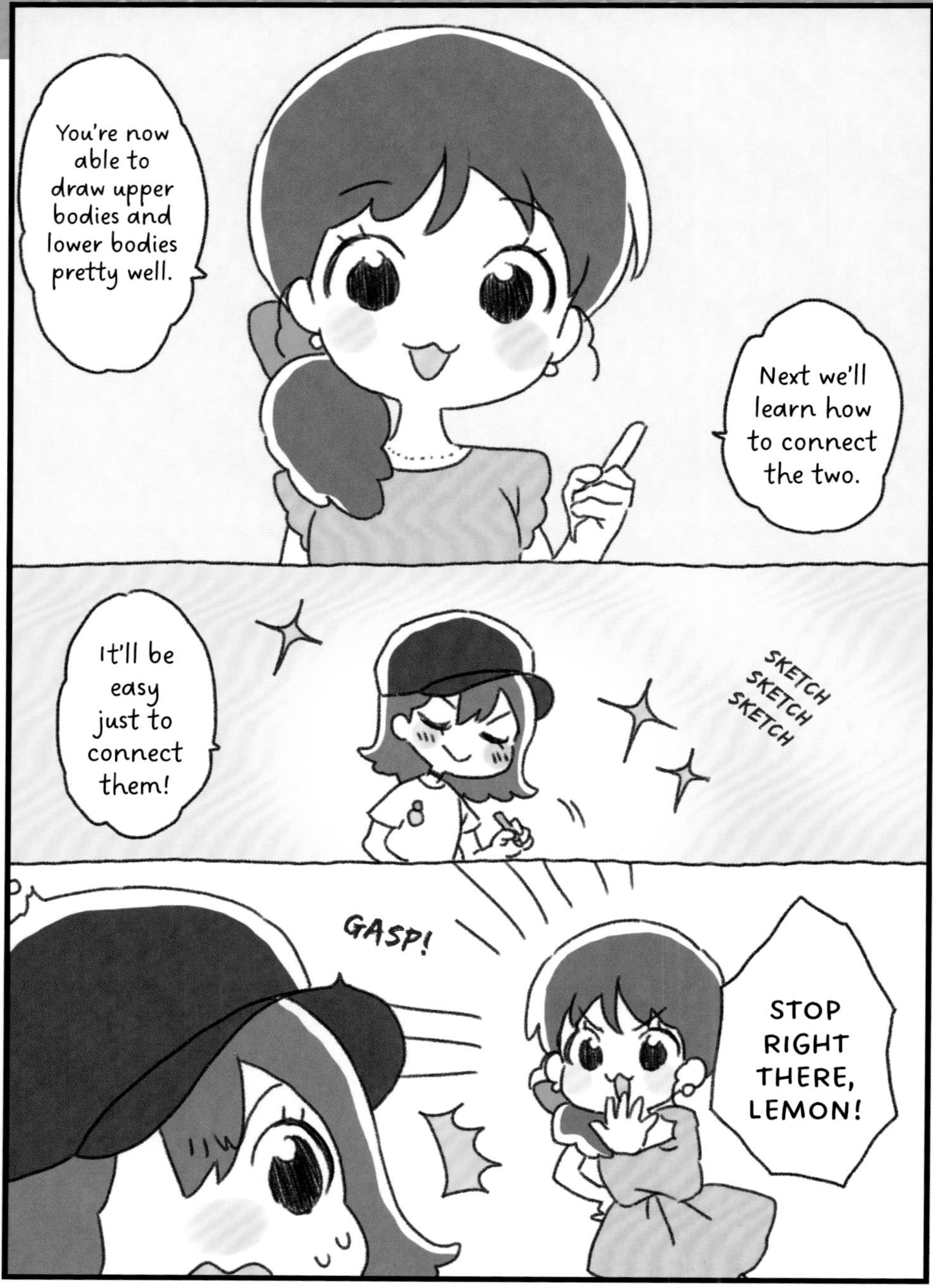

You're now able to draw upper bodies and lower bodies pretty well.
Next we'll learn how to connect the two.
It'll be easy just to connect them!
SKETCH SKETCH SKETCH
GASP!
STOP RIGHT THERE, LEMON!

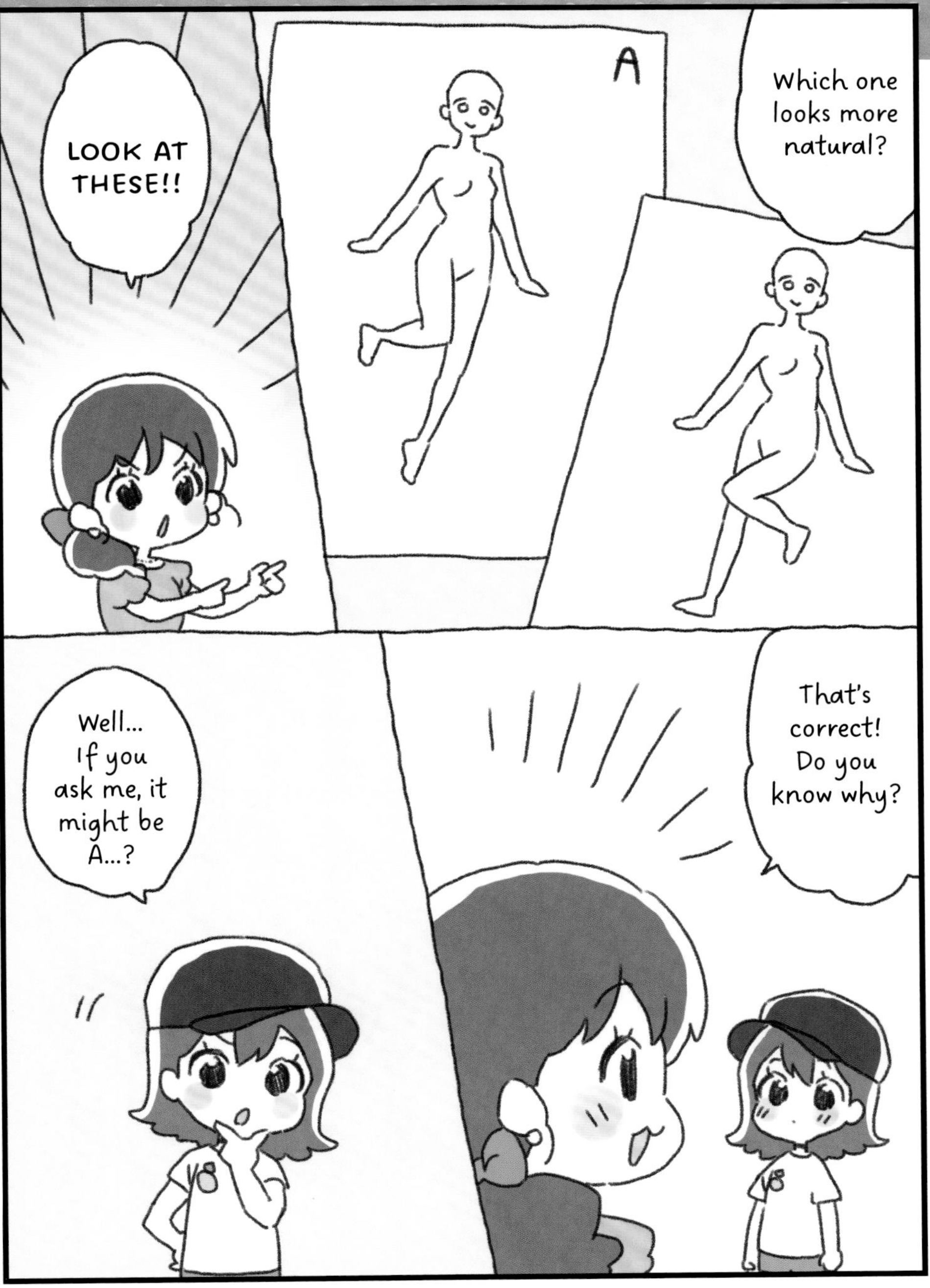
LOOK AT THESE!!
A
Which one looks more natural?
Well... If you ask me, it might be A...?
That's correct! Do you know why?

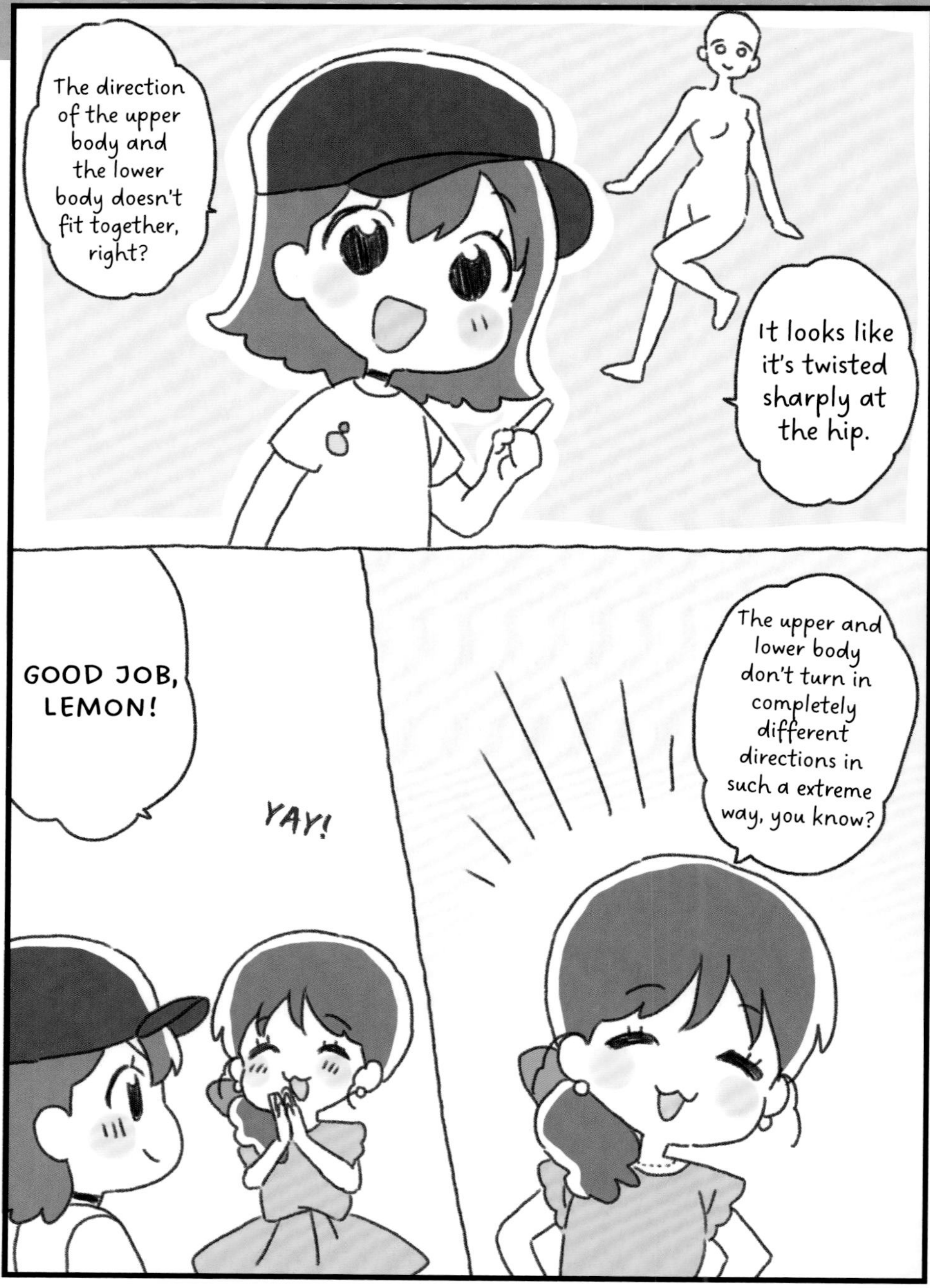
The direction of the upper body and the lower body doesn't fit together, right?
It looks like it's twisted sharply at the hip.
GOOD JOB, LEMON!
YAY!
The upper and lower body don't turn in completely different directions in such a extreme way, you know?

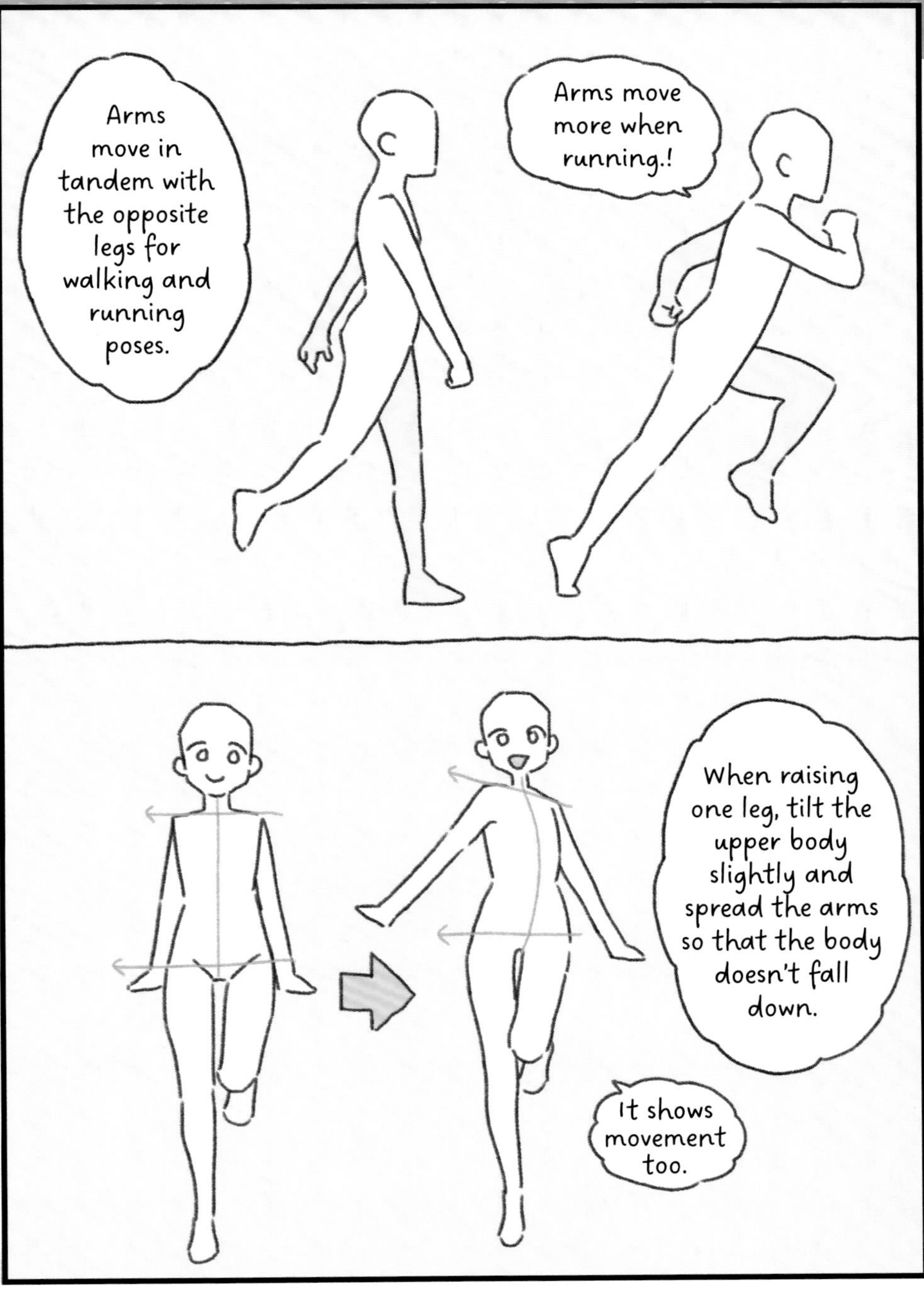
Arms move in tandem with the opposite legs for walking and running poses.
Arms move more when running.!
When raising one leg, tilt the upper body slightly and spread the arms so that the body doesn't fall down.
It shows movement too.

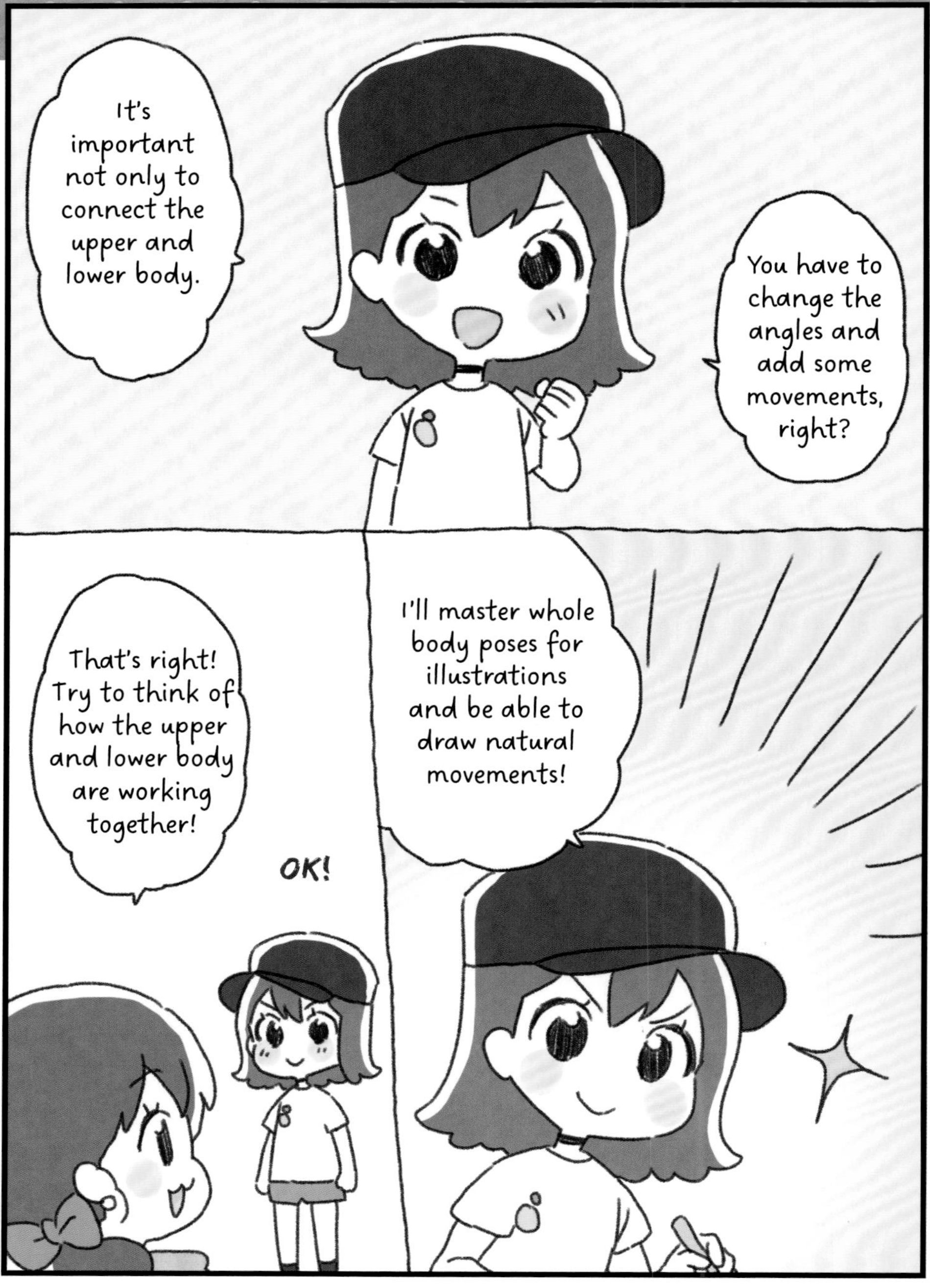
It's important not only to connect the upper and lower body.
You have to change the angles and add some movements, right?
That's right! Try to think of how the upper and lower body are working together!
OK!
I'll master whole body poses for illustrations and be able to draw natural movements!

## — SUMMARY —

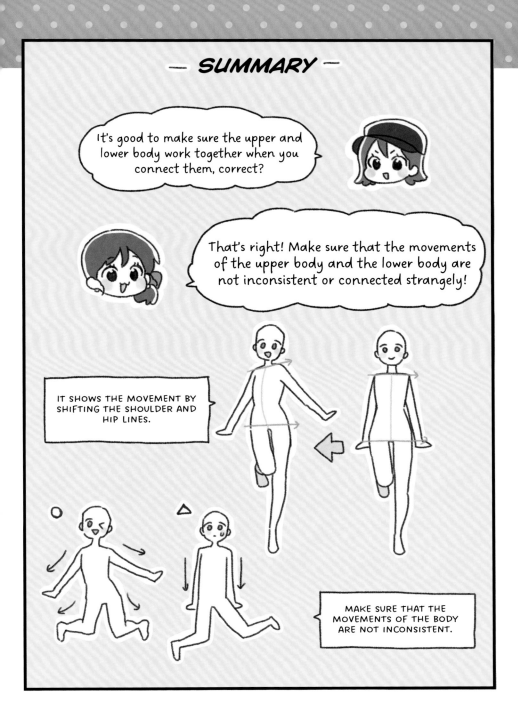

It's good to make sure the upper and lower body work together when you connect them, correct?

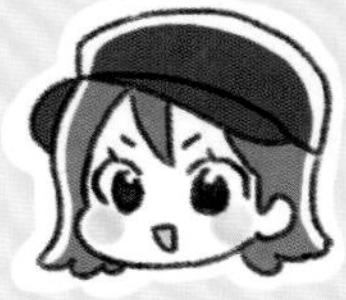

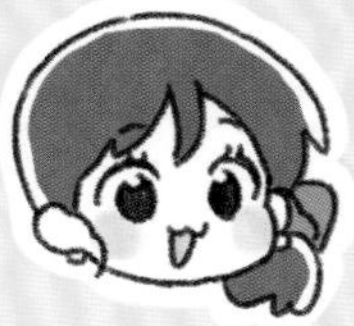

That's right! Make sure that the movements of the upper body and the lower body are not inconsistent or connected strangely!

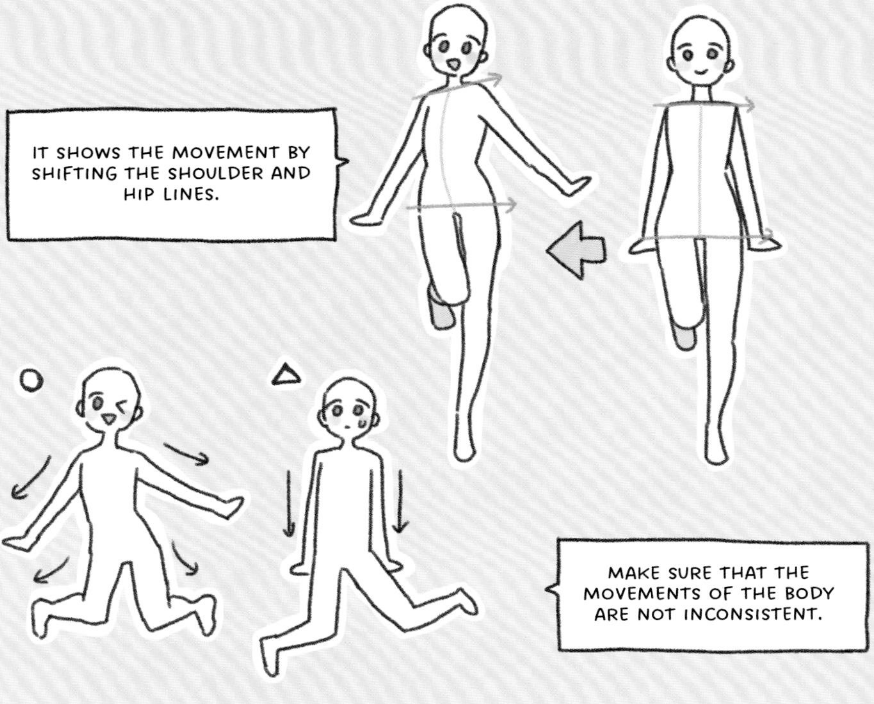
IT SHOWS THE MOVEMENT BY SHIFTING THE SHOULDER AND HIP LINES.
MAKE SURE THAT THE MOVEMENTS OF THE BODY ARE NOT INCONSISTENT.

# DON'T DRAW WITH YOUR IMAGINATION!

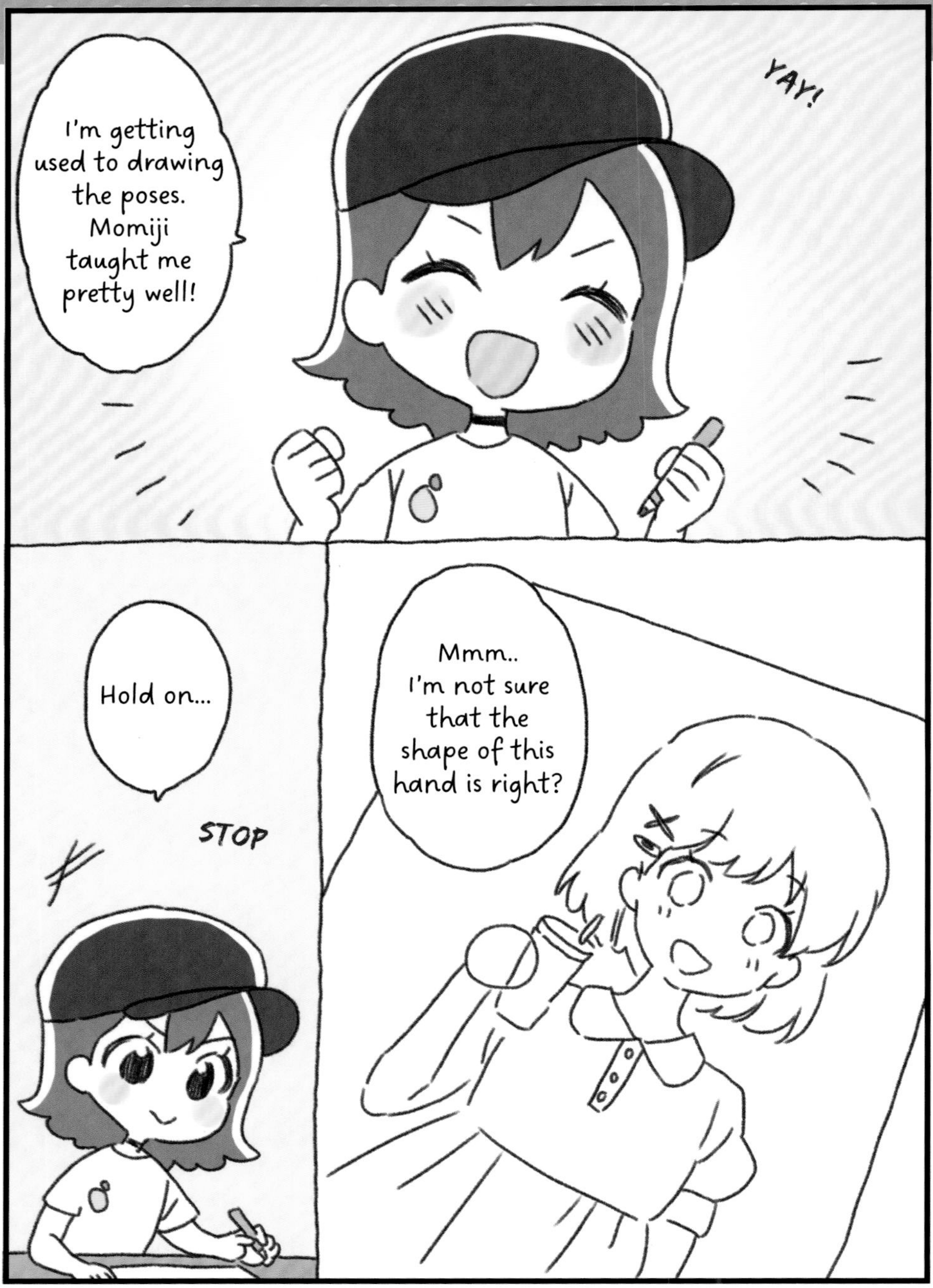
I'm getting used to drawing the poses. Momiji taught me pretty well!
YAY!
Hold on...
STOP
Mmm.. I'm not sure that the shape of this hand is right?

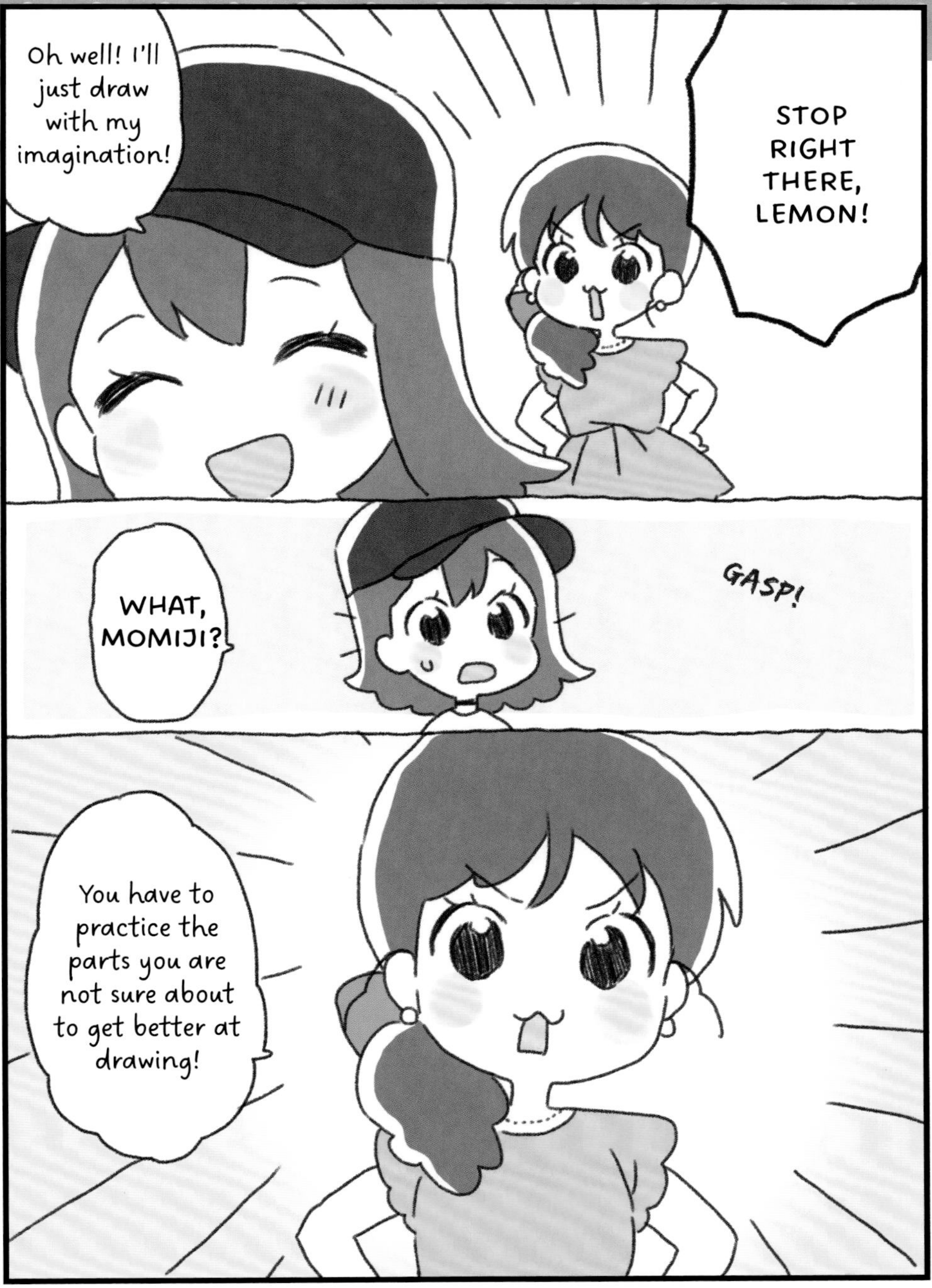
Oh well! I'll just draw with my imagination!
STOP RIGHT THERE, LEMON!
GASP!
WHAT, MOMIJI?
You have to practice the parts you are not sure about to get better at drawing!

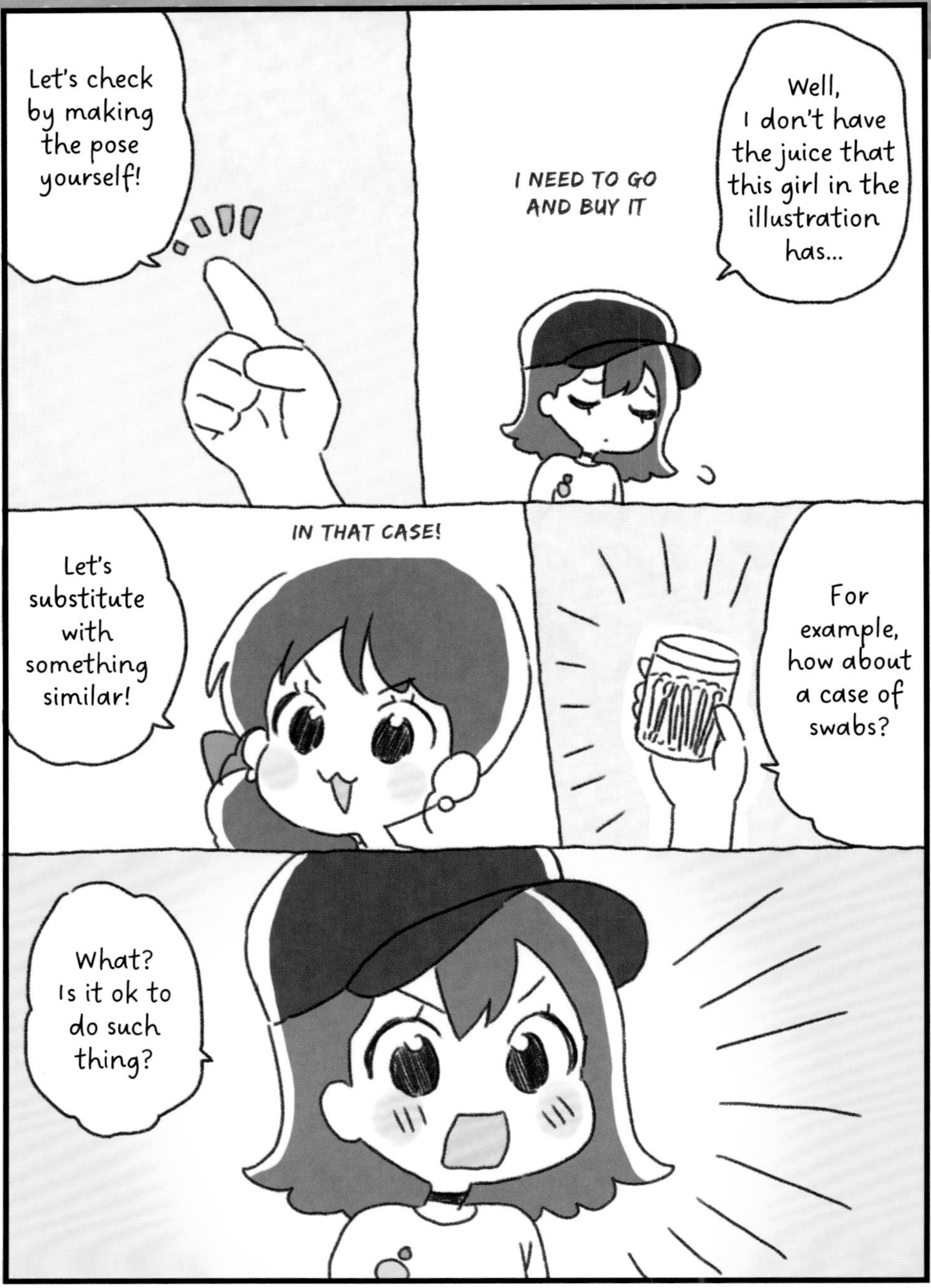
Let's check by making the pose yourself!
Well, I don't have the juice that this girl in the illustration has...
I NEED TO GO AND BUY IT
IN THAT CASE!
Let's substitute with something similar!
For example, how about a case of swabs?
What? Is it ok to do such thing?

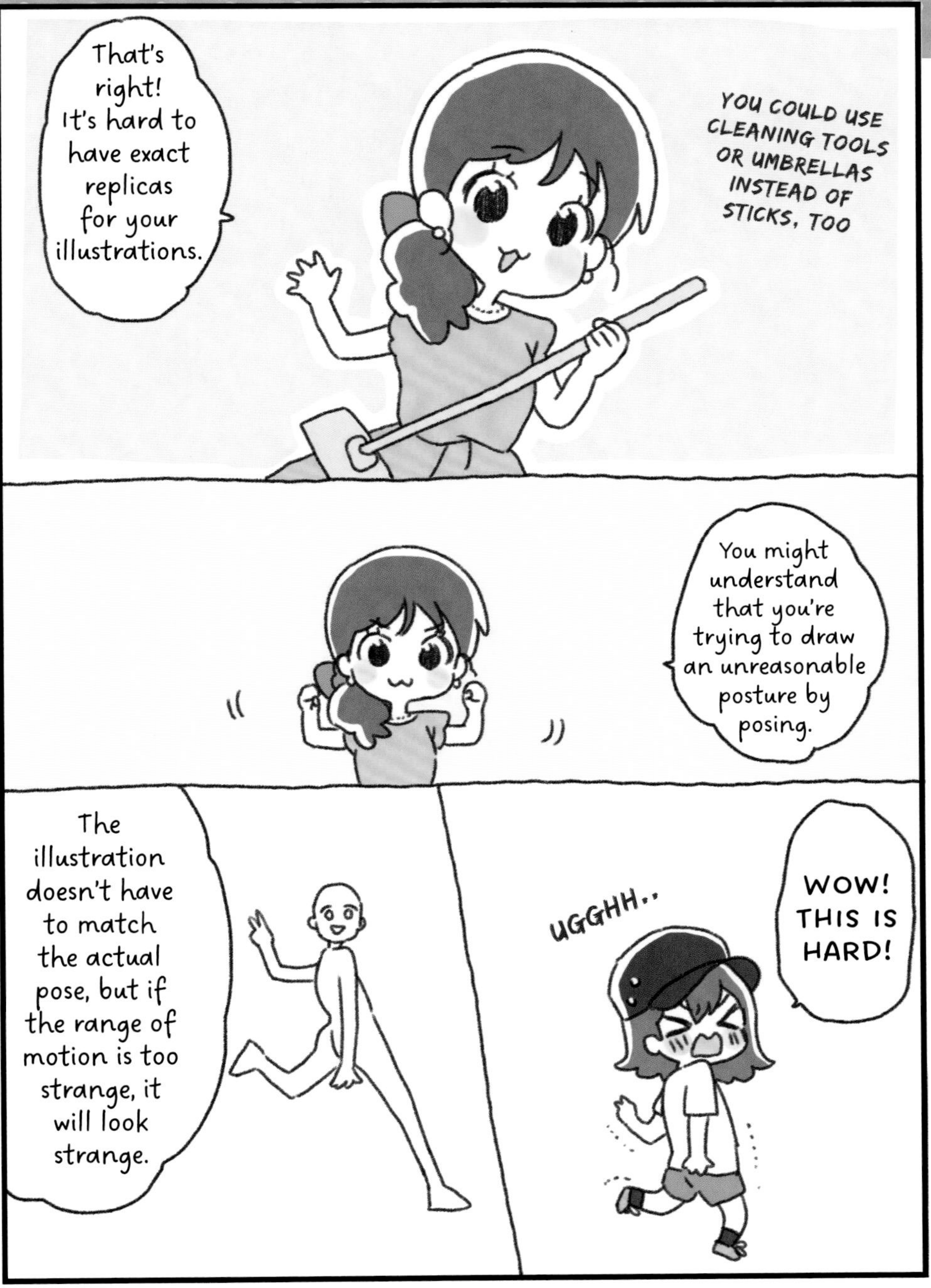
That's right! It's hard to have exact replicas for your illustrations.
YOU COULD USE CLEANING TOOLS OR UMBRELLAS INSTEAD OF STICKS, TOO
You might understand that you're trying to draw an unreasonable posture by posing.
The illustration doesn't have to match the actual pose, but if the range of motion is too strange, it will look strange.
UGGHH..
WOW! THIS IS HARD!

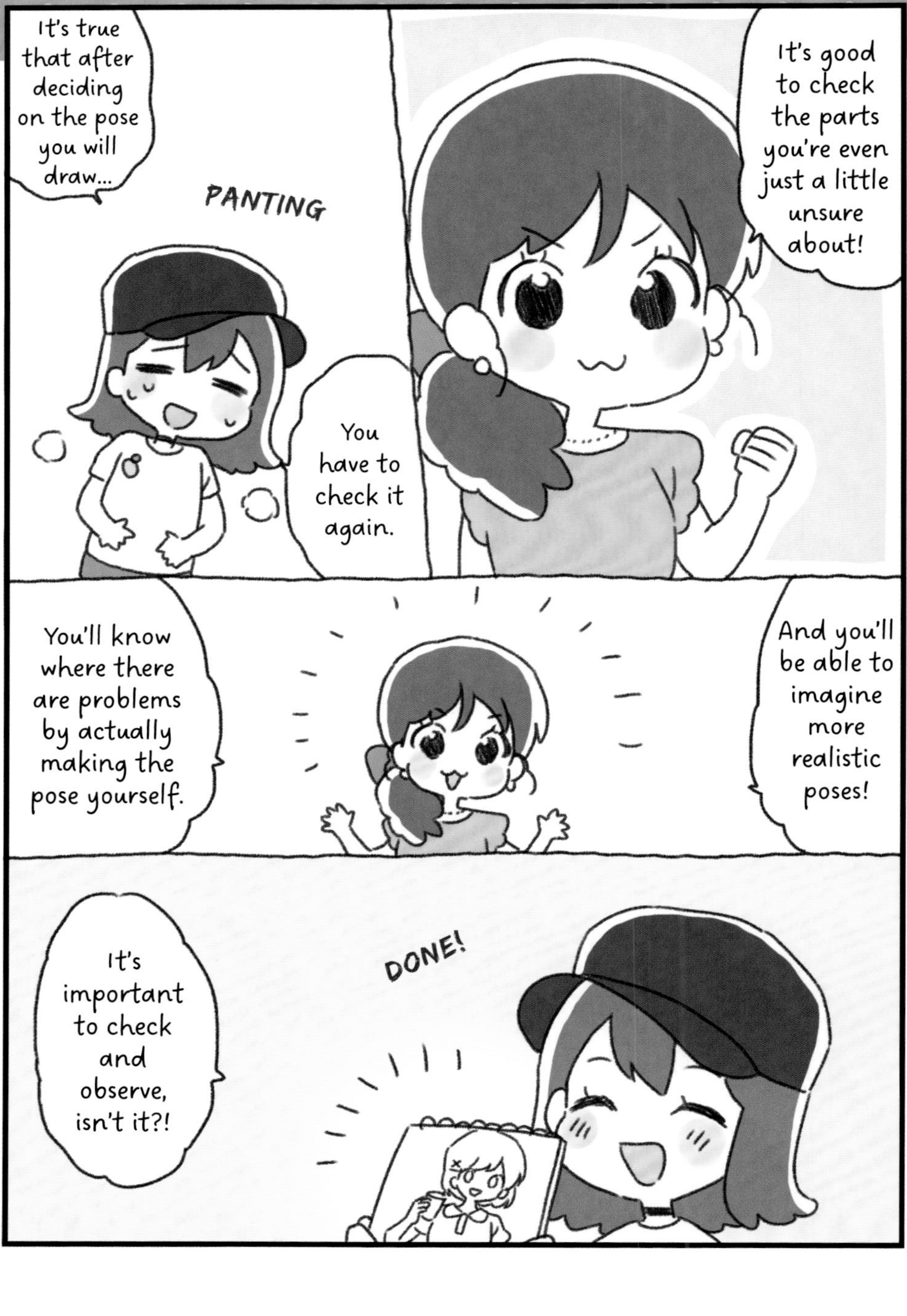
It's true that after deciding on the pose you will draw...
PANTING
You have to check it again.
It's good to check the parts you're even just a little unsure about!
You'll know where there are problems by actually making the pose yourself.
And you'll be able to imagine more realistic poses!
It's important to check and observe, isn't it?!
DONE!

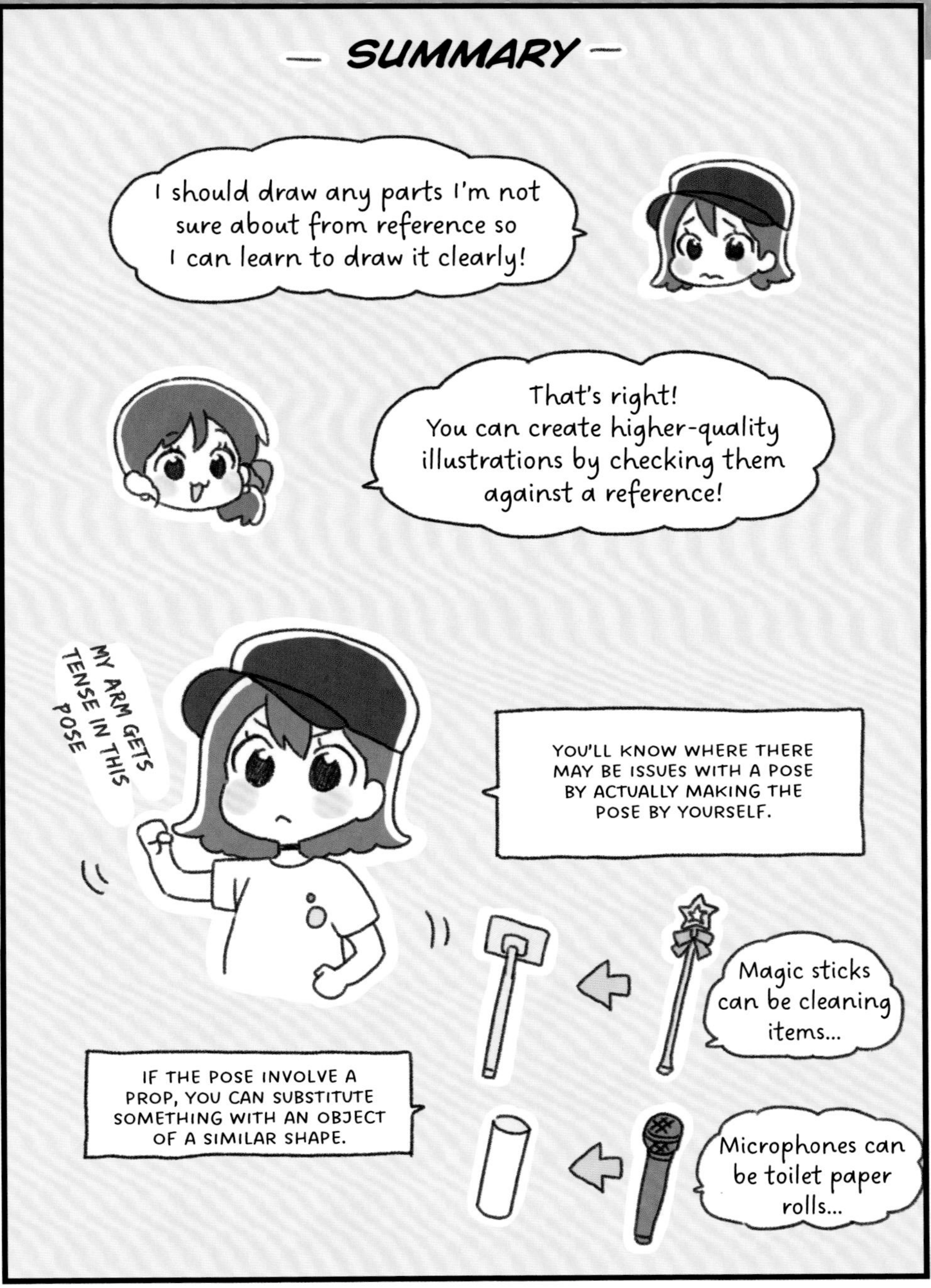
SUMMARY
I should draw any parts I'm not sure about from reference so I can learn to draw it clearly!
That's right! You can create higher-quality illustrations by checking them against a reference!
MY ARM GETS TENSE IN THIS POSE
YOU'LL KNOW WHERE THERE MAY BE ISSUES WITH A POSE BY ACTUALLY MAKING THE POSE BY YOURSELF.
Magic sticks can be cleaning items...
IF THE POSE INVOLVE A PROP, YOU CAN SUBSTITUTE SOMETHING WITH AN OBJECT OF A SIMILAR SHAPE.
Microphones can be toilet paper rolls...

# CENTER OF GRAVITY AND CONTRAPPOSTO

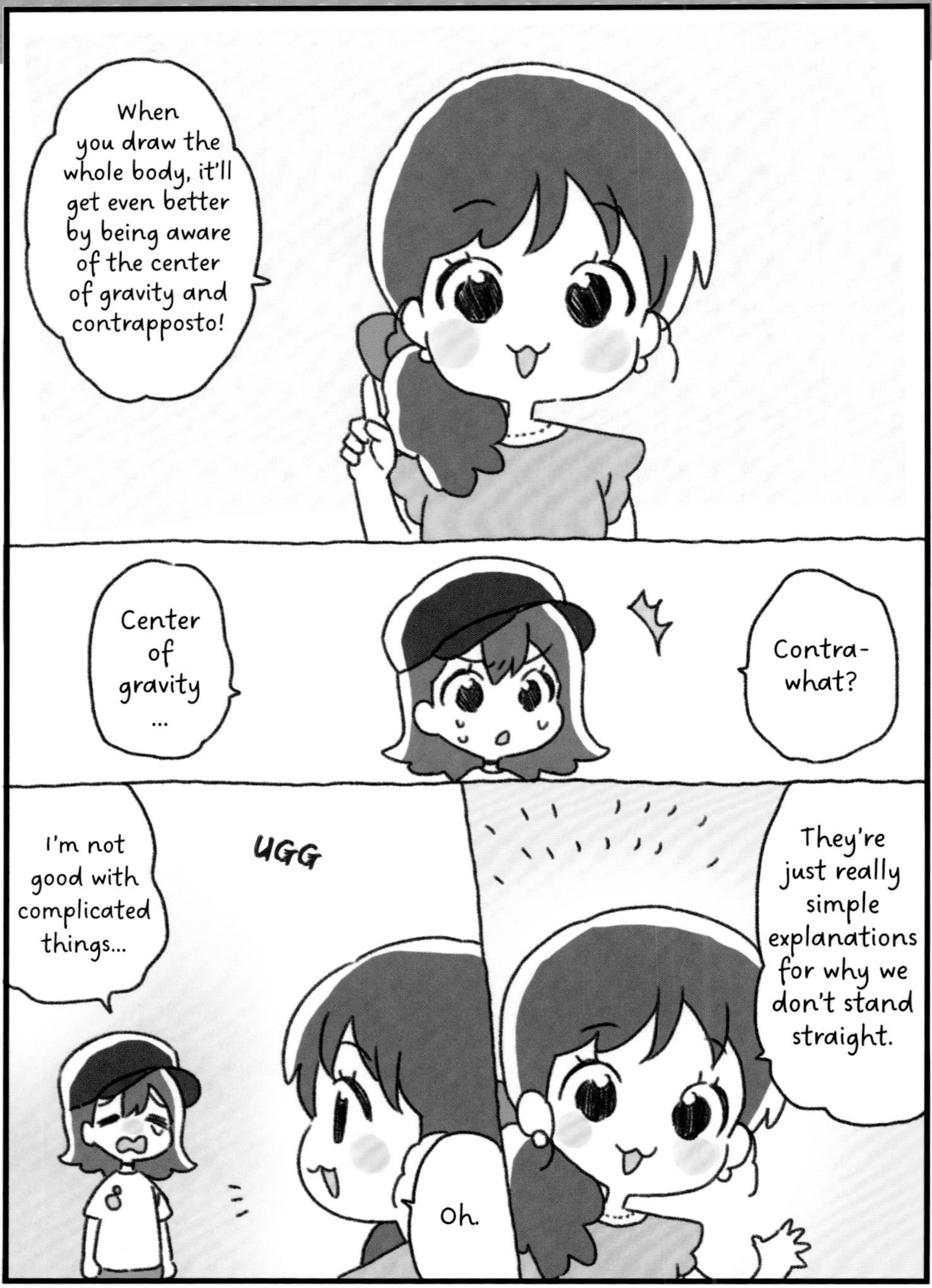

When you draw the whole body, it'll get even better by being aware of the center of gravity and contrapposto!
Center of gravity ...
Contra-what?
I'm not good with complicated things...
UGG
They're just really simple explanations for why we don't stand straight.
Oh.

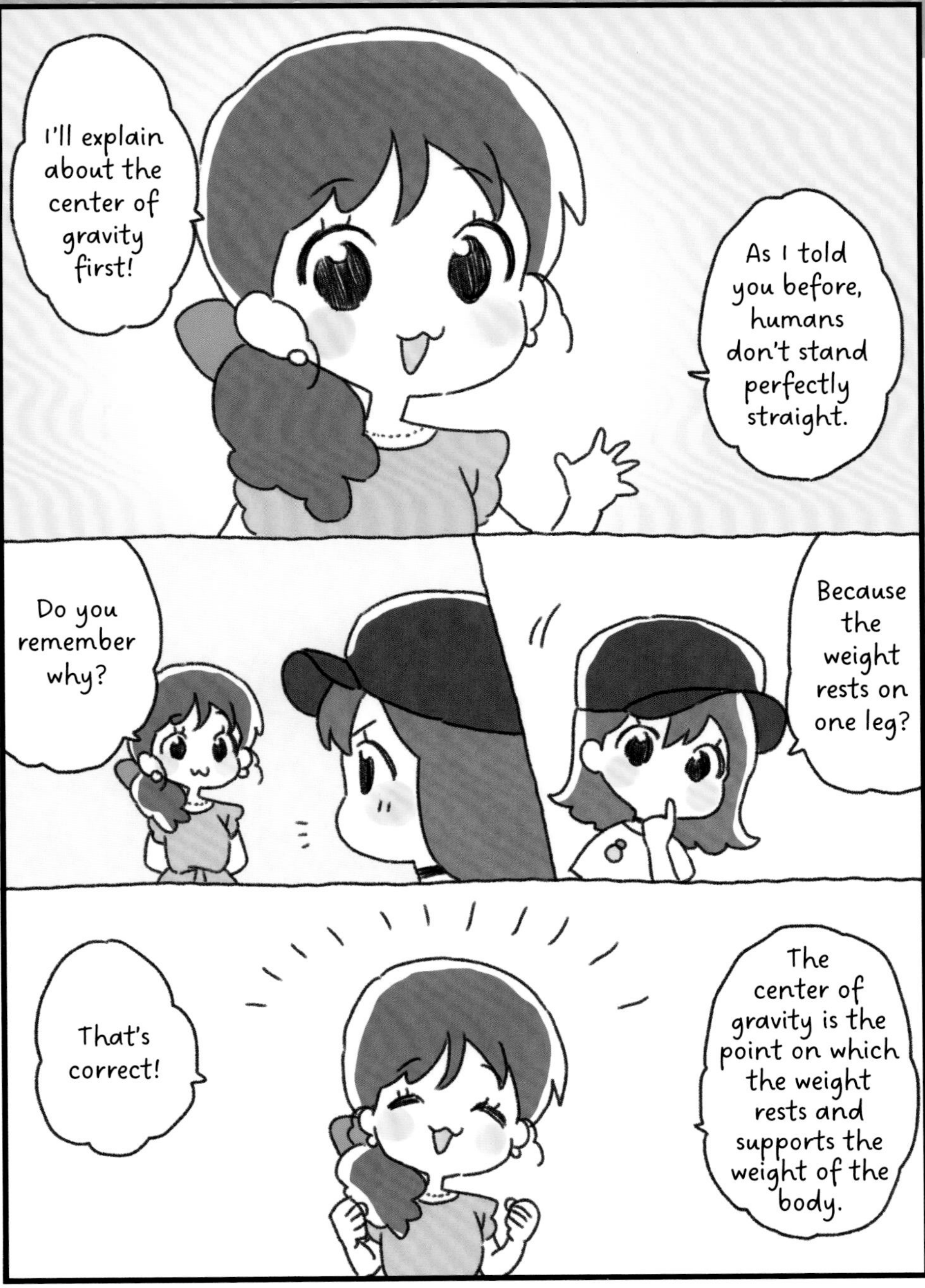
I'll explain about the center of gravity first!
As I told you before, humans don't stand perfectly straight.
Do you remember why?
Because the weight rests on one leg?
That's correct!
The center of gravity is the point on which the weight rests and supports the weight of the body.

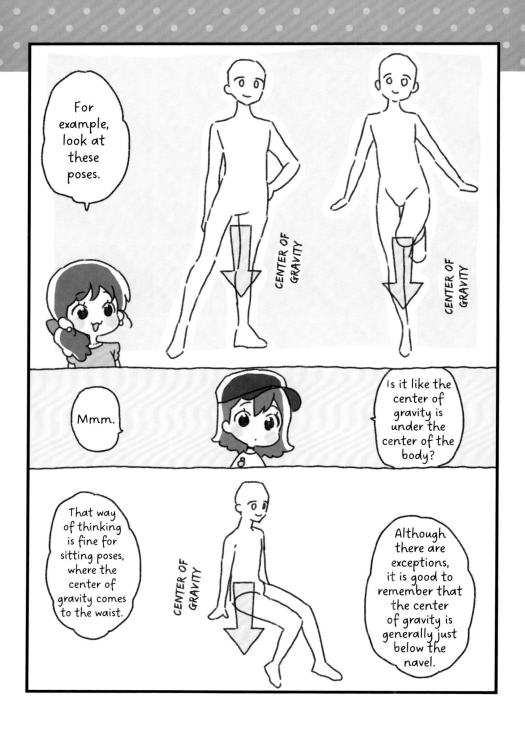

For example, look at these poses.

CENTER OF GRAVITY

CENTER OF GRAVITY

Mmm.

Is it like the center of gravity is under the center of the body?

That way of thinking is fine for sitting poses, where the center of gravity comes to the waist.

CENTER OF GRAVITY

Although there are exceptions, it is good to remember that the center of gravity is generally just below the navel.

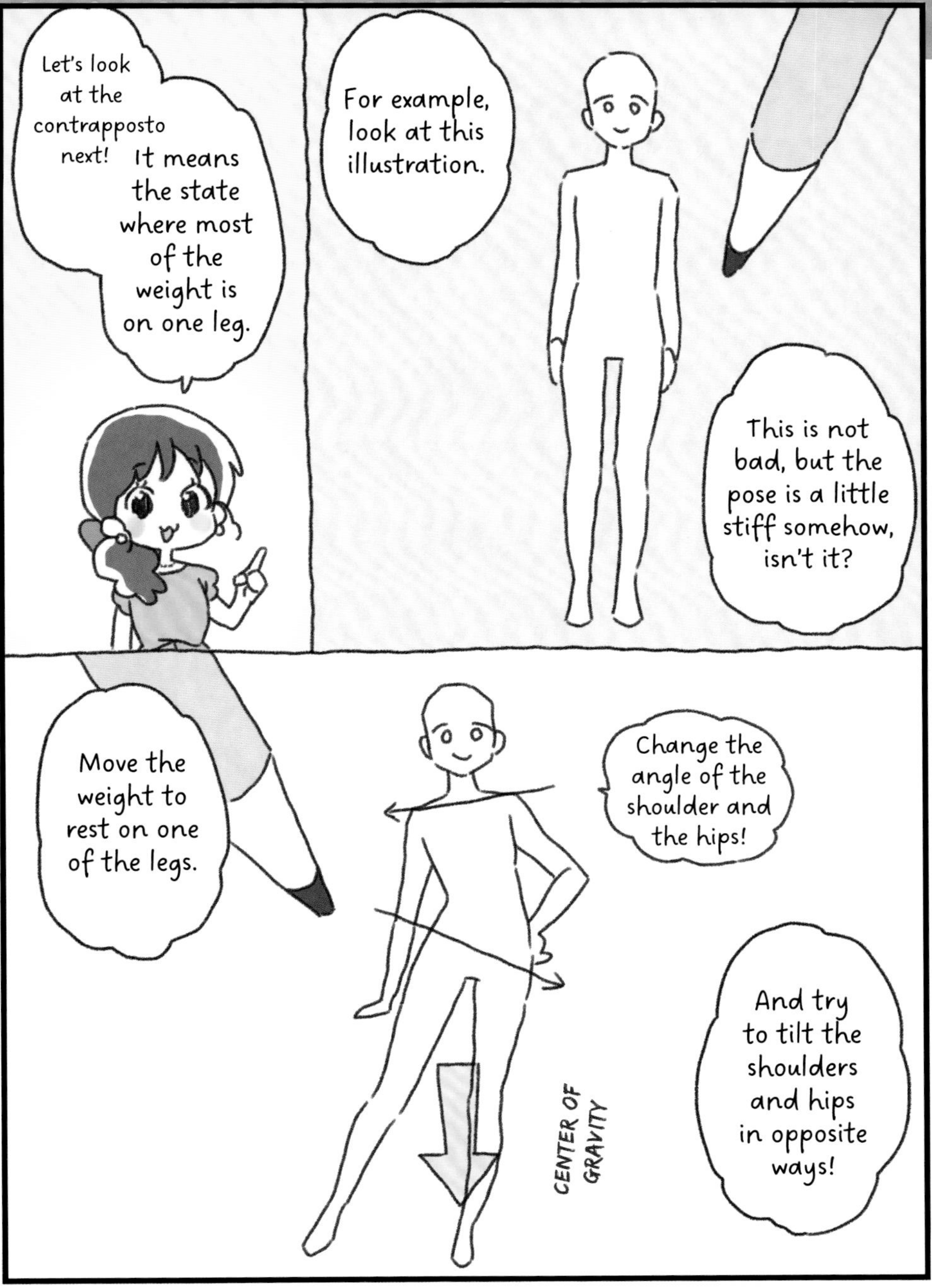
Let's look at the contrapposto next!
It means the state where most of the weight is on one leg.
For example, look at this illustration.
This is not bad, but the pose is a little stiff somehow, isn't it?
Move the weight to rest on one of the legs.
Change the angle of the shoulder and the hips!
CENTER OF GRAVITY
And try to tilt the shoulders and hips in opposite ways!

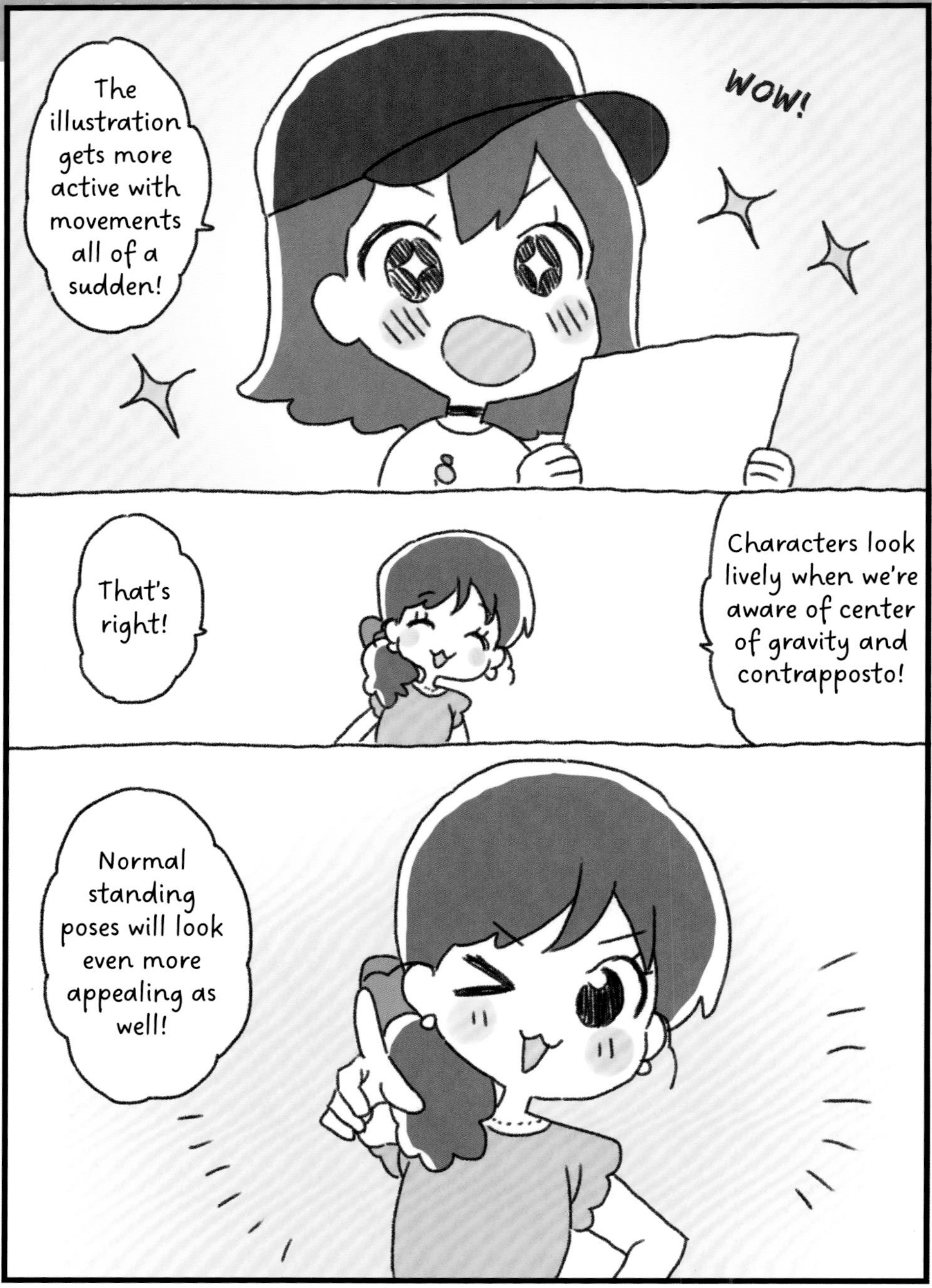
The illustration gets more active with movements all of a sudden!
WOW!
Characters look lively when we're aware of center of gravity and contrapposto!
That's right!
Normal standing poses will look even more appealing as well!

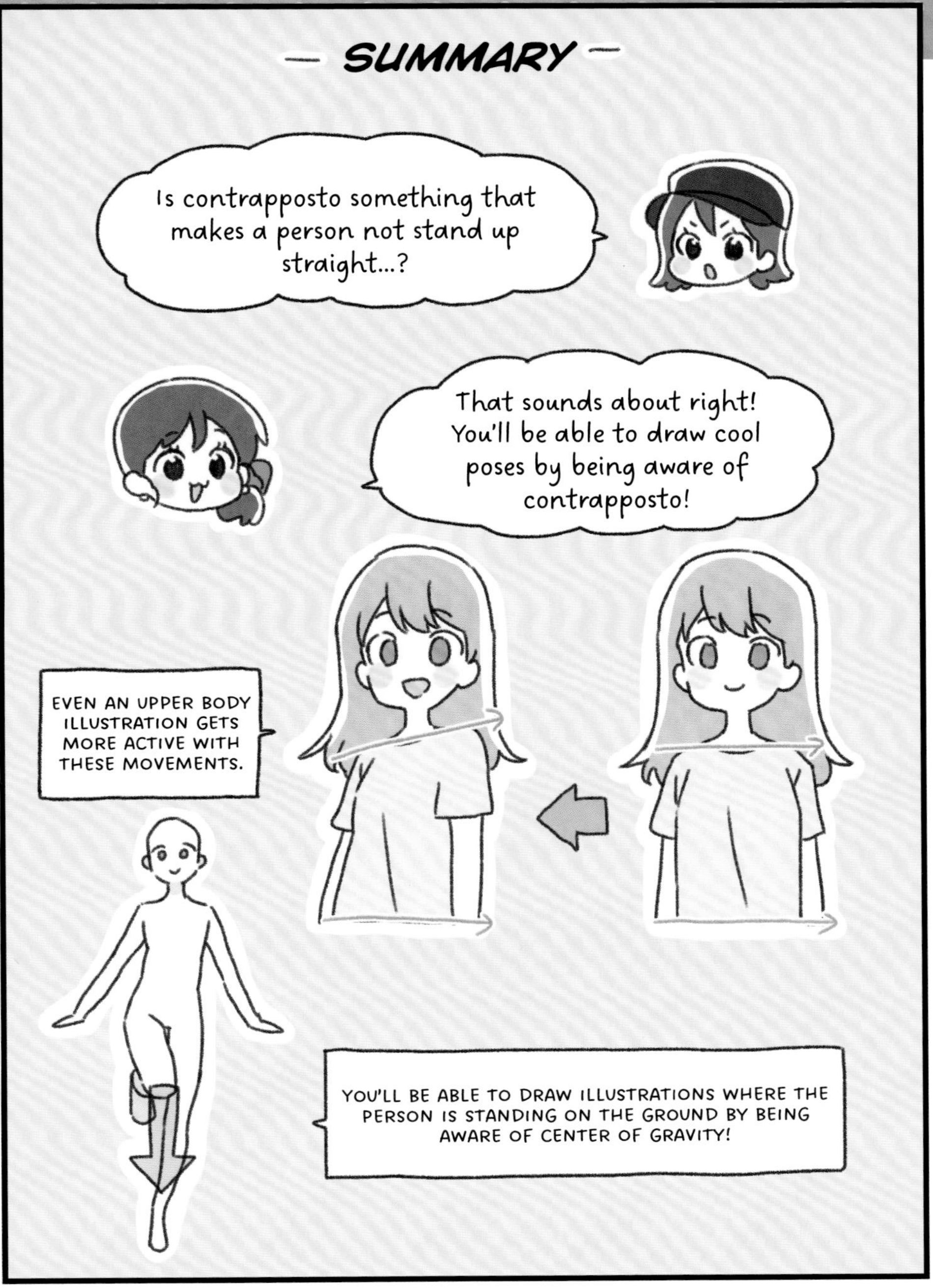
SUMMARY
Is contrapposto something that makes a person not stand up straight...?
That sounds about right! You'll be able to draw cool poses by being aware of contrapposto!
EVEN AN UPPER BODY ILLUSTRATION GETS MORE ACTIVE WITH THESE MOVEMENTS.
YOU'LL BE ABLE TO DRAW ILLUSTRATIONS WHERE THE PERSON IS STANDING ON THE GROUND BY BEING AWARE OF CENTER OF GRAVITY!

# REVIEW THE WHOLE DRAWING

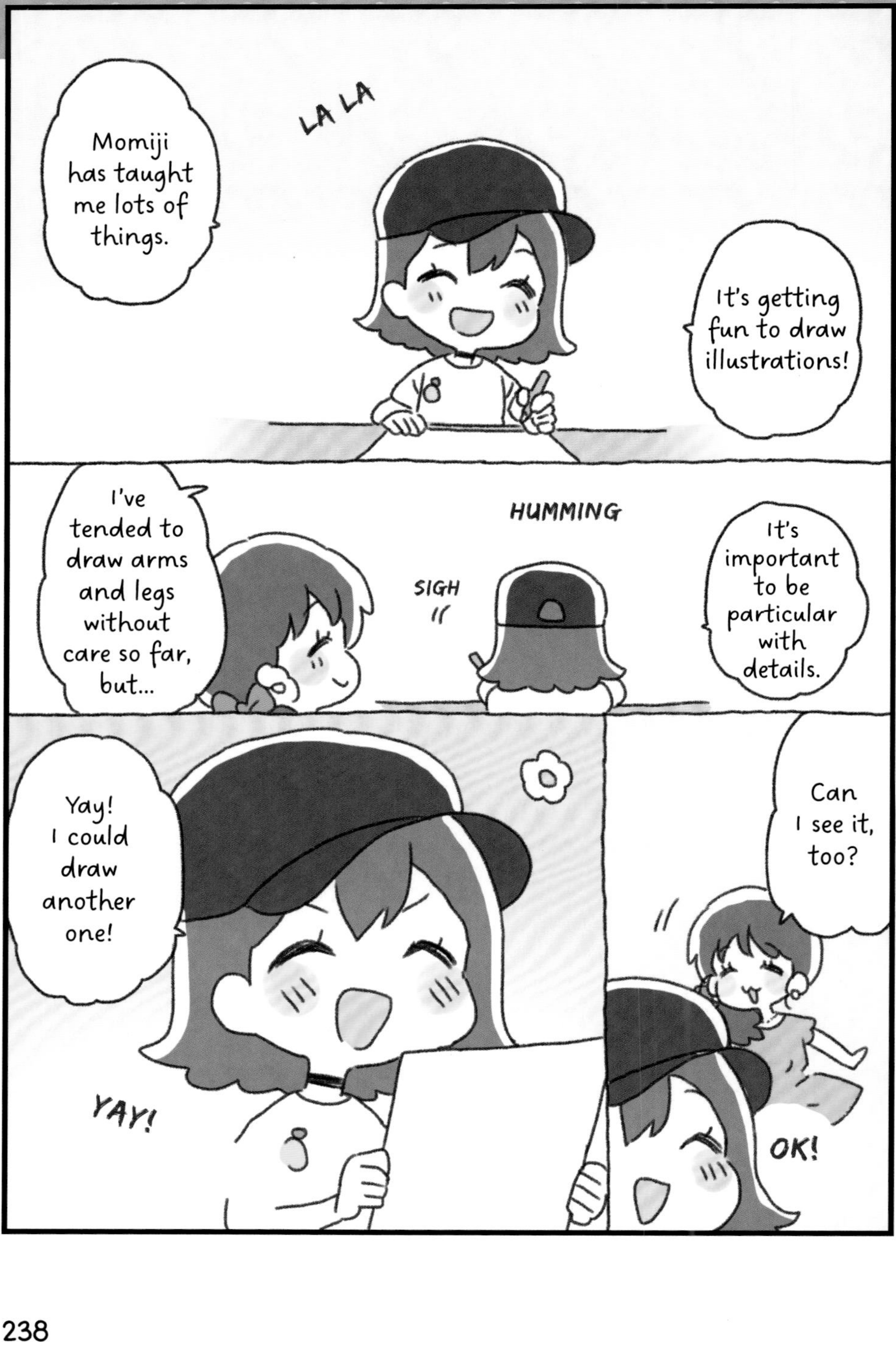
LA LA
Momiji has taught me lots of things.
It's getting fun to draw illustrations!
I've tended to draw arms and legs without care so far, but...
HUMMING
SIGH
It's important to be particular with details.
Yay! I could draw another one!
YAY!
Can I see it, too?
OK!

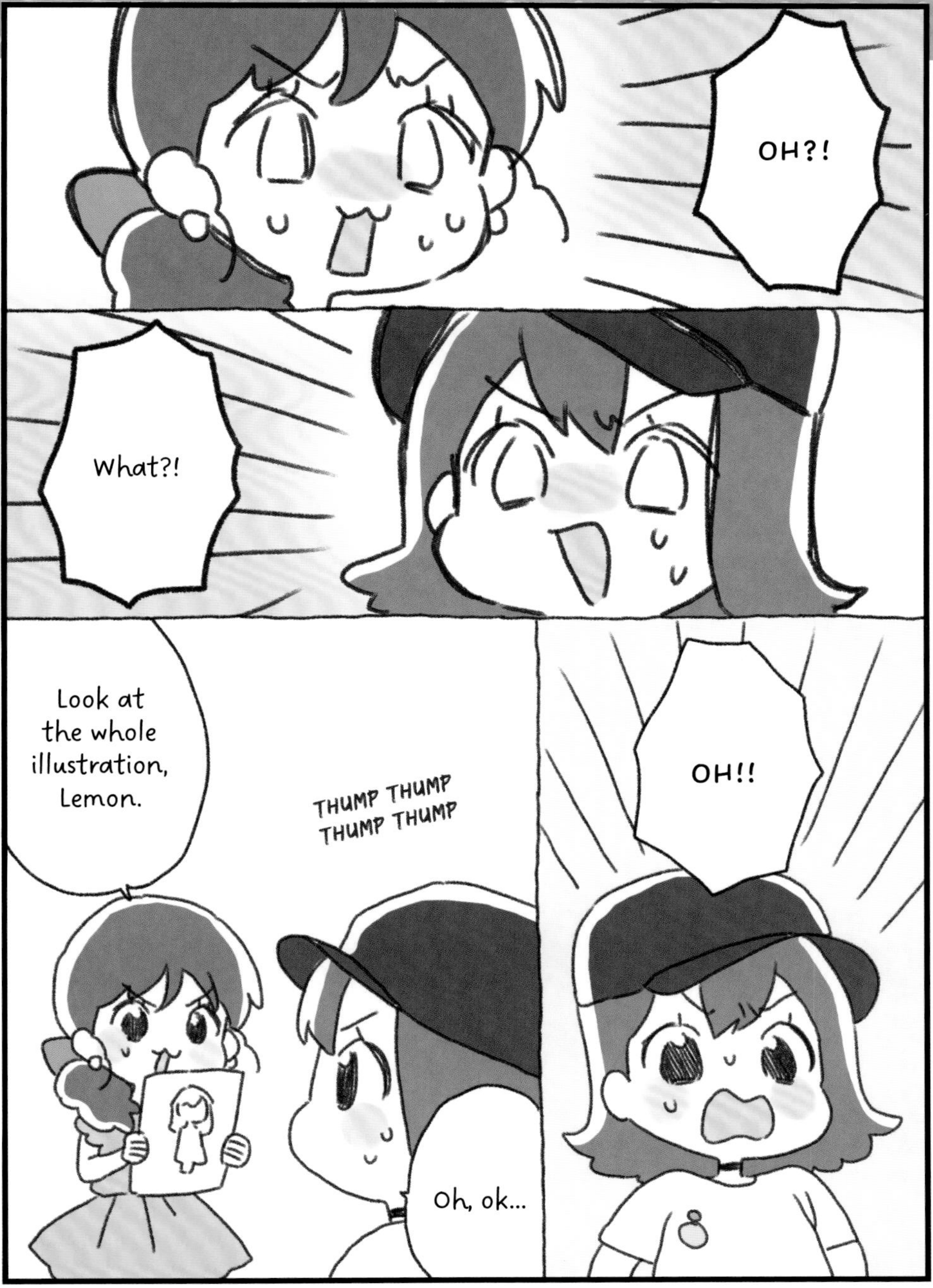
OH?!
What?!
Look at the whole illustration, Lemon.
THUMP THUMP THUMP THUMP
Oh, ok...
OH!!

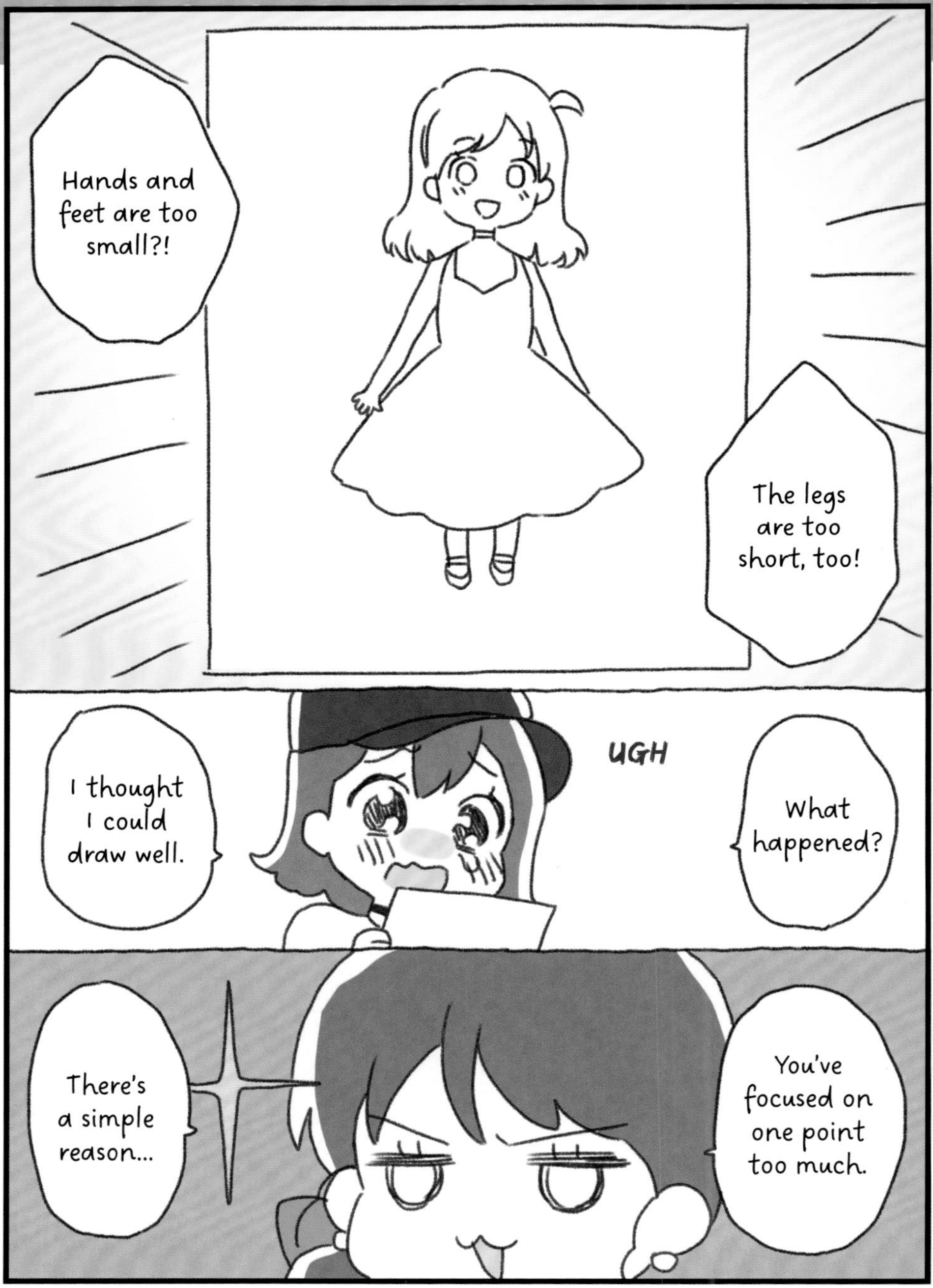
Hands and feet are too small?!
The legs are too short, too!
I thought I could draw well.
UGH
What happened?
There's a simple reason...
You've focused on one point too much.

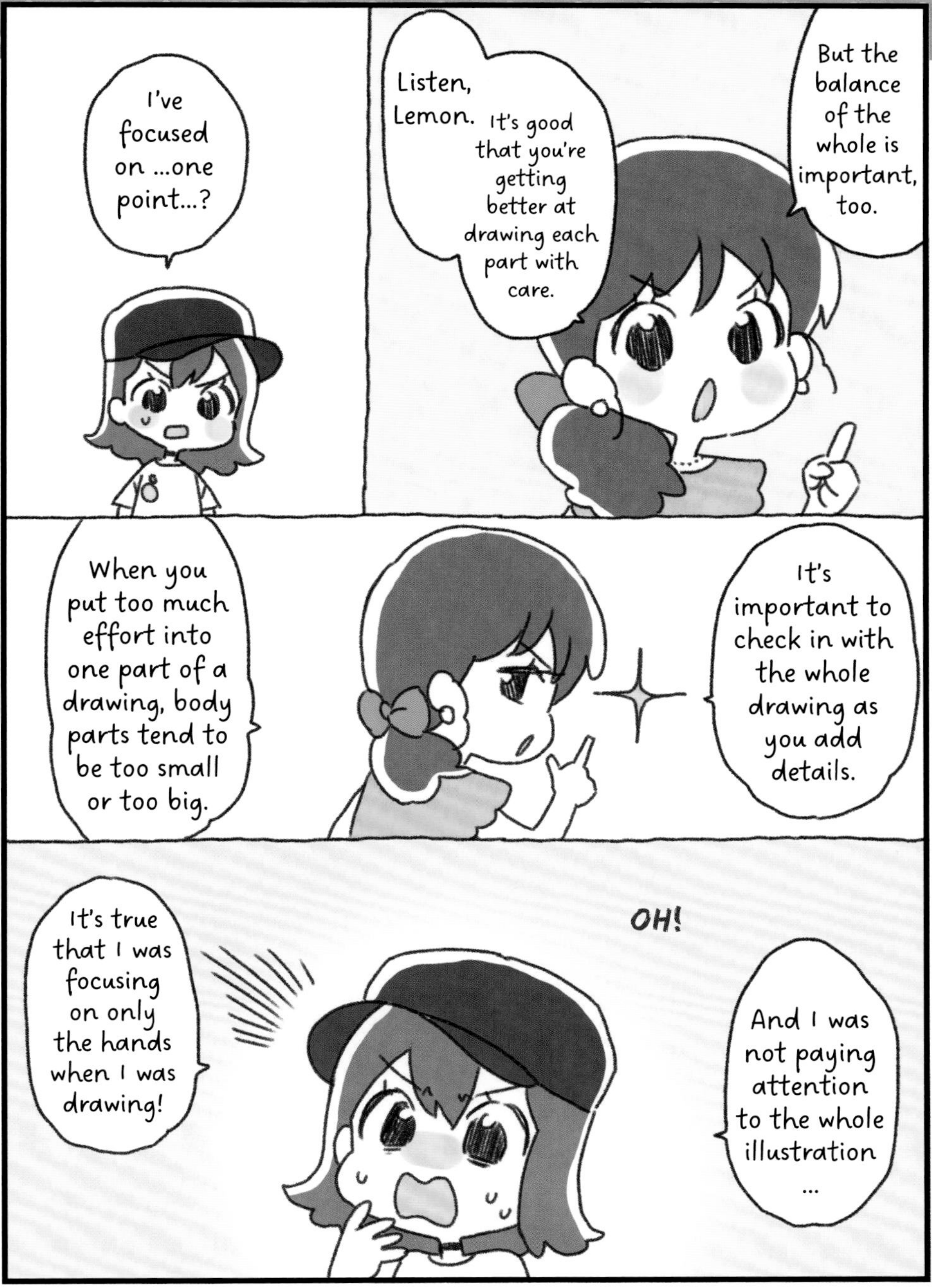
I've focused on ...one point...?
Listen, Lemon.
It's good that you're getting better at drawing each part with care.
But the balance of the whole is important, too.
When you put too much effort into one part of a drawing, body parts tend to be too small or too big.
It's important to check in with the whole drawing as you add details.
OH!
It's true that I was focusing on only the hands when I was drawing!
And I was not paying attention to the whole illustration ...

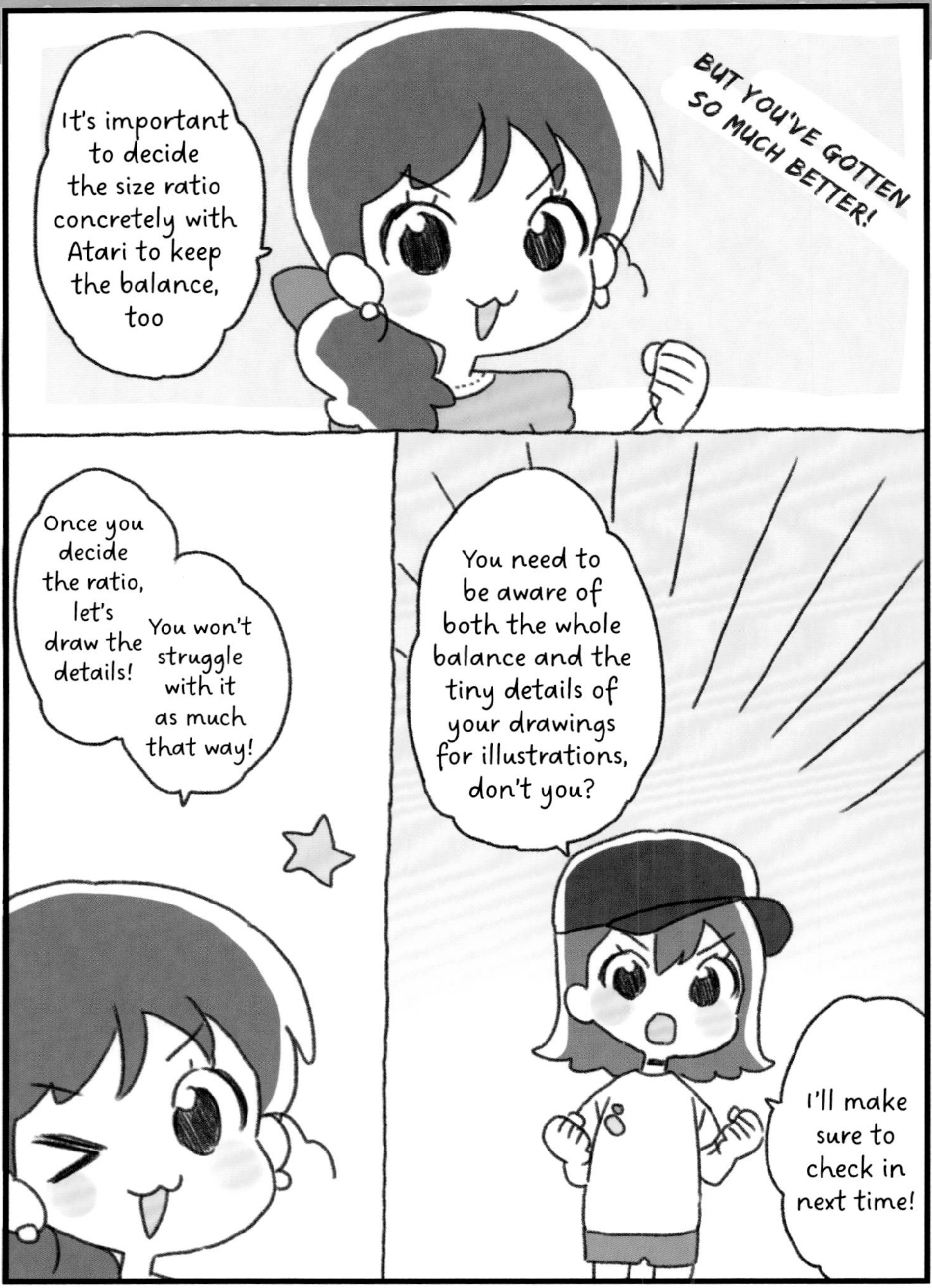
It's important to decide the size ratio concretely with Atari to keep the balance, too
BUT YOU'VE GOTTEN SO MUCH BETTER!
Once you decide the ratio, let's draw the details!
You won't struggle with it as much that way!
You need to be aware of both the whole balance and the tiny details of your drawings for illustrations, don't you?
I'll make sure to check in next time!

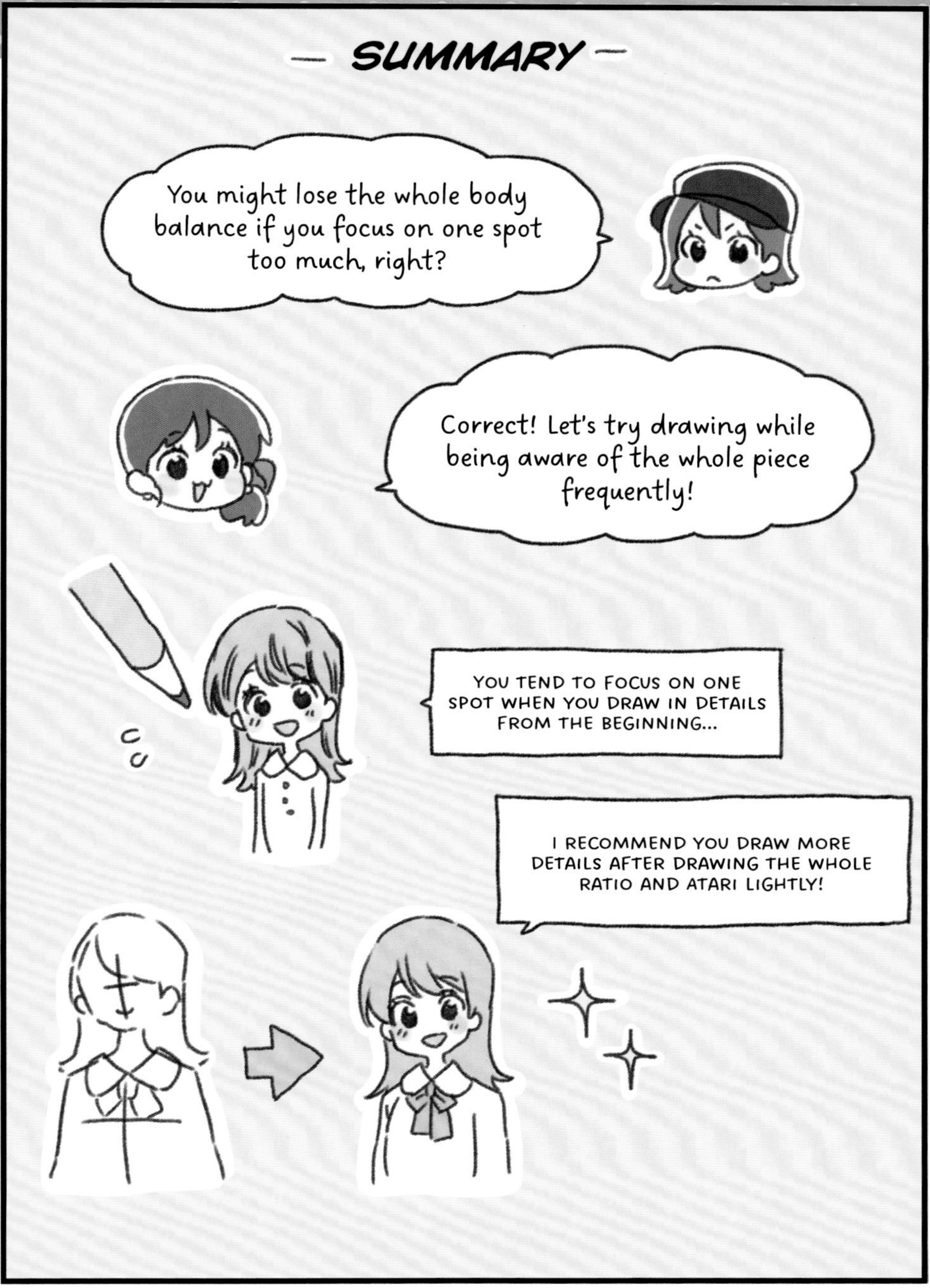
SUMMARY
You might lose the whole body balance if you focus on one spot too much, right?
Correct! Let's try drawing while being aware of the whole piece frequently!
YOU TEND TO FOCUS ON ONE SPOT WHEN YOU DRAW IN DETAILS FROM THE BEGINNING...
I RECOMMEND YOU DRAW MORE DETAILS AFTER DRAWING THE WHOLE RATIO AND ATARI LIGHTLY!

# CONSIDER THE GROUND UNDER THE FEET

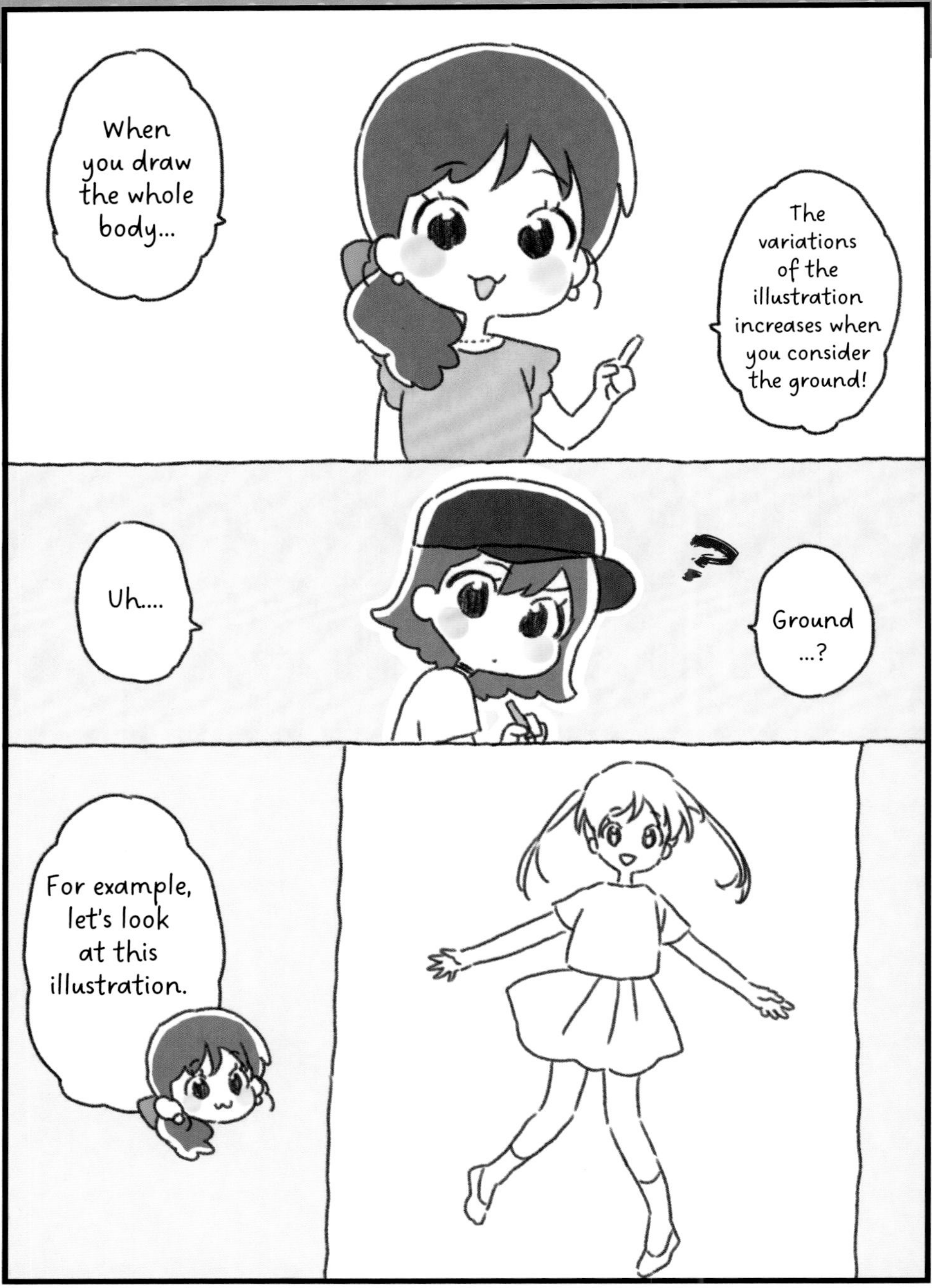
When you draw the whole body...
The variations of the illustration increases when you consider the ground!
Uh....
Ground ...?
For example, let's look at this illustration.

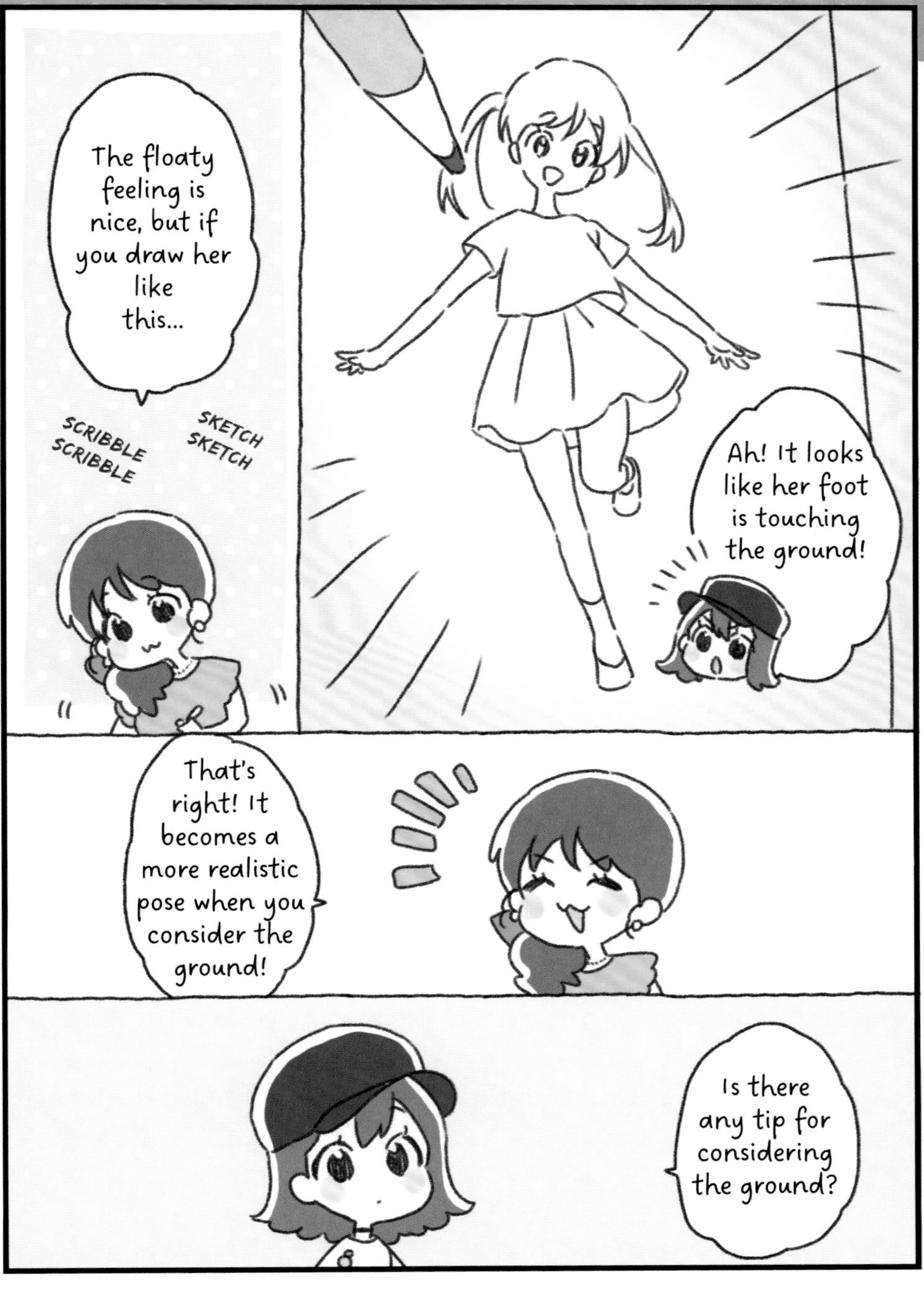
The floaty feeling is nice, but if you draw her like this...
SCRIBBLE SCRIBBLE
SKETCH SKETCH
Ah! It looks like her foot is touching the ground!
That's right! It becomes a more realistic pose when you consider the ground!
Is there any tip for considering the ground?

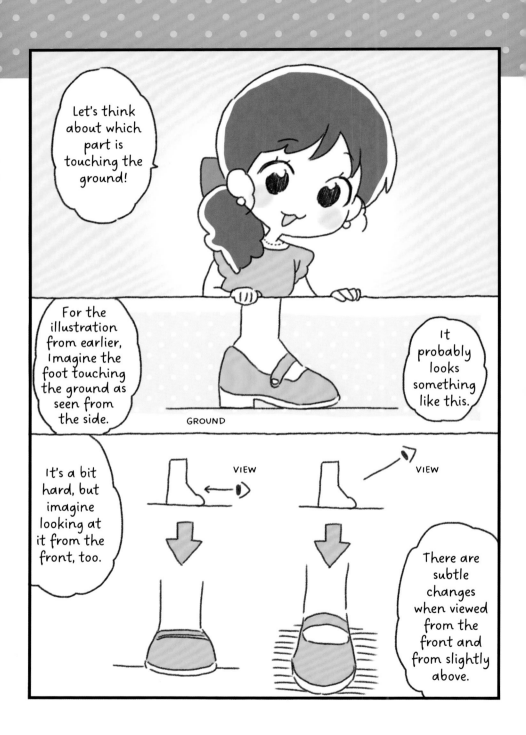

Let's think about which part is touching the ground!

For the illustration from earlier, Imagine the foot touching the ground as seen from the side.

GROUND

It probably looks something like this.

It's a bit hard, but imagine looking at it from the front, too.

VIEW

VIEW

There are subtle changes when viewed from the front and from slightly above.

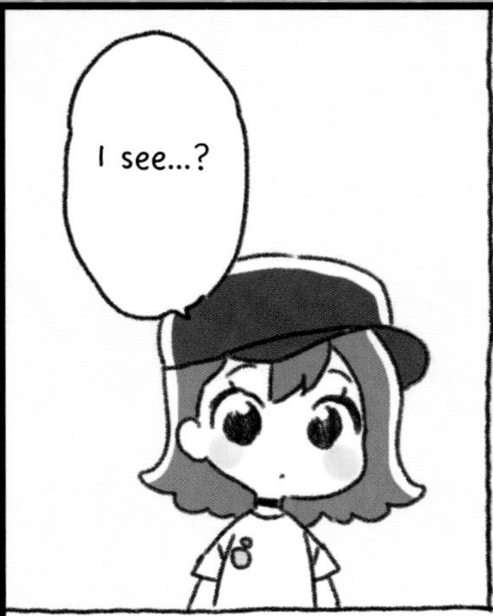
I see...?

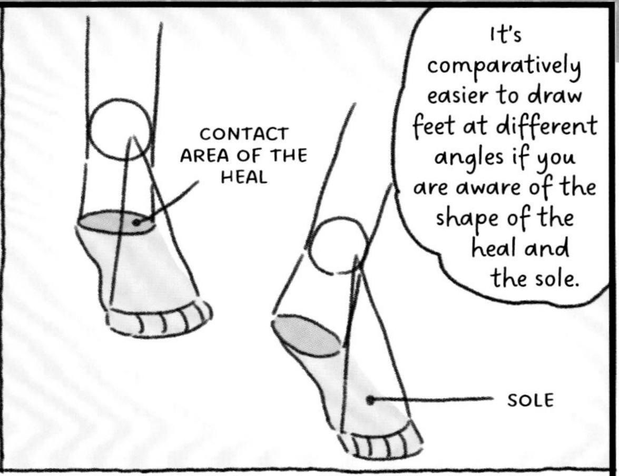
CONTACT AREA OF THE HEAL
It's comparatively easier to draw feet at different angles if you are aware of the shape of the heal and the sole.
SOLE

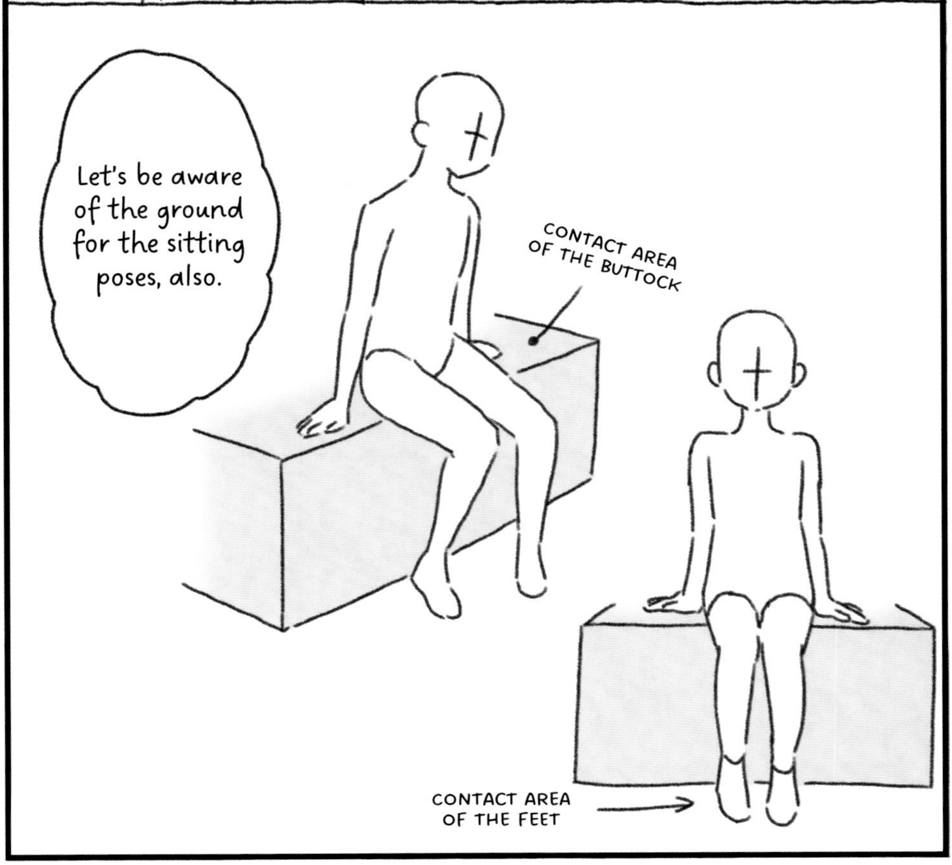
Let's be aware of the ground for the sitting poses, also.
CONTACT AREA OF THE BUTTOCK
CONTACT AREA OF THE FEET

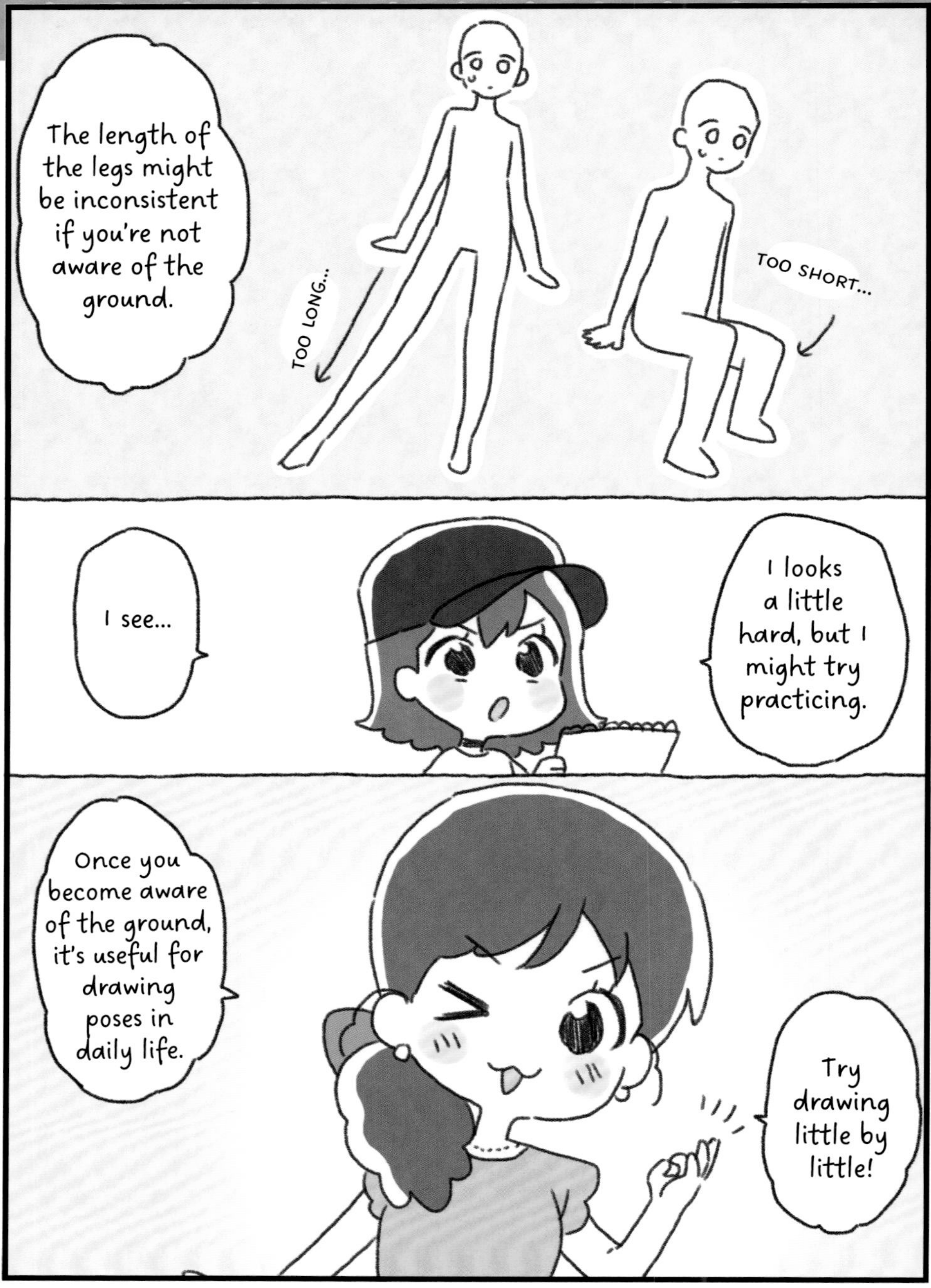
The length of the legs might be inconsistent if you're not aware of the ground.
TOO LONG...
TOO SHORT...
I looks a little hard, but I might try practicing.
I see...
Once you become aware of the ground, it's useful for drawing poses in daily life.
Try drawing little by little!

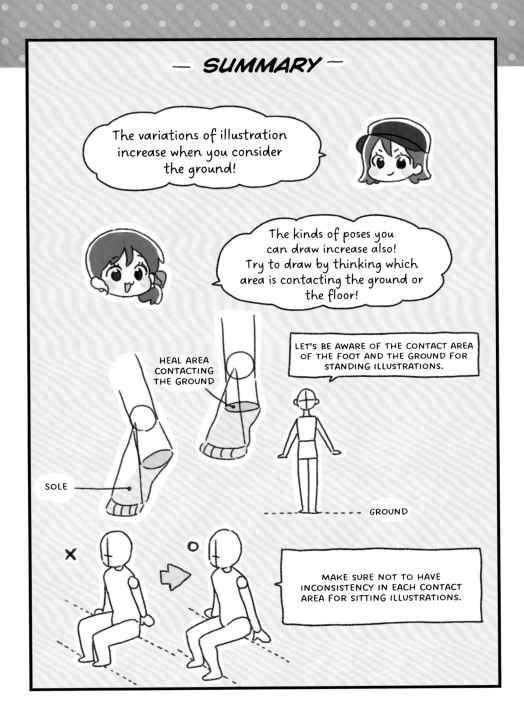

## — SUMMARY —

The variations of illustration increase when you consider the ground!

The kinds of poses you can draw increase also! Try to draw by thinking which area is contacting the ground or the floor!

HEAL AREA CONTACTING THE GROUND

LET'S BE AWARE OF THE CONTACT AREA OF THE FOOT AND THE GROUND FOR STANDING ILLUSTRATIONS.

SOLE

GROUND

MAKE SURE NOT TO HAVE INCONSISTENCY IN EACH CONTACT AREA FOR SITTING ILLUSTRATIONS.

# HOW TO DRAW ANGLED POSES

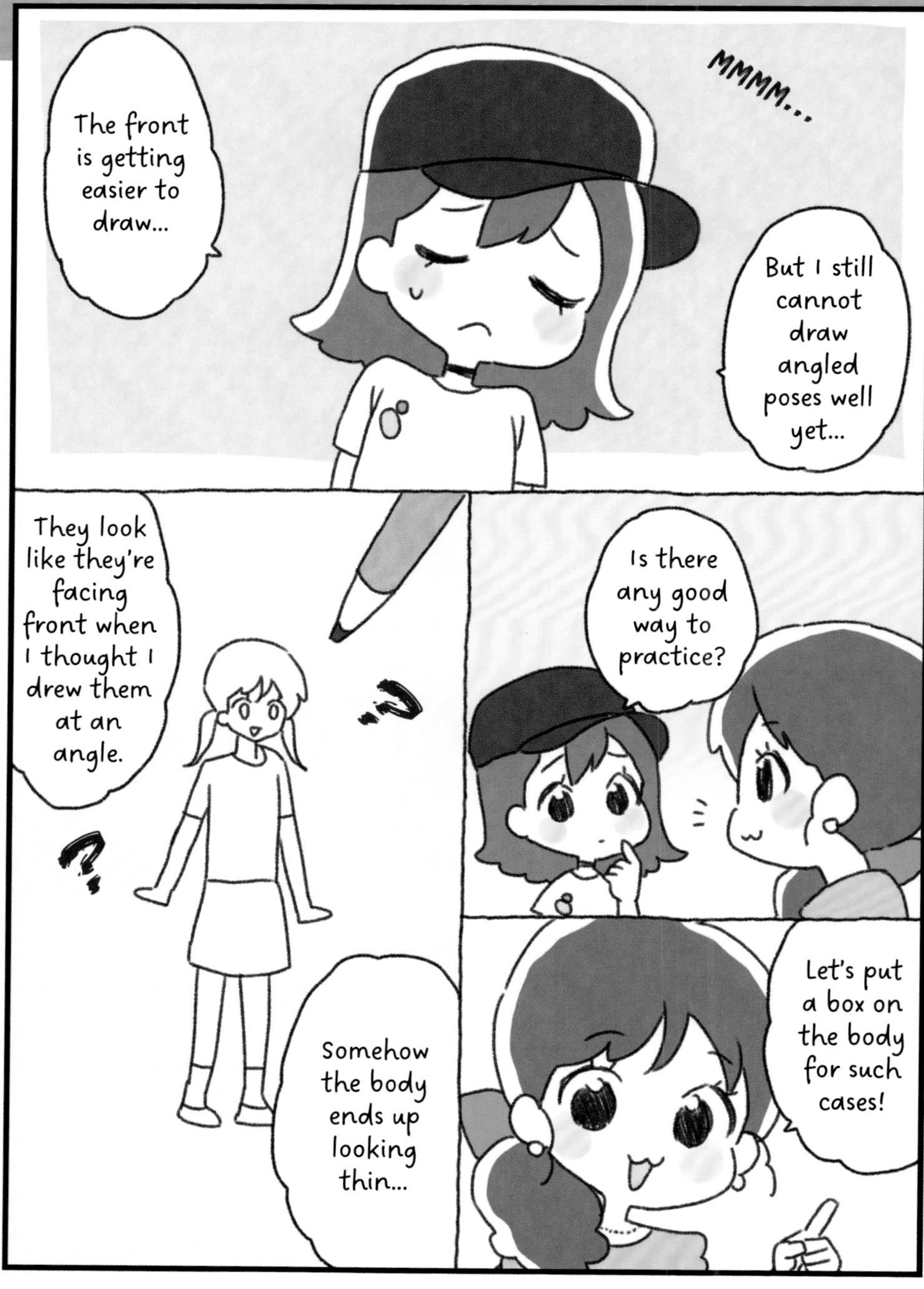

The front is getting easier to draw...
MMMM...
But I still cannot draw angled poses well yet...
They look like they're facing front when I thought I drew them at an angle.
Is there any good way to practice?
Somehow the body ends up looking thin...
Let's put a box on the body for such cases!

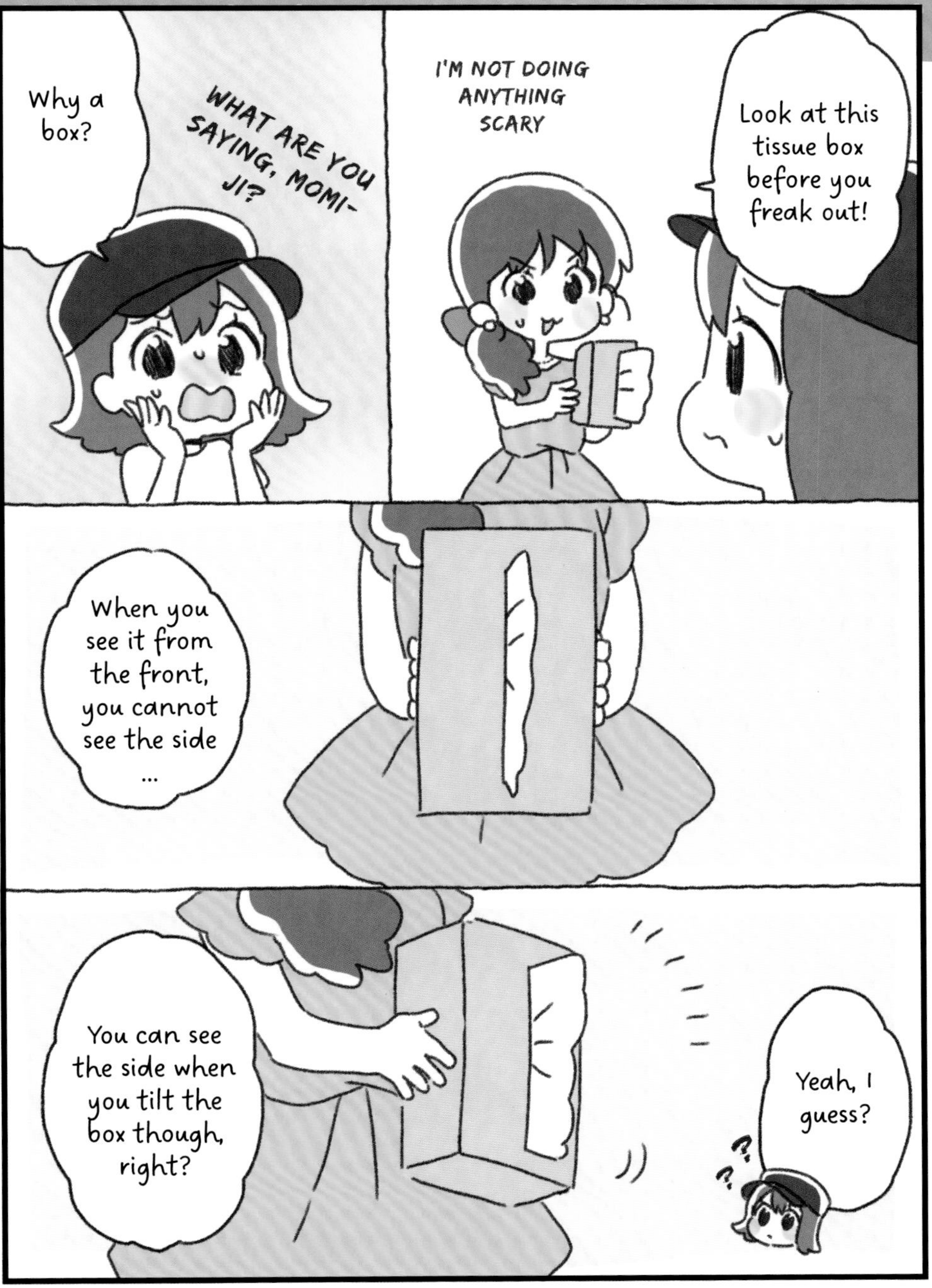
Why a box?
WHAT ARE YOU SAYING, MOMI-JI?
I'M NOT DOING ANYTHING SCARY
Look at this tissue box before you freak out!
When you see it from the front, you cannot see the side ...
You can see the side when you tilt the box though, right?
Yeah, I guess?

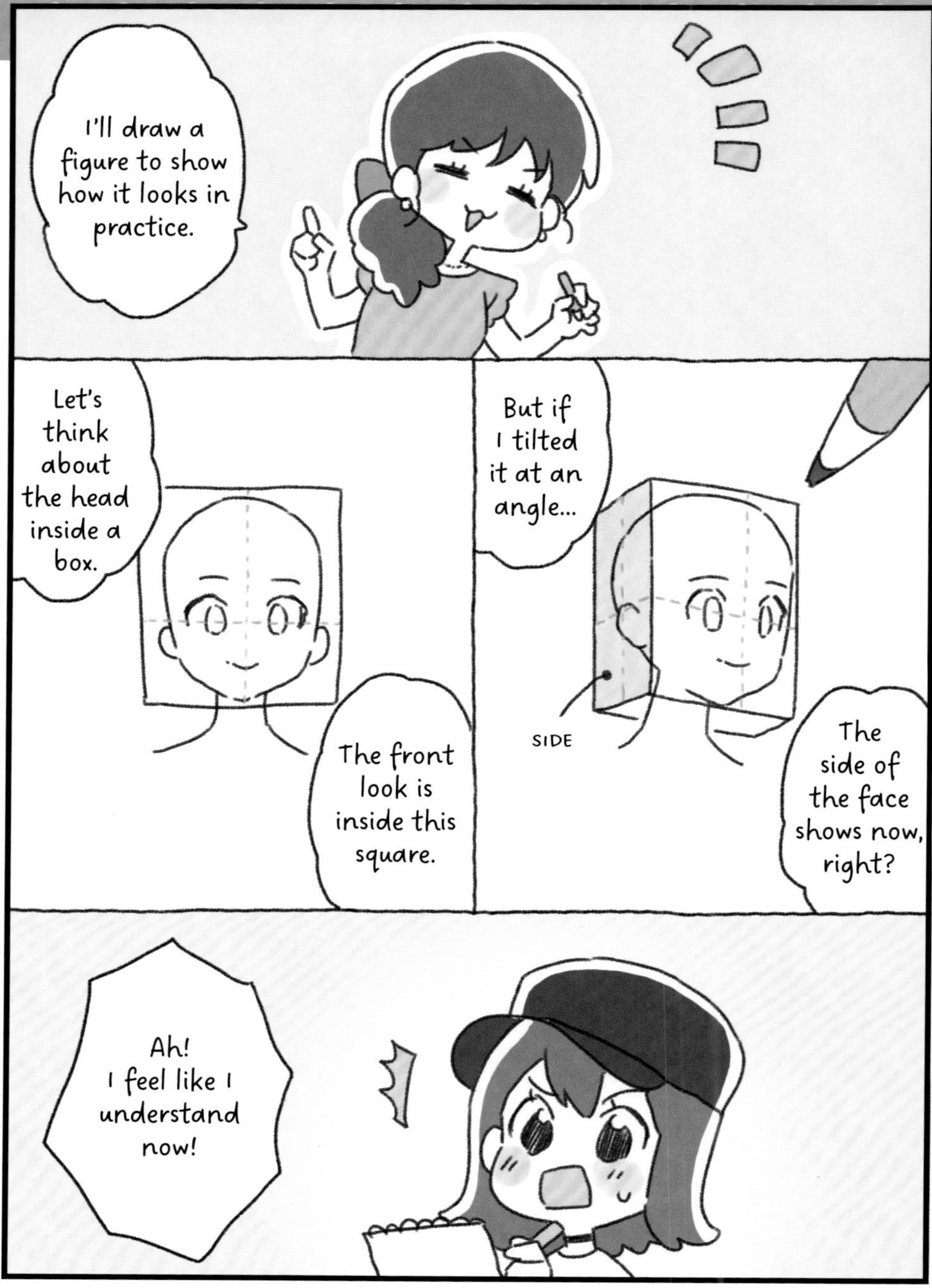

I'll draw a figure to show how it looks in practice.
Let's think about the head inside a box.
The front look is inside this square.
But if I tilted it at an angle...
SIDE
The side of the face shows now, right?
Ah! I feel like I understand now!

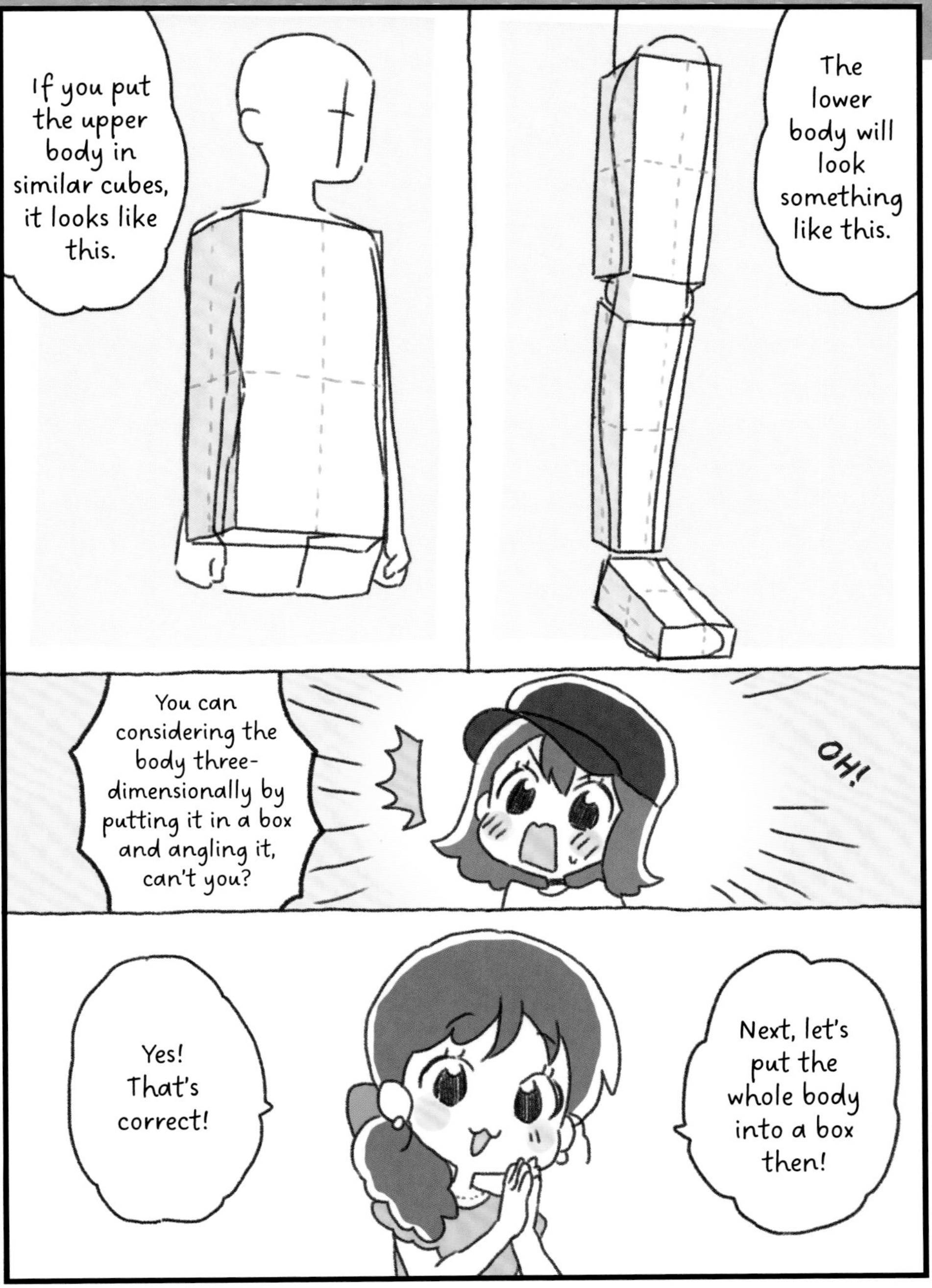
If you put the upper body in similar cubes, it looks like this.
The lower body will look something like this.
You can considering the body three-dimensionally by putting it in a box and angling it, can't you?
OH!
Yes! That's correct!
Next, let's put the whole body into a box then!

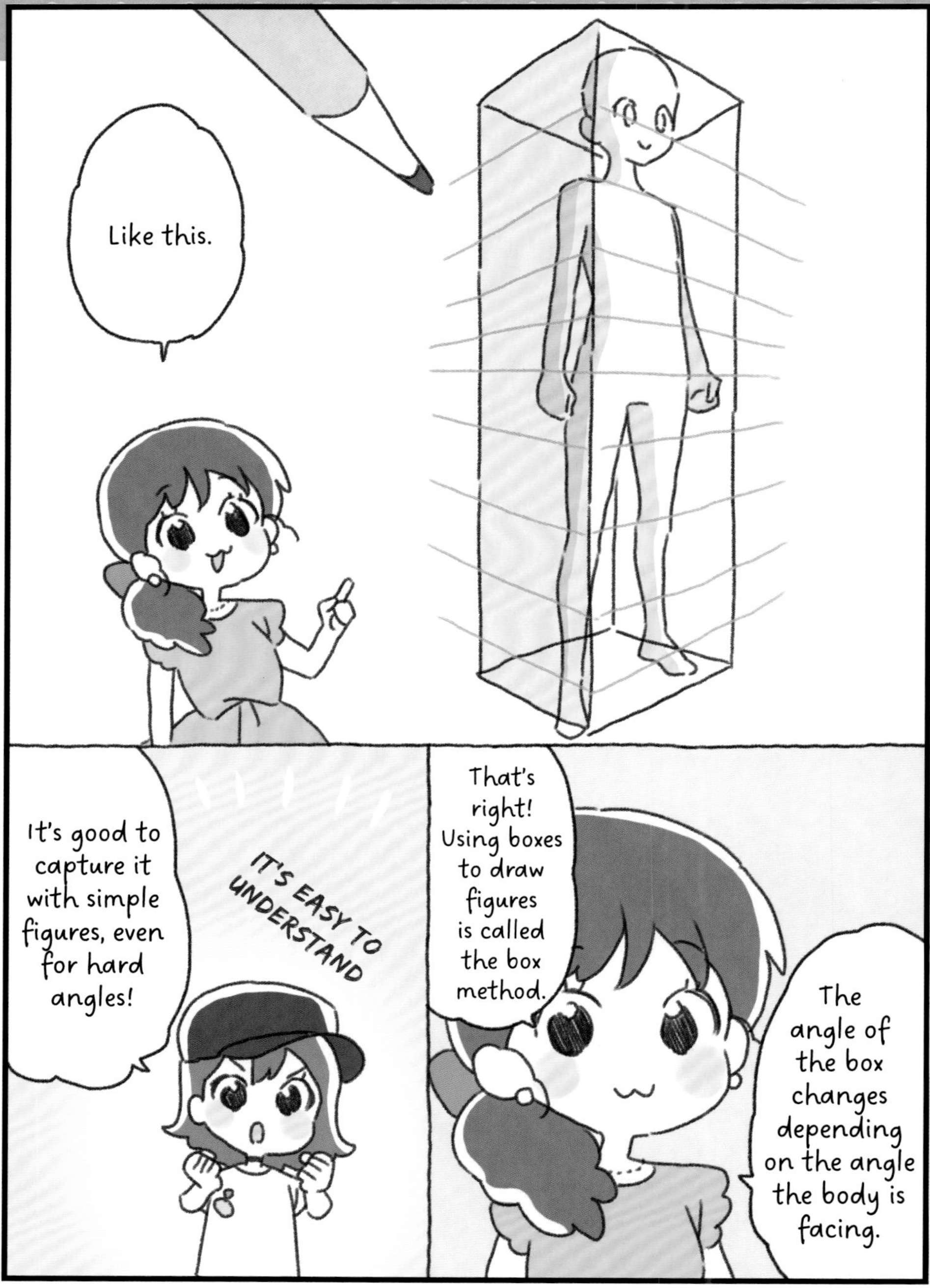
Like this.
It's good to capture it with simple figures, even for hard angles!
IT'S EASY TO UNDERSTAND
That's right! Using boxes to draw figures is called the box method.
The angle of the box changes depending on the angle the body is facing.

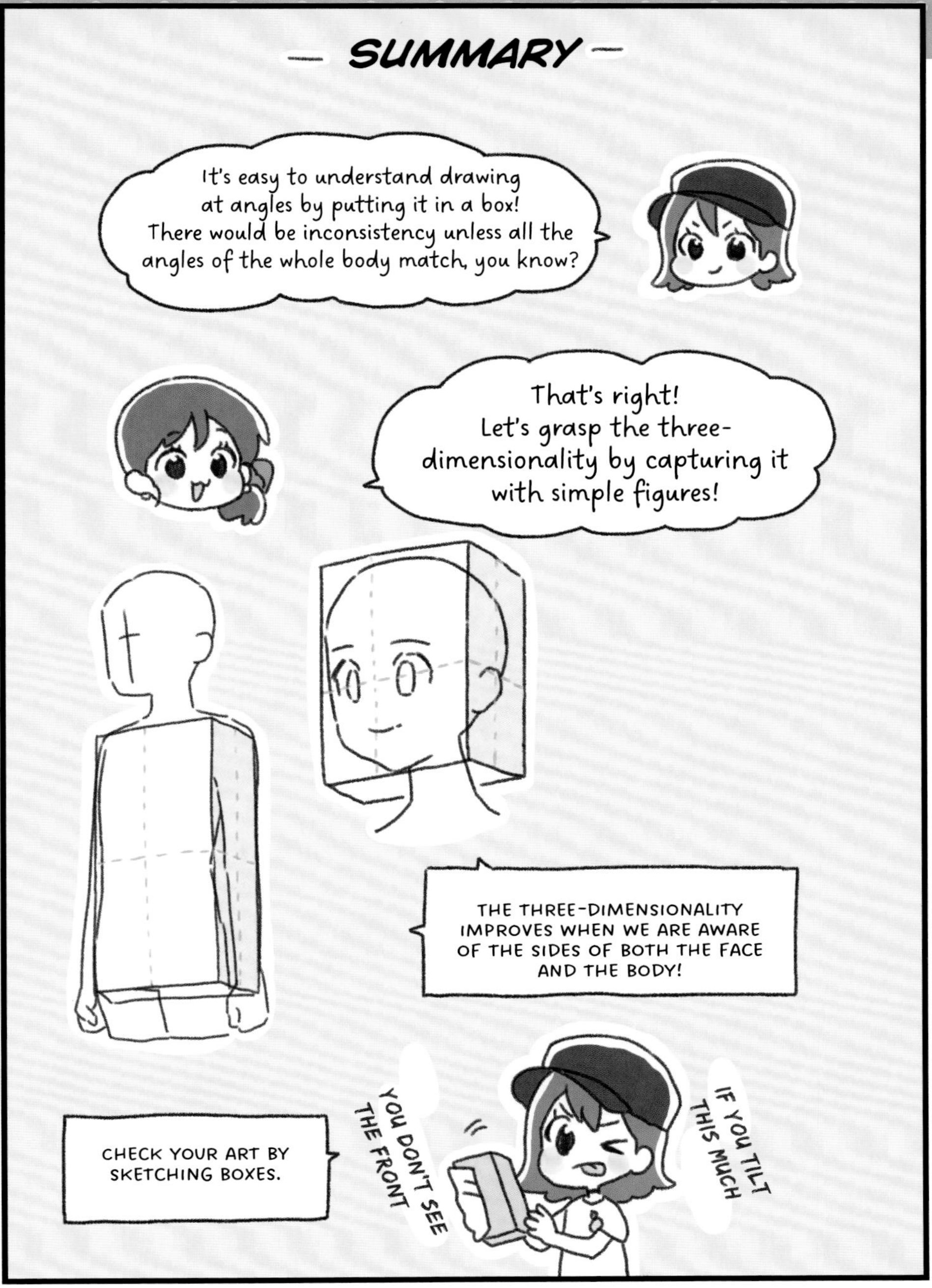
SUMMARY
It's easy to understand drawing at angles by putting it in a box! There would be inconsistency unless all the angles of the whole body match, you know?
That's right! Let's grasp the three-dimensionality by capturing it with simple figures!
THE THREE-DIMENSIONALITY IMPROVES WHEN WE ARE AWARE OF THE SIDES OF BOTH THE FACE AND THE BODY!
CHECK YOUR ART BY SKETCHING BOXES.
YOU DON'T SEE THE FRONT
IF YOU TILT THIS MUCH

# HOW TO SHOW POSES

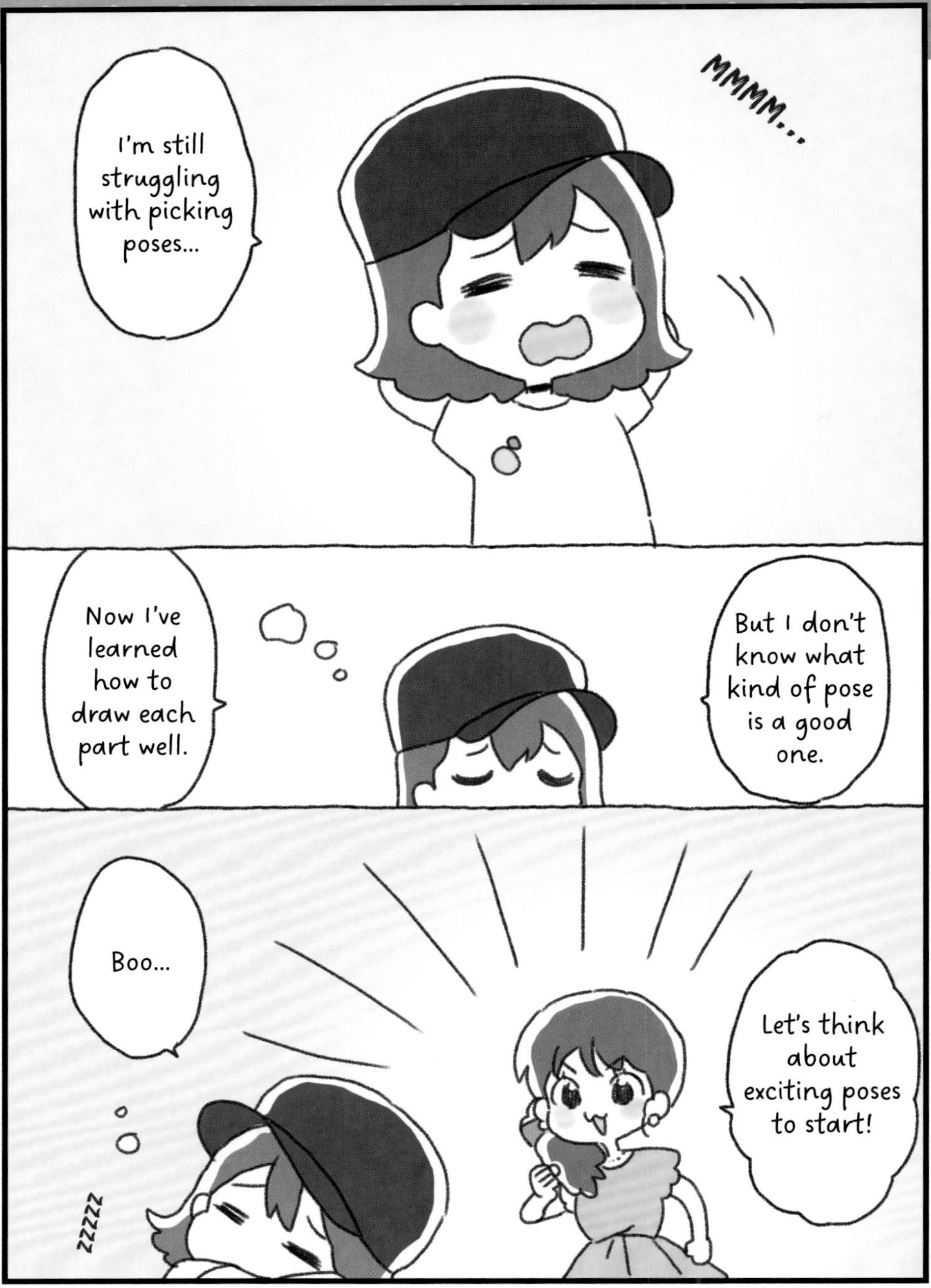
I'm still struggling with picking poses...
MMMM...
Now I've learned how to draw each part well.
But I don't know what kind of pose is a good one.
Boo...
Let's think about exciting poses to start!
ZZZZZ

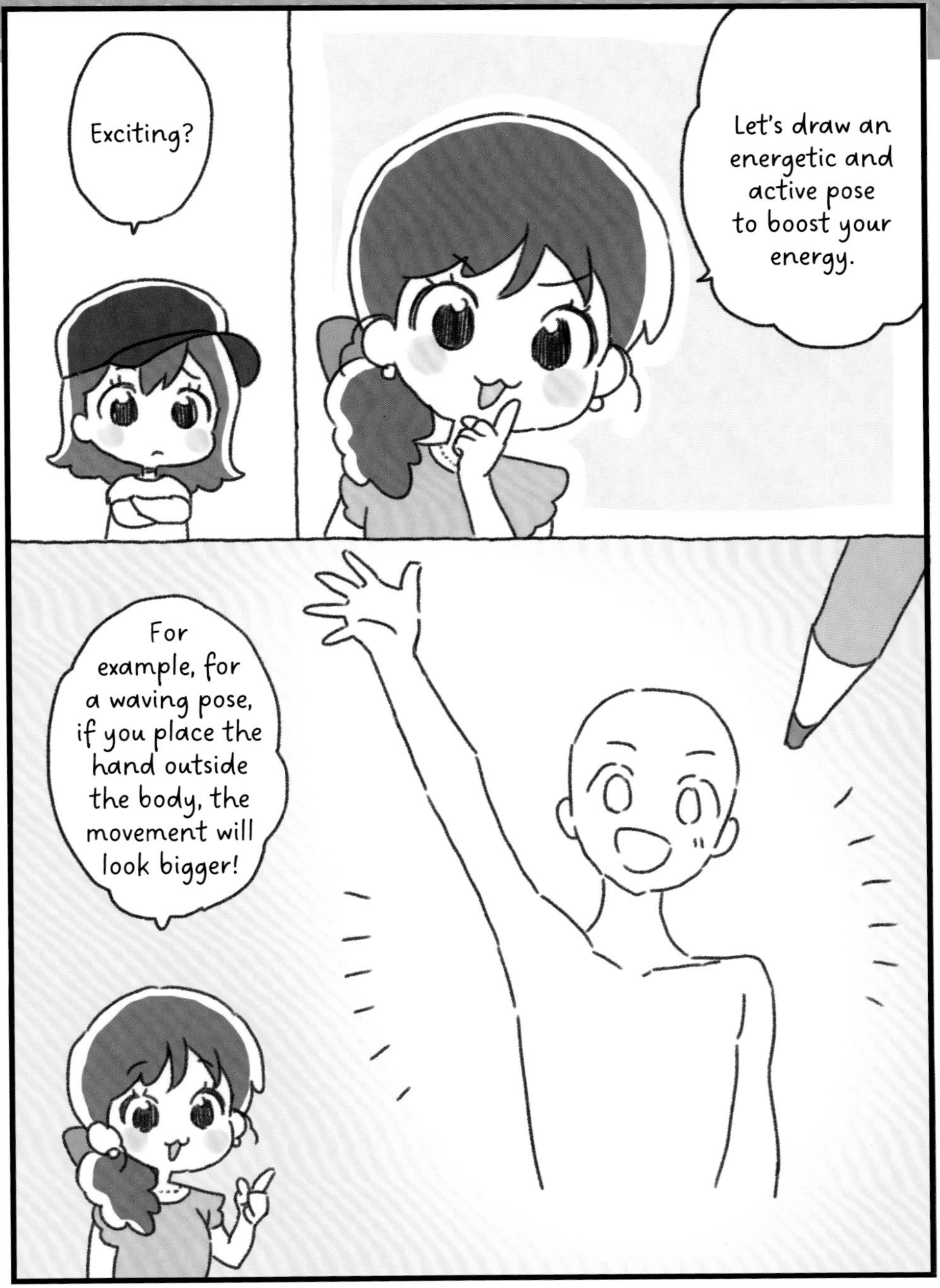
Let's draw an energetic and active pose to boost your energy.
Exciting?
For example, for a waving pose, if you place the hand outside the body, the movement will look bigger!

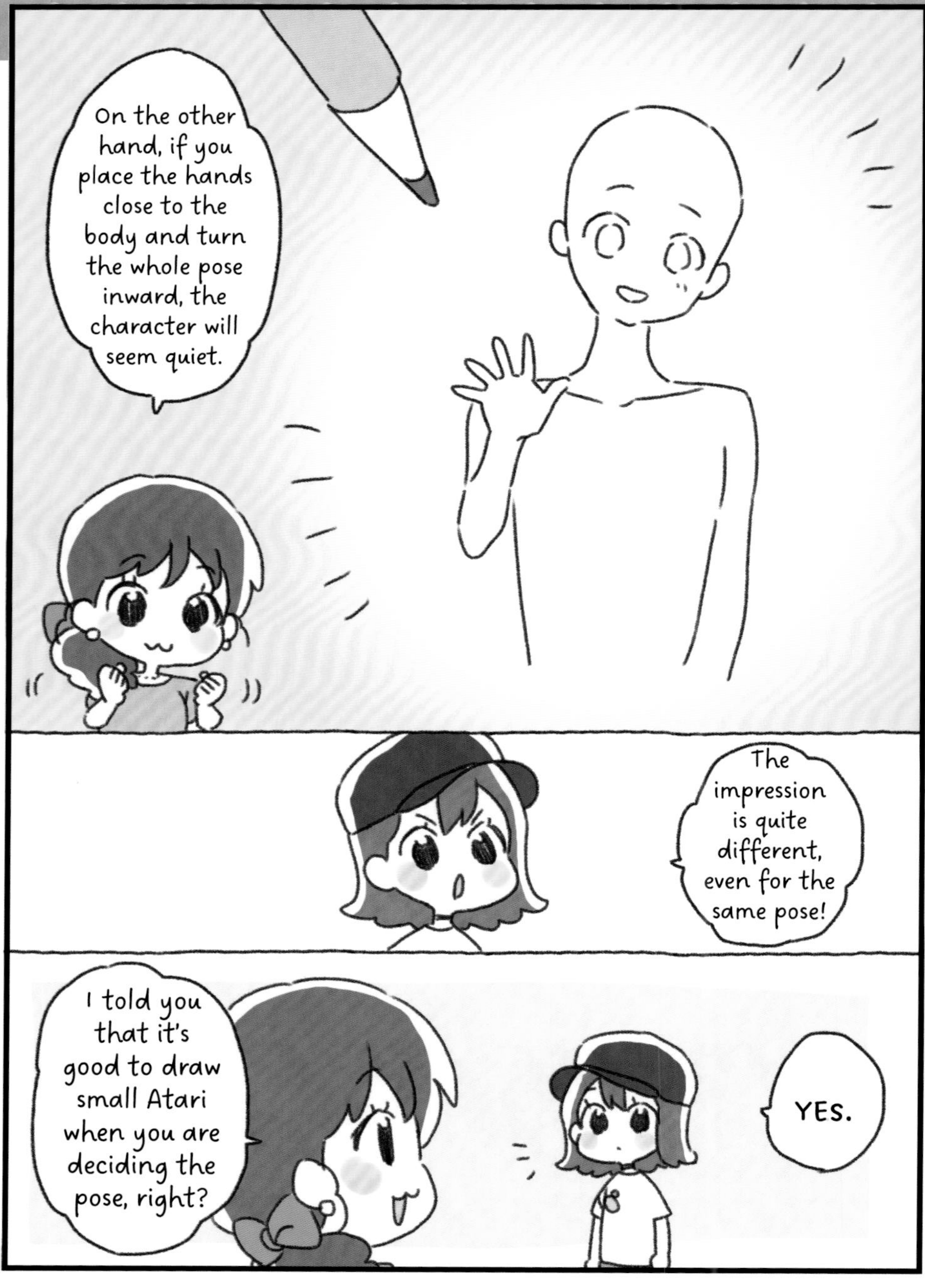
On the other hand, if you place the hands close to the body and turn the whole pose inward, the character will seem quiet.
The impression is quite different, even for the same pose!
I told you that it's good to draw small Atari when you are deciding the pose, right?
YES.

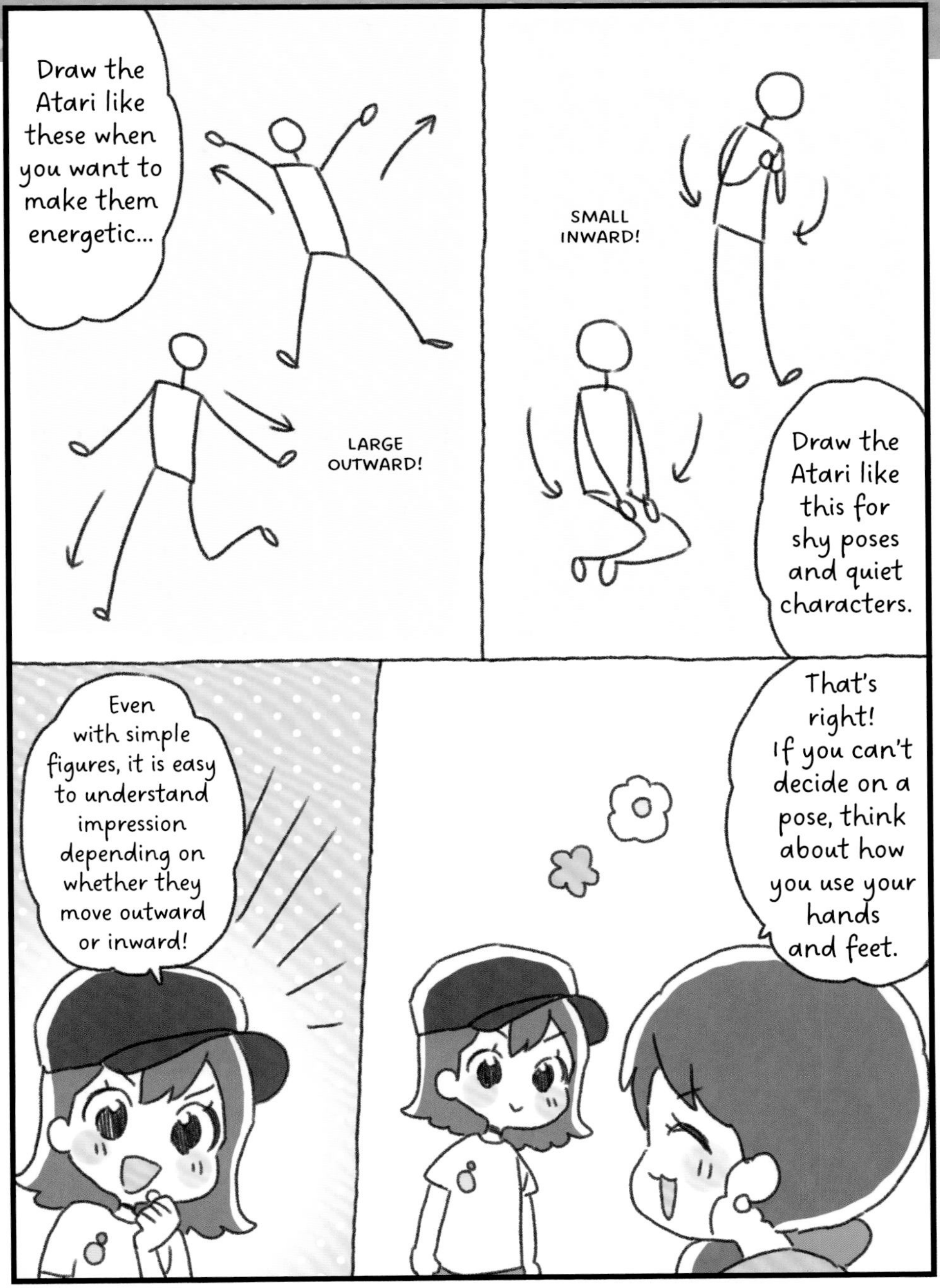
Draw the Atari like these when you want to make them energetic...
LARGE OUTWARD!
SMALL INWARD!
Draw the Atari like this for shy poses and quiet characters.
Even with simple figures, it is easy to understand impression depending on whether they move outward or inward!
That's right! If you can't decide on a pose, think about how you use your hands and feet.

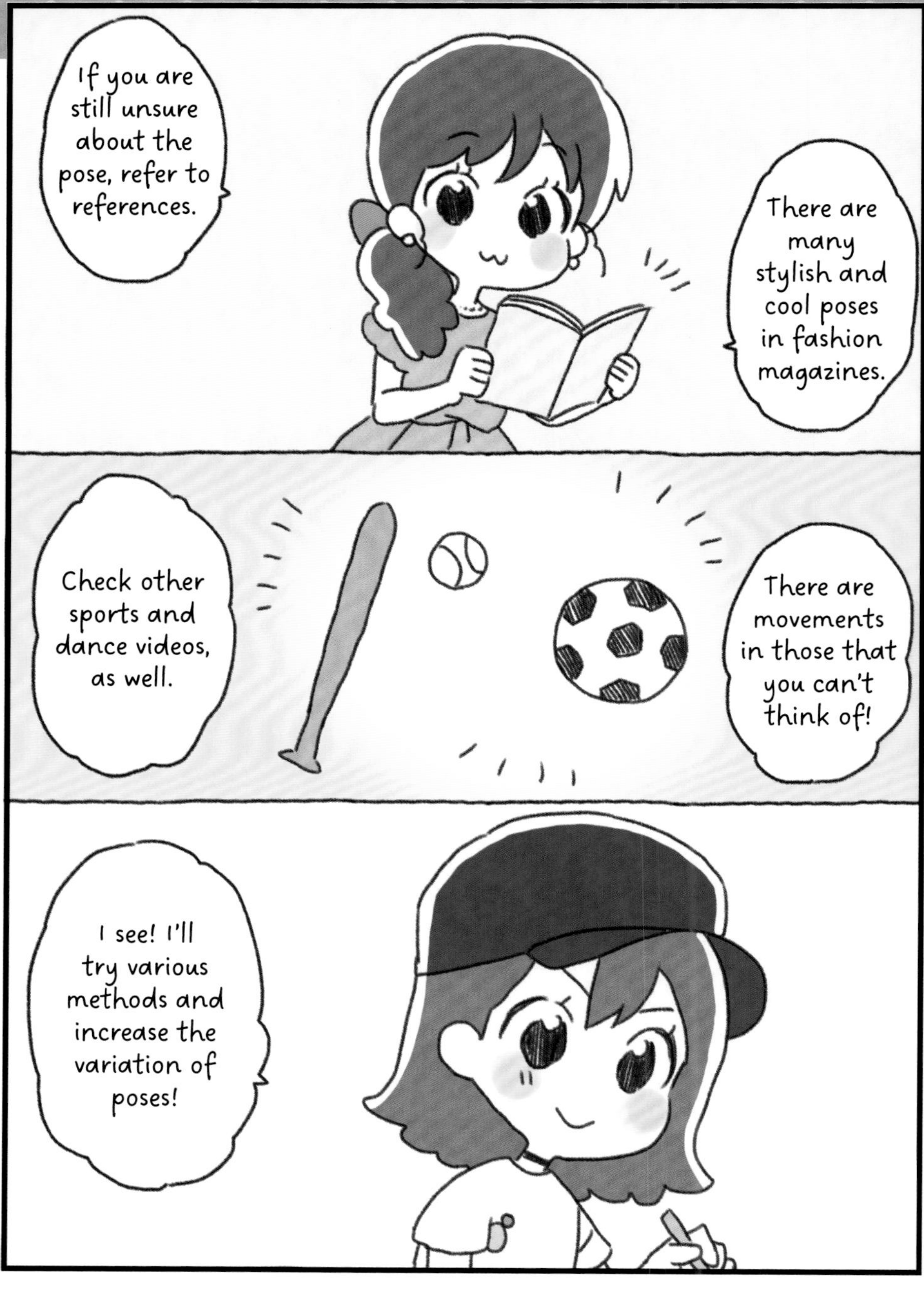
If you are still unsure about the pose, refer to references.
There are many stylish and cool poses in fashion magazines.
Check other sports and dance videos, as well.
There are movements in those that you can't think of!
I see! I'll try various methods and increase the variation of poses!

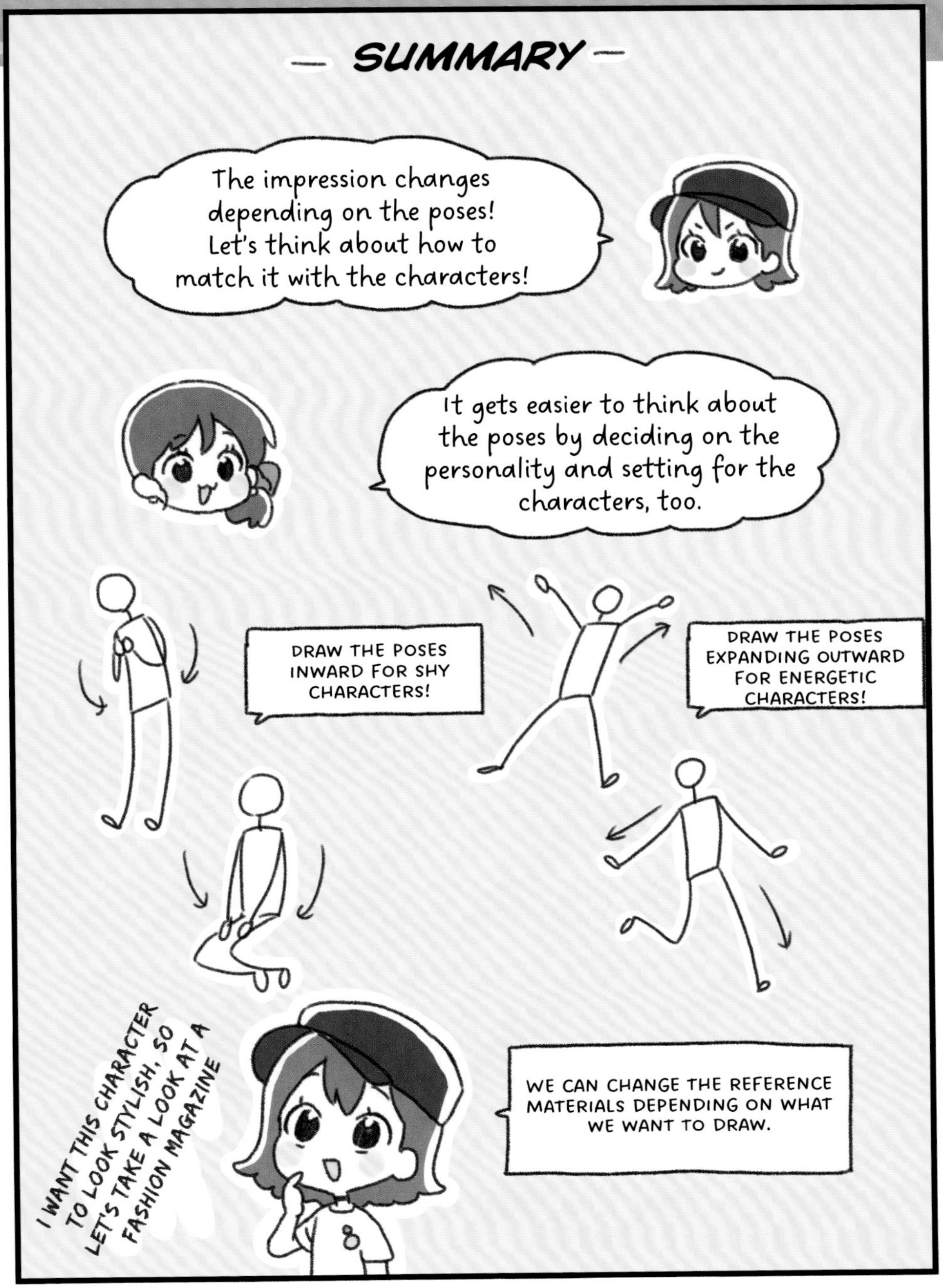
SUMMARY
The impression changes depending on the poses! Let's think about how to match it with the characters!
It gets easier to think about the poses by deciding on the personality and setting for the characters, too.
DRAW THE POSES INWARD FOR SHY CHARACTERS!
DRAW THE POSES EXPANDING OUTWARD FOR ENERGETIC CHARACTERS!
I WANT THIS CHARACTER TO LOOK STYLISH, SO LET'S TAKE A LOOK AT A FASHION MAGAZINE
WE CAN CHANGE THE REFERENCE MATERIALS DEPENDING ON WHAT WE WANT TO DRAW.

# POSES AND COMPOSITION

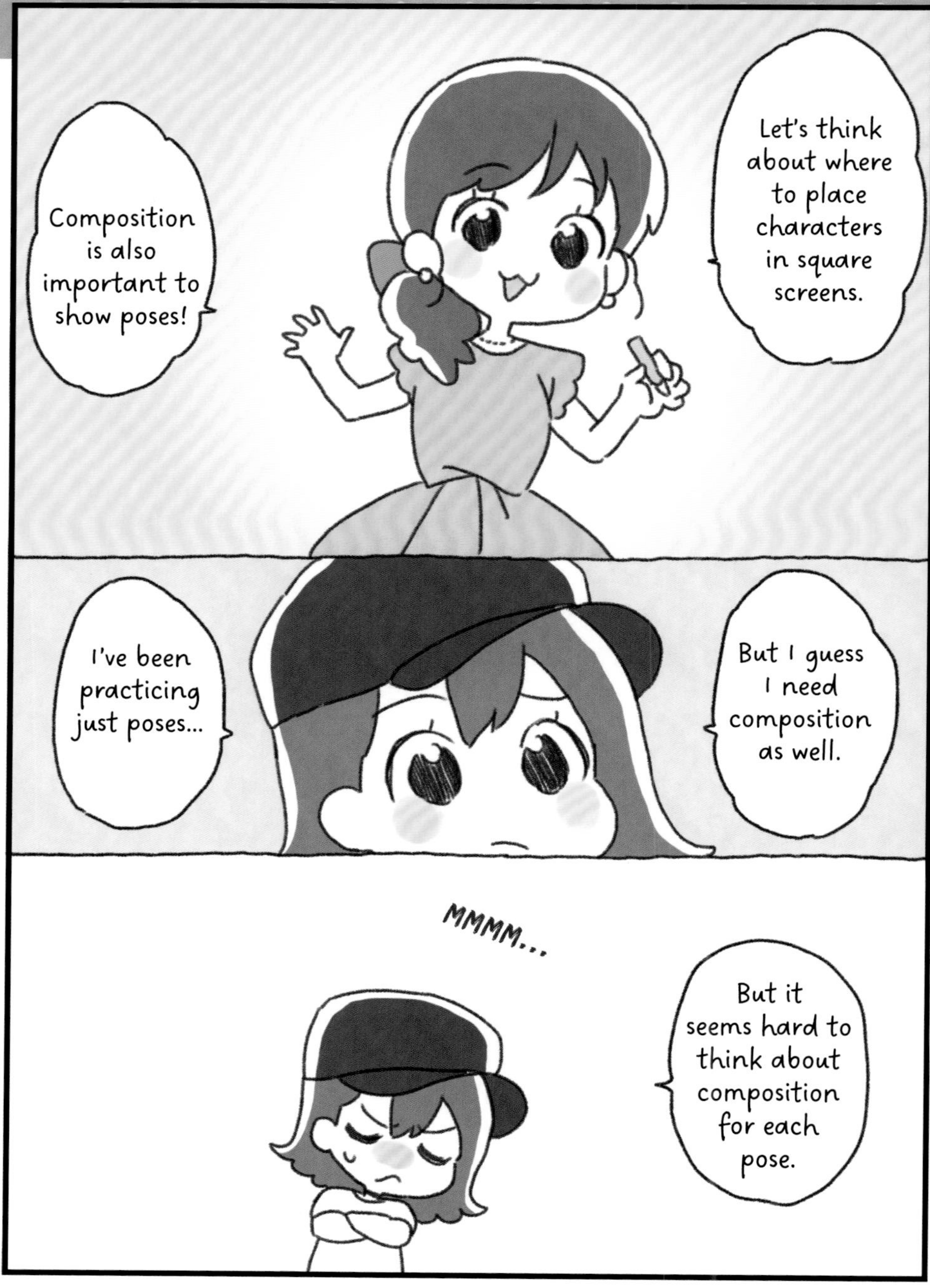
Composition is also important to show poses!
Let's think about where to place characters in square screens.
I've been practicing just poses...
But I guess I need composition as well.
MMMM...
But it seems hard to think about composition for each pose.

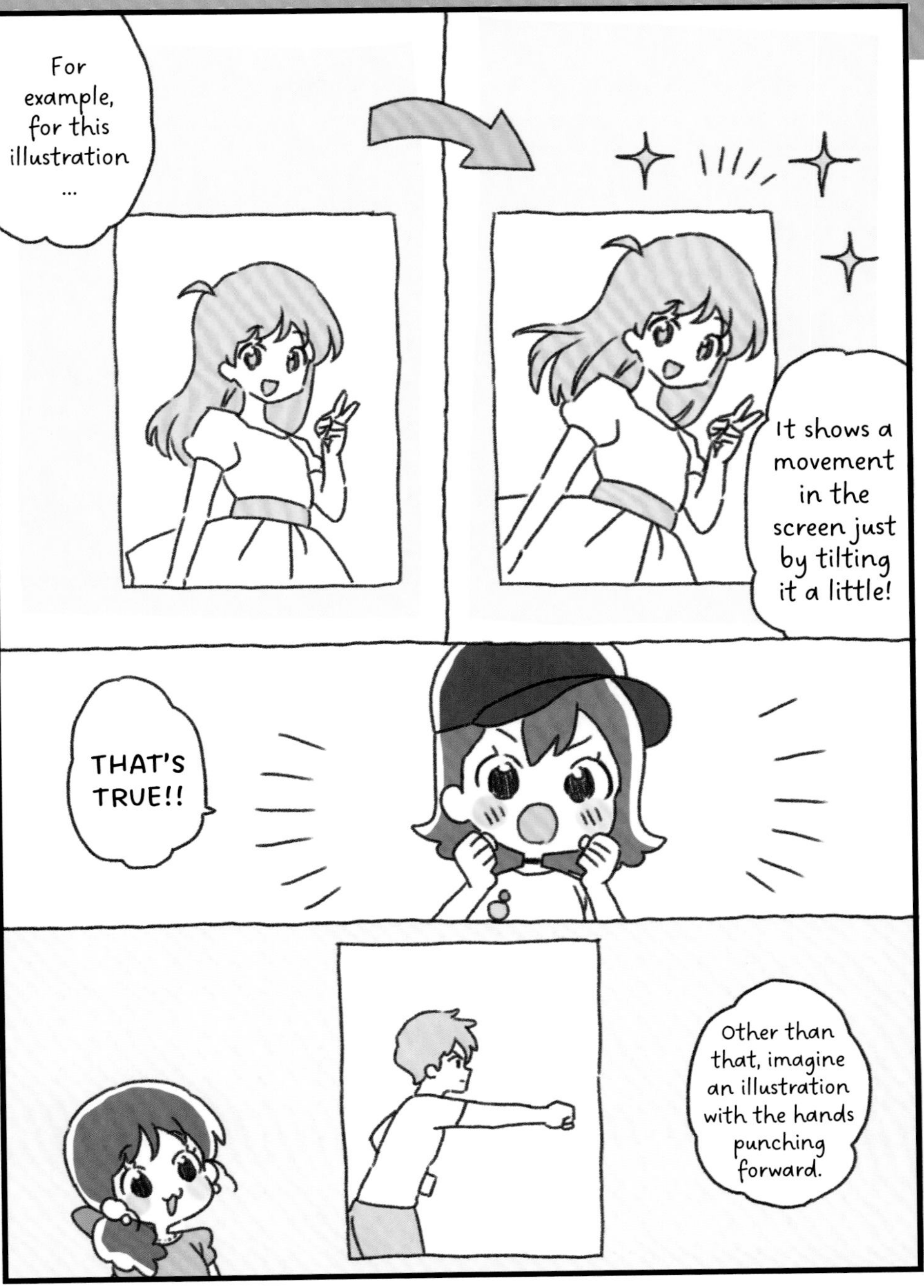
For example, for this illustration ...
It shows a movement in the screen just by tilting it a little!
THAT'S TRUE!!
Other than that, imagine an illustration with the hands punching forward.

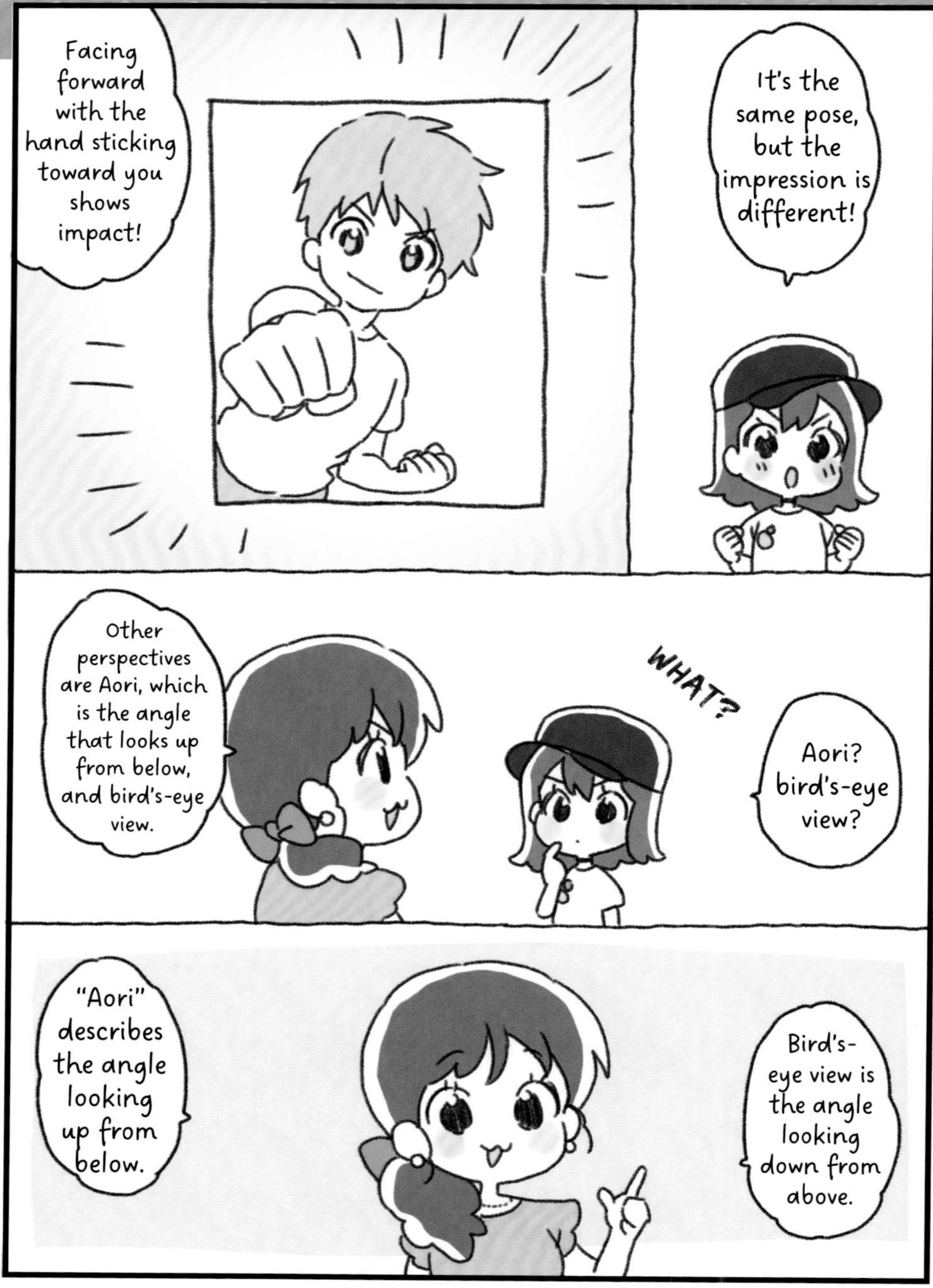
Facing forward with the hand sticking toward you shows impact!
It's the same pose, but the impression is different!
Other perspectives are Aori, which is the angle that looks up from below, and bird's-eye view.
WHAT?
Aori? bird's-eye view?
"Aori" describes the angle looking up from below.
Bird's-eye view is the angle looking down from above.

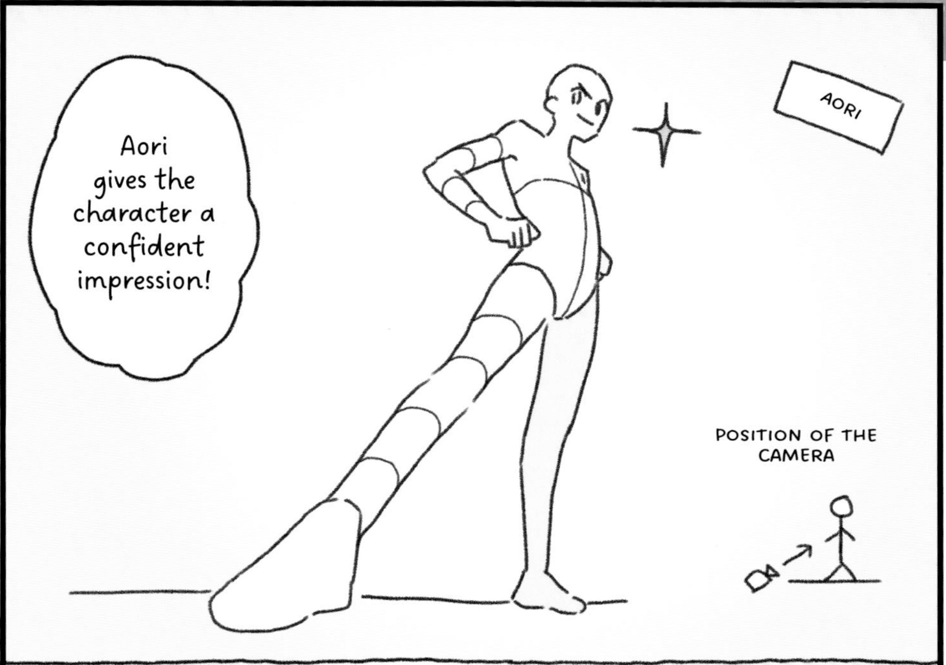
Aori gives the character a confident impression!
AORI
POSITION OF THE CAMERA

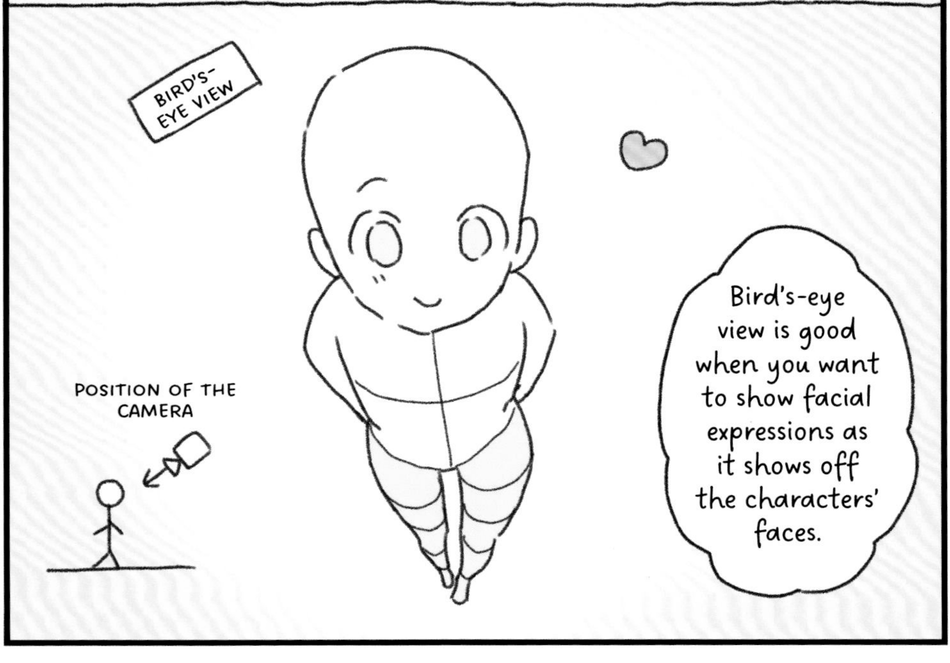
BIRD'S-EYE VIEW
POSITION OF THE CAMERA
Bird's-eye view is good when you want to show facial expressions as it shows off the characters' faces.

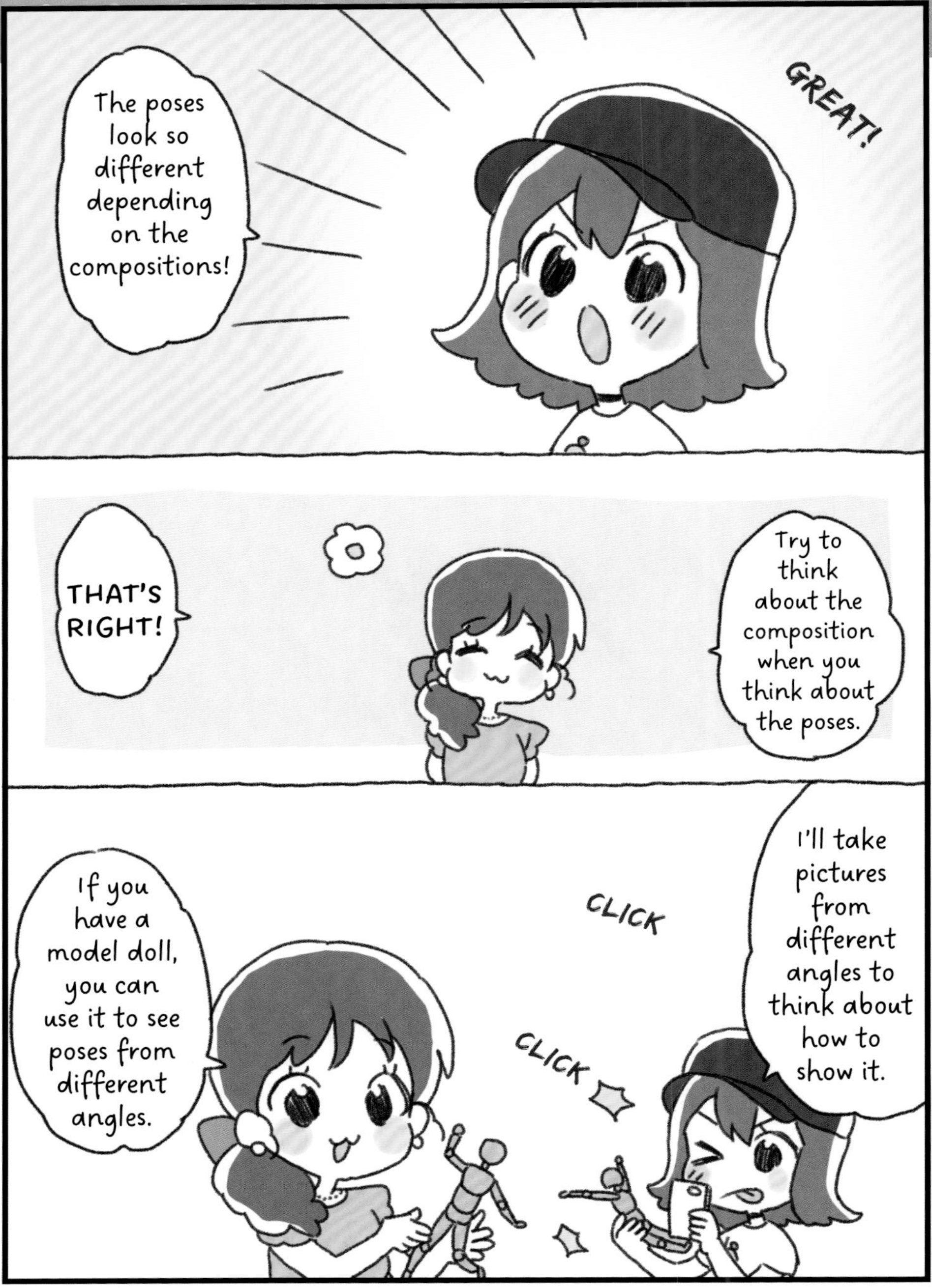
GREAT!
The poses look so different depending on the compositions!
THAT'S RIGHT!
Try to think about the composition when you think about the poses.
I'll take pictures from different angles to think about how to show it.
CLICK
CLICK
If you have a model doll, you can use it to see poses from different angles.

## SUMMARY

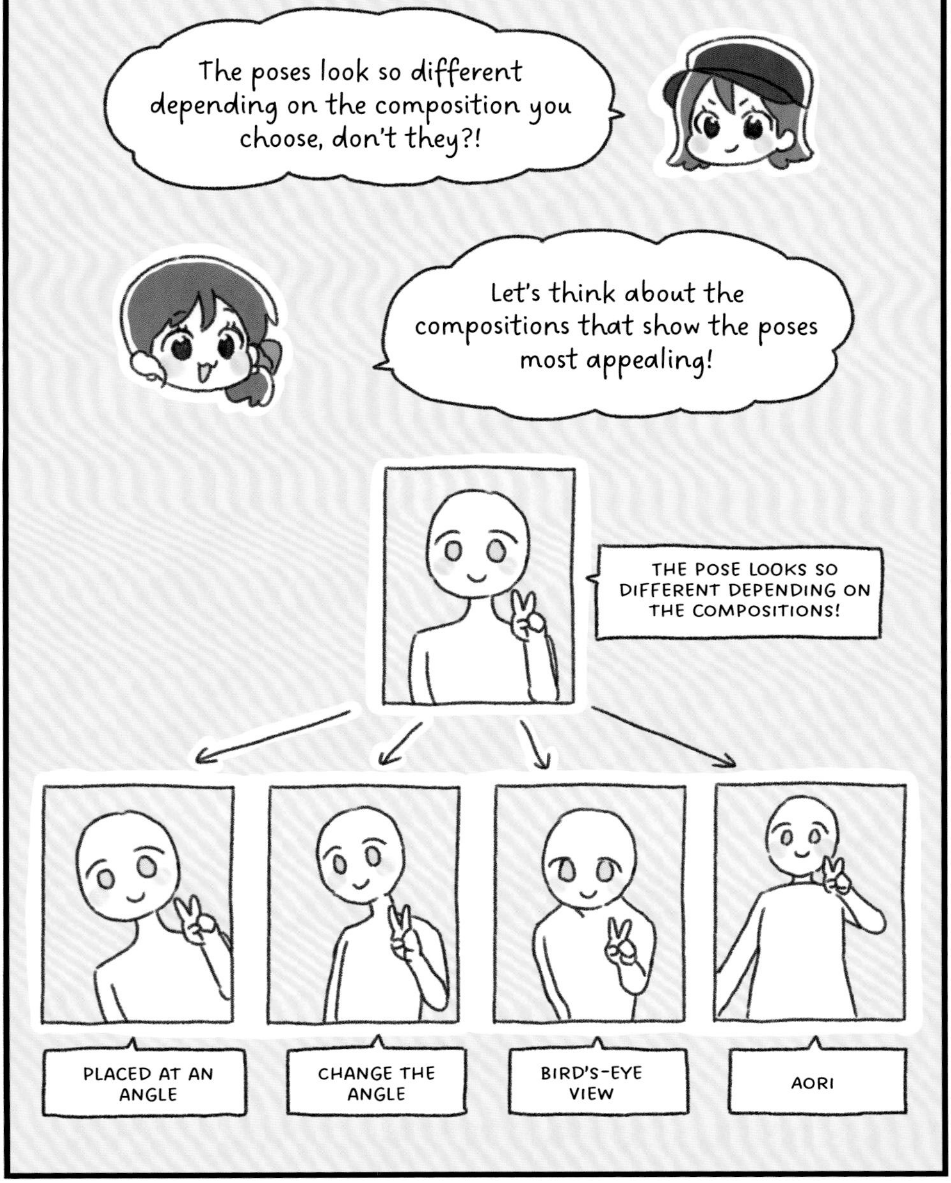
The poses look so different depending on the composition you choose, don't they?!
Let's think about the compositions that show the poses most appealing!
THE POSE LOOKS SO DIFFERENT DEPENDING ON THE COMPOSITIONS!
PLACED AT AN ANGLE
CHANGE THE ANGLE
BIRD'S-EYE VIEW
AORI

# AORI AND BIRD'S-EYE VIEW

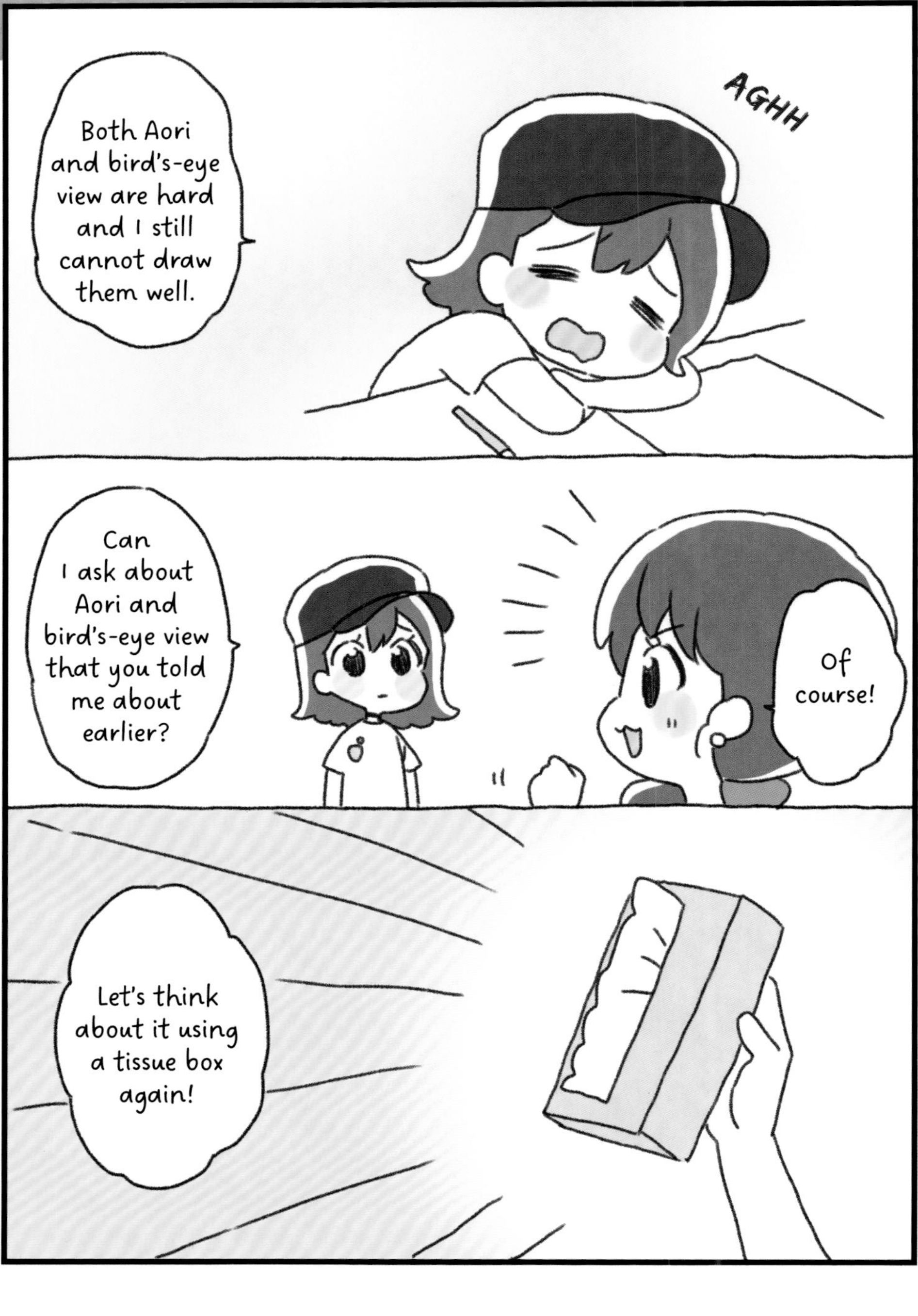
Both Aori and bird's-eye view are hard and I still cannot draw them well.
AGHH
Can I ask about Aori and bird's-eye view that you told me about earlier?
Of course!
Let's think about it using a tissue box again!

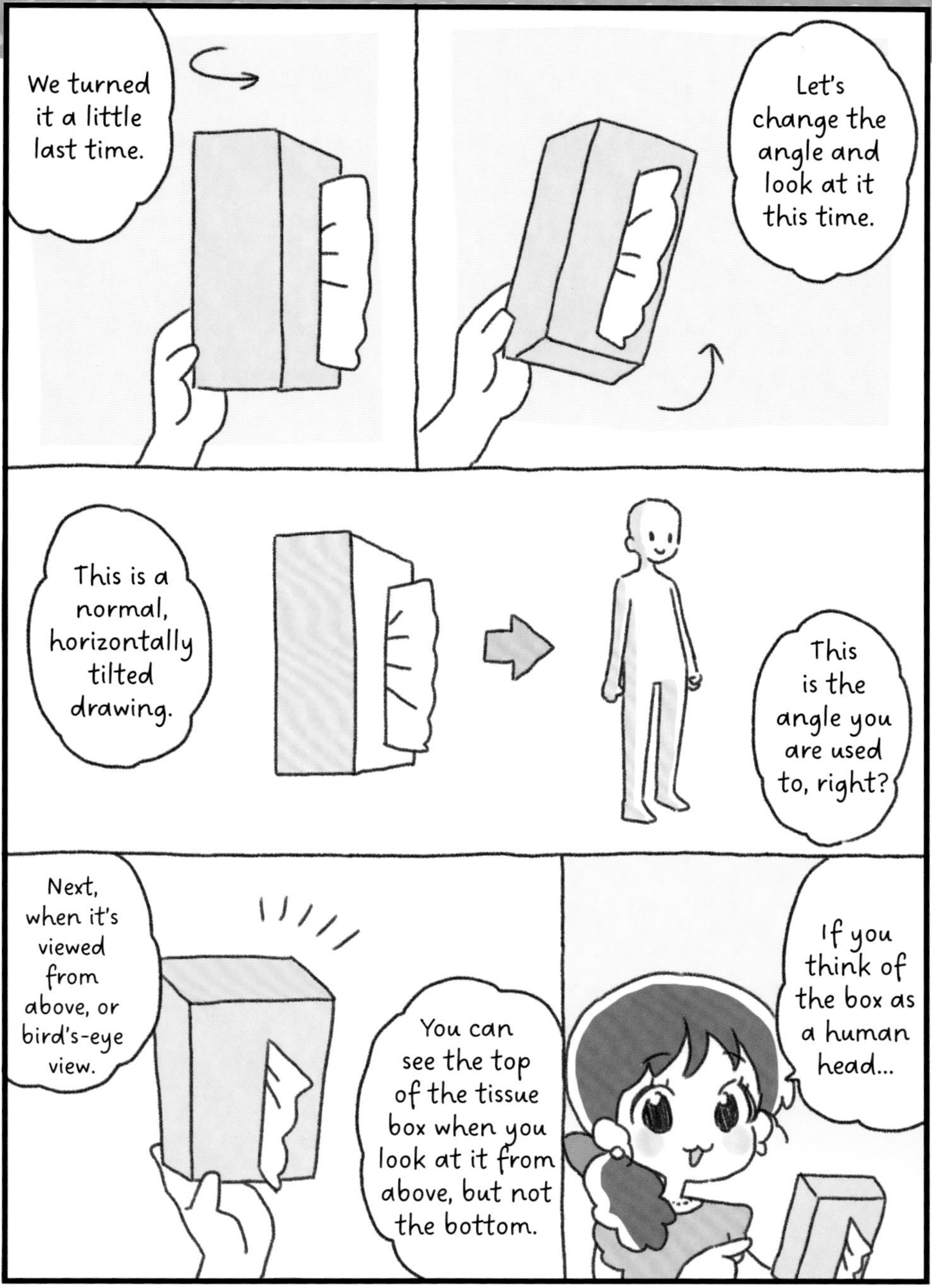
We turned it a little last time.
Let's change the angle and look at it this time.
This is a normal, horizontally tilted drawing.
This is the angle you are used to, right?
Next, when it's viewed from above, or bird's-eye view.
You can see the top of the tissue box when you look at it from above, but not the bottom.
If you think of the box as a human head...

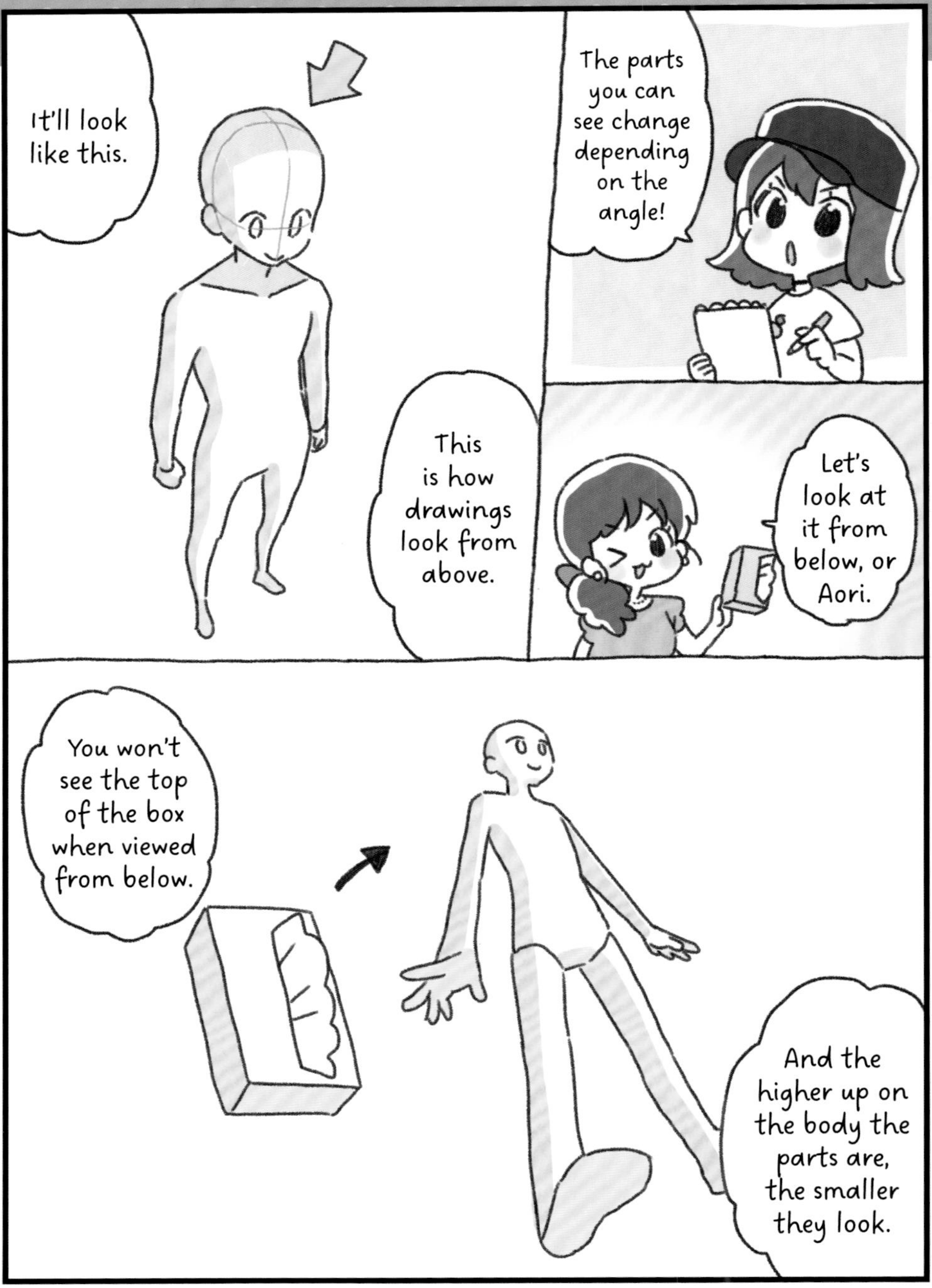
It'll look like this.
The parts you can see change depending on the angle!
This is how drawings look from above.
Let's look at it from below, or Aori.
You won't see the top of the box when viewed from below.
And the higher up on the body the parts are, the smaller they look.

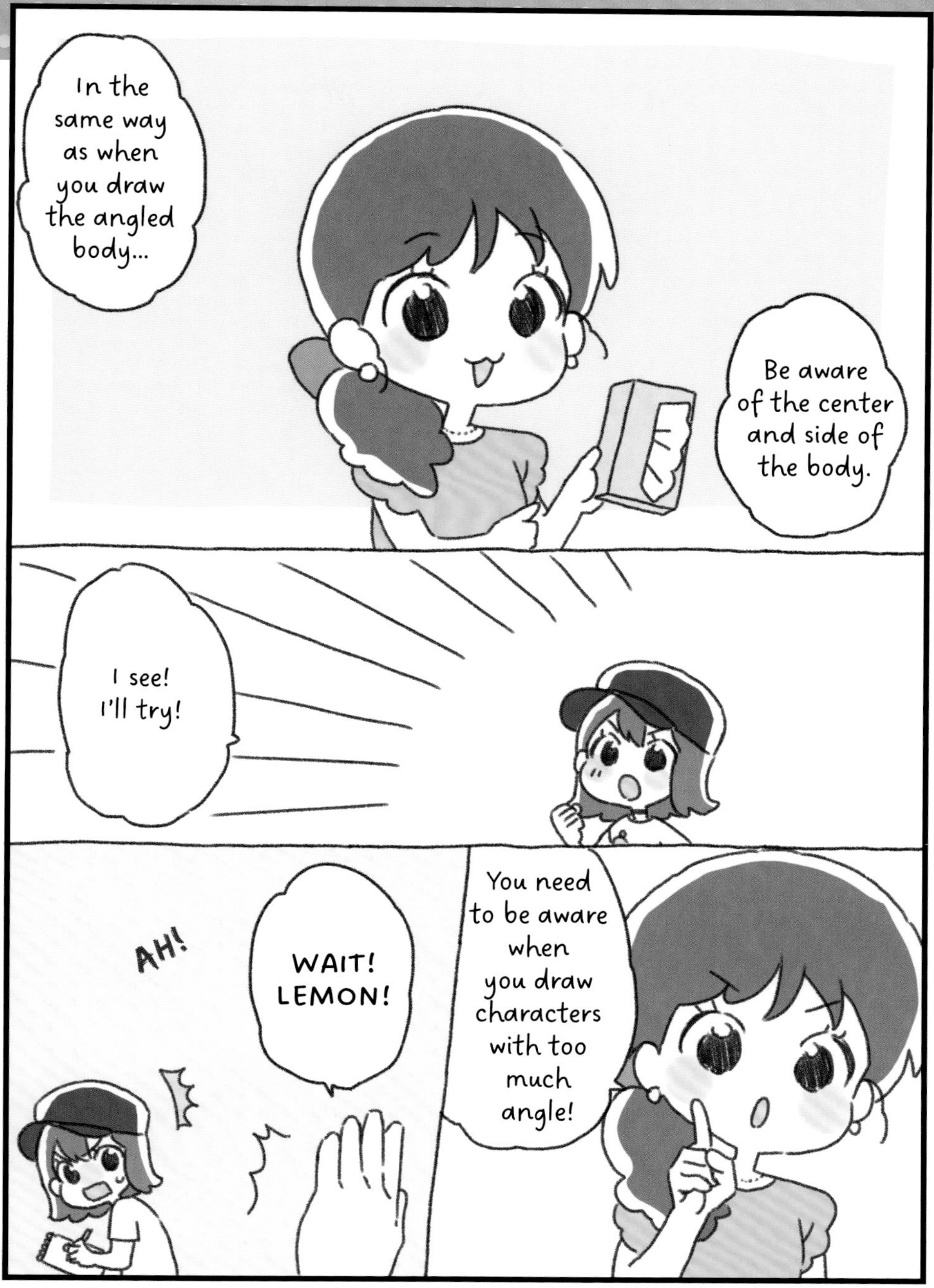
In the same way as when you draw the angled body...
Be aware of the center and side of the body.
I see! I'll try!
AH!
WAIT! LEMON!
You need to be aware when you draw characters with too much angle!

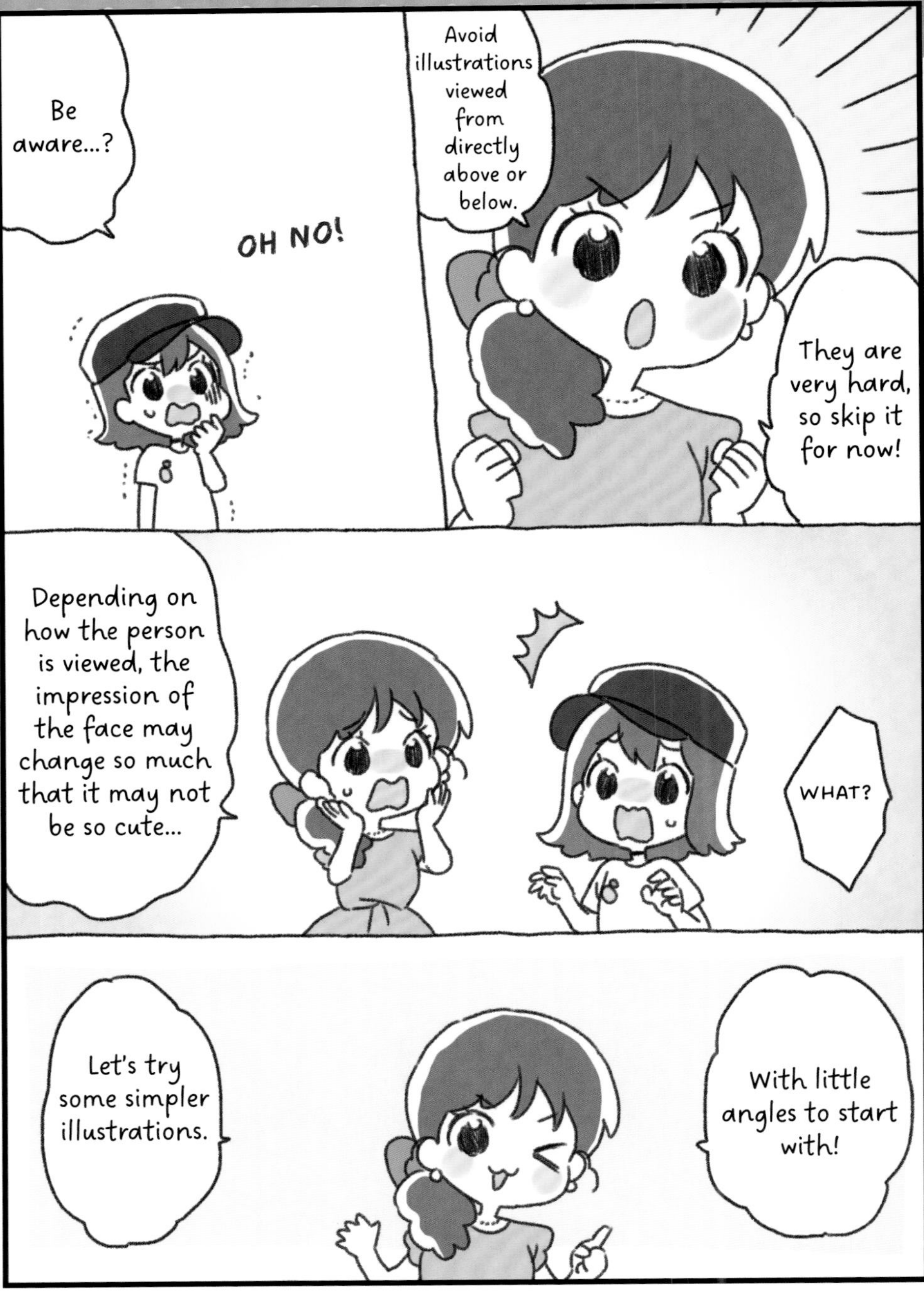
Be aware...?
OH NO!
Avoid illustrations viewed from directly above or below.
They are very hard, so skip it for now!
Depending on how the person is viewed, the impression of the face may change so much that it may not be so cute...
WHAT?
Let's try some simpler illustrations.
With little angles to start with!

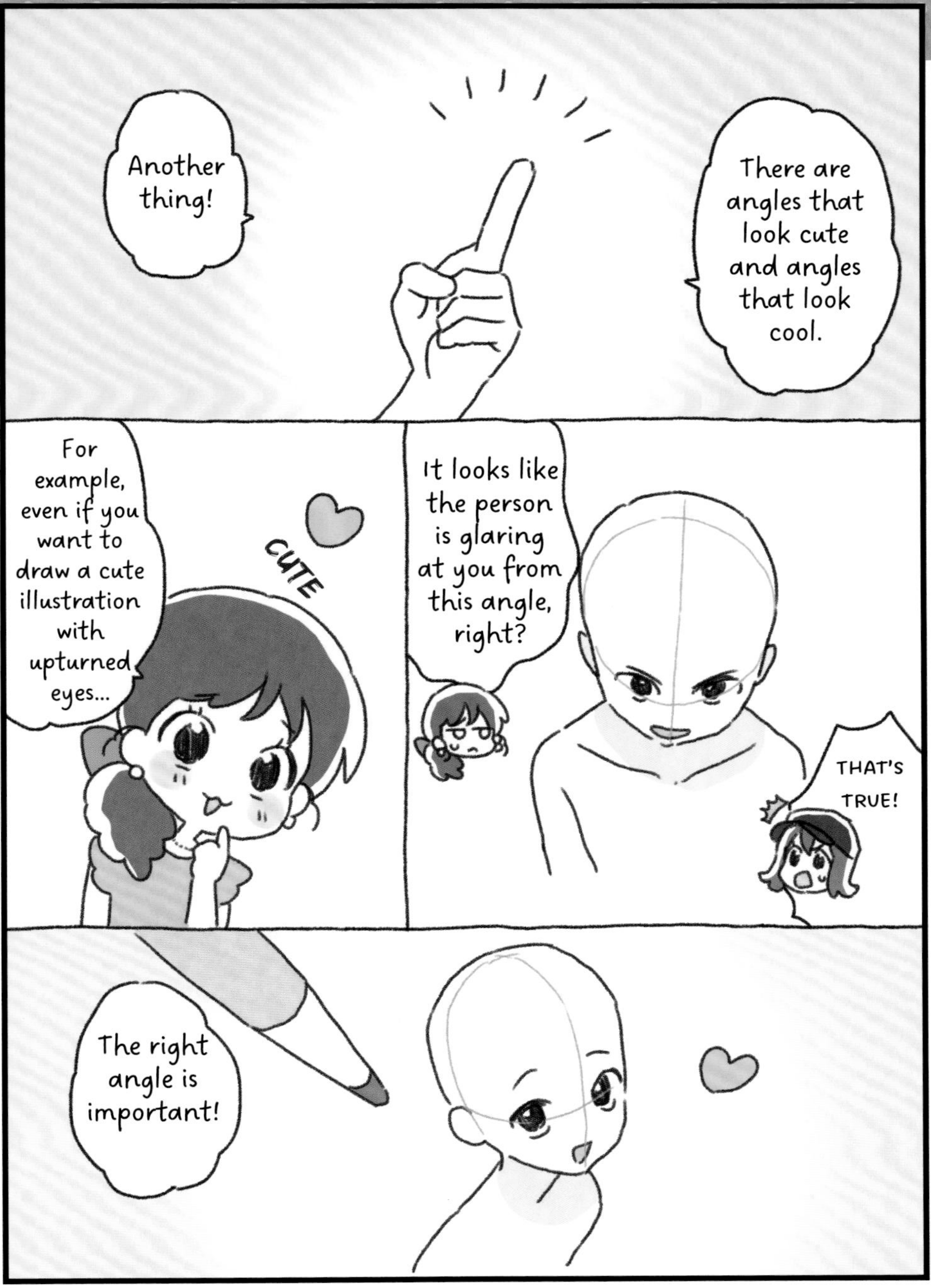
Another thing!
There are angles that look cute and angles that look cool.
For example, even if you want to draw a cute illustration with upturned eyes...
CUTE
It looks like the person is glaring at you from this angle, right?
THAT'S TRUE!
The right angle is important!

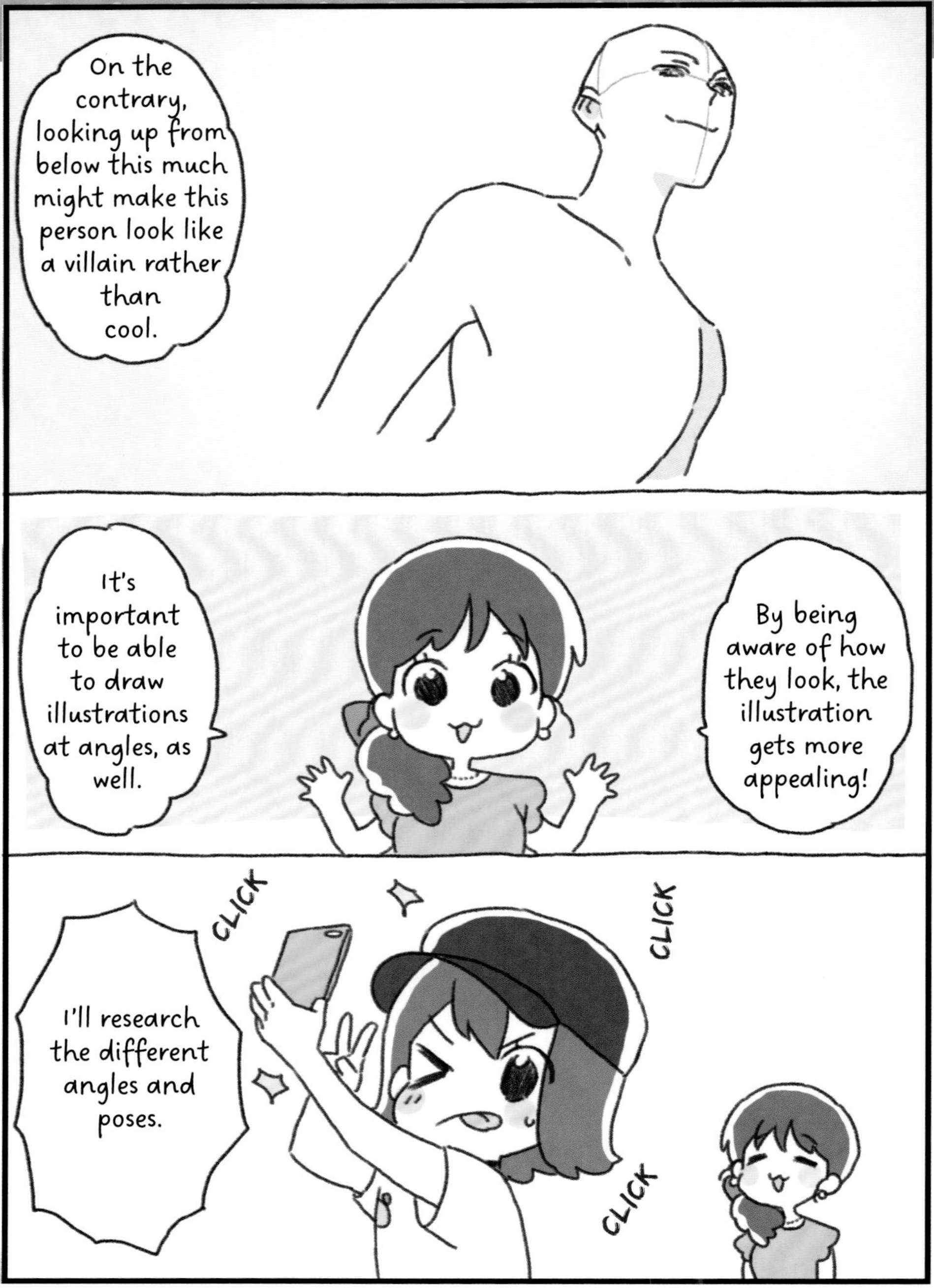
On the contrary, looking up from below this much might make this person look like a villain rather than cool.
It's important to be able to draw illustrations at angles, as well.
By being aware of how they look, the illustration gets more appealing!
CLICK
CLICK
I'll research the different angles and poses.
CLICK

## — SUMMARY —

It's hard to draw bodies at an angle, but it's important to keep the characteristics of Aori and bird's-eye view in mind!

That's right!
Whenever you think something is hard, it's easy to use simple figures to solve the problem!

LET'S REMEMBER HOW BIRD'S-EYE AND AORI VIEW LOOK.

THE TOP PART SHOWS.

THE BOTTOM PART SHOWS.

LET'S FIND THE RIGHT ANGLE FOR EACH POSE.

HOW ABOUT THIS ANGLE

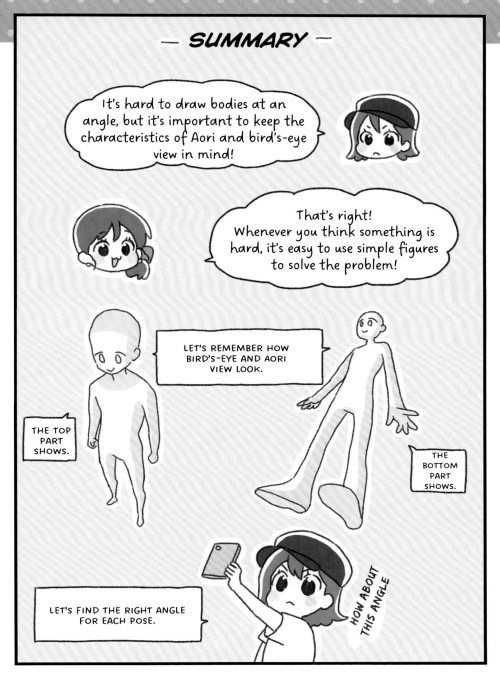

# EXTRA TIPS FOR DRAWING AORI AND BIRD'S-EYE VIEW

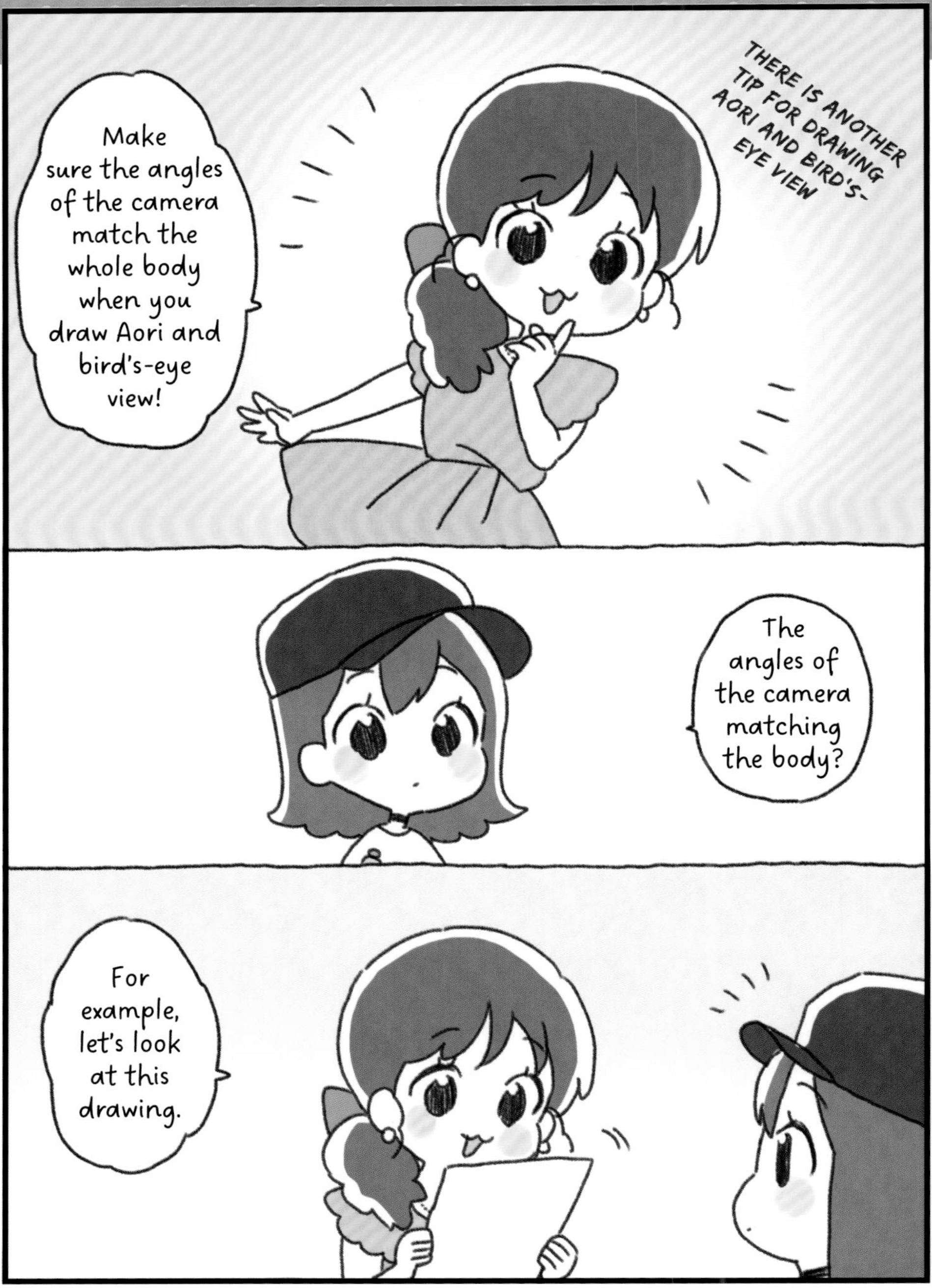
Make sure the angles of the camera match the whole body when you draw Aori and bird's-eye view!
THERE IS ANOTHER TIP FOR DRAWING AORI AND BIRD'S-EYE VIEW
The angles of the camera matching the body?
For example, let's look at this drawing.

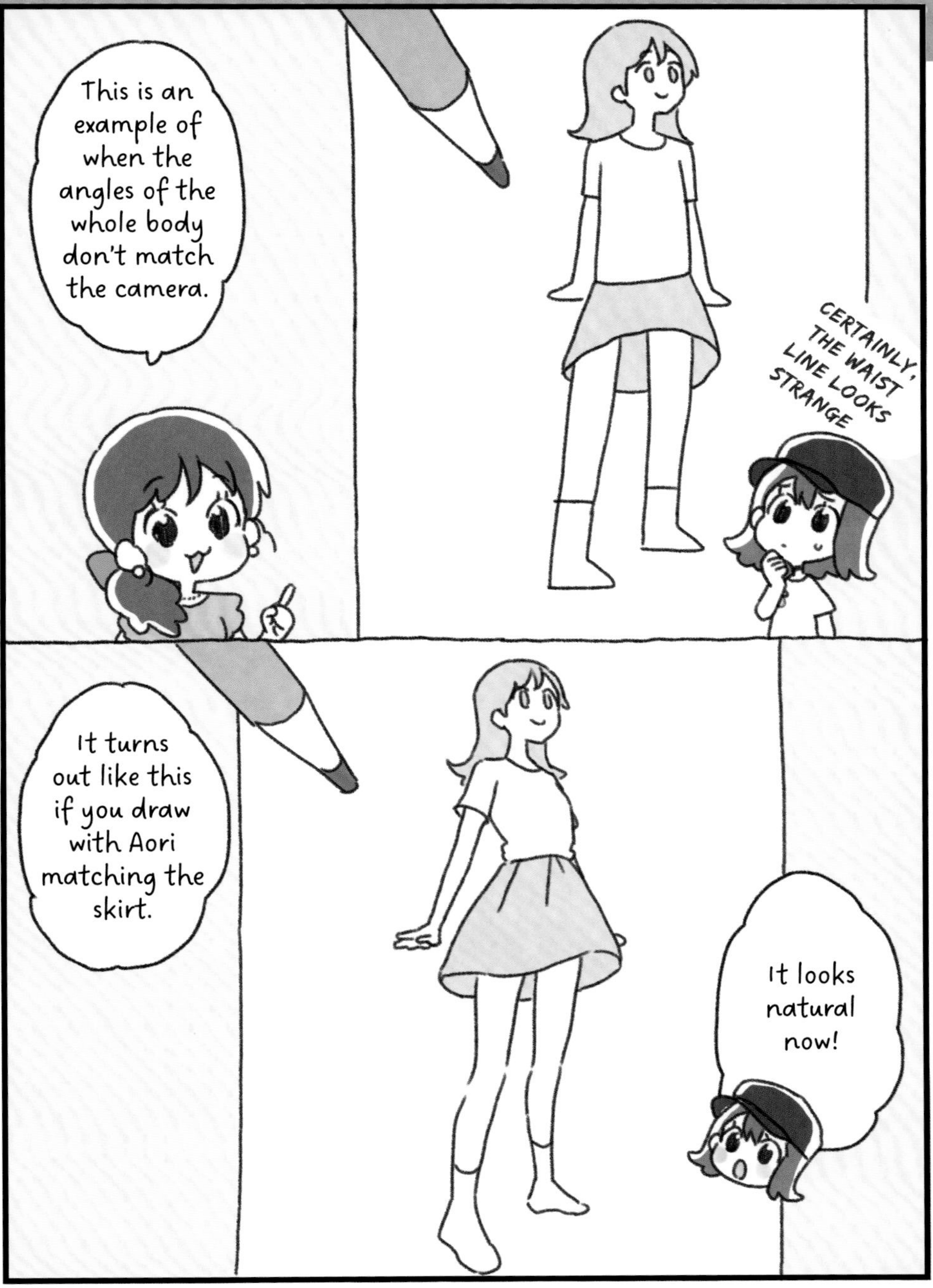
This is an example of when the angles of the whole body don't match the camera.
CERTAINLY, THE WAIST LINE LOOKS STRANGE
It turns out like this if you draw with Aori matching the skirt.
It looks natural now!

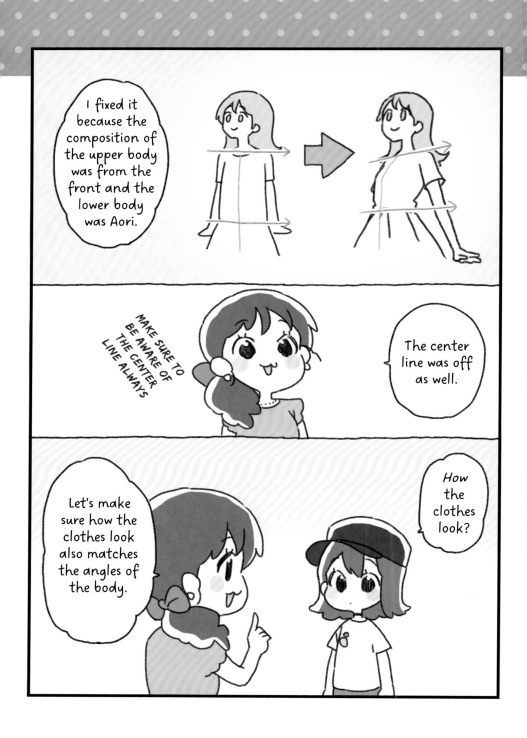

I fixed it because the composition of the upper body was from the front and the lower body was Aori.

MAKE SURE TO BE AWARE OF THE CENTER LINE ALWAYS

The center line was off as well.

Let's make sure how the clothes look also matches the angles of the body.

How the clothes look?

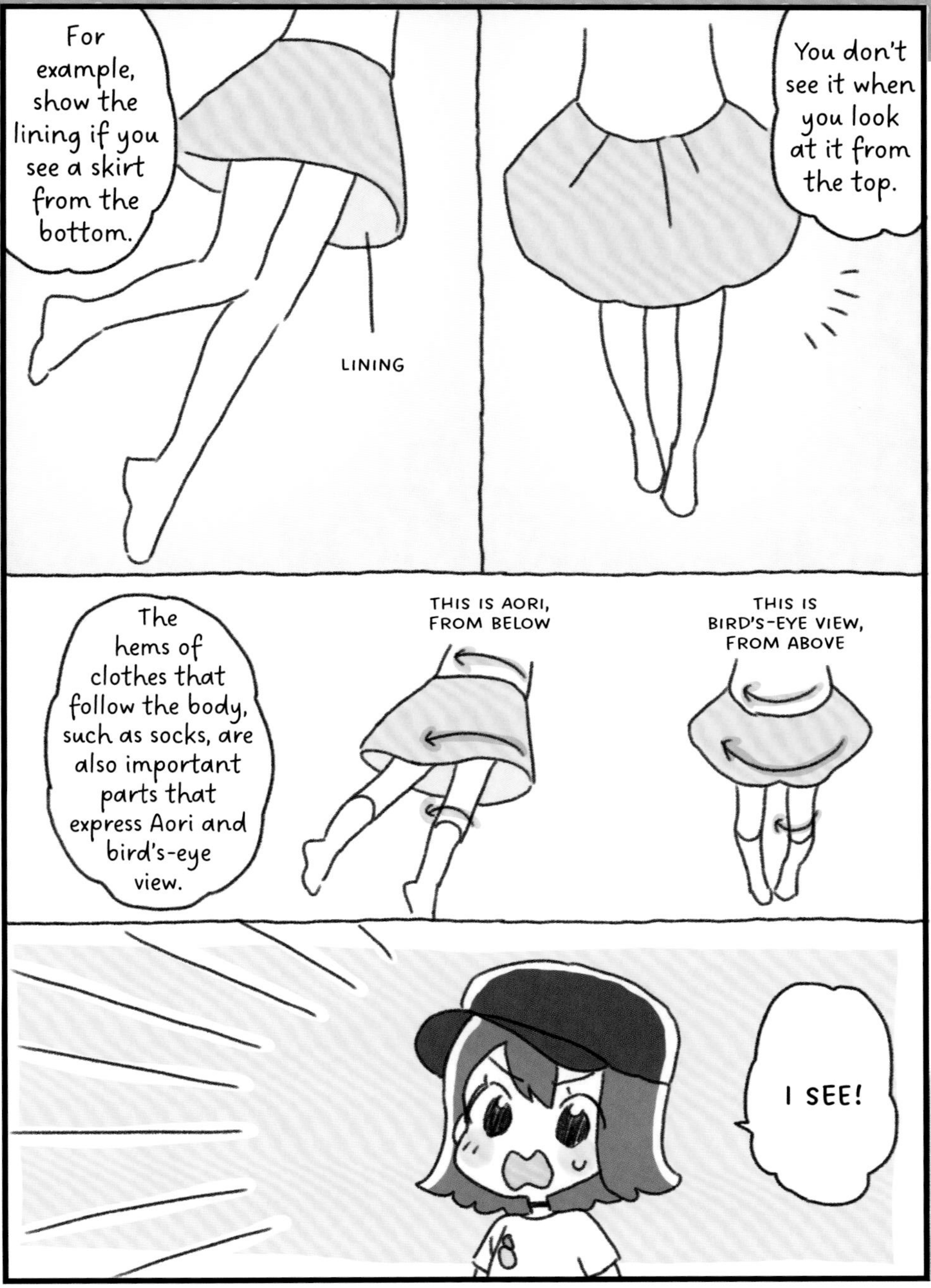
For example, show the lining if you see a skirt from the bottom.
LINING
You don't see it when you look at it from the top.
The hems of clothes that follow the body, such as socks, are also important parts that express Aori and bird's-eye view.
THIS IS AORI, FROM BELOW
THIS IS BIRD'S-EYE VIEW, FROM ABOVE
I SEE!

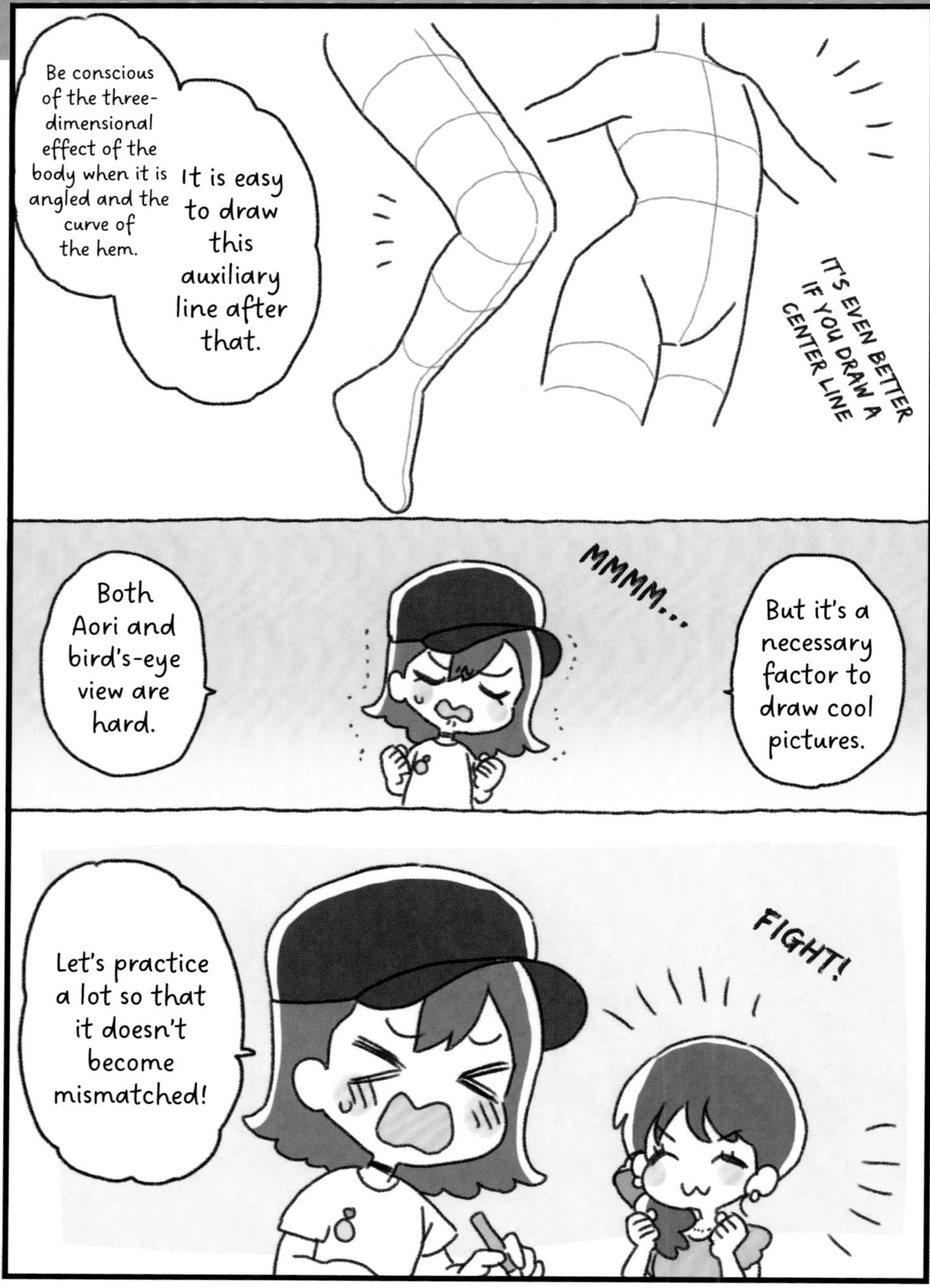
Be conscious of the three-dimensional effect of the body when it is angled and the curve of the hem.
It is easy to draw this auxiliary line after that.
IT'S EVEN BETTER IF YOU DRAW A CENTER LINE
Both Aori and bird's-eye view are hard.
MMMM...
But it's a necessary factor to draw cool pictures.
Let's practice a lot so that it doesn't become mismatched!
FIGHT!

## — *SUMMARY* —

It's hard to notice when drawing, but I tend to end up drawing parts mismatched when I check the whole body...

It's difficult to notice the differences if you are focusing on one spot too much!
Make sure to check frequently!

BIRD'S-EYE VIEW

AORI

YOU CAN EXPRESS AORI AND BIRD'S-EYE VIEW BY DRAWING A CURVED LINE FACING UPWARDS OR DOWNWARDS.

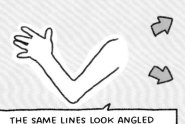

THE SAME LINES LOOK ANGLED DIFFERENTLY WHEN YOU DRAW THREE-DIMENSIONAL LINES.

# MOVEMENTS OF THE HAIR AND CLOTHES

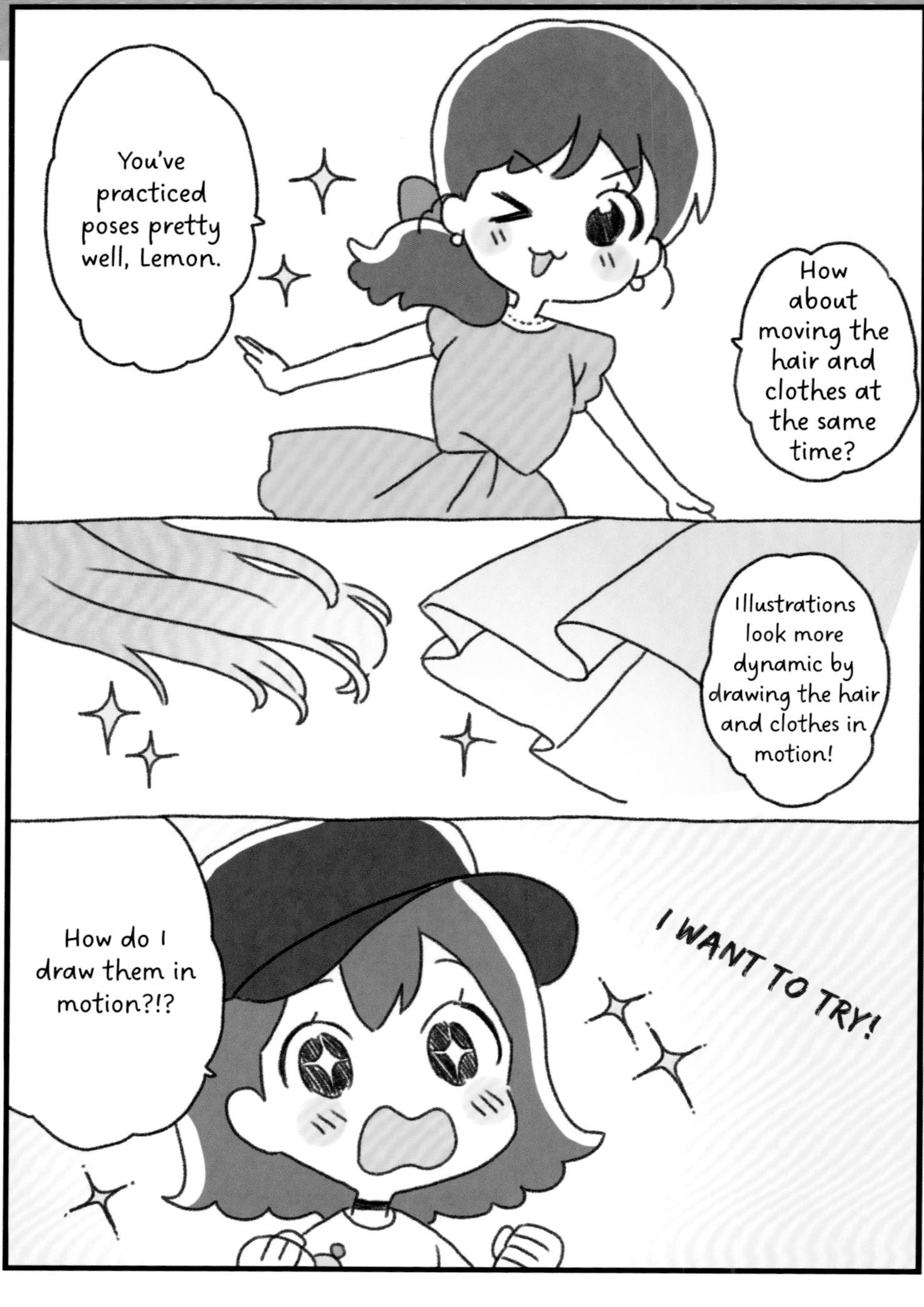
You've practiced poses pretty well, Lemon.
How about moving the hair and clothes at the same time?
Illustrations look more dynamic by drawing the hair and clothes in motion!
How do I draw them in motion?!?
I WANT TO TRY!

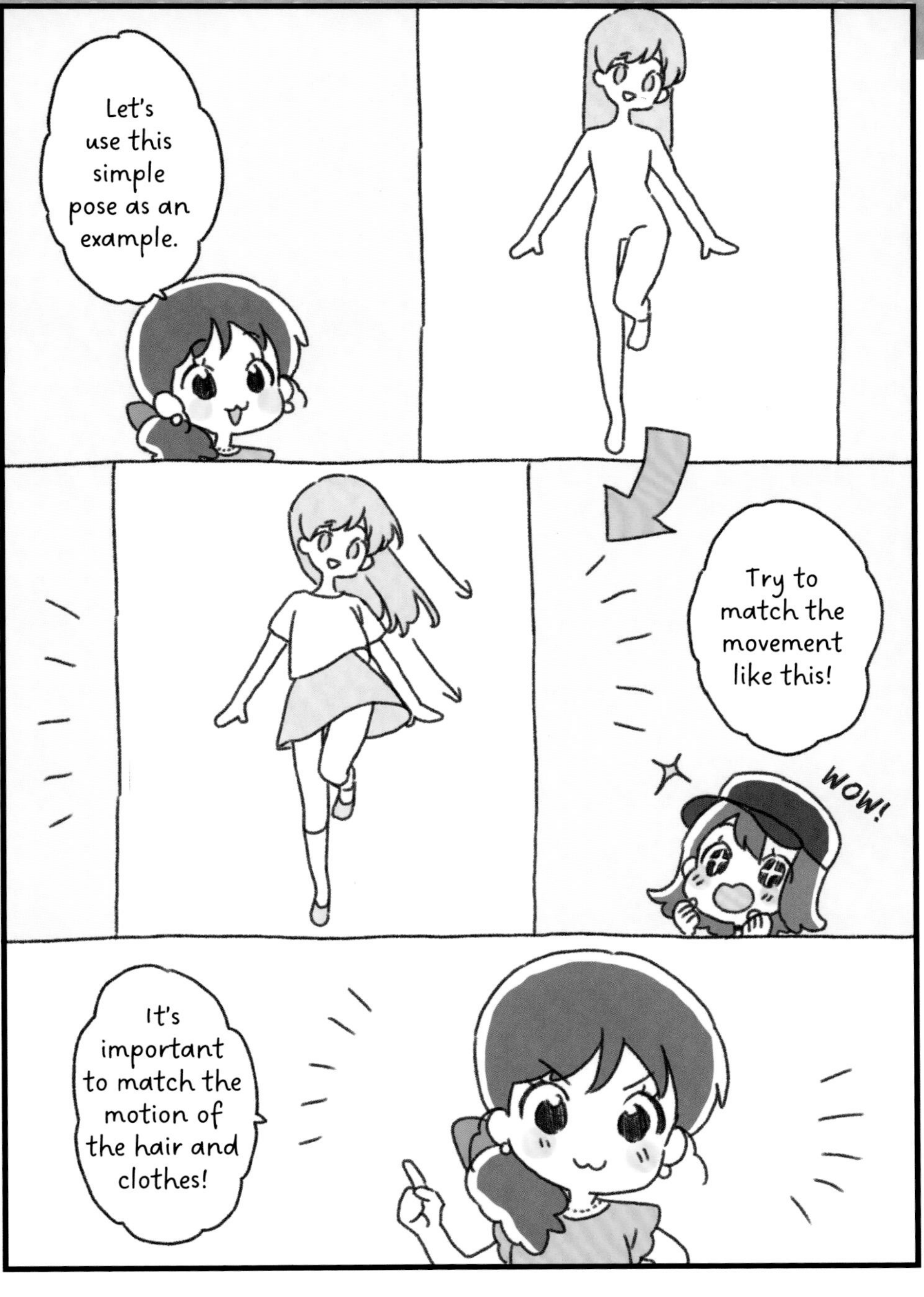
Let's use this simple pose as an example.
Try to match the movement like this!
WOW!
It's important to match the motion of the hair and clothes!

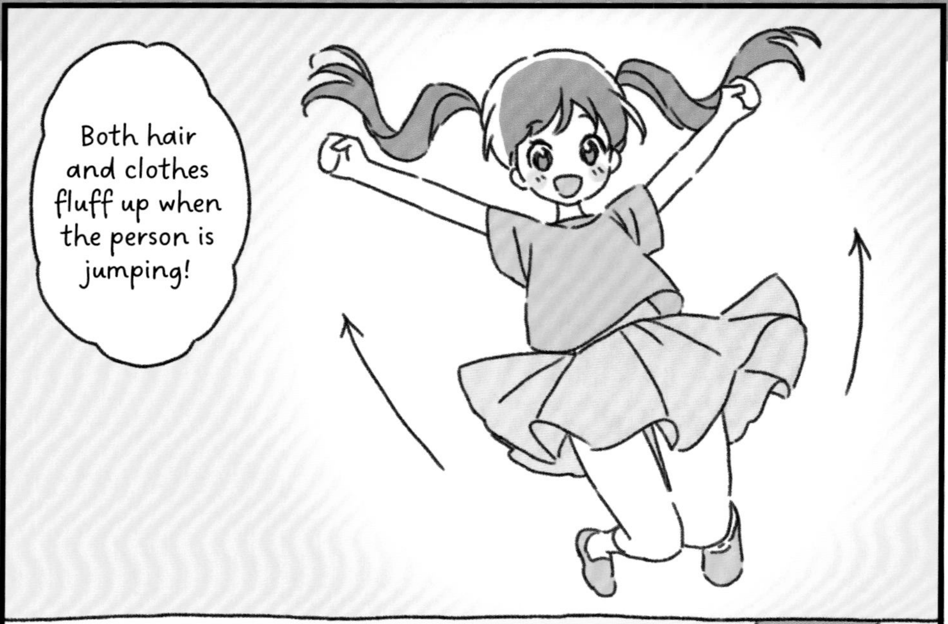
Both hair and clothes fluff up when the person is jumping!

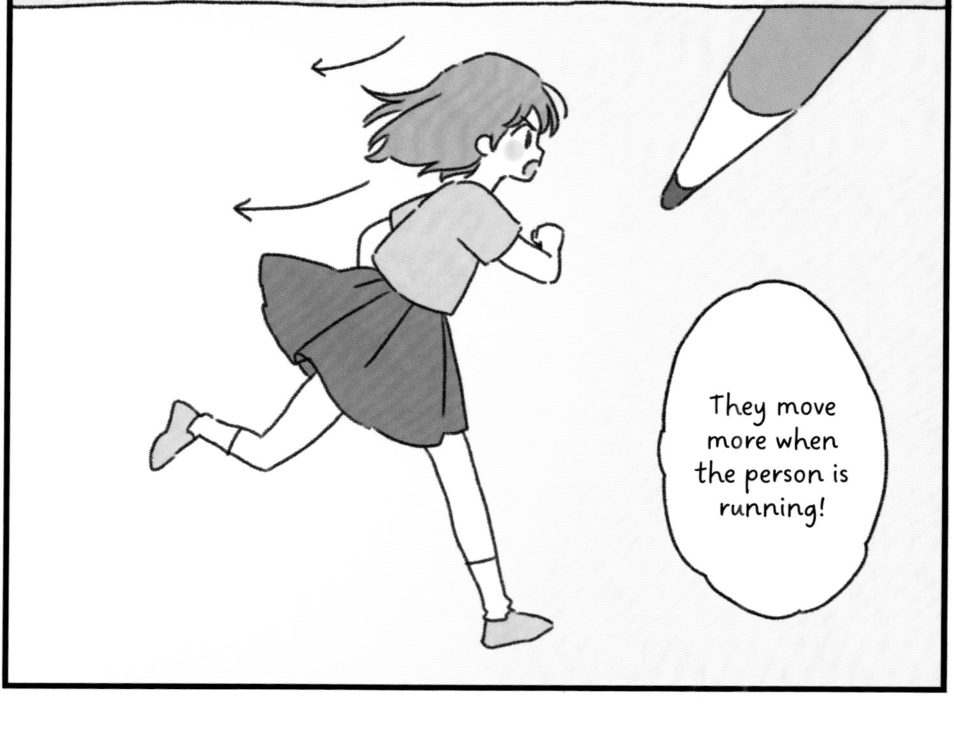
They move more when the person is running!

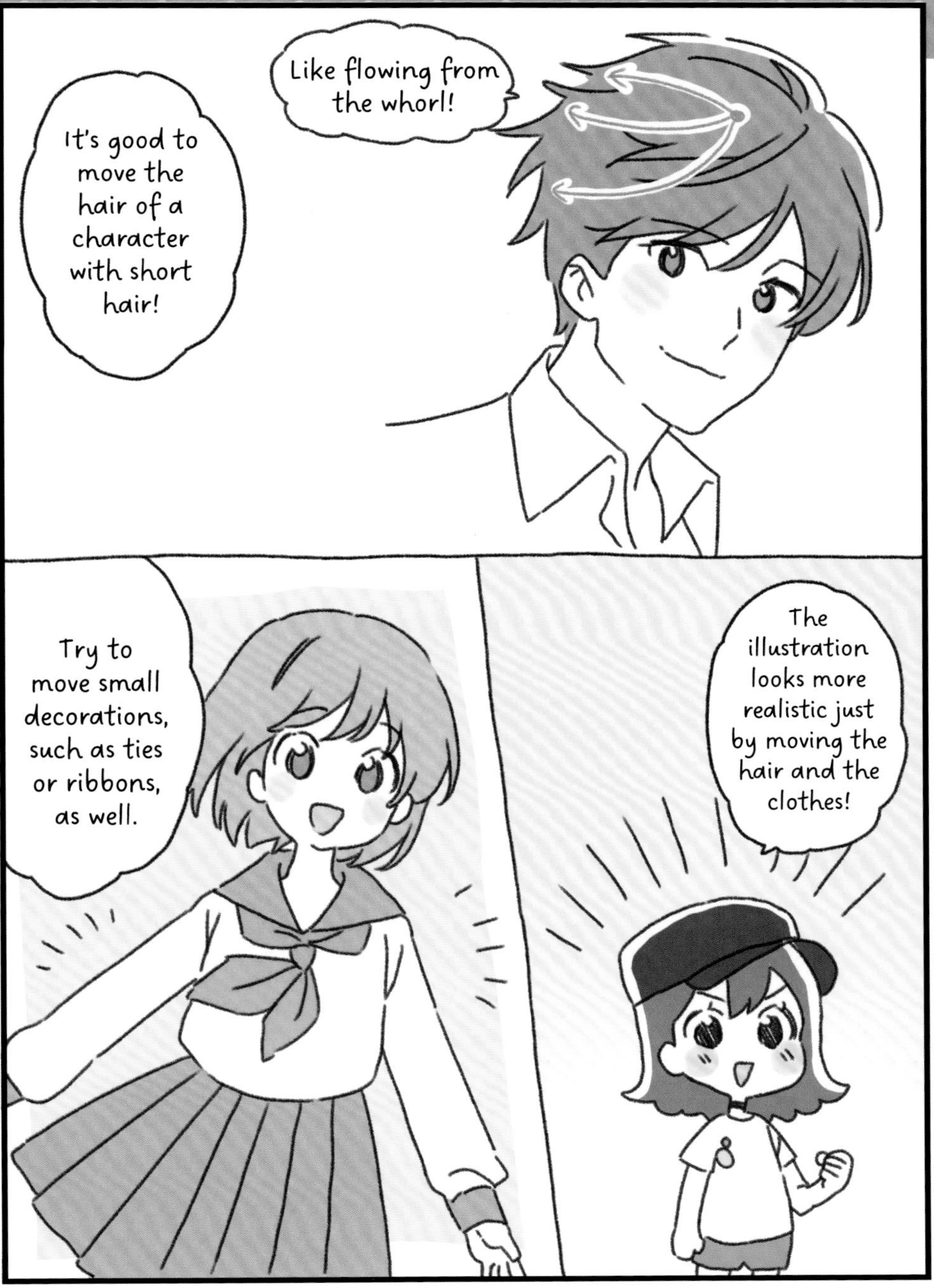
It's good to move the hair of a character with short hair!
Like flowing from the whorl!
Try to move small decorations, such as ties or ribbons, as well.
The illustration looks more realistic just by moving the hair and the clothes!

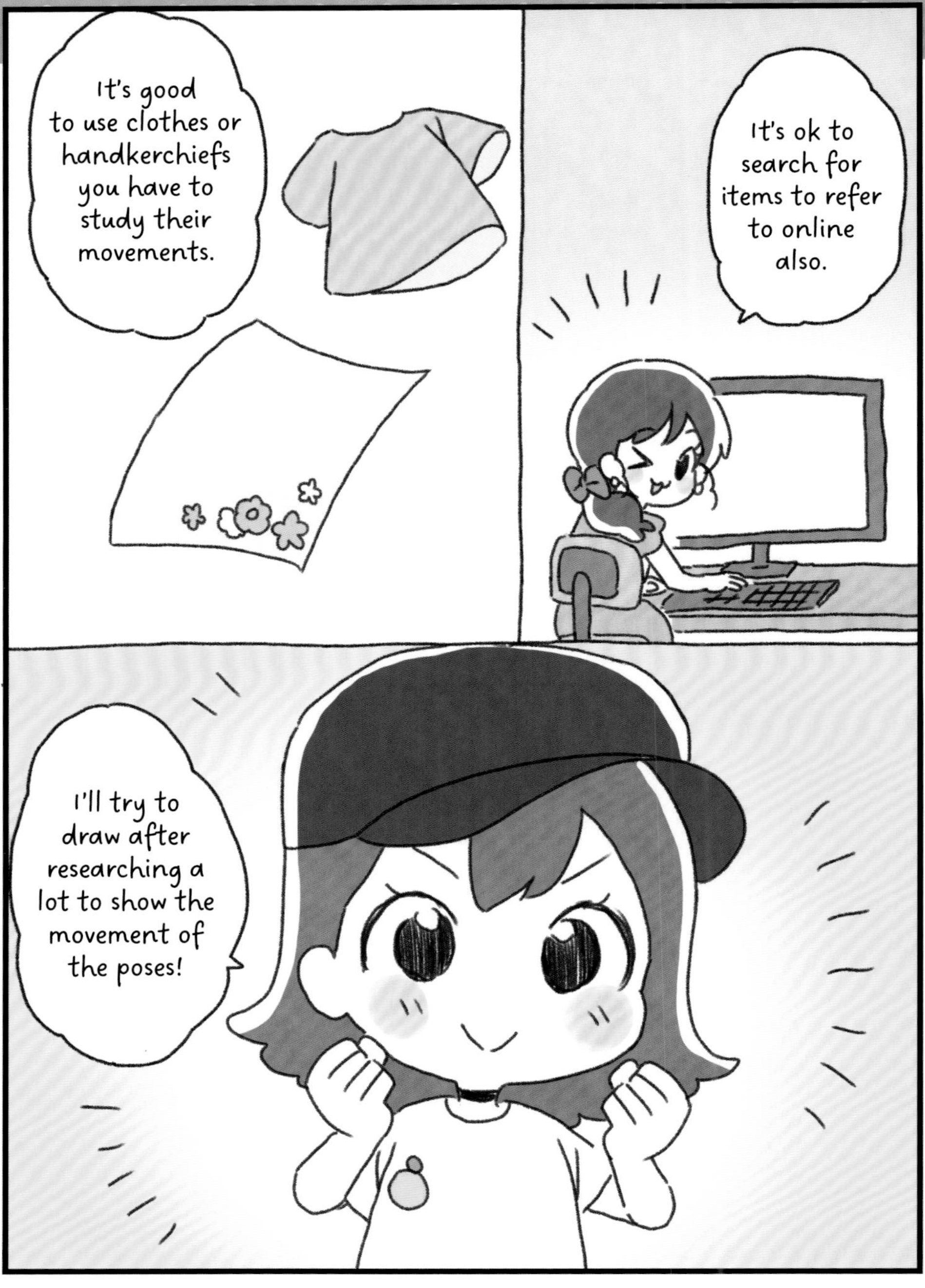
It's good to use clothes or handkerchiefs you have to study their movements.
It's ok to search for items to refer to online also.
I'll try to draw after researching a lot to show the movement of the poses!

# — *SUMMARY* —

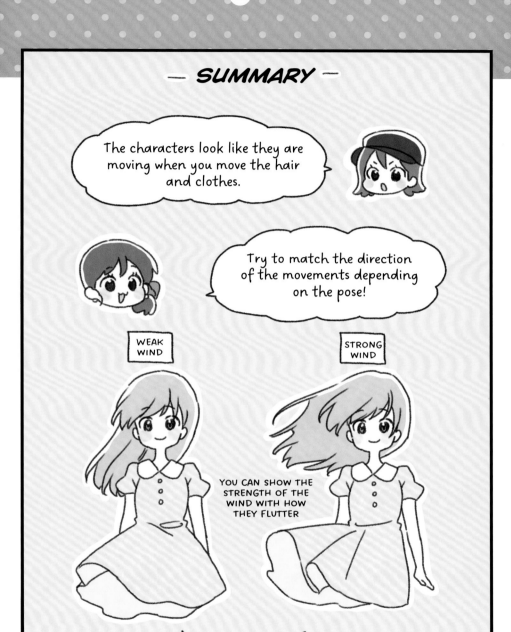

The characters look like they are moving when you move the hair and clothes.

Try to match the direction of the movements depending on the pose!

WEAK WIND

STRONG WIND

YOU CAN SHOW THE STRENGTH OF THE WIND WITH HOW THEY FLUTTER

DEPENDING ON THE THICKNESS AND MATERIAL OF THE CLOTH, THE WAY IT FLUTTERS WILL ALSO CHANGE.

# MOMIJI'S TIPS
# TO BE ABLE TO DRAW DIFFERENT POSES

I want to be able to draw different poses, but what kind of ways of practicing are there?

I'll tell you a few things I recommend!

## TRACE THE MATERIAL PATTERNS AND MEMORIZE PROPORTIONS AND SHAPES FIRST

TRY TO TRACE AND DRAW TO CHECK THE BALANCE FIRST. YOU'LL FIND OUT THINGS SUCH AS: THE HANDS ARE BIGGER THAN I THOUGHT... HOW THE UNEVENNESS OF THE LEGS LOOKS LIKE, ETC....

CURVED LIKE THIS!

WRINKLED LIKE THAT!

### COPY PHOTOS

BY COPYING PHOTOS, YOU'LL BECOME MORE AWARE OF THE RATIOS OR THE BALANCE WITHOUT TRACING.

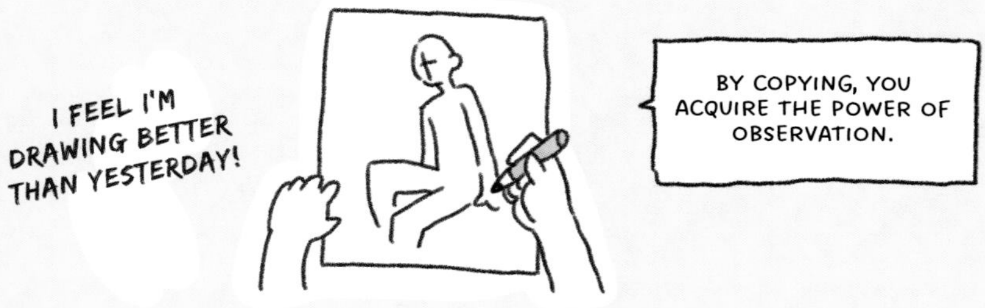

I FEEL I'M DRAWING BETTER THAN YESTERDAY!

BY COPYING, YOU ACQUIRE THE POWER OF OBSERVATION.

### TRY TO DRAW BY OBSERVING PEOPLE AROUND YOU

I ALSO RECOMMEND HAVING YOUR FAMILY AND FRIENDS POSE FOR YOU, OR TO SKETCH AT A CAFE OR A PARK. PHOTOS ARE TWO-DIMENSIONAL, BUT BY LOOKING AT THE REAL THING, IT IS EASY TO VISUALIZE THE THREE-DIMENSIONAL EFFECT.

### COPY YOUR FAVORITE ILLUSTRATION

LET'S OBSERVE HOW THE HUMAN BODY IS UNIQUE BY COPYING NOT ONLY PHOTOS, BUT ALSO ILLUSTRATIONS.

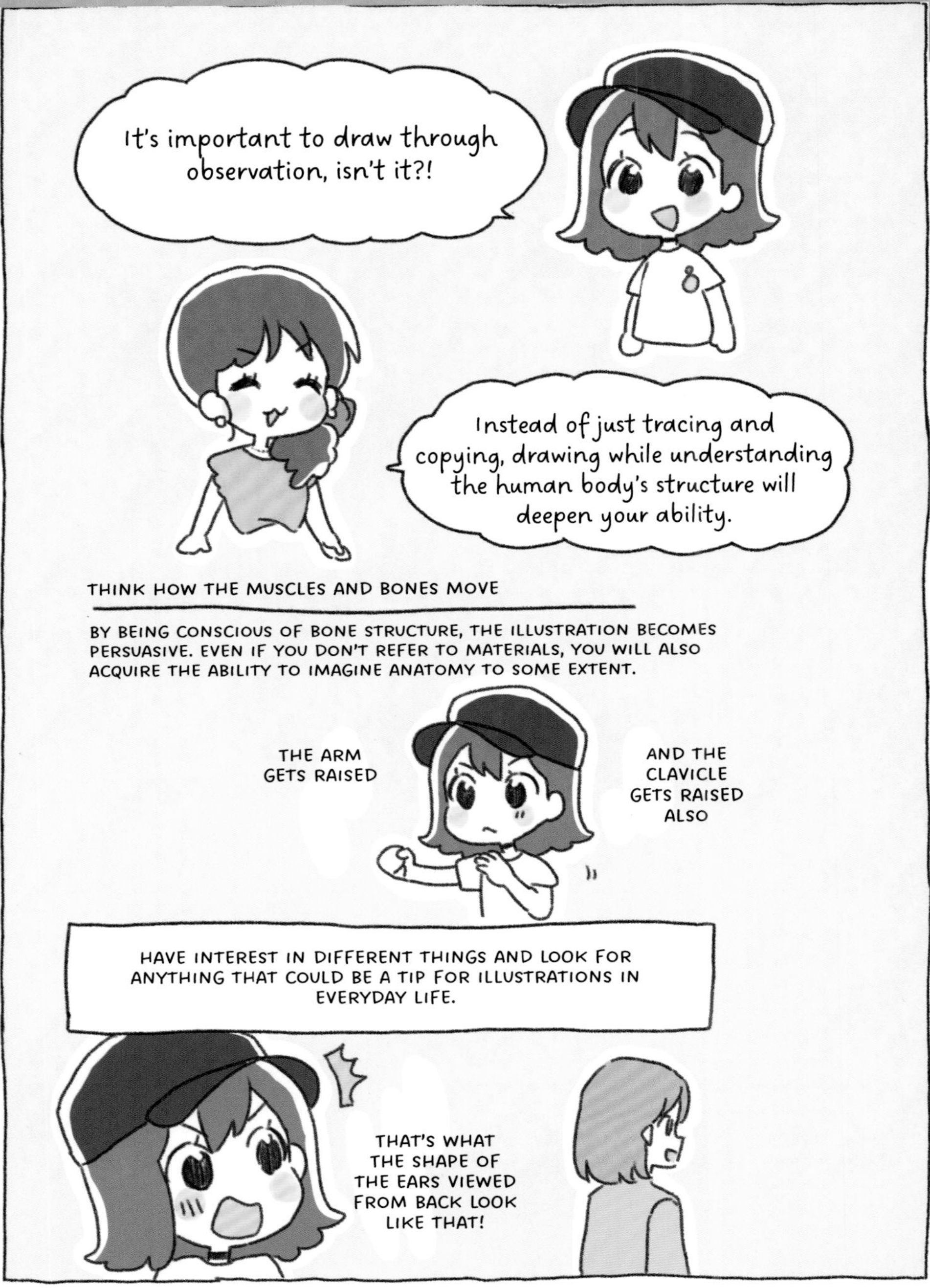

It's important to draw through observation, isn't it?!
Instead of just tracing and copying, drawing while understanding the human body's structure will deepen your ability.
THINK HOW THE MUSCLES AND BONES MOVE
BY BEING CONSCIOUS OF BONE STRUCTURE, THE ILLUSTRATION BECOMES PERSUASIVE. EVEN IF YOU DON'T REFER TO MATERIALS, YOU WILL ALSO ACQUIRE THE ABILITY TO IMAGINE ANATOMY TO SOME EXTENT.
THE ARM GETS RAISED
AND THE CLAVICLE GETS RAISED ALSO
HAVE INTEREST IN DIFFERENT THINGS AND LOOK FOR ANYTHING THAT COULD BE A TIP FOR ILLUSTRATIONS IN EVERYDAY LIFE.
THAT'S WHAT THE SHAPE OF THE EARS VIEWED FROM BACK LOOK LIKE THAT!

CHAPTER

**5**

# WHEN YOU CANNOT COME UP WITH POSES

# THE BASIC POSES

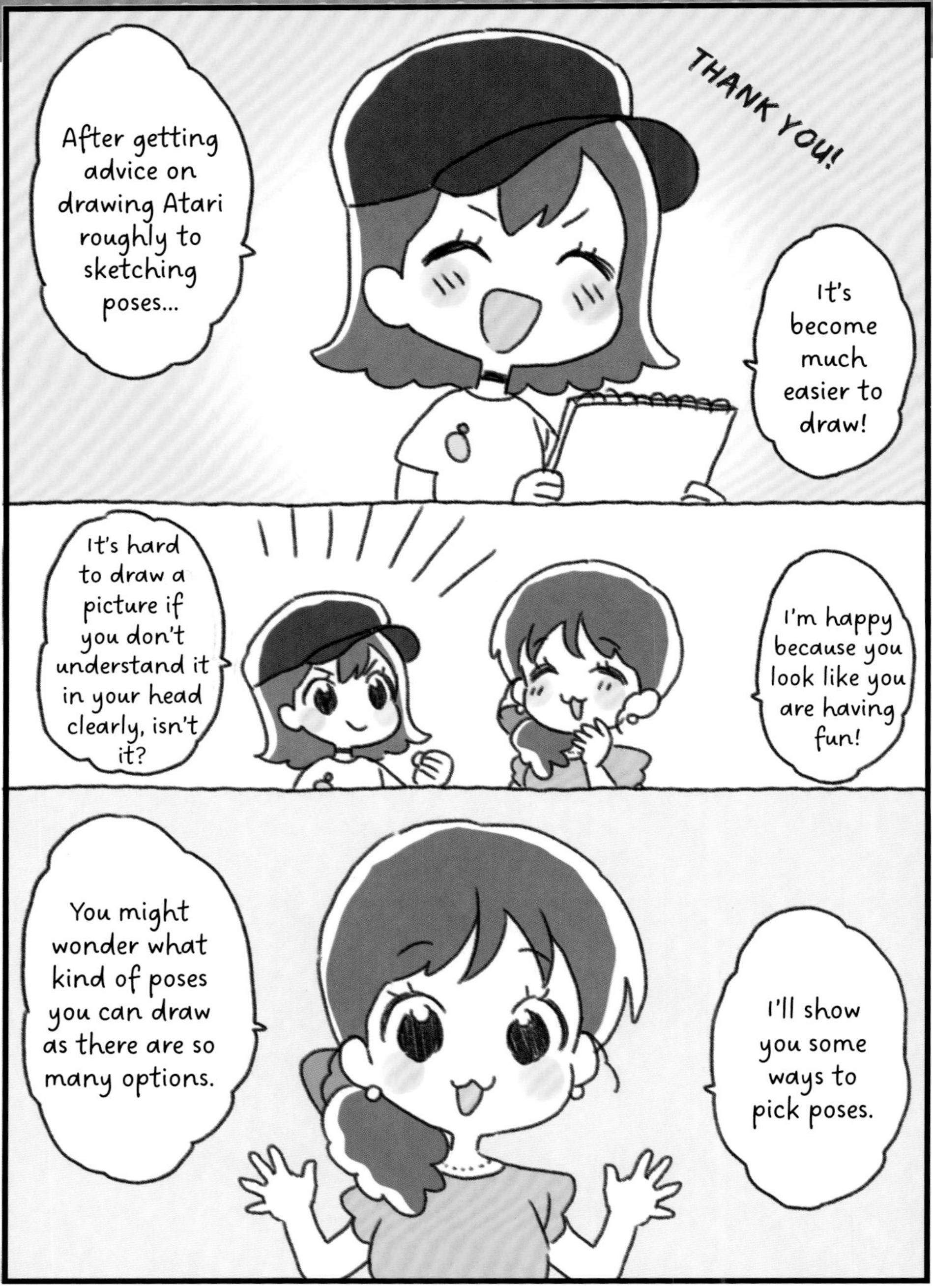
After getting advice on drawing Atari roughly to sketching poses...
THANK YOU!
It's become much easier to draw!
It's hard to draw a picture if you don't understand it in your head clearly, isn't it?
I'm happy because you look like you are having fun!
You might wonder what kind of poses you can draw as there are so many options.
I'll show you some ways to pick poses.

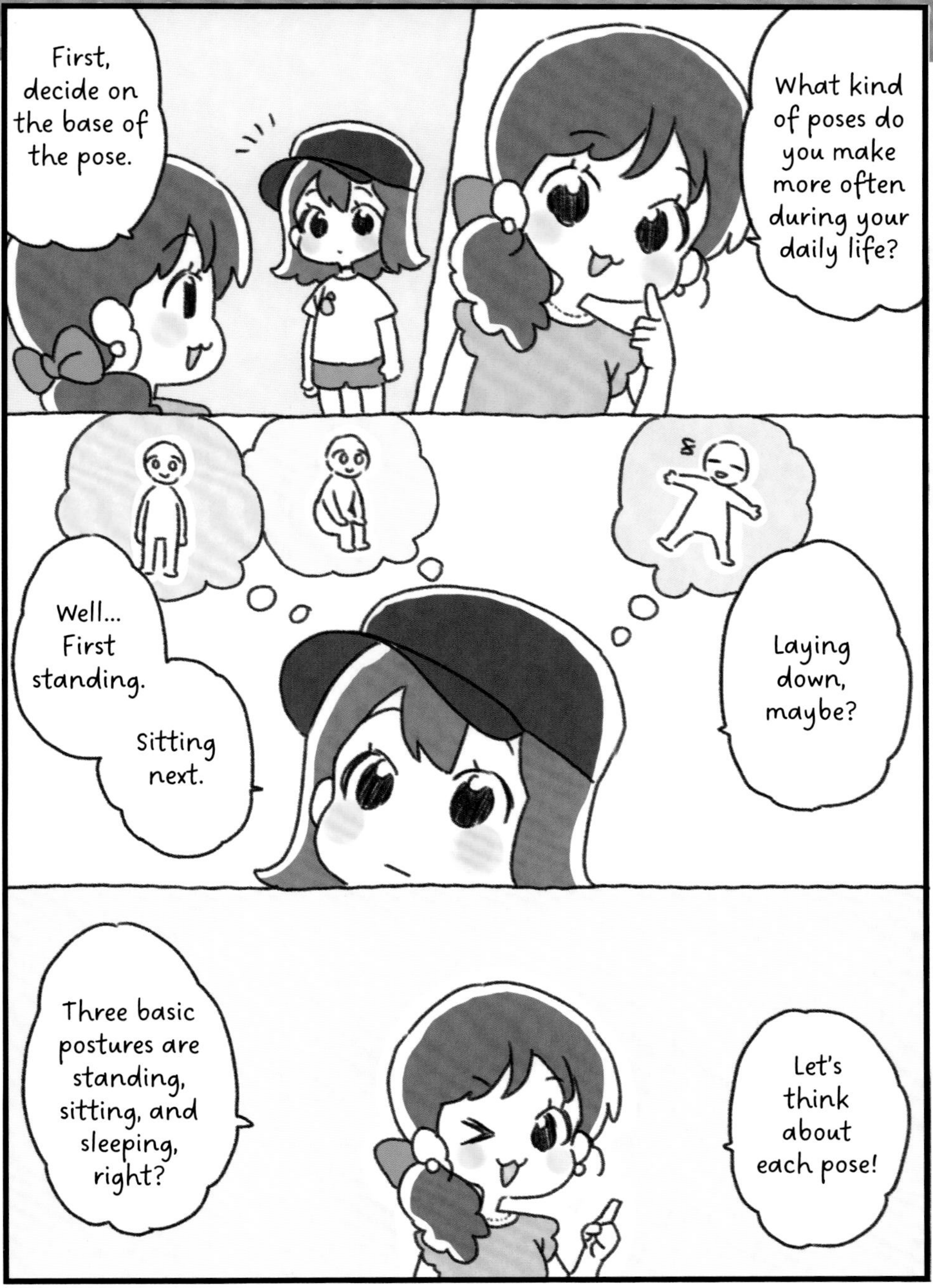

First, decide on the base of the pose.
What kind of poses do you make more often during your daily life?
Well... First standing.
Sitting next.
Laying down, maybe?
Three basic postures are standing, sitting, and sleeping, right?
Let's think about each pose!

# STANDING POSES

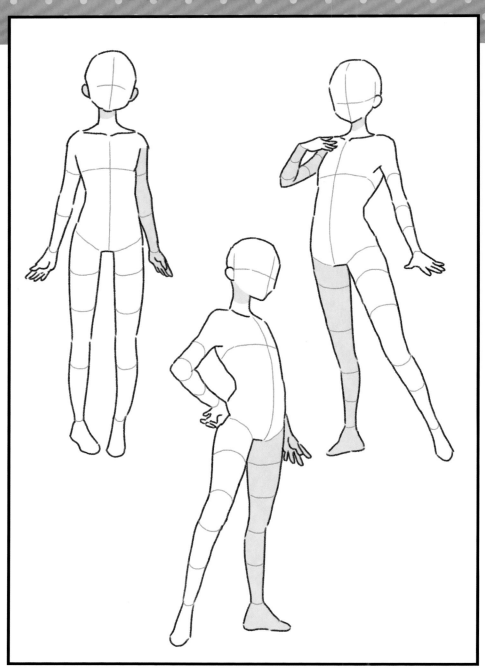

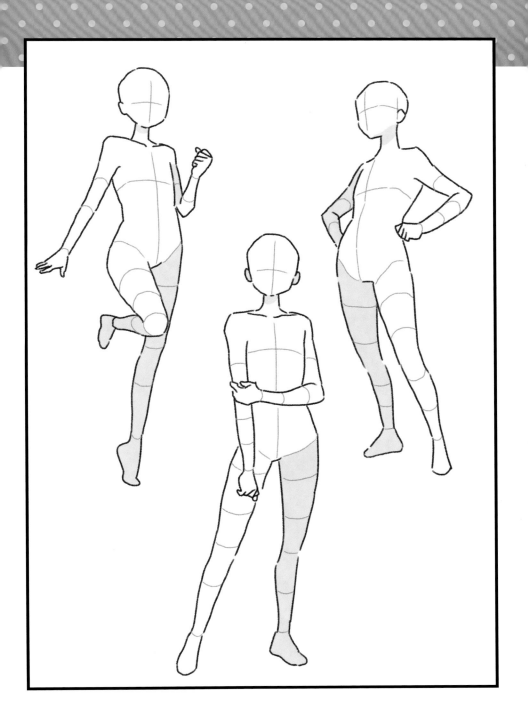

# SITTING POSES

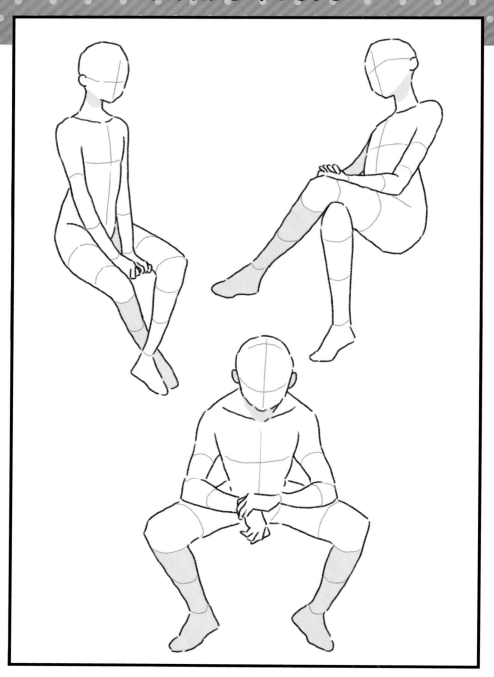

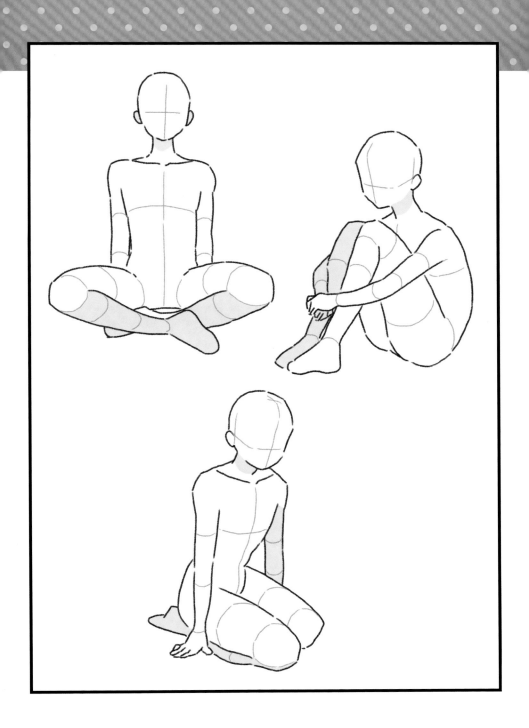

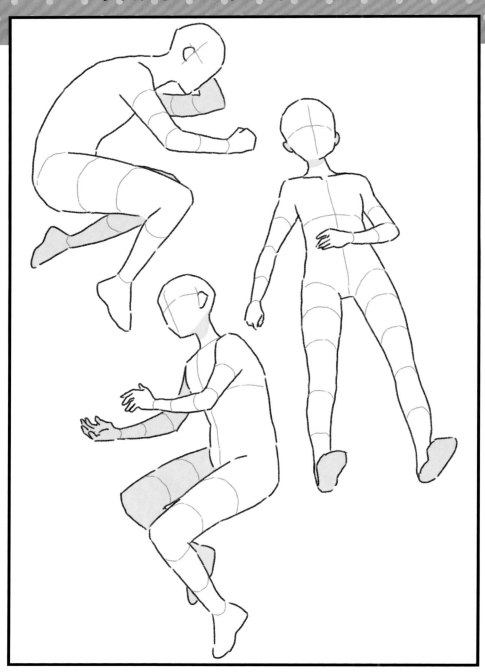

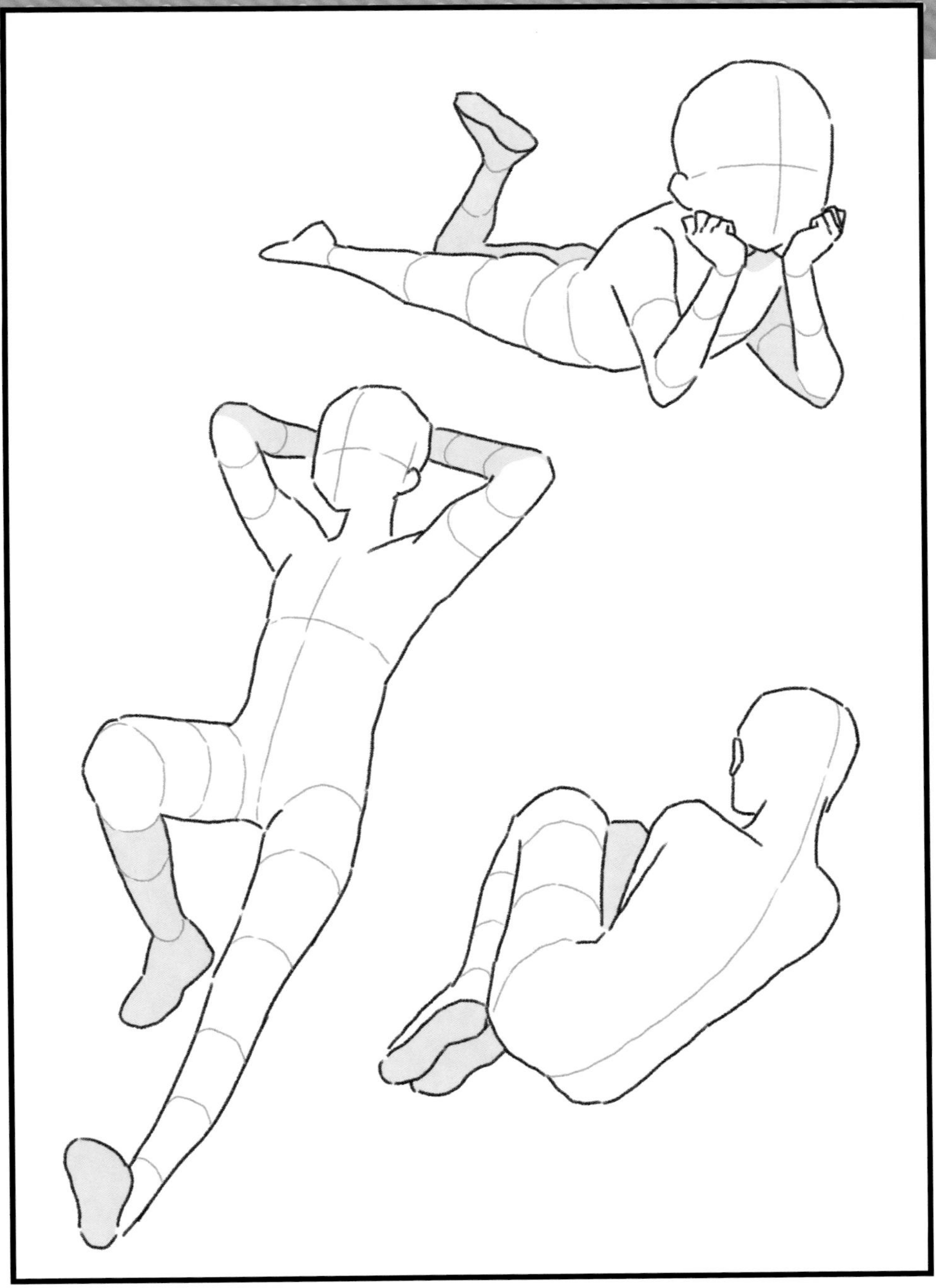

# DECIDE ON A POSE BASED ON THE CHARACTER'S EMOTIONS

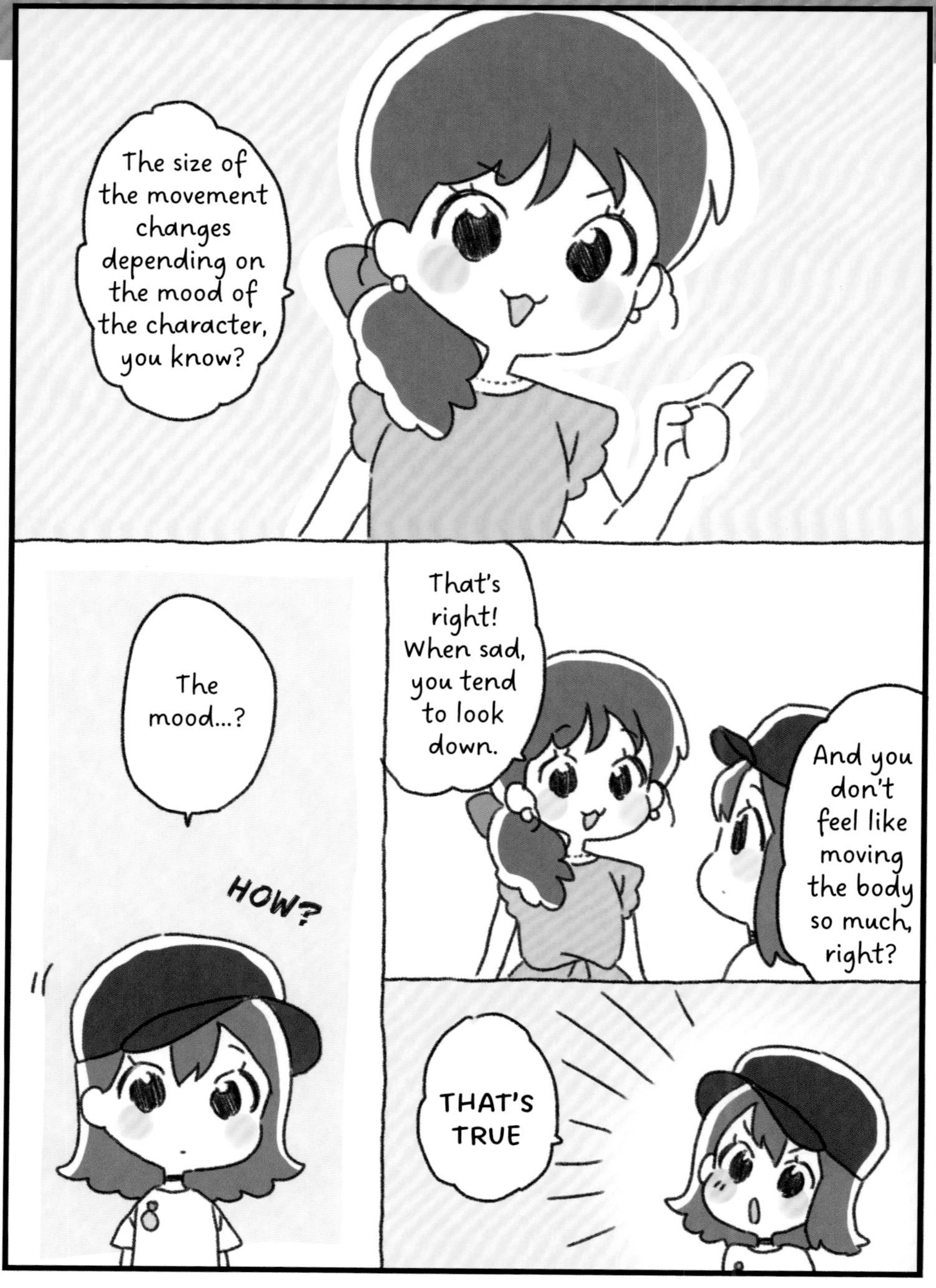
The size of the movement changes depending on the mood of the character, you know?
The mood...?
HOW?
That's right! When sad, you tend to look down.
And you don't feel like moving the body so much, right?
THAT'S TRUE

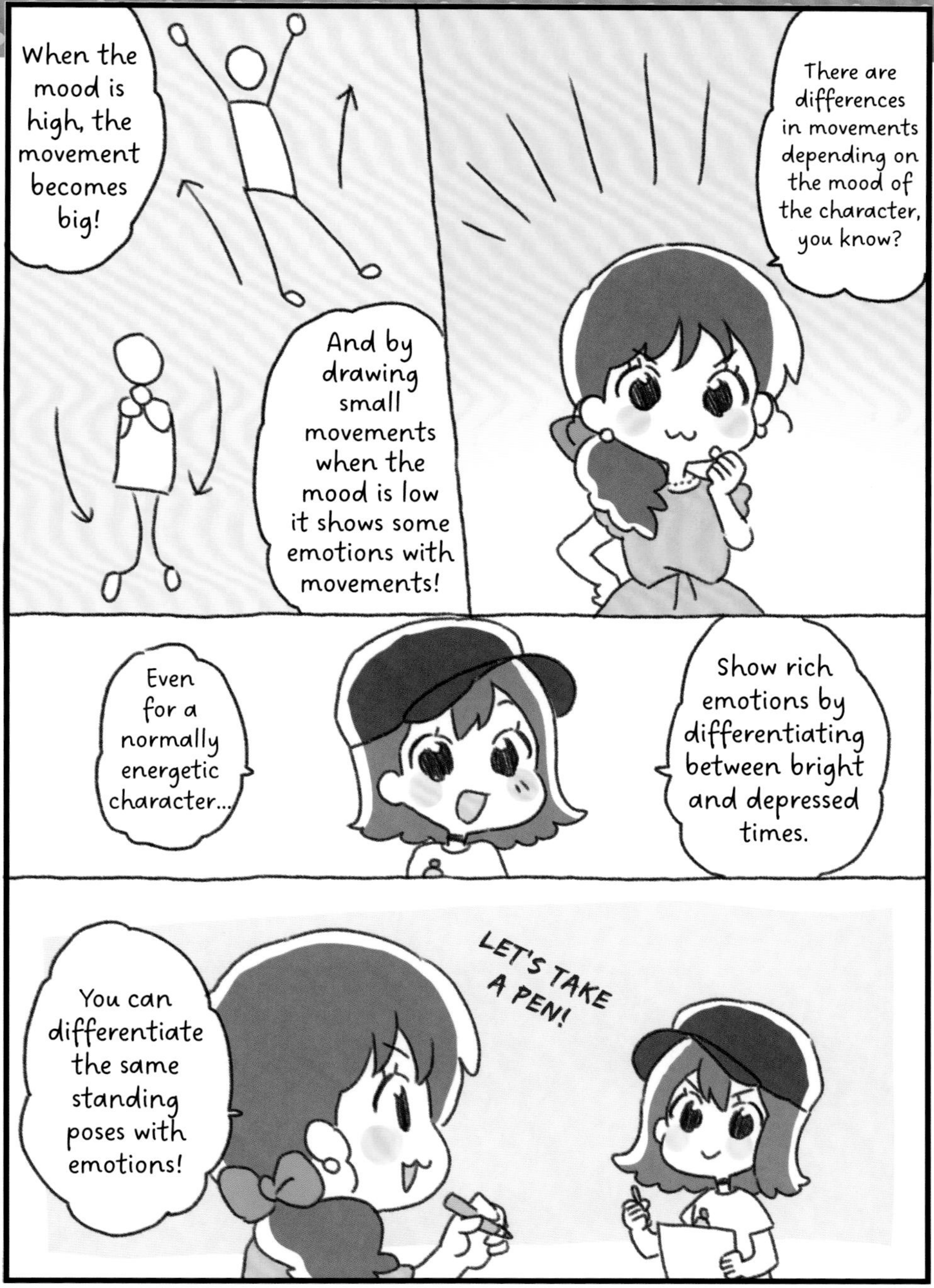
There are differences in movements depending on the mood of the character, you know?
When the mood is high, the movement becomes big!
And by drawing small movements when the mood is low it shows some emotions with movements!
Show rich emotions by differentiating between bright and depressed times.
Even for a normally energetic character...
LET'S TAKE A PEN!
You can differentiate the same standing poses with emotions!

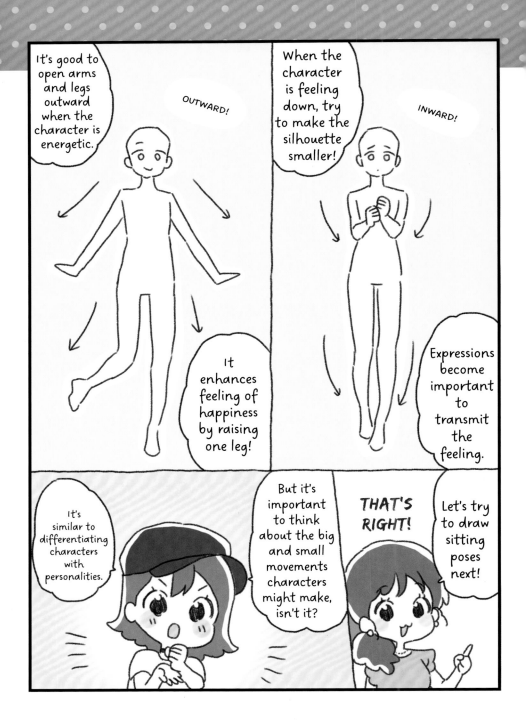

It's good to open arms and legs outward when the character is energetic.

OUTWARD!

It enhances feeling of happiness by raising one leg!

When the character is feeling down, try to make the silhouette smaller!

INWARD!

Expressions become important to transmit the feeling.

It's similar to differentiating characters with personalities.

But it's important to think about the big and small movements characters might make, isn't it?

THAT'S RIGHT!

Let's try to draw sitting poses next!

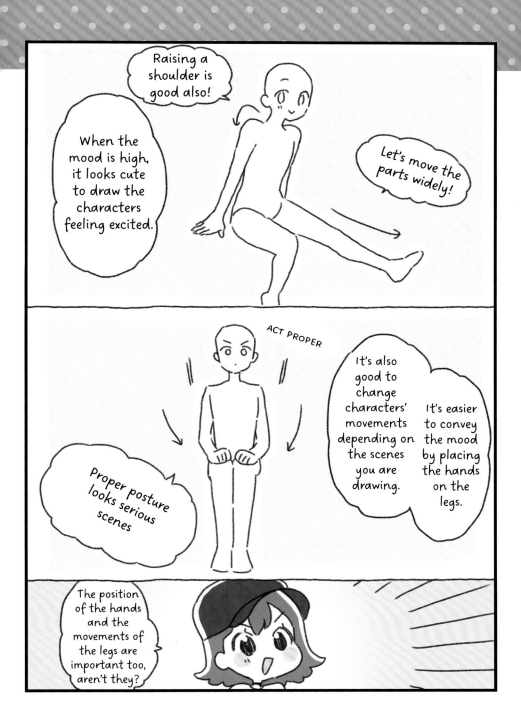

Raising a shoulder is good also!

When the mood is high, it looks cute to draw the characters feeling excited.

Let's move the parts widely!

ACT PROPER

It's also good to change characters' movements depending on the scenes you are drawing.

It's easier to convey the mood by placing the hands on the legs.

Proper posture looks serious scenes

The position of the hands and the movements of the legs are important too, aren't they?

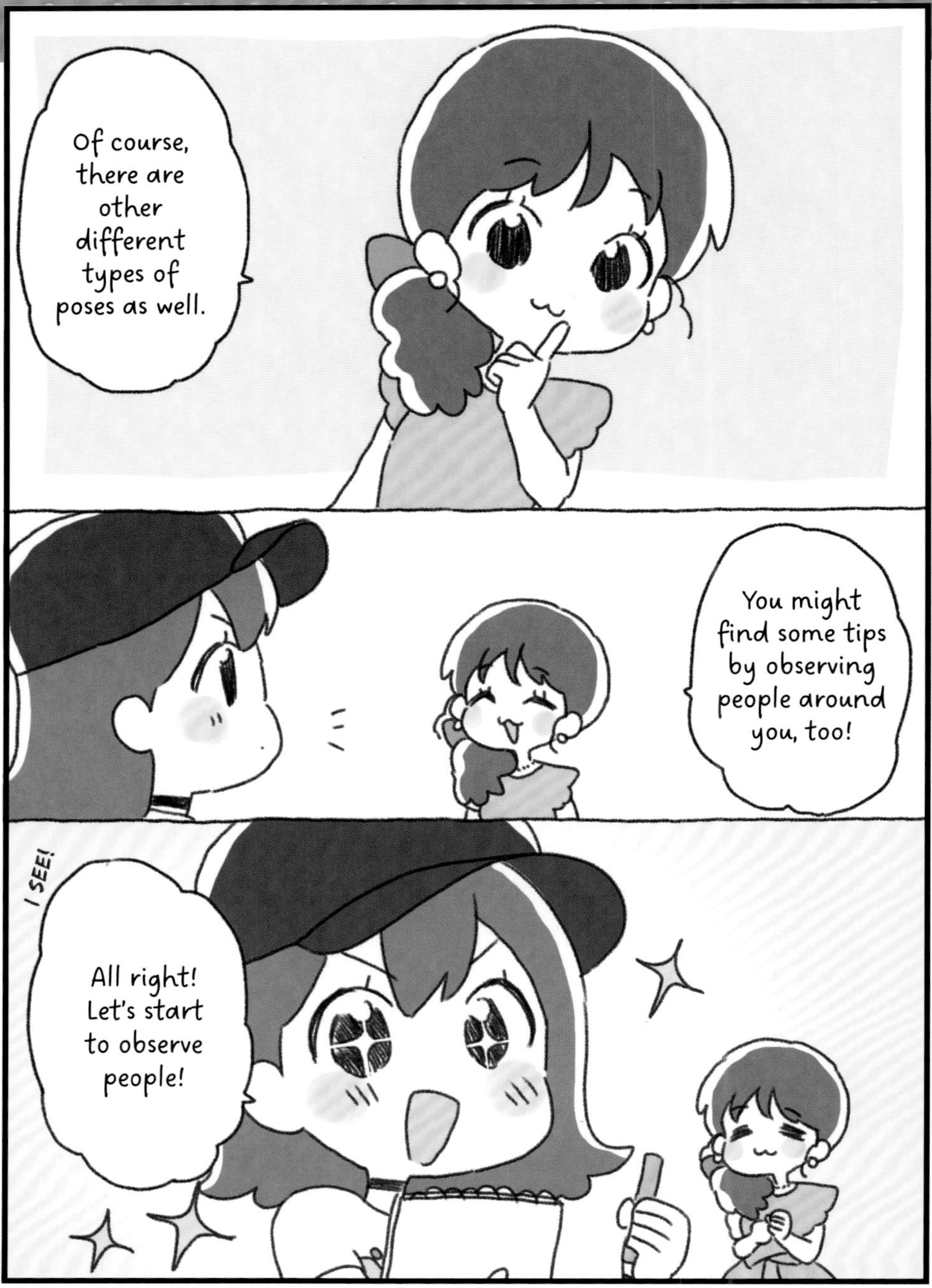
Of course, there are other different types of poses as well.
You might find some tips by observing people around you, too!
I SEE!
All right! Let's start to observe people!

## SUMMARY

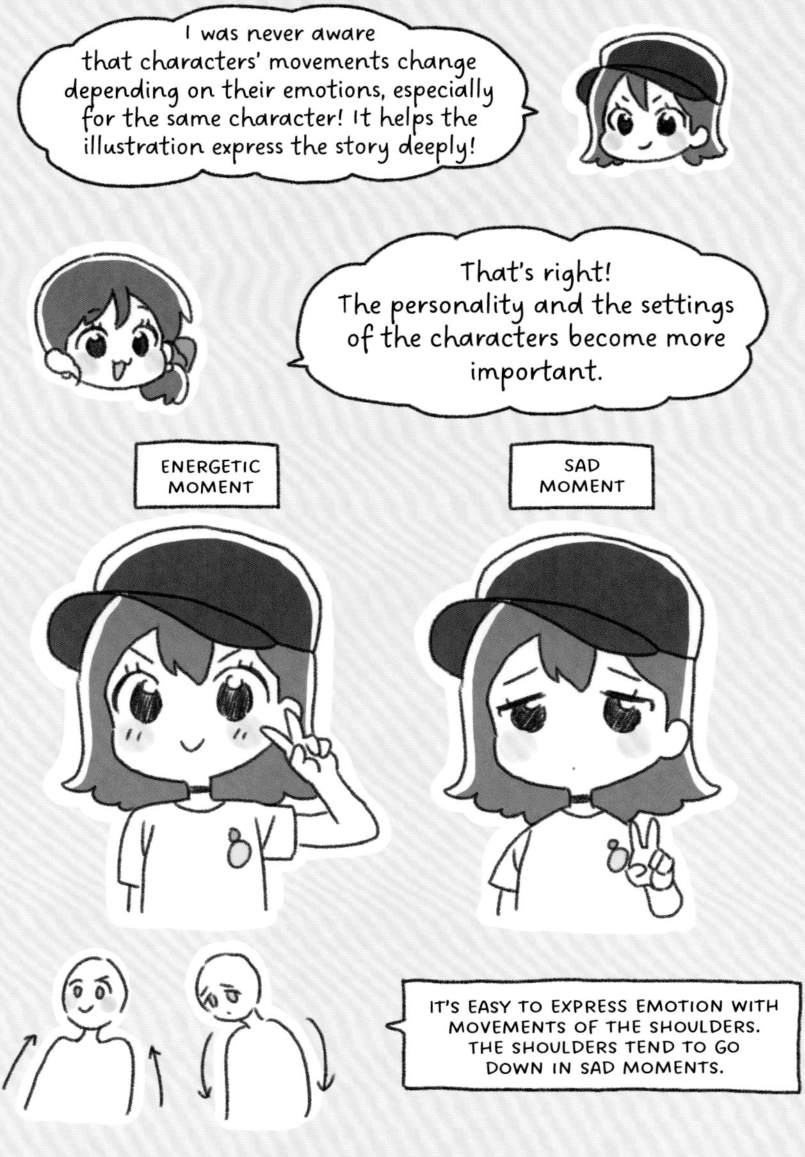
I was never aware that characters' movements change depending on their emotions, especially for the same character! It helps the illustration express the story deeply!
That's right! The personality and the settings of the characters become more important.
ENERGETIC MOMENT
SAD MOMENT
IT'S EASY TO EXPRESS EMOTION WITH MOVEMENTS OF THE SHOULDERS. THE SHOULDERS TEND TO GO DOWN IN SAD MOMENTS.

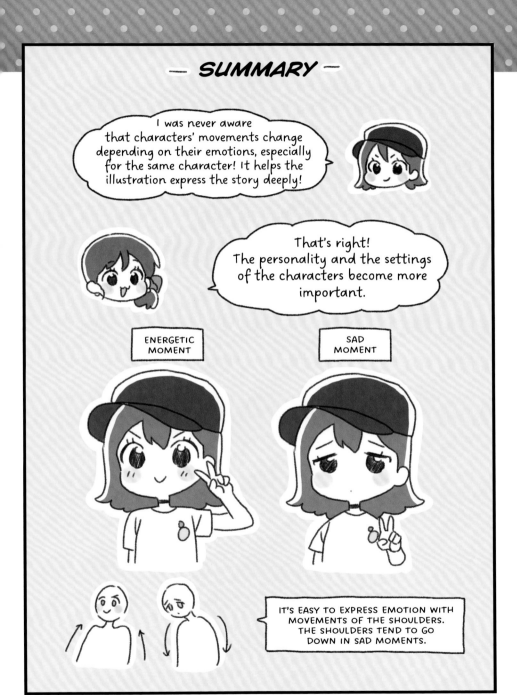

# CONSIDER THE CHARACTER'S GESTURES

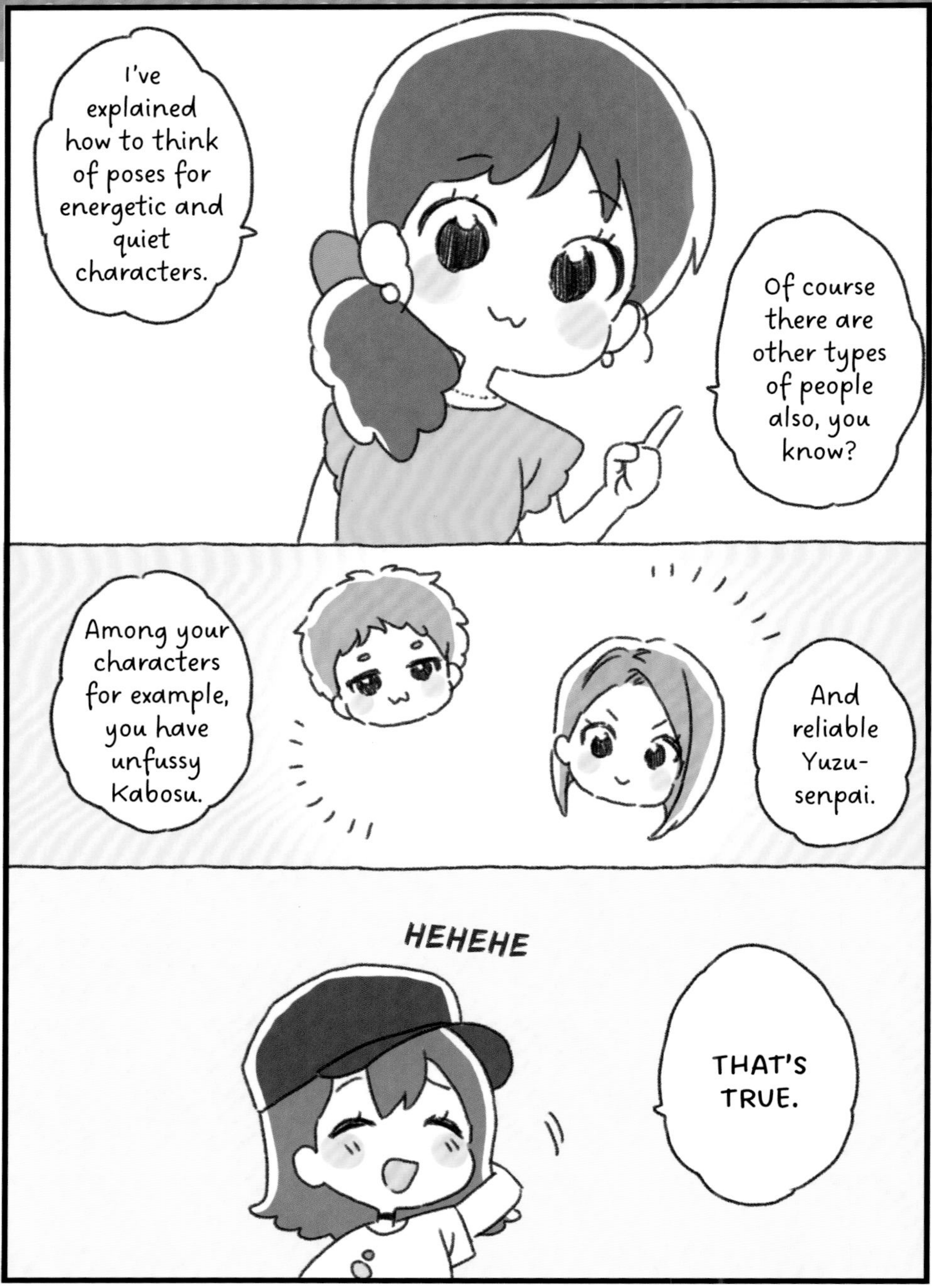
I've explained how to think of poses for energetic and quiet characters.
Of course there are other types of people also, you know?
Among your characters for example, you have unfussy Kabosu.
And reliable Yuzu-senpai.
HEHEHE
THAT'S TRUE.

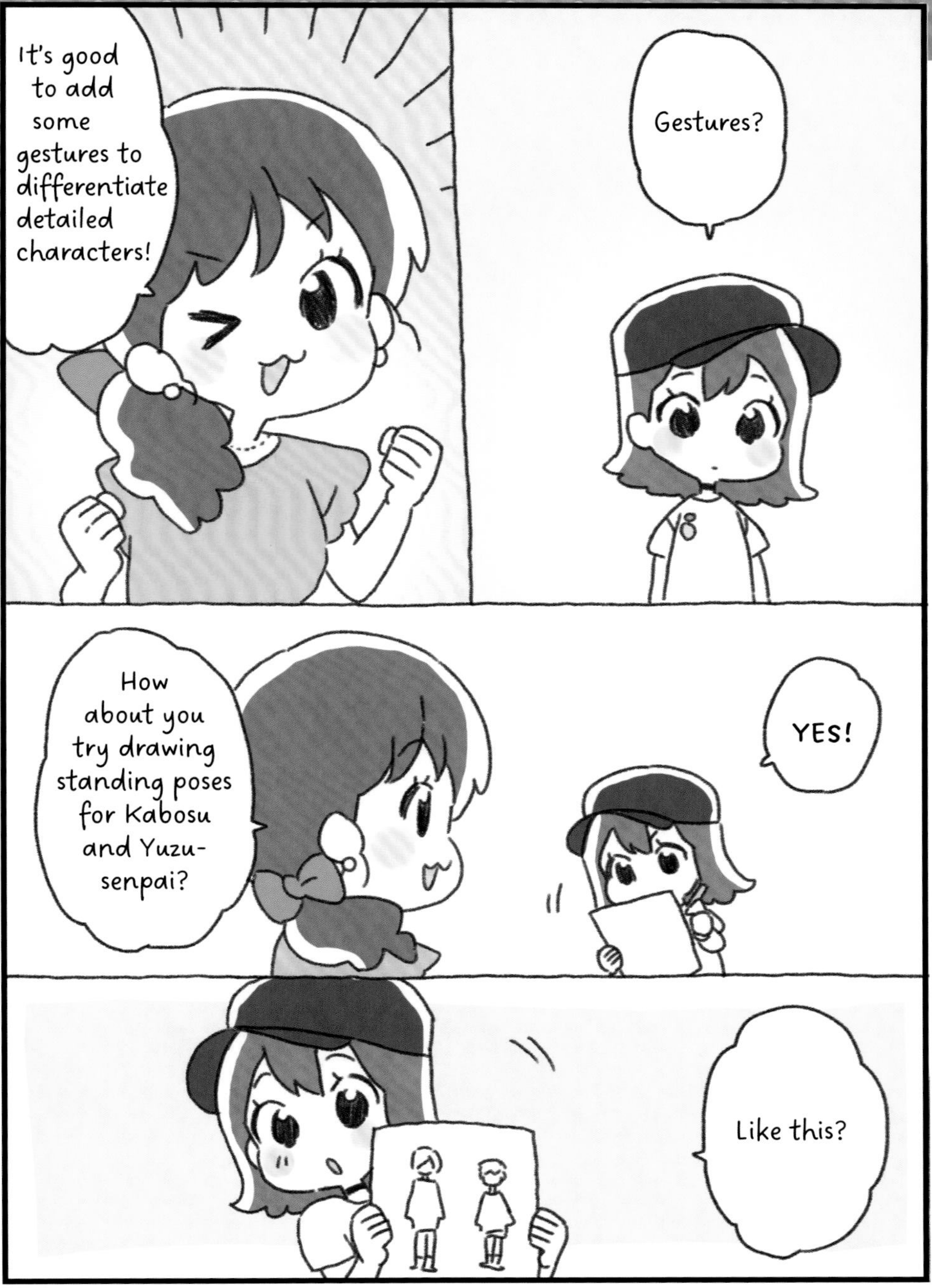
It's good to add some gestures to differentiate detailed characters!
Gestures?
How about you try drawing standing poses for Kabosu and Yuzu-senpai?
YES!
Like this?

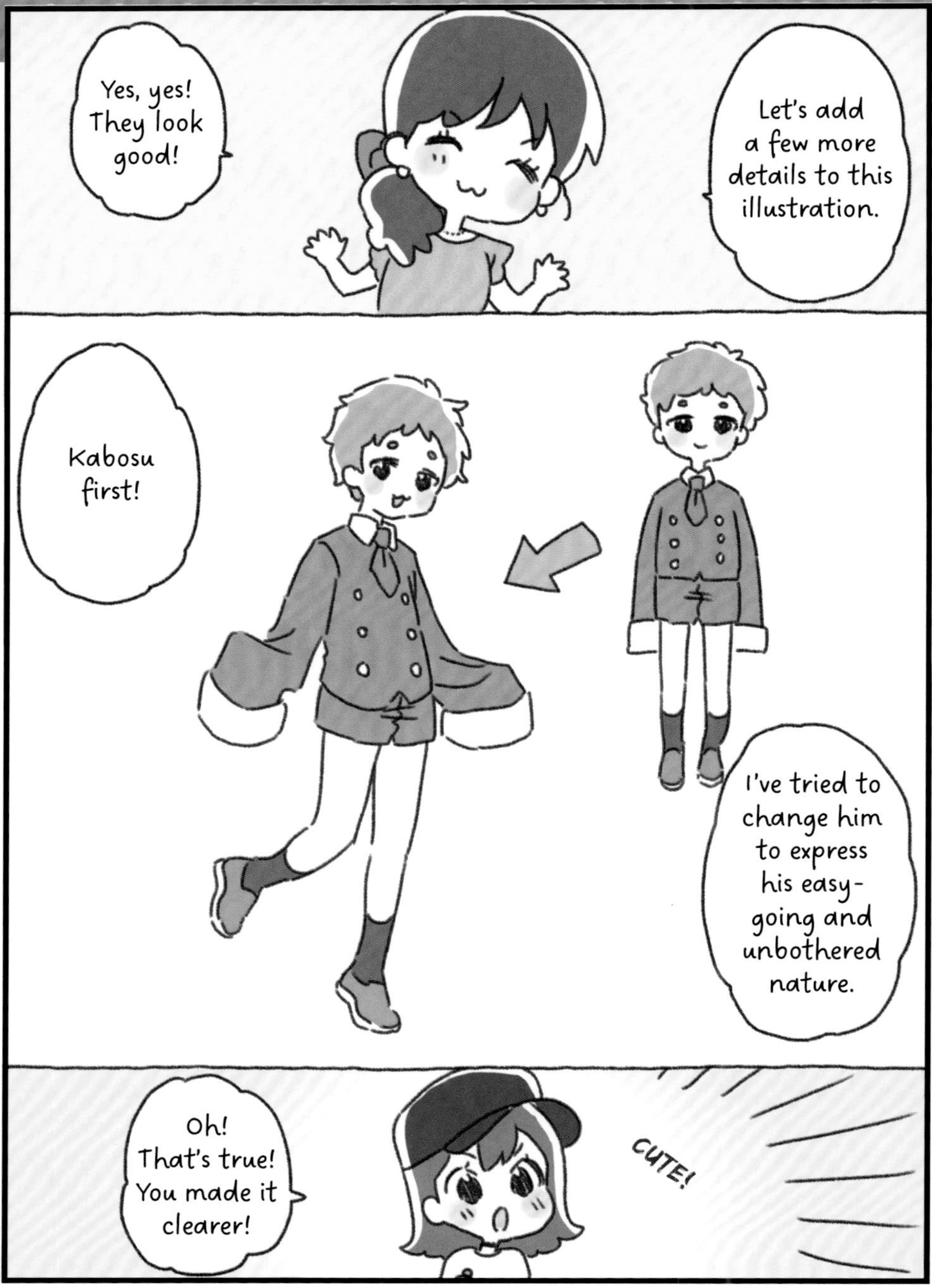
Let's add a few more details to this illustration.
Yes, yes! They look good!
I've tried to change him to express his easy-going and unbothered nature.
Kabosu first!
CUTE!
Oh! That's true! You made it clearer!

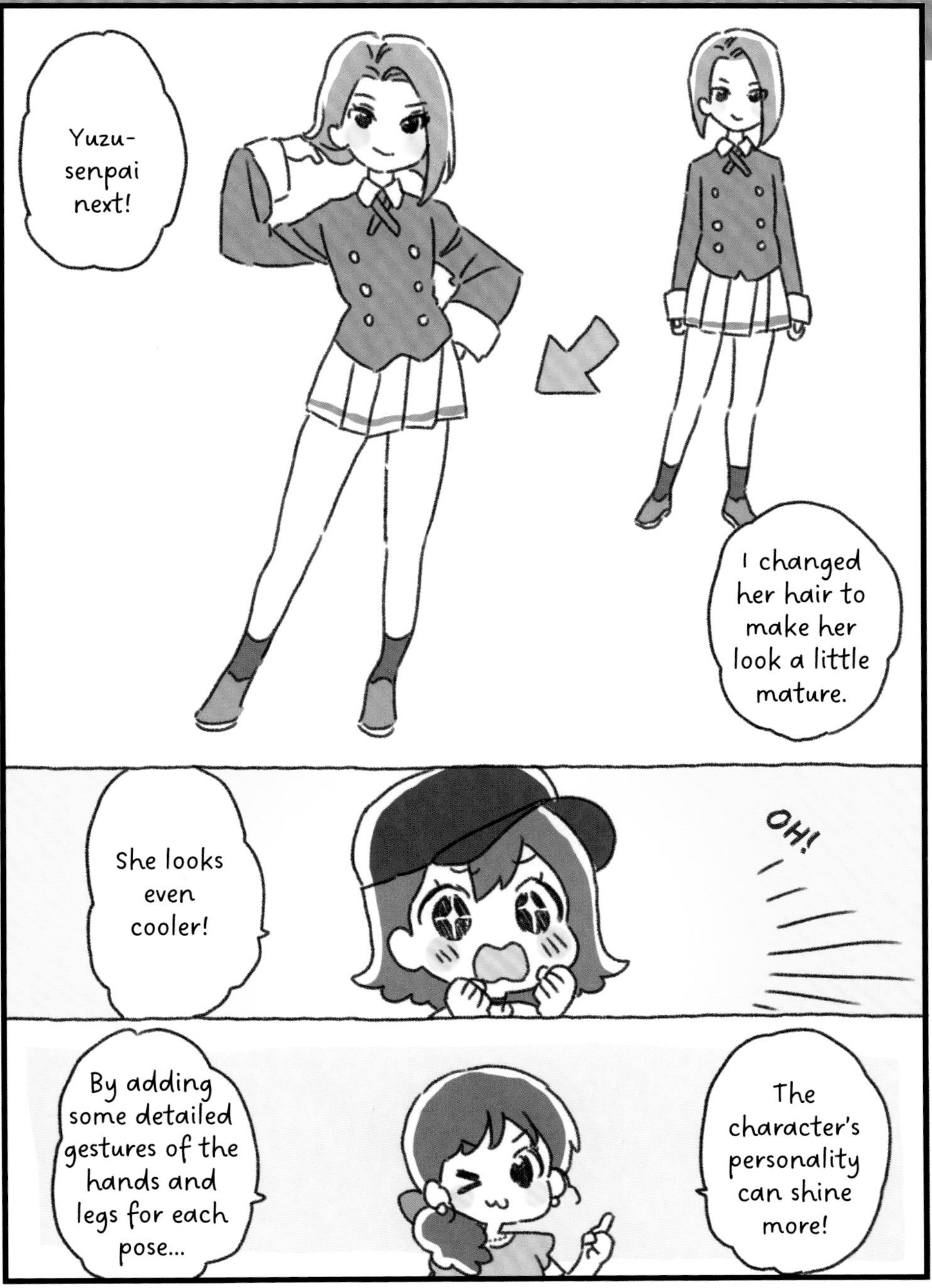
Yuzu-senpai next!
I changed her hair to make her look a little mature.
She looks even cooler!
OH!
By adding some detailed gestures of the hands and legs for each pose...
The character's personality can shine more!

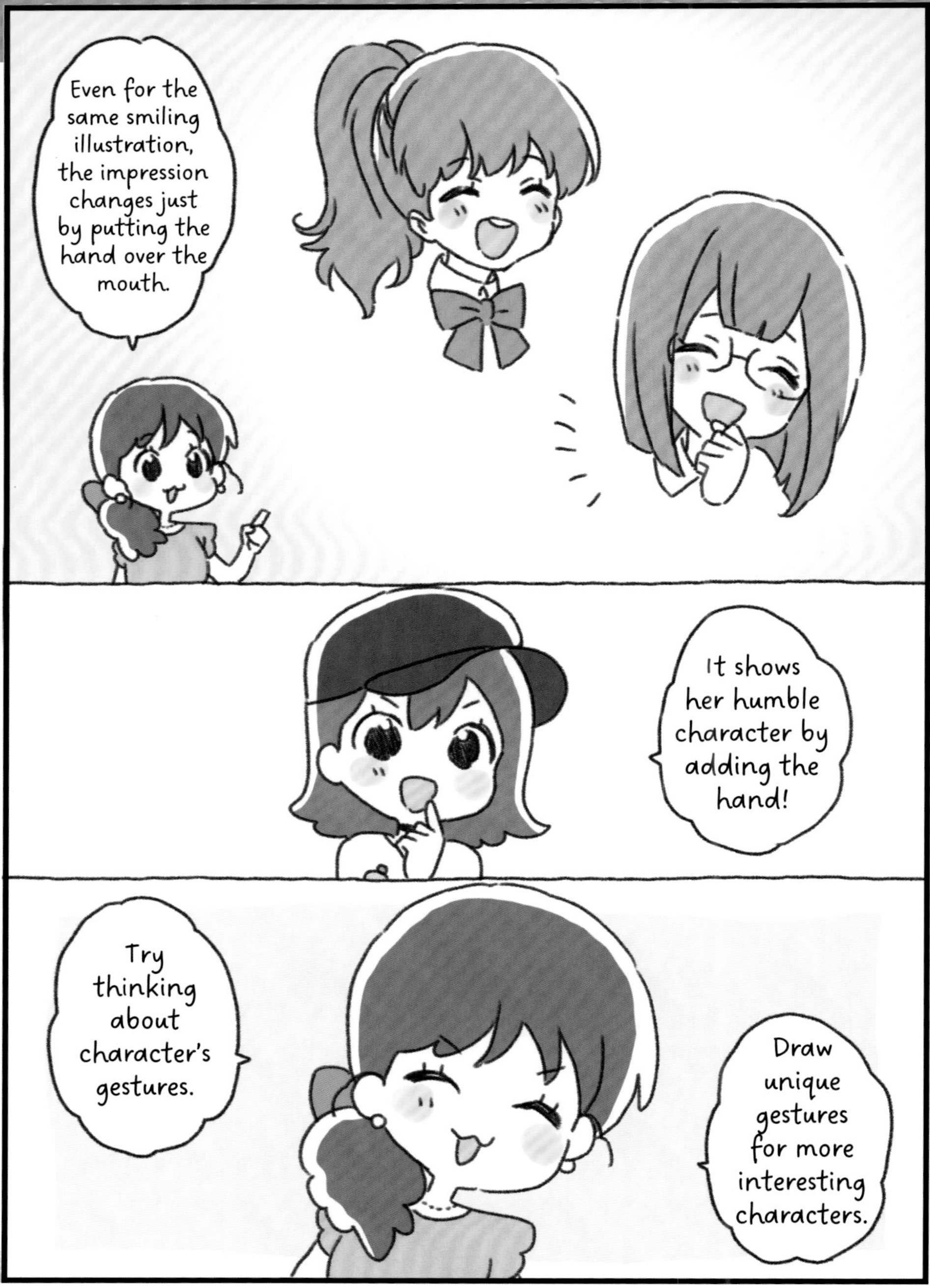
Even for the same smiling illustration, the impression changes just by putting the hand over the mouth.
It shows her humble character by adding the hand!
Try thinking about character's gestures.
Draw unique gestures for more interesting characters.

## LEVEL UP

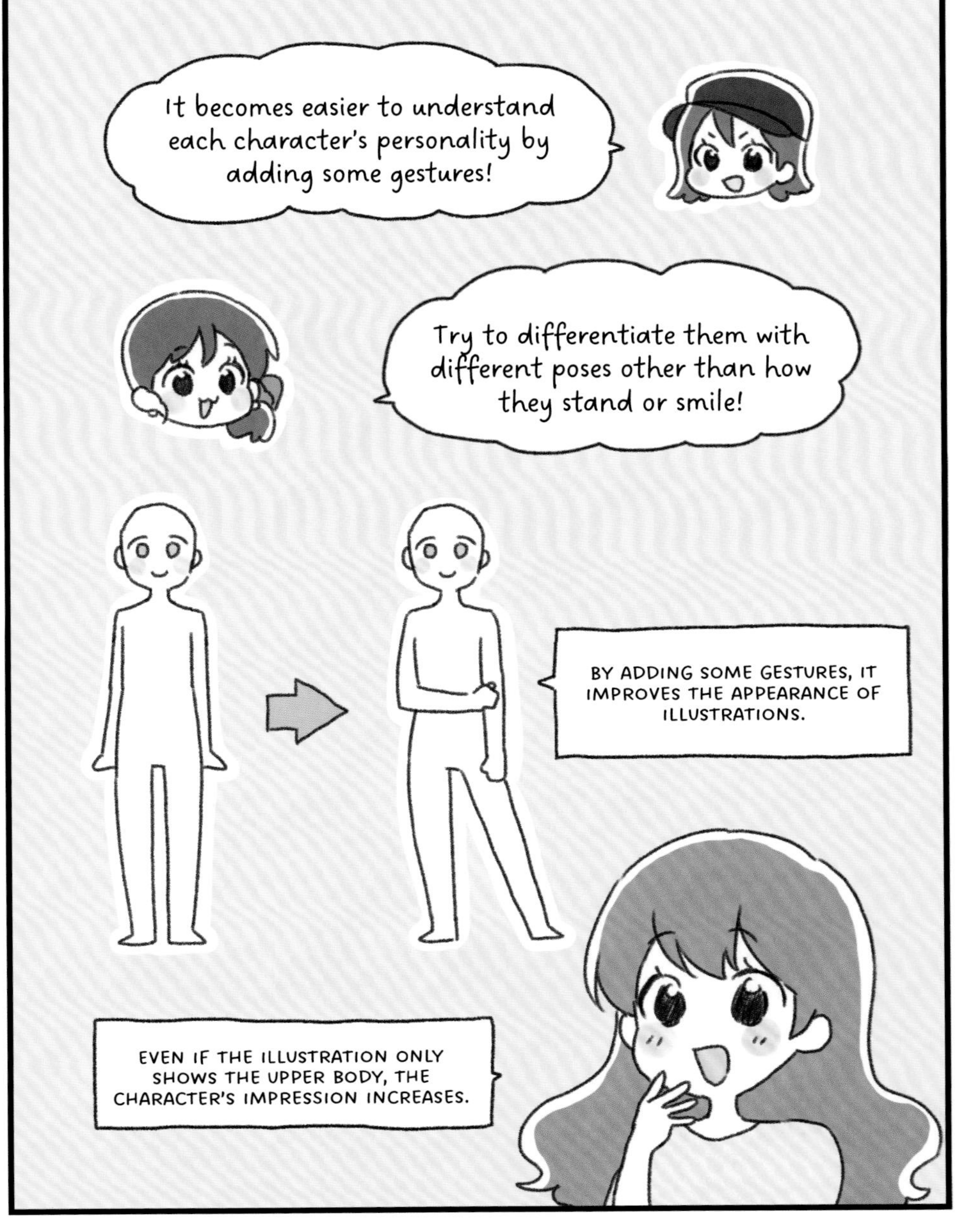
It becomes easier to understand each character's personality by adding some gestures!
Try to differentiate them with different poses other than how they stand or smile!
BY ADDING SOME GESTURES, IT IMPROVES THE APPEARANCE OF ILLUSTRATIONS.
EVEN IF THE ILLUSTRATION ONLY SHOWS THE UPPER BODY, THE CHARACTER'S IMPRESSION INCREASES.

## THINKING ABOUT POSES ACCORDING TO THE SCENES

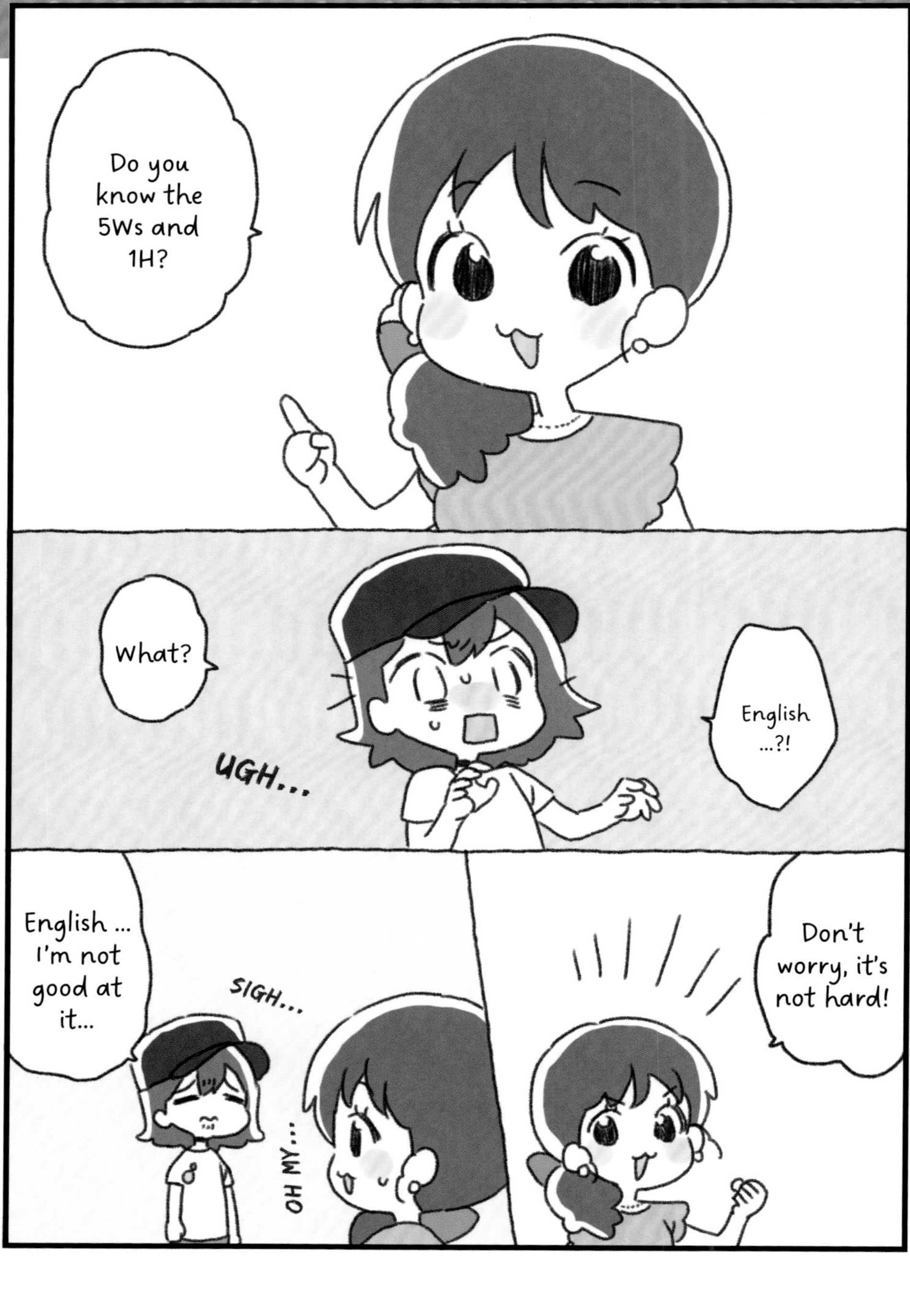
Do you know the 5Ws and 1H?
What?
English ...?!
UGH...
English ... I'm not good at it...
SIGH...
OH MY...
Don't worry, it's not hard!

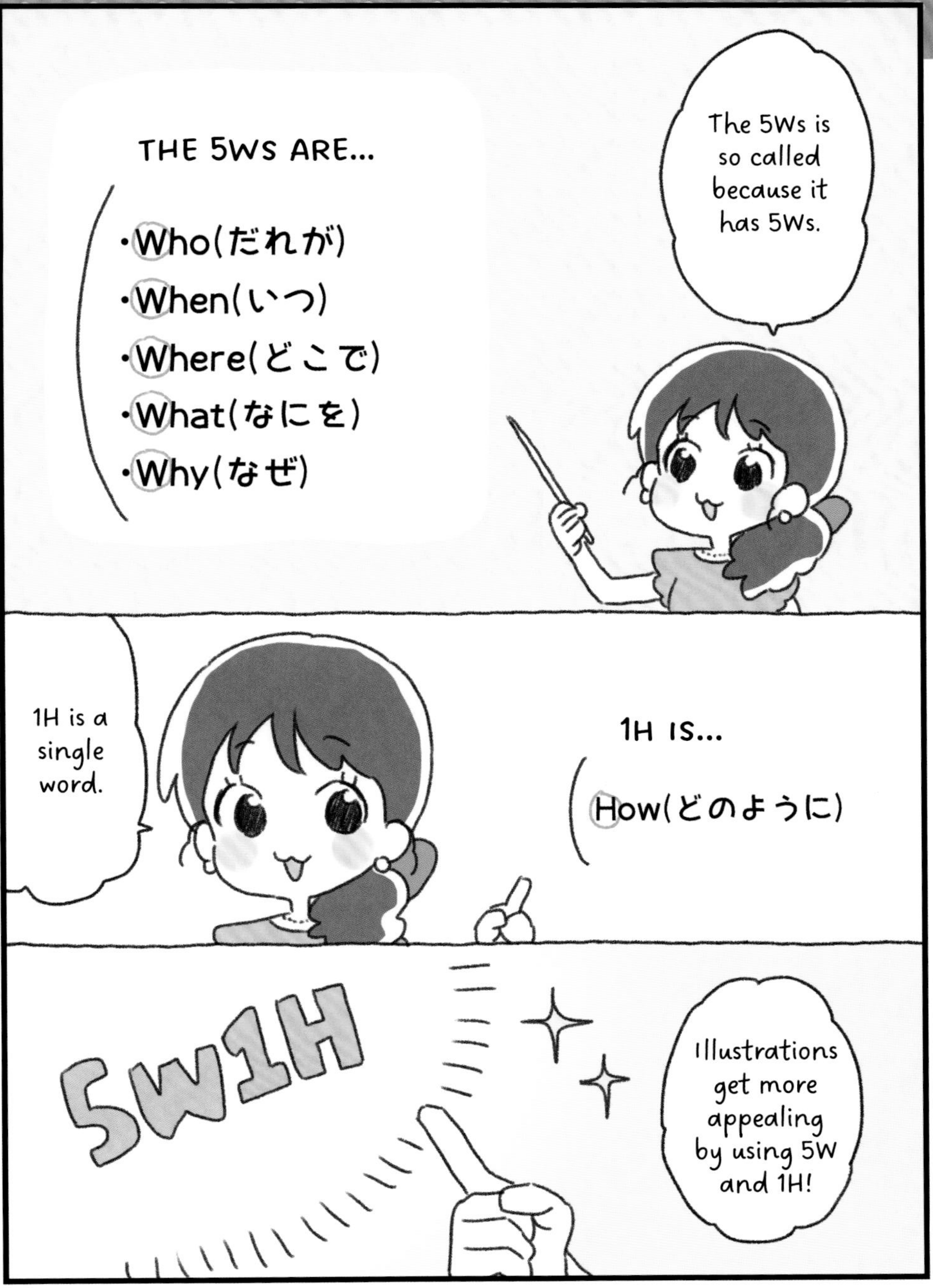
The 5Ws is so called because it has 5Ws.
THE 5WS ARE...
·Who(だれが)
·When(いつ)
·Where(どこで)
·What(なにを)
·Why(なぜ)
1H is a single word.
1H IS...
How(どのように)
5W1H
Illustrations get more appealing by using 5W and 1H!

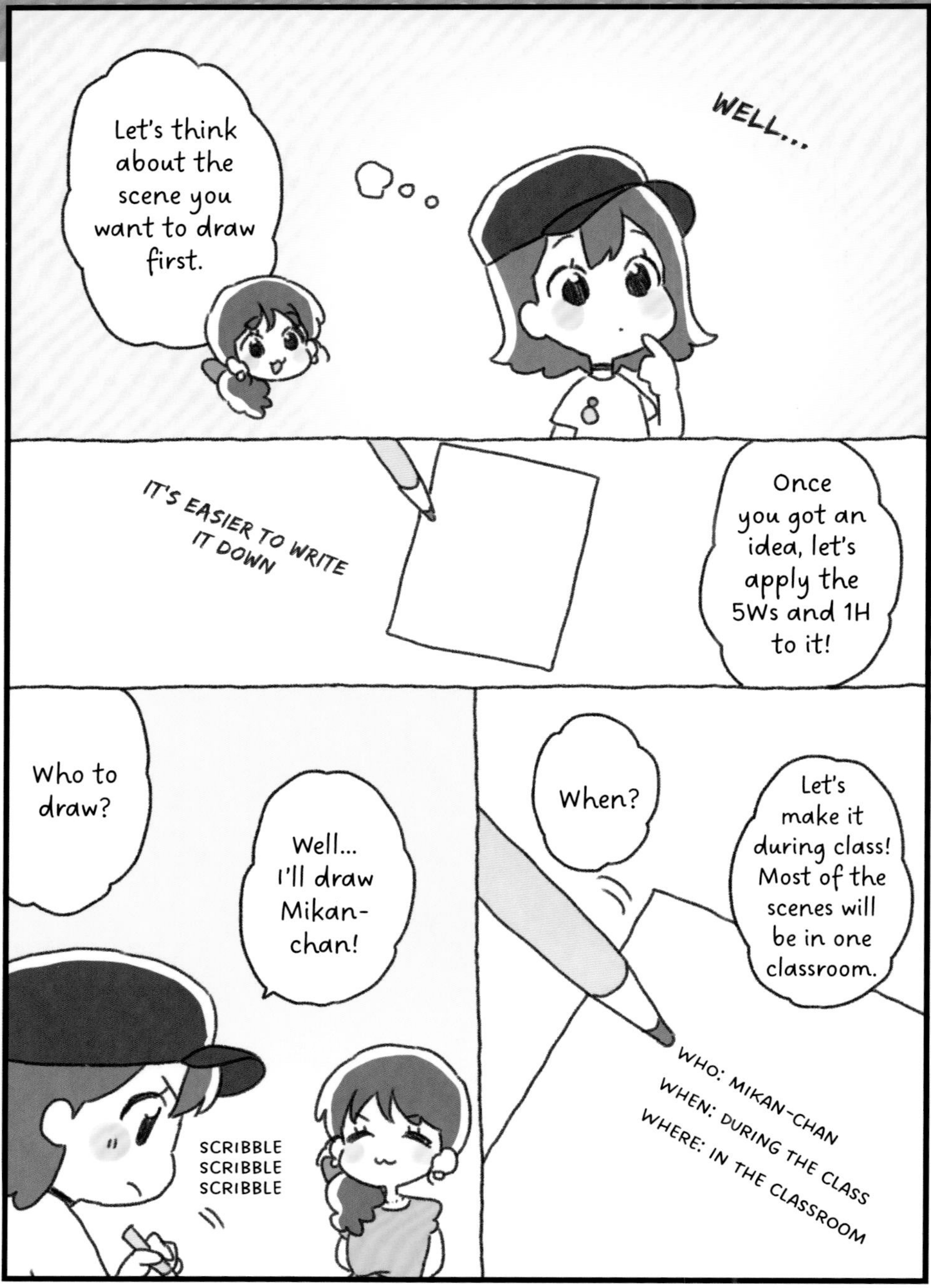
Let's think about the scene you want to draw first.
WELL...
IT'S EASIER TO WRITE IT DOWN
Once you got an idea, let's apply the 5Ws and 1H to it!
Who to draw?
Well... I'll draw Mikan-chan!
SCRIBBLE SCRIBBLE SCRIBBLE
When?
Let's make it during class! Most of the scenes will be in one classroom.
WHO: MIKAN-CHAN
WHEN: DURING THE CLASS
WHERE: IN THE CLASSROOM

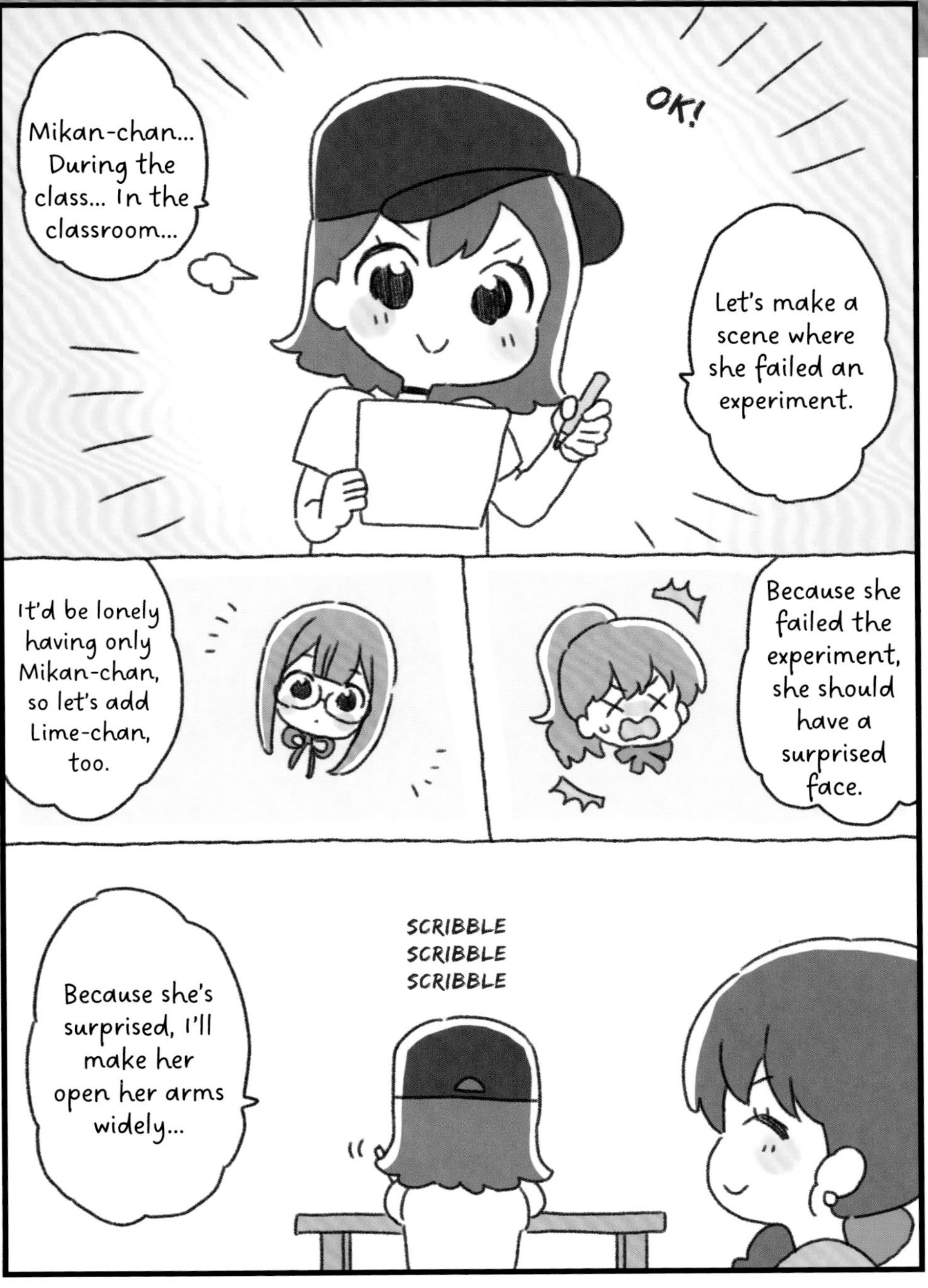
Mikan-chan... During the class... In the classroom...
OK!
Let's make a scene where she failed an experiment.
It'd be lonely having only Mikan-chan, so let's add Lime-chan, too.
Because she failed the experiment, she should have a surprised face.
Because she's surprised, I'll make her open her arms widely...
SCRIBBLE
SCRIBBLE
SCRIBBLE

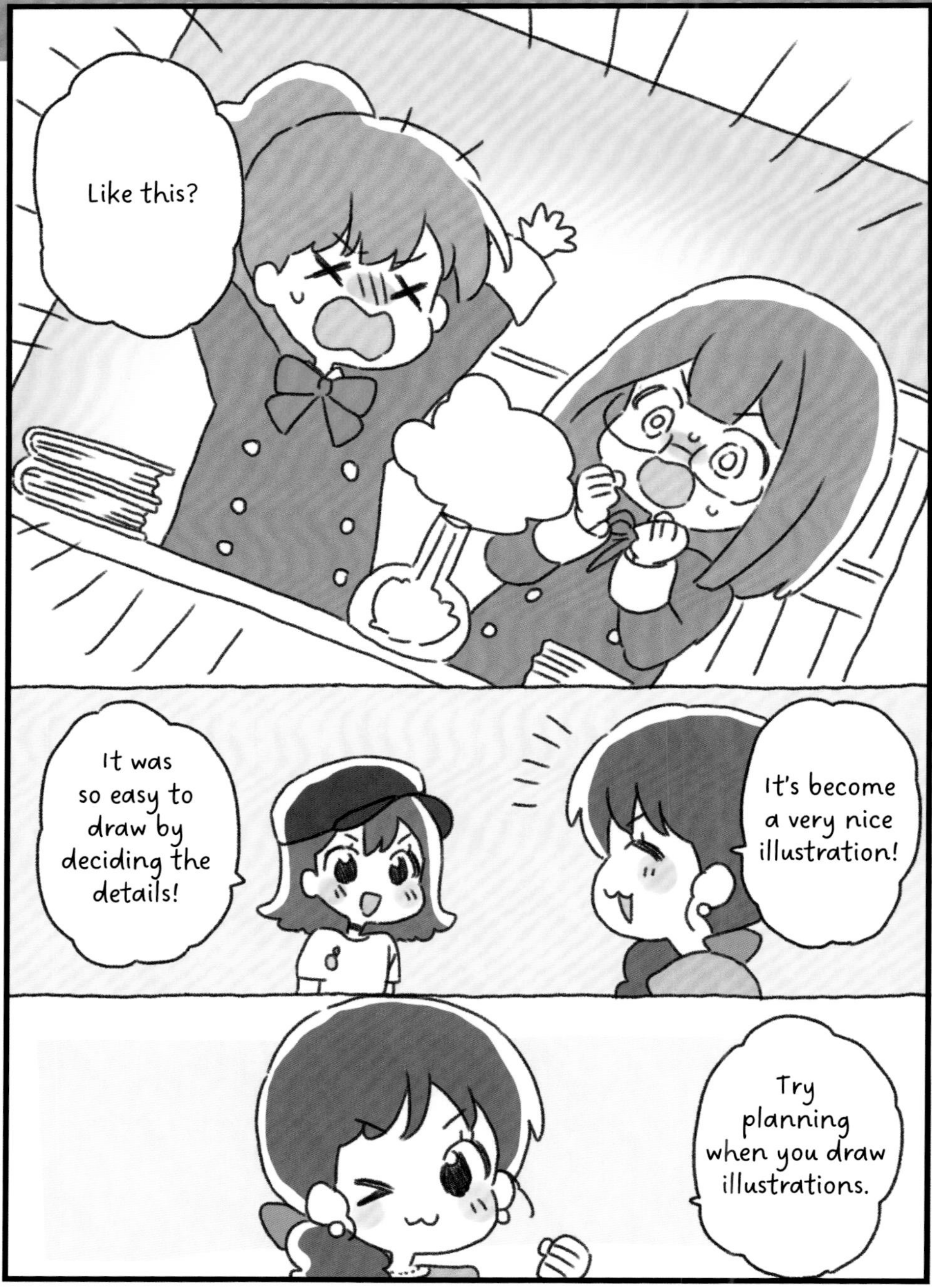
Like this?
It was so easy to draw by deciding the details!
It's become a very nice illustration!
Try planning when you draw illustrations.

## — SUMMARY —

It's easy to draw illustrations for a story by thinking about the 5Ws and 1H!

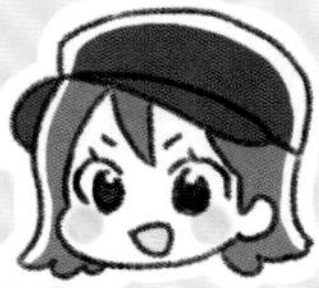

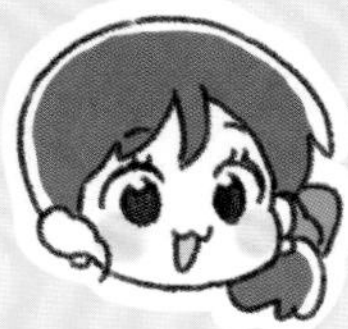

As the number of elements increases the density increases as well, and the illustration becomes more gorgeous, you know?

### 5Ws 1H

- Who(だれが)
- When(いつ)
- Where(どこで)
- What(なにを)
- Why(なぜ)

How(どのように)

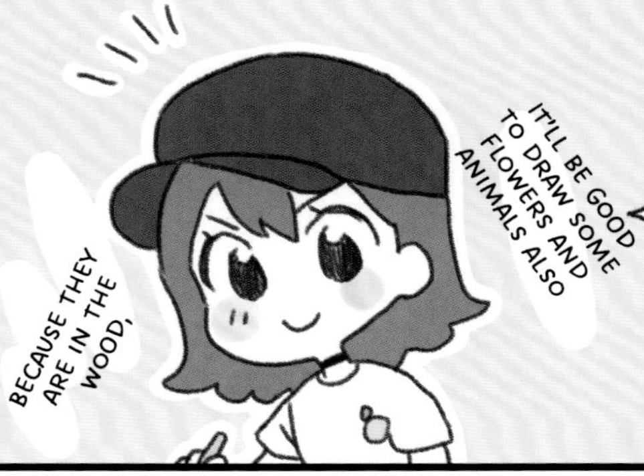
BECAUSE THEY ARE IN THE WOOD,
IT'LL BE GOOD TO DRAW SOME FLOWERS AND ANIMALS ALSO

LET'S INCREASE THE ELEMENTS OF EACH ILLUSTRATION BY ASSOCIATING FROM ONE IDEA TO ANOTHER.

## CONSIDER THE SCENE'S TIMELINE

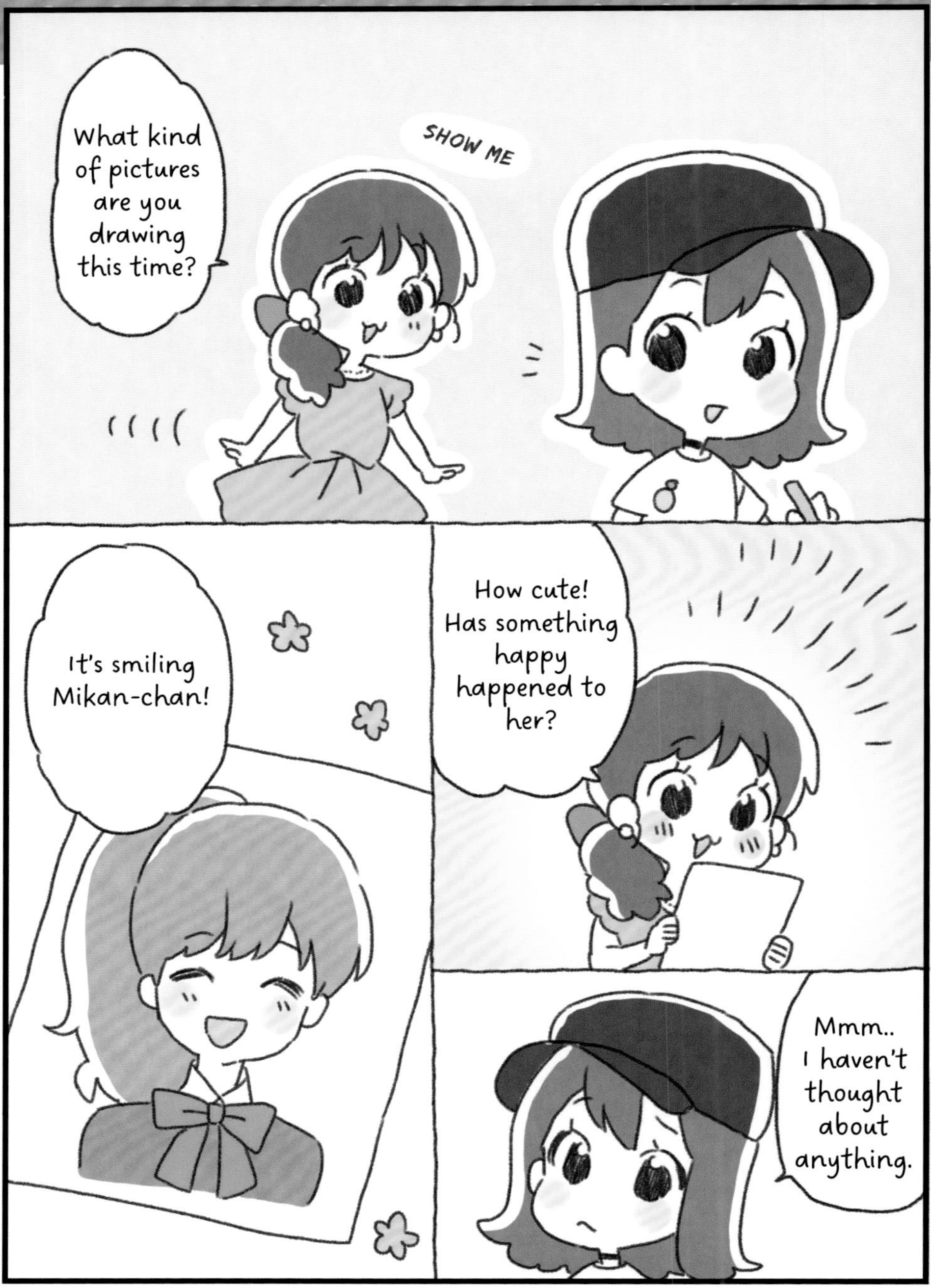
What kind of pictures are you drawing this time?
SHOW ME
It's smiling Mikan-chan!
How cute! Has something happy happened to her?
Mmm.. I haven't thought about anything.

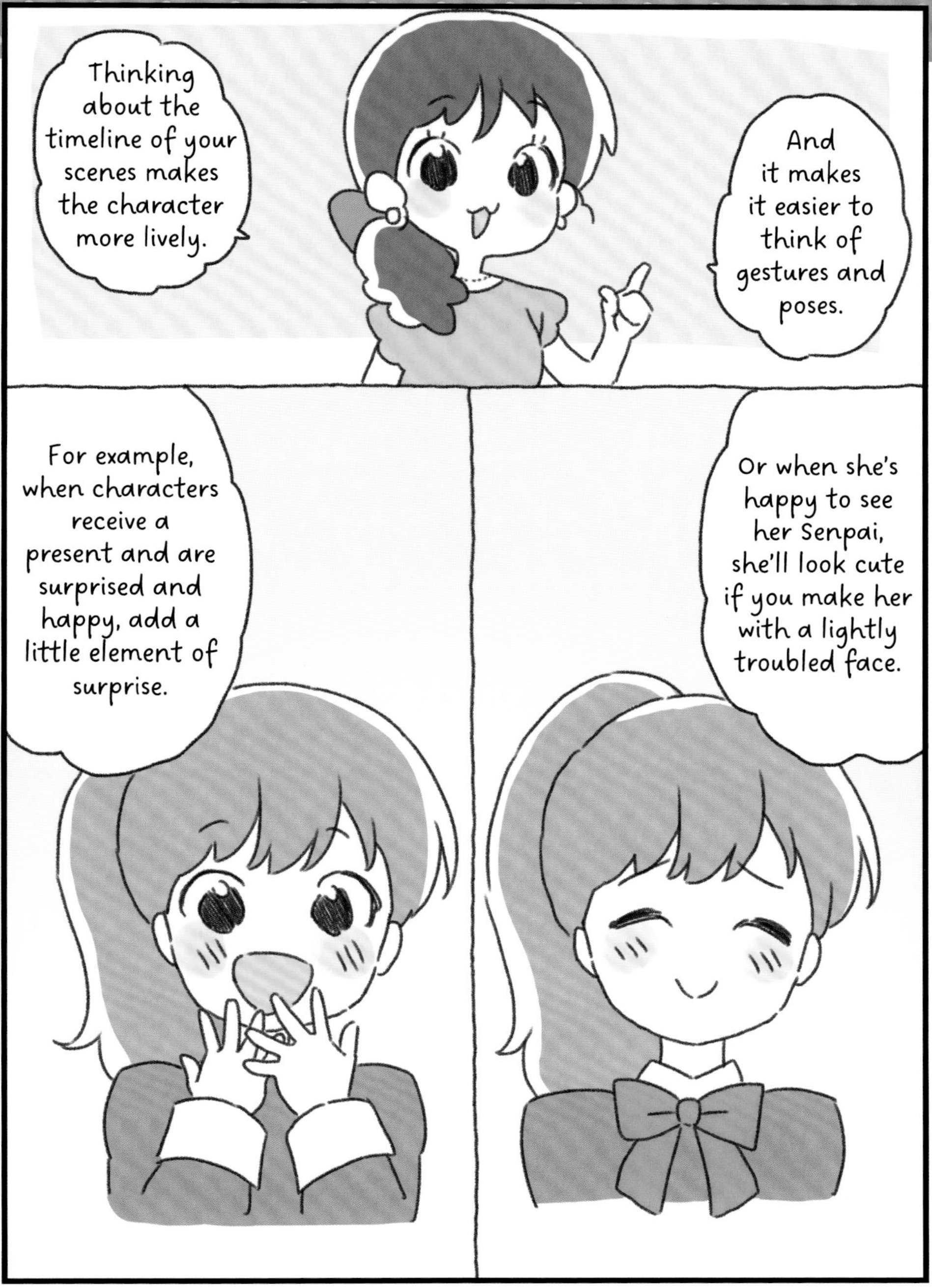
Thinking about the timeline of your scenes makes the character more lively.
And it makes it easier to think of gestures and poses.
For example, when characters receive a present and are surprised and happy, add a little element of surprise.
Or when she's happy to see her Senpai, she'll look cute if you make her with a lightly troubled face.

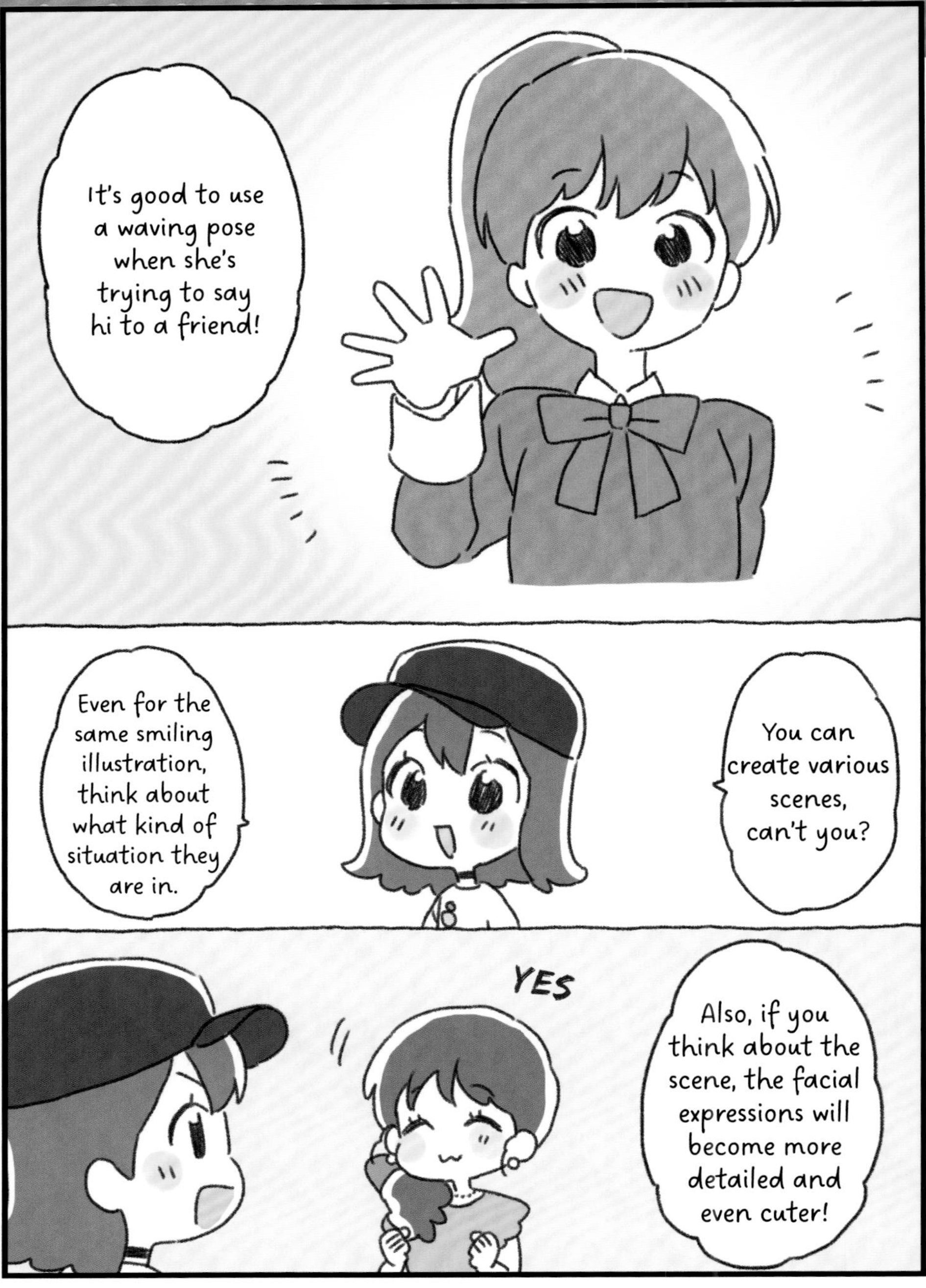
It's good to use a waving pose when she's trying to say hi to a friend!
Even for the same smiling illustration, think about what kind of situation they are in.
You can create various scenes, can't you?
YES
Also, if you think about the scene, the facial expressions will become more detailed and even cuter!

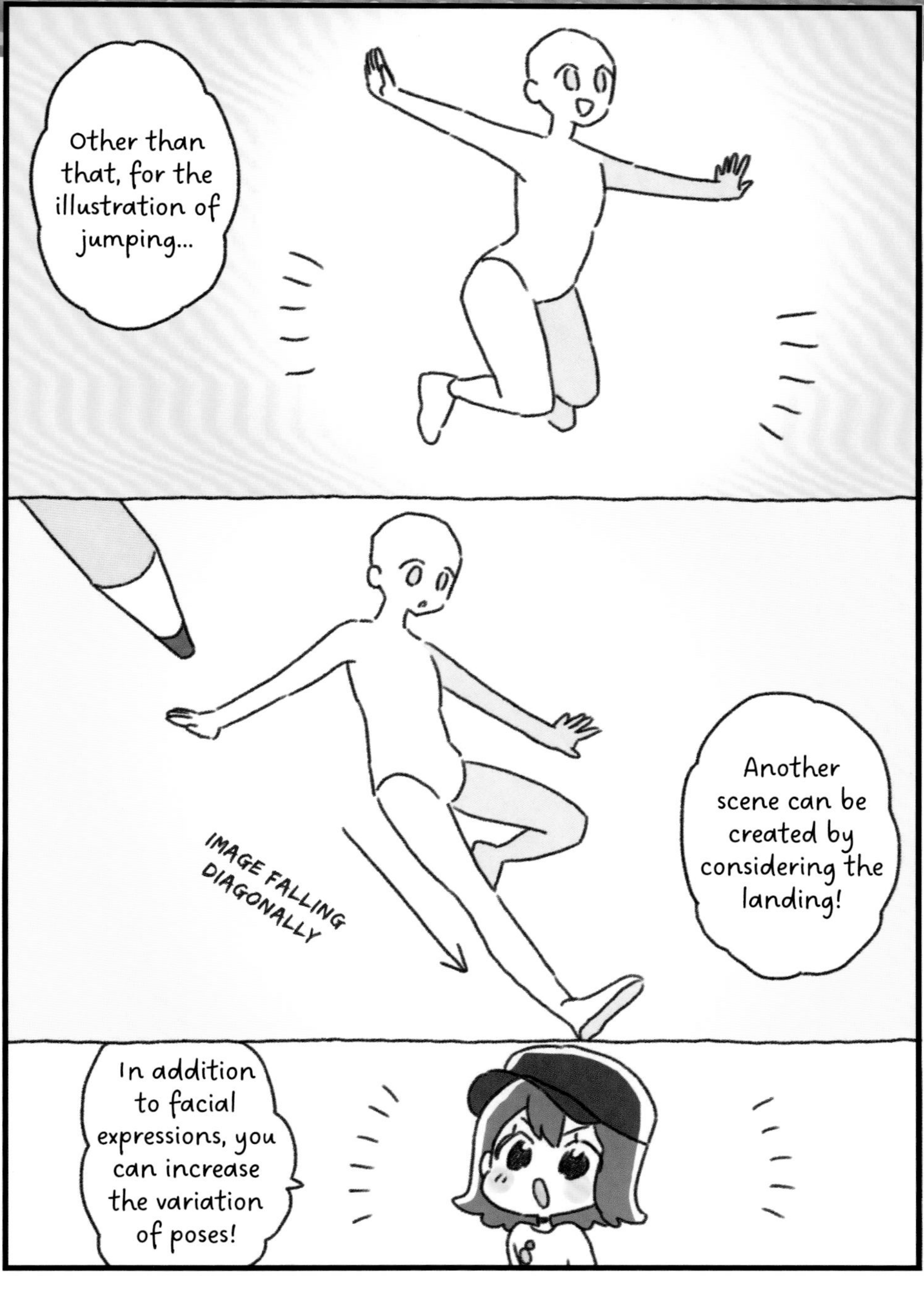
Other than that, for the illustration of jumping...
Another scene can be created by considering the landing!
IMAGE FALLING DIAGONALLY
In addition to facial expressions, you can increase the variation of poses!

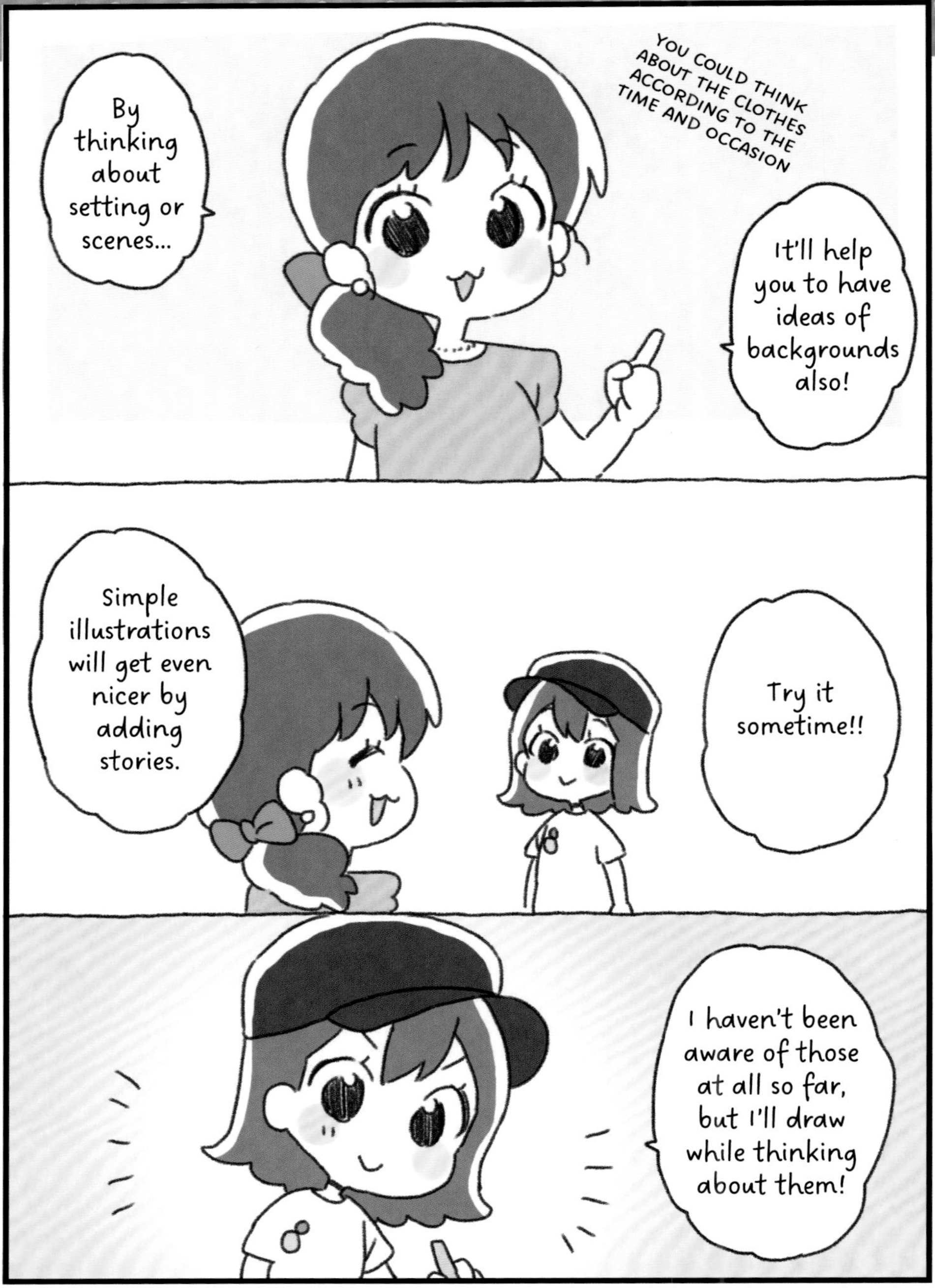
By thinking about setting or scenes...
YOU COULD THINK ABOUT THE CLOTHES ACCORDING TO THE TIME AND OCCASION
It'll help you to have ideas of backgrounds also!
Simple illustrations will get even nicer by adding stories.
Try it sometime!!
I haven't been aware of those at all so far, but I'll draw while thinking about them!

# — *SUMMARY* —

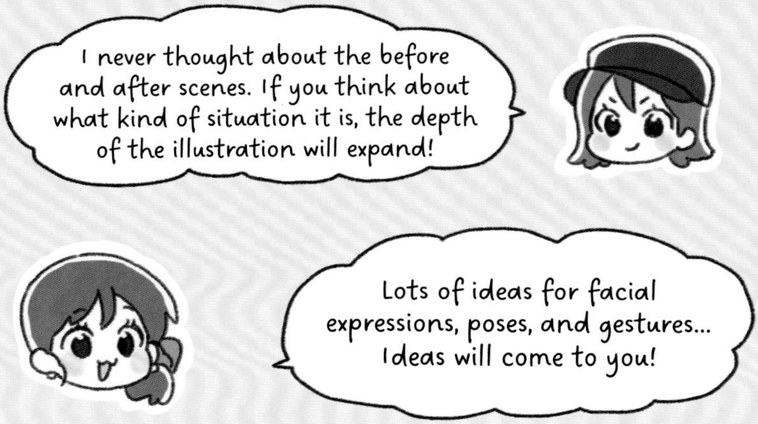

I never thought about the before and after scenes. If you think about what kind of situation it is, the depth of the illustration will expand!

Lots of ideas for facial expressions, poses, and gestures... Ideas will come to you!

EXPRESSIONS AND GESTURES CHANGE DEPENDING ON THE SCENES BEFORE AND AFTER!

DEGREES OF EXPRESSION

# SAMPLE POSES

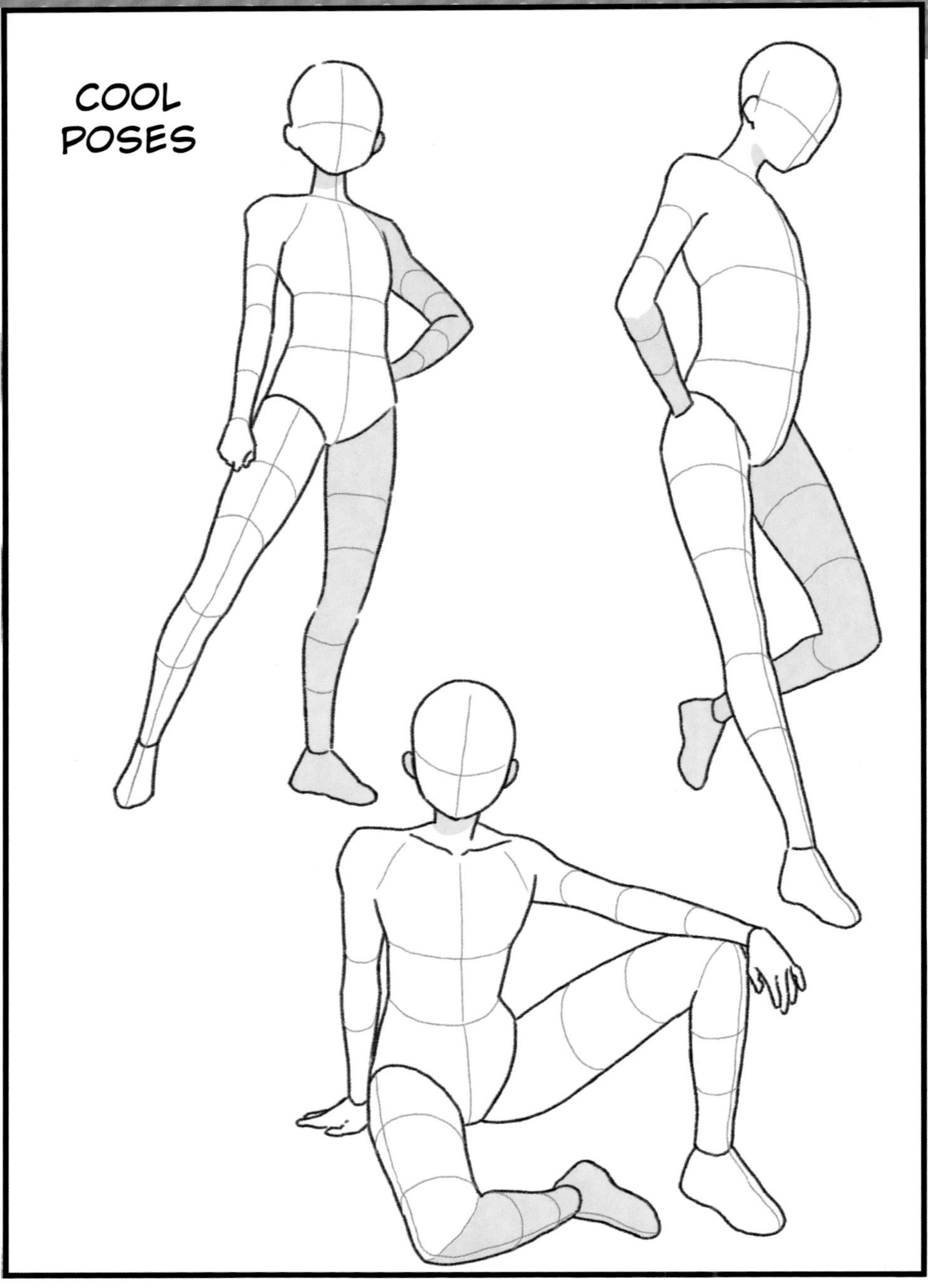
COOL POSES

# CUTE POSES

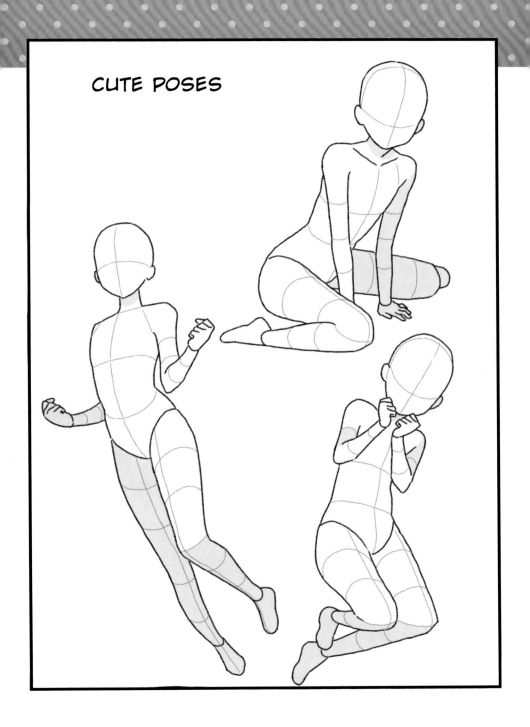

# FIGHTING POSES

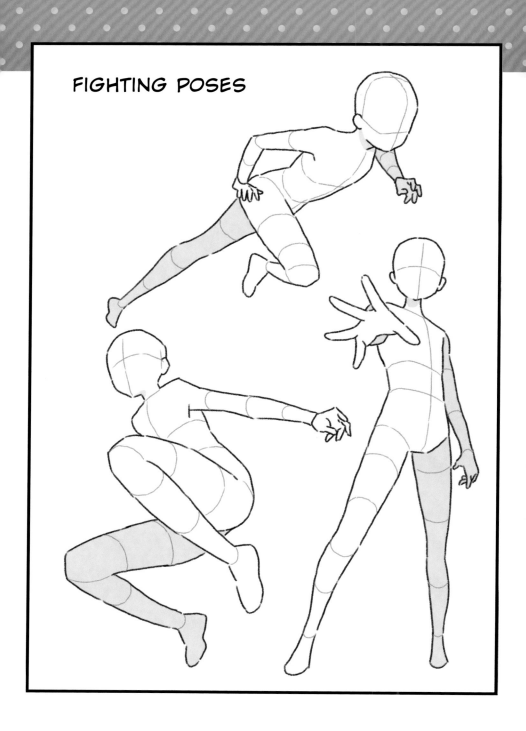

# DANCING POSES

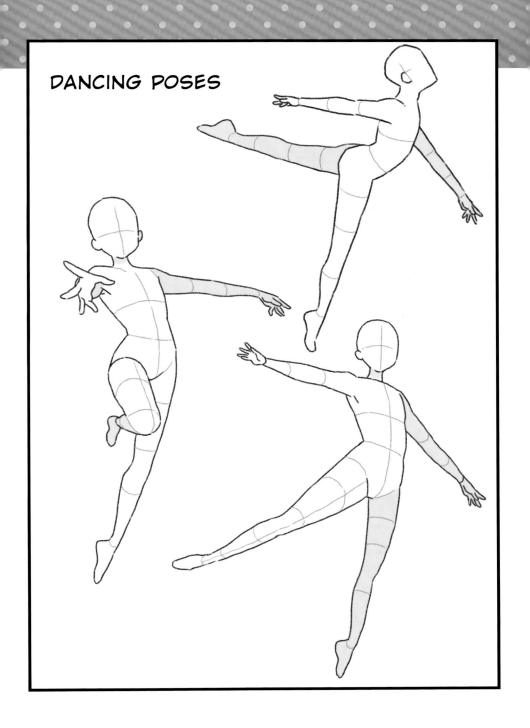

# REVIEW YOUR FINISHED DRAWINGS

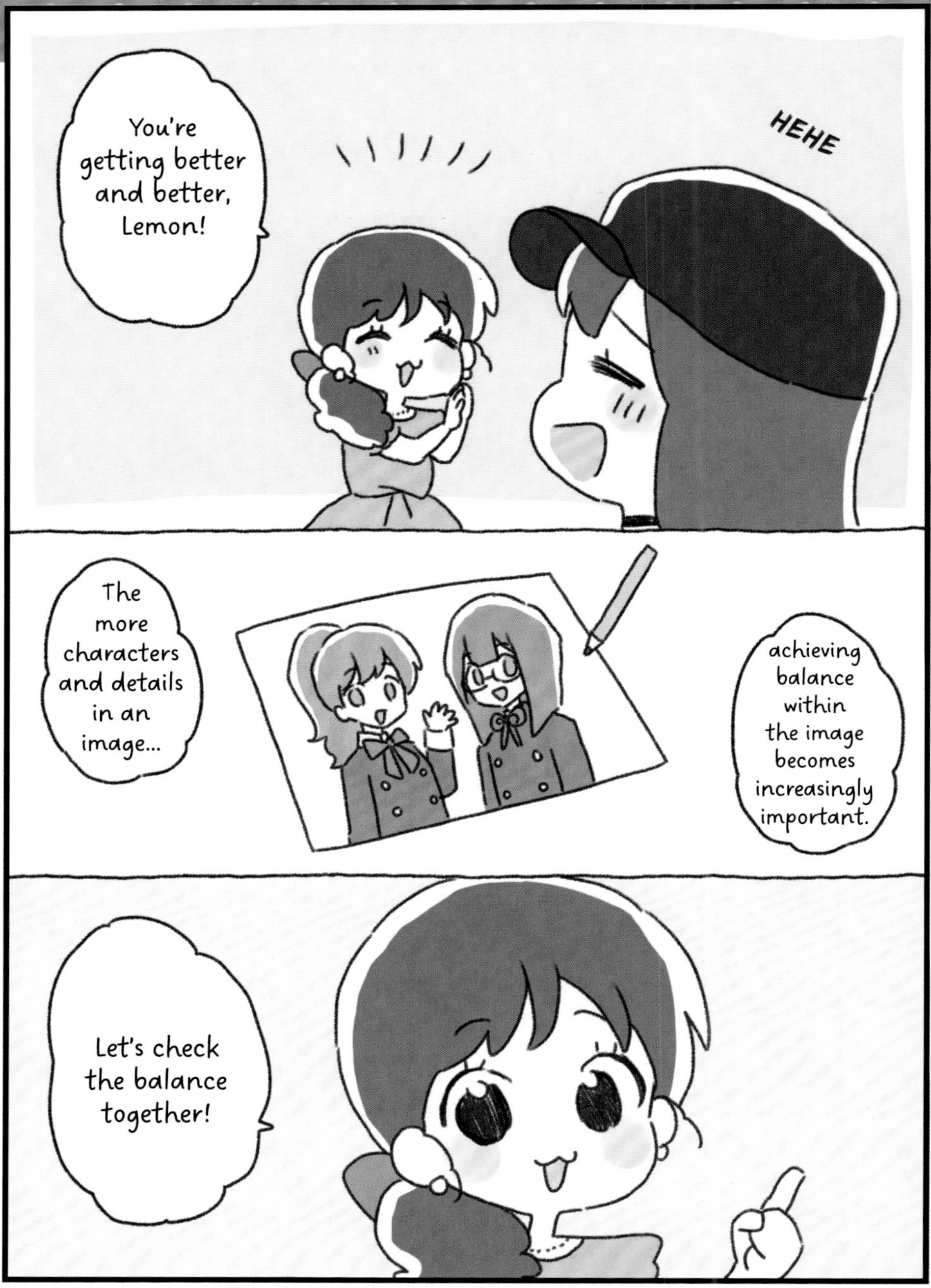
You're getting better and better, Lemon!
HEHE
The more characters and details in an image...
achieving balance within the image becomes increasingly important.
Let's check the balance together!

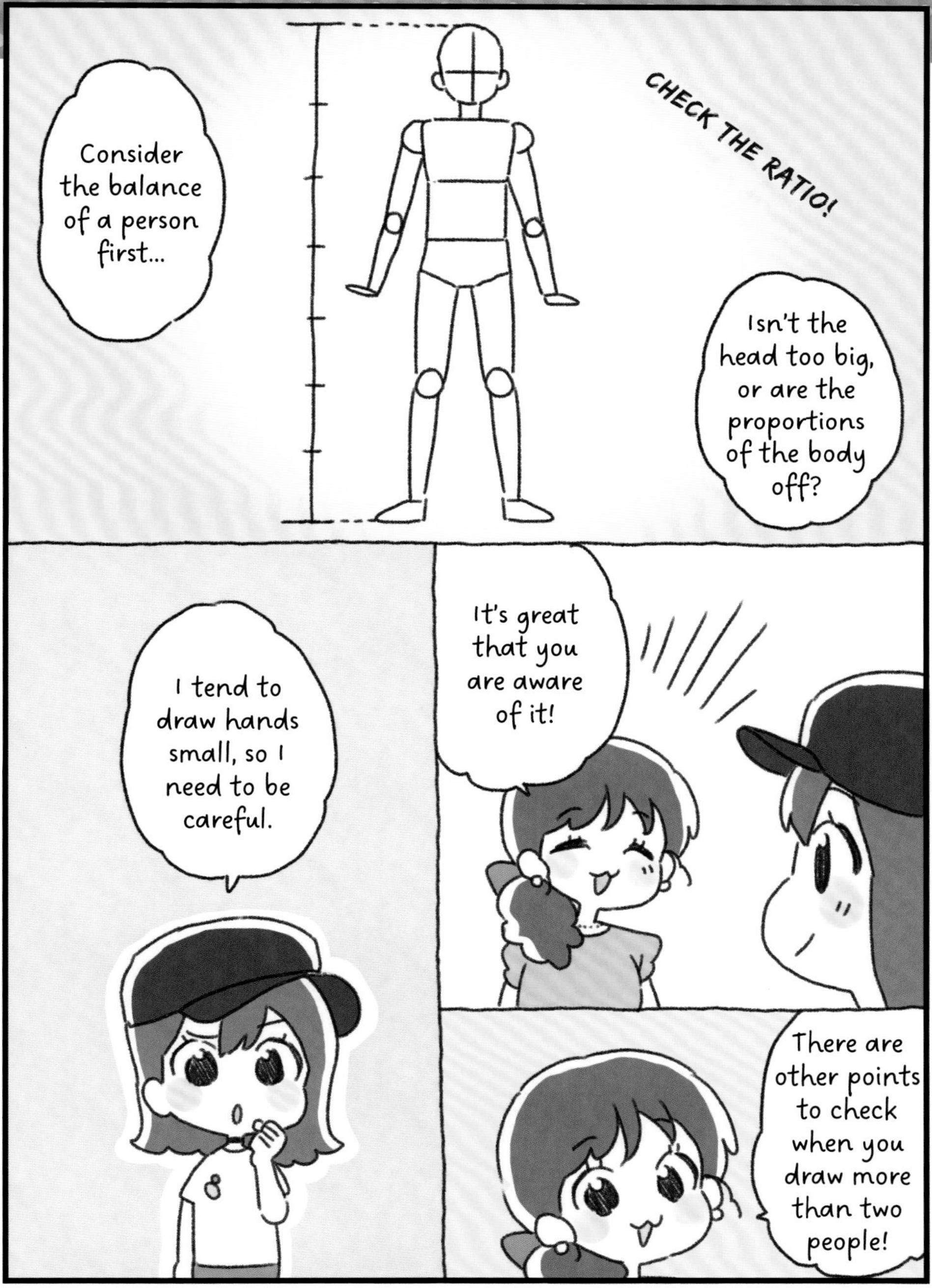
Consider the balance of a person first...
CHECK THE RATIO!
Isn't the head too big, or are the proportions of the body off?
I tend to draw hands small, so I need to be careful.
It's great that you are aware of it!
There are other points to check when you draw more than two people!

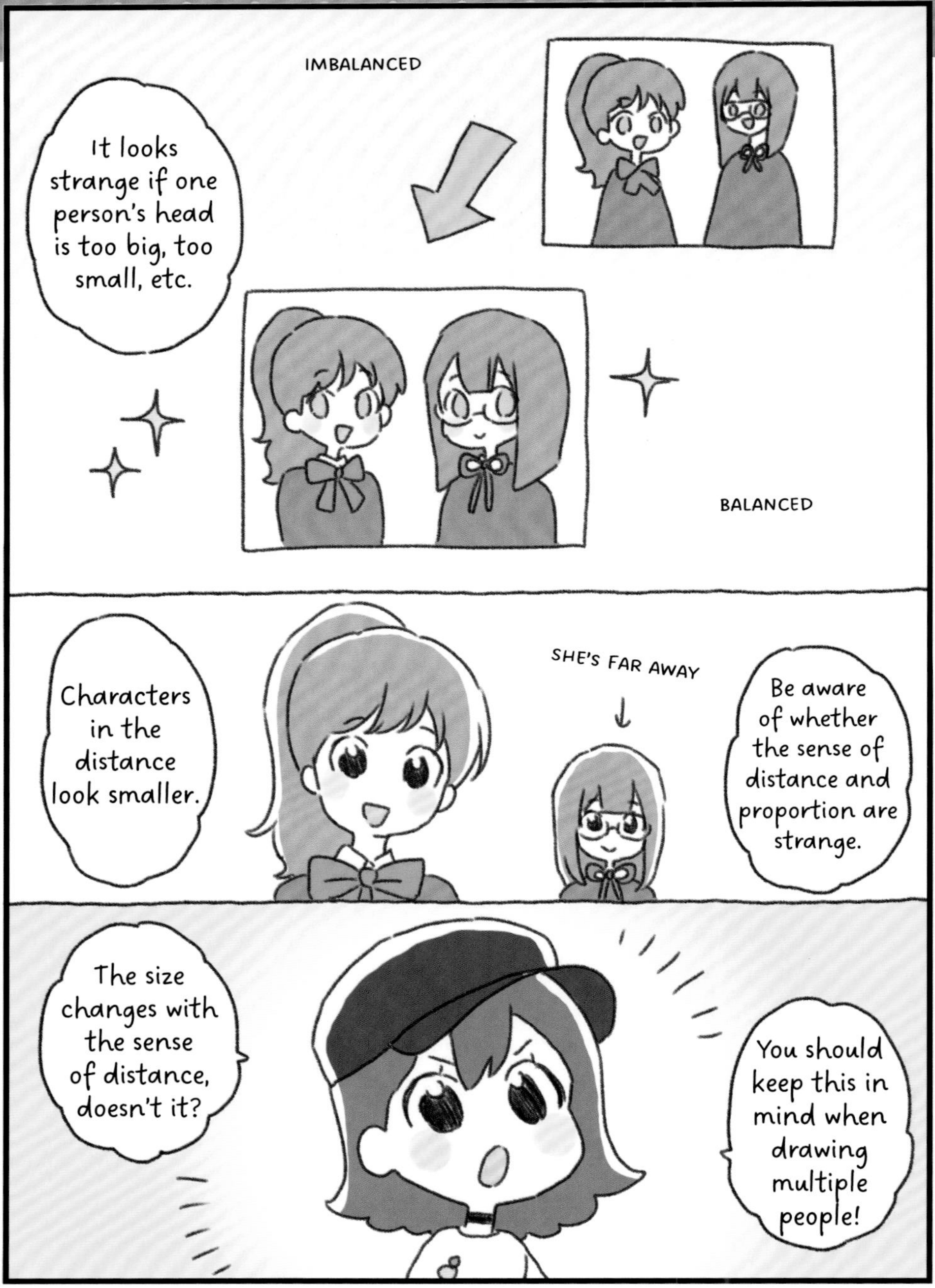
IMBALANCED
It looks strange if one person's head is too big, too small, etc.
BALANCED
Characters in the distance look smaller.
SHE'S FAR AWAY
Be aware of whether the sense of distance and proportion are strange.
The size changes with the sense of distance, doesn't it?
You should keep this in mind when drawing multiple people!

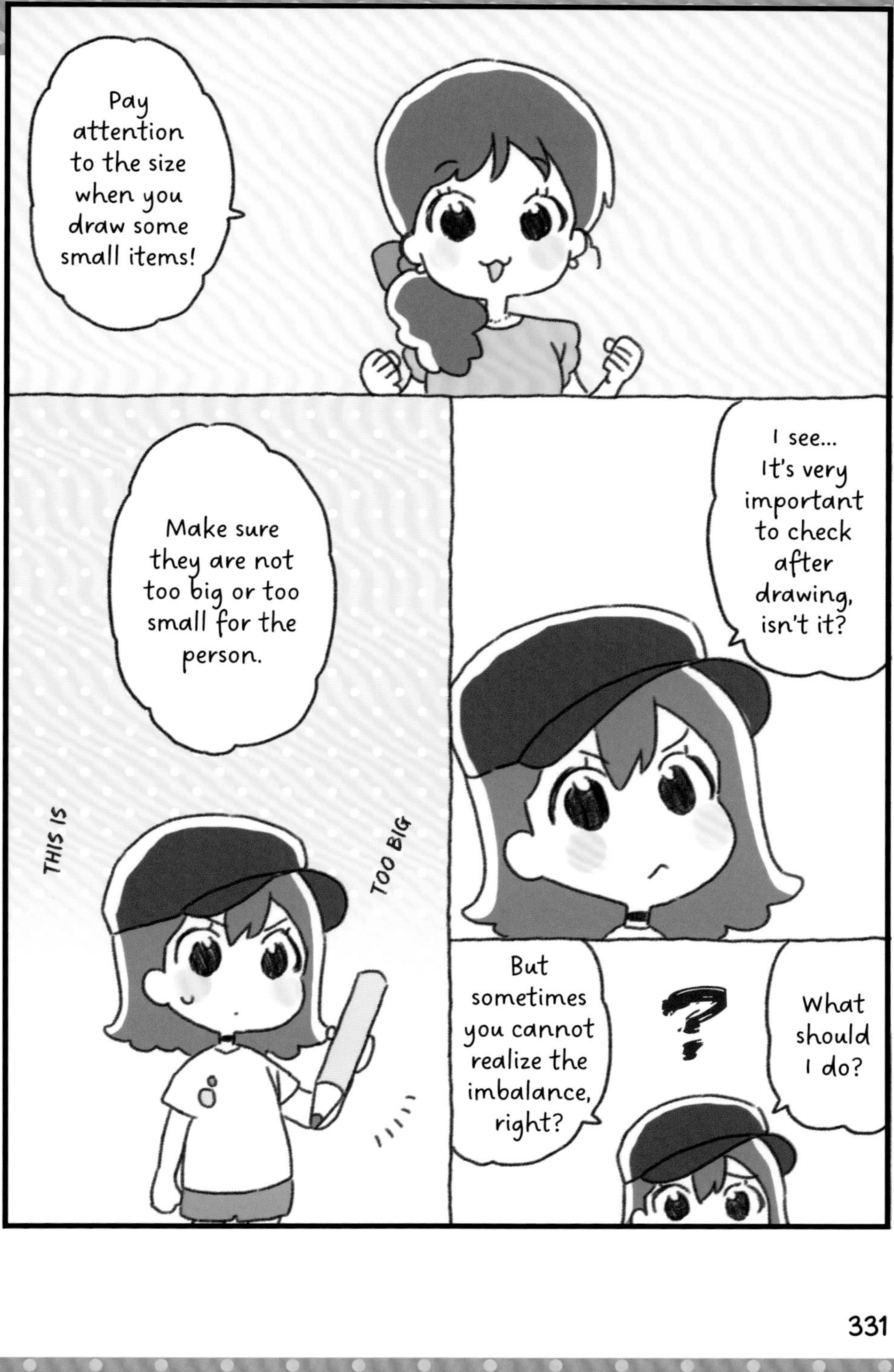
Pay attention to the size when you draw some small items!
Make sure they are not too big or too small for the person.
THIS IS TOO BIG
I see... It's very important to check after drawing, isn't it?
But sometimes you cannot realize the imbalance, right?
?
What should I do?

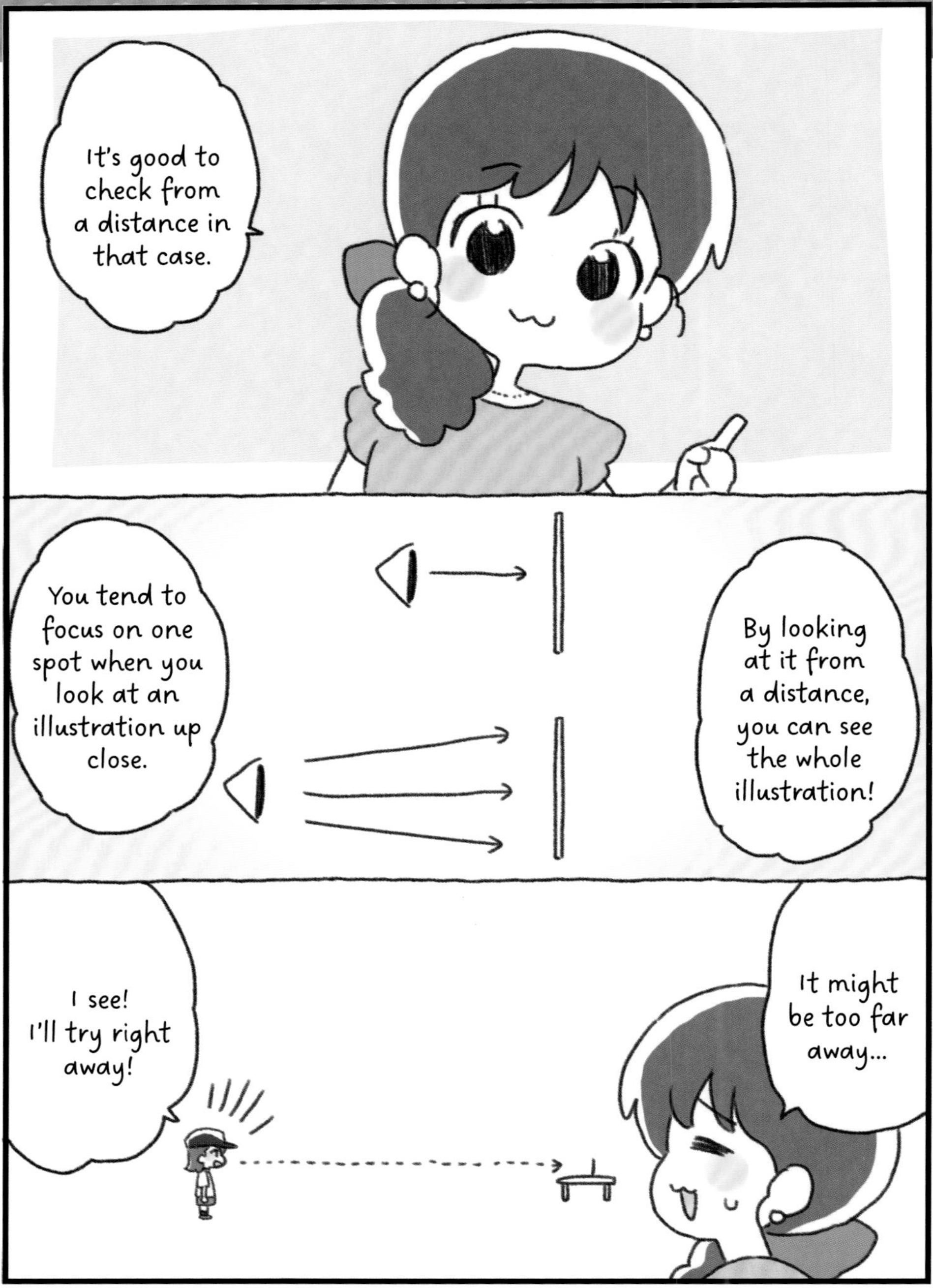
It's good to check from a distance in that case.
You tend to focus on one spot when you look at an illustration up close.
By looking at it from a distance, you can see the whole illustration!
I see! I'll try right away!
It might be too far away...

# — *SUMMARY* —

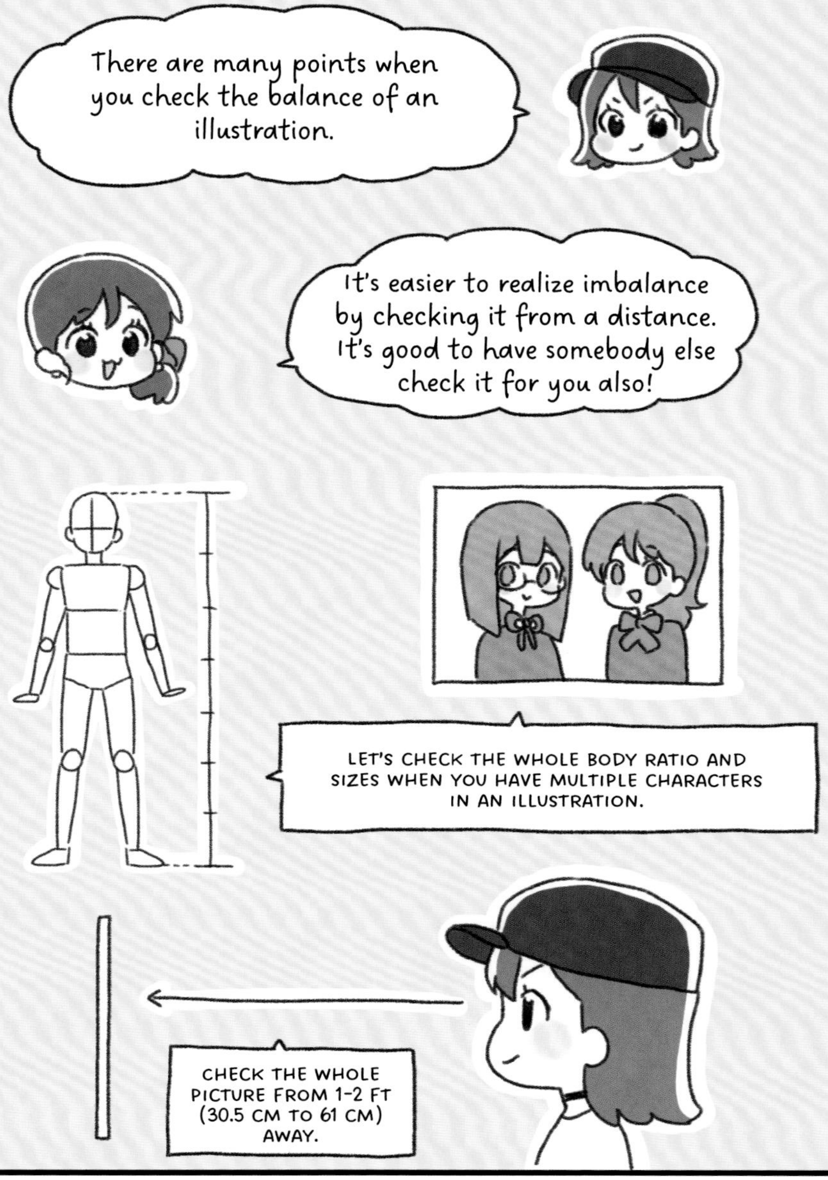

There are many points when you check the balance of an illustration.

It's easier to realize imbalance by checking it from a distance. It's good to have somebody else check it for you also!

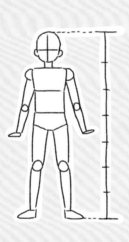

LET'S CHECK THE WHOLE BODY RATIO AND SIZES WHEN YOU HAVE MULTIPLE CHARACTERS IN AN ILLUSTRATION.

CHECK THE WHOLE PICTURE FROM 1–2 FT (30.5 CM TO 61 CM) AWAY.

# EPILOGUE

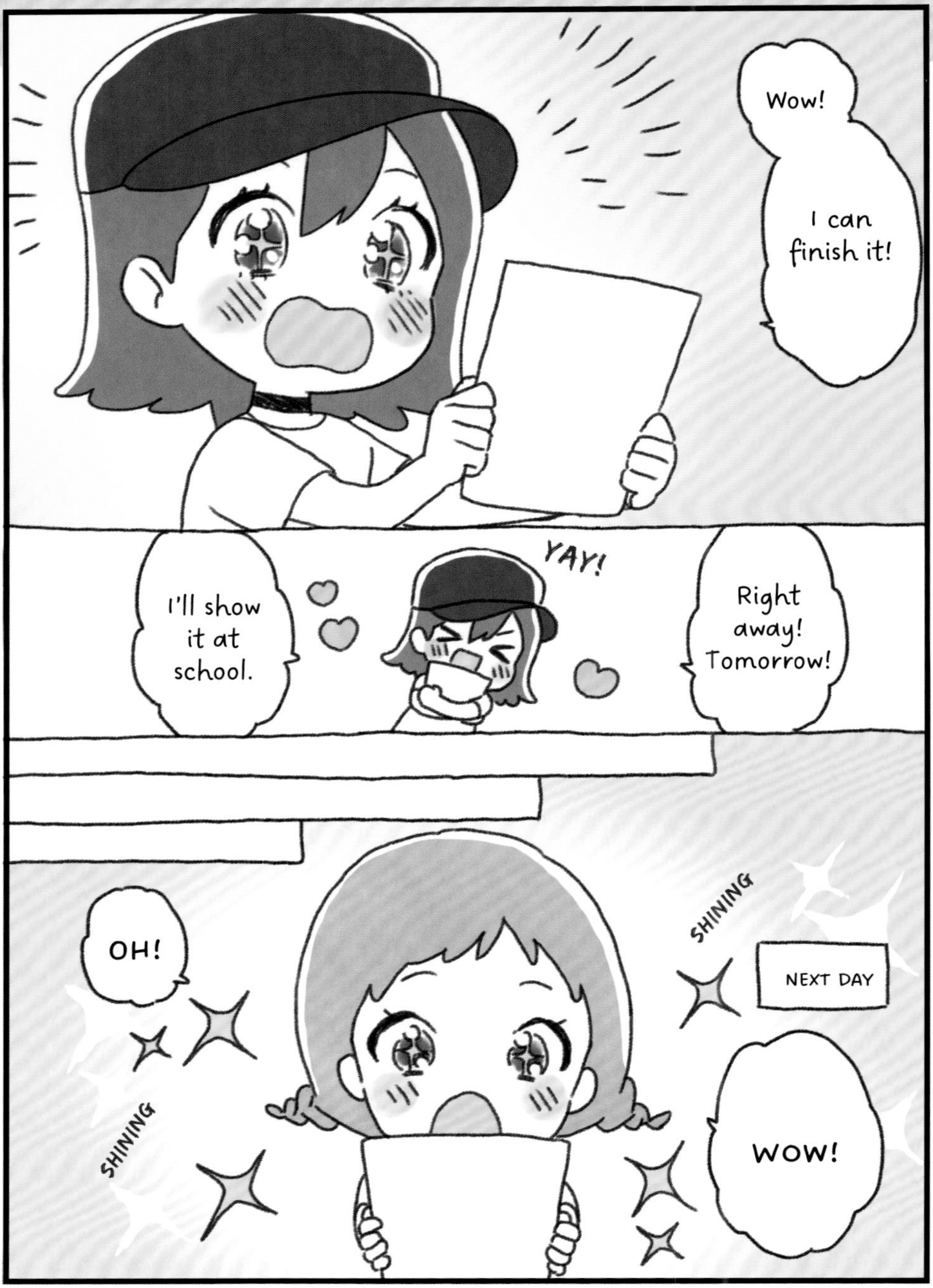
Wow!
I can finish it!
YAY!
I'll show it at school.
Right away! Tomorrow!
NEXT DAY
OH!
SHINING
SHINING
WOW!

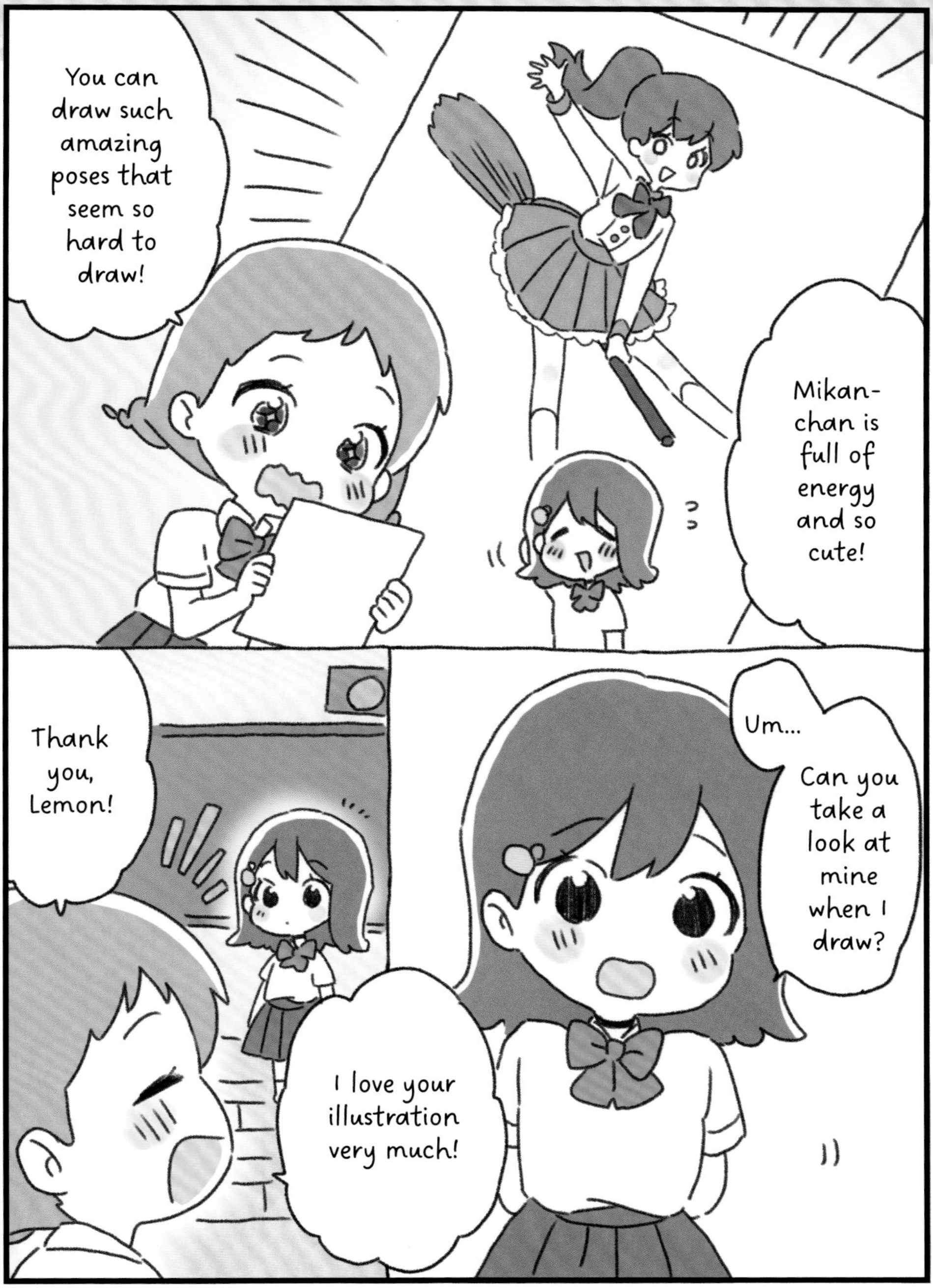
You can draw such amazing poses that seem so hard to draw!
Mikan-chan is full of energy and so cute!
Thank you, Lemon!
Um...
Can you take a look at mine when I draw?
I love your illustration very much!

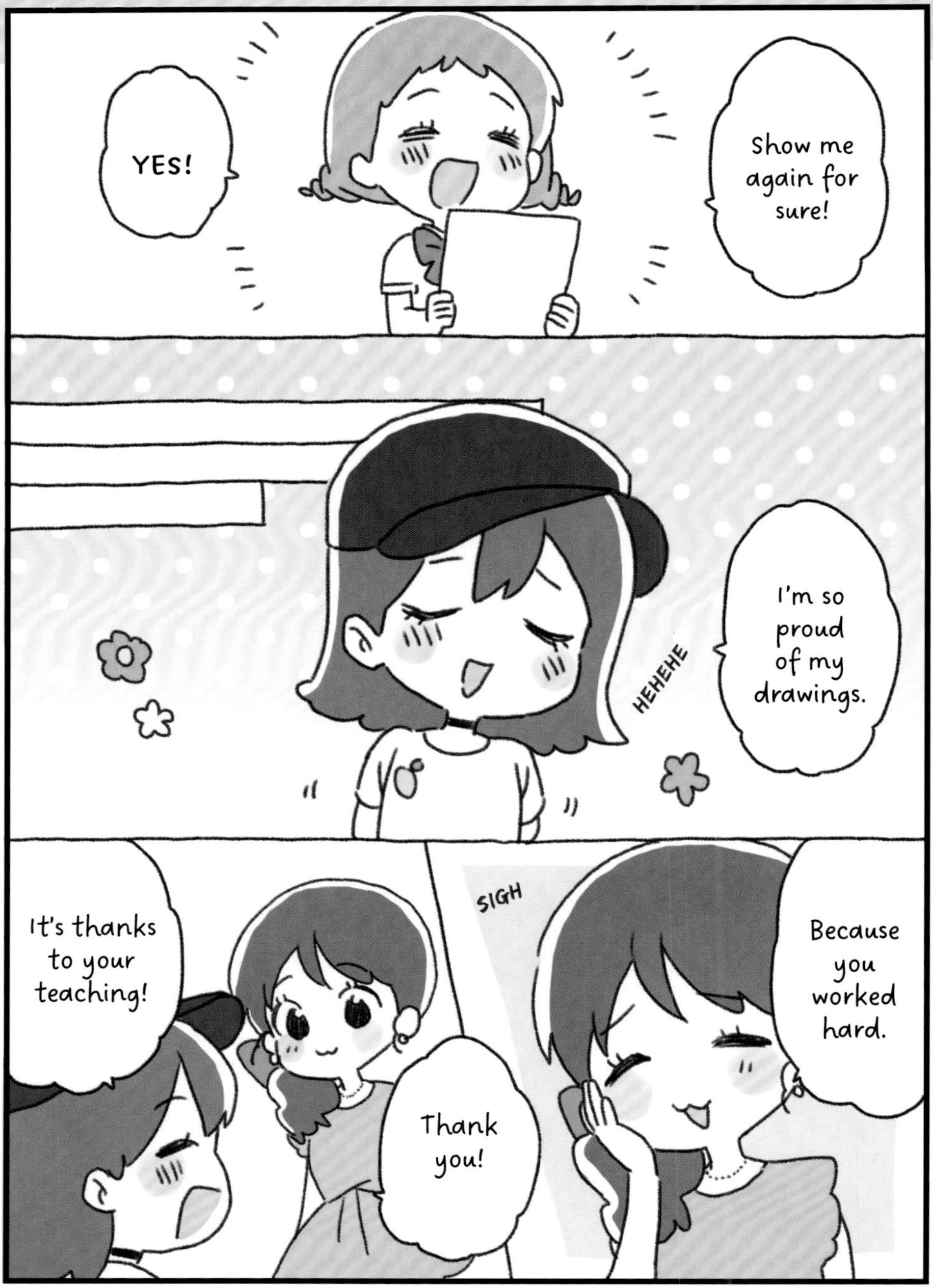
YES!
Show me again for sure!
I'm so proud of my drawings.
HEHEHE
It's thanks to your teaching!
SIGH
Because you worked hard.
Thank you!

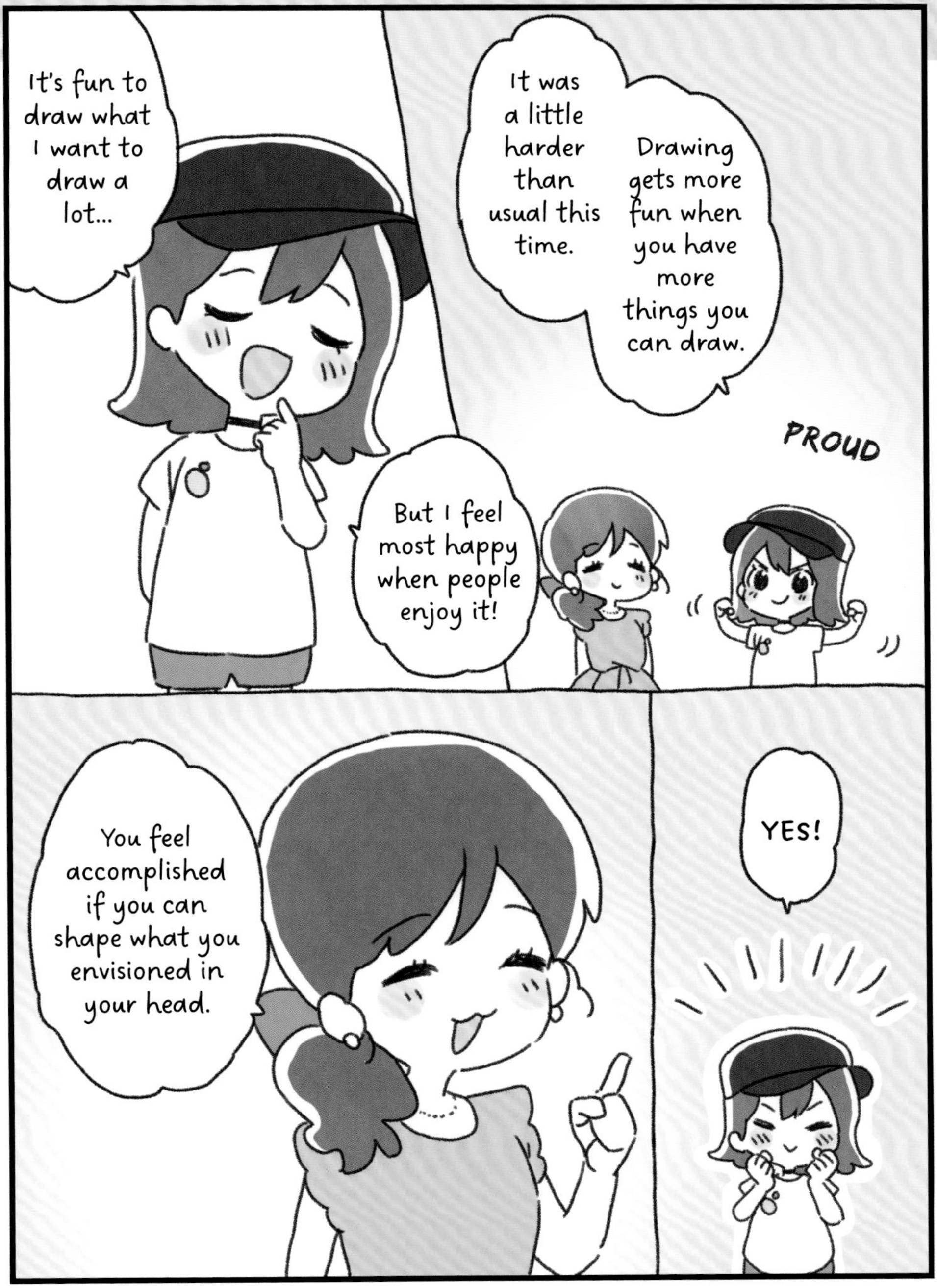
It's fun to draw what I want to draw a lot...
It was a little harder than usual this time.
Drawing gets more fun when you have more things you can draw.
PROUD
But I feel most happy when people enjoy it!
You feel accomplished if you can shape what you envisioned in your head.
YES!

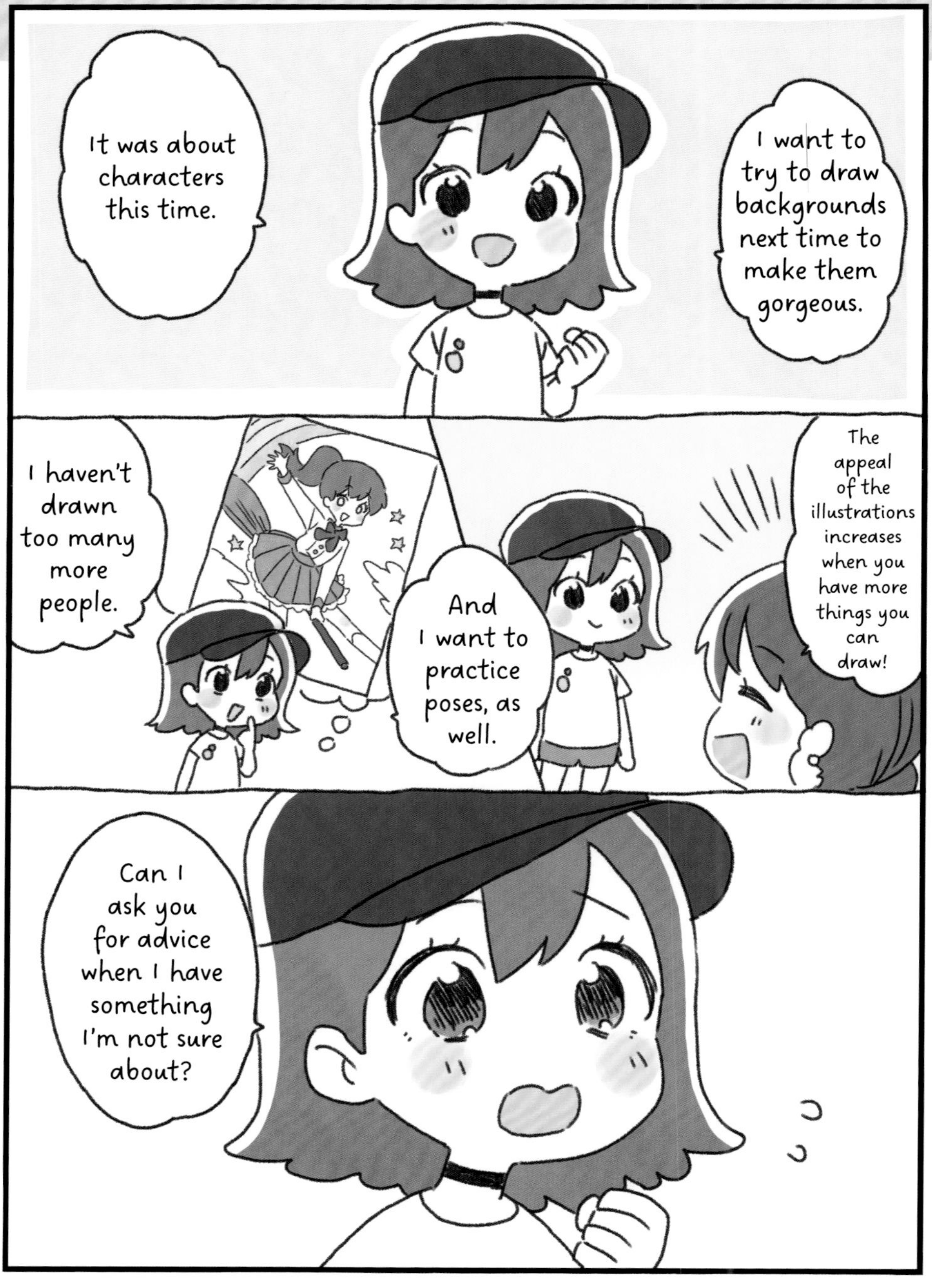
It was about characters this time.
I want to try to draw backgrounds next time to make them gorgeous.
I haven't drawn too many more people.
And I want to practice poses, as well.
The appeal of the illustrations increases when you have more things you can draw!
Can I ask you for advice when I have something I'm not sure about?

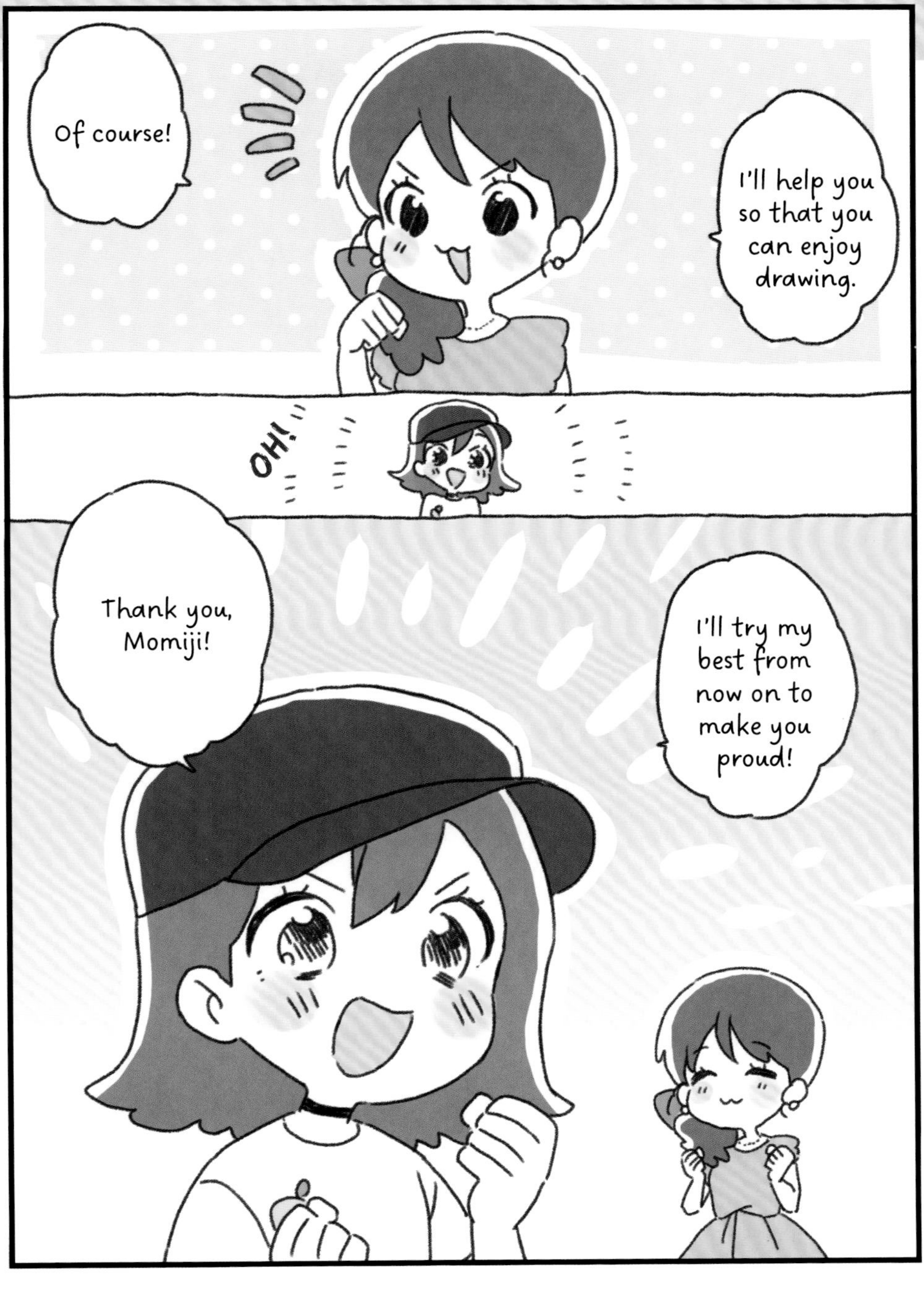
Of course!
I'll help you so that you can enjoy drawing.
OH!
Thank you, Momiji!
I'll try my best from now on to make you proud!

# POSTSCRIPT

How was the third book in the Lemon-chan series?

Illustration gets a different kind of appeal when you draw while thinking about bones and muscles!

I think that you can enjoy learning by practicing drawing your favorite parts first.

It's most important to have fun while drawing.

If you get tired, take a rest.

Try collecting the necessary knowledge according to your own pattern!

I hope that Lemon, Momiji, and I can help you enjoy drawing even a little more.

### YUYU KOUHARA

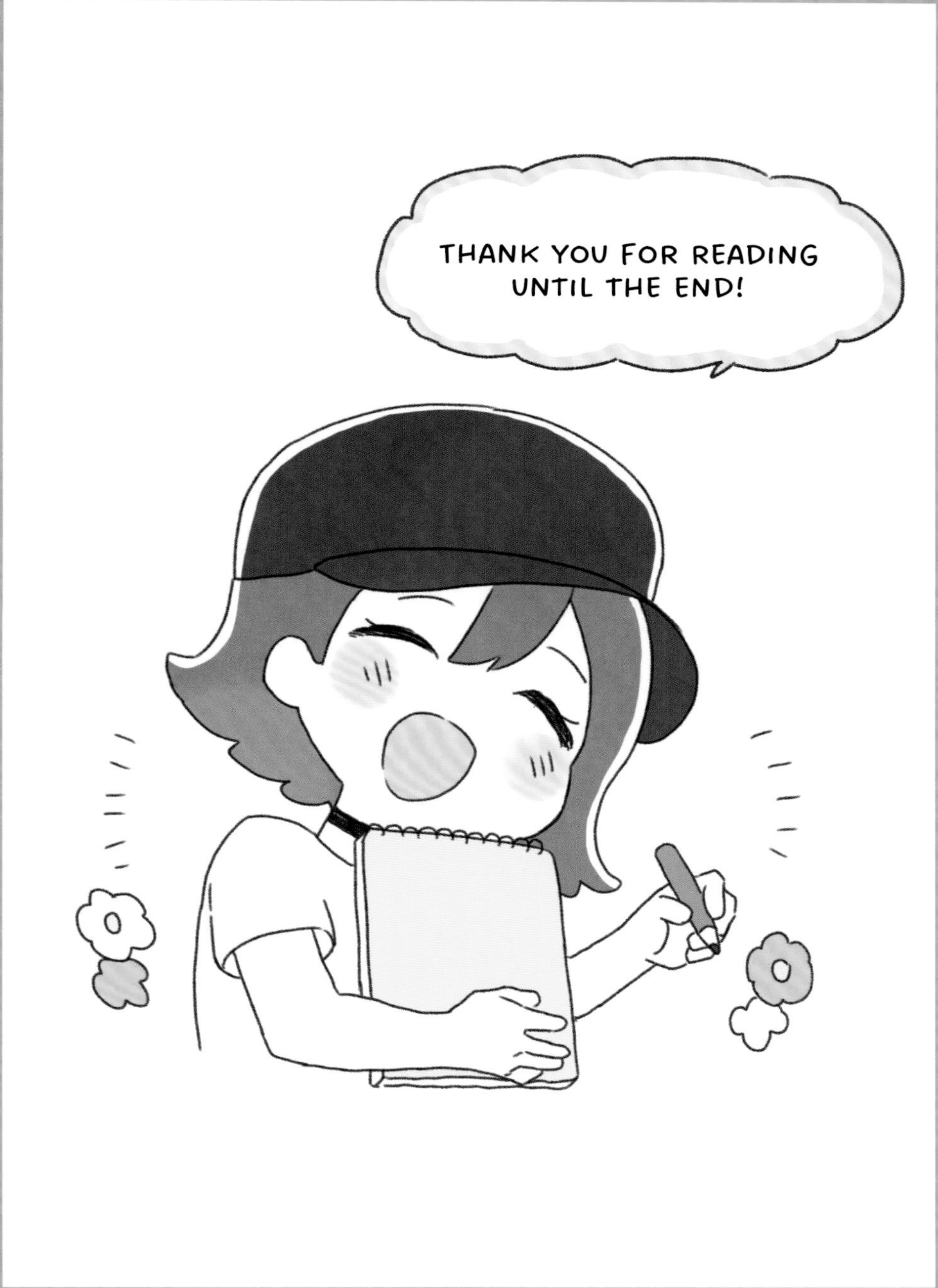
THANK YOU FOR READING
UNTIL THE END!

# ALSO AVAILABLE

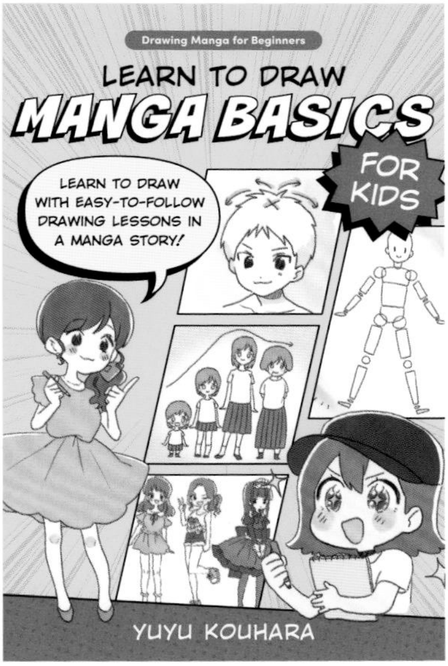
Drawing Manga for Beginners
LEARN TO DRAW
MANGA BASICS
FOR KIDS
LEARN TO DRAW WITH EASY-TO-FOLLOW DRAWING LESSONS IN A MANGA STORY!
YUYU KOUHARA

978-0-7603-8548-7

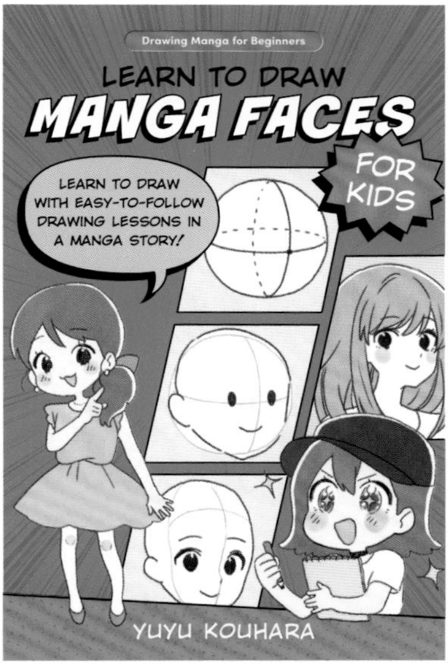
Drawing Manga for Beginners
LEARN TO DRAW
MANGA FACES
FOR KIDS
LEARN TO DRAW WITH EASY-TO-FOLLOW DRAWING LESSONS IN A MANGA STORY!
YUYU KOUHARA

978-0-7603-8550-0

**Quarto.com**

© 2023 Quarto Publishing Group USA Inc.

Originally published in Japan by PIE International
Under the title *Manga de Wakariyasui! Lemon-chan Kyarano Pozuga Kakeruyouni Naritai*
© 2022 Kouhara Yuyu / Enomoto Office / PIE International

Original Japanese Edition Creative Staff:
Author: Yuyu Kouhara
Draft: Aki Enomoto (Enomoto Office)
Project cooperation: Ayane Torii (Enomoto Office), Asuka Nishida (Enomoto Office)
Design: Akiko Shiba, Mai Kato (PIE Graphics)
Coordination: Kaoru Takahashi
English translation rights arranged through PIE International, Japan

First Published in USA in 2023 by Quarry Books, an imprint of The Quarto Group,
100 Cummings Center, Suite 265-D, Beverly, MA 01915, USA.
T (978) 282-9590 F (978) 283-2742

Quarry Books titles are also available at discount for retail, wholesale, promotional, and bulk
purchase. For details, contact the Special Sales Manager by email at specialsales@quarto.com
or by mail at The Quarto Group, Attn: Special Sales Manager, 100 Cummings Center, Suite 265-D,
Beverly, MA 01915, USA.

10 9 8 7 6 5 4 3 2 1

ISBN: 978-0-7603-8549-4

Digital edition published in 2023
eISBN: 978-0-7603-8622-4

Library of Congress Cataloging-in-Publication Data available

English translation: Mayumi Anzai

Printed in China